COLORADO MOUNTAIN COLLEGE
PR1175.E51875
SP
Emerson, Ralph Waldo
Parnassus;
1 03 0000095
W9-DHH-027

PARNASSUS.

PARNASSUS

EDITED BY

RALPH WALDO EMERSON

"Oh, how fair fruit may you to mortal man
From Wisdom's garden give!"—GASCOIGNE.

SBN 512-00172-3
LIBRARY OF CONGRESS CATALOG CARD
NUMBER 12-1642

This volume is a photographic reprint of the Second Edition
published in 1875 in Boston by James R. Osgood & Co.

First Garrett Press Edition Published 1969

Manufactured in the United States of America

PREFACE.

This volume took its origin from an old habit of copying any poem or lines that interested me into a blank book. In many years, my selections filled the volume, and required another; and still the convenience of commanding all my favorites in one album, instead of searching my own and other libraries for a desired song or verse, and the belief that what charmed me probably might charm others, suggested the printing of my enlarged selection. I know the convenience and merits of the existing anthologies, and the necessity of printing in every collection many masterpieces which all English-speaking men have agreed in admiring. Each has its merits; but I have found that the best of these collections do not contain certain gems of pure lustre, whilst they admit many of questionable claim. The voluminous octavos of Anderson and Chalmers have the same fault of too much mass and too little genius; and even the more select "Golden Treasury" of Mr. Palgrave omits too much that I cannot spare. I am aware that no two readers would make the same selection. Of course, I shall gladly hail with the public a better collection than mine.

Poetry teaches the enormous force of a few words, and, in proportion to the inspiration, checks loquacity. It requires that splendor of expression which carries with it the proof of great thoughts. Great thoughts insure musical expressions. Every word should be the right word. The poets are they who see that spiritual is greater than any material force, that thoughts rule the world. The great poets are judged by the frame of mind they induce; and to them, of all men, the severest criticism is due.

Some poems I have inserted for their historical importance; some, for their weight of sense; some, for single couplets or lines, perhaps even for a word; some, for magic of style; and I have admitted verses, which, in their structure, betray a defect of poetic ear, but have a wealth of truth which ought to have created melody. I know the peril of didactics to kill poetry, and that Wordsworth runs fearful risks to save his mental experiences. Some poems are external, like Moore's, and have only a superficial melody: others, like Chaucer's, have such internal music as to forgive a roughness to the modern ear, which, in the mouth of the bard, his contemporaries probably did not detect. To Chaucer may be well applied the word of Heraclitus, that "Harmony latent is of greater value than that which is patent."

There are two classes of poets, — the poets by education and practice, these we respect; and poets by nature, these we love. Pope is the best type of the one class: he had all the advantage that taste and wit could give him, but never rose to grandeur or to pathos. Milton had all its advantages, but was also poet born. Chaucer, Shakspeare, Jonson (despite all the pedantic lumber he dragged with him), Herbert, Herrick, Collins, Burns, — of the other. Then there are poets who rose slowly, and wrote badly, and had yet a true calling, and, after a hundred failures, arrived at pure power; as Wordsworth, encumbered for years with childish whims, but at last, by his religious insight, lifted to genius.

Scott was a man of genius, but only an accomplished rhymer (poet on the same terms as the Norse bards and minstrels), admirable chronicler, and master of the ballad, but never crossing the threshold of the epic, where Homer, Dante, Shakspeare, and Milton dwell.

The task of selection is easiest in poetry. What a signal convenience is fame! Do we read all authors to grope our way to the best? No; but the world selects for us the best, and we select from these our best.

Chaucer fulfils the part of the poet, possesses the advantage of being the most cultivated man of his time, and so speaks always sovereignly and cheerfully. Often the poetic nature, being too susceptible, is over-acted on by others. The religious sentiment teaching the immensity of every moment, the indifference of magnitude, the present is all, the soul is God; — this lesson is great and greatest. Yet this, also, has limits for humanity. One must not seek to dwell in ethereal contemplation: so should the man decline into a monk, and stop short of his possible enlargement. The intellect is cheerful.

Chaucer's antiquity ought not to take him out of the hands of intelligent readers. No lover of poetry can spare him, or should grudge the short study required to command the archaisms of his English, and the skill to read the melody of his verse. His matter is excellent, his story told with vivacity, and with equal skill in the pathos and in triumph. I think he has lines of more force than any English writer, except Shakspeare. If delivered by an experienced reader, the verses will be found musical as well as wise, and fertile in invention. He is always strong, facile, and pertinent, and with what vivacity of style through all the range of his pictures, comic or tragic! He knows the language of joy and of despair.

Of Shakspeare what can we say, but that he is and remains an exceptional mind in the world; that a universal poetry began and ended with him; and that mankind have required the three hundred and ten years since his birth to familiarize themselves with his supreme genius? I should like to have the Academy of Letters propose a prize for an essay on Shakspeare's poem, "*Let the bird of loudest lay*," and the "*Threnos*" with which it closes; the aim of the essay being to explain, by a historical research into the poetic myths and tendencies of the age in which it was written, the frame and allusions of the poem. I have not seen Chester's "*Love's Martyr*," and "the Additional Poems" (1601), in which it appeared. Perhaps that book will suggest all the explanation this poem requires. To unassisted readers, it would appear to be a lament on the death of a poet, and of his poetic mistress. But the poem is so quaint, and charming in diction, tone, and allusions, and in its perfect metre and harmony, that I would gladly have the fullest illustration yet attainable. I consider this piece a good example of the rule, that there is a poetry for bards proper, as well as a poetry for the world of readers. This poem, if published for the first time, and without a known author's name, would find no general reception. Only the poets would save it.

To the modern reader, Ben Jonson's plays have lost their old attraction; but his occasional poems are full of heroic thought, and his songs are among the best in the language. His life interests us from the wonderful circle of companions with whom he lived,—with Camden, Shakspeare, Beaumont, Fletcher, Bacon, Chapman, Herbert, Herrick, Cowley, Suckling, Drayton, Donne, Carew, Selden,—and by whom he was honored. Cowley tells us, "I must not forget Ben's reading: it was delicious: never was poetry married to more exquisite music:" and the Duchess of Newcastle relates, that her husband, himself a good reader, said he "never heard any man read well but Ben Jonson."

Spence reports, that Pope said to him, "Crashaw is a worse sort of Cowley: Herbert is lower than Crashaw,"—an opinion which no reader of their books at this time will justify. Crashaw, if he be the translator of the 'Sospetto d'Herode,' has written masterly verses never learned from Cowley, some of which I have transcribed; and Herbert is the psalmist dear to all who love religious poetry with exquisite refinement of thought. So much piety was never married to so much wit. Herbert identifies himself with Jèwish genius, as Michael Angelo did when carving or painting prophets and patriarchs, not merely old men in robes and beards, but with the sanctity and the character of the Pentateuch and the prophecy conspicuous in them. His wit and his piety are genuine, and are sure to make a lifelong friend of a good reader.

Herrick is the lyric poet, ostentatiously choosing petty subjects, petty names for each piece, and disposing of his theme in a few lines, or in a couplet; is never dull, and is the master of miniature painting. On graver themes, in his "Sacred Numbers," he is equally successful.

Milton's "Paradise Lost" goes so surely with the Bible on to every book-shelf, that I have not cited a line; but I could not resist the insertion of the "Comus," and the "Lycidas," which are made of pure poetry, and have contented myself with extracts from the grander scenes of "Samson Agonistes."

The public sentiment of the reading world was long divided on the merits of Wordsworth. His early poems were written on a false theory of poetry; and the critics denounced them as childish. He persisted long to write after his own whim; and, though he arrived at unexpected power, his readers were never safe from a childish return upon himself and an unskilful putting-forward of it. How different from the absolute concealment of Shakspeare in all his miraculous dramas, and even in his love-poems, in which, of course, the lover must be perpetually present, but always by thought, and never by his buttons or pitifulness! Montaigne is delightful in his egotism. Byron is always egotistic, but interesting thereby, through the taste and genius of his confession or his defiance.

Wordsworth has the merit of just moral perception, but not that of deft poetic execution. How would Milton curl his lip at such slipshod newspaper style! Many of his poems, as, for example, "The Rylstone Doe," might be all improvised: nothing of Milton, nothing of Marvell, of Herbert, of Dryden, could be. These are verses such as many country gentlemen could write; but few would think of claiming the poet's laurel on their merit. Pindar, Dante, Shakspeare, whilst they have the just and open soul, have also the eye to see the dimmest star, the serratures of every leaf, the test objects of the microscope, and then the tongue to utter the same things in words that engrave them on the ears of all mankind.

The poet demands all gifts, and not one or two only. Like the electric rod, he must reach from a point nearer to the sky than all surrounding objects, down to the earth, and into the wet soil, or neither is of use. The poet must not only converse with pure thought, but he must demonstrate it almost to the senses. His words must be pictures: his verses must be spheres and cubes, to be seen and handled. His fable must be a good story, and its meaning must hold as pure truth. In the debates on the Copyright Bill, in the English parliament, Mr. Sergeant Wakley, the coroner, quoted Wordsworth's poetry in derision, and asked the roaring House of Commons, "what that meant, and whether a man should have a public reward for writing such stuff?"—Homer, Horace, Milton, and Chaucer would defy the coroner. Whilst they have wisdom to the wise, he would see that to the external they have external meaning. Coleridge rightly said that "poetry must first be good sense, as a palace might well be magnificent, but first it must be a house." Wordsworth is open to ridicule of this kind; and yet, though satisfied if he can suggest to a sympathetic mind his own mood, and though setting a private and exaggerated value on his compositions, and taking the public to task for not admiring his poetry, he is really a master of the English language; and his best poems evince a power of diction that is no more rivalled by his contemporaries than is his poetic insight. But his capital merit is, that he has done more for the sanity of his generation than any other writer.

"Laodamia" is almost entitled to that eminence in his literary performance which Landor gave it when he said, that "Wordsworth had now written a poem which might be fitly read in Elysium, and the gods and heroes might gather round to listen." I count that and the "Ode on Immortality" as the best.

Wordsworth has a religious value for his thoughts; but his inspirations are casual and insufficient, and he persists in writing after they are gone. No great poet needs so much a severely critical selection of the noble numbers from the puerile into which he often falls. Leigh Hunt said of him, that "he was a fine lettuce with too many outer leaves."

Byron's rare talent is conspicuously partial. He has not sweetness, nor solid knowledge, nor lofty aim. He had a rare skill for rhythm, unmatched facility of expression, a firm, ductile thread of gold. His rhymes do not suggest any restraint, but the utmost freedom, as the rules of the dance do not fetter the good dancer, but exhibit his natural grace. In his isolation he is starved for a purpose; and finding no material except of romance, — first, of corsairs, and Oriental robbers and harems, and, lastly, of satire, — he revenges himself on society for its supposed distrust of him, by cursing it, and throwing himself on the side of its destroyers. His life was wasted; and its only result was this brilliant gift of song with which he soothed his chosen exile. I do not know that it can retain for another generation the charm it had for his contemporaries; but the security with which he pours these perfectly modulated verses to any extent, without any sacrifice of sense for the sake of metre, surprises the reader.

Tennyson has incomparable felicity in all poetic forms, surpassing in melody also, and is a brave, thoughtful Englishman, unmatched in rhythmic power and variety. The thoroughness with which the fable has been thought out, as in the account of the supreme influence of Arthur on his knights, is only one of his triumphs. The passion of love in his "Maud" found a new celebration, which woke delight wherever the English language is known; the "Dirge of Wellington" was a more magnificent monument than any or all of the histories that record that commander's life. Then the variety of his poems discloses the wealth and the health of his mind. Nay, some of his words are poems.

The selections from American writers are necessarily confined to the present century; but some of them have secured a wide fame. Some of them are recent, and have yet to earn their laurels. I have inserted only one of the remarkable poems of Forceythe Willson, a young Wisconsin poet of extraordinary promise, who died very soon after this was written. The poems of a lady who contents herself with the initials H. H. in her book published in Boston (1874) have rare merit of thought and expression, and will reward the reader for the careful attention which they require. The poem of "Sir Pavon and Saint Pavon," by another hand, has a dangerous freedom of style, but carries in it rare power and pathos.

The imagination wakened brings its own language, and that is always musical. It may or may not have rhyme or a fixed metre; but it will always have its special music or tone. Whatever language the bard uses, the secret of tone is at the heart of the poem. Every great master is such by this power, — Chaucer and Shakspeare and Raleigh and Milton and Collins and Burns and Byron and Tennyson and Wolfe. The true inspiration always brings it. Perhaps it cannot be analyzed; but we all yield to it. It is the life of the good ballads; it is in the German hymns which Wesley translated; it is in the "Marseillaise" of Rouget de Lisle; it gave their value to the chants of the old Romish and of the English Church; and it is the only account we can give of their wonderful power on the people. Poems may please by their talent and ingenuity; but, when they charm us, it is because they have this quality, for this is the union of nature with thought.

R. W. E.

CONTENTS

NATURE.

LAND. — SEA. — SKY.

		PAGE.
Argument of his Book	*Herrick*	3
At Sea	*J. T. Trowbridge*	48
Barberry-Bush, The	*Jones Very*	32
Bird, The	*W. Allingham*	36
Birds of Killingworth, The	*Longfellow*	11
Blossoms, To	*Herrick*	33
Bothie of Tober na Vuolich, From the	*Clough*	20
Boy Poet, The	*Wordsworth*	27
Breeding Lark	*Arthur Boar*	36
Cave of Staffa	*Wordsworth*	42
Cloud, The	*Shelley*	46
Coral Grove, The	*J. G. Percival*	39
Corinna's going a-Maying	*Herrick*	10
Country Life, The	*Herrick*	15
Dawn	*Shakspeare*	5
Daffodills, To	*Herrick*	33
Daffodils	*Wordsworth*	33
Death of the Flowers, The	*Bryant*	29
Death of the Old Year, The	*Tennyson*	24
Diamond, The	*J. J. G Wilkinson*	34
Dover Cliffs	*Shakspeare*	8
Drop of Dew, A	*A Marvell*	47
Eagle, The	*Tennyson*	38
Earth-Spirit, The	*W. E. Channing*	27
Evening, Ode to	*Collins*	43
Evening Star, To the	*Wordsworth*	44
First of May	*Wordsworth*	9
Flight of the Wild Geese	*Channing*	37
Flowers	*Shakspeare*	29
Flowers at Cave of Staffa	*Wordsworth*	42
Fox and Cock	*Chaucer*	16
Fringed Gentian, To the	*Bryant*	30
Garden, The	*Marvell*	25
Grasshopper, The	*Richard Lovelace*	16
Haze	*H. D. Thoreau*	48
Herb Rosemary, To the	*H. K. White*	32
Hillside Cot, The	*Channing*	7
Hope	*Campbell*	45
Joanna, To	*Wordsworth*	17
Il Penseroso	*Milton*	18
Lachin y Gair	*Byron*	26
L'Allegro	*Milton*	4
Landscape	*Tennyson*	9
Liberty	*Wordsworth*	33
Lost in the Snow	*Thomson*	23
May	*Ben Jonson*	9
Milky Way, The	*Chaucer*	45
Mist	*Thoreau*	48
Moonlight	*Shakspeare*	43
Morning	*Shakspeare*	6
Morning in the Mountains	*Wordsworth*	8

Mountain, The . . . . Channing 6
Nature . . . . Ben Jonson 3
Nature . . . . James Beattie 3
Night and Death . . . . J. Blanco White . . . 44
Night . . . . Beattie 3
Night . . . . Shakspeare 34
Nightingale, The . . . . Keats 34
Nightingale . . . . Thomson 34
Nightingale, The . . . . R. Barnefield 35
Nightingale's Death-Song, The . . . . Hemans 35
Nightingale's Song, The . . . . . . T. H. Bayly 35
Ocean . . . . Charles Sprague 38
Ocean . . . . Pollok 38
Osmunda Regalis, The . . . . Wordsworth 32
Out and Inward Bound . . . . . . Shakspeare 40
Pass of Kirkstone, The . . . . . . Wordsworth 28
Primrose, The . . . . Herrick 32
Rainbow, To the . . . . Campbell 46
Rainbow, The . . . . Byron 46
Rivulet, The . . . . Bryant 25
Sea . . . . Byron 39
Sea-Shell, Inscription on a . . . . . . Landor 40
Sea Song . . . . Channing 38
Sea Song . . . . A. Cunningham 39
September, 1819 . . . . Wordsworth 34
Skating . . . . Wordsworth 22
Skylark, To a . . . . Shelley 36
Skylark, To the . . . . Wordsworth 36
Smoke . . . . Thoreau 47
Snow . . . . Wordsworth 22
Solitude . . . . Byron 28
Song of the Emigrants in Bermuda . . . . Marvell 41
Song of the Stars . . . . Bryant 44
Sonnet: "Full many a glorious morning" . . Shakspeare 6
Storm, The . . . . Byron 42
Sunflower, The . . . . W. Blake 29
Sunset . . . . Byron 42
Swimming . . . . Byron 21
Tacking Ship off Shore . . . . . . Walter Mitchel 40
Tintern Abbey . . . . Wordsworth 29
Trees . . . . Spenser 30
Waterfowl, To a . . . . Bryant 37
Winter: a Dirge . . . . Burns 22
Winter Night, A . . . . Burns 24
Yew-Trees . . . . Wordsworth 31

HUMAN LIFE.

Home. — Woman. — Love. — Friendship. — Manners. — Holy Days. — Holidays.

Anathemata . . . . F. B. Sanborn 59
Apology for having loved before . . . . . E. Waller 63
Ariadne . . . . Chaucer 75
Athulf and Ethilda . . . . Henry Taylor 70
Babe, The . . . . Sir Wm. Jones (Trans.) . 56
Beauty . . . . Spenser 84
Bride, The . . . . Spenser 67
Bride, The . . . . Suckling 68
Charmer, My . . . . Waller 87
Child, To a . . . . N P. Willis 57
Children's Hour, The . . . . Longfellow 57
Common Sense . . . . Shakspeare 76
Corinne, To . . . . Mrs. Hemans 51
Cotter's Saturday Night, The . . . . . Burns 53
Divided . . . . Jean Ingelow 80
Duchesse Blanche . . . . Chaucer 60
Ecstasy, The . . . . John Donne 70
Elizabeth of Bohemia . . . . Wotton 66
Freedom in Dress . . . . Ben Jonson 87

Genevieve . . . . . *Coleridge* 73
Gentility . . . . . *Chaucer* 83
Girdle, On a . . . . . *Waller* 73
Give me the Old . . . . . *Messinger* 57
Home . . . . . *Wordsworth* 51
Honoria . . . . . *Coventry Patmore* 59
Hymn to the Graces . . . . . *Herrick* 86
If Thou wert by my Side, my Love . . . . . *Heber* 53
I'll never love thee more . . . . . *Montrose* 63
Inborn Royalty . . . . . *Shakspeare* 83
Lady's Yes, The . . . . . *E. B. Browning* 64
Last Farewell, The . . . . . *E. B. E.* 51
Lily of Nithsdale, The . . . . . *A. Cunningham* 75
Lines on leaving Europe . . . . . *N. P. Willis* 51
Love . . . . . *Donne* 62
Love against Love . . . . . *D. A. Wasson* 83
Love at First Sight . . . . . *Beaumont and Fletcher* 71
Lucasta, To . . . . . *Lovelace* 63
Lucy . . . . . *Wordsworth* 62
Maud . . . . . *Tennyson* 72
My Mother's Picture . . . . . *Cowper* 52
Othello's Defence . . . . . *Shakspeare* 69
Outgrown . . . . . *Julia R. C. Dorr* 64
Peasant's Return, The . . . . . *William Barnes* 75
Playmate, The . . . . . *Whittier* 79
Pilot's Daughter, The . . . . . *Allingham* 77
Poetry of Dress, The . . . . . *Herrick* 87
Portrait, The . . . . . *Heywood* 65
Qua Cursum Ventus . . . . . *Clough* 82
Queen, The . . . . . *Patmore* 63
Rosaline . . . . . *T. Lodge* 72
Rose of the World, The . . . . . *Patmore* 58
Sentences . . . . . *Patmore* 76
She walks in Beauty . . . . . *Byron* 59
Silvia, To . . . . . *Herrick* 58
Song: "See the Chariot at hand" . . . . . *Ben Jonson* 73
Song: "How near to Good is what is Fair" . . . . . *Ben Jonson* 87
Sonnet: "How oft when thou" . . . . . *Shakspeare* 73
Sonnet: "Let me not to the Marriage" . . . . . *Shakspeare* 77
Sonnet: "So am I as the Rich" . . . . . *Shakspeare* 78
Sonnet: "To me Fair Friend" . . . . . *Shakspeare* 86
Sundered . . . . . *Sidney H. Morse* 82
Sympathy . . . . . *Thoreau* 78
Thou hast sworn by thy God, my Jeanie . . . . . *A. Cunningham* 66
Tribute, The . . . . . *Coventry Patmore* 66
True Love . . . . . *Shakspeare* 62
Una and the Lion . . . . . *Spenser* 85
Venus, To . . . . . *Beaumont and Fletcher* 72
Viola disguised, and the Duke . . . . . *Shakspeare* 68
Virginia . . . . . *Chaucer* 67
When I do count the Clock . . . . . *Shakspeare* 86
Woman . . . . . *Prof. Wilson (Trans.)* 58
Wood-Fire, The . . . . . *E. S. H.* 56

INTELLECTUAL.

MEMORY. — INSPIRATION. — IMAGINATION. — FANCY. — MUSIC. — ART. — BEAUTY. — MOODS.

Æolian Harp . . . . . *Allingham* 130
Alexander's Feast . . . . . *Dryden* 130
Art and Nature . . . . . *Shakspeare* 132
Cathedral . . . . . *Congreve* 133
Compliment to Queen Elizabeth . . . . . *Shakspeare* 124
Comus: a Mask . . . . . *Milton* 104
Critic, To the . . . . . *Tennyson* 133
Cuckow and the Nightingale . . . . . *Chaucer* 97
Dædalus . . . . . *Sterling* 132
Dreams . . . . . *Scott* 122
Fantasy . . . . . *Ben Jonson* 123

Fairies	*Warton*	126
Fame	*Ben Jonson*	101
Flower, The	*George Herbert*	95
Foresight	*Shakspeare*	92
Harp, To the	*Drayton*	130
Hurts of Time	*Byron*	138
Inspiration	*Burns*	95
Inspiration	*Thoreau*	94
Kilmeny	*James Hogg*	120
King Lear	*Shakspeare*	102
Kubla Khan	*Coleridge*	126
Locksley Hall	*Tennyson*	134
Memory	*Tennyson*	92
Memory	*Channing*	92
Moods	*Sir J. Suckling*	139
Morning	*Allingham*	94
Muse, The	*George Wither*	96
Music, To	*Mrs. Hemans*	130
Music	*Keats*	128
Music	*W. Strode*	127
Mythology	*Coleridge*	120
Not Every Day Fit for Verse	*Herrick*	93
Ode to Himself	*Ben Jonson*	93
Orpheus with his Flute	*Shakspeare*	127
Passions, The: an Ode for Music	*Collins*	128
Phœnix and Turtle Dove	*Shakspeare*	123
Pleasures of Imagination	*Akenside*	99
Poet, The	*C. S. T.*	95
Poet, The	*Chaucer*	96
Poet's Mood	*Beaumont and Fletcher*	138
Praise of Homer, The	*George Chapman*	93
Prayer to Apollo	*Chaucer*	96
Queen Mab	*Shakspeare*	125
Questionings	*F. H. Hedge*	91
Rabia	*J. F. Clarke* (*Trans.*)	140
Romeo's Presage	*Shakspeare*	122
Scale of Minds	*Wordsworth*	98
Ships at Sea	*R. B. Coffin*	122
Socrates	*Young*	94
Song from Gypsies' Metamorphoses	*Ben Jonson*	125
Song of Fionnuala, The	*Moore*	126
Sonnet: "O how much more doth"	*Shakspeare*	133
Sonnet: "From you have I been"	*Shakspeare*	133
Sonnet on First Looking into Chapman's Homer	*Keats*	94
Soul's Errand, The	*Raleigh*	139
St. Cecilia's Day	*Dryden*	127
Steamboats, Viaducts, and Railways	*Wordsworth*	98
Supplication, A	*Cowley*	129
Thought	*H. H.*	91
Ulysses	*Tennyson*	101
Under the Portrait of Milton	*Dryden*	99
White Island, The	*Herrick*	123
Outline	*Wordsworth*	102
Writing Verses	*Burns*	95

CONTEMPLATIVE. — MORAL. — RELIGIOUS.

MAN. — VIRTUE. — HONOR. — TIME. — FATE. — SLEEP. — DREAMS. — LIFE. — DEATH. — IMMORTALITY. — HYMNS AND ODES.

Abou Ben Adhem	*Leigh Hunt*	158
Affliction	*Herbert*	184
Angels, The	*Drummond*	190
An Honest Man's Fortune	*John Fletcher*	155
Before Sleep	*Sir T. Browne*	185
Burning Babe, The	*Southwell*	191
Celinda	*Lord Herbert*	172
Character	*Coleridge*	154
Church Porch, The	*Herbert*	145
Christmas	*Tennyson*	192
Christmas Carol, The	*Wordsworth*	191

Christmas Hymn	*Milton*	187
Come Morir	*S. G. W.*	166
Confession	*Herbert*	150
Consolers, The	*S. G. W.*	150
Death's Final Conquest	*James Shirley*	167
Dependence	*Cowper*	182
Destiny	*Chaucer*	152
Divine Love	*Wesley (Trans.)*	177
Duty, Ode to	*Wordsworth*	149
Easter	*Herbert*	192
Elegy Written in a Country Churchyard	*Gray*	169
Elixir, The	*Herbert*	181
English Channel	*Wordsworth*	144
Eton College	*Gray*	148
Euthanasia	*Henry More*	173
Forecast	*Chaucer*	153
Forecast	*Bailey*	153
Good Omens	*Shakspeare*	152
Gratefulness	*Herbert*	184
Hamlet's Soliloquy	*Shakspeare*	160
Happy Life, The	*Wotton*	146
Honest Poverty	*Burns*	147
Honor	*Wordsworth*	144
Humility	*R. M. Milnes*	145
Hymn to Christ, A	*Donne*	180
Hymn to God, My God, in my Sickness	*Donne*	186
Hymn: "Lord, when I quit this Earthly Stage"	*Watts*	185
Hyperion: "As Heaven and Earth are Fairer"	*Keats*	143
Immortality	*Wordsworth*	173
Immortal Mind, The	*Byron*	172
Inscription on Melrose Abbey	*Anonymous*	161
Inscription on a Wall in St. Edmund's Church, in Lombard St., London	*Anonymous*	162
Inscription in Marble in the Parish Church of Faversham, in Agro Cantiano	*Anonymous*	162
Joy	*H. H.*	157
Knowing the Heart of Man is Set to be	*Daniel*	
Laodamia	*Wordsworth*	162
Life	*Herbert*	151
Life	*Mrs. Barbauld*	169
Life	*Longfellow*	149
Life and Death	*Shakspeare*	161
Life and Death	*Shakspeare*	161
Litany to the Holy Spirit	*Herrick*	186
Love and Humility	*Henry More*	176
Man	*Herbert*	143
Matins	*Herrick*	185
Moravian Hymn	*John Wesley*	178
My Legacy	*H. H.*	177
My Mind to Me a Kingdom is	*Byrd*	154
Narayena: Spirit of God	*Sir. Wm. Jones (Trans.)*	180
New Prince, New Pomp	*Southwell*	191
Old Man's Funeral, The	*Bryant*	167
Orthodoxy	*W. Blake*	158
Peace	*Herbert*	157
Penitence	*Young*	180
Pilgrimage	*Sir W. Raleigh*	160
Poet's Hope, A	*W. E. Channing*	153
Praise to God	*Mrs. Barbauld*	183
Prayers	*Shakspeare*	159
Providence	*Herbert*	182
Providence	*Cowper*	182
Psalm XCIII.	*Sir Philip Sidney*	178
Psalm XVIII.	*Sternhold*	182
Psalm CXXXIX.	*Sir Philip Sidney*	178
Pulley, The	*Herbert*	144
Quip, The	*Herbert*	147
Retreat, The	*Henry Vaughan*	173
Revolutions	*Shakspeare*	152
Satan	*Richard Crashaw*	179
Seven Ages, The	*Shakspeare*	151
Shepherds, The	*Drummond*	190
Shield, The	*S. G. W.*	150

Sin . . . . . . Herbert 159
Sing unto the Lord . . . . . Sir Philip Sidney . . 181
Skeptic, The . . . . . . Wordsworth 152
Skull, The . . . . . . Byron 171
Sleep . . . . . . Shakspeare 160
Sleep . . . . . . Young 160
Stanzas written in the Churchyard of Richmond, Yorkshire . . . . . Herbert Knowles . . . 167
Star-Song, The . . . . . . Herrick 190
Strangers, The . . . . . . Jones Very 159
Sun-Dial . . . . . . Montgomery 151
Thanatopsis . . . . . . Bryant 168
That Each Thing is hurt of Itself . . . . Anonymous 154
The Spacious Firmament on High . . . . Addison 180
Tithonus . . . . . . Tennyson 165
To Be no More . . . . . . Milton 169
Touchstone, The . . . . . . Allingham 158
Two went up into the Temple to pray . . . . Richard Crashaw . . . 180
Undertaking, The . . . . . . Donne 154
Virtue . . . . . . Herbert 147
Wayfarers . . . . . . E. Hooper 159
Wisdom . . . . . . Coventry Patmore . . . 146

HEROIC.

Patriotic. — Historic. — Political.

Abraham Lincoln . . . . . . Tom Taylor 254
Antony over the Dead Body of Cæsar . . . . Shakspeare 205
Ariadne's Farewell . . . . . . H. H. 202
Bannockburn . . . . . . Burns 219
Bard, The . . . . . . Gray 215
Battle Hymn of the Republic . . . . . Julia Ward Howe . . . 230
Battle of the Baltic . . . . . . Campbell 220
Battle on St. Crispian's Day . . . . . Shakspeare 211
Bay Fight, The . . . . . . H. H. Brownell . . . 248
Boadicea . . . . . . Cowper 212
Bonduca . . . . . . Beaumont and Fletcher . . 213
Bunker Hill . . . . . . G. Mellen 226
Cassius . . . . . . Shakspeare 203
Chicago . . . . . . Bret Harte 261
Chivalry . . . . . . Ben Jonson 199
Christian Militant . . . . . . Herrick 198
Commemoration Ode . . . . . . Lowell 258
Constancy . . . . . . Herbert 195
Coronation . . . . . . H. H. 202
Cromwell and King Charles . . . . . Marvell 219
Cumberland, The . . . . . . Longfellow 239
Defiance . . . . . . Scott 218
Entrance of Columbus into Barcelona . . . . G. Mellen 225
Epistle to a Friend to persuade him to the Wars . Ben Jonson 196
Flag, The . . . . . . Julia Ward Howe . . . 236
George Washington 226
Greeting to "The George Griswold" . . . . Punch 227
Happy Warrior, The . . . . . . Wordsworth 196
Henry V.'s Audience of French Ambassadors . Shakspeare 210
Heroism . . . . . . Coleridge (Trans.) . . . 195
Hohenlinden . . . . . . Campbell 223
Hotspur's Quarrel with Henry IV. . . . . Shakspeare 207
Hotspur . . . . . . Shakspeare 208
Ichabod . . . . . . Whittier 227
Indians . . . . . . Charles Sprague . . . 225
In State . . . . . . Forceythe Wilson . . . 255
In the Fight . . . . . . Tennyson 228
Jephthah's Daughter . . . . . . Byron 203
John Brown of Osawatomie . . . . . E. C. Stedman . . . 227
King Richard's Soliloquy . . . . . Shakspeare 211
Landing of the Pilgrim Fathers, The . . . . Mrs. Hemans 225
Lochiel's Warning . . . . . . Campbell 217
Lost Leader, The . . . . . . Robert Browning . . . 224
Loyal Woman's No, A . . . . . . Lucy Larcom 246

Maryland	*J. R. Randall*	230
Mason and Slidell	*Lowell*	234
Master Spirit, The	*George Chapman*	198
Murat	*Byron*	223
Never or Now	*O. W. Holmes*	232
Ode on Decorating the Graves of the Confederate Soldiers	*Henry Timrod*	258
Old Ironsides	*O. W. Holmes*	226
On the Late Massacre in Piemont	*Milton*	195
Port Royal, At	*Whittier*	231
Prayer, The	*Tennyson*	198
Requiem	*George Lunt*	257
Royalty	*D. A. Wasson*	198
Samson Agonistes	*Milton*	199
Schill	*Wordsworth*	222
Scotland	*Burns*	220
Song of Saul before his Last Battle	*Byron*	203
Sonnet: "Alas! what boots the long"	*Wordsworth*	221
Sonnet: "It is not to be thought of that"	*Wordsworth*	223
Speech of the Dauphin	*Shakspeare*	207
Sunthin in a Pastoral Line	*Lowell*	240
Thought of a Briton on the Subjugation of Switzerland	*Wordsworth*	221
Vision, The	*Burns*	219
Warden of the Cinque Ports, The	*Longfellow*	224
Washers of the Shroud, The	*Lowell*	237
Waterloo	*Byron*	222
Westward the Star of Empire	*G. Berkley*	225
What the Birds said	*Whittier*	246
Ye Mariners of England	*Campbell*	221

PORTRAITS. — PERSONAL. — PICTURES.

Addison, Portrait of	*Pope*	271
Agassiz, Fiftieth Birthday of	*Longfellow*	280
A King	*Robert Browning*	282
Alexander Pope, Lines to	*David Lewis*	272
Ben Jonson, Ode to	*Herrick*	270
Black Prince, The	*Shakspeare*	266
Burial of Moses	*Mrs. Alexander*	290
Campbell, To	*Moore*	276
Caliph's Encampment, The	*Moore*	286
Cleopatra	*Shakspeare*	283
Coriolanus	*Shakspeare*	265
Coriolanus at Antium	*Shakspeare*	266
Countess of Rutland, To the	*Ben Jonson*	269
Cowley's Epigram on Sir Francis Drake	*Ben Jonson (Trans.)*	268
Destruction of Sennacherib, The	*Byron*	282
Elegy on Mistress Elizabeth Drury	*Donne*	273
Entrance of Bolingbroke into London	*Shakspeare*	285
Epigram	*Ben Jonson*	269
Epitaph on Shakspeare	*Milton*	268
Epitaph: "Underneath this sable hearse"	*Ben Jonson*	269
Epitaph: "Underneath this stone doth lye"	*Ben Jonson*	268
Execution, The	*Byron*	284
Fare Thee Well	*Byron*	277
Fop, The	*Shakspeare*	286
Forging of the Anchor, The	*S. Fergusson*	287
George Peabody, To	*O. W. Holmes*	282
Gladiator, The	*Byron*	283
Henry V.	*Shakspeare*	267
Ice Palace, The	*Cowper*	288
Lines in a Lady's Album	*Daniel Webster*	281
Love of England	*Byron*	277
Lucy, Countess of Bedford, On	*Ben Jonson*	268
Man of Ross The	*Pope*	272
Milton, To	*Wordsworth*	274
Mountain Daisy, To a	*Burns*	279
Mouse, To a	*Burns*	278
Nebuchadnezzar	*Gower*	265
Nestor to Hector	*Shakspeare*	265

No More . . . . *Byron* 278
On his Blindness . . . . *Milton* 271
Outward Bound . . . . *Byron* 276
Palm and Pine . . . . *Milnes* 289
Prayer to Ben Jonson . . . . *Herrick* 269
Prisoner of Chillon, The . . . . *Byron* 283
Rob Roy's Grave . . . . *Wordsworth* 274
Santa Filomena . . . . *Longfellow* 280
Siege of Corinth . . . . *Byron* 284
Sir Henry Vane, To . . . . *Milton* 271
Sir Philip Sidney . . . . *Matthew Royden* 268
Soldier's Dream, The . . . . *Campbell* 289
Sonnet: "O for my sake do you with fortune chide!" *Shakspeare* 271
Sonnet, on his being arrived to the age of twenty-three . . . . *Milton* 270
Spenser at Court . . . . *Spenser* 267
Stanzas, "Though the day of my destiny's over" *Byron* 276
To live Merrily and to trust to Good Verses . . *Herrick* 269
Wants of Man, The . . . . *J. Q. Adams* 280
When the Assault was intended to the City . . *Milton* 274
William Sidney on his Birthday, To . . . . *Ben Jonson* 269

NARRATIVE POEMS AND BALLADS.

Alfred the Harper . . . . *Sterling* 298
Alice Brand . . . . *Scott* 334
Allen-a-Dale . . . . *Scott* 363
Amy Wentworth . . . . *Whittier* 380
Auld Robin Gray . . . . *Lady Anne Lindsay* . . . 383
Battle of Harlaw . . . . *Scott* 301
Boy of Egremond, The . . . . *Wordsworth* 339
Braes of Yarrow, The . . . . *W. Hamilton* 412
Bristowe Tragedy . . . . *T. Chatterton* 343
Bruce and the Abbot . . . . *Scott* 415
Child Dyring . . . . *Scott* 336
Children in the Wood . . . . *Anonymous* 337
Chimney-Sweep, The . . . . *E. S. H.* 339
Crowning of Arthur, The . . . . *Tennyson* 296
Drowned Lovers, The . . . . *Anonymous* 321
Duchess May, Rhyme of . . . . *E. B. Browning* 404
Earl o' Quarterdeck, The . . . . *George MacDonald* 318
Fair Annie . . . . *Scott* 384
Fair Helen . . . . *Anonymous* 411
Fidelity . . . . *Wordsworth* 326
Fitz Traver's Song . . . . *Scott* 364
Friar of Orders Gray . . . . *Scott* 349
Garci Perez de Vargas . . . . *Lockhart* 300
Gate of Camelot, The . . . . *Tennyson* 294
Gay Goss-Hawk, The . . . . *Scott* 361
George Nidiver . . . . *Anonymous* 327
Glenara . . . . *Campbell* 363
Glenlogie . . . . *Smith's Scottish Minstrel* . 360
Græme and Bewick . . . . *Scott* 350
Griselda . . . . *Chaucer* 385
Heir of Linne, The . . . . *Percy's Reliques* 307
Helvellyn . . . . *Scott* 326
High Tide on the Coast of Lincolnshire, The . . *Jean Ingelow* 340
House of Busyrane . . . . *Spenser* 293
How they brought the Good News from Ghent to Aix *Robert Browning* 355
Island, The . . . . *Byron* 377
King John and the Abbot of Canterbury . . . *Percy's Reliques* 352
Kinmont Willie . . . . *Scott* 301
Lady Clara Vere de Vere . . . . *Tennyson* 365
Lady Clare . . . . *Tennyson* 381
Lady Geraldine's Courtship . . . . . . *E. B. Browning* 366
Lake of the Dismal Swamp, The . . . . . . *Moore* 335
Lochinvar . . . . *Scott* 356
Mass, The . . . . *Scott* 349
Œnone; or, the Choice of Paris . . . . . *Tennyson* 375
Relief of Lucknow, The . . . . *Robert Lowell* 311
Rhotruda . . . . *Tuckerman* 357

Rosabelle	*Scott*	414
Sally from Coventry, The	*Anonymous*	354
Sea-Cave, The	*Byron*	378
Skipper Ireson's Ride	*Whittier*	304
Siege and Conquest of Alhama	*Byron*	310
Sir Andrew Barton	*Anonymous*	312
Sir Patrick Spens	*Anonymous*	317
Sir Pavon and St. Pavon	*Sarah H. Palfrey*	417
Song of the Tonga-Islanders	*Anonymous*	380
Svend Vonved	*George Borrow (Trans.)*	328
Telling the Bees	*Whittier*	414
Vision of Belshazzar	*Byron*	416
Waly, Waly, but Love be Bonny	*Anonymous*	383
Wild Huntsman, The	*Scott (Trans.)*	330
William of Cloudeslé	*Anonymous*	306
Winstanley	*Jean Ingelow*	322
Wreck of "The Grace of Sunderland"	*Jean Ingelow*	320

SONGS.

Althea, To	*Lovelace*	445
Araby's Daughter	*Moore*	435
Ariel's Song	*Shakspeare*	440
Auld Lang Syne	*Burns*	439
A Weary Lot is Thine	*Scott*	448
Banks of Doon, The	*Burns*	447
Blow, Blow, thou Winter Wind	*Shakspeare*	439
Boatie Rows, The	*Anonymous*	437
Bonny Dundee	*Scott*	449
Bridal of Andalla, The	*Lockhart*	447
Brignall Banks	*Scott*	449
Bugle-Song, The	*Tennyson*	441
Canadian Boat-Song	*Moore*	436
Celia, To	*Ben Jonson*	445
Ceres, Song to	*Leigh Hunt*	434
Clan-Alpine, Song of	*Scott*	450
Come Away, Come Away, Death	*Shakspeare*	439
County Guy	*Scott*	442
Disdain Returned	*Thomas Carew*	446
Dying Bard, The	*Scott*	451
Full Fathom Five thy Father Lies	*Shakspeare*	441
Garden Song	*Tennyson*	444
Goldilocks	*Jean Ingelow*	443
Go, Lovely Rose!	*Waller*	443
Hark, Hark, the Lark!	*Shakspeare*	441
Hero to Leander	*Tennyson*	448
Jeanie Morrison	*Motherwell*	438
John Anderson, My Jo	*Burns*	438
Love	*Samuel Daniel*	446
Love's Young Dream	*Moore*	446
Manly Heart, The	*G. Wither*	446
Mary Donnelly	*Allingham*	434
Masque of Pleasure and Virtue	*Ben Jonson*	433
Night Piece: to Julia	*Herrick*	445
Night-Sea, The	*Harriet Prescott*	448
Of A' the Airts	*Burns*	442
Oft in the Stilly Night	*Moore*	438
O my Luve's like a Red, Red Rose	*Burns*	443
Pibroch of Donuil Dhu	*Scott*	450
River Song	*F. B. Sanborn*	442
Rose, To the	*Herrick*	443
Sailor, The	*Allingham*	436
Song of Echo	*Ben Jonson*	441
Song	*Milton*	441
Song from Jason	*William Morris*	442
Song from Neptune's Triumph	*Ben Jonson*	434
Song: "Shake off your heavy trance"	*Beaumont and Fletcher*	433
Song: "When Daisies Pied"	*Shakspeare*	440
Take, O Take Those Lips away	*Shakspeare*	444

Tell Me where is Fancy Bred . . . . *Shakspeare* 441
Thekla's Song . . . . (*Trans.*) 447
The Harp that once through Tara's Halls . . . . *Moore* 435
There's Nae Luck about the House . . . . . *W. J. Mickle* 437
Under the Greenwood-Tree . . . . *Shakspeare* 440

DIRGES AND PATHETIC POEMS.

Braes of Yarrow, The . . . . *J. Logan* 456
Burial of Sir John Moore at Corunna, The . . . . *Charles Wolfe* 466
Coronach . . . . *Scott* 461
Departed . . . . *Wordsworth* 471
Deserted House, The . . . . *Tennyson* 457
Dion . . . . *Wordsworth* 475
Dirge for Dorcas . . . . *Herrick* 461
Dirge: "He is gone — is dust" . . . . . . *Coleridge* (*Trans.*) . . . 459
Dirge in Cymbeline . . . . *Collins* 460
Epitaph from Simonides . . . . *Anonymous* 463
Fear no More the Heat o' th' Sun . . . . . . *Shakspeare* 461
For Thou hast Passed All Change of Human Life . *A. S. Gage* . . . . .
He's Gane . . . . *Burns* 458
Hosea Biglow's Lament . . . . *Lowell* 476
Laborer, The . . . . *John Clare* 456
Lachrimæ; or, Mirth turned to Mourning . . . . *Herrick* 455
Lament for James, Earl of Glencairn . . . . *Burns* 458
Lament of Mary Queen of Scots on the Approach of Spring . . . . *Burns* 456
Lines written at Grasmere on Tidings of the Approaching Death of Charles James Fox . . . . . *Wordsworth* 463
Lycidas . . . . *Milton* 467
Lykewake Dirge . . . . *Anon.* 459
Murdered Traveller, The . . . . *Bryant* 457
Nymph Mourning her Fawn, The . . . . . . *Marvell* 455
Ode: "How sleep the brave who sink to rest" . . *Collins* 459
Ode on the Death of the Duke of Wellington . . *Tennyson* 464
Ode on the Death of Thomson . . . . *Collins* 462
Ode on the Consecration of Sleepy-Hollow Cemetery *F. B. Sanborn* 462
On Sir Philip Sidney . . . . *Fulke Greville, Lord Brooke* 467
On the Loss of the "Royal George" . . . . . *Cowper* 463
Othello's Last Words . . . . *Shakspeare* 476
Sleepy Hollow . . . . *Channing* 460
Thyrsis . . . . *Matthew Arnold* 471
Winding-Sheet, To his . . . . *Herrick* 458

COMIC AND HUMOROUS.

Satirical.

Atheism . . . . *Clough* 497
Chiquita . . . . *Bret Harte* 502
Collusion between a Alegaiter and a Water-Snaik . *George H. Derby* 491
Contentment . . . . *Holmes* 499
Cosmic Egg, The . . . . *Anonymous* 505
Dorothy Q. . . . . *Holmes* 498
Fight over the Body of Keitt, The . . . . . *Punch* 500
Her Letter . . . . *Bret Harte* 495
His Answer to "Her Letter" . . . . *Bret Harte* 496
Holy Willie's Prayer . . . . *Burns* 481
Jove and the Souls . . . . *Swift* 502
Mignonette . . . . *Bartlett* 505
Old Cove, The . . . . *H. H. Brownell* 502
Origin of Didactic Poetry, The . . . . . . *Lowell* 483
Plain Language from Truthful James . . . . . *Bret Harte* 504
Puritans . . . . *Butler* 501
Rudolph, The Headsman . . . . *Holmes* 503
Tam O'Shanter . . . . *Burns* 484
The Courtin' . . . . *Lowell* 494
The Deacon's Masterpiece; or, The Wonderful One-Hoss-Shay . . . . *Holmes* 492

The Friend of Humanity and the Knife-Grinder . *Canning* 504
To the Devil . . . . *Burns* 483
To the Unco Guid; or, the Rigidly Righteous . . *Burns* 482
Witch of Fife, The . . . . *Hogg* 487

POETRY OF TERROR.

Apparition, The . . . . *Byron* 514
Clarence's Dream . . . . *Shakspeare* 511
Corsair, The . . . . *Byron* 512
Crime . . . . *Shakspeare* 510
Hesitation . . . . *Shakspeare* 512
Incantation from Manfred . . . . *Byron* 512
I see Men's Judgments are . . . . *Shakspeare* 511
Macbeth is ripe for shaking . . . . *Shakspeare* 510
Manfred . . . . *Byron* 513
Merciful Heaven . . . . *Shakspeare* 511
Remorse . . . . *Shakspeare* 510
Song of the Parcæ . . . . *Goethe trans. by Frothingham* 510
Thea . . . . *Keats* 509
The Gods are Just . . . . *Shakspeare* 511
This Army led by a Delicate and Tender Prince . *Shakspeare* 512
Tiger, The . . . . *William Blake* 509
To beguile the time . . . . *Shakspeare* . . . .
Turner . . . . *J. J. G. Wilkinson* 509
When we in our viciousness grow hard . . . . *Shakspeare* 510

ORACLES AND COUNSELS.

Good Counsel. — Supreme Hours.

Antony and the Soothsayer . . . . *Shakspeare* 519
Beware . . . . *Scott* 517
Cleopatra's Resolution . . . . *Shakspeare* 521
Courage . . . . *Shakspeare* 520
Each and all . . . . *Shakspeare* 520
Faith . . . . *Mrs. Kemble* 518
Firmness . . . . *Shakspeare* 521
Good Heart . . . . *Burns* 518
Guidance . . . . *Shakspeare* 521
Human Life . . . . *Shakspeare* 521
If men be worlds . . . . *Donne* 517
Knowing the heart of man . . . . *Daniel* 517
Mine honesty and I begin to square . . . . . *Shakspeare* 521
Mother's Blessing . . . . *Shakspeare* 520
O how feeble is man's power . . . . *Donne* 517
Opportunity . . . . *Shakspeare* 517
Saturn . . . . *Keats* 518
The flighty purpose never is o'ertook . . . . *Shakspeare* 520
The Nobly Born . . . . *E. S H.* 518
The recluse hermit . . . . *Donne* 517
There is a history . . . . *Shakspeare* 517
There is a mystery . . . . *Shakspeare* 517
True Dignity . . . . *Wordsworth* 520
Trust . . . . *Wordsworth* 521
Ulysses and Achilles . . . . *Shakspeare* 518

INDEX OF AUTHORS.

ADAMS, JOHN QUINCY.
Born in Quincy, Mass., 1767; *died* 1848.
The Wants of Man 280

ADDISON, JOSEPH.
Born in Wiltshire, Eng., 1672; *died* 1719.
The Spacious Firmament 180

AKENSIDE, MARK.
Born in Newcastle-upon-Tyne, 1721; *died* 1770.
Pleasures of Imagination 99

ALEXANDER, MRS.
Burial of Moses 290

ALLINGHAM, WILLIAM.
Born in Ireland.
Mary Donnelly 434
Morning 94
The Æolian Harp 130
The Bird 36
The Pilot's Daughter 77
The Sailor 436
The Touchstone 158

ARNOLD, MATTHEW.
Born in England, 1822.
Thyrsis 471

BARBAULD, ANNA LÆTITIA.
Born in Leicestershire, Eng., 1743; *died* 1825.
Life 169
Praise to God 183

BAILEY, PHILIP JAMES.
Born in Nottingham, Eng., 1816.
Forecast 153

BARNEFIELD, RICHARD.
Born in England.
The Nightingale 35

BARNES, WILLIAM.
Born in Dorsetshire.
The Peasant's Return 75

BARTLETT, GEORGE B.
Mignonette 515

BAYLEY, THOMAS HAYNES.
Born near Bath, Eng., 1797; *died* 1839.
Nightingale's Song 35

BEATTIE, JAMES.
Born in Scotland, 1735; *died* 1803.
Nature 3
Night 3

BEAUMONT AND FLETCHER.
Francis Beaumont born in Leicestershire, 1586; *died* 1616. *John Fletcher born in Northamptonshire*, 1576; *died in London*, 1625.
Bonduca 213
Love at First Sight 71
Poet's Mood 138
Song: "Shake off your heavy trance," 433
To Venus 72

BERKELEY, GEORGE.
Born in Ireland, 1684; *died* 1573.
Verse: "Westward the Star of Empire" 225

BLAKE, WILLIAM.
Born in London, 1757; *died* 1828.
Orthodoxy 158
The Sunflower 29
The Tiger 509

BOAR, ARTHUR.
The Breeding Lark 36

BORROW, GEORGE.
Born in England, 1803.
Svend Vonved 328

BROWNE, SIR THOMAS.
Born in London, 1605; *died* 1682.
Before Sleep 185

BROWNELL, HENRY HOWARD.
Born in Connecticut, 1820; *died* 1872.
The Bay Fight 248
The Old Cove 502

BROWNING, ELIZABETH BARRETT.
Born in London, 1809; *died in Florence*, 1861.
Lady Geraldine's Courtship . . . 366
Rhyme of the Duchess May . . 404
The Lady's Yes 64

BROWNING, ROBERT.
Born in Camberwell, near London, 1812.
A King 282
How they brought the Good News from Ghent to Aix 355
The Lost Leader 224

BRYANT, WILLIAM CULLEN.
Born in Cummington, Mass., 1794.
Death of the Flowers 29
Song of the Stars 44
Thanatopsis 168
The Murdered Traveller . . . 457
The Old Man's Funeral 167
The Rivulet. 25
To a Waterfowl 37
To the Fringed Gentian . . . 30

BURNS, ROBERT.
Born near Ayr, Scotland, 1759; *died* 1796.
Auld Lang Syne 439
Banks of Doon 447
Bannockburn 219
He's Gane 458
Holy Willie's Prayer 481
Honest Poverty 147
Inspiration 95
John Anderson, my Jo 438
Lament for James, Earl of Glencairn . 458
Lament of Mary, Queen of Scots . 456
Of a' the Airts the Wind can Blau . 442
Oh, my Luve's like a Red, Red Rose . 443
Scotland 220
Tam O' Shanter 484
The Cotter's Saturday Night . . . 53
The Good Heart 518
The Vision 219
To a Mountain Daisy 279
To a Mouse 278
To the Devil 483
To the Unco Guid 482
Winter 22
Winter Night 24
Writing Verses 95

BUTLER, SAMUEL.
Born in Worcestershire, 1612; *died in London*, 1680.
Puritans 501

BYRD, WILLIAM.
Born in England, about 1540; *died* 1623.
My Minde to me a Kingdom is . . 154

BYRON, GEORGE GORDON (LORD).
Born in London, 1788; *died in Greece*, 1824.
Destruction of Sennacherib 282
Fare Thee Well 277
Hurts of Time 138
Incantation, from Manfred . . 512
Island (The Sea Cave) 378
Jephthah's Daughter 203
Lachin y Gair 26
Love of England 277
Manfred 512
Murat 223
No More 278
Outward Bound 276
She Walks in Beauty 59
Siege and Conquest of Alhama . . 310
Siege of Corinth 284
Solitude 28
Song of Saul before his Last Battle . 203
Stanzas: "Though the day of" . 276
Sunset 42
Swimming 21
The Apparition 514
The Corsair 512
The Execution 284
The Gladiator 283
The Immortal Mind 172
The Island 377
The Prisoner of Chillon 283
The Rainbow 46
The Sea 39
The Skull 171
The Storm 42
Vision of Belshazzar 416
Waterloo 222

CALIDASA.
Supposed to have lived about 50 *B. C.*
The Babe (Sir William Jones's translation) 56
Woman (Prof. Wilson's translation) . 58

CAMPBELL, THOMAS.
Born in Glasgow, 1777; *died in Boulogne*, 1844.
Battle of the Baltic 220
Glenara 363
Hohenlinden 223
Hope 45
Lochiel's Warning 217
To the Rainbow 46
The Soldier's Dream 289
Ye Mariners of England 221

CANNING, GEORGE.
Born in London, 1770; *died in Chiswick*, 1827.
The Knife-Grinder 504

CAREW, THOMAS.
Born in Devonshire, Eng., 1589; *died* 1639.
Disdain Returned 446

CHANNING, WILLIAM ELLERY.
Born in Boston.
Memory 92
Sea Song 38
Sleepy Hollow 460
The Earth-Spirit 27
The Flight of the Wild Geese . . 37
The Hillside Cot 7
The Mountain 6
The Poet's Hope 153

CHAPMAN, GEORGE.
Born in England, 1557; *died in London*, 1634.
The Master Spirit 198
The Praise of Homer 93

CHATTERTON, THOMAS.
Born in Bristol, Eng., 1752; *died* 1770.
Bristowe Tragedy 343

CHAUCER, GEOFFREY.
Born in London, 1328; *died* 1400.
Ariadne 75
Destiny 152
Duchesse Blanche 60
Forecast 153
Fox and Cock 16
Gentility 83
Griselda 385
Prayer to Apollo 96
The Cuckow and the Nightingale . . 97
The Milky Way 45
The Poet 96
Virginia 67

CLARE, JOHN.
Born in England, 1793; *died* 1864.
The Laborer 456

CLARKE, JAMES FREEMAN.
Born in Boston.
Rabia (translation) 140

CLOUGH, ARTHUR HUGH.
Born in Liverpool, 1819; *died in Florence*, 1861.
Atheism 497
Bathing; from The Bothie of Tober na Vuolich 20
Qua Cursum Ventus 82

COFFIN, R. B.
Born in America.
Ships at Sea 122

COLERIDGE, SAMUEL TAYLOR.
Born in Devonshire, Eng., 1772; *died* 1834.
Character (trans. from Schiller) . . 154
Dirge: He is gone — is dust (trans. from Schiller) 459
Genevieve 73
Heroism (trans. from Schiller) . . 195
Kubla Khan 126
Mythology (trans. from Schiller) . 120

COLLINS, WILLIAM.
Born in Chichester, Eng., 1720; *died* 1756.
Dirge in Cymbeline 460
Ode: "How sleep the brave" . . 459
Ode on the Death of Thomson . . 462
Ode to Evening 43
The Passions 128

CONGREVE, WILLIAM.
Born near Leeds, Eng., 1670; *died* 1729.
The Cathedral 133

COWLEY, ABRAHAM.
Born in London, 1618; *died* 1667.
A Supplication 129
Epigram on Drake (trans. by Ben Jonson) 268

COWPER, WILLIAM.
Born in Hertfordshire, Eng., 1731; *died* 1800.
Boadicea 212
Dependence 182
Loss of "The Royal George" . . 463
My Mother's Picture 52
Providence 182
The Ice Palace 288

CRASHAW, RICHARD.
Born in England; died 1650.
Satan 179
Two went up into the Temple to Pray . 180

CUNNINGHAM, ALLAN.
Born in Blackwood, Scotland, 1784; *died* 1842.
Sea-Song: A wet sheet and a flowing sea 39
The Lily of Nithsdale 75
Thou hast sworn by thy God, my Jeanie, 66

DANIEL, SAMUEL.
Born in Taunton, Eng., 1562; *died* 1619.
Knowing the Heart of Man is set to be, 517
Love 446

DERBY, GEORGE H. (John Phœnix).
Born in Massachusetts.
A Collusion between a Alegaiter and a Water-Snaik 491

DONNE, JOHN.
Born in London, 1573; *died* 1631.
Elegy on Mistress Elizabeth Drury . 273
Ecstasy 70
Hymn to God, my God, in my Sickness, 186
Hymn to Christ 180
If Men be Worlds 517
Love 62
Oh, how feeble is Man's Power . . 517
The Recluse Hermit 517
The Undertaking 154

DORR, JULIA C. R.
Born in America.
Outgrown 64

DRAYTON, MICHAEL.
Born in England, 1563; *died* 1631.
The Harp 130

DRUMMOND, WILLIAM.
Born in Scotland, 1585; *died* 1649.
The Angels 190
The Shepherds 190

DRYDEN, JOHN.
Born in Northamptonshire, Eng., 1631; *died* 1700.
Alexander's Feast 130
St. Cecilia's Day 127
Under the Portrait of Milton . . 99

EMERSON, EDWARD BLISS.
Born in Boston, 1805; *died in Porto Rico*, 1834.
The Last Farewell 51

FERGUSSON, SAMUEL.
Born in Ireland, about 1805.
Forging of the Anchor 287

FROTHINGHAM, N. L.
Born in Boston, 1793; *died* 1870.
Translation of Goethe's Song of the Parcæ 510

GOWER, JOHN.
Born in England, 1320; *died* 1402.
Nebuchadnezzar 265

GRAY, THOMAS.
Born in London, 1716; *died* 1771.
Elegy Written in a Country Churchyard, 169
Eton College 148
The Bard 215

GREVILLE, FULKE (LORD BROOKE).
Born in England, 1554; *died* 1628.
On Sir Philip Sidney 467

HAMILTON, WILLIAM.
Born in Bangour, Scotland, 1704; *died* 1754.
Braes of Yarrow 412

HARTE, BRET.
Chicago 261
Chiquita 502
Her Letter 495
His Answer to her Letter . . . 496
Plain Language from Truthful James 504

HEBER, REGINALD.
Born in Cheshire, Eng., 1783; *died* 1826.
If thou wert by my side, my Love . . 53

HEDGE, FREDERIC H.
Born in Cambridge, Mass., 1805.
Questionings 91

HEMANS, FELICIA.
Born in Liverpool, Eng., 1794; *died* 1835.
Landing of the Pilgrim Fathers . . 225
Music 130
Nightingale's Death Song . . . 35
To Corinne 51

HERBERT, GEORGE.
Born in Wales in 1593; *died* 1632.
Affliction 184
Confession 150
Constancy 195
Easter 192
Gratefulness 184
Life 151
Man 143
Peace 157
Providence 182
Sin 159
The Church Porch 145
The Elixir 181
The Flower 95
The Pulley 144
The Quip 147
Virtue 147

HERBERT, EDWARD (LORD OF CHERBURY).
Born in London, 1591; *died* 1648.
Celinda 172

HERRICK, ROBERT.
Born in London, 1591; *died* 1674.
Argument of his Book 3
Christian Militant 198
Corinna's going a-Maying 10
Country Life 15
Dirge for Dorcas 461
Hymn to the Graces 86
Lachrimæ; or, Mirth turned to Mourning 455
Litany to the Holy Spirit 186
Matins 185
Night Piece to Julia 445
Not Every Day fit for Verse . . . 93
Ode to Ben Jonson 270
Prayer to Ben Jonson 269
Poetry of Dress 87
Star Song 190
The Primrose 32
The Rose 443
The White Island 123
To Blossoms 33
To Daffodills 33
To his Winding Sheet 458
To Live Merrily and to Trust to Good Verses 269
To Silvia 58

HEYWOOD, JOHN.
Born in England; died 1565.
The Portrait 65

HOGG, JAMES.
Born in Ettrick, Scotland, 1772; *died* 1835.
Kilmeny 120
The Witch of Fife 487

HOLMES, OLIVER WENDELL.
Born in Cambridge, Mass., 1809.
Contentment 499
Dorothy Q. 498
Never or Now 232
Old Ironsides 226
Rudolph the Headsman 503
The Deacon's Masterpiece; or, The Wonderful One-Hoss-Shay . 492
To George Peabody 282

HOWE, JULIA WARD.
Born in New York.
Battle Hymn of the Republic . . 230
The Flag 236

HUNT, LEIGH.
Born in Middlesex, Eng., 1784; *died* 1859.
Abou Ben Adhem 158
Song to Ceres 434

E. S. H.
The Chimney Sweep 339
The Nobly Born 518
The Wood Fire 56
Wayfarers 159

H. H.
Ariadne's Farewell 202
Coronation 202
Joy 157
My Legacy 176
Thought 91

INGELOW, JEAN.
Born in England, 1825.
Divided 80
Goldilocks 443
High Tide on the Coast of Lincolnshire 340
Winstanley 322
Wreck of the "Grace of Sunderland" 320

JONES, SIR WILLIAM.
Born in London, 1746; *died* 1794.
Narayena, Spirit of God (translation) . 180
The Babe (translation from Calidasa) . 56

JONSON, BEN.
Born in London, 1574; *died* 1637.
Chivalry 199
Epigram 269
Epigram (trans.) 268

JONSON, BEN (*continued*).
Epistle to a Friend to Persuade Him to the Wars 196
Epitaph: "Underneath this sable hearse" 269
Epitaph: "Underneath this stone doth lye" 268
Fame 101
Fantasy 123
Freedom in Dress 87
May 9
Masque of Pleasure and Virtue . . 433
Nature 3
Ode to Himself 93
On Lucy, Countess of Bedford . . 268
Song: "How near to good is what is fair" 87
Song: "The owl is abroad" . . . 125
Song of Echo 441
Song: "See the chariot at hand" . 73
Song: "Spring all the graces of the age" 434
To Celia 445
To the Countess of Rutland . . . 269
To William Sidney, on his Birthday 269

KEATS, JOHN.
Born in London, 1796; *died* 1820.
Hyperion: "As heaven and earth are fairer" 143
Hyperion (Music) 128
Hyperion (Saturn, as he walked into the midst) 518
Hyperion (Thea) 509
On First Looking into Chapman's Homer 94
The Nightingale 34

KEMBLE, MRS. FRANCES ANNE.
Born in London, about 1811.
Faith 518

KNOWLES, HERBERT.
Born in England.
Written in the Churchyard of Richmond, Yorkshire . . . 167

LANDOR, WALTER SAVAGE.
Born in Warwickshire, Eng., 1775; *died* 1864
Inscription on a Sea-Shell . . . 40

LARCOM, LUCY.
Born in Massachusetts.
A Loyal Woman's No 248

LEWIS, DAVID.
Lines to Alexander Pope 272

LINDSAY, LADY ANNE.
Born in Scotland, 1750: *died in London,* 1825.
Auld Robin Gray 383

LOCKHART, JOHN GIBSON.
Born in Glasgow, Scotland, 1792: *died* 1854.
Bridal of Andalla 447
Garci Perez de Vargas 300

LODGE, THOMAS.
Born in England, 1556; *died* 1625.
Rosaline 72

LOGAN, JOHN.
Born in Scotland, 1748; *died* 1788.
The Braes of Yarrow 456

LONGFELLOW, HENRY WADSWORTH.
Born in Portland, Me., 1807.
Agassiz, on the Fiftieth Birthday of . 280
Life 149
Santa Filomena 280
The Birds of Killingworth . . . 11
The Children's Hour 57
The Cumberland 239
The Warden of the Cinque Ports . 224

LOVELACE, RICHARD.
Born in Kent, Eng., 1618; *died* 1658.
To Althea 445
To Lucasta 63
The Grasshopper 16

LOWELL, JAMES RUSSELL.
Born in Cambridge, Mass., 1819.
Commemoration Ode 258
Hosea Biglow's Lament 476
Mason and Slidell 234
Origin of Didactic Poetry 483
Sunthin' in a Pastoral Line . . . 240
The Courtin' 494
The Washers of the Shroud . . . 237

LOWELL, ROBERT T. S.
Born in Boston, Mass., 1816.
The Relief of Lucknow 311

LUNT, GEORGE.
Born in Newburyport, Mass., 1803.
Requiem: "Breathe, trumpets, breathe" 257

MACDONALD, GEORGE.
Born in Scotland.
The Earl o' Quarterdeck . . . 318

MARVELL, ANDREW.
Born in England, 1620; *died* 1678.
A Drop of Dew 47
Cromwell and King Charles . . . 219
The Garden 25
The Nymph Mourning her Fawn . 455
Song of the Emigrants in Bermuda . 41

MELLEN, GRENVILLE.
Born in America, 1799; *died* 1841.
Bunker Hill 226
Entrance of Columbus into Barcelona 225

MESSINGER, ROBERT HINCKLEY.
Born in Boston, Mass., about 1807.
Give me the Old 57

MICKLE, WILLIAM JULIUS.
Born in Dumfries-shire, Scotland, 1734; *died* 1788.
There's Nae Luck about the House . 437

MILNES, RICHARD MONCKTON (LORD HOUGHTON).
Born in Yorkshire, Eng., 1809.
Humility 145
The Palm and the Pine 289

MILTON, JOHN.
Born in London, 1608; *died* 1674.
Christmas Hymn 187
Comus 104
Epitaph on Shakspeare 268
Il Penseroso 18
L'Allegro 4
Lycidas 467
Samson Agonistes 199
Song: "Sweet Echo" 441
On His being Arrived at the Age of Twenty-three 270
Sonnet on his Blindness 271
Sonnet on the Late Massacre in Piemont 195
Sonnet to Sir Harry Vane . . . 271
To Be no More 169
When the Assault was intended to the City 274

MITCHEL, WALTER.
Born in America.
Tacking Ship off Shore 40

MONTGOMERY, JAMES.
Born in Irvine, Scotland, 1771; *died* 1834.
The Sun-Dial 151

MONTROSE (JAMES GRAHAME), MARQUIS OF.
Born in Montrose, Scotland, 1612; *executed* 1650.
I'll never Love Thee more . . . 63

MOORE, THOMAS.
Born in Dublin, 1779; *died* 1852.
Araby's Daughter 435
Canadian Boat-Song 436
Harp that once through Tara's Halls . 435
Lake of the Dismal Swamp . . 335
Love's Young Dream 446
Oft in the Stilly Night 438
Song of Fionnuala 126
To Campbell 276
The Caliph's Encampment . . . 286

MORE, HENRY.
Born in Grantham, Eng., 1614; *died* 1687.
Euthanasia 173
Love and Humility 176

MORRIS, WILLIAM.
Born in England.
Song from Jason: "I know a little garden close" 442

MORSE, SIDNEY H.
Born in America.
Sundered 82

MOTHERWELL, WILLIAM.
Born in Scotland, 1797; *died* 1835.
Jeanie Morrison 438

PALFREY, SARA H. [E. FOXTON.]
Born in America.
Sir Pavon and Saint Pavon . . 417

PATMORE, COVENTRY.
Born in Essex, Eng., 1823.
Honoria 59
Sentences 76
The Queen 63
The Rose of the World . . . 58
The Tribute 66
Wisdom 146

PERCIVAL, JAMES GATES.
Born in Berlin, Conn., 1795; *died* 1856.
The Coral Grove 39

PERCY'S RELIQUES.
Heir of Linne 307
King John and the Abbot of Canterbury 352

POLLOK, ROBERT.
Born in Renfrewshire, Scotland, 1799; *died* 1827.
The Ocean 38

POPE, ALEXANDER.
Born in London, 1688; *died* 1744.
Man of Ross 272
Portrait of Addison 271

LONDON PUNCH.
Abraham Lincoln 254
A Greeting to the "George Griswold," 227
Fight over the Dead Body of Keitt . 500

RALEIGH, SIR WALTER.
Born in Budleigh, Eng., 1552; *beheaded* 1618.
Pilgrimage 160
The Soul's Errand. 139

RANDALL JAMES R.
Maryland 230

ROYDON, MATTHEW.
On Sir Philip Sidney 268

SANBORN, F. B.
Born in America.
Anathemata 59
River Song 442
Ode written for the Consecration of Sleepy Hollow Cemetery . . 462

SCHILLER (see COLERIDGE).
Born in Germany.

SCOTT, SIR WALTER.
Born in Edinburgh, 1771; *died* 1832.
Allen-a-Dale 363
Alice Brand 334
A Weary Lot is Thine 448
Battle of Harlaw 301
Beware 517
Bonny Dundee 449
Brignall Banks 449
Bruce and the Abbot 415
Child Dyring 336
Clan Alpine 450
Coronach 461
County Guy 442
Defiance 218
Dreams 122
Fair Helen 411
Fitz Travers' Song 364
Friar of Orders Gray 349
Græme and Bewick 350
Helvellyn 326
Kinmont Willie 301
Lochinvar 356
Pibroch of Donuil Dhu 450
Rosabelle 414
The Dying Bard 451
The Gay Goss-Hawk 361
The Mass 349
Wild Huntsman 330

SHAKSPEARE, WILLIAM.
Born in Stratford-on-Avon, Eng., 1564; *died* 1616.
Antony and the Soothsayer . . . 519
Antony over the Dead Body of Cæsar . 205
Ariel's Song 440
Art and Nature 132
Battle of St. Crispian's Day . . . 211
Blow, Blow, thou Winter Wind . 439
Bolingbroke's Entrance into London 285
Cassius 203
Clarence's Dream 511
Cleopatra 283
Cleopatra's Resolution 521
Come Away, Come Away, Death . 439
Common Sense 76
Compliment to Queen Elizabeth . 124
Coriolanus 265
Courage 520
Crime 510
Dawn 5
Dover Cliffs 8
Each and All 520
Fear no More the Heat o' the Sun 461
Firmness 521
Flowers 29
Fop 286
Foresight 92
Full Fathoms Five thy Father Lies . 441
Good Omens 152
Guidance 521

SHAKSPEARE, WILLIAM (*continued.*)

Hamlet's Soliloquy 160
Hark, Hark, the Lark! 441
Henry V. 267
Henry V.'s Audience of French Ambassadors 210
Hesitation 512
Hotspur 208
Hotspur's Quarrel with Henry IV. . 207
Human Life 521
Inborn Royalty 83
I See Men's Judgments 511
King Lear 102
King Richard's Soliloquy . . . 211
Life and Death 161
Macbeth is Ripe for Shaking . . . 510
Merciful Heaven! 511
Moonlight 43
Morning 6
Mother's Blessing 520
Nestor to Hector 265
Night 34
Opportunity 517
Oracle: "Mine honesty and I" . . 521
Oracle: "The flighty purpose" . . 520
Oracle: "There is a mystery in the," 517
Oracle: "There is a history" . . 517
Oracle: "We must not stint" . . . 521
Orpheus with his Lute 127
Othello's Defence 69
Othello's Last Words 476
Outward and Inward Bound . . 40
Prayers 159
Phœnix and Turtle-Dove 123
Queen Mab 125
Remorse 510
Revolutions 152
Romeo's Presage 122
Seven Ages 151
Sleep 160
Sonnet: "From you have I been absent" 133
Sonnet: "Full many a glorious morning" 6
Sonnet: "How oft when thou my music" 73
Sonnet: "Let me not to the marriage," 77
Sonnet: "Oh, for my sake" . . 271
Sonnet: "Oh, how much more doth". 133
Sonnet: "So am I as the rich" . . 78
Sonnet: "To me, fair friend" . . 86
Sonnet: "When I do count the clock" 86
Speech of the Dauphin 207
Take, O Take those Lips away . . 444
Tell me where is Fancy Bred . . 441
The Black Prince 266
The Gods are Just 511
This Army Led by a Delicate and Tender Prince 512
To Beguile Time 510
True Love 62
Ulysses and Achilles 518
Under the Greenwood Tree . . . 440
Viola Disguised, and the Duke . . 68
When Daisies Pied and Violets Blue . 440
When we in our Viciousness grow Hard, 510

SHELLEY, PERCY BYSSHE.

Born in Sussex, Eng., 1792; *died* 1822.

The Cloud 46
To the Skylark 36

SHIRLEY, JAMES.

Born in London, about 1594; *died* 1666.

Death's Final Conquest 167

SIDNEY, SIR PHILIP.

Born in Penhurst Kent, Eng., 1554; *died* 1586.

Psalm XCIII. 178
Psalm CXXXIX. 178
Psalm XCVI. 181

SIMONIDES.

Born in Julis, Island of Ceos, B.C. 554.

Epitaph 463

SOUTHWELL, ROBERT.

Born in England, 1556; *executed* 1595.

New Prince, New Pomp 191
The Burning Babe 191

SPENSER, EDMUND.

Born in London, 1553; *died* 1599.

Beauty 84
House of Busyrane 293
Spenser at Court 267
The Bride 67
Trees 30
Una and the Lion 85

SPOFFORD, HARRIET PRESCOTT.

Born in America.

The Night Sea 448

SPRAGUE, CHARLES.

Born in Boston, Mass., 1791.

The Indians 225
The Ocean 38

STEDMAN, EDMUND CLARENCE.

Born in America.

John Brown of Osawatomie . . . 227

STERLING, JOHN,

Born in the Island of Bute, 1806; *died* 1844.

Alfred the Harper 298
Dædalus 132

STERNHOLD, THOMAS.

Born in England; died 1549.

Psalm XVIII. 182

STRODE, WILLIAM.

Born in England, 1600; *died* 1644.

Music 127

SUCKLING, SIR JOHN.

Born in Whitton, Eng., 1609; *died* 1641.

Moods 139
The Bride 68

SWIFT, JONATHAN.
Born in Dublin, 1667; *died* 1745.
Jove and the Souls 502

TAYLOR, HENRY.
Born in England, about 1800.
Athulf and Ethilda 70

TAYLOR, TOM.
Born in England, 1817.
Abraham Lincoln 254

TENNYSON, ALFRED.
Born in Lincolnshire, Eng., 1810.
Bugle Song 441
Christmas 192
Crowning of Arthur 296
Death of the Old Year 24
Eagle, The 38
Gate of Camelot 294
Hero to Leander 448
In the Fight 223
Lady Clara Vere de Vere 365
Lady Clare 381
Landscape 9
Locksley Hall 134
Maud 72
Maud: "The Garden Song" . . . 444
Memory 92
Ode on the Death of the Duke of Wellington 464
Œnone; or, the Choice of Paris . . 375
The Deserted House 457
The Prayer 198
Tithonus 165
To the Critic 133
Ulysses 101

C. S. T.
The Poet 95

TERSTEEGEN, GERHARD (see JOHN WESLEY).
Born in Westphalia, Germany, 1697.

THOMSON, JAMES.
Born in Roxburghshire, Scotland, 1700; *died* 1748.
Lost in the Snow 23
The Nightingale 34

THOREAU, HENRY DAVID.
Born in Concord, Mass., 1817; *died* 1862.
Haze 48
Inspiration 94
Mist 48
Smoke 47
Sympathy 78

TIMROD, HENRY.
Born 1829; *died in South Carolina*, 1867.
Ode sung on the Occasion of decorating the Graves of the Confederate Dead, at Magnolia Cemetery, Charleston, S.C. 258

TUCKERMAN, FREDERIC GORDON.
Born in 1821; *died* 1873.
Rhotruda 357

TROWBRIDGE, J. T.
Born in New York, 1827.
At Sea 48

VAUGHAN, HENRY.
Born in Newton, Eng., 1621; *died* 1695.
The Retreat 173

VERY, JONES.
Born in Salem, Mass., about 1812.
The Barberry-Bush 32
The Strangers 159

WALLER, EDMUND.
Born in Colehill, Eng., 1605; *died* 1687.
Apology for having Loved Before . . 63
Go, Lovely Rose 443
On a Girdle 73
My Charmer 87

WARTON, THOMAS.
Born in Basingstoke, Eng., 1728; *died* 1687.
The Fairies 126

WASSON, DAVID A.
Born in America.
Love against Love 83
Royalty 198

WATTS, ISAAC.
Born in Southampton, Eng., 1674; *died* 1748.
Hymn: "Lord, when I quit this earthly stage" 185

WEBSTER, DANIEL.
Born in Salisbury, N.H., 1782; *died* 1852.
Lines Written in a Lady's Album . 281

WESLEY, JOHN.
Born in Lincolnshire, Eng., 1703; *died* 1795.
Translation of Tersteegen's Divine Love 177
Moravian Hymn 178

WHITE, JOSEPH BLANCO.
Born in Spain, about 1773; *died in England*, 1840.
Night and Death 44

WHITE, HENRY KIRKE.
Born in Nottingham, Eng., 1785; *died* 1806.
To the Herb Rosemary 32

WHITTIER, JOHN GREENLEAF.
Born in Haverhill, Mass., 1808.

Amy Wentworth 380
At Port Royal 231
Ichabod 227
Skipper Ireson's Ride 304
Telling the Bees 414
The Playmate 79
What the Birds said 246

WILKINSON, JAMES JOHN GARTH.
Born in London, about 1812.

The Diamond 34
Turner 509

WILLIS, NATHANIEL PARKER.
Born in Portland, Me., 1807; *died* 1867.

Lines on Leaving Europe 51
To a Child 57

WILSON, JOHN.
Born in Scotland, 1785; *died* 1854.

Translation of Calidasa's Woman . 58

WILLSON, FORCEYTHE.
Born in Little Genesee, N. Y., 1837; *died in Alfred Centre, N. Y.*, 1867.

In State 255

WITHER, GEORGE.
Born in Bentworth, Eng., 1588; *died* 1667.

The Manly Heart 446
The Muse 96

WOLFE, CHARLES.
Born in Ireland, 1791; *died* 1823.

Burial of Sir John Moore 466

WORDSWORTH, WILLIAM.
Born in Cockermouth, Eng., 1770; *died* 1850.

Cave of Staffa 42
Christmas Carol 191
Daffodils 33
Departed 471
Dion 475
English Channel 144
Fidelity 326
First of May 9
Flowers at the Cave of Staffa . . . 42
Home 51
Honor 144
Immortality 173
Laodamia 162
Liberty 33
Lines written on Tidings of the Approaching Death of Charles James Fox 463
Lucy 62
Morning in the Mountains 8

WORDSWORTH, WILLIAM (*continued*).

Ode to Duty 149
Osmunda Regalis 32
Outline 102
Pass of Kirkstone 28
Rob Roy's Grave 274
Scale of Minds 98
Schill 222
September, 1819 34
Skating 22
Snow 22
Sonnet: "Alas! what boots the long." 221
Sonnet: "It is not to be thought of" 223
Steamboats, Viaducts, and Railways . 98
The Boy of Egremond 339
The Boy Poet 27
The Evening Star 44
The Happy Warrior 196
The Skeptic 152
Thought of a Briton on the Subjugation of Switzerland 221
Tintern Abbey 29
To Milton 274
To the Skylark 36
To Joanna 17
True Dignity 520
Trust 521
Yew-Trees 31

WOTTON, SIR HENRY.
Born in England, 1568; *died* 1639.

Elizabeth of Bohemia 66
The Happy Life 146

YOUNG, EDWARD.
Born in Hampshire, Eng., 1684; *died* 1765.

Penitence 180
Sleep 160
Socrates 94

ANONYMOUS.

Boatie Rows 437
Children in the Wood 337
Come Morir 166
Epitaph from Simonides 463
Fair Annie (Scott's version) . . . 384
George Nidiver 327
George Washington 226
Glenlogie (Smith's Scottish Minstrelsy) 360
Inscription on a Wall in St. Edmund's Church in Lombard Street, London 162
Inscription in the Parish Church in Faversham in Agro Cantiano . 162
Inscription in Melrose Abbey . . . 161
Lykewake Dirge 459
Sir Andrew Barton (old ballads) . 312
Sir Patrick Spens (old ballads) . . 317
Song of the Tonga-Islanders . . . 380
That each Thing is Hurt of Itself . . 154
The Consolers 150
The Cosmic Egg 505
The Drowned Lovers (Buchan) . . . 321
The Sally from Coventry 354
The Shield 150
Waly, Waly, but Love be Bonny (tea-table miscellany) 383
William of Cloudeslé 306

I.

NATURE.

LAND. — SEA. — SKY.

"Nature the vicar of the Almightie Lord." — CHAUCER.

NATURE.

ARGUMENT OF HIS BOOK.

I SING of brooks, of blossoms, birds, and bowers,
Of April, May, of June, and July-flowers;
I sing of May-poles, hock-carts, wassails, wakes,
Of bride-grooms, brides, and of their bridal-cakes.
I write of youth, of love, and have access
By these, to sing of cleanly wantonness;
I sing of dews, of rains, and, piece by piece,
Of balm, of oil, of spice, and ambergrece.
I sing of times trans-shifting; and I write
How roses first came red, and lilies white.
I write of groves, of twilights, and I sing
The court of Mab, and of the fairie king.
I write of Hell; I sing, and ever shall,
Of Heaven, and hope to have it after all.

HERRICK.

NATURE.

O HOW canst thou renounce the boundless store
Of charms which Nature to her votary yields!
The warbling woodland, the resounding shore,
The pomp of groves, and garniture of fields;
All that the genial ray of morning gilds,
And all that echoes to the song of even,
All that the mountain's sheltering bosom shields,
And all the dread magnificence of heaven,
O how canst thou renounce, and hope to be forgiven!

JAMES BEATTIE.

NIGHT.

'TIS night, and the landscape is lovely no more;
I mourn, but, ye woodlands, I mourn not for you;
For morn is approaching, your charms to restore,
Perfumed with fresh fragrance, and glittering with dew:
Nor yet for the ravage of winter I mourn;
Kind Nature the embryo blossom will save,
But when shall spring visit the mouldering urn!
O when shall day dawn on the night of the grave!

JAMES BEATTIE.

NATURE.

How young and fresh am I to-night,
To see't kept day by so much light,
And twelve of my sons stand in their Maker's sight!
Help, wise Prometheus, something must be done,
To show they are the creatures of the sun.
That each to other
Is a brother,
And Nature here no stepdame, but a mother.

Come forth, come forth, prove all the numbers then,
That make perfection up, and may absolve you men.
But show thy winding ways and arts,
Thy risings, and thy timely starts
Of stealing fire from ladies' eyes and hearts.
Those softer circles are the young man's heaven,
And there more orbs and planets are than seven.
To know whose motion
Were a notion
As worthy of youth's study, as devotion.
Come forth, come forth! prove all the time will gain,
For Nature bids the best, and never bade in vain.

BEN JONSON.

L'ALLEGRO.

HENCE, loathed Melancholy,
Of Cerberus and blackest Midnight born!
In Stygian cave forlorn,
'Mongst horrid shapes, and shrieks, and sights unholy,
Find out some uncouth cell,
Where brooding Darkness spreads his jealous wings,
And the night-raven sings;
There under ebon shades, and low-brow'd rocks,
As ragged as thy locks,
In dark Cimmerian desert ever dwell.
But come, thou Goddess fair and free,
In heav'n y-clep'd Euphrosyne,
And by men, heart-easing Mirth,
Whom lovely Venus at a birth,
With two sister Graces more,
To ivy-crowned Bacchus bore;
Or whether (as some sager sing)
The frolic wind that breathes the spring,
Zephyr with Aurora playing,
As he met her once a-Maying;
There on beds of violets blue,
And fresh-blown roses washed in dew,
Fill'd her with thee, a daughter fair,
So buxom, blithe, and debonair.
Haste thee, Nymph, and bring with thee
Jest, and youthful Jollity,
Quips, and Cranks, and wanton Wiles,
Nods, and Becks, and wreathèd Smiles,
Such as hang on Hebe's cheek,
And love to live in dimple sleek;
Sport that wrinkled Care derides,
And Laughter holding both his sides.
Come, and trip it as ye go,
On the light fantastic toe;
And in thy right hand lead with thee
The mountain nymph, sweet Liberty;
And if I give thee honor due,
Mirth, admit me of thy crew,
To live with her, and live with thee,
In unreprovèd pleasures free;
To hear the lark begin his flight,
And singing startle the dull night
From his watch-tower in the skies,
Till the dappled dawn doth rise;
Then to come in spite of sorrow,
And at my window bid good morrow,
Through the sweetbrier, or the vine,
Or the twisted eglantine:
While the cock with lively din
Scatters the rear of Darkness thin,
And to the stack, or the barn-door,
Stoutly struts his dames before:
Oft listening how the hounds and horn
Cheerly rouse the slumbering morn,
From the side of some hoar hill,
Through the high wood echoing shrill:
Some time walking, not unseen,
By hedge-row elms, on hillocks green,
Right against the eastern gate,
Where the great sun begins his state,
Robed in flames, and amber light,
The clouds in thousand liveries dight;
While the ploughman near at hand
Whistles o'er the furrowed land,
And the milkmaid singeth blithe,
And the mower whets his scythe,
And every shepherd tells his tale
Under the hawthorn in the dale.
Straight mine eye hath caught new pleasures
Whilst the landscape round it measures;
Russet lawns, and fallows gray,
Where the nibbling flocks do stray;
Mountains, on whose barren breast
The laboring clouds do often rest;
Meadows trim with daisies pied,
Shallow brooks, and rivers wide;

Towers and battlements it sees
Bosomed high in tufted trees,
Where perhaps some beauty lies,
The cynosure of neighboring eyes;
Hard by, a cottage chimney smokes,
From betwixt two aged oaks,
Where Corydon and Thyrsis met,
Are at their savory dinner set
Of herbs, and other country messes,
Which the neat-handed Phillis dresses;
And then in haste her bow'r she leaves,
With Thestylis to bind the sheaves;
Or, if the earlier season lead,
To the tann'd haycock in the mead.
Sometimes with secure delight
The upland hamlets will invite,
When the merry bells ring round,
And the jocund rebecs sound
To many a youth, and many a maid,
Dancing in the checker'd shade;
And young and old come forth to play
On a sunshine holiday,
Till the livelong daylight fail.
Then to the spicy nut-brown ale,
With stories told of many a feat,
How fairy Mab the junkets eat;
She was pincht and pull'd, she said,
And he by friar's lanthorn led,
Tells how the drudging Goblin sweat,
To earn his cream-bowl duly set,
When in one night, ere glimpse of morn,
His shadowy flail hath thresh'd the corn
That ten day-laborers could not end;
Then lies him down the lubbar fiend,
And stretch'd out all the chimney's length,
Basks at the fire his hairy strength,
And crop-full out of doors he flings,
Ere the first cock his matin rings.
Thus done the tales, to bed they creep,
By whispering winds soon lull'd asleep.
Tower'd cities please us then,
And the busy hum of men,
Where throngs of knights and barons bold
In weeds of peace high triumphs hold,
With store of ladies, whose bright eyes
Rain influence, and judge the prize
Of wit, or arms, while both contend
To win her grace whom all commend.
There let Hymen oft appear
In saffron robe, with taper clear,
And pomp, and feast, and revelry,
With mask, and antique pageantry,
Such sights as youthful poets dream
On summer eves by haunted stream.
Then to the well-trod stage anon,
If Jonson's learned sock be on,
Or sweetest Shakspeare, Fancy's child,
Warble his native wood-notes wild.
  And ever against eating cares,
Lap me in soft Lydian airs,
Married to immortal verse,
Such as the meeting soul may pierce,
In notes, with many a winding bout
Of linkèd sweetness long drawn out,
With wanton heed, and giddy cunning,
The melting voice through mazes running,
Untwisting all the chains that tie
The hidden soul of harmony;
That Orpheus' self may heave his head
From golden slumber on a bed
Of heapt Elysian flowers, and hear
Such strains as would have won the ear
Of Pluto, to have quite set free
His half regain'd Eurydice.
  These delights if thou canst give,
Mirth, with thee I mean to live.

MILTON.

DAWN.

Juliet.—Wilt thou be gone? It is not yet near day,
It was the nightingale, and not the lark,
That pierced the fearful hollow of thine ear:
Nightly she sings on yon pomegranate tree:
Believe me, love, it was the nightingale.

Romeo.—It was the lark, the herald of the morn,
No nightingale: look, love, what envious streaks
Do lace the severing clouds in yonder east:

Night's candles are burnt out, and jocund day
Stands tiptoe on the misty mountain-tops;
I must be gone and live, or stay and die.

SHAKSPEARE.

MORNING.

THIS castle hath a pleasant seat; the air
Nimbly and sweetly recommends itself
Unto our gentle senses.

This guest of summer,
The temple-haunting martlet, does approve,
By his lov'd mansionry, that the heaven's breath
Smells wooingly here: no jutty, frieze, buttress,
Nor coigne of vantage, but this bird hath made
His pendent bed, and procreant cradle: Where they
Most breed and haunt, I have observ'd the air
Is delicate.

SHAKSPEARE: *Macbeth.*

SONNET.

FULL many a glorious morning have I seen
Flatter the mountain-tops with sovereign eye,
Kissing with golden face the meadows green,
Gilding pale streams with heavenly alchemy.
Anon permit the basest clouds to ride
With ugly rack on his celestial face,
And from the forlorn world his visage hide,
Stealing unseen to west with this disgrace:
Even so my sun one early morn did shine
With all triumphant splendor on my brow;
But out! alack! he was but one hour mine,
The region cloud hath mask'd him from me now.
Yet him for this my love no whit disdaineth;
Suns of the world may stain, when heaven's sun staineth.

SHAKSPEARE.

THE MOUNTAIN.

. . . ONCE we built our fortress where you see
Yon group of spruce-trees sidewise on the line
Where the horizon to the eastward bounds, —
A point selected by sagacious art,
Where all at once we viewed the Vermont hills,
And the long outlines of the mountain-ridge,
Ever-renewing, changeful every hour.
Strange, a few cubits raised above the plain,
And a few tables of resistless stone
Spread round us, with that rich delightful air,
Draping high altars in cerulean space,
Could thus enchant the being that we are!
Those altars, where the airy element
Flows o'er in new perfection, and reveals
Its constant lapsing (never stillness all),
As a mother's kiss, touching the bright spruce-foliage;
And in her wise distilment the soft rain,
Trickling below the sphagnum that o'erlays
The plateau's slope, is led to the ravine,
And so electrified by her pure breath,
As if in truth the living water famed
Recorded in John's mythus, who first dashed
Ideal baptism on Jordan's shore.

In this sweet solitude, the Mountain's life,
At morn and eve, at rise and hush of day,
I heard the wood-thrush sing in the white spruce.
The living water, the enchanted air

So mingling in its crystal clearness there
A sweet, peculiar grace from both, — this song,
Voice of the lonely mountain's favorite bird!
These steeps inviolate by human art,
Centre of awe, raised over all that man
Would fain enjoy, and consecrate to one,
Lord of the desert and of all beside,
Consorting with the cloud, the echoing storm,
When like a myriad bowls the mountain wakes
In all its alleys one responsive roar;
And sheeted down the precipice, all light
Tumble the momentary cataracts, —
The sudden laughter of the mountain-child.

. . . .

On the mountain-peak
I marked the sage at sunset, where he mused,
Forth looking on the continent of hills;
While from his feet the five long granite spurs
That bind the centre to the valley's side,
(The spokes from this strange middle to the wheel)
Stretched in the fitful torrent of the gale,
Bleached on the terraces of leaden cloud
And passages of light, — Sierras long
In archipelagoes of mountain sky,
Where it went wandering all the livelong year.
He spoke not, yet methought I heard him say,
"All day and night the same; in sun or shade,
In summer flames, and the jagged, biting knife
That hardy winter splits upon the cliff, —
From earliest time the same.
One mother and one father brought us forth
Thus gazing on the summits of the days,
Nor wearied yet when generations fade.
The crystal air, the hurrying light, the night,
Always the day that never seems to end,
Always the night whose day does never set;
One harvest and one reaper, ne'er too ripe,
Sown by the self-preserver, free from mould,
And builded in these granaries of heaven,
This ever-living purity of air,
In these perpetual centres of repose
Still softly rocked."

W. E. Channing.

THE HILLSIDE COT.

And here the hermit sat, and told his beads,
And stroked his flowing locks, red as the fire,
Summed up his tale of moon and sun and star:
"How blest are we," he deemed, "who so comprise
The essence of the whole, and of ourselves,
As in a Venice flask of lucent shape,
Ornate of gilt Arabic, and inscribed
With Suras from Time's Koran, live and pray,
More than half grateful for the glittering prize,
Human existence! If I note my powers,
So poor and frail a toy, the insect's prey,
Itched by a berry, festered by a plum,
The very air infecting my thin frame
With its malarial trick, whom every day
Rushes upon and hustles to the grave,
Yet raised by the great love that broods o'er all
Responsive, to a height beyond all thought."
He ended as the nightly prayer and fast
Summoned him inward. But I sat and heard

The night-hawks rip the air above my head,
Till midnight, o'er the warm, dry, dewless rocks;
And saw the blazing dog-star droop his fire,
And the low comet, trailing to the south,
Bend his reverted gaze, and leave us free.

CHANNING.

"HERE let us live and spend away our lives,"
Said once Fortunio, "while below, absorbed,
The riotous careering race of man,
Intent on gain or war, pour out their news.
Let us bring in a chosen company,
Like that the noblest of our beauteous maids
Might lead, — unequalled Margaret, herself
The summary of good for all our state;
Composedly thoughtful, genial, yet reserved,
Pure as the wells that dot the ravine's bed,
And lofty as the stars that pierce her skies.
Here shall she reign triumphant, and preside
With gentle prudence o'er the camp's wild mood,
Summoning forth much order from what else
Surely must prove unsound."

CHANNING.

MORNING IN THE MOUNTAINS.

O THEN what soul was his, when, on the tops
Of the high mountains, he beheld the sun
Rise up, and bathe the world in light! He looked —
Ocean and earth, the solid frame of earth
And ocean's liquid mass, beneath him lay
In gladness and deep joy. The clouds were touched,
And in their silent faces did he read
Unutterable love. Sound needed none,
Nor any voice of joy; his spirit drank
The spectacle; sensation, soul, and form
All melted into him; they swallowed up
His animal being; in them did he live,
And by them did he live; they were his life.
In such access of mind, in such high hour
Of visitation from the living God,
Thought was not; in enjoyment it expired.
No thanks he breathed, he proffered no request;
Rapt into still communion that transcends
The imperfect offices of prayer and praise,
His mind was a thanksgiving to the power
That made him; it was blessedness and love.

WORDSWORTH.

DOVER CLIFFS.

COME on, sir; here's the place: — stand still. — How fearful
And dizzy 'tis, to cast one's eye so low!
The crows and choughs, that wing the midway air,
Show scarce so gross as beetles: half way down
Hangs one that gathers samphire; dreadful trade!
Methinks he seems no bigger than his head:
The fishermen, that walk upon the beach,
Appear like mice; and yond' tall anchoring bark
Diminish'd to her cock; her cock, a buoy
Almost too small for sight: the murmuring surge,
That on the unnumber'd idle pebbles chafes,
Cannot be heard so high: — I'll look no more;
Lest my brain turn, and the deficient sight
Topple down headlong.

SHAKSPEARE.

LANDSCAPE.

CALM and still light on yon great plain
That sweeps with all its autumn bowers,
And crowded farms and lessening towers,
To mingle with the bounding main.

TENNYSON.

MAY.

WHENCE is it that the air so sudden clears,
And all things in a moment turn so mild?
Whose breath or beams have got proud Earth with child
Of all the treasure that great Nature's worth,
And makes her every minute to bring forth?
How comes it winter is so quite forced hence
And locked up under ground? That every sense
Hath several objects, trees have got their heads,
The fields their coats, that now the shining meads
Do boast the paunce, the lily, and the rose,
And every flower doth laugh as Zephyr blows?
That seas are now more even than the land;
The rivers run as smoothèd by his hand;
Only their heads are crispèd by his stroke.
How plays the yearling, with his brow scarce broke,
Now in the open grass, and frisking lambs
Make wanton salts about their dry-sucked dams,
Who to repair their bags do rob the fields.
How is't each bough a several music yields?
The lusty throstle, early nightingale,
Accord in tune though vary in their tale.
The chirping swallow, called forth by the sun,
And crested lark, doth his division run.
The yellow bees the air with murmur fill,
The finches carol and the turtles bill;—
Whose power is this? What god? Behold a King,
Whose presence maketh this perpetual spring,
The glories of which spring grow in that bower,
And are the marks and beauties of his power.

BEN JONSON.

FIRST OF MAY.

WHILE from the purpling east departs
  The star that led the dawn,
Blithe Flora from her couch upstarts,
  For May is on the lawn.
A quickening hope, a freshening glee,
  Foreran the expected power,
Whose first-drawn breath, from bush and tree,
  Shakes off that pearly shower.

All Nature welcomes her whose sway
  Tempers the year's extremes;
Who scattereth lustres o'er noonday,
  Like morning's dewy gleams;
While mellow warble, sprightly trill,
  The tremulous heart excite;
And hums the balmy air to still
  The balance of delight.

Time was, blest Power! when youths and maids
  At peep of dawn would rise,
And wander forth, in forest glades
  Thy birth to solemnize.
Though mute the song — to grace the rite
  Untouched the hawthorn bough,
Thy spirit triumphs o'er the slight;
  Man changes, but not thou!

Thy feathered lieges bill and wings
  In love's disport employ.
Warmed by thy influence, creeping things
  Awake to silent joy:

Queen art thou still for each gay plant
Where the slim wild deer roves;
And served in depths where fishes haunt
Their own mysterious groves.

. . . .

And if, on this thy natal morn,
The pole, from which thy name
Hath not departed, stands forlorn
Of song and dance and game,
Still from the village-green a vow
Aspires to thee addrest,
Wherever peace is on the brow,
Or love within the breast.

Yes! where love nestles thou canst teach
The soul to love the more;
Hearts also shall thy lessons reach
That never loved before.
Stript is the haughty one of pride,
The bashful freed from fear,
While rising, like the ocean-tide,
In flows the joyous year.

Hush, feeble lyre! weak words, refuse
The service to prolong!
To yon exulting thrush the Muse
Intrusts the imperfect song;
His voice shall chant, in accents clear,
Throughout the livelong day,
Till the first silver star appear,
The sovereignty of May.

Wordsworth.

CORINNA'S GOING A-MAYING.

Get up, get up, for shame; the blooming Morn
Upon her wings presents the god unshorn.
See how Aurora throws her fair
Fresh-quilted colors through the air;
Get up, sweet slug-a-bed, and see
The dew bespangling herb and tree.
Each flower has wept, and bow'd toward the east,
Above an hour since, yet you not drest,
Nay! not so much as out of bed;
When all the birds have matins said,
And sung their thankful hymns; 'tis sin,
Nay, profanation to keep in,
When as a thousand virgins on this day
Spring, sooner than the lark, to fetch in May.

Rise, and put on your foliage, and be seen
To come forth, like the spring-time fresh and green,
And sweet as Flora. Take no care
For jewels for your gowne or haire;
Feare not, the leaves will strew
Gems in abundance upon you;
Besides, the childhood of the day has kept,
Against you come, some orient pearls unwept.
Come, and receive them while the light
Hangs on the dew-locks of the night;
And Titan on the eastern hill
Retires himself, or else stands stiil
Till you come forth. Wash, dresse, be briefe in praying;
Few beads are best, when once we go a-Maying.

Come, my Corinna, come; and coming, mark
How each field turns a street, each street a park
Made green, and trimm'd with trees; see how
Devotion gives each house a bough,
Or branch; each porch, each doore, ere this,
An ark, a tabernacle is,
Made up of white-thorn neatly interwove;
As if here were those cooler shades of love.
And sin no more, as we have done, by staying;
But, my Corinna, come, let's go a-Maying.

Herrick.

THE BIRDS OF KILLINGWORTH.

It was the season when through all the land
The merle and mavis build, and building sing
Those lovely lyrics written by His hand
Whom Saxon Cædmon calls the Blithe-heart King;
When on the boughs the purple buds expand,
The banners of the vanguard of the Spring;
And rivulets, rejoicing, rush and leap,
And wave their fluttering signals from the steep.

The robin and the bluebird, piping loud,
Filled all the blossoming orchards with their glee;
The sparrows chirped as if they still were proud
Their race in Holy Writ should mentioned be;
And hungry crows, assembled in a crowd,
Clamored their piteous prayer incessantly,
Knowing who hears the ravens cry, and said,
"Give us, O Lord, this day our daily bread!"

Across the Sound the birds of passage sailed,
Speaking some unknown language, strange and sweet
Of tropic isle remote, and, passing, hailed
The village with the cheers of all their fleet;
Or, quarrelling together, laughed and railed
Like foreign sailors landed in the street
Of seaport town, and with outlandish noise
Of oaths and gibberish frightening girls and boys.

Thus came the jocund Spring in Killingworth,
In fabulous days, some hundred years ago;
And thrifty farmers, as they tilled the earth,
Heard with alarm the cawing of the crow,
That mingled with the universal mirth,
Cassandra-like, prognosticating woe:
They shook their heads, and doomed with dreadful words
To swift destruction the whole race of birds.

And a town-meeting was convened straightway
To set a price upon the guilty heads
Of these marauders, who, in lieu of pay,
Levied black-mail upon the garden-beds
And cornfields, and beheld without dismay
The awful scarecrow, with his fluttering shreds, —
The skeleton that waited at their feast,
Whereby their sinful pleasure was increased.

Then from his house, a temple painted white,
With fluted columns, and a roof of red,
The Squire came forth, — august and splendid sight! —
Slowly descending, with majestic tread,
Three flights of steps, nor looking left nor right,
Down the long street he walked, as one who said,
"A town that boasts inhabitants like me
Can have no lack of good society."

The Parson, too, appeared, a man austere,
The instinct of whose nature was to kill;
The wrath of God he preached from year to year,
And read with fervor Edwards on the Will:
His favorite pastime was to slay the deer
In summer on some Adirondack hill:

E'en now, while walking down the rural lane,
He lopped the wayside lilies with his cane.

From the Academy, whose belfry crowned
The Hill of Science with its vane of brass,
Came the Preceptor, gazing idly round,
Now at the clouds, and now at the green grass,
And all absorbed in reveries profound
Of fair Almira in the upper class,
Who was, as in a sonnet he had said,
As pure as water, and as good as bread.

And next the Deacon issued from his door,
In his voluminous neck-cloth, white as snow;
A suit of sable bombazine he wore:
His form was ponderous, and his step was slow;
There never was so wise a man before:
He seemed the incarnate "Well, I told you so!"
And to perpetuate his great renown,
There was a street named after him in town.

These came together in the new town-hall,
With sundry farmers from the region round:
The Squire presided, dignified and tall,
His air impressive and his reasoning sound.
Ill fared it with the birds, both great and small;
Hardly a friend in all that crowd they found,
But enemies enough, who every one
Charged them with all the crimes beneath the sun.

When they had ended, from his place apart
Rose the Preceptor, to redress the wrong,
And, trembling like a steed before the start,
Looked round bewildered on the expectant throng;
Then thought of fair Almira, and took heart
To speak out what was in him, clear and strong,
Alike regardless of their smile or frown,
And quite determined not to be laughed down.

"Plato, anticipating the reviewers,
From his republic banished without pity
The poets: in this little town of yours,
You put to death, by means of a committee,
The ballad-singers and the troubadours,
The street-musicians of the heavenly city,
The birds, who make sweet music for us all
In our dark hours, as David did for Saul.

"The thrush, that carols at the dawn of day
From the green steeples of the piny wood;
The oriole in the elm; the noisy jay,
Jargoning like a foreigner at his food;
The bluebird balanced on some topmost spray,
Flooding with melody the neighborhood;
Linnet and meadow-lark, and all the throng
That dwell in nests, and have the gift of song, —

"You slay them all! and wherefore? For the gain
Of a scant handful, more or less, of wheat,
Or rye, or barley, or some other grain,
Scratched up at random by industrious feet
Searching for worm or weevil after rain,
Or a few cherries, that are not so sweet
As are the songs these uninvited guests
Sing at their feast with comfortable breasts.

"Do you ne'er think what wondrous beings these?
Do you ne'er think who made them, and who taught
The dialect they speak, where melodies
Alone are the interpreters of thought?
Whose household words are songs in many keys,
Sweeter than instrument of man e'er caught!
Whose habitations in the tree-tops even
Are half-way houses on the road to heaven!

"Think, every morning when the sun peeps through
The dim, leaf-latticed windows of the grove,
How jubilant the happy birds renew
Their old melodious madrigals of love!
And when you think of this, remember, too,
'Tis always morning somewhere, and above
The awakening continents, from shore to shore,
Somewhere the birds are singing evermore.

"Think of your woods and orchards without birds!
Of empty nests that cling to boughs and beams,
As in an idiot's brain remembered words
Hang empty 'mid the cobwebs of his dreams!
Will bleat of flocks or bellowing of herds
Make up for the lost music, when your teams
Drag home the stingy harvest, and no more
The feathered gleaners follow to your door?

"What! would you rather see the incessant stir
Of insects in the windrows of the hay,
And hear the locust and the grasshopper
Their melancholy hurdy-gurdies play?
Is this more pleasant to you than the whirr
Of meadow-lark, and its sweet roundelay,
Or twitter of little fieldfares, as you take
Your nooning in the shade of bush and brake?

"You call them thieves and pillagers; but know
They are the wingèd wardens of your farms,
Who from the cornfields drive the insidious foe,
And from your harvests keep a hundred harms;
Even the blackest of them all, the crow,
Renders good service as your man-at-arms,
Crushing the beetle in his coat of mail,
And crying havoc on the slug and snail.

"How can I teach your children gentleness,
And mercy to the weak, and reverence
For Life, which, in its weakness or excess,
Is still a gleam of God's omnipotence,
Or Death, which, seeming darkness, is no less
The selfsame light, although averted hence,
When by your laws, your actions, and your speech,
You contradict the very things I teach?"

With this he closed; and through the audience went
A murmur like the rustle of dead leaves;
The farmers laughed and nodded, and some bent
Their yellow heads together like their sheaves:
Men have no faith in fine-spun sentiment
Who put their trust in bullocks and in beeves.
The birds were doomed; and, as the record shows,
A bounty offered for the head of crows.

There was another audience out of reach,
  Who had no voice nor vote in making laws,
But in the papers read his little speech,
  And crowned his modest temples with applause:
They made him conscious, each one more than each,
  He still was victor, vanquished in their cause:
Sweetest of all the applause he won from thee,
O fair Almira at the Academy!

And so the dreadful massacre began:
  O'er fields and orchards, and o'er woodland crests,
The ceaseless fusillade of terror ran.
  Dead fell the birds, with blood-stains on their breasts,
Or wounded crept away from sight of man,
  While the young died of famine in their nests:
A slaughter to be told in groans, not words,
The very St. Bartholomew of birds!

The Summer came, and all the birds were dead;
  The days were like hot coals; the very ground
Was burned to ashes: in the orchards fed
  Myriads of caterpillars, and around
The cultivated fields and garden-beds
  Hosts of devouring insects crawled, and found
No foe to check their march, till they had made
The land a desert without leaf or shade.

Devoured by worms, like Herod, was the town,
  Because, like Herod, it had ruthlessly
Slaughtered the Innocents. From the trees spun down
  The canker-worms upon the passers-by, —
Upon each woman's bonnet, shawl, and gown,
  Who shook them off with just a little cry:
They were the terror of each favorite walk,
The endless theme of all the village-talk.

The farmers grew impatient; but a few
  Confessed their error, and would not complain;
For, after all, the best thing one can do,
  When it is raining, is to let it rain.
Then they repealed the law, although they knew
  It would not call the dead to life again:
As school-boys, finding their mistake too late,
Draw a wet sponge across the accusing slate.

That year in Killingworth the Autumn came
  Without the light of his majestic look,
The wonder of the falling tongues of flame,
  The illumined pages of his Dooms-Day Book.
A few lost leaves blushed crimson with their shame,
  And drowned themselves despairing in the brook,
While the wild wind went moaning everywhere,
Lamenting the dead children of the air.

But the next Spring, a stranger sight was seen,
  A sight that never yet by bard was sung,
As great a wonder as it would have been,
  If some dumb animal had found a tongue:
A wagon overarched with evergreen,
  Upon whose boughs were wicker cages hung,
All full of singing-birds, came down the street,
Filling the air with music, wild and sweet.

From all the country round these birds were brought
  By order of the town, with anxious quest,

And, loosened from their wicker prison, sought
In woods and fields the places they loved best,
Singing loud canticles, which many thought
Were satires to the authorities addressed;
While others, listening in green lanes, averred
Such lovely music never had been heard.

But blither still and louder carolled they
Upon the morrow, for they seemed to know
It was the fair Almira's wedding-day;
And everywhere, around, above, below,
When the Preceptor bore his bride away,
Their songs burst forth in joyous overflow,
And a new heaven bent over a new earth
Amid the sunny farms of Killingworth.

LONGFELLOW.

THE COUNTRY LIFE.

SWEET country life, to such unknown,
Whose lives are others, not their own;
But, serving courts and cities, be
Less happy, less enjoying thee.
Thou never plough'st the ocean's foame
To seek and bring rough pepper home;
Nor to the Eastern Ind dost rove
To bring from thence the scorched clove;
Nor, with the loss of thy loved rest,
Bring'st home the ingot from the west:
No, thy ambitious masterpiece
Flies no thought higher than a fleece;
Or to pay thy hinds, and cleere
All scores, and so to end the yeare:
But walk'st about thine own dear bounds,
Not envying others' larger grounds;
For well thou know'st, 'tis not the extent
Of land makes life, but sweet content.
When now the cock, the ploughman's horne,
Calls forth the lily-wristed morne;
Then to thy cornfields thou dost go,
Which, though well soyl'd, yet thou dost know,
That the best compost for the lands
Is the wise master's feet and hands:
There at the plough thou find'st thy teame,
With a hind whistling there to them;
And cheer'st them up, by singing how
The kingdom's portion is the plough;
This done, then to the enameled meads
Thou go'st, and as thy foot there treads,
Thou seest a present godlike power
Imprinted in each herbe and flower;
And smell'st the breath of great-eyed kine,
Sweet as the blossoms of the vine:
Here thou behold'st thy large sleek neat
Unto the dew-laps up in meat;
And as thou look'st, the wanton steere,
The heifer, cow, and oxe draw neare,
To make a pleasing pastime there:
These seen, thou go'st to view thy flocks
Of sheep, safe from the wolf and fox,
And find'st their bellies there as full
Of short sweet grass, as backs with wool;
And leav'st them, as they feed and fill,
A shepherd piping on a hill.
For sports, for pageantrie, and playes,
Thou hast thy eves and holydayes;
On which the young men and maids meet
To exercise their dancing feet,
Tripping the comely country round,
With daffodils and daisies crowned.
Thy wakes, thy quintels, here thou hast,
Thy May-poles, too, with garlands grac't,
Thy morris-dance, thy Whitsun ale,
Thy shearing-feast, which never faile,

Thy harvest home, thy wassail bowle,
That's tost up after fox i' th' hole,
Thy mummeries, thy twelf-tide kings
And queenes, thy Christmas revellings,
Thy nut-browne mirth, thy russet wit,
And no man pays too deare for it:
To these thou hast thy times to goe,
And trace the hare i' th' treacherous snow;
Thy witty wiles to draw and get
The larke into the trammel net;
Thou hast thy cockrood and thy glade
To take the precious pheasant made;
Thy lime-twigs, snares, and pit-falls then
To catch the pilfering birds, not men.
O happy life! if that their good
The husbandmen but understood;
Who all the day themselves do please,
And younglings with such sports as these;
And, lying down, have nought to affright
Sweet sleep, that makes more short the night.

HERRICK.

FOX AND COCK.

Now wol I turn unto my tale agen.
The silly widow and her doughtren two,
Herden these hennés cry and maken wo,
And out of dorés sterten they anon,
And saw the fox toward the wode is gon,
And bare upon his back the cock away:
They criden out! "Harow and wala wa!
A ha! the fox!" and after him they ran,
And eke with stavés many another man;
Ran Colle our dog, and Talbot, and Gerlond;
And Malkin, with her distaf in her hond;
Ran cow and calf, and eke the very hogges
So feared were for barking of the dogges.
And shouting of the men and women eke,
They ronnen so, them thought hir hertes breke.
They yelleden as fendés don in Helle:
The dokès crieden as men wold hem quelle:
The gees for fere flewen over the trees,
Out of the hive came the swarme of bees,
So hideous was the noise, a benedicite!
Certes he Jakke Straw, and his meinie,
Ne maden never shoutés half so shrill,
When that they wolden any Fleming kill,
As thilké day was made upon the fox.
Of brass they broughten beemés and of box,
Of horn and bone, in which they blew and pouped,
And therwithal they shriekèd and they houped;
It seemed, as the Heven shuldé falle.

CHAUCER: *Nuns' Priest's Tale.*

THE GRASSHOPPER.

TO MY NOBLE FRIEND, MR. CHARLES COTTON.

ODE.

O THOU that swing'st upon the waving ear
Of some well-filled oaten beard,
Drunk every night with a delicious tear
Dropt thee from heaven, where now thou art reared.

The joys of earth and air are thine entire
That with thy feet and wings dost hop and fly,
And when thy poppy works thou dost retire,
To thy carved acorn-bed to lie.

Up with the day, the Sun thou welcom'st then,
Sport'st in the gilt plaits of his beams,
And all these merry days mak'st merry men
Thyself and melancholy streams.

But ah! the sickle! golden ears are cropt;
Ceres and Bacchus bid good-night;
Sharp frosty fingers all your flowers have topt,
And what scythes spared winds shave off quite.

Poor verdant fool! and now green ice, thy joys
Large and as lasting as thy perch of grass
Bid us lay in 'gainst winter rain, and poise
Their floods with an o'erflowing glass.

Thou best of men and friends, we will create
A genuine summer in each other's breast;
And spite of this cold time and frozen fate,
Thaw us a warm seat to our rest.

Our sacred hearths shall burn eternally
As vestal flames; the North-wind, he
Shall strike his frost-stretched wings, dissolve, and fly
This Ætna in epitome.

Dropping December shall come weeping in,
Bewail th' usurping of his reign;
But when in showers of old Greek* we begin,
Shall cry, he hath his crown again!

Night as clear Hesper shall our tapers whip
From the light casements where we play,
And the dark hag from her black mantle strip,
And stick there everlasting day.

Thus richer than untempted kings are we,
That asking nothing, nothing need;
Though lord of all what seas embrace, yet he
That wants himself is poor indeed.

RICHARD LOVELACE.

* Greek wine.

TO JOANNA.

As it befell,
One summer morning we had walked abroad
At break of day, Joanna and myself.
'Twas that delightful season when the broom,
Full-flowered, and visible on every steep,
Along the copses runs in veins of gold.
Our pathway led us on to Rotha's banks;
And when we came in front of that tall rock
That eastward looks, I there stopped short, and stood
Tracing the lofty barrier with my eye
From base to summit; such delight I found
To note in shrub and tree, in stone and flower,
That intermixture of delicious hues,
In one impression, by connecting force
Of their own beauty, imaged in the heart.
When I had gazed perhaps two minutes' space,
Joanna, looking in my eyes, beheld
That ravishment of mine, and laughed aloud.
The Rock, like something starting from a sleep,
Took up the Lady's voice, and laughed again;
That ancient Woman seated on Helm-crag
Was ready with her cavern; Hammar-scar,
And the tall Steep of Silver-how, sent forth
A noise of laughter; southern Loughrigg heard,
And Fairfield answered with a mountain tone;
Helvellyn far into the clear blue sky

Carried the Lady's voice, — old Skiddaw blew
His speaking-trumpet; back out of the clouds
Of Glaramara southward came the voice;
And Kirkstone tossed it from his misty head.
"Now whether" (said I to our cordial friend,
Who in the hey-day of astonishment
Smiled in my face), "this were in simple truth
A work accomplished by the brotherhood
Of ancient mountains, or my ear was touched
With dreams and visionary impulses
To me alone imparted, sure I am
That there was a loud uproar in the hills."
And while we both were listening, to my side
The fair Joanna drew, as if she wished
To shelter from some object of her fear.
And hence long afterwards, when eighteen moons
Were wasted, as I chanced to walk alone
Beneath this rock, at sunrise, on a calm
And silent morning, I sat down, and there,
In memory of affections old and true,
I chiselled out in those rude characters
Joanna's name deep in the living stone;
And I and all who dwell by my fireside
Have called the lovely rock, "Joanna's Rock."

WORDSWORTH.

IL PENSEROSO.

HENCE, vain deluding joys,
The brood of Folly without father bred,
How little you bestead,
Or fill the fixed mind with all your toys!
Dwell in some idle brain,
And fancies fond with gaudy shapes possess,
As thick and numberless
As the gay motes that people the sunbeams,
Or likest hovering dreams
The fickle pensioners of Morpheus' train.
But hail thou Goddess, sage and holy,
Hail divinest Melancholy,
Whose saintly visage is too bright
To hit the sense of human sight,
And therefore to our weaker view
O'erlaid with black, staid Wisdom's hue;
Black, but such as in esteem
Prince Memnon's sister might beseem,
Or that starr'd Ethiop queen that strove
To set her beauty's praise above
The Sea-Nymphs, and their powers offended:
Yet thou art higher far descended;
Thee bright-hair'd Vesta, long of yore,
To solitary Saturn bore;
His daughter she (in Saturn's reign,
Such mixture was not held a stain).
Oft in glimmering bowers and glades
He met her, and in secret shades
Of woody Ida's inmost grove,
While yet there was no fear of Jove.
Come, pensive Nun, devout and pure,
Sober, steadfast, and demure,
All in a robe of darkest grain,
Flowing with majestic train,
And sable stole of cyprus-lawn,
Over thy decent shoulders drawn.
Come, but keep thy wonted state,
With even step, and musing gait,
And looks commercing with the skies,
Thy rapt soul sitting in thine eyes:
There held in holy passion still,
Forget thyself to marble, till
With a sad leaden downward cast
Thou fix them on the earth as fast:
And join with thee calm Peace, and Quiet,
Spare Fast, that oft with Gods doth diet,
And hears the Muses in a ring
Aye round about Jove's altar sing:
And add to these retired Leisure,
That in trim gardens takes his pleasure;
But first, and chiefest, with thee bring,

Him that yon soars on golden wing,
Guiding the fiery-wheeled throne,
The Cherub Contemplation;
And the mute Silence hist along,
'Less Philomel will deign a song,
In her sweetest, saddest plight,
Smoothing the rugged brow of night,
While Cynthia checks her dragon yoke,
Gently o'er th' accustomed oak;
Sweet bird, that shunn'st the noise of folly,
Most musical, most melancholy!
Thee, chauntress, oft the woods among
I woo, to hear thy even-song;
And missing thee, I walk unseen
On the dry smooth-shaven green,
To behold the wandering moon,
Riding near her highest noon,
Like one that had been led astray
Through the heav'n's wide pathless way;
And oft, as if her head she bow'd,
Stooping through a fleecy cloud.
Oft on a plat of rising ground,
I hear the far-off curfew sound,
Over some wide-water'd shore,
Swinging slow with sullen roar;
Or, if the air will not permit,
Some still removèd place will fit,
Where glowing embers through the room
Teach light to counterfeit a gloom;
Far from all resort of mirth,
Save the cricket on the hearth,
Or the bellman's drowsy charm,
To bless the doors from nightly harm:
Or let my lamp at midnight hour
Be seen in some high lonely tow'r,
Where I may oft outwatch the Bear,
With thrice-great Hermes, or unsphere
The spirit of Plato, to unfold
What worlds, or what vast regions hold
The immortal mind, that hath forsook
Her mansion in this fleshly nook:
And of those Demons that are found
In fire, air, flood, or under ground,
Whose power hath a true consent
With planet, or with element.
Sometime let gorgeous Tragedy
In sceptred pall come sweeping by,
Presenting Thebes, or Pelops' line,
Or the tale of Troy divine,
Or what (though rare) of later age
Ennobled hath the buskin'd stage.
But, O sad Virgin, that thy power
Might raise Musæus from his bower,
Or bid the soul of Orpheus sing
Such notes as warbled to the string,
Drew iron tears down Pluto's cheek,
And made Hell grant what love did seek.
Or call up him that left half told
The story of Cambuscan bold,
Of Camball, and of Algarsife,
And who had Canacé to wife,
That own'd the virtuous ring and glass,
And of the wondrous horse of brass,
On which the Tartar king did ride;
And if aught else great bards beside,
In sage and solemn tunes have sung,
Of turneys and of trophies hung,
Of forests, and enchantments drear,
Where more is meant than meets the ear.
Thus Night oft see me in thy pale career,
Till civil-suited Morn appear,
Not trick'd and frounc'd as she was wont
With the Attic boy to hunt,
But kerchiefed in a comely cloud,
While rocking winds are piping loud,
Or usher'd with a shower still,
When the gust hath blown his fill,
Ending on the rustling leaves,
With minute drops from off the eaves.
And when the sun begins to fling
His flaring beams, me, Goddess, bring
To archèd walks of twilight groves,
And shadows brown that Sylvan loves
Of pine, or monumental oak,
Where the rude axe with heavèd stroke
Was never heard the Nymphs to daunt,
Or fright them from their hallow'd haunt.
There in close covert by some brook,
Where no profaner eye may look,
Hide me from day's garish eye,
While the bee with honied thigh,
That at her flowery work doth sing,
And the waters murmuring
With such consort as they keep,

Entice the dewy-feather'd Sleep;
And let some strange mysterious dream
Wave at his wings in aery stream
Of lively portraiture display'd,
Softly on my eyelids laid.
And as I wake, sweet music breathe
Above, about, or underneath,
Sent by some Spirit to mortals good,
Or the unseen Genius of the wood.
But let my due feet never fail
To walk the studious cloisters pale,
And love the high embowèd roof,
With antique pillars massy proof,
And storied windows richly dight,
Casting a dim religious light:
There let the pealing organ blow,
To the full voic'd quire below,
In service high, and anthems clear,
As may with sweetness, through mine ear,
Dissolve me into ecstasies,
And bring all heav'n before mine eyes.
And may at last my weary age
Find out the peaceful hermitage,
The hairy gown and mossy cell,
Where I may sit and rightly spell
Of every star that heav'n doth show,
And every herb that sips the dew;
Till old experience do attain
To something like prophetic strain.
These pleasures Melancholy give,
And I with thee will choose to live.

MILTON.

FROM THE BOTHIE OF TOBER NA VUOLICH.

THERE is a stream, I name not its name, lest inquisitive tourist
Hunt it, and make it a lion, and get it at last into guide-books,
Springing far off from a loch unexplored in the folds of great mountains,
Falling two miles through rowan and stunted alder, enveloped
Then for four more in a forest of pine, where broad and ample
Spreads, to convey it, the glen with heathery slopes on both sides:
Broad and fair the stream, with occasional falls and narrows;
But, where the glen of its course approaches the vale of the river,
Met and blocked by a huge interposing mass of granite,
Scarce by a channel deep-cut, raging up and raging onward,
Forces its flood through a passage so narrow a lady would step it,
There, across the great rocky wharves, a wooden bridge goes,
Carrying a path to the forest; below, three hundred yards, say
Lower in level some twenty-five feet, through flats of shingle,
Stepping-stones and a cart-track cross in the open valley.
But in the interval here the boiling, pent-up water
Frees itself by a final descent, attaining a basin,
Ten feet wide and eighteen long, with whiteness and fury
Occupied partly, but mostly pellucid, pure, a mirror;
Beautiful there for color derived from green rocks under;
Beautiful, most of all, where beads of foam uprising
Mingle their clouds of white with the delicate hue of the stillness.
Cliff over cliff for its sides, with rowan and pendent birch-boughs,
Here it lies, unthought of above at the bridge and pathway,
Still more enclosed from below by wood and rocky projection.
You are shut in, left alone with yourself and perfection of water,
Hid on all sides, left alone with yourself and the goddess of bathing.
Here, the pride of the plunger, you stride the fall and clear it;
Here, the delight of the bather, you roll in beaded sparklings,
Here into pure green depth drop down from lofty ledges.
Hither, a month agone, they had come, and discovered it; hither
(Long a design, but long unaccountably left unaccomplished),
Leaving the well-known bridge and pathway above to the forest,
Turning below from the track of the carts over stone and shingle,

Piercing a wood, and skirting a narrow and natural causeway
Under the rocky wall that hedges the bed of the streamlet,
Rounded a craggy point, and saw on a sudden before them
Slabs of rock, and a tiny beach, and perfection of water,
Picture-like beauty, seclusion sublime, and the goddess of bathing.
There they bathed, of course, and Arthur, the glory of headers,
Leapt from the ledges with Hope, he twenty feet, he thirty;
There, overbold, great Hobbes from a ten-foot height descended,
Prone, as a quadruped, prone with hands and feet protending;
There in the sparkling champagne, ecstatic, they shrieked and shouted.
"Hobbes's gutter," the Piper entitles the spot, profanely,
Hope "the Glory" would have, after Arthur, the glory of headers:
But, for before they departed, in shy and fugitive reflex
Here in the eddies and there did the splendor of Jupiter glimmer,
Adam adjudged it the name of Hesperus, star of the evening.
Hither, to Hesperus, now, the star of evening above them,
Come in their lonelier walk the pupils twain and Tutor;
Turned from the track of the carts, and passing the stone and shingle,
Piercing the wood, and skirting the stream by the natural causeway,
Rounded the craggy point, and now at their ease looked up; and
Lo, on the rocky ledge, regardant, the Glory of headers,
Lo, on the beach, expecting the plunge, not cigarless, the Piper.—
And they looked, and wondered, incredulous, looking yet once more.
Yes, it was he, on the ledge, bare-limbed, an Apollo, down-gazing,
Eying one moment the beauty, the life, ere he flung himself in it,
Eying through eddying green waters the green tinting floor underneath them,
Eying the bead on the surface, the bead, like a cloud, rising to it,
Drinking in, deep in his soul, the beautiful hue and the clearness,
Arthur, the shapely, the brave, the unboasting, the glory of headers;
Yes, and with fragrant weed, by his knapsack, spectator and critic,
Seated on slab by the margin, the Piper, the Cloud-compeller.

CLOUGH.

SWIMMING.

How many a time have I
Cloven, with arm still lustier, breast more daring,
The wave all roughened; with a swimmer's stroke
Flinging the billows back from my drenched hair,
And laughing from my lip the audacious brine,
Which kissed it like a wine-cup, rising o'er
The waves as they arose, and prouder still
The loftier they uplifted me; and oft,
In wantonness of spirit, plunging down
Into their green and glassy gulfs, and making
My way to shells and seaweed, all unseen
By those above, till they waxed fearful; then
Returning with my grasp full of such tokens
As showed that I had searched the deep; exulting,
With a far-dashing stroke, and drawing deep
The long-suspended breath, again I spurned
The foam which broke around me, and pursued
My track like a sea-bird.—I was a boy then.

BYRON.

SKATING.

— In the frosty season, when the sun
Was set, and, visible for many a mile,
The cottage windows through the twilight blazed,
I heeded not the summons: happy time
It was indeed for all of us; for me
It was a time of rapture. Clear and loud
The village clock tolled six. I wheel'd about,
Proud and exulting, like an untired horse
That cares not for its home. All shod with steel,
We hiss'd along the polish'd ice in games
Confederate, imitative of the chase
And woodland pleasures, — the resounding horn,
The pack loud-bellowing, and the hunted hare.
So through the darkness and the cold we flew,
And not a voice was idle: with the din
Meanwhile the precipices rang aloud;
The leafless trees and every icy crag
Tingled like iron; while the distant hills
Into the tumult sent an alien sound
Of melancholy, not unnoticed, while the stars,
Eastward, were sparkling clear, and in the west
The orange sky of evening died away.

Not seldom from the uproar I retired
Into a silent bay, or sportively
Glanced sideway, leaving the tumultuous throng,
To cut across the image of a star
That gleam'd upon the ice; and oftentimes,
When we had given our bodies to the wind,
And all the shadowy banks on either side
Came sweeping through the darkness, spinning still
The rapid line of motion, then at once
Have I, reclining back upon my heels,
Stopp'd short; yet still the solitary cliffs
Wheel'd by me, even as if the earth had roll'd
With visible motion her diurnal round.
Behind me did they stretch in solemn train,
Feebler and feebler, and I stood and watch'd
Till all was tranquil as a summer sea.

WORDSWORTH.

WINTER. — A DIRGE.

THE wintry west extends his blast,
  And hail and rain does blaw;
Or the stormy north sends driving forth
  The blinding sleet and snaw:
While tumbling brown, the burn comes down,
  And roars frae bank to brae;
And bird and beast in covert rest,
  And pass the heartless day.

"The sweeping blast the sky o'ercast,"
  The joyless winter-day,
Let others fear, to me more dear
  Than all the pride of May;
The tempest's howl, it soothes my soul,
  My griefs it seems to join;
The leafless trees my fancy please,
  Their fate resembles mine!

Thou Power Supreme, whose mighty scheme
  These woes of mine fulfil,
Here, firm, I rest. they must be best,
  Because they are thy will.
Then all I want (oh, do thou grant
  This one request of mine!)
Since to enjoy thou dost deny,
  Assist me to resign!

BURNS.

SNOW.

FLEET the Tartar's reinless steed,
But fleeter far the pinions of the wind,
Which from Siberia's caves the monarch freed,

And sent him forth, with squadrons of his kind,
And bade the snow their ample backs bestride,
And to the battle ride:
No pitying voice commands a halt,
No courage can repel the dire assault:
Distracted, spiritless, benumbed, and blind,
Whole legions sink, and, in an instant, find
Burial and death: look for them, and descry,
When morn returns, beneath the clear blue sky,
A soundless waste, a trackless vacancy!

WORDSWORTH.

LOST IN THE SNOW.

THE snows arise; and, foul and fierce,
All winter drives along the darkened air:
In his own loose-revolving fields the swain
Disastered stands; sees other hills ascend,
Of unknown joyless brow; and other scenes,
Of horrid prospect, shag the trackless plain:
Nor finds the river, nor the forest, hid
Beneath the formless wild, but wanders on
From hill to dale, still more and more astray:
Impatient flouncing through the drifted heaps,
Stung with the thoughts of home; the thoughts of home
Rush on his nerves, and call their vigor forth
In many a vain attempt. How sinks his soul!
What black despair, what horror, fills his heart!
When, for the dusky spot which fancy feigned
His tufted cottage rising through the snow,
He meets the roughness of the middle waste,
Far from the track, and bless'd abode of man;
While round him night resistless closes fast,
And every tempest, howling o'er his head,
Renders the savage wilderness more wild.
Then throng the busy shapes into his mind,
Of covered pits unfathomably deep,
A dire descent! beyond the power of frost;
Of faithless bogs; of precipices huge,
Smoothed up with snow; and what is land unknown,
What water, of the still unfrozen spring,
In the loose marsh or solitary lake,
Where the fresh fountain from the bottom boils.
These check his fearful steps; and down he sinks
Beneath the shelter of the shapeless drift,
Thinking o'er all the bitterness of death;
Mixed with the tender anguish Nature shoots
Through the wrung bosom of the dying man,
His wife, his children, and his friends unseen.
In vain for him th'officious wife prepares
The fire fair-blazing, and the vestment warm;
In vain his little children, peeping out
Into the mingling storm, demand their sire,
With tears of artless innocence. Alas!
Nor wife, nor children, more shall he behold;
Nor friends, nor sacred home. On every nerve
The deadly Winter seizes; shuts up sense,
And, o'er his inmost vitals creeping cold,
Lays him along the snows a stiffened corse,
Stretched out, and bleaching in the northern blast.

THOMSON.

A WINTER NIGHT.

When biting Boreas, fell and doure,
Sharp shivers thro' the leafless bow'r;
When Phœbus gies a short-liv'd glow'r
Far south the lift,
Dim dark'ning thro' the flaky show'r,
Or whirlin' drift:

Ae night the storm the steeples rocked,
Poor labor sweet in sleep was locked,
While burns, wi' snawy wreaths up-chocked,
Wild-eddying swirl,
Or thro' the mining outlet bocked,
Down headlong hurl.

Listening, the doors an' winnocks rattle.
I thought me on the ourie cattle,
Or silly sheep, wha bide this brattle
O' winter war,
And thro' the drift, deep-lairing sprattle
Beneath a scar.

Ilk happing bird, wee, helpless thing,
That, in the merry months o' spring,
Delighted me to hear thee sing,
What comes o' thee?
Whare wilt thou cow'r thy chitt'ring wing,
An' close thy e'e?

E'en you on murd'ring errands toil'd,
Lone from your savage homes exiled,
The blood-stained roost, and sheep-cote spoiled,
My heart forgets,
While pitiless the tempest wild
Sore on you beats.

Now Phœbe, in her midnight reign,
Dark muffled, viewed the dreary plain;
Still crowding thoughts, a pensive train,
Rose in my soul,
While on my ear this plaintive strain,
Slow, solemn, stole:—

"O ye! who, sunk in beds of down,
Feel not a want but what yourselves create,
Think for a moment on his wretched fate,
Whom friends and fortune quite disown!
Ill satisfied keen Nature's clamorous call,
Stretched on his straw, he lays himself to sleep,
While thro' the ragged roof and chinky wall,
Chill o'er his slumbers piles the drifty heap!"

. . : . . . .

I heard nae mair, for Chanticleer
Shook off the pouthery snaw,
And hailed the morning with a cheer,—
A cottage-rousing craw!

Burns.

THE DEATH OF THE OLD YEAR.

Full knee-deep lies the winter snow,
And the winter winds are wearily sighing:
Toll ye the church-bell sad and slow,
And tread softly, and speak low,
For the old year lies a-dying.
Old year, you must not die;
You came to us so readily,
You lived with us so steadily,
Old year, you shall not die.

He lieth still: he doth not move:
He will not see the dawn of day.
He hath no other life above.
He gave me a friend, and a true true-love,
And the New-year will take 'em away.
Old year, you must not go;
So long as you have been with us,
Such joy as you have seen with us,
Old year, you shall not go.

He frothed his bumpers to the brim;

A jollier year we shall not see.
But though his eyes are waxing dim,
And though his foes speak ill of him,
He was a friend to me.
Old year, you shall not die;
We did so laugh and cry with you,
I've half a mind to die with you,
Old year, if you must die.

He was full of joke and jest;
But all his merry quips are o'er:
To see him die, across the waste
His son and heir doth ride post-haste;
But he'll be dead before.
Every one for his own.
The night is starry and cold, my friend,
And the New-year blithe and bold, my friend,
Comes up to take his own.

How hard he breathes! over the snow
I heard just now the crowing cock.
The shadows flicker to and fro;
The cricket chirps; the light burns low:
'Tis nearly twelve o'clock.
Shake hands, before you die.
Old year, we'll dearly rue for you:
What is it we can do for you?
Speak out before you die.

His face is growing sharp and thin.
Alack! our friend is gone.
Close up his eyes: tie up his chin:
Step from the corpse, and let him in
That standeth there alone,
And waiteth at the door.
There's a new foot on the floor, my friend,
And a new face at the door, my friend,
A new face at the door.

TENNYSON.

THE RIVULET.

AND I shall sleep; and on thy side,
As ages after ages glide,
Children their early sports shall try,
And pass to hoary age, and die.
But thou, unchanged from year to year,
Gayly shalt play and glitter here:
Amid young flowers and tender grass
Thy endless infancy shalt pass;
And, singing down thy narrow glen,
Shalt mock the fading race of men.

BRYANT.

THE GARDEN.

How vainly men themselves amaze,
To win the palm, the oak, or bays,
And their incessant labors see
Crowned from some single herb or tree,
Whose short and narrow-vergèd shade
Does prudently their toils upbraid;
While all the flowers and trees do close,
To weave the garlands of repose!

Fair Quiet, have I found thee here,
And Innocence, thy sister dear?
Mistaken long, I sought you then
In busy companies of men.
Your sacred plants, if here below,
Only among the plants will grow:
Society is all but rude
To this delicious solitude.

No white nor red was ever seen
So amorous as this lovely green.
Fond lovers, cruel as their flame,
Cut in these trees their mistress' name:
Little, alas! they know or heed
How far these beauties her exceed!
Fair trees! where'er your barks I wound,
No name shall but your own be found.

When we have run our passion's heat,
Love hither makes his best retreat.
The gods, who mortal beauty chase,
Still in a tree did end their race;
Apollo hunted Daphne so,
Only that she might laurel grow;
And Pan did after Syrinx speed,
Not as a nymph, but for a reed.

What wondrous life is this I lead!
Ripe apples drop about my head;
The luscious clusters of the vine
Upon my mouth do crush their wine;

The nectarine, and curious peach,
Into my hands themselves do reach;
Stumbling on melons, as I pass,
Insnared with flowers, I fall on grass.

Meanwhile the mind, from pleasure less,
Withdraws into its happiness, —
The mind, that ocean where each kind
Does straight its own resemblance find,
Yet it creates, transcending these,
Far other worlds and other seas,
Annihilating all that's made
To a green thought in a green shade.

Here at the fountain's sliding foot,
Or at some fruit-tree's mossy root,
Casting the body's vest aside,
My soul into the boughs does glide:
There, like a bird, it sits and sings,
Then whets and claps its silver wings,
And, till prepared for longer flight,
Waves in its plumes the various light.

Such was that happy garden-state,
While man there walked without a mate:
After a place so pure and sweet,
What other help could yet be meet!
But 'twas beyond a mortal's share
To wander solitary there:
Two paradises are in one,
To live in paradise alone.

How well the skilful gardener drew
Of flowers and herbs this dial new,
Where, from above, the milder sun
Does through a fragrant zodiac run,
And, as it works, the industrious bee
Computes its time as well as we!
How could such sweet and wholesome hours
Be reckoned but with herbs and flowers?

MARVELL.

LACHIN Y GAIR.

AWAY, ye gay landscapes, ye gardens of roses!
In you let the minions of luxury rove;
Restore me the rocks where the snowflake reposes,
For still they are sacred to freedom and love:
Yet, Caledonia, beloved are thy mountains,
Round their white summits though elements war,
Though cataracts foam, 'stead of smooth-flowing fountains,
I sigh for the valley of dark Loch na Gair.

Ah! there my young footsteps in infancy wandered;
My cap was the bonnet, my cloak was the plaid;
On chieftains long perished, my memory pondered,
As daily I strode through the pine-covered glade;
I sought not my home till the day's dying glory
Gave place to the rays of the bright polar star;
For Fancy was cheered by traditional story
Disclosed by the natives of dark Loch na Gair.

"Shades of the dead! have I not heard your voices
Rise on the night-rolling breath of the gale?"
Surely the soul of the hero rejoices,
And rides on the wind o'er his own Highland vale:
Round Loch na Gair, while the stormy mist gathers,
Winter presides in his cold icy car;
Clouds there encircle the forms of my fathers:
They dwell in the tempests of dark Loch na Gair.

"Ill-starred, though brave, did no visions foreboding
Tell you that Fate had forsaken your cause?"
Ah! were you destined to die at Culloden,
Victory crowned not your fall with applause;
Still were you happy; in death's early slumber
You rest with your clan, in the caves of Braemar,

The pibroch resounds to the piper's loud number,
Your deeds on the echoes of dark Loch na Gair.

Years have rolled on, Loch na Gair, since I left you;
Years must elapse ere I tread you again;
Nature of verdure and flowers has bereft you,
Yet still are you dearer than Albion's plain:
England! thy beauties are tame and domestic
To one who has roved on the mountains afar;
Oh for the crags that are wild and majestic,
The steep-frowning glories of dark Loch na Gair!

BYRON.

THE BOY-POET.

THERE was a boy; ye knew him well, ye cliffs
And islands of Winander! Many a time,
At evening, when the earliest stars began
To move along the edges of the hills,
Rising or setting, would he stand alone,
Beneath the trees, or by the glimmering lake;
And there, with fingers interwoven, both hands
Pressed closely palm to palm and to his mouth
Uplifted, he, as through an instrument,
Blew mimic hootings to the silent owls,
That they might answer him. And they would shout
Across the watery vale, and shout again,
Responsive to his call, with quivering peals,
And long halloos and screams, and echoes loud
Redoubled and redoubled; concourse wild
Of mirth and jocund din! And when it chanced
That pauses of deep silence mocked his skill,
Then, sometimes, in that silence, while he hung
Listening, a gentle shock of mild surprise
Has carried far into his heart the voice
Of mountain torrents; or the visible scene
Would enter unawares into his mind
With all its solemn imagery, its rocks,
Its woods, and that uncertain heaven, received
Into the bosom of the steady lake.

WORDSWORTH.

THE EARTH-SPIRIT.

I HAVE woven shrouds of air
In a loom of hurrying light,
For the trees which blossoms bear,
And gilded them with sheets of bright;
I fall upon the grass like love's first kiss;
I make the golden flies and their fine bliss;
I paint the hedgerows in the lane,
And clover white and red the pathways bear;
I laugh aloud in sudden gusts of rain
To see the ocean lash himself in air;
I throw smooth shells and weeds along the beach,
And pour the curling waves far o'er the glossy reach;
Swing birds' nests in the elms, and shake cool moss
Along the aged beams, and hide their loss.
The very broad rough stones I gladden too;
Some willing seeds I drop along their sides,
Nourish the generous plant with freshening dew,
Till there where all was waste, true joy abides.
The peaks of aged mountains, with my care
Smile in the red of glowing morn elate;

I bind the caverns of the sea with hair,
Glossy, and long, and rich as kings' estate;
I polish the green ice, and gleam the wall
With the white frost, and leaf the brown trees tall.

CHANNING.

THE PASS OF KIRKSTONE.

WITHIN the mind strong fancies work,
A deep delight the bosom thrills,
Oft as I pass along the fork
Of these fraternal hills,
Where, save the rugged road, we find
No appanage of human kind,
Nor hint of man; if stone or rock
Seem not his handiwork to mock
By something cognizably shaped;
Mockery, or model roughly hewn,
And left as if by earthquake strewn,
Or from the flood escaped:
Altars for Druid service fit;
(But where no fire was ever lit,
Unless the glow-worm to the skies
Thence offer nightly sacrifice,)
Wrinkled Egyptian monument;
Green moss-grown tower; or hoary tent;
Tents of a camp that never shall be raised —
On which four thousand years have gazed!

II.

Ye ploughshares sparkling on the slopes!
Ye snow-white lambs that trip
Imprisoned 'mid the formal props
Of restless ownership!
Ye trees, that may to-morrow fall
To feed the insatiate prodigal!
Lawns, houses, chattels, groves, and fields,
All that the fertile valley shields;
Wages of folly, baits of crime,
Of life's uneasy game the stake,
Playthings that keep the eyes awake
Of drowsy, dotard Time, —
O care! O guilt! O vales and plains,
Here, 'mid his own unvexed domains,
A genius dwells, that can subdue
At once all memory of You, —
Most potent when mists veil the sky, —
Mists that distort and magnify;
While the coarse rushes to the sweeping breeze
Sigh forth their ancient melodies!

III.

List to those shriller notes! that march
Perchance was on the blast,
When, through this height's inverted arch,
Rome's earliest legion passed!
They saw, adventurously impelled,
And older eyes than theirs beheld,
This block, and yon, whose church-like frame
Gives to this savage pass its name.
Aspiring Road! that lov'st to hide
Thy daring in a vapory bourn,
Not seldom may the hour return
When thou shalt be my guide.

WORDSWORTH.

SOLITUDE.

THERE is a pleasure in the pathless woods;
There is a rapture on the lonely shore;
There is society where none intrudes,
By the deep sea, and music in its roar:
I love not man the less, but nature more,
From these our interviews, in which I steal
From all I may be, or have been before,
To mingle with the universe, and feel
What I can ne'er express, yet cannot all conceal.

Roll on, thou deep and dark-blue ocean, roll!
Ten thousand fleets sweep over thee in vain:
Man marks the earth with ruin: his control
Stops with the shore: upon the watery plain

The wrecks are all thy deed, nor
doth remain
A shadow of man's ravage, save his
own,
When, for a moment, like a drop of
rain,
He sinks into thy depths with bubbling groan,
Without a grave, unknelled, uncoffined, and unknown.

BYRON: *Childe Harold.*

TINTERN ABBEY.

I HAVE learned
To look on Nature, not as in the
hour
Of thoughtless youth, but hearing
oftentimes
The still, sad music of humanity,
Not harsh nor grating, though of
ample power
To chasten and subdue. And I
have felt
A presence that disturbs me with
the joy
Of elevated thoughts; a sense sub-
lime
Of something far more deeply inter-
fused,
Whose dwelling is the light of set-
ting suns,
And the round ocean, and the living
air,
And the blue sky, and in the mind
of man, —
A motion and a spirit, that impels
All thinking things, all objects of all
thought,
And rolls through all things. There-
fore am I still
A lover of the meadows, and the
woods,
And mountains, and of all that we
behold
From this green earth; of all the
mighty world
Of eye and ear, both what they half
create,
And what perceive; well pleased to
recognize
In Nature and the language of the
sense
The anchor of my purest thoughts.

WORDSWORTH.

FLOWERS.

O PROSERPINA,
For the flowers now, that frighted,
thou let'st fall
From Dis's wagon! daffodils,
That come before the swallow dares,
and take
The winds of March with beauty;
violets dim,
But sweeter than the lids of Juno's
eyes,
Or Cytherea's breath; pale prim-
roses,
That die unmarried, ere they can
behold
Bright Phœbus in his strength, a
malady
Most incident to maids; bold ox-lips,
and
The crown-imperial; lilies of all
kinds,
The flower-de-luce being one! O,
these I lack,
To make you garlands of; and my
sweet friend,
To strew him o'er and o'er!

SHAKSPEARE: *Winter's Tale.*

THE SUNFLOWER.

AH, sunflower! weary of time,
Who countest the steps of the sun,
Seeking after that sweet golden
clime,
Where the traveller's journey is
done;

Where the youth pined away with
desire,
And the pale virgin shrouded in
snow,
Arise from their graves, and aspire
Where my sunflower wishes to go.

WILLIAM BLAKE.

THE DEATH OF THE FLOWERS.

THE melancholy days are come, the
saddest of the year,
Of wailing winds, and naked woods,
and meadows brown and sear.
Heaped in the hollows of the grove,
the withered leaves lie dead:
They rustle to the eddying gust, and
to the rabbit's tread.

The robin and the wren are flown, and from the shrubs the jay;
And from the wood-top calls the crow, through all the gloomy day.

Where are the flowers, the fair young flowers, that lately sprang and stood,
In brighter light and softer airs, a beauteous sisterhood?
Alas! they all are in their graves: the gentle race of flowers
Are lying in their lowly beds, with the fair and good of ours.
The rain is falling where they lie; but the cold November rain
Calls not, from out the gloomy earth, the lovely ones again.

The wind-flower and the violet, they perished long ago;
And the brier-rose and the orchis died amid the summer glow;
But on the hill the golden-rod, and the aster in the wood,
And the yellow sunflower by the brook, in autumn beauty stood,
Till fell the frost from the clear, cold heaven, as falls the plague on men,
And the brightness of their smile was gone from upland, glade, and glen.

And now when comes the calm mild day, as still such days will come,
To call the squirrel and the bee from out their winter home;
When the sound of dropping nuts is heard, though all the trees are still,
And twinkle in the smoky light the waters of the rill,—
The south wind searches for the flowers whose fragrance late he bore,
And sighs to find them in the wood and by the stream no more.
And then I think of one who in her youthful beauty died,
The fair, meek blossom that grew up, and faded by my side:
In the cold moist earth we laid her when the forest cast the leaf,
And we wept that one so lovely should have a life so brief;
Yet not unmeet it was, that one, like that young friend of ours,
So gentle and so beautiful, should perish with the flowers.

BRYANT.

TO THE FRINGED GENTIAN.

THOU blossom bright with autumn dew,
And colored with the heaven's own blue,
That openest, when the quiet light
Succeeds the keen and frosty night.

Thou comest not when violets lean
O'er wandering brooks and springs unseen,
Or columbines, in purple drest,
Nod o'er the ground-bird's hidden nest.

Thou waitest late, and com'st alone,
When woods are bare, and birds are flown,
And frosts and shortening days portend
The aged year is near its end.

Then doth thy sweet and quiet eye
Look through its fringes to the sky,
Blue, blue, as if that sky let fall
A flower from its cerulean wall.

I would that thus, when I shall see
The hour of death draw near to me,
Hope, blossoming within my heart,
May look to heaven as I depart.

BRYANT.

TREES.

A SHADIE grove not far away they spied,
That promist ayde the tempest to withstand;
Whose loftie trees, yclad with sommers pride,
Did spred so broad, that heaven's light did hide,
Not perceable with power of any starr;
And all within were pathes and alleies wide,

With footing worne, and leading inward far:
Faire harbour that them seems; so in they entred are.

And forth they passe, with pleasure forward led,
Joying to heare the birdes' sweete harmony,
Which therein shrouded from the tempest dred,
Seemed in their song to scorne the cruell sky.
Much can they praise the trees so straight and high,
The sayling pine; the cedar proud and tall;
The vine-propp elme; the poplar never dry;
The builder oake, sole king of forrests all;
The aspine good for staves; the cypresse funerall;

The laurell meed of mightie conquerours
And poets sage; the fir that weepeth still;
The willow, worne of forlorne paramours;
The yew, obedient to the bender's will;
The birch for shaftes; the sallow for the mill;
The mirrhe sweet-bleeding in the bitter wound;
The warlike beech; the ash for nothing ill;
The fruitful olive; and the platane round;
The carver holme; the maple, seldom inward sound.

SPENSER.

YEW-TREES.

THERE is a yew-tree, pride of Lorton Vale,
Which to this day stands single in the midst
Of its own darkness, as it stood of yore:
Not loath to furnish weapons for the bands
Of Umfraville or Percy ere they marched
To Scotland's heaths; or those that crossed the sea,
And drew their sounding bows at Azincour;
Perhaps at earlier Crecy, or Poictiers.
Of vast circumference and gloom profound
This solitary tree! a living thing
Produced too slowly ever to decay;
Of form and aspect too magnificent
To be destroyed. But worthier still of note
Are those fraternal Four of Borrowdale,
Joined in one solemn and capacious grove;
Huge trunks! and each particular trunk a growth
Of intertwisted fibres serpentine
Up-coiling, and inveterately convolved;
Nor uninformed with fantasy, and looks
That threaten the profane; a pillared shade,
Upon whose grassless floor of red-brown hue,
By sheddings from the pining umbrage tinged
Perennially; beneath whose sable roof
Of boughs, as if for festal purpose, decked
With unrejoicing berries, ghostly shapes
May meet at noontide; Fear, and trembling Hope,
Silence, and Foresight; Death the Skeleton,
And Time the Shadow; there to celebrate,
As in a natural temple scattered o'er
With altars undisturbed of mossy stone,
United worship; or in mute repose
To lie, and listen to the mountain flood
Murmuring from Glaramara's inmost caves.

WORDSWORTH.

THE OSMUNDA REGALIS.

Often, trifling with a privilege
Alike indulged to all, we paused, one
now,
And now the other, to point out,
perchance
To pluck, some flower or water-weed
too fair
Either to be divided from the place
On which it grew, or to be left alone
To its own beauty. Many such there
are,
Fair ferns and flowers, and chiefly
that tall fern,
So stately, of the queen Osmunda
named;
Plant lovelier, in its own retired abode
On Grasmere's beach, than Naiad by
the side
Of Grecian brook, or Lady of the
Mere,
Sole-sitting by the shores of old ro-
mance.

Wordsworth.

THE BARBERRY-BUSH.

The bush that has most briers and
bitter fruit:
Wait till the frost has turned its
green leaves red,
Its sweetened berries will thy palate
suit,
And thou mayst find e'en there a
homely bread.
Upon the hills of Salem scattered
wide,
Their yellow blossoms gain the eye
in spring;
And, straggling e'en upon the turn-
pike's side,
Their ripened branches to your hand
they bring.
I've plucked them oft in boyhood's
early hour,
That then I gave such name, and
thought it true;
But now I know that other fruit as
sour
Grows on what now thou callest *me*
and *you:*
Yet wilt thou wait, the autumn that
I see
Will sweeter taste than these red
berries be.

Jones Very.

TO THE HERB ROSEMARY.

Sweet-scented flower! who art
wont to bloom
On January's front severe,
And o'er the wintry desert drear
To waft thy waste perfume!
Come, thou shalt form my nosegay
now,
And I will bind thee round my brow;
And as I twine the mournful
wreath,
I'll weave a melancholy song,
And sweet the strain shall be, and
long, —
The melody of death.

Come, funeral flower! who lov'st to
dwell
With the pale corse in lonely
tomb,
And throw across the desert gloom
A sweet decaying smell.
Come, press my lips, and lie with
me
Beneath the lowly alder-tree,
And we will sleep a pleasant sleep,
And not a care shall dare in-
trude
To break the marble solitude,
So peaceful and so deep.

And hark! the wind-god, as he flies,
Moans hollow in the forest trees,
And, sailing on the gusty breeze,
Mysterious music dies.
Sweet flower! that requiem wild
is mine;
It warns me to the lonely shrine,
The cold turf altar of the dead;
My grave shall be in yon lone
spot,
Where as I lie, by all forgot,
A dying fragrance thou wilt o'er my
ashes shed.

H. K. White.

THE PRIMROSE.

Ask me why I send you here
This sweet Infanta of the yeere?
Ask me why I send to you
This Primrose, thus bepearl'd with
dew?
I will whisper to your eares,
The sweets of love are mixt with
tears.

Ask me why this flower does show
So yellow-green and sickly too?
Ask me why the stalk is weak
And bending, yet it doth not break?
I will answer, these discover
What fainting hopes are in a lover.

HERRICK.

TO DAFFODILLS.

FAIRE Daffodills, we weep to see
You haste away so soone;
As yet the early rising sun
Has not attain'd his noone.
Stay, stay,
Untill the hasting day
Has run
But to the even-song;
And, having pray'd together, we
Will goe with you along.

We have short time to stay as you,
We have as short a spring;
As quick a growth to meet decay,
As you, or any thing.
We die
As your hours doe, and drie
Away,
Like to the summer's raine;
Or as the pearles of morning's dew,
Ne'er to be found againe.

HERRICK.

DAFFODILS.

I WANDERED lonely as a cloud
That floats on high o'er vales and hills,
When all at once I saw a crowd,
A host, of golden daffodils;
Beside the lake, beneath the trees,
Fluttering, dancing in the breeze.

Continuous as the stars that shine
And twinkle on the milky way,
They stretched in never-ending line
Along the margin of a bay:
Ten thousand saw I at a glance,
Tossing their heads in sprightly dance.

The waves beside them danced; but they
Outdid the sparkling waves in glee:
A poet could not but be gay
In such a jocund company:
I gazed, and gazed, but little thought
What wealth the show to me had brought:

For oft, when on my couch I lie
In vacant or in pensive mood,
They flash upon that inward eye
Which is the bliss of solitude;
And then my heart with pleasure fills,
And dances with the daffodils.

WORDSWORTH.

TO BLOSSOMS.

FAIR pledges of a fruitful tree,
Why do ye fall so fast?
Your date is not so past,
But you may stay yet here a while
To blush and gently smile,
And go at last.

What, were ye born to be
An hour or half's delight,
And so to bid good-night?
'Twas pity Nature brought ye forth
Merely to show your worth,
And lose you quite.

But you are lovely leaves, where we
May read how soon things have
Their end, though ne'er so brave:
And after they have shown their pride
Like you, a while, they glide
Into the grave.

HERRICK.

LIBERTY.

WHO can divine what impulses from God
Reach the caged lark, within a town abode,
From his poor inch or two of daisied sod?
Oh, yield him back his privilege! No sea
Swells like the bosom of a man set free:
A wilderness is rich with liberty.

Roll on, ye spouting whales, who die or keep
Your independence in the fathomless deep!
Spread, tiny Nautilus, the living sail;
Dive, at thy choice, or brave the freshening gale!
If unreproved the ambitious eagle mount
Sunward to seek the daylight in its fount,
Bays, gulfs, and ocean's Indian width, shall be,
Till the world perishes, a field for thee!

WORDSWORTH.

NIGHT.

COME, seeling night,
Skarf up the tender eye of pitiful day,
And, with thy bloody and invisible hand,
Cancel, and tear to pieces, that great bond
Which keeps me pale! — Light thickens; and the crow
Makes wing to the rooky wood.

SHAKSPEARE: *Macbeth.*

THE DIAMOND.

STAR of the flowers, and flower of the stars,
And earth of the earth, art thou!
And darkness hath battles, and light hath wars
That pass in thy beautiful brow.

The eye of the ground thus was planted by heaven,
And the dust was new wed to the sun,
And the monarch went forth, and the earth-star was given,
That should back to the heaven-star run.

So in all things it is: the first origin lives,
And loves his life out to his flock;
And in dust, and in matter, and nature, he gives
The spirit's last spark to the rock.

J. J. G. WILKINSON.

SEPTEMBER.

1819.

AND, sooth to say, yon vocal grove
Albeit uninspired by love,
By love untaught to ring,
May well afford to mortal ear
An impulse more profoundly dear
Than music of the spring.

But list! though winter's storms be nigh,
Unchecked is that soft harmony:
There lives Who can provide
For all his creatures; and in him,
Even like the radiant Seraphim,
These Choristers confide.

WORDSWORTH.

NIGHTINGALE.

OFT when, returning with her loaded bill,
Th' astonish'd mother finds a vacant nest,
By the hard hand of unrelenting clown
Robb'd; to the ground the vain provision falls;
Her pinions ruffle, and low-drooping scarce
Can bear the mourner to the poplar shade;
Where, all abandoned to despair, she sings
Her sorrows thro' the night; and on the bough
Sole-sitting, still at every dying fall
Takes up again her lamentable strain
Of winding woe, till, wide around, the woods
Sigh to her song, and with her wail resound.

THOMSON.

THE NIGHTINGALE.

THOU wast not born for death, immortal bird!
No hungry generations tread thee down;
The voice I hear this passing night was heard
In ancient days by emperor and clown,—

Perhaps the selfsame song that found a path
Through the sad heart of Ruth, when, sick for home,
She stood in tears amid the alien corn;
The same that oft-times hath
Charmed magic casements, opening on the foam
Of perilous seas, in faery lands forlorn.

KEATS.

THE NIGHTINGALE.

As it fell upon a day
In the merry month of May,
Sitting in a pleasant shade
Which a grove of myrtles made,
Beasts did leap, and birds did sing,
Trees did grow, and plants did spring,
Every thing did banish moan,
Save the nightingale alone.
She, poor bird, as all forlorn,
Leaned her breast against a thorn,
And there sung the dolefulest ditty,
That to hear it was great pity.
Fie, fie, fie! now would she cry;
Tereu, tereu, by and by:
That to hear her so complain
Scarce I could from tears refrain;
For her griefs so lively shown
Made me think upon mine own.
Ah, thought I, thou mourn'st in vain,
None takes pity on thy pain:
Senseless trees, they cannot hear thee,
Ruthless beasts, they will not cheer thee;
King Pandiva, he is dead,
All thy friends are lapp'd in lead:
All thy fellow-birds do sing
Careless of thy sorrowing;
Even so, poor bird, like thee,
None alive will pity me.

R. BARNEFIELD.

THE NIGHTINGALE'S SONG.

ROUND my own pretty rose I have hovered all day,
I have seen its sweet leaves one by one fall away:
They are gone, they are gone; but I go not with them,
I linger to weep o'er its desolate stem.

They say if I rove to the south I shall meet
With hundreds of roses more fair and more sweet;
But my heart, when I'm tempted to wander, replies,
Here my first love, my last love, my only love lies.

When the last leaf is withered, and falls to the earth,
The false one to southerly climes may fly forth;
But truth cannot fly from his sorrows: he dies,
Where his first love, his last love, his only love lies.

T. H. BAYLY.

THE NIGHTINGALE'S DEATH-SONG.

MOURNFULLY, sing mournfully,
And die away my heart!
The rose, the glorious rose, is gone,
And I, too, will depart.

The skies have lost their splendor,
The waters changed their tone,
And wherefore, in the faded world,
Should music linger on?

Where is the golden sunshine,
And where the flower-cup's glow?
And where the joy of the dancing leaves,
And the fountain's laughing flow?

Tell of the brightness parted,
Thou bee, thou lamb at play!
Thou lark, in thy victorious mirth!
Are ye, too, passed away?

With sunshine, with sweet odor,
With every precious thing,
Upon the last warm southern breeze,
My soul its flight shall wing.

Alone I shall not linger
When the days of hope are past,
To watch the fall of leaf by leaf,
To wait the rushing blast.

Triumphantly, triumphantly,
  Sing to the woods, I go!
For me, perchance, in other lands
  The glorious rose may blow.

No more, no more, sing mournfully!
  Swell high, then break, my heart!
The rose, the royal rose, is gone,
  And I, too, will depart.

HEMANS.

THE BIRD.

"BIRDIE, Birdie, will you, pet?
Summer is far and far away yet.
You'll have silken quilts and a velvet bed,
And a pillow of satin for your head."

"I'd rather sleep in the ivy wall:
No rain comes through, though I hear it fall;
The sun peeps gay at dawn of day,
And I sing, and wing away, away!"

"O Birdie, Birdie, will you, pet?
Diamond stones and amber and jet
We'll string on a necklace fair and fine,
To please this pretty bird of mine."

"Oh! thanks for diamonds, and thanks for jet;
But here is something daintier yet, —
A feather necklace, round and round,
That I would not sell for a thousand pound!"

"O Birdie, Birdie, won't you, pet?
We'll buy you a dish of silver fret,
A golden cup and an ivory seat,
And carpets soft beneath your feet."

"Can running water be drunk from gold?
Can a silver dish the forest hold?
A rocking twig is the finest chair,
And the softest paths lie through the air:
Good-by, good-by, to my lady fair."

ALLINGHAM.

TO THE SKY-LARK.

ETHEREAL minstrel, pilgrim of the sky!
Dost thou despise the earth where cares abound?
Or, while the wings aspire, are heart and eye
Both with thy nest upon the dewy ground? —
Thy nest, which thou canst drop into at will,
Those quivering wings composed, that music still!

To the last point of vision, and beyond,
Mount, daring warbler! That love-prompted strain,
'Twixt thee and thine a never-failing bond,
Thrills not the less the bosom of the plain;
Yet might'st thou seem, proud privilege! to sing
All independent of the leafy spring.

Leave to the nightingale her shady wood;
A privacy of glorious light is thine,
Whence thou dost pour upon the world a flood
Of harmony, with instinct more divine;
Type of the wise, who soar, but never roam,
True to the kindred points of heaven and home.

WORDSWORTH.

TO A SKY-LARK.

LIKE a poet hidden
  In the light of thought,
Singing hymns unbidden,
  Till the world is wrought
To sympathy with hopes and fears it heeded not.

SHELLEY.

BREEDING LARK.

I MUST go furnish up
A nest I have begun,
And will return and bring ye meat,
As soon as it is done.

Then up she clambe the clouds
With such a lusty lay,
That it rejoiced her younglings' heart,
As in their nest they lay.

ARTHUR BOAR.

FLIGHT OF THE WILD GEESE.

Rambling along the marshes,
On the bank of the Assabet,
Sounding myself as to how it went,
Praying that I might not forget,
And all uncertain
Whether I was in the right,
Toiling to lift Time's curtain,
And if I burnt the strongest light;
Suddenly,
High in the air,
I heard the travelled geese
Their overture prepare.

Stirred above the patent ball,
The wild geese flew,
Nor near so wild as that doth me befall,
Or, swollen Wisdom, you.

In the front there fetched a leader,
Him behind the line spread out,
And waved about,
As it was near night,
When these air-pilots stop their flight.

Cruising off the shoal dominion
Where we sit,
Depending not on their opinion,
Nor hiving sops of wit;
Geographical in tact,
Naming not a pond or river,
Pulled with twilight down in fact,
In the reeds to quack and quiver,
There they go,
Spectators at the play below,
Southward in a row.

Cannot laud and map the stars
The indifferent geese,
Nor taste the sweetmeats in odd jars,
Nor speculate and freeze;
Rancid weasands need be well,
Feathers glossy, quills in order,
Starts this train, yet rings no bell;
Steam is raised without recorder.

"Up, my feathered fowl, all," —
Saith the goose commander,
"Brighten your bills, and flirt your pinions,
My toes are nipped, — let us render
Ourselves in soft Guatemala,
Or suck puddles in Campeachy,
Spitzbergen-cake cuts very frosty,
And the tipple is not leechy.

"Let's brush loose for any creek,
There lurk fish and fly,
Condiments to fat the weak,
Inundate the pie.
Flutter not about a place,
Ye concomitants of space!"

Mute the listening nations stand
On that dark receding land;
How faint their villages and towns,
Scattered on the misty downs!
A meeting-house
Appears no bigger than a mouse.

How long?
Never is a question asked,
While a throat can lift the song,
Or a flapping wing be tasked.

All the grandmothers about
Hear the orators of Heaven,
Then put on their woollens stout,
And cower o'er the hearth at even;
And the children stare at the sky,
And laugh to see the long black line so high!

Then once more I heard them say, —
"'Tis a smooth, delightful road
Difficult to lose the way,
And a trifle for a load."

'Twas our forte to pass for this
Proper sack of sense to borrow
Wings and legs, and bills that clatter,
And the horizon of To-morrow.

Channing.

TO A WATERFOWL.

Whither, 'midst falling dew,
While glow the heavens with the last steps of day?
Far through their rosy depths dost thou pursue
Thy solitary way?

Vainly the fowler's eye
Might mark thy distant flight to do thee wrong,
As, darkly painted on the crimson sky,
Thy figure floats along.

Seek'st thou the plashy brink
Of weedy lake, or marge of river wide,

Or where the rocking billows rise
and sink
On the chafed ocean-side?

There is a Power whose care
Teaches thy way along that pathless
coast, —
The desert and illimitable air, —
Lone wandering, but not lost.

All day thy wings have fanned
At that far height the cold, thin
atmosphere,
Yet stoop not, weary, to the welcome
land,
Though the dark night is near.

And soon that toil shall end,
Soon shalt thou find a summer home,
and rest,
And scream among thy fellows:
reeds shall bend,
Soon, o'er thy sheltered nest.

Thou'rt gone, the abyss of heaven
Hath swallowed up thy form; yet
on my heart
Deeply hath sunk the lesson thou
hast given,
And shall not soon depart.

He who, from zone to zone,
Guides through the boundless sky
thy certain flight,
In the long way that I must tread
alone
Will lead my steps aright.

BRYANT.

THE EAGLE.

HE clasps the crag with hookèd
hands;
Close to the sun in lonely lands,
Ringed with the azure world, he
stands.

The wrinkled sea beneath him crawls:
He watches from his mountain walls,
And like a thunderbolt he falls.

TENNYSON.

OCEAN.

GREAT Ocean! strongest of crea-
tion's sons,
Unconquerable, unreposed, untired,
That rolled the wild, profound, eter-
nal bass
In nature's anthem, and made mu-
sic such
As pleased the ear of God! original,
Unmarred, unfaded work of Deity!
And unburlesqued by mortal's puny
skill;
From age to age enduring, and un-
changed,
Majestical, inimitable, vast,
Loud uttering satire, day and night,
on each
Succeeding race, and little pompous
work
Of man; unfallen, religious, holy sea!
Thou bowedst thy glorious head to
none, fearedst none,
Heardst none, to none didst honor,
but to God
Thy Maker, only worthy to receive
Thy great obeisance.

POLLOK.

OCEAN.

SEE living vales by living waters
blessed,
Their wealth see earth's dark caverns
yield,
See Ocean roll in glory dressed,
For all a treasure, and round all a
shield.

CHARLES SPRAGUE.

SEA SONG.

OUR boat to the waves go free,
By the bending tide, where the
curled wave breaks,
Like the track of the wind on the
white snowflakes:
Away, away! 'Tis a path o'er the sea.

Blasts may rave, — spread the sail,
For our spirits can wrest the power
from the wind,
And the gray clouds yield to the
sunny mind,
Fear not we the whirl of the gale.

Waves on the beach, and the wild
sea-foam,
With a leap, and a dash, and a sudden cheer,

Where the seaweed makes its bending home,
And the sea-birds swim on the crests so clear,
Wave after wave, they are curling o'er,
While the white sand dazzles along the shore.

CHANNING.

SEA SONG.

A WET SHEET AND A FLOWING SEA.

A WET sheet and a flowing sea,
A wind that follows fast,
And fills the white and rustling sail,
And bends the gallant mast.
And bends the gallant mast, my boys,
While, like the eagle free,
Away the good ship flies, and leaves
Old England on the lee.

There's tempest in yon hornèd moon,
And lightning in yon cloud;
And hark, the music, mariners!
The wind is wakening loud.
The wind is wakening loud, my boys,
The lightning flashes free;
The hollow oak our palace is,
Our heritage the sea.

ALLAN CUNNINGHAM.

SEA.

O'ER the glad waters of the dark-blue sea,
Our thoughts as boundless, and our souls as free,
Far as the breeze can bear, the billows foam,
Survey our empire, and behold our home!
These are our realms, no limits to their sway;
Our flag the sceptre all who meet obey.
Ours the wild life in tumult still to range
From toil to rest, and joy in every change.
Oh! who can tell? not thou, luxurious slave!
Whose soul would sicken o'er the heaving wave;
Not thou, vain lord of wantonness and ease!
Whom slumber soothes not, pleasure cannot please, —
Oh! who can tell, save he whose heart hath tried,
And danced in triumph o'er the waters wide,
The exulting sense, the pulse's maddening play,
That thrills the wanderer of that trackless way?

BYRON: *Corsair*.

THE CORAL GROVE.

DEEP in the wave is a coral grove,
Where the purple mullet and gold-fish rove;
Where the sea-flower spreads its leaves of blue,
That never are wet with falling dew,
But in bright and changeful beauty shine
Far down in the green and glassy brine.
The floor is of sand, like the mountain drift,
And the pearl-shells spangle the flinty snow:
From coral rocks the sea-plants lift
Their boughs, where the tides and billows flow;
The water is calm and still below,
For the winds and the waves are absent there,
And the sands are bright as the stars that glow
In the motionless fields of upper air:
There with its waving blade of green,
The sea-flag streams through the silent water,
And the crimson leaf of the dulse is seen
To blush like a banner bathed in slaughter:
There with a light and easy motion
The fan coral sweeps through the clear deep sea;
And the yellow and scarlet tufts of ocean
Are bending like corn on the upland lea;
And life, in rare and beautiful forms,
Is sporting amid those bowers of stone.

And is safe, when the wrathful spirit of storms
Has made the top of the waves his own:
And when the ship from his fury flies,
When the myriad voices of ocean roar,
When the wind-god frowns in the murky skies,
And demons are waiting the wreck on the shore,
Then, far below, in the peaceful sea,
The purple mullet and gold-fish rove,
Where the waters murmur tranquilly
Through the bending twigs of the coral grove.

PERCIVAL.

INSCRIPTION ON A SEA SHELL.

PLEASED we remember our august abodes,
And murmur as the ocean murmurs there.

LANDOR.

OUT AND INWARD BOUND.

ALL things that are,
Are with more spirit chasèd than enjoy'd.
How like a younker or a prodigal
The scarfèd bark puts from her native bay,
Hugg'd and embracèd by the strumpet wind!
How like the prodigal doth she return
With over-weather'd ribs, and ragged sails,
Lean, rent, and beggar'd by the strumpet wind!

SHAKSPEARE.
Merchant of Venice. Act ii. Sc. 6.

TACKING SHIP OFF SHORE.

The weather-leech of the topsail shivers,
The bow-lines strain, and the lee-shrouds slacken,
The braces are taut, the lithe boom quivers,
And the waves with the coming squall-cloud blacken.

Open one point on the weather-bow,
Is the light-house tall on Fire Island Head?
There's a shade of doubt on the captain's brow,
And the pilot watches the heaving lead.

I stand at the wheel, and with eager eye,
To sea and to sky and to shore I gaze,
Till the muttered order of "*Full and by!*"
Is suddenly changed for "*Full for stays!*"

The ship bends lower before the breeze,
As her broadside fair to the blast she lays;
And she swifter springs to the rising seas,
As the pilot calls, "*Stand by for stays!*"

It is silence all, as each in his place,
With the gathered coil in his hardened hands,
By tack and bowline, by sheet and brace,
Waiting the watchword impatient stands.

And the light on Fire Island Head draws near,
As, trumpet-winged, the pilot's shout
From his post on the bowsprit's heel I hear,
With the welcome call of "*Ready! About!*"

No time to spare! It is touch and go;
And the captain growls, "Down, helm! hard down!"
As my weight on the whirling spokes I throw,
While heaven grows black with the storm-cloud's frown.

High o'er the knight-heads flies the spray,
As we meet the shock of the plunging sea;

And my shoulder stiff to the wheel I lay,
As I answer, "*Ay, ay, sir! Ha-a-rd a lee!*"

With the swerving leap of a startled steed
The ship flies fast in the eye of the wind,
The dangerous shoals on the lee recede,
And the headland white we have left behind.

The topsails flutter, the jibs collapse,
And belly and tug at the groaning cleats;
The spanker slats, and the mainsail flaps;
And thunders the order, "*Tacks and sheets!*"

'Mid the rattle of blocks and the tramp of the crew,
Hisses the rain of the rushing squall:
The sails are aback from clew to clew,
And now is the moment for, "Mainsail, haul!"

And the heavy yards, like a baby's toy,
By fifty strong arms are swiftly swung:
She holds her way, and I look with joy
For the first white spray o'er the bulwarks flung.

"*Let go, and haul!*" 'Tis the last command,
And the head-sails fill to the blast once more:
Astern and to leeward lies the land,
With its breakers white on the shingly shore.

What matters the reef, or the rain, or the squall?
I steady the helm for the open sea;
The first mate clamors, "Belay there, all!"
And the captain's breath once more comes free.

And so off shore let the good ship fly;
Little care I how the gusts may blow,
In my fo'castle bunk, in a jacket dry,
Eight bells have struck and my watch is below.

WALTER MITCHEL.

SONG OF THE EMIGRANTS IN BERMUDA.

WHERE the remote Bermudas ride
In the ocean's bosom unespied,
From a small boat that rowed along,
The listening winds received this song:—
"What should we do but sing His praise,
That led us through the watery maze
Where He the huge sea-monsters wracks,
That lift the deep upon their backs,
Unto an isle so long unknown,
And yet far kinder than our own?
He lands us on a grassy stage,
Safe from the storms, and prelate's rage:
He gave us this eternal spring
Which here enamels every thing,
And sends the fowls to us in care
On daily visits through the air.
He hangs in shades the orange bright,
Like golden lamps in a green night,
And does in the pomegranates close
Jewels more rich than Ormus shows:
He makes the figs our mouths to meet,
And throws the melons at our feet;
But apples, plants of such a price,
No tree could ever bear them twice.
With cedars chosen by his hand
From Lebanon he stores the land;
And makes the hollow seas that roar
Proclaim the ambergris on shore.
He cast (of which we rather boast)
The gospel's pearl upon our coast;
And in these rocks for us did frame
A temple where to sound his name.
Oh! let our voice his praise exalt
Till it arrive at heaven's vault,
Which then perhaps rebounding may
Echo beyond the Mexique bay."
Thus sung they in the English boat
A holy and a cheerful note:
And all the way, to guide their chime,
With falling oars they kept the time.

A. MARVELL.

CAVE OF STAFFA.

Thanks for the lessons of this spot, fit school
For the presumptuous thoughts that would assign
Mechanic laws to agency divine,
And, measuring heaven by earth, would overrule
Infinite power. The pillared vestibule,
Expanding yet precise, the roof embowed,
Might seem designed to humble man, when proud
Of his best workmanship by plan and tool.
Down-bearing with his whole Atlantic weight
Of tide and tempest on the structure's base,
And flashing upwards to its topmost height,
Ocean has proved its strength, and of its grace
In calms is conscious, finding for his freight
Of softest music some responsive place.

WORDSWORTH.

FLOWERS ON THE TOP OF THE PILLARS AT THE ENTRANCE OF THE CAVE.

Hope smiled when your nativity was cast,
Children of summer! Ye fresh flowers that brave
What summer here escapes not, the fierce wave,
And whole artillery of the western blast.
Battering the temple's front, its long-drawn nave
Smiting, as if each moment were their last.
But ye, bright flowers, on frieze and architrave
Survive, and once again the pile stands fast,
Calm as the universe, from specular towers
Of heaven contemplated by spirits pure —
Suns and their systems, diverse yet sustained
In symmetry, and fashioned to endure,
Unhurt, the assaults of time with all his hours,
As the supreme Artificer ordained.

WORDSWORTH.

THE STORM.

The sky is changed; and such a change! O night,
And storm, and darkness, ye are wondrous strong,
Yet lovely in your strength, as is the light
Of a dark eye in woman! Far along,
From peak to peak, the rattling crags among,
Leaps the live thunder! Not from one lone cloud,
But every mountain now hath found a tongue,
And Jura answers, through her misty shroud,
Back to the joyous Alps, who call to her aloud!

BYRON.

SUNSET.

The moon is up, and yet it is not night:
Sunset divides the sky with her; a sea
Of glory streams along the Alpine height
Of blue Friuli's mountains; heaven is free
From clouds, but of all colors seems to be
Melted to one vast Iris of the west,
Where the day joins the past eternity;
While, on the other hand, meek Dian's crest
Floats through the azure air, an island of the blest.

A single star is at her side, and reigns
With her o'er half the lovely heaven; but still
Yon sunny sea heaves brightly, and remains
Rolled o'er the peak of the far Rhœtian hill,

As day and night contending were
until
Nature reclaimed her order:
gently flows
The deep-dyed Brenta, where
their hues instil
The odorous purple of a new-born
rose,
Which streams upon her stream,
and glassed within it glows,

Filled with the face of heaven,
which, from afar,
Comes down upon the waters; all
its hues,
From the rich sunset to the rising
star,
Their magical variety diffuse:
And now they change; a paler
shadow strews
Its mantle o'er the mountains:
parting day
Dies like the dolphin, whom each
pang imbues
With a new color as it gasps away,
The last still loveliest, till 'tis gone
—and all is gray.

BYRON.

MOONLIGHT.

How sweet the moonlight sleeps
upon this bank!
Here will we sit, and let the sounds
of music
Creep in your ears: soft stillness,
and the night,
Become the touches of sweet harmony.
Sit, Jessica: look, how the floor of
heaven
Is thick inlaid with patines of bright
gold:
There's not the smallest orb which
thou behold'st,
But in his motion like an angel sings,
Still quiring to the young-ey'd
cherubims.

SHAKSPEARE.

ODE TO EVENING.

If aught of oaten stop, or pastoral
song,
May hope, chaste Eve, to soothe thy
modest ear,
Like thy own brawling springs,
Thy springs, and dying gales;

O nymph reserved, while now the
bright-haired sun
Sits in yon western tent, whose cloudy
skirts,
With brede ethereal wove,
O'erhang his wavy bed:

Now air is hush'd, save where the
weak-eyed bat
With short shrill shriek flits by on
leathern wing;
Or where the beetle winds
His small but sullen horn,

As oft he rises 'midst the twilight
path,
Against the pilgrim borne in heedless
hum:
Now teach me, maid composed,
To breathe some softened strain,

Whose numbers, stealing through thy
darkening vale,
May not unseemly with its stillness
suit;
As, musing slow, I hail
Thy genial loved return!

For when thy folding-star arising
shows
His paly circlet, at his warning lamp
The fragrant Hours and Elves
Who slept in buds the day,

And many a Nymph who wreathes
her brows with sedge,
And sheds the freshening dew, and,
lovelier still,
The pensive Pleasures sweet,
Prepare thy shadowy car.

Then let me rove some wild and
healthy scene;
Or find some ruin, 'midst its dreary
dells,
Whose walls more awful nod
By thy religious gleams.

Or, if chill blustering winds, or driving rain,
Prevent my willing feet, be mine the
hut,
That from the mountain's side,
Views wilds, and swelling floods,

And hamlets brown, and dim-discovered spires;
And hears their simple bell, and marks o'er all
Thy dewy fingers draw
The gradual dusky veil.

While Spring shall pour his showers, as oft he wont,
And bathe thy breathing tresses, meekest Eve!
While Summer loves to sport
Beneath thy lingering light;

While sallow Autumn fills thy lap with leaves;
Or Winter, yelling through the troublous air,
Affrights thy shrinking train,
And rudely rends thy robes;

So long, regardful of the quiet rule,
Shall Fancy, Friendship, Science, smiling Peace,
Thy gentlest influence own,
And love thy favorite name!

COLLINS.

NIGHT AND DEATH.

MYSTERIOUS Night! when our first Parent knew
Thee, from report divine, and heard thy name,
Did he not tremble for this lovely Frame,
This glorious canopy of Light and Blue?
Yet 'neath a curtain of translucent dew,
Bathed in the rays of the great setting Flame,
Hesperus with the Host of Heaven came,
And lo! Creation widened on Man's view.
Who could have thought such Darkness lay concealed
Within thy beams, O Sun! or who could find,
Whilst flower, and leaf, and insect stood revealed,
That to such countless Orbs thou mad'st us blind!
Why do we then shun Death with anxious strife?
If Light can thus deceive, wherefore not Life?

J. BLANCO WHITE.

TO THE EVENING STAR.

SINCE the Sun,
The absolute, the world-absorbing one,
Relinquished half his empire to the host
Emboldened by thy guidance, holy star,
Holy as princely, who that looks on thee,
Touching, as now, in thy humility
The mountain borders of this seat of care,
Can question that thy countenance is bright,
Celestial power, as much with love as light?

WORDSWORTH.

SONG OF THE STARS.

WHEN the radiant morn of creation broke,
And the world in the smile of God awoke,
And the empty realms of darkness and death
Were moved through their depths by his mighty breath,
And orbs of beauty and spheres of flame
From the void abyss by myriads came, —
In the joy of youth as they darted away,
Through the widening wastes of space to play,
Their silver voices in chorus rung,
And this was the song the bright ones sung.

"Away, away, through the wide, wide sky, —
The fair blue fields that before us lie, —
Each sun with the worlds that round him roll,
Each planet poised on her turning pole;

With her isles of green and her clouds of white,
And her waters that lie like fluid light.

"For the Source of Glory uncovers his face,
And the brightness o'erflows unbounded space;
And we drink, as we go, the luminous tides
In our ruddy air and our blooming sides:
Lo, yonder the living splendors play;
Away, on our joyous path, away!

"Look, look, through our glittering ranks afar,
In the infinite azure, star after star,
How they brighten and bloom as they swiftly pass!
How the verdure runs o'er each rolling mass!
And the path of the gentle winds is seen,
Where the small waves dance, and the young woods lean.

"And see, where brighter day-beams pour,
How the rainbows hang in the sunny shower;
And the morn and eve, with their pomp of hues,
Shift o'er the bright planets and shed their dews;
And 'twixt them both, o'er the teeming ground,
With her shadowy cone the night goes round!

"Away, away! in our blossoming bowers,
In the soft air wrapping these spheres of ours,
In the seas and fountains that shine with morn,
See, love is brooding, and life is born,
And breathing myriads are breaking from night,
To rejoice like us, in motion and light.

"Glide on in your beauty, ye youthful spheres,
To weave the dance that measures the years;
Glide on, in the glory and gladness sent,
To the farthest wall of the firmament, —
The boundless visible smile of Him,
To the veil of whose brow your lamps are dim."

BRYANT.

THE MILKY WAY.

"Lo," quoth he, "cast up thine eye,
See yonder, lo! the galaxie,
The which men clepe the Milky Way,
For it is white; and some parfay
Callen it Watling streete,
That once was brent with the hete,
When the Sunne's sonne the rede,
That hight Phaeton, would lead
Algate his father's cart, and gie.*
"The cart horses gan well aspie,
That he could no governaunce,
And gan for to leape and praunce,
And bear him up, and now down,
Till he saw the Scorpioun,
Which that in Heaven a signe is yet,
And for feré lost his wit
Of that, and let the reynés gone
Of his horses, and they anone
Soone up to mount, and downe descend,
Till both air and Earthé brend,
Till Jupiter, lo! at the last
Him slew, and fro the carté cast.

CHAUCER.

HOPE.

At summer eve, when heaven's aërial bow
Spans with bright arch the glittering hills below,
Why to yon mountain turns the musing eye,
Whose sunbright summit mingles with the sky?
Why do those cliffs of shadowy tint appear
More sweet than all the landscape smiling near? —
'Tis distance lends enchantment to the view,
And robes the mountain in its azure hue.

CAMPBELL.

* Guide.

TO THE RAINBOW.

Triumphal arch, that fill'st the sky
  When storms prepare to part,
I ask not proud philosophy
  To teach me what thou art.

Still seem as to my childhood's sight,
  A midway station given,
For happy spirits to alight
  Betwixt the earth and heaven.

Can all that optics teach unfold
  Thy form to please me so,
As when I dreamed of gems and gold
  Hid in thy radiant bow?

And yet, fair bow, no fabling dreams,
  But words of the Most High,
Have told why first thy robe of beams
  Was woven in the sky.

When o'er the green, undeluged earth
  Heaven's covenant thou didst shine,
How came the world's gray fathers forth
  To watch thy sacred sign!

And when its yellow lustre smiled
  O'er mountains yet untrod,
Each mother held aloft her child
  To bless the bow of God.

Methinks, thy jubilee to keep,
  The first-made anthem rang
On earth, delivered from the deep,
  And the first poet sang.

The earth to thee her incense yields,
  The lark thy welcome sings,
When, glittering in the freshened fields,
  The snowy mushroom springs.

How glorious is thy girdle cast
  O'er mountain, tower, and town,
Or mirrored in the ocean vast,
  A thousand fathoms down!

As fresh in yon horizon dark,
  As young thy beauties seem,
As when the eagle from the ark
  First sported in thy beam.

For, faithful to its sacred page,
  Heaven still rebuilds thy span;
Nor lets the type grow pale with age,
  That first spoke peace to man.

Campbell.

THE RAINBOW.

Now overhead a rainbow, bursting through
  The scattering clouds, shone, spanning the dark sea,
Resting its bright base on the quivering blue;
  And all within its arch appeared to be
Clearer than that without; and its wide hue
  Waxed broad and waving, like a banner free,
Then changed like to a bow that's bent, and then
Forsook the dim eyes of those shipwrecked men.

It changed, of course; a heavenly chameleon,
  The airy child of vapor and the sun,
Brought forth in purple, cradled in vermilion,
  Baptized in molten gold, and swathed in dun,
Glittering like crescents o'er a Turk's pavilion,
  And blending every color into one.

Byron.

THE CLOUD.

I sift the snow on the mountains below,
  And their great pines groan aghast;
And all the night 'tis my pillow white,
  While I sleep in the arms of the blast.

That orbèd maiden, with white fire laden,
  Whom mortals call the moon,
Glides glimmering o'er my fleece-like floor,
  By the midnight breezes strewn;
And wherever the beat of her unseen feet,

Which only the angels hear,
May have broken the woof of my tent's thin roof,
The stars peep behind her and peer;
And I laugh to see them whirl and flee,
Like a swarm of golden bees,
When I widen the rent in my wind-built tent,
Till the calm rivers, lakes, and seas,
Like strips of the sky fallen through me on high
Are each paved with the moon and these.

I am the daughter of earth and water,
And the nursling of the sky;
I pass through the pores of the ocean and shores;
I change, but I cannot die.
For after the rain, when with never a stain,
The pavilion of heaven is bare,
And the winds and sunbeams, with their convex gleams,
Build up the blue dome of air,
I silently laugh at my own cenotaph,
And out of the caverns of rain,
Like a child from the womb, like a ghost from the tomb,
I arise and unbuild it again.

SHELLEY.

A DROP OF DEW.

SEE how the orient dew,
Shed from the bosom of the morn
Into the blowing roses,
(Yet careless of its mansion new,
For the clear region where 'twas born,)
Round in itself encloses
And, in its little globe's extent,
Frames, as it can, its native element.
How it the purple flower does slight,
Scarce touching where it lies,
But gazing back upon the skies,
Shines with a mournful light,
Like its own tear,
Because so long divided from the sphere.
Restless it rolls, and insecure,
Trembling, lest it grow impure;
Till the warm sun pities its pain,
And to the skies exhales it back again.

So the soul, that drop, that ray,
Of the clear fountain of eternal day,
Could it within the human flower be seen,
Remembering still its former height,
Shuns the sweet leaves, and blossoms green,
And, recollecting its own light,
Does, in its pure and circling thoughts, express
The greater heaven in a heaven less.
In how coy a figure wound,
Every way it turns away,
So the world excluding round,
Yet receiving in the day,
Dark beneath, but bright above,
Here disdaining, there in love.
How loose and easy hence to go;
How girt and ready to ascend;
Moving but on a point below,
It all about does upwards bend.
Such did the manna's sacred dew distil,
White and entire, although congealed and chill;
Congealed on earth; but does, dissolving, run
Into the glories of the almighty sun.

MARVELL.

SMOKE.

LIGHT-WINGED Smoke! Icarian bird,
Melting thy pinions in thy upward flight;
Lark without song, and messenger of dawn,
Circling above the hamlets as thy nest;
Or else, departing dream, and shadowy form
Of midnight vision, gathering up thy skirts;
By night star-veiling, and by day
Darkening the light and blotting out the sun;
Go thou, my incense, upward from this hearth,
And ask the gods to pardon this clear flame.

THOREAU.

MIST.

Low-anchored cloud,
Newfoundland air,
Fountain-head and source of rivers,
Dew-cloth, dream-drapery,
And napkin spread by fays;
Drifting meadow of the air,
Where bloom the daisied banks and
violets,
And in whose fenny labyrinth
The bittern booms and heron wades;
Spirit of lakes and seas and rivers, —
Bear only perfumes and the scent
Of healing herbs to just men's fields.

Thoreau.

HAZE.

Woof of the fen, ethereal gauze,
Woven of Nature's richest stuffs,
Visible heat, air-water, and dry sea,
Last conquest of the eye;
Toil of the day displayed, sun-dust,
Aerial surf upon the shores of earth,
Ethereal estuary, frith of light,
Breakers of air, billows of heat,
Fine summer spray on inland seas;
Bird of the sun, transparent-winged,
Owlet of noon, soft-pinioned,
From heath or stubble rising without
song, —
Establish thy serenity o'er the fields.

Thoreau.

AT SEA.

The night is made for cooling shade,
For silence, and for sleep;
And when I was a child, I laid
My hands upon my breast, and prayed,
And sank to slumbers deep:
Childlike as then I lie to-night,
And watch my lonely cabin-light.

Each movement of the swaying lamp
Shows how the vessel reels:
As o'er her deck the billows tramp,
And all her timbers strain and cramp
With every shock she feels.
It starts and shudders, while it burns,
And in its hingèd socket turns.

Now swinging slow and slanting low,
It almost level lies;
And yet I know, while to and fro
I watch the seeming pendule go
With restless fall and rise,
The steady shaft is still upright,
Poising its little globe of light.

O hand of God! O lamp of peace!
O promise of my soul!
Though weak, and tossed, and ill at
ease,
Amid the roar of smiting seas,
The ship's convulsive roll,
I own with love and tender awe
Yon perfect type of faith and law.

A heavenly trust my spirit calms,
My soul is filled with light:
The Ocean sings his solemn psalms,
The wild winds chant: I cross my
palms,
Happy as if to-night
Under the cottage roof again
I heard the soothing summer rain.

J. T. Trowbridge.

II.

HUMAN LIFE.

HOME. — WOMAN. — LOVE. — FRIENDSHIP. — MANNERS. — BEAUTY.

"The privates of man's heart—
They speken and sound in his ear
As though they loud winds were." — Gower.

HUMAN LIFE.

HOME.

'Tis not in battles that from youth we train
The governor who must be wise and good,
And temper with the sternness of the brain
Thoughts motherly, and meek as womanhood.
Wisdom doth live with children round her knees:
Books, leisure, perfect freedom, and the talk
Man holds with week-day man in the hourly walk
Of the mind's business: these are the degrees
By which true Sway doth mount; this is the stalk
True Power doth grow on; and her rights are these.

Wordsworth.

TO CORINNE.

Happy, happier far than thou
With the laurel on thy brow,
She that makes the humblest hearth
Lovely but to one on earth!

Hemans.

LINES ON LEAVING EUROPE.

Bright flag at yonder tapering mast,
Fling out your field of azure blue;
Let star and stripe be westward cast,
And point as Freedom's eagle flew!
Strain home! O lithe and quivering spars!
Point home, my country's flag of stars!

My mother, in thy prayer to-night
There come new words and warmer tears;
On long, long darkness breaks the light,
Comes home the loved, the lost for years.
Sleep safe, O wave-worn mariner!
Fear not to-night, or storm or sea:
The ear of Heaven bends low to *her!*
He comes to shore who sails with me.
The wind-tossed spider needs no token
How stands the tree when lightnings blaze;
And, by a thread from heaven unbroken,
I know my mother lives and prays.

N. P. Willis.

THE LAST FAREWELL.

Farewell, ye lofty spires
That cheered the holy light!
Farewell, domestic fires
That broke the gloom of night!
Too soon these spires are lost,
Too fast we leave the bay,
Too soon by ocean tost
From hearth and home away,
Far away, far away.

Farewell, the busy town,
The wealthy and the wise,
Kind smile and honest frown
From bright, familiar eyes.
All these are fading now;
Our brig hastes on her way;
Her unremembering prow
Is leaping o'er the sea,
Far away, far away.

Farewell, my mother fond,
Too kind, too good to me,
Nor pearl, nor diamond
Would pay my debt to thee;
But even thy kiss denies
Upon my cheek to stay.
The winged vessel flies,
And billows round her play,
Far away, far away.

Farewell, my brothers true,
My betters, yet my peers,
How desert without you
My few and evil years!
But though aye one in heart,
Together sad or gay,
Rude ocean doth us part,
We separate to-day,
Far away, far away.

Farewell I breathe again
To dim New England's shore:
My heart shall beat not when
I pant for thee no more.
In yon green palmy isle,
Beneath the tropic ray,
I murmur never while
For thee and thine I pray:
Far away, far away.

E. B. E.

MY MOTHER'S PICTURE.

My mother, when I learned that thou wast dead,
Say, wast thou conscious of the tears I shed?
Hovered thy spirit o'er thy sorrowing son, —
Wretch even then, life's journey just begun?
I heard the bell tolled on thy burial-day;
I saw the hearse that bore thee slow away;
And, turning from my nursery-window, drew
A long, long sigh, and wept a last adieu!
But was it such? It was. Where thou art gone,
Adieus and farewells are a sound unknown;
May I but meet thee on that peaceful shore,
The parting word shall pass my lips no more.
Thy maidens, grieved themselves at my concern,
Oft gave me promise of thy quick return:
What ardently I wished, I long believed,
And, disappointed still, was still deceived, —
By expectation every day beguiled,
Dupe of tomorrow even from a child.
Thus many a sad tomorrow came and went,
Till, all my stock of infant sorrows spent,
I learned at last submission to my lot;
But, though I less deplored thee, ne'er forgot.
Where once we dwelt, our name is heard no more;
Children not thine have trod my nursery floor;
And where the gardener Robin, day by day,
Drew me to school along the public way, —
Delighted with my bawble coach, and wrapped
In scarlet mantle warm, and velvet cap, —
Could Time, his flight reversed, restore the hours
When, playing with thy vesture's tissued flowers, —
The violet, the pink, the jessamine, —
I pricked them into paper with a pin,
(And thou wast happier than myself the while —
Wouldst softly speak, and stroke my head, and smile,)
Could those few pleasant days again appear,
Might one wish bring them, would I wish them here?
But no! What here we call our life is such,
So little to be loved, and thou so much,
That I should ill requite thee to constrain
Thy unbound spirit into bonds again.

COWPER.

IF THOU WERT BY MY SIDE, MY LOVE.

If thou wert by my side, my love,
How fast would evening fail,
In green Bengala's palmy grove,
Listening the nightingale!

I miss thee, when, by Gunga's stream,
My twilight steps I guide,
But most beneath the lamp's pale beam
I miss thee from my side.

But when at morn and eve the star
Beholds me on my knee,
I feel, though thou art distant far,
Thy prayers ascend for me.

Then on, then on, where duty leads!
My course be onward still,
O'er broad Hindostan's sultry meads,
O'er bleak Almorah's hill.

That course nor Delhi's kingly gates,
Nor mild Malwah detain;
For sweet the bliss us both awaits
By yonder western main.

Thy towers, Bombay, gleam bright, they say,
Across the dark blue sea;
But ne'er were hearts so light and gay
As then shall meet in thee!

Heber.

THE COTTER'S SATURDAY NIGHT.

. . . .

November chill blaws loud wi' angry sugh;
The short'ning winter-day is near a close;
The miry beasts retreating frae the pleugh;
The black'ning trains o' craws to their repose;
The toil-worn Cotter frae his labor goes,
This night his weekly moil is at an end,
Collects his spades, his mattocks, and his hoes,
Hoping the morn in ease and rest to spend,
And weary, o'er the moor, his course does hameward bend.

At length his lonely cot appears in view,
Beneath the shelter of an aged tree;
Th' expectant wee-things, toddlin stacher thro',
To meet their Dad, wi' flichterin noise an' glee.
His wee bit ingle, blinkin bonnily,
His clane hearth-stane, his thriftie wifie's smile,
The lisping infant prattling on his knee,
Does all his weary carking cares beguile,
An' makes him quite forget his labor an' his toil.

. . . .

Wi' joy unfeign'd brothers and sisters meet,
An' each for other's welfare kindly spiers:
The social hours, swift-winged, unnoticed fleet;
Each tells the uncos that he sees or hears;
The parents, partial, eye their hopeful years,
Anticipation forward points the view.
The mother, wi' her needle and her shears,
Gars auld claes look amaist as weel's the new;
The father mixes a' wi' admonition due.

Their master's an' their mistress's command,
The younkers a' are warnèd to obey;
And mind their labors wi' an eydent hand,
And ne'er, tho' out o' sight, to jauk or play:
"And, oh! be sure to fear the Lord alway,
And mind your duty, duly, morn and night!
Lest in temptation's path ye gang astray,

Implore his counsel and assisting might:
They never sought in vain that sought the Lord aright!"

But, hark! a rap comes gently to the door;
Jenny, wha kens the meaning o' the same,
Tells how a neebor lad cam o'er the moor,
To do some errands, and convoy her hame.
The wily mother sees the conscious flame
Sparkle in Jenny's e'e, and flush her cheek;
Wi' heart-struck anxious care, inquires his name,
While Jenny hafflins is afraid to speak;
Weel pleas'd the mother hears, it's nae wild worthless rake.

Wi' kindly welcome Jenny brings him ben;
A strappan youth; he takes the mother's eye;
Blythe Jenny sees the visit's no ill ta'en;
The father cracks of horses, pleughs, and kye.
The youngster's artless heart o'erflows wi' joy,
But, blate and laithfu', scarce can weel behave;
The woman, wi' a woman's wiles, can spy
What makes the youth sae bashfu' an' sae grave;
Weel pleas'd to think her bairn's respected like the lave.

O happy love! where love like this is found!
O heart-felt raptures! bliss beyond compare!
I've pacèd much this weary, mortal round,
And sage experience bids me this declare —
"If Heav'n a draught of heav'nly pleasure spare,
One cordial in this melancholy vale,
'Tis when a youthful, loving, modest pair,
In other's arms breathe out the tender tale,
Beneath the milk-white thorn that scents the ev'ning gale!"

. . . .

But now the supper crowns their simple board,
The halesome parritch, chief o' Scotia's food:
The soupe their only hawkie does afford,
That 'yont the hallan snugly chows her cood;
The dame brings forth in complimental mood,
To grace the lad, her weel-hain'd kebbuck, fell,
And aft he's prest, and aft he calls it gude;
The frugal wifie, garrulous, will tell
How 'twas a towmond auld, sin' lint was i' the bell.

The cheerful supper done, wi' serious face,
They, round the ingle, form a circle wide;
The sire turns o'er, wi' patriarchal grace,
The big ha'-Bible, ance his father's pride:
His bonnet rev'rently is laid aside,
His lyart haffets wearing thin an' bare;
Those strains that once did sweet in Zion glide,
He wales a portion with judicious care;
And "Let us worship God!" he says, with solemn air.

They chant their artless notes in simple guise;
They tune their hearts, by far the noblest aim;
Perhaps "Dundee's" wild warbling measures rise,
Or plaintive "Martyrs," worthy of the name;
Or noble "Elgin" beats the heav'nward flame,
The sweetest far of Scotia's holy lays:
Compar'd with these, Italian trills are tame;

The tickled ears no heart-felt raptures raise;
Nae unison hae they with our Creator's praise.

The priest-like father reads the sacred page,
How Abram was the friend of God on high;
Or Moses bade eternal warfare wage
With Amalek's ungracious progeny;
Or how the royal Bard did groaning lie
Beneath the stroke of Heaven's avenging ire:
Or Job's pathetic plaint, and wailing cry;
Or rapt Isaiah's wild, seraphic fire;
Or other holy seers that tune the sacred lyre.

Perhaps the Christian volume is the theme,
How guiltless blood for guilty man was shed;
How He, who bore in Heaven the second name,
Had not on earth whereon to lay his head:
How his first followers and servants sped;
The precepts sage they wrote to many a land:
How he, who lone in Patmos banished,
Saw in the sun a mighty angel stand;
And heard great Babylon's doom pronounced by Heaven's command.

Then kneeling down, to Heaven's Eternal King,
The saint, the father, and the husband prays:
Hope "springs exulting on triumphant wing,"
That thus they all shall meet in future days:
There ever bask in uncreated rays,
No more to sigh, or shed the bitter tear,
Together hymning their Creator's praise,
In such society, yet still more dear;
While circling time moves round in an eternal sphere.

Compar'd with this, how poor religion's pride,
In all the pomp of method, and of art,
When men display to congregations wide
Devotion's ev'ry grace, except the heart!
The Power, incens'd, the pageant will desert,
The pompous strain, the sacerdotal stole;
But haply, in some cottage far apart,
May hear, well pleas'd, the language of the soul;
And in his book of life the inmates poor enrol.

Then homeward all take off their sev'ral way;
The youngling cottagers retire to rest:
The parent-pair their secret homage pay,
And proffer up to Heaven the warm request,
That He who stills the raven's clam'rous nest,
And decks the lily fair in flow'ry pride,
Would, in the way his wisdom sees the best,
For them and for their little ones provide;
But chiefly in their hearts with grace divine preside.

From scenes like these old Scotia's grandeur springs,
That makes her lov'd at home, rever'd abroad:
Princes and lords are but the breath of kings;
"An honest man's the noblest work of God:"
And certes, in fair virtue's heavenly road,
The cottage leaves the palace far behind;
What is a lordling's pomp? a cumbrous load,
Disguising oft the wretch of human kind,
Studied in arts of hell, in wickedness refin'd!

O Scotia! my dear, my native soil!
For whom my warmest wish to Heaven is sent!

Long may thy hardy sons of rustic toil
Be blest with health, and peace, and sweet content!
And, oh, may Heaven their simple lives prevent
From luxury's contagion, weak and vile!
Then, howe'er crowns and coronets be rent,
A virtuous populace may rise the while,
And stand a wall of fire around their much-lov'd isle.

O Thou! who pour'd the patriotic tide
That stream'd thro' Wallace's undaunted heart;
Who dar'd to nobly stem tyrannic pride,
Or nobly die, the second glorious part,
(The patriot's God, peculiarly Thou art,
His friend, inspirer, guardian, and reward!)
O never, never Scotia's realm desert;
But still the patriot, and the patriot-bard,
In bright succession raise, her ornament and guard!

BURNS.

THE BABE.

NAKED on parents' knees, a newborn child,
Weeping thou sat'st when all around thee smiled:
So live, that, sinking to thy last long sleep,
Thou then mayst smile while all around thee weep.

SIR WILLIAM JONES:
Translated from Calidasa.

THE WOOD-FIRE.

THIS bright wood-fire,
So like to that which warmed and lit
My youthful days, — how doth it flit
Back on the periods nigher!
Re-lighting and re-warming with its glow
The bright scenes of my youth, — all gone out now.
How eagerly its flickering blaze doth catch
On every point now wrapped in time's deep shade!
Into what wild grotesqueness by its flash
And fitful checkering is the picture made!
When I am glad or gay,
Let me walk forth into the brilliant sun,
And with congenial rays be shone upon:
When I am sad, or thought-bewitched would be,
Let me glide forth in moonlight's mystery,
But never, while I live this changeful life,
This past and future with all wonders rife,
Never, bright flame, may be denied to me
Thy dear, life-imaging, close sympathy.
What but my hopes shot upwards e'er so bright?
What but my fortunes sank so low in night?
Why art thou banished from our hearth and hall,
Thou who art welcomed and beloved by all?
Was thy existence then too fanciful
For our life's common light, who are so dull?
Did thy bright gleam mysterious converse hold
With our congenial souls? secrets too bold?
Well, we are safe and strong; for now we sit
Beside a hearth where no dim shadows flit;
Where nothing cheers nor saddens, but a fire
Warms feet and hands, nor does to more aspire;
By whose compact, utilitarian heap,
The present may sit down and go to sleep,
Nor fear the ghosts who from the dim past walked,
And with us by the unequal light of the old wood-fire talked.

E. S. H.

GIVE ME THE OLD.

I.

Old wine to drink!
Ay, give the slippery juice
That drippeth from the grape thrown loose
Within the tun;
Plucked from beneath the cliff
Of sunny-sided Teneriffe,
And ripened 'neath the blink
Of India's sun!
Peat whiskey hot,
Tempered with well-boiled water!
These make the long night shorter,
Forgetting not
Good stout old English porter.

II.

Old wood to burn!—
Ay, bring the hillside beech
From where the owlets meet and screech,
And ravens croak;
The crackling pine, and cedar sweet;
Bring too a clump of fragrant peat,
Dug 'neath the fern;
The knotted oak,
A fagot too, perhap,
Whose bright flame, dancing, winking,
Shall light us at our drinking;
While the oozing sap
Shall make sweet music to our thinking.

III.

Old books to read!
Ay, bring those nodes of wit,
The brazen-clasped, the vellum-writ,
Time-honored tomes!
The same my sire scanned before,
The same my grandsire thumbèd o'er,
The same his sire from college bore,
The well-earned meed
Of Oxford's domes:
Old *Homer* blind,
Old *Horace*, rake *Anacreon*, by
Old *Tully*, *Plautus*, *Terence* lie;
Mort *Arthur's* olden minstrelsie,
Quaint *Burton*, quainter *Spenser*, ay!
And *Gervase Markham's* venerie—
Nor leave behind
The Holy Book by which we live and die.

IV.

Old friends to talk!
Ay, bring those chosen few,
The wise, the courtly, and the true,
So rarely found;
Him for my wine, him for my stud,
Him for my easel, distich, bud
In mountain walk!
Bring *Walter* good:
With soulful *Fred;* and learned *Will*,
And thee, my *alter ego*, (dearer still
For every mood).

R. H. MESSINGER.

TO A CHILD.

I WOULD that thou might always be
As innocent as now,
That time might ever leave as free
Thy yet unwritten brow.
I would life were all poetry
To gentle measure set,
That nought but chastened melody
Might stain thine eye of jet,
Nor one discordant note be spoken,
Till God the cunning harp had broken.
I fear thy gentle loveliness,
Thy witching tone and air,
Thine eye's beseeching earnestness
May be to thee a snare.
The silver stars may purely shine,
The waters taintless flow;
But they who kneel at woman's shrine
Breathe on it as they bow.

N. P. WILLIS.

THE CHILDREN'S HOUR.

BETWEEN the dark and the daylight,
When the night is beginning to lower,
Comes a pause in the day's occupations
That is known as the children's hour.

I hear in the chamber above me
The patter of little feet,
The sound of a door that is opened,
And voices soft and sweet.

From my study I see in the lamplight,
Descending the broad hall-stair,

Grave Alice and laughing Allegra,
  And Edith with golden hair.

A whisper, and then a silence;
  Yet I know by their merry eyes
They are plotting and planning together
  To take me by surprise.

A sudden rush from the stairway,
  A sudden raid from the hall:
By three doors left unguarded
  They enter my castle wall.

They climb up into my turret
  O'er the arms and back of my chair;
If I try to escape, they surround me:
  They seem to be everywhere.

They almost devour me with kisses;
  Their arms about me intwine,
Till I think of the Bishop of Bingen
  In his Mouse-Tower on the Rhine.

Do you think, O blue-eyed banditti!
  Because you have scaled the wall,
Such an old mustache as I am
  Is not a match for you all?

I have you fast in my fortress,
  And will not let you depart,
But put you down into the dungeons
  In the Round Tower of my heart.

And there will I keep you forever, —
  Yes, forever and a day,
Till the walls shall crumble to ruin,
  And moulder in dust away.

LONGFELLOW.

WOMAN.

THERE in the fane a beauteous creature stands,
The first best work of the Creator's hands,
Whose slender limbs inadequately bear
A full-orbed bosom and a weight of care;
Whose teeth like pearls, whose lips like cherries, show,
And fawn-like eyes still tremble as they glow.

WILSON:
Translated from Calidasa.

TO SILVIA.

I AM holy while I stand
  Circum-crost by thy pure hand;
But when that is gone, again
  I, as others, am profane.

HERRICK.

THE ROSE OF THE WORLD.

I.

Lo, when the Lord made north and south,
  And sun and moon ordained, he,
Forth bringing each by word of mouth
  In order of its dignity,
Did man from the crude clay express
  By sequence, and, all else decreed,
He formed the woman; nor might less
  Than Sabbath such a work succeed.

II.

And still with favor singled out,
  Marred less than man by mortal fall,
Her disposition is devout,
  Her countenance angelical.
No faithless thought her instinct shrouds,
  But fancy checkers settled sense,
Like alteration of the clouds
  On noonday's azure permanence.
Pure courtesy, composure, ease,
  Declare affections nobly fixed,
And impulse sprung from due degrees
  Of sense and spirit sweetly mixed.
Her modesty, her chiefest grace,
  The cestus clasping Venus' side,
Is potent to deject the face
  Of him who would affront its pride.
Wrong dares not in her presence speak,
  Nor spotted thought its taint disclose
Under the protest of a cheek
  Outbragging Nature's boast, the rose.
In mind and manners how discreet!
  How artless in her very art!
How candid in discourse! how sweet
  The concord of her lips and heart!

How (not to call true instinct's bent
  And woman's very nature harm),
How amiable and innocent
  Her pleasure in her power to charm!
How humbly careful to attract,
  Though crowned with all the soul desires,
Connubial aptitude exact,
  Diversity that never tires!

COVENTRY PATMORE.

SHE WALKS IN BEAUTY.

SHE walks in beauty, like the night
  Of cloudless climes and starry skies;
And all that's best of dark and bright
  Meet in her aspect and her eyes:
Thus mellowed to that tender light
  Which heaven to gaudy day denies.

One shade the more, one ray the less,
  Had half impaired the nameless grace
Which waves in every raven tress,
  Or softly lightens o'er her face,
Where thoughts serenely sweet express
  How pure, how dear, their dwelling-place.

And on that cheek, and o'er that brow,
  So soft, so calm, yet eloquent,
The smiles that win, the tints that glow,
  But tell of days in goodness spent,
A mind at peace with all below,
  A heart whose love is innocent.

BYRON.

ANATHEMATA.

"O maiden! come into port bravely, or sail with God the seas."

WITH joys unknown, with sadness unconfessed,
The generous heart accepts the passing year,
Finds duties dear, and labor sweet as rest,
And for itself knows neither care nor fear.

Fresh as the morning, earnest as the hour
That calls the noisy world to grateful sleep,
Our silent thought reveres the nameless power
That high seclusion round thy life doth keep:
So feigned the poets, did Diana love
To smile upon her darlings while they slept;
Serene, untouched, and walking far above
The narrow ways wherein the many crept,
Along her lonely path of luminous air
She glided, of her brightness unaware.

Yet if they said she heeded not the hymn
Of shepherds gazing heavenward from the moor;
Or homeward sailors, when the waters dim
Flashed with long splendors, widening toward the shore;
Nor wondering eyes of children cared to see;
Or glowing face of happy lover, upturned,
As late he wended from the trysting-tree,
Lit by the kindly lamp in heaven that burned;
And heard unmoved the prayer of wakeful pain,
Or consecrated maiden's holy vow, —
Believe them not: they sing the song in vain;
For so it never was, and is not now.
Her heart was gentle as her face was fair,
With grace and love and pity dwelling there.

F. B. SANBORN.

HONORIA.

I WATCHED her face, suspecting germs
  Of love: her farewell showed me plain
She loved, on the majestic terms
  That she should not be loved again.
She was all mildness; yet t'was writ
  Upon her beauty legibly,

"He that's for heaven itself unfit,
Let him not hope to merit me."

. . . .

And though her charms are a strong law
Compelling all men to admire,
They are so clad with lovely awe,
None but the noble dares desire.

He who would seek to make her his,
Will comprehend that souls of grace
Own sweet repulsion, and that 'tis
The quality of their embrace

To be like the majestic reach
Of coupled suns, that, from afar,
Mingle their mutual spheres, while each
Circles the twin obsequious star:

And in the warmth of hand to hand,
Of heart to heart, he'll vow to note
And reverently understand
How the two spirits shine remote;

And ne'er to numb fine honor's nerve,
Nor let sweet awe in passion melt,
Nor fail by courtesies to observe
The space which makes attraction felt;

Nor cease to guard like life the sense
Which tells him that the embrace of love
Is o'er a gulf of difference
Love cannot sound, nor death remove.

COVENTRY PATMORE.

DUCHESSE BLANCHE.

It happed that I came on a day
Into a place, there that I say,
Truly the fairest companey
Of ladies that ever man with eye
Had seen together in one place, —
Shall I clepe it hap or grace?
Among these ladies thus each one
Sooth to say I saw one
That was like none of the rout,
For I dare swear without doubt,
That as the summer's Sunne bright
Is fairer, clearer, and hath more light
Than any other planet in Heaven,
The moone, or the starres seven,
For all the world, so had she
Surmounten them all of beauty,
Of manner, and of comeliness,
Of stature, and of well set gladnesse,
Of goodly heed, and so well besey,[1] —
Shortly what shall I more say,
By God, and by his holowes[2] twelve,
It was my sweet, right all herselve.
She had so stedfast countenance
In noble port and maintenance,
And Love that well harde my bone[3]
Had espied me thus soone,
That she full soone in my thought
As, help me God, so was I caught
So suddenly that I ne took
No manner counsel but at her look,
And at my heart for why her eyen
So gladly I trow mine heart, seyen
That purely then mine own thought
Said, 'Twere better to serve her for nought
Than with another to be well.

I saw her dance so comely,
Carol and sing so swetely,
Laugh and play so womanly,
And look so debonairly,
So goodly speak, and so friendly,
That certes I trow that evermore
N'as seen so blissful a treasore,
For every hair on her head,
Sooth to say, it was not red,
Nor neither yellow nor brown it n'as,
Methought most like gold it was,
And such eyen my lady had,
Debonnaire, good, glad, and sad,
Simple, of good mokel,[4] not too wide,
Thereto her look was not aside,
Nor overtwhart, but beset so well
It drew and took up every dell.
All that on her 'gan behold
Her eyen seemed anon she would
Have mercy, — folly wenden[5] so,
But it was never the rather do.
It was no counterfeited thing
It was her own pure looking
That the goddess Dame Nature
Had made them open by measure
And close; for, were she never so glad
Her looking was not foolish sprad[6]
Nor wildly, though that she played;
But ever methought her eyen said

[1] Beseen, appearing.
[2] Saints.
[3] Boon, petition.
[4] Quantity.
[5] Thought.
[6] Spread.

By God my wrath is all forgive.
Therewith her list so well to live,
That dulness was of her adrad,
She n'as too sober ne too glad;
In all thinges more measure
Had never I trowe creature,
But many one with her look she hurt,
And that sat her full little at herte:
For she knew nothing of their thought,
But whether she knew, or knew it not,
Alway she ne cared for them a stree;[1]
To get her love no near n'as he
That woned[2] at home, than he in Inde,
The foremost was alway behinde;
But good folk over all other
She loved as man may his brother,
Of which love she was wonder large,
In skilful places that bear charge:
But what a visage had she thereto,
Alas! my heart is wonder wo
That I not can describen it; —
Me lacketh both English and wit
For to undo it at the full.
And eke my spirits be so dull
So great a thing for to devise,
I have not wit that can suffice
To comprehend her beauté,
But thus much I dare saine, that she
Was white, ruddy, fresh, and lifely hued,
And every day her beauty newed.
And nigh her face was alderbest;[3]
For, certes, Nature had such lest
To make that fair, that truly she
Was her chief patron of beauté,
And chief example of all her worke
And moulter:[4] for, be it never so derke,
Methinks I see her evermo,
And yet, moreover, though all tho
That ever lived were now alive,
Not would have founde to descrive
In all her face a wicked sign, —
For it was sad, simple, and benign.
And such a goodly sweet speech
Had that sweet, my life's leech,
So friendly, and so well y-grounded
Upon all reason, so well founded,
And so treatable to all good,
That I dare swear well by the rood,
Of eloquence was never found
So sweet a sounding faconde,[5]
Nor truer tongued nor scornèd less,
Nor bét[6] could heal, that, by the Mass
I durst swear, though the Pope it sung,

[1] Straw.
[2] Lived.
[3] Best of all.
[4] Monster.
[5] Eloquence.
[6] Better.

There was never yet through her tongue
Man or woman greatly harmèd
As for her was all harm hid,
No lassie flattering in her worde,
That, purely, her simple record
Was found as true as any bond,
Or truth of any man'es hand.

Her throat, as I have now memory,
Seemed as a round tower of ivory,
Of good greatness, and not too great,
And fair white she hete[7]
That was my lady's name right,
She was thereto fair and bright,
She had not her name wrong,
Right fair shoulders, and body long
She had, and armes ever lith
Fattish, fleshy, not great therewith,
Right white hands and nailès red
Round breasts, and of good brede[8]
Her lippes were; a straight flat back,
I knew on her none other lack,
That all her limbs were pure snowing
In as far as I had knowing.
Thereto she could so well play
What that her list, that I dare say
That was like to torch bright
That every man may take of light
Enough, and it hath never the less
Of manner and of comeliness.
Right so fared my lady dear
For every wight of her mannere
Might catch enough if that he would
If he had eyes her to behold
For I dare swear well if that she
Had among ten thousand be,
She would have been at the best,
A chief mirror of all the feast
Though they had stood in a row
To men's eyen that could know,
For whereso men had played or waked,
Methought the fellowship as naked
Without her, that I saw once
As a crown without stones.
Truely she was to mine eye
The solein[9] phœnix of Araby,
For there liveth never but one,
Nor such as she ne know I none.
To speak of goodness, truely she
Had as much debonnairte
As ever had Hester in the Bible,
And more, if more were possible;
And sooth to say therewithal
She had a wit so general,

[7] Was called.
[8] Breadth.
[9] Sole.

So well inclinèd to all good
That all her wit was set by the rood,
Without malice, upon gladness,
And thereto I saw never yet a less
Harmful than she was in doing.
I say not that she not had knowing
What harm was, or else she
Had known no good, so thinketh me:
And truly, for to speak of truth
But she had had, it had been ruth,
Therefore she had so much her dell
And I dare say, and swear it well
That Truth himself over all and all
Had chose his manor principal
In her that was his resting place;
Thereto she had the moste grace
To have stedfast perseverance
And easy attempre governance
That ever I knew or wist yet
So pure suffraunt was her wit.

CHAUCER.

LUCY.

THREE years she grew in sun and shower;
Then Nature said, " A lovelier flower
On earth was never sown;
This child I to myself will take;
She shall be mine, and I will make
A lady of my own.

"Myself will to my darling be
Both law and impulse; and with me
The girl, in rock and plain,
In earth and heaven, in glade and bower,
Shall feel an overseeing power
To kindle or restrain.

"The floating clouds their state shall lend
To her; for her the willow bend:
Nor shall she fail to see,
Even in the motions of the storm,
Grace that shall mould the maiden's form
By silent sympathy.

"The stars of midnight shall be dear
To her; and she shall lean her ear
In many a secret place
Where rivulets dance their wayward round;
And beauty, born of murmuring sound,
Shall pass into her face.

"And vital feelings of delight
Shall rear her form to stately height,
Her virgin bosom swell:
Such thoughts to Lucy I will give,
While she and I together live
Here in this happy dell."

WORDSWORTH.

LOVE.

THOU art not gone, being gone, where'er thou art
Thou leav'st in him thy watchful eyes, in him thy loving heart.

DONNE.

TRUE LOVE.

I THINK not on my father,
And these great tears grace his remembrance more
Than those I shed for him. What was he like?
I have forgot him: my imagination
Carries no favor in it, but Bertram's.
I am undone: there is no living, none,
If Bertram be away. It were all one,
That I should love a bright, particular star,
And think to wed it, he is so above me:
In his bright radiance and collateral light
Must I be comforted, not in his sphere.
The ambition in my love thus plagues itself.
The hind that would be mated by the lion
Must die for love. 'Twas pretty, though a plague,
To see him every hour; to sit and draw
His archèd brows, his hawking eye, his curls,
In our heart's table; heart, too capable
Of every line and trick of his sweet favor:
But now he's gone, and my idolatrous fancy
Must sanctify his relics.

SHAKSPEARE.

THE QUEEN.

I.

To heroism and holiness
  How hard it is for man to soar,
But how much harder to be less
  Than what his mistress loves him for!
He does with ease what do he must,
  Or lose her, and there's nought debarred
From him who's called to meet her trust,
  And credit her desired regard.
Ah, wasteful woman! she that may
  On her sweet self set her own price,
Knowing he cannot choose but pay;
  How has she cheapened paradise,
How given for nought her priceless gift,
  How spoiled the bread, and spilled the wine,
Which, spent with due, respective thrift,
  Had made brutes men, and men divine.

II.

O queen! awake to thy renown,
  Require what 'tis our wealth to give,
And comprehend and wear the crown
  Of thy despised prerogative!
I who in manhood's name at length
  With glad songs come to abdicate
The gross regality of strength,
  Must yet in this thy praise abate,
That through thine erring humbleness
  And disregard of thy degree,
Mainly, has man been so much less
  Than fits his fellowship with thee.
High thoughts had shaped the foolish brow,
  The coward had grasped the hero's sword,
The vilest had been great, hadst thou,
  Just to thyself, been worth's reward:
But lofty honors undersold
  Seller and buyer both disgrace;
And favor that makes folly bold
  Puts out the light in virtue's face.

COVENTRY PATMORE.

I'LL NEVER LOVE THEE MORE.

MY dear and only love, I pray
  That little world of thee
Be governed by no other sway
  But purest monarchy:
For if confusion have a part,
  Which virtuous souls abhor,
And hold a synod in thy heart,
  I'll never love thee more.

As Alexander I will reign,
  And I will reign alone:
My thoughts did evermore disdain
  A rival on my throne.
He either fears his fate too much,
  Or his deserts are small,
Who dares not put it to the touch,
  To gain or lose it all.

But, if no faithless action stain
  Thy love and constant word,
I'll make thee famous by my pen,
  And glorious by my sword.
I'll serve thee in such noble ways
  As ne'er was known before;
I'll deck and crown thy head with bays,
  And love thee more and more.

MARQUIS OF MONTROSE.

TO LUCASTA.

TELL me not, sweet, I am unkind,
  That from the nunnery
Of thy chaste breast and quiet mind,
  To war and arms I fly.

True, a new mistress now I chase,
  The first foe in the field;
And with a stronger faith embrace
  A sword, a horse, a shield.

Yet this inconstancy is such
  As you too shall adore;
I could not love thee, dear, so much,
  Loved I not honor more.

RICHARD LOVELACE.

APOLOGY FOR HAVING LOVED BEFORE.

THEY that never had the use
Of the grape's surprising juice,
To the first delicious cup
All their reason render up:

Neither do, nor care to, know,
Whether it be best or no.

So they that are to love inclined,
Sway'd by chance, nor choice or art,
To the first that's fair or kind,
Make a present of their heart:
Tis not she that first we love,
But whom dying we approve.

To man, that was in th' evening made,
Stars gave the first delight;
Admiring in the gloomy shade
Those little drops of light.

Then, at Aurora, whose fair hand
Removed them from the skies,
He gazing toward the east did stand,
She entertained his eyes.

But when the bright sun did appear,
All those he 'gan despise;
His wonder was determin'd there.
And could no higher rise.

He neither might nor wished to know
A more refulgent light;
For that (as mine your beauties now),
Employed his utmost sight.

EDMUND WALLER.

THE LADY'S YES.

"YES!" I answered you last night:
"No!" this morning, sir, I say.
Colors seen by candle-light
Will not look the same by day.

When the tabors played their best,
Lamps above, and laughs below,
Love me sounded like a jest,
Fit for *Yes*, or fit for *No!*

Call me false; or call me free;
Vow, whatever light may shine,
No man on thy face shall see
Any grief for change on mine.

Yet the sin is on us both:
Time to dance is not to woo;
Wooer light makes fickle troth,
Scorn of *me* recoils on *you*.

Learn to win a lady's faith
Nobly as the thing is high,
Bravely as for life and death,
With a loyal gravity.

Lead her from the festive boards;
Point her to the starry skies;
Guard her by your faithful words,
Pure from courtship's flatteries.

By your truth she shall be true,
Ever true, as wives of yore,
And her *Yes*, once said to you,
Shall be Yes for evermore.

ELIZABETH BARRETT BROWNING.

OUTGROWN.

NAY, you wrong her my friend, she's not fickle; her love she has simply outgrown:
One can read the whole matter, translating her heart by the light of one's own.

Can you bear me to talk with you frankly? There is much that my heart would say;
And you know we were children together, have quarrelled and "made up" in play.

And so, for the sake of old friendship, I venture to tell you the truth, —
As plainly, perhaps, and as bluntly, as I might in our earlier youth.

Five summers ago, when you wooed her, you stood on the selfsame plane,
Face to face, heart to heart, never dreaming your souls could be parted again.

She loved you at that time entirely, in the bloom of her life's early May;
And it is not her fault, I repeat it, that she does not love you to-day.

Nature never stands still, nor souls either: they ever go up or go down;

And hers has been steadily soaring — but how has it been with your own?

She has struggled and yearned and aspired, grown purer and wiser each year:
The stars are not farther above you in yon luminous atmosphere!

For she whom you crowned with fresh roses, down yonder, five summers ago,
Has learned that the first of our duties to God and ourselves is to grow.

Her eyes they are sweeter and calmer; but their vision is clearer as well:
Her voice has a tenderer cadence, but is pure as a silver bell.

Her face has the look worn by those who with God and his angels have talked:
The white robes she wears are less white than the spirits with whom she has walked.

And you? Have you aimed at the highest? Have you, too, aspired and prayed?
Have you looked upon evil unsullied? Have you conquered it undismayed?

Have you, too, grown purer and wiser, as the months and the years have rolled on?
Did you meet her this morning rejoicing in the triumph of victory won?

Nay, hear me! The truth cannot harm you. When to-day in her presence you stood,
Was the hand that you gave her as white and clean as that of her womanhood?

Go measure yourself by her standard; look back on the years that have fled:
Then ask, if you need, why she tells you that the love of her girlhood is dead.

She cannot look down to her lover: her love like her soul, aspires;
He must stand by her side, or above her, who would kindle its holy fires.

Now farewell! For the sake of old friendship I have ventured to tell you the truth,
As plainly, perhaps, and as bluntly, as I might in our earlier youth.

JULIA C. R. DORR.

THE PORTRAIT.

GIVE place, ye ladies, and begone,
Boast not yourselves at all:
For here at hand approacheth one
Whose face will stain you all.

The virtue of her lively looks
Excels the precious stone:
I wish to have none other books
To read or look upon.

In each of her two crystal eyes
Smileth a naked boy:
It would you all in heart suffice
To see that lamp of joy.

I think Nature hath lost the mould
Where she her shape did take;
Or else I doubt if Nature could
So fair a creature make.

In life she is Diana chaste,
In truth Penelope;
In word and eke in deed steadfast:
What will you more we say?

If all the world were sought so far,
Who could find such a wight?
Her beauty twinkleth like a star
Within the frosty night.

Her rosial color comes and goes
With such a comely grace,
More ruddier too, than in the rose
Within her lovely face.

At Bacchus' feast none shall her meet,
Nor at no wanton play,
Nor gazing in an open street,
Nor gadding as astray.

The modest mirth that she doth use
Is mixt with shamefastness;
All vice she doth wholly refuse,
And hateth idleness.

O Lord! it is a world to see
How virtue can repair
And deck in her such honesty,
Whom Nature made so fair!

How might I do to get a graffe
Of this unspotted tree?
For all the rest are plain but chaff,
Which seem good corn to be.

HEYWOOD.

THE TRIBUTE.

No splendor 'neath the sky's proud dome
But serves for her familiar wear;
The far-fetch'd diamond finds its home
Flashing and smouldering in her hair;
For her the seas their pearls reveal;
Art and strange lands her pomp supply
With purple, chrome, and cochineal,
Ochre, and lapis lazuli;
The worm its golden woof presents;
Whatever runs, flies, dives, or delves,
All doff for her their ornaments,
Which suit her better than themselves;
And all, by this their power to give
Proving her right to take, proclaim
Her beauty's clear prerogative
To profit so by Eden's blame.

COVENTRY PATMORE.

ELIZABETH OF BOHEMIA.

You meaner beauties of the night,
That poorly satisfy our eyes
More by your number than your light, —
You common people of the skies,
What are you when the sun shall rise?

Ye violets that first appear,
By your pure purple mantles known,
Like the proud virgins of the year,
As if the spring were all your own, —
What are you when the rose is blown?

Ye curious chanters of the wood,
That warble forth dame Nature's lays,
Thinking your voices understood
By your weak accents, — what's your praise
When Philomel her voice shall raise?

So when my mistress shall be seen,
In form and beauty of her mind,
By virtue first, then choice, a queen,
Tell me if she was not design'd
Th' eclipse and glory of her kind.

SIR HENRY WOTTON.

THOU HAST SWORN BY THY GOD, MY JEANIE.

Thou hast sworn by thy God, my Jeanie,
By that pretty white hand o' thine,
And by a' the lowing stars in heaven,
That thou wad aye be mine!
And I hae sworn by my God, my Jeanie,
And by that kind heart o' thine,
By a' the stars sown thick owre heaven,
That thou shalt aye be mine!

Then foul fa' the hands that wad loose sic bands,
And the heart that wad part sic luve!
But there's nae hand can loose my band,
But the finger o' Him above.
Though the wee wee cot maun be my bield,
And my clothing ne'er sa mean,
I wad lap me up rich i' the faulds o' luve, —
Heaven's armfu' o' my Jean.

Her white arm wad be a pillow for me
Fu' safter than the down;
And Luve wad winnow owre us his kind kind wings,

An' sweetly I'd sleep an' sound.
Come here to me, thou lass o' my
luve!
Come here and kneel wi me!
The morn is fu' o' the presence o'
God,
And I canna pray without thee.

The morn wind is sweet 'mang the
beds o' new flowers,
The wee birds sing kindlie and hie;
Our gudeman leans o'er his kale
yard dyke,
And a blythe auld bodie is he.
The Beuk maun be ta'en when the
carle comes hame,
Wi the holy psalmodie;
And thou maun speak o' me to thy
God,
And I will speak o' thee.

CUNNINGHAM.

VIRGINIA.

THIS knight a doughter hadde by
his wif.
No children had he mo in all his lif.
Faire was this maid in excellent
beautee
Aboven every wight that man may
see:
For nature hath with soveraine dili-
gence
Yformed hire in so gret excellence,
As though she wolde sayn, lo, I
Nature,
Thus can I forme and peint a crea-
ture,
Whan that me list; who can me
contrefete?
Pigmalion? not, though he ay forge
and bete,
Or grave, or peinte: for I dare wel
sain,
Apelles, Xeuxis, shulden werche
in vain,
Other to grave, or peinte, or forge,
or bete,
If they presumed me to contrefete.
For he that is the Former principal,
Hath maked me his vicaire general
To forme and peinten erthly crea-
tures
Right as me list, and eche thing in
my cure is
Under the mone, that may wane
and waxe.
And for my werk right nothing wol
I axe;
My lord and I ben ful of one accord.
I made her to the worship of my Lord.

CHAUCER.

THE BRIDE.

Lo! where she comes along with
portly pace,
Like Phœbe from her chamber of
the east,
Arising forth to run her mighty race,
Clad all in white, that seems a virgin
best.
So well it her beseems, that ye would
ween
Some angel she had been.
Her long, loose yellow locks, like
golden wire,
Sprinkled with pearl, and pearling
flowers atween,
Do like a golden mantle her attire;
And being crownèd with a garland
green,
Seem like some maiden queen.
Her modest eyes abashèd to behold
So many gazers as on her do stare,
Upon the lowly ground affixèd are;
Ne dare lift up her countenance too
bold,
But blush to hear her praises sung
so loud,
So far from being proud.
Nathless do ye still loud her praises
sing,
That all the woods may answer, and
your echo ring.

Tell me, ye merchants' daughters,
did ye see
So fair a creature in your town be-
fore?
So sweet, so lovely, and so mild as
she,
Adorned with Beauty's grace and
Virtue's store?
Her goodly eyes like sapphires, shin-
ing bright,
Her forehead ivory white,
Her cheeks like apples which the
sun hath rudded,
Her lips like cherries charming men
to bite,
Her breast like to a bowl of cream
uncrudded,
Her paps like lilies budded,

Her snowy neck like to a marble tower;
And all her body like a palace fair,
Ascending up with many a stately stair
To Honor's seat and Chastity's sweet bower.

Why stand ye still, ye virgins, in amaze,
Upon her so to gaze,
Whilst ye forget your former lay to sing,
To which the woods did answer, and your echo ring.

SPENSER.

THE BRIDE.

HER finger was so small the ring
Would not stay on which they did bring, —
It was too wide a peck;
And, to say truth, — for out it must, —
It looked like the great collar — just —
About our young colt's neck.

Her feet beneath her petticoat,
Like little mice stole in and out,
As if they feared the light;
But O, she dances such a way!
No sun upon an Easter day
Is half so fine a sight.

Her cheeks so rare a white was on,
No daisy makes comparison;
Who sees them is undone;
For streaks of red were mingled there,
Such as are on a Cath'rine pear,
The side that's next the sun.

Her lips were red; and one was thin,
Compared to that was next her chin,
Some bee had stung it newly;
But, Dick, her eyes so guard her face,
I durst no more upon them gaze,
Than on the sun in July.

Her mouth so small, when she does speak
Thou'dst swear her teeth her words did break,
That they might passage get;
But she so handled still the matter,
They came as good as ours, or better,
And are not spent a whit.

SIR JOHN SUCKLING.

VIOLA DISGUISED AND THE DUKE.

Duke. — Once more, Cesario,
Get thee to yon same sovereign cruelty:
The parts that fortune hath bestow'd upon her,
Tell her, I hold as giddily as fortune;
But 'tis that miracle and queen of gems,
That nature pranks her in, attracts my soul.
Viola. — But if she cannot love you, sir?
Duke. — I cannot be so answer'd.
Vio. — Sooth, but you must.
Say, that some lady, as perhaps there is,
Hath for your love as great a pang of heart
As you have for Olivia: you cannot love her;
You tell her so; must she not, then, be answer'd?
Duke. — There is no woman's sides
Can bide the beating of so strong a passion
As love doth give my heart: no woman's heart
So big, to hold so much; they lack retention.
Alas! their love may be call'd appetite, —
No motion of the liver, but the palate, —
That suffer forfeit, cloyment, and revolt;
But mine is all as hungry as the sea,
And can digest as much: make no compare
Between that love a woman can bear me,
And that I owe Olivia.
Vio. — Ay, but I know, —
Duke. — What dost thou know?
Vio. — Too well what love women to men may owe:
In faith, they are as true of heart as we.

My father had a daughter lov'd a man,
As it might be, perhaps, were I a woman,
I should your lordship.
Duke. — And what's her history?
Vio. — A blank, my lord. She never told her love,
But let concealment, like a worm i' the bud,
Feed on her damask cheek; she pin'd in thought;
And with a green and yellow melancholy,
She sat like patience on a monument,
Smiling at grief. Was not this love indeed?
We men may say more, swear more; but indeed
Our shows are more than will; for still we prove
Much in our vows, but little in our love.
Duke. — But died thy sister of her love, my boy?
Vio. — I am all the daughters of my father's house,
And all the brothers too.

SHAKSPEARE.

OTHELLO'S DEFENCE.

Most potent, grave, and reverend signiors,
My very noble and approved good masters,
That I have ta'en away this old man's daughter,
It is most true; true, I have married her;
The very head and front of my offending
Hath this extent, no more. Rude am I in my speech,
And little bless'd with the set phrase of peace.
For since these arms of mine had seven years' pith,
Till now some nine moons wasted, they have used
Their dearest action in the tented field:
And little of this great world can I speak,
More than pertains to feats of broil and battle;
And therefore little shall I grace my cause
In speaking for myself. Yet, by your gracious patience,
I will a round unvarnished tale deliver
Of my whole course of love; what drugs, what charms,
What conjuration, and what mighty magic,
(For such proceeding I am charged withal,)
I won his daughter with.

Her father loved me, oft invited me;
Still questioned me the story of my life,
From year to year; the battles, sieges, fortunes,
That I have passed.
I ran it through, even from my boyish days,
To the very moment that he bade me tell it:
Wherein I spoke of most disastrous chances,
Of moving accidents, by flood and field;
Of hairbreadth scapes in the imminent deadly breach;
Of being taken by the insolent foe,
And sold to slavery; of my redemption thence,
And portance in my travel's history:
Wherein of antres vast, and deserts idle,
Rough quarries, rocks, and hills whose heads touch heaven,
It was my hint to speak, such was the process:
And of the Cannibals that each other eat,
The Anthropophagi, and men whose heads
Do grow beneath their shoulders. These things to hear
Would Desdemona seriously incline:
But still the house affairs would draw her thence;
Which ever as she could with haste despatch,
She'd come again, and with a greedy ear
Devour up my discourse: which, I observing,
Took once a pliant hour, and found good means

To draw from her a prayer of earnest heart,
That I would all my pilgrimage dilate,
Whereof by parcels she had something heard,
But not intentively: I did consent;
And often did beguile her of her tears,
When I did speak of some distressful stroke
That my youth suffer'd. My story being done,
She gave me for my pains a world of sighs:
She swore, — in faith, 'twas strange, 'twas passing strange;
'Twas pitiful, 'twas wondrous pitiful:
She wished she had not heard it; yet she wished
That heaven had made her such a man; she thank'd me;
And bade me, if I had a friend that loved her,
I should but teach him how to tell my story,
And that would woo her. Upon this hint, I spake:
She loved me for the dangers I had passed,
And I loved her that she did pity them.
This only is the witchcraft I have used:
Here comes the lady, let her witness it.

SHAKSPEARE.

ATHULF AND ETHILDA.

Athulf. — Appeared
The princess with that merry child Prince Guy:
He loves me well, and made her stop and sit,
And sate upon her knee, and it so chanced
That in his various chatter he denied
That I could hold his hand within my own
So closely as to hide it: this being tried
Was proved against him; he insisted then
I could not by his royal sister's hand
Do likewise. Starting at the random word,
And dumb with trepidation, there I stood
Some seconds as bewitched; then I looked up,
And in her face beheld an orient flush
Of half-bewildered pleasure: from which trance
She with an instant ease resumed herself,
And frankly, with a pleasant laugh, held out
Her arrowy hand.
I thought it trembled as it lay in mine,
But yet her looks were clear, direct, and free,
And said that she felt nothing.
Sidroc. — And what felt'st thou?
Athulf. — A sort of swarming, curling, tremulous tumbling,
As though there were an ant-hill in my bosom.
I said I was ashamed. — Sidroc, you smile,
If at my folly, well! But if you smile,
Suspicious of a taint upon my heart,
Wide is your error, and you never loved.

HENRY TAYLOR.

THE ECSTASY.

WHERE, like a pillow on a bed,
A pregnant bank swelled up to rest
The violet's declining head,
Sate we on one another's breast.
Our hands were firmly cemented
By a fast balm which thence did spring,
Our eye-beams twisted, and did thread
Our eyes upon one double string,
So to ingraft our hands as yet
Was all the means to make us one,
And pictures in our eyes to get
Was all our propagation.
As 'twixt two equal armies Fate
Suspends uncertain victory,
Our souls (which to advance our state
Were gone out) hung 'twixt her and me.

And whilst our souls negotiate there,
We like sepulchral statues lay:
All day the same our postures were,
And we said nothing all the day.
If any, so by love refined,
That he soul's language understood,
And by good love were grown all mind,
Within convenient distance stood,
He, (though he knew not which soul spoke,
Because both meant, both spoke the same,)
Might thence a new concoction take,
And part far purer than he came.
This ecstasy doth unperplex,
We said, and tell us what we love;
We see by this it was not sex,
We see, we saw not what did move:
But as all several souls contain
Mixture of things they know not what,
Love these mixed souls doth mix again,
And makes both one, each this and that.
A single violet transplant,
The strength, the color, and the size
(All which before was poor and scant,)
Redoubles still and multiplies.
When love with one another so
Interanimates two souls,
That abler soul which thence doth flow
Defects of loveliness controls.
We then, who are this new soul, know
Of what we are composed and made:
For the atoms of which we grow
Are soul, whom no change can invade.
But, O alas! so long, so far
Our bodies why do we forbear?
They are ours, though not we. We are
The Intelligences, they the spheres:
We owe them thanks, because they thus
Did us to us at first convey,
Yielded their sense's force to us,
Nor are dross to us, but allay.
On man Heaven's influence works not so,
But that it first imprints the Air;
For soul into the soul may flow,
Though it to body first repair.
As our blood labors to beget
Spirits as like souls as it can,
Because such fingers need to knit
That subtile knot which makes us man:
So must pure lovers' souls descend
To affections and to faculties,
Which sense may reach and apprehend;
Else a great Prince in prison lies.
To our bodies turn we then, and so
Weak men on love revealed may look;
Love's mysteries in souls do grow,
But yet the body is the book.
And if some lover such as we
Have heard this dialogue of one,
Let him still mark us, he shall see
Small change when we're to bodies grown.

DONNE.

LOVE AT FIRST SIGHT.

SITTING in my window,
Pointing my thoughts in lawn, I saw a god,
(I thought, but it was you,) enter our gates;
My blood flew out and back again, as fast
As I had prest it forth, and sucked it in,
Like breath; then was I called away in haste
To entertain you. Never was a man
Heaved from a sheepcot to a sceptre, raised
So high in thoughts as I: you left a kiss
Upon these lips, then, which I mean to keep
From you forever. I did hear you talk
Far above singing; after you were gone,
I grew acquainted with my heart, and searched
What stirred it so. Alas! I found it love.

BEAUMONT AND FLETCHER: *Philaster.*

MAUD.

I.

A VOICE by the cedar-tree,
In the meadow under the Hall!
She is singing an air that is known
to me,
A passionate ballad gallant and gay,
A martial song like a trumpet's call!
Singing alone in the morning of life,
In the happy morning of life and of
May,
Singing of men that in battle array,
Ready in heart and ready in hand,
March with banner and bugle and fife
To the death, for their native land.

II.

Maud with her exquisite face,
And wild voice pealing up to the
sunny sky,
And feet like sunny gems on an
English green;
Maud in the light of her youth and
her grace,
Singing of Death, and of Honor that
cannot die,
Till I well could weep for a time so
sordid and mean,
And myself so languid and base.

III.

Silence, beautiful voice,
Be still, for you only trouble the mind
With a joy in which I cannot rejoice,
A glory I shall not find.
Still! I will hear you no more;
For your sweetness hardly leaves me
a choice
But to move to the meadow, and fall
before
Her feet on the meadow grass, and
adore,
Not her, who is neither courtly nor
kind,
Not her, not her, but a voice.

TENNYSON.

TO VENUS.

O DIVINE star of Heaven,
Thou in power above the seven;
Thou, O gentle Queen, that art
Curer of each wounded heart,
Thou the fuel, and the flame;
Thou in heaven, and here, the same;
Thou the wooer, and the wooed;
Thou the hunger, and the food;
Thou the prayer, and the prayed;
Thou what is or shall be said.

BEAUMONT AND FLETCHER.

ROSALINE.

LIKE to the clear in highest sphere
Where all imperial glory shines,
Of selfsame color is her hair,
Whether unfolded, or in twines:
Heigh ho, fair Rosaline!
Her eyes are sapphires set in snow,
Resembling Heaven by every wink;
The Gods do fear whereas they glow,
And I do tremble when I think
Heigh ho, would she were mine!

Her cheeks are like the blushing
cloud
That beautifies Aurora's face,
Or like the silver crimson shroud
That Phœbus' smiling looks doth
grace;
Heigh ho, fair Rosaline!
Her lips are like two budded roses
Whom ranks of lilies neighbor nigh,
Within which bounds she balm en-
closes
Apt to entice a deity:
Heigh ho, would she were mine!

Her neck is like a stately tower
Where Love himself imprisoned lies,
To watch for glances every hour
From her divine and sacred eyes:
Heigh ho, fair Rosaline!
Her paps are centres of delight,
Her breasts are orbs of heavenly
frame,
Where Nature moulds the dew of
light
To feed perfection with the same:
Heigh ho, would she were mine!

With orient pearl, with ruby red,
With marble white, with sapphire
blue,
Her body every way is fed,
Yet soft in touch and sweet in view:
Heigh ho, fair Rosaline!
Nature herself her shape admires;
The Gods are wounded in her sight;
And Love forsakes his heavenly fires,

And at her eyes his brand doth light:
Heigho, would she were mine!

Then muse not, Nymphs, though I bemoan
The absence of fair Rosaline,
Since for a fair there's fairer none,
Nor for her virtues so divine:
Heigh ho, fair Rosaline;
Heigh ho, my heart! would God that she were mine!

T. LODGE.

SONG.

SEE the chariot at hand here of Love,
Wherein my lady rideth!
Each that draws is a swan or a dove,
And well the car Love guideth.
As she goes, all hearts do duty
Unto her beauty,
And enamoured do wish so they might
But enjoy such a sight;
That they still were to run by her side,
Through swords, through seas, whither she would ride.

Do but look on her eyes, they do light
All that Love's world compriseth:
Do but look on her hair, it is bright
As Love's star when it riseth:
Do but mark, her forehead's smoother
Than words that soothe her.
And from her arched brows such a grace
Sheds itself through the face,
As alone there triumphs to the life
All the gain, all the good of the element's strife.

Have you seen a bright lily grow,
Before rude hands have touched it?
Have you marked but the fall o' the snow
Before the soil hath smutched it?
Have you felt the wool of the Beaver?
Or Swan's down ever?
Or have smelt of the bud of the brier?
Or the Nard in the fire?
Or have tasted the bag of the bee?
O so white, O so soft, O so sweet is she!

BEN JONSON.

ON A GIRDLE.

THAT which her slender waist confined
Shall now my joyful temples bind:
No monarch but would give his crown
His arms might do what this has done.

A narrow compass! and yet there
Dwelt all that's good and all that's fair:
Give me but what this ribband bound,
Take all the rest the Sun goes round.

WALLER.

SONNET.

How oft, when thou, my music, music play'st,
Upon that blessed wood whose motion sounds
With thy sweet fingers, when thou gently sway'st
The wiry concord that mine ear confounds,
Do I envy those jacks, that nimble leap
To kiss the tender inward of thy hand,
Whilst my poor lips, which should that harvest reap,
At the wood's boldness by thee blushing stand!
To be so tickled, they would change their state
And situation with those dancing chips,
O'er whom thy fingers walk with gentle gait,
Making dead wood more bless'd than living lips.
Since saucy jacks so happy are in this,
Give them thy fingers, me thy lips to kiss.

SHAKSPEARE.

GENEVIEVE.

ALL thoughts, all passions, all delights,
Whatever stirs this mortal frame,
All are but ministers of Love,
And feed his sacred flame.

Oft in my waking dreams do I
Live o'er again that happy hour,
When midway on the mount I lay,
Beside the ruined tower.

The moonshine, stealing o'er the scene,
Had blended with the lights of eve;
And she was there, my hope, my joy,
My own dear Genevieve!

She leaned against the armèd man,
The statue of the armèd knight;
She stood and listened to my lay,
Amid the lingering light.

Few sorrows hath she of her own,
My hope, my joy, my Genevieve!
She loves me best, whene'er I sing
The songs that make her grieve.

I played a soft and doleful air,
I sang an old and moving story, —
An old rude song, that suited well
That ruin wild and hoary.

She listened with a flitting blush,
With downcast eyes and modest grace;
For well she knew I could not choose
But gaze upon her face.

I told her of the Knight that wore
Upon his shield a burning brand;
And that for ten long years he wooed
The Lady of the Land.

I told her how he pined; and ah!
The deep, the low, the pleading tone
With which I sang another's love
Interpreted my own.

She listened with a fitting blush,
With downcast eyes, and modest grace;
And she forgave me that I gazed
Too fondly on her face.

But when I told the cruel scorn
That crazed that bold and lovely Knight,
And that he crossed the mountain-woods,
Nor rested day nor night;

That sometimes from the savage den,
And sometimes from the darksome shade,
And sometimes starting up at once
In green and sunny glade,

There came and looked him in the face
An angel beautiful and bright;
And that he knew it was a Fiend,
This miserable Knight!

And that, unknowing what he did,
He leaped amid a murderous band,
And saved from outrage worse than death
The Lady of the Land;

And how she wept, and clasped his knees;
And how she tended him in vain,
And ever strove to expiate
The scorn that crazed his brain;

And that she nursed him in a cave;
And how his madness went away,
When on the yellow forest leaves
A dying man he lay; —

His dying words, — but when I reached
That tenderest strain of all the ditty,
My faltering voice and pausing harp
Disturbed her soul with pity.

All impulses of soul and sense
Had thrilled my guileless Genevieve;
The music and the doleful tale,
The rich and balmy eve;

And hopes, and fears that kindle hope,
An undistinguishable throng,
And gentle wishes, long subdued,
Subdued and cherished long.

She wept with pity and delight,
She blushed with love and virgin shame;
And like the murmur of a dream,
I heard her breathe my name.

Her bosom heaved: she stept aside,
As conscious of my look she stept;
Then suddenly, with timorous eye
She fled to me and wept.

She half enclosed me with her arms,
She pressed me with a meek embrace;
And, bending back her head, looked up,
And gazed upon my face.

'Twas partly love, and partly fear,
And partly 'twas a bashful art,
That I might rather feel, than see,
The swelling of her heart.

I calmed her fears, and she was calm,
And told her love with virgin pride;
And so I won my Genevieve,
My bright and beauteous bride.

COLERIDGE.

THE LILY OF NITHSDALE.

SHE's gane to dwall in heaven, my lassie,
She's gane to dwall in heaven;
Ye're ower pure, quoth the voice of God,
For dwalling out of heaven!

O what'll she do in heaven, my lassie?
O what'll she do in heaven? —
She'll mix her ain thoughts with angels' sangs,
An' make them mair meet for heaven.

Low there thou lies, my lassie,
Low there thou lies;
A bonnier form ne'er went to the yird,
Nor frae it will arise!

Fu' soon I'll follow thee, lassie,
Fu' soon I'll follow thee;
Thou left me nought to covet ahin',
But took gudness' self wi' thee.

I looked on thy death-cold face, my lassie,
I looked on thy death-cold face;
Thou seemed a lilie new cut i' the bud,
An' fading in its place.

I looked on thy death-shut eye, my lassie,
I looked on thy death-shut eye;
An' a lovelier light in the brow of heaven
Fell time shall ne'er destroy.

Thy lips were ruddy and calm, my lassie,
Thy lips were ruddy and calm;
But gane was the holy breath of heaven
To sing the evening psalm.

There's nought but dust now mine, lassie,
There's nought but dust now mine;
My saul's wi thee in the cauld grave,
An' why should I stay behin'?

CUNNINGHAM.

THE PEASANT'S RETURN.

AND passing here through evening dew,
He hastened happy to her door,
But found the old folk only two
With no more footsteps on the floor
To walk again below the skies
Where beaten paths do fall and rise.

For she wer gone from earthly eyes
To be a-kept in darksome sleep
Until the good again do rise
A joy to souls they left to weep.
The rose were dust that bound her brow;
The moth did eat her Sunday cape;
Her frock were out of fashion now;
Her shoes were dried up out of shape.

WILLIAM BARNES.

ARIADNE.

BUT I wol turne againe to Ariadne,
That is with slepe for werinesse ytake,
Ful sorrowfully her herté may awake.
Alas, for thee, mine herté hath pité;
Right in the dawning tho awaketh she,
And gropeth in the bed, and found right nought:
"Alas," (quoth she) "that ever I was wrought, —

I am betrayed," and her haire to rent,
And to the strandé barefote fast she went,
And cried: "Theseus, mine herté swete,
Where be ye, that I may not with you mete?
And mighte thus with beestes ben yslaine."
  The hollow rockés answerede her againe,
No man she saw, and yet shone the Moone,
And hie upon a rocké she went soone,
And sawe his bargé sayling in the sea,
Cold woxe her herte, and righte thus said she:
  "Meker then ye find I the beestes wilde."
Hath he not sinne, that he her thus begilde?
She cried, "O turne againe for routhe and sinne,
Thy bargé hath not all his meinie in,"
Her kerchefe on a pole sticked she,
Ascaunce he should it well ysee,
And him remembre that she was behind,
And turne againe, and on the stronde her find.
  But all for nought, — his way he is ygone,
And down she fell a swone upon a stone,
And up she riste, and kissed in all her care
The steppés of his feete, there he hath fare,
And to her bed right thus she spek-eth tho:
  "Thou bed," (quod she) "that hast received two,
Thou shalt answere of two, and not of one,
Where is the greater parte, away ygone?
  Alas, where shall I wretched wight become?
For though so be that boté none here come,
Home to my countrey dare I not for drede.
I can my selfe in this case not yrede."
  What should I tellé more her com-plaining,
It is so long, it were an heavy thing?
In her epistle, Naso telleth all,
But shortly to the endé tell I shall,
The goddes have her holpen for pité,
And, in the signe of Taurus, men may see
The stonés of her crowné shiné clere, —
I will no more speake of this ma-tere.

CHAUCER.

COMMON SENSE.

SECOND THOUGHT.

My mistress's eyes are nothing like the sun;
Coral is far more red than her lips' red;
If snow be white, why then her breasts are dun;
If hairs be wires, black wires grow on her head.
I have seen roses damask'd red and white,
But no such roses see I in her cheeks;
And in some perfumes is there more delight
Than in the breath that from my mistress reeks.
I love to hear her speak, — yet well I know
That music hath a far more pleasing sound;
I grant I never saw a goddess go, —
My mistress, when she walks, treads on the ground;
  And yet by Heaven, I think my love as rare
  As any she belie'd with false compare.

SHAKSPEARE.

SENTENCES

'Tis truth, (although this truth's a star
  Too deep-enskied for all to see),
As poets of grammar, lovers are
  The well-heads of morality.

"Keep measure in love?" More light befall
Thy sanctity, and make it less!
Be sure I will not love at all
Where I may not love with excess.

Who is the happy husband? He
Who, scanning his unwedded life,
Thanks Heaven, with a conscience free,
'Twas faithful to his future wife.

COVENTRY PATMORE.

SONNET.

LET me not to the marriage of true minds
Admit impediments. Love is not love
Which alters when it alteration finds,
Or bends with the remover to remove;
O no; it is an ever-fixèd mark,
That looks on tempests, and is never shaken;
It is the star to every wandering bark,
Whose worth's unknown, although his height be taken.
Love's not Time's fool, though rosy lips and cheeks
Within his bending sickle's compass come;
Love alters not with his brief hours and weeks,
But bears it out even to the edge of doom.
If this be error, and upon me proved,
I never writ, nor no man ever loved.

SHAKSPEARE.

THE PILOT'S DAUGHTER.

O'ER western tides the fair Spring Day
Was smiling back as it withdrew,
And all the harbor, glittering gay,
Returned a blithe adieu;
Great clouds above the hills and sea
Kept brilliant watch, and air was free
Where last lark firstborn star shall greet,—
When, for the crowning vernal sweet,
Among the slopes and crags I meet
The pilot's pretty daughter.

Round her gentle, happy face,
Dimpled soft, and freshly fair,
Danced with careless ocean grace
Locks of auburn hair:
As lightly blew the veering wind,
They touched her cheeks, or waved behind,
Unbound, unbraided, and unlooped;
Or when to tie her shoe she stooped,
Below her chin the half-curls drooped,
And veiled the pilot's daughter.

Rising, she tossed them gayly back,
With gesture infantine and brief,
To fall around as soft a neck
As the wild-rose's leaf.
Her Sunday frock of lilac shade
(That choicest tint) was neatly made,
And not too long to hide from view
The stout but noway clumsy shoe,
And stockings' smoothly-fitting blue,
That graced the pilot's daughter.

With look half timid and half droll,
And then with slightly downcast eyes,
And blush that outward softly stole,
Unless it were the skies
Whose sun-ray shifted on her cheek,
She turned when I began to speak;
But 'twas a brightness all her own
That in her firm light step was shown,
And the clear cadence of her tone;
The pilot's lovely daughter.

Were it my lot (the sudden wish)
To hand a pilot's oar and sail,
Or haul the dripping moonlight mesh,
Spangled with herring-scale;
By dying stars, how sweet 'twould be,
And dawn-blow freshening the sea,
With weary, cheery pull to shore,
To gain my cottage home once more,
And clasp, before I reach the door,
My love, the pilot's daughter.

This element beside my feet
Allures, a tepid wine of gold;
One touch, one taste, dispels the cheat
'Tis salt and nipping cold:
A fisher's hut, the scene perforce

Of narrow thoughts and manners coarse,
Coarse as the curtains that beseem
With net-festoons the smoky beam,
Would never lodge my favorite dream,
E'en with my pilot's daughter.

To the large riches of the earth,
Endowing men in their own spite,
The *poor*, by privilege of birth,
Stand in the closest right.
Yet not alone the palm grows dull
With clayey delve and watery pull:
And this for me; — or hourly pain.
But could I sink and call it gain?
Unless a pilot true, 'twere vain
To wed a pilot's daughter.

Like *her*, perhaps? — but ah! I said,
Much wiser leave such thoughts alone.
So may thy beauty, simple maid,
Be mine, yet all thine own.
Joined in my free contented love
With companies of stars above;
Who, from their throne of airy steep,
Do kiss these ripples as they creep
Across the boundless, darkening deep, —
Low voiceful wave! hush soon to sleep
The gentle pilot's daughter.

ALLINGHAM.

SONNET.

So am I as the rich, whose blessed key
Can bring him to his sweet up-lockèd treasure.
The which he will not every hour survey,
For blunting the fine point of seldom pleasure.
Therefore are feasts so solemn and so rare,
Since seldom coming, in the long year set,
Like stones of worth they thinly placed are,
Or captain jewels in the carcanet.
So is the time that keeps you, as my chest,
Or as the wardrobe which the robe doth hide,
To make some special instant special-blest,
By new unfolding his imprison'd pride.
Blessèd are you, whose worthiness gives scope,
Being had, to triumph, being lack'd, to hope.

SHAKSPEARE.

SYMPATHY.

LATELY, alas! I knew a gentle boy,
Whose features all were cast in Virtue's mould,
As one she had designed for Beauty's toy,
But after manned him for her own stronghold.

On every side he open was as day,
That you might see no lack of strength within;
For walls and ports do only serve alway
For a pretence to feebleness and sin.

Say not that Cæsar was victorious,
With toil and strife who stormed the House of Fame,
In other sense this youth was glorious,
Himself a kingdom whereso'er he came.

No strength went out to get him victory,
When all was income of its own accord;
For where he went none other was to see,
But all were parcel of their noble lord.

He forayed like the subtle haze of summer,
That stilly shows fresh landscapes to our eyes,
And revolutions works without a murmur,
Or rustling of a leaf beneath the skies.

So was I taken unawares by this,
I quite forgot my homage to confess;
Yet now am forced to know, though hard it is,
I might have loved him, had I loved him less.

Each moment as we nearer drew to each,
A stern respect withheld us further yet,
So that we seemed beyond each other's reach,
And less acquainted than when first we met.

We two were one while we did sympathize,
So could we not the simplest bargain drive;
And what avails it, now that we are wise,
If absence doth this doubleness contrive?

Eternity may not the chance repeat;
But I must tread my single way alone,
In sad remembrance that we once did meet,
And know that bliss irrevocably gone.

The spheres henceforth my elegy shall sing,
For elegy has other subject none;
Each strain of music in my ears shall ring
Knell of departure from that other one.

Make haste and celebrate my tragedy;
With fitting strain resound, ye woods and fields;
Sorrow is dearer in such case to me
Than all the joys other occasion yields.

Is't then too late the damage to repair?
Distance, forsooth, from my weak grasp has reft
The empty husk, and clutched the useless tare,
But in my hands the wheat and kernel left.

If I but love that virtue which he is,
Though it be scented in the morning air,
Still shall we be truest acquaintances,
Nor mortals know a sympathy more rare.

THOREAU.

MY PLAYMATE.

THE pines were dark on Ramoth hill,
Their song was soft and low;
The blossoms in the sweet May wind
Were falling like the snow.

The blossoms drifted at our feet,
The orchard birds sang clear:
The sweetest and the saddest day
It seemed of all the year.

For, more to me than birds or flowers,
My playmate left her home,
And took with her the laughing spring,
The music and the bloom.

She kissed the lips of kith and kin,
She laid her hand in mine:
What more could ask the bashful boy
Who fed her father's kine?

She left us in the bloom of May:
The constant years told o'er
Their seasons with as sweet May morns;
But she came back no more.

I walk with noiseless feet the round
Of uneventful years:
Still o'er and o'er I sow the spring
And reap the autumn ears.

She lives where all the golden year
Her summer roses blow:
The dusky children of the sun
Before her come and go.

There haply with her jewelled hands
She smooths her silken gown,—
No more the homespun lap wherein
I shook the walnuts down.

The wild grapes wait us by the brook,
The brown nuts on the hill,
And still the May-day flowers make sweet
The woods of Follymill.

The lilies blossom in the pond;
The bird builds in the tree;
The dark pines sing on Ramoth hill
The slow song of the sea.

I wonder if she thinks of them,
And how the old time seems;
If ever the pines of Ramoth wood
Are sounding in her dreams.

I see her face, I hear her voice:
Does she remember mine?
And what to her is now the boy
Who fed her father's kine?

What cares she that the orioles build
For other eyes than ours;
That other hands with nuts are filled,
And other laps with flowers?

O playmate in the golden time!
Our mossy seat is green;
Its fringing violets blossom yet;
The old trees o'er it lean.

The winds so sweet with birch and fern
A sweeter memory blow;
And there in spring the veeries sing
The song of long ago.

And still the pines of Ramoth wood
Are moaning like the sea, —
The moaning of the sea of change
Between myself and thee.

WHITTIER.

DIVIDED.

I.

AN empty sky, a world of heather,
Purple of foxglove, yellow of broom;
We two among them wading together,
Shaking out honey, treading perfume.

Crowds of bees are giddy with clover,
Crowds of grasshoppers skip at our feet,
Crowds of larks at their matins hang over,
Thanking the Lord for a life so sweet.

Flusheth the rise with her purple favor,
Gloweth the cleft with her golden ring,
'Twixt the two brown butterflies waver,
Lightly settle, and sleepily swing.

We two walk till the purple dieth,
And short dry grass under foot is brown,
But one little streak at a distance lieth
Green like a ribbon to prank the down.

II.

Over the grass we stepped unto it,
And God he knoweth how blithe we were!
Never a voice to bid us eschew it:
Hey the green ribbon that showed so fair!

Hey the green ribbon! we kneeled beside it,
We parted the grasses dewy and sheen:
Drop over drop there filtered and slided
A tiny bright beck that trickled between.

Tinkle, tinkle, sweetly it sung to us,
Light was our talk as of faëry bells;
Faëry wedding-bells faintly rung to us
Down in their fortunate parallels.

Hand in hand while the sun peered over,
We lapped the grass on that youngling spring;
Swept back its rushes, smoothed its clover,
And said, "Let us follow it westering."

III.

A dappled sky, a world of meadows,
Circling above us the black rooks fly
Forward, backward; lo their dark shadows
Flit on the blossoming tapestry;

Flit on the beck; for her long grass parteth
As hair from a maid's bright eyes blown back:
And, lo, the sun like a lover darteth
His flattering smile on her wayward track.

Sing on! we sing in the glorious weather
Till one steps over the tiny strand,
So narrow, in sooth, that still together
On either brink we go hand in hand.

The beck grows wider, the hands must sever.
On either margin, our songs all done,
We move apart, while she singeth ever,
Taking the course of the stooping sun.

He prays, "Come over," — I may not follow;
I cry, "Return," — but he cannot come:
We speak, we laugh, but with voices hollow;
Our hands are hanging, our hearts are numb.

IV.

A breathing sigh, a sigh for answer,
A little talking of outward things:
The careless beck is a merry dancer,
Keeping sweet time to the air she sings.

A little pain when the beck grows wider;
"Cross to me now; for her wavelets swell;"
"I may not cross," — and the voice beside her
Faintly reacheth, though heeded well.

No backward path; ah! no returning;
No second crossing that ripple's flow:
"Come to me now, for the west is burning;
Come ere it darkens." — "Ah, no! ah, no!"

Then cries of pain, and arms outreaching,
The beck grows wider and swift and deep:
Passionate words as of one beseeching:
The loud beck drowns them: we walk, and weep.

V.

A yellow moon in splendor drooping,
A tired queen with her state oppressed,
Low by rushes and swordgrass stooping,
Lies she soft on the waves at rest.

The desert heavens have felt her sadness;
Her earth will weep her some dewy tears;
The wild beck ends her tune of gladness,
And goeth stilly as soul that fears.

We two walk on in our grassy places
On either marge of the moonlit flood,
With the moon's own sadness in our faces,
Where joy is withered, blossom and bud.

VI.

A shady freshness, chafers whirring;
A little piping of leaf-hid birds;
A flutter of wings, a fitful stirring;
A cloud to the eastward snowy as curds.

Bare grassy slopes where kids are tethered,
Round valleys like nests all fernylined,
Round hills, with fluttering tree-tops feathered,
Swell high in their freckled robes behind.

A rose-flush tender, a thrill, a quiver,
When golden gleams to the treetops glide;
A flashing edge for the milk-white river,
The beck, a river — with still sleek tide.

Broad and white, and polished as silver
On she goes under fruit-laden trees:
Sunk in leafage cooeth the culver,
And 'plaineth of love's disloyal ties.

Glitters the dew, and shines the river,
Up comes the lily and dries her bell;
But two are walking apart forever,
And wave their hands for a mute farewell.

VII.

A braver swell, a swifter sliding;
The river hasteth, her banks recede.
Wing-like sails on her bosom gliding
Bear down the lily, and drown the reed.

Stately prows are rising and bowing
(Shouts of mariners winnow the air),
And level sands for banks endowing
The tiny green ribbon that showed so fair.

While, O my heart! as white sails shiver,
And clouds are passing, and banks stretch wide,
How hard to follow, with lips that quiver,
That moving speck on the far-off side.

Farther, farther; I see it, know it —
My eyes brim over, it melts away:
Only my heart to my heart shall show it
As I walk desolate day by day.

VIII.

And yet I know past all doubting, truly, —
A knowledge greater than grief can dim, —
I know, as he loved, he will love me duly, —
Yea better, e'en better than I love him.

And as I walk by the vast calm river,
The awful river so dread to see,
I say, "Thy breadth and thy depth forever
Are bridged by his thoughts that cross to me."

JEAN INGELOW.

QUA CURSUM VENTUS.

As ships becalmed at eve, that lay
With canvas drooping, side by side,
Two towers of sail at dawn of day
Are scarce, long leagues apart, descried;

When fell the night, upsprung the breeze,
And all the darkling hours they plied,
Nor dreamt but each the selfsame seas
By each was cleaving, side by side:

E'en so — but why the tale reveal
Of those whom, year by year unchanged,
Brief absence joined anew to feel,
Astounded, soul from soul estranged?

At dead of night their sails were filled,
And onward each rejoicing steered:
Ah, neither blame, for neither willed,
Or wist, what first with dawn appeared!

To veer, how vain! On, onward strain,
Brave barks! In light, in darkness too,
Through winds and tides one compass guides, —
To that, and your own selves, be true.

But O blithe breeze, and O great seas,
Though ne'er, that earliest parting past,
On your wide plain they join again,
Together lead them home at last!

One port, methought, alike they sought,
One purpose hold where'er they fare, —
O bounding breeze, O rushing seas,
At last, at last, unite them there!

CLOUGH.

SUNDERED.

I CHALLENGE not the oracle
That drove you from my board:
I bow before the dark decree
That scatters as I hoard.

You vanished like the sailing ship
  That rides far out at sea.
I murmur as your farewell dies
  And your form floats from me;

Ah! ties are sundered in this hour:
  No tide of fortune rare
Shall bring the heart I owned before,
  And my love's loss repair.

When voyagers make a foreign port,
  And leave their precious prize,
Returning home they bear for freight
  A bartered merchandise.

Alas! When you come back to me,
  And come not as of yore,
But with your alien wealth and peace,
  Can we be lovers more?

I gave you up to go your ways,
  O you whom I adored!
Love hath no ties, but Destiny
  Shall cut them with a sword.

SIDNEY H. MORSE.

LOVE AGAINST LOVE.

As unto blowing roses summer dews,
Or morning's amber to the tree-top choirs,
So to my bosom are the beams that use
To rain on me from eyes that love inspires.
Your love, — vouchsafe it, royal-hearted Few,
And I will set no common price thereon,
O, I will keep, as heaven his holy blue,
Or night her diamonds, that dear treasure won.
But aught of inward faith must I forego,
Or miss one drop from truth's baptismal hand,
Think poorer thoughts, pray cheaper prayers, and grow
Less worthy trust, to meet your heart's demand, —
Farewell! Your wish I for your sake deny:
Rebel to love in truth to love am I.

D. A. WASSON.

INBORN ROYALTY.

O THOU goddess,
Thou divine Nature, how thyself thou blazon'st
In these two princely boys! They are as gentle
As zephyrs, blowing below the violet,
Not wagging his sweet head: and yet as rough,
Their royal blood enchafed, as the rud'st wind,
That by the top doth take the mountain pine,
And make him stoop to the vale. 'Tis wonderful
That an invisible instinct should frame them
To royalty unlearned; honor untaught;
Civility not seen from other; valor,
That wildly grows in them, but yields a crop
As if it had been sowed!

SHAKSPEARE: *Cymbeline.*

GENTILITY.

BUT for ye speken of such gentillesse,
As is descended out of old richesse,
That therfore shullen ye be gentilmen, —
Such arrogance n'is not worth an hen.
  Look who that is most virtuous alway,
Prive and apart, and most entendeth aye
To do the gentil dedés that he can,
And take him for the greatest gentilman.
Christ wol we claime of him our gentillesse,
Not of our elders for their old richesse:
For though they gave us all their heritage,
For which we claim to be of high parage,
Yet may they not bequethen, for no thing,
To none of us, their virtuous living,
That made them gentilmen callèd to be,
And bade us follow them in such degree.

"Wel can the wise poet of Florence,
That highté Dant, speken of this sentence:
Lo, in such maner rime is Dante's tale.
Ful selde upriseth by his branches smale
Prowesse of man, for God of his goodnesse
Will that we claime of him our gentillesse:
For of our elders may we nothing claime
But temporal thing, that man may hurt and maime.
"Eke every wight wot this as wel as I,
If gentillesse were planted naturelly
Unto a certain linage down the line,
Prive and apart, then wol they never fine
To don of gentillesse the faire office,
They mighten do no vilanie or vice.
"Take fire and beare it into the derkest hous
Betwixt this and the mount of Caucasus,
And let men shut the dorés, and go thenne,
Yet wol the fire as faire lie and brenne
As twenty thousand men might it behold;
His office naturel ay wol it hold,
Up peril of my lif, til that it die.
"Here may ye see wel, how that genterie
Is not annexed to possession,
Sith folk ne don their operation
Alway, as doth the fire, lo, in his kind,
For God it wot, men may full often find
A lordé's son do shame and vilanie.
And he that wol have prize of his genterie,
For he was boren of a gentil house,
And had his elders noble and virtuous,
And n'ill himselven do no gentil dedes,
Ne folwe his gentil auncestrie, that dead is,
He n'is not gentil, be he duke or erl;
For vilains' sinful dedés make a churl.
For gentillesse n'is but the renomee
Of thine auncestres, for their high bountée,
Which is a strange thing to thy persone:
Thy gentillesse cometh fro God alone.
Than cometh our very gentillesse of grace,
It was no thing bequethed us with our place.

CHAUCER.

BEAUTY.

So every spirit, as it is most pure,
And hath in it the more of heavenly light,
So it the fairer body doth procure
To habit in, and it more fairly dight
With cheerful grace and amiable sight;
For of the soul the body form doth take;
For soul is form, and doth the body make.

Therefore wherever that thou dost behold
A comely corpse, with beauty fair endued,
Know this for certain, that the same doth hold
A beauteous soul, with fair conditions thewed,
Fit to receive the seed of virtue strewed;
For all that fair is, is by nature good;
That is a sign to know the gentle blood.

Yet oft it falls that many a gentle mind
Dwells in deformèd tabernacle drowned,
Either by chance, against the course of kind,
Or through unaptnesse in the substance found,
Which it assumèd of some stubborne ground,
That will not yield unto her form's direction,
But is perform'd with some foul imperfection.

And oft it falls (aye me, the more to
rue!)
That goodly beauty, albeit heavenly
born,
Is foul abus'd, and that celestial hue,
Which doth the world with her delight adorn,
Made but the bait of sin, and sinners' scorn,
Whilst every one doth seek and sue
to have it,
But every one doth seek but to deprave it.

Yet nathëmore is that faire beauty's
blame,
But theirs that do abuse it unto ill:
Nothing so good, but that through
guilty shame
May be corrupt, and wrested unto
will:
Nathelesse the soule is fair and
beauteous still,
However fleshe's fault it filthy make;
For things immortal no corruption
take.

SPENSER.

UNA AND THE LION.

ONE day, nigh weary of the irksome
way,
From her unhasty beast she did
alight;
And on the grass her dainty limbs
did lay,
In secret shadow far from all men's
sight;
From her fair head her fillet she undight,
And laid her stole aside; her angel's
face
As the great eye of heaven shined
bright,
And made a sunshine in the shady
place;
Did never mortal eye behold such
heavenly grace.

It fortunèd, out of the thickest wood
A ramping lion rushèd suddenly,
Hunting full greedy after savage
blood.
Soon as the royal virgin he did spy,
With gaping mouth at her ran greedily,
To have at once devoured her tender
corse;
But to the prey when as he drew
more nigh,
His bloody rage assuagèd with remorse,
And with the sight amazed, forgat
his furious force.

Instead thereof, he kissed her weary
feet,
And licked her lily hands with fawning tongue,
As he her wrongèd innocence did
weet.
Oh! how can beauty master the
most wrong,
And simple truth subdue avenging
strong!
Whose yielded pride and proud submission,
Still dreading death, when she had
markèd long,
Her heart 'gan melt in great compassion,
And drizzling tears did shed for pure
affection.

"The lion, lord of every beast in
field,"
Quoth she, "his princely puissance
doth abate,
And mighty proud to humble weak
does yield
Forgetful of the hungry rage, which
late
Him pricked, in pity of my sad estate:—
But he, my lion, and my noble lord,
How does he find in cruel heart to
hate
Her that him loved, and ever most
adored
As the god of my life? Why hath
he me abhorred?"

Redounding tears did choke th' end
of her plaint,
Which softly echoed from the neighbor wood;
And sad to see her sorrowful constraint
The kingly beast upon her gazing
stood;
With pity calmed, down fell his angry mood.
At last, in close heart shutting up
her pain,

Arose the virgin, born of heavenly brood,
And to her snowy palfrey got again
To seek her strayed champion if she might attain.

The lion would not leave her desolate,
But with her went along, as a strong guard
Of her chaste person, and a faithful mate.
Still, when she slept, he kept both watch and ward;
And, when she waked, he waited diligent,
With humble service to her will prepared:
From her fair eyes he took commandment
And ever by her looks conceivèd her intent.

SPENSER.

WHEN I DO COUNT THE CLOCK.

WHEN I do count the clock that tells the time,
And see the brave day sunk in hideous night;
When I behold the violet past prime,
And sable curls all silvered o'er with white;
When lofty trees I see barren of leaves,
Which erst from heat did canopy the herd,
And summer's green, all girded up in sheaves,
Borne on the bier with white and bristly beard;
Then of thy beauty do I question make,
That thou among the wastes of time must go,
Since sweets and beauties do themselves forsake,
And die as fast as they see others grow;
And nothing 'gainst Time's scythe can make defence,
Save breed, to brave him when he takes thee hence.

SHAKSPEARE.

SONNET.

To me, fair friend, you never can be old,
For as you were, when first your eye I eyed,
Such seems your beauty still. Three winters cold
Have from the forest shook three summers' pride;
Three beauteous springs to yellow autumn turned,
In process of the seasons have I seen,
Three April perfumes in three hot Junes burned,
Since first I saw you fresh which yet are green.
Ah! yet doth beauty, like a dial-hand,
Steal from his figure, and no pace perceived;
So your sweet hue, which methinks still doth stand,
Hath motion, and mine eye may be deceived.
For fear of which, hear this, thou age unbred,
Ere you were born, was beauty's summer dead.

SHAKSPEARE.

TRUTH needs no color with his color fixed,
Beauty no pencil, beauty's truth to lay;
But best is best, if never intermix'd.

SHAKSPEARE.

HYMN TO THE GRACES.

WHEN I love, as some have told,
Love I shall when I am old,
O ye Graces! make me fit
For the welcoming of it.
Clean my rooms as temples be,
To entertain that deity;
Give me words wherewith to woo,
Suppling and successful too;
Winning postures, and withal,
Manners each way musical;
Sweetnesse to allay my sour
And unsmooth behavior:
For I know you have the skill
Vines to prune, though not to kill;
And of any wood ye see,
You can make a Mercury.

HERRICK.

SONG.

How near to good is what is fair,
Which we no sooner see,
But with the lines and outward air
Our senses taken be.
We wish to see it still, and prove
What ways we may deserve;
We court, we praise, we more than love,
We are not grieved to serve.

BEN JONSON.

MY CHARMER.

SWEETNESS, truth, and every grace
Which time and use are wont to teach,
The eye may in a moment reach
And read distinctly in her face.

Some other nymphs with colors faint
And pencil slow, may Cupid paint,
And a weak heart in time destroy;
She has a stamp, and prints the boy.

WALLER.

THE POETRY OF DRESS.

A sweet disorder in the dress
Kindles in clothes a wantonness:—
A lawn about the shoulders thrown
Into a fine distraction,—
An erring lace, which here and there
Inthralls the crimson stomacher,—
A cuff neglectful, and thereby
Ribbons to flow confusedly,—
A winning wave, deserving note,
In the tempestuous petticoat,—
A careless shoe-string, in whose tie
I see a wild civility,—
Do more bewitch me, than when art
Is too precise in every part.

HERRICK.

FREEDOM IN DRESS.

STILL to be neat, still to be drest,
As you were going to a feast;
Still to be powdered, still perfumed,—
Lady, it is to be presumed,
Though art's hid causes are not found,
All is not sweet, all is not sound.

Give me a look, give me a face,
That makes simplicity a grace;
Robes loosely flowing, hair as free,—
Such sweet neglect more taketh me
Than all the adulteries of art;
They strike mine eyes, but not my heart.

BEN JONSON.

III.

INTELLECTUAL.

MEMORY. — INSPIRATION. — IMAGINATION. FANCY. — MUSIC. — ART. — MOODS.

"Quotque aderant vates, rebar adesse Deos." — OVID.

"By pain of heart, now checked, and now impelled,
The intellectual power from words to things
Went sounding on, — a dim and perilous way." — WORDSWORTH.

INTELLECTUAL.

THOUGHT.

O Messenger, art thou the king, or I?
Thou dalliest outside the palace gate
Till on thine idle armor lie the late
And heavy dews: the morn's bright, scornful eye
Reminds thee; then, in subtle mockery,
Thou smilest at the window where I wait,
Who bade thee ride for life. In empty state
My days go on, while false hours prophesy
Thy quick return; at last, in sad despair,
I cease to bid thee, leave thee free as air;
When lo, thou stand'st before me glad and fleet,
And lay'st undreamed-of treasures at my feet.
Ah! messenger, thy royal blood to buy,
I am too poor. Thou art the king, not I.

H. H.

QUESTIONINGS.

Hath this world, without me wrought,
Other substance than my thought?
Lives it by my sense alone,
Or by essence of its own,
Will its life, with mine begun,
Cease to be when that is done,
Or another consciousness
With the selfsame forms impress?

Doth yon fire-ball, poised in air,
Hang by my permission there?
Are the clouds that wander by
But the offspring of mine eye,
Born with every glance I cast,
Perishing when that is past?
And those thousand, thousand eyes,
Scattered through the twinkling skies,
Do they draw their life from mine,
Or, of their own beauty shine?

Now I close my eyes, my ears,
And creation disappears;
Yet if I but speak the word,
All creation is restored.
Or — more wonderful — within,
New creations do begin;
Hues more bright and forms more rare,
Than reality doth wear,
Flash across my inward sense,
Born of the mind's omnipotence.

Soul! that all informest, say!
Shall these glories pass away?
Will those planets cease to blaze
When these eyes no longer gaze?
And the life of things be o'er,
When these pulses beat no more?

Thought! that in me works and lives, —
Life to all things living gives, —
Art thou not thyself, perchance,
But the universe in trance?
A reflection inly flung
By that world thou fanciedst sprung
From thyself, — thyself a dream, —
Of the world's thinking thou the theme?

Be it thus, or be thy birth
From a source above the earth, —
Be thou matter, be thou mind,
In thee alone myself I find,
And through thee alone, for me,

Hath this world reality.
Therefore, in thee will I live,
To thee all myself will give,
Losing still, that I may find
This bounded self in boundless mind.

F. H. Hedge.

MEMORY.

In sweet dreams softer than unbroken rest
Thou leddest by the hand thine infant Hope.
The eddying of her garments caught from thee
The light of thy great presence; and the cope
 Of the half-attained futurity,
 Though deep not fathomless,
Was cloven with the million stars which tremble
O'er the deep mind of dauntless infancy.

. . . .

Sure she was nigher to heaven's spheres,
Listening the lordly music flowing from
 The illimitable years.

Tennyson.

MEMORY.

TO ——

I hear thy solemn anthem fall,
 O richest song, upon my ear,
That clothes thee in thy golden pall,
 As this wide sun flows on the mere.

Away — 'tis Autumn in the land,
 Though Summer decks the green pine's bough,
Its spires are plucked by thy white hand, —
 I see thee standing by me now.

I dress thee in the withered leaves,
 Like forests when their day is done,
I bear thee as the wain its sheaves,
 Which crisply rustle in the sun.

A thousand flowers enchant the gale
 With perfume sweet as love's first kiss,
And odors in the landscape sail,
 And charm the sense with sudden bliss.

But Fate, who metes a different way
 To me, since I was falsely sold,
Hath gray-haired turned the sunny day,
 Bent its high form, and made it old.

Come Time, come Death, and blot my doom
 With feller woes, if they be thine;
Clang back thy gates, sepulchral tomb,
 And match thy barrenness with mine.

O moaning wind along the shore,
 How faint thy sobbing accents come!
Strike on my heart with maddest roar,
 Thou meet'st no discord in this home.

Sear, blistering sun, these temple veins;
 Blind, icy moon, these coldest eyes;
And drench me through, ye winter rains, —
 Swell, if ye can, my miseries.

Those dark deep orbs are meeting mine,
 That white hand presses on my brow,
That soft, sweet smile I know, 'tis thine, —
 I see thee standing by me now.

W. E. Channing.

FORESIGHT.

 No man is the lord of any thing
Till he communicate his parts to others,
Nor doth he of himself know them for aught
Till he behold them formed in the applause
Where they are extended, which, like an arch, reverberates
The voice again; or like a gate of steel,
Fronting the sun, receives and renders back
His figure and his heart.

Shakspeare.

ODE TO HIMSELF.

WHERE dost thou careless lie
  Buried in ease and sloth?
Knowledge that sleeps, doth die:
And this security,
  It is the common moth
That eats on wits and arts, and so destroys them both.

Are all the Aonian springs
  Dried up.? lies Thespia waste?
Doth Clarius' harp want strings?
That not a nymph now sings?
  Or droop they as disgraced
To see their seats and bowers by chattering pies defaced?

If hence thy silence be,
  As 'tis too just a cause, —
Let this thought quicken thee;
Minds that are great and free
  Should not on fortune pause;
'Tis crown enough to virtue still, her own applause.

BEN JONSON.

NOT EVERY DAY FIT FOR VERSE.

'TIS not every day that I
Fitted am to prophesy;
No, but when the spirit fills
The fantastic pannicles,
Full of fire, then I write
As the Godhead doth indite.
Thus inraged, my lines are hurled,
Like the Sibyl's through the world:
Look how next the holy fire
Either slakes, or doth retire;
So the fancy cools, till when
That brave spirit comes agen.

HERRICK.

THE PRAISE OF HOMER.

O! 'TIS wondrous much
Though nothing prosed, that the right virtuous touch
Of a well written soul to virtue moves.
Nor have we souls to purpose, if their loves
Of fitting objects be not so inflamed.
How much, then, were this kingdom's main soul maimed
To want this great inflamer of all powers
That move in human souls! All realms but yours
Are honored with them, and hold blest that State
That have his works to read and contemplate,
In which humanity to her height is raised;
Which all the world, yet none enough hath praised.
Seas, earth, and heaven, he did in verse comprise,
Outsung the Muses, and did equalize
Their King Apollo; being so far from cause
Of princes' light thoughts, that their gravest laws
May find stuff to be fashioned by his lines.
Through all the pomp of kingdoms still he shines,
And graceth all his gracers. Then let lie
Your lutes and viols, and more loftily
Make the heroics of your Homer sung;
To drums and trumpets set his angel tongue;
And, with the princely sport of hawks you use,
Behold the kingly flight of his high muse,
And see how, like the Phœnix, she renews
Her age and starry feathers in your sun,
Thousands of years attending; every one
Blowing the holy fire, throwing in
Their seasons, kingdoms, nations, that have been
Subverted in them; laws, religions, all
Offered to change, and greedy funeral,
Yet still your Homer lasting, living, reigning,
And proves how firm Truth builds in poets feigning.

GEORGE CHAPMAN.

SONNET.

ON FIRST LOOKING INTO CHAPMAN'S HOMER.

Much have I travelled in the realms of gold,
And many goodly states and kingdoms seen;
Round many western islands have I been,
Which bards in fealty to Apollo hold.
Oft of one wide expanse had I been told
That deep-browed Homer ruled as his demesne:
Yet did I never breathe its pure serene
Till I heard Chapman speak out loud and bold:
Then felt I like some watcher of the skies
When a new planet swims into his ken;
Or like stout Cortez, when with eagle eyes
He stared at the Pacific, — and all his men
Looked at each other with a wild surmise —
Silent, upon a peak in Darien.

Keats.

SOCRATES.

Night is fair Virtue's immemorial friend.
The conscious moon through every distant age
Has held a lamp to Wisdom, and let fall
On Contemplation's eye her purging ray.
The famed Athenian, he who wooed from heaven
Philosophy the fair, to dwell with men,
And form their manners, not inflame their pride;
While o'er his head, as fearful to molest
His laboring mind, the stars in silence slide,
And seem all gazing on their future guest,
See him soliciting his ardent suit,
In private audience; all the livelong night
Rigid in thought and motionless he stands,
Nor quits his theme or posture, till the sun
Disturbs his nobler intellectual beam,
And gives him to the tumult of the world.

Young.

MORNING.

Sleep is like death, and after sleep,
The world seems new begun,
Its earnestness all clear and deep,
Its true solution won:
White thoughts stand luminous and firm,
Like statues in the sun.
Refreshed from supersensuous founts,
The soul to purer vision mounts.

Allingham.

INSPIRATION.

If with light head erect I sing,
Though all the Muses lend their force,
From my poor love of any thing,
The verse is weak and shallow as its source.

But if with bended neck I grope,
Listening behind me for my wit,
With faith superior to hope,
More anxious to keep back than forward it;

Making my soul accomplice there
Unto the flame my heart hath lit,
Then will the verse forever wear, —
Time cannot bend the line which God has writ.

I hearing get, who had but ears,
And sight, who had but eyes before;
I moments live, who lived but years,
And truth discern, who knew but learning's lore.

Now chiefly is my natal hour,
And only now my prime of life,
Of manhood's strength it is the flower,
'Tis peace's end, and war's beginning strife.

It comes in summer's broadest noon,
By a gray wall, or some chance place,
Unseasoning time, insulting June,
And vexing day with its presuming face.

I will not doubt the love untold
Which not my worth nor want hath bought,
Which wooed me young, and wooed me old,
And to this evening hath me brought.

THOREAU.

THE POET.

THOU hast learned the woes of all the world
From thine own longings and lone tears,
And now thy broad sails are unfurled
And all men hail thee with loud cheers.

The flowing sunlight is thy home,
The billows of the sea are thine,
To all the nations shalt thou roam,
Through every heart thy love shall shine.

The subtlest thought that finds its goal
Far, far beyond the horizon's verge,—
Oh! shoot it forth on arrows bold
The thoughts of men on, on, to urge.

Toil not to free the slave from chains,
Think not to give the laborer rest, —
Unless rich beauty fill the plains
The free man wanders still unblest.

All men can dig and hew rude stone,
But thou must carve the frieze above,
And columned high through thee alone
Shall rise our frescoed homes of love.

C. S. T.

INSPIRATION.

THE Muse, nae poet ever fand her,
Till by himsel' he learned to wander,
Adown some trotting burn's meander,
And no think lang;
O sweet to stray and pensive ponder
A heartfelt sang!

BURNS.

THE FLOWER.

How fresh, O Lord, how sweet and clean
Are thy returns! even as the flowers in spring;
To which, besides their own demean,
The late-past frosts tributes of pleasure bring.
Grief melts away
Like snow in May,
As if there were no such cold thing.

Who would have thought my shrivelled heart
Could have recovered greenness?
It was gone
Quite underground; as flowers depart
To see their mother root, when they have blown;
Where they together
All the hard weather,
Dead to the world, keep house unknown.

And now in age I bud again,
After so many deaths I live and write;
I once more smell the dew and rain,
And relish versing: O my only light,
It cannot be
That I am he
On whom thy tempests fell all night.

HERBERT.

WRITING VERSES.

JUST now I've ta'en a fit of rhyme,
My barmy noddle's working prime,
My fancy yerkit up sublime
Wi' hasty summons:
Hae ye a leisure moment's time
To hear what's comin'?

Some rhyme a neebor's name to lash;
Some rhyme (vain thought!) for needfu' cash;
Some rhyme to court the countra clash,

An' raise a din;
For me, an aim I never fash!
I rhyme for fun.

The star that rules my luckless lot,
Has fated me the russet coat,
An' damned my fortune to the groat;
But in requit,
Has blessed me wi' a random shot
O' countra wit.

BURNS.

THE MUSE.

THE Muse doth tell me where to borrow
Comfort in the midst of sorrow;
Makes the desolatest place
To her presence be a grace;
And the blackest discontents
Be her fairest ornaments.
In my former days of bliss,
Her divine skill taught me this,
That, from every thing I saw,
I could some invention draw;
And raise pleasure to her height,
Through the meanest object's sight.
By the murmur of a spring,
Or the least bough's rustling,
By a daisy, whose leaves spread,
Shut, when Titan goes to bed,
Or a shady bush, or tree,
She could more infuse in me,
Than all Nature's beauties can
In some other wiser man.
By her help, I also now
Make this churlish place allow
Some things that may sweeten gladness,
In the very gall of sadness.
The dull loneness, the black shade,
That these hanging vaults have made;
The strange music of the waves
Beating on these hollow caves;
This black den which rocks emboss
Overgrown with eldest moss;
The rude portals which give light
More to terror than delight
This my chamber of Neglect,
Walled about with Disrespect;
From all these, and this dull air,
A fit object for despair,
She hath taught me by her might
To draw comfort and delight.
Therefore, thou best earthly bliss,
I will cherish thee for this;
Poesy, thou sweet'st content,
That e'er Heaven to mortals lent,
Though they as a trifle leave thee,
Whose dull thoughts cannot conceive thee,
Though thou be to them a scorn
Who to nought but earth are born;
Let my life no longer be
Than I am in love with thee.

GEORGE WITHER.

THE POET.

AND also, beau sire, of other things,
That is, thou hasté no tidings
Of Lové's folk, if they be glade,
Ne of nothing elsé that God made,
And not only fro far countree,
That no tidings come to thee,
Not of thy very neighbors,
That dwellen almost at thy dores,
Thou hearest neither that ne this,
For when thy labor all done is,
And hast made all thy reckonings
Instead of rest and of new things,
Thou goest home to thine house anone,
And also dumbé as a stone,
Thou sittest at another booke,
Till fully dazèd is thy looke,
And livest thus as an hermite.

CHAUCER.

PRAYER TO APOLLO.

GOD of science and of light,
Apollo through thy greate might,
This littell last booke now thou gie,*
Now that I will for maistrie,
Here art potenciall be shewde,
But for the rime is light and lewde,
Yet make it somewhat agreeable,
Though some verse fayle in a sillable,
And that I do no diligence,
To shewe craft, but sentence,
And if divine vertue thou
Wilt helpe me to shewe now,
That in my heed ymarked is,
Lo, that is for to meanen this,
The House of Fame for to discrive,—
Thou shalt see me go as blive†
Unto the next laurel I see
And kisse it, for it is thy tree,
Now enter in my brest anon.

CHAUCER.

* Guide. † Quickly.

THE CUCKOW AND THE NIGHTINGALE.

I CAME to a laund of white and green,
So faire one had I never in been,
The ground was green, ypowdred with daisie,
The flowres and the gróvés like hy,
All greene and white, was nothing eles seene.

There sate I downe among the faire flowres,
And saw the birds trip out of hir bowrs,
There as they rested them all the night,
They were so joyfull of the dayés light,
They began of May for to done honours.

They coud that service all by rote,
There was many a lovely note,
Some sung loud as they had plainèd,
And some in other manner voice yfainèd,
And some all out with the full throte.

They proyned hem, and made them right gay,
And daunceden, and leapten on the spray,
And evermore two and two in fere,
Right so as they had chosen them to yere
In Februere, upon saint Valentine's day.

And the river that I sate upon,
It made such a noise as it ran,
Accordaunt with the birdés harmony,
Methought it was the best melody
That might ben yheard of any mon.

And for delite, I wote never how
I fell in such a slomber and a swow,
Not all asleepe, ne fully waking,
And in that swow me thought I heard sing
The sorry bird, the lewd cuckow.

And that was on a tree right fast by,
But who was then evill apaid but I?
"Now God" (quod I) "that died on the crois
Yeve sorrow on thee, and on thy lewde vois,
Full little joy have I now of thy cry."

And as I with the cuckow thus gan chide,
I heard in the next bush beside
A nightingale so lustely sing,
That with her cleré voice she madé ring
Through all the greene wood wide.

"Ah, good nightingalé" (quoth I then)
"A little hast thou ben too longé hen,*
For here hath been the lewd cuckow,
And songen songs rather than hast thou,
I pray to God evil fire her bren."

But now I wol you tell a wonder thing,
As long as I lay in that swowning,
Me thought I wist what the birds meant,
And what they said, and what was their intent,
And of their speech I had good knowing.

There heard I the nightingalé say,
"Now, good cuckow, go somewhere away,
And let us that can singen dwellen here,
For every wight escheweth thee to hear,
Thy songs be so elengé in good fay."

"What" (quod she) "what may thee ailen now,
It thinketh me, I sing as well as thou,
For my song is both true and plaine,
And though I cannot crakell so in vaine,
As thou dost in thy throte, I wot never how.

"And every wight may understandé mee,
But nightingale so may they not done thee;
For thou hast many a nice queint cry,
I have thee heard saine, *ocy*, *ocy*,
How might I know what that should be?"

* Hence.

"Ah foole," (quod she,) "wist thou not what it is
When that I say, *ocy*, *ocy*, *ywis?*
Then meané I that I would wonder faine
That all they were shamefully yslaine
That meanen ought againé love amiss.

"And also I would that all tho were dede
That thinké not in love their life to lede,
For whoso that wol not the God of love serve,
I dare well say, he worthy is to sterve,
And for that skill, *ocy*, *ocy*, I grede."

CHAUCER.

STEAMBOATS, VIADUCTS, AND RAILWAYS.

MOTIONS and means, on land and sea at war
With old poetic feeling, not for this,
Shall ye, by poets even, be judged amiss!
Nor shall your presence, howsoe'er it mar
The loveliness of Nature, prove a bar
To the mind's gaining that prophetic sense
Of future change, that point of vision whence
May be discovered what in soul ye are.
In spite of all that beauty may disown
In your harsh features, Nature doth embrace
Her lawful offspring in man's art; and Time,
Pleased with your triumphs o'er his brother Space,
Accepts from your bold hands the proffered crown
Of hope, and smiles on you with cheer sublime.

WORDSWORTH.

SCALE OF MINDS.

"HERE might I pause, and bend in reverence
To Nature, and the power of human minds;
To men as they are men within themselves.
How oft high service is performed within,
When all the external man is rude in show:
Not like a temple rich with pomp and gold,
But a mere mountain chapel that protects
Its simple worshippers from sun and shower!
Of these, said I, shall be my song; of these,
If future years mature me for the task,
Will I record the praises, making verse
Deal boldly with substantial things, — in truth
And sanctity of passion speak of these,
That justice may be done, obeisance paid
Where it is due. Thus haply shall I teach,
Inspire, through unadulterated ears
Pour rapture, tenderness, and hope; my theme
No other than the very heart of man,
As found among the best of those who live,
Not unexalted by religious faith,
Nor uninformed by books, good books, though few,
In Nature's presence: thence may I select
Sorrow that is not sorrow, but delight,
And miserable love that is not pain
To hear of, for the glory that redounds
Therefrom to human kind, and what we are.
Be mine to follow with no timid step
Where knowledge leads me; it shall be my pride
That I have dared to tread this holy ground,
Speaking no dream, but things oracular,
Matter not lightly to be heard by those
Who to the letter of the outward promise
Do read the invisible soul: by men adroit
In speech, and for communion with the world
Accomplished, minds whose faculties are then

Most active when they are most eloquent,
And elevated most when most admired.
Men may be found of other mould than these;
Who are their own upholders, to themselves
Encouragement, and energy, and will;
Expressing liveliest thoughts in lively words,
As native passion dictates. Others, too,
There are, among the walks of homely life,
Still higher, men for contemplation framed;
Shy, and unpractised in the strife of phrase.
Meek men, whose very souls perhaps would sink
Beneath them, summoned to such intercourse.
Theirs is the language of the heavens, the power,
The thought, the image, and the silent joy:
Words are but under-agents in their souls;
When they are grasping with their greatest strength
They do not breathe among them; this I speak
In gratitude to God, who feeds our hearts
For his own service, knoweth, loveth us,
When we are unregarded by the world."

WORDSWORTH.

UNDER THE PORTRAIT OF MILTON.

THREE Poets, in three distant ages born,
Greece, Italy, and England did adorn.
The first in loftiness of thought surpassed;
The next in majesty; in both the last.
The force of Nature could no further go:
To make a third she joined the former two.

DRYDEN.

PLEASURES OF IMAGINATION.

As Memnon's marble harp renowned of old
By fabling Nilus, to the quivering touch
Of Titan's ray, with each repulsive string
Consenting, sounded through the warbling air
Unbidden strains; e'en so did Nature's hand
To certain species of external things
Attune the finer organs of the mind;
So the glad impulse of congenial powers,
Or of sweet sound, or fair-proportioned form,
The grace of motion, or the bloom of light,
Thrills through imagination's tender frame,
From nerve to nerve; all naked and alive
They catch the spreading rays; till now the soul
At length discloses every tuneful spring,
To that harmonious movement from without,
Responsive. Then the inexpressive strain
Diffuses its enchantment; Fancy dreams
Of sacred fountains and Elysian groves,
And vales of bliss; the Intellectual Power
Bends from his awful throne a wondering ear,
And smiles; the passions gently soothed away,
Sink to divine repose, and love and joy
Alone are waking; love and joy serene
As airs that fan the summer. O attend,
Whoe'er thou art whom these delights can touch,
Whose candid bosom the refining love
Of nature warms; O, listen to my song,
And I will guide thee to her favorite walks,
And teach thy solitude her voice to hear,
And point her loveliest features to thy view.

Say, why was man so eminently raised
Amid the vast creation; why ordained
Through life and death to dart his piercing eye,
With thoughts beyond the limits of his frame,
But that the Omnipotent might send him forth
In sight of mortal and immortal powers,
As on a boundless theatre to run
The great career of justice; to exalt
His generous aim to all diviner deeds;
To chase each partial purpose from his breast;
And through the mists of passion and of sense,
And through the tossing tide of chance and pain,
To hold his course unfaltering, while the voice
Of Truth and Virtue, up the steep ascent
Of nature, calls him to his high reward,
The applauding smile of heaven? else wherefore burns,
In mortal bosoms, this unquenched hope
That breathes from day to day sublimer things,
And mocks possession? wherefore darts the mind,
With such resistless ardor to embrace
Majestic forms; impatient to be free,
Spurning the gross control of wilful might;
Proud of the strong contention of her toils;
Proud to be daring? Who but rather turns
To heaven's broad fire his unconstrained view,
Than to the glimmering of a waxen flame?
Who that, from Alpine heights, his laboring eye
Shoots round the wide horizon to survey
Nilus or Ganges rolling his broad tide
Through mountains, plains, through empires black with shade,
And continents of sand, — will turn his gaze
To mark the windings of a scanty rill
That murmurs at his feet? The high-born soul
Disdains to rest her heaven-aspiring wing
Beneath its native quarry. Tired of earth
And this diurnal scene, she springs aloft,
Through fields of air pursues the flying storm;
Rides on the volleyed lightning through the heavens;
Or, yoked with whirlwinds and the northern blast,
Sweeps the long track of day. Then high she soars
The blue profound, and hovering o'er the sun
Beholds him pouring the redundant stream
Of light: beholds the unrelenting sway
Bend the reluctant planets to absolve
The fated rounds of time. Thence far effused
She darts her swiftness up the long career
Of devious comets; through its burning signs
Exulting circles the perennial wheel
Of nature, and looks back on all the stars,
Whose blended light, as with a milky zone,
Invests the orient. Now amazed she views
The empyreal waste, where happy spirits hold,
Beyond this concave heaven, their calm abode;
And fields of radiance, whose unfading light
Has travelled the profound six thousand years,
Nor yet arrived in sight of mortal things.

. . . . . .

Nature's care, to all her children just,
With richer treasures and an ampler state,
Endows at large whatever happy man
Will deign to use them. His the city's pomp,
The rural honors his: whate'er adorns

The princely dome, the column and the arch,
The breathing marbles and the sculptured gold,
Beyond the proud possessor's narrow claim,
His tuneful breast enjoys. For him the Spring
Distils her dews, and from the silken gem
His lucid leaves unfolds; for him the hand
Of Autumn tinges every fertile branch
With blooming gold, and blushes like the morn.
Each passing Hour sheds tribute from her wings,
And still new beauties meet his lonely walk,
And loves unfelt attract him.

. . . .

Look, then, abroad through Nature, to the range
Of planets, suns, and adamantine spheres,
Wheeling unshaken through the Void immense,
And speak, O man! does this capacious scene
With half that kindling majesty dilate
Thy strong conception, as when Brutus rose
Refulgent from the stroke of Cæsar's fate,
Amid the crowd of patriots; and his arm
Aloft extending, like eternal Jove,
When guilt brings down the thunder, called aloud
On Tully's name, and shook his crimson steel,
And bade the Father of his Country, hail!
For lo! the tyrant prostrate in the dust,
And Rome again is free!

AKENSIDE.

FAME.

HER house is all of Echo made
Where never dies the sound;
And as her brows the clouds invade,
Her feet do strike the ground.

BEN JONSON.

ULYSSES.

IT little profits that an idle king
By this still hearth, among these barren crags,
Matched with an aged wife, I mete and dole
Unequal laws unto a savage race
That hoard, and sleep, and feed, and know not me.
I cannot rest from travel: I will drink
Life to the lees: all times I have enjoyed
Greatly, have suffered greatly, both with those
That loved me, and alone; on shore, and when
Through scudding drifts the rainy Hyades
Vext the dim sea: I am become a name;
For always roaming with a hungry heart
Much have I seen and known; cities of men
And manners, climates, councils, governments,
Myself not least, but honored of them all;
And drunk delight of battle with my peers,
Far on the ringing plains of windy Troy.
I am a part of all that I have met;
Yet all experience is an arch wherethrough
Gleams that untravelled world, whose margin fades
Forever and forever when I move.
How dull it is to pause, to make an end,
To rust unburnished, not to shine in use!
As though to breathe were life. Life piled on life
Were all too little, and of one to me
Little remains: but every hour is saved
From that eternal silence, something more,
A bringer of new things; and vile it were
For some three suns to store and hoard myself,
And this gray spirit yearning in desire
To follow knowledge like a sinking star

Beyond the utmost bound of human thought.
This is my son, mine own Telemachus,
To whom I leave the sceptre and the isle —
Well loved of me, discerning to fulfil
This labor, by slow prudence to make mild
A rugged people, and through soft degrees
Subdue them to the useful and the good.
Most blameless is he, centred in the sphere
Of common duties, decent not to fail
In offices of tenderness, and pay
Meet adoration to my household gods,
When I am gone. He works his work, I mine.
There lies the port: the vessel puffs her sail:
There gloom the dark broad seas. My mariners,
Souls that have toiled, and wrought, and thought with me, —
That ever with a frolic welcome took
The thunder and the sunshine, and opposed
Free hearts, free foreheads, — you and I are old;
Old age hath yet his honor and his toil;
Death closes all: but something ere the end,
Some work of noble note, may yet be done
Not unbecoming men that strove with Gods.
The lights begin to twinkle from the rocks:
The long day wanes: the slow moon climbs: the deep
Moans round with many voices. Come, my friends,
'Tis not too late to seek a newer world.
Push off, and sitting well in order, smite
The sounding furrows; for my purpose holds
To sail beyond the sunset, and the baths
Of all the western stars, until I die.
It may be that the gulfs will wash us down:
It may be we shall touch the Happy Isles,
And see the great Achilles, whom we knew.
Though much is taken, much abides; and though
We are not now that strength which in old days
Moved earth and heaven; that which we are, we are;
One equal temper of heroic hearts,
Made weak by time and fate, but strong in will
To strive, to seek, to find, and not to yield.

TENNYSON.

KING LEAR.

O Heavens,
If you do love old men, if your sweet sway
Allow obedience, if yourselves are old,
Make it your cause; send down, and take my part!

SHAKSPEARE.

RUMBLE thy belly-full! Spit, fire! spout, rain!
Nor rain, wind, thunder, fire, are my daughters:
I tax not you, you elements, with unkindness,
I never gave you kingdom, called you children;
You owe me no subscription; why then, let fall
Your horrible pleasure; here I stand your slave,
A poor infirm, weak, and despised old man; —
But yet I call you servile ministers,
That have with two pernicious daughters joined
Your high-engendered battles 'gainst a head
So old and white as this. O! O! 'tis foul!

SHAKSPEARE.

OUTLINE.

OF Truth, of Grandeur, Beauty, Love, and Hope,
And melancholy Fear subdued by Faith;
Of blessed consolations in distress;
Of moral strength, and intellectual power;

Of joy in widest commonalty spread;
Of the individual Mind that keeps her own
Inviolate retirement, subject there
To Conscience only, and the law supreme
Of that Intelligence which governs all —
I sing: — "fit audience let me find, though few!"
So prayed, more gaining than he asked, the Bard
In holiest mood. Urania, I shall need
Thy guidance, or a greater Muse, if such
Descend to earth or dwell in highest heaven!
For I must tread on shadowy ground, must sink
Deep, and, aloft ascending, breathe in worlds
To which the heaven of heavens is but a veil.
All strength, all terror, single or in bands,
That ever was put forth in personal form —
Jehovah, with his thunder, and the choir
Of shouting Angels, and the empyreal thrones, —
I pass them unalarmed. Not Chaos, not
The darkest pit of lowest Erebus,
Nor aught of blinder vacancy, scooped out
By help of dreams, can breed such fear and awe
As fall upon us often when we look
Into our Minds, into the Mind of Man, —
My haunt, and the main region of my song.
Beauty — a living Presence of the earth,
Surpassing the most fair ideal Forms
Which craft of delicate Spirits doth compose
From earth's materials — waits upon my steps;
Pitches her tents before me as I move,
An hourly neighbor. Paradise, and groves
Elysian, Fortunate Fields, — like those of old
Sought in the Atlantic main, — why should they be
A history only of departed things,
Or a mere fiction of what never was?
For the discerning intellect of Man,
When wedded to this goodly universe
In love and holy passion, shall find these
A simple produce of the common day.
I, long before the blissful hour arrives,
Would chant, in lonely peace, the spousal verse
Of this great consummation: — and, by words
Which speak of nothing more than what we are,
Would I arouse the sensual from their sleep
Of Death, and win the vacant and the vain
To noble raptures; while my voice proclaims
How exquisitely the individual Mind
(And the progressive powers, perhaps no less,
Of the whole species) to the external World
Is fitted: — and how exquisitely, too —
(Theme this but little heard of among men —)
The external World is fitted to the Mind;
And the creation (by no lower name
Can it be called) which they with blended might
Accomplish: — this is our high argument.
Such grateful haunts foregoing, if I oft
Must turn elsewhere, to travel near the tribes
And fellowships of men, and see ill sights
Of madding passions mutually inflamed;
Must hear Humanity in fields and groves
Pipe solitary anguish; or must hang
Brooding above the fierce confederate storm
Of sorrow, barricaded evermore
Within the walls of cities, — may these sounds
Have their authentic comment; that even these
Hearing, I be not downcast or forlorn!

Descend, prophetic spirit! that inspir'st
The human Soul of universal earth,
Dreaming on things to come; and dost possess
A metropolitan temple in the hearts
Of mighty Poets: upon me bestow
A gift of genuine insight; that my Song
With star-like virtue in its place may shine,
Shedding benignant influence, and secure,
Itself, from all malevolent effect
Of those mutations that extend their sway
Throughout the nether sphere! And if with this
I mix more lowly matter; with the thing
Contemplated, describe the Mind and Man
Contemplating; and who, and what he was, —
The transitory Being that beheld
This Vision; when and where, and how he lived; —
Be not this labor useless. If such theme
May sort with highest objects, then — dread Power!
Whose gracious favor is the primal source
Of all illumination, — may my Life
Express the image of a better time,
More wise desires, and simpler manners; nurse
My Heart in genuine freedom: — all pure thoughts
Be with me; — so shall thy unfailing love
Guide and support and cheer me to the end!

WORDSWORTH.

COMUS, A MASK.

THE FIRST SCENE DISCOVERS A WILD WOOD.

The ATTENDANT SPIRIT *descends or enters.*

BEFORE the starry threshold of Jove's court
My mansion is, where those immortal shapes
Of bright aerial spirits live insphered
In regions mild of calm and serene air,
Above the smoke and stir of this dim spot
Which men call Earth, and with low-thoughted care
Confined and pestered in this pinfold here,
Strive to keep up a frail and feverish being,
Unmindful of the crown that virtue gives,
After this mortal change, to her true servants,
Amongst the enthronèd Gods on sainted seats.
Yet some there be that by due steps aspire
To lay their just hands on that golden key
That opes the palace of eternity;
To such my errand is; and, but for such,
I would not soil these pure ambrosial weeds
With the rank vapors of this sin-worn mould.
But to my task. Neptune, besides the sway
Of every salt flood, and each ebbing stream,
Took in by lot 'twixt high and nether Jove
Imperial rule of all the sea-girt isles,
That like to rich and various gems inlay
The unadornèd bosom of the deep;
Which he, to grace his tributary Gods,
By course commits to several government,
And gives them leave to wear their sapphire crowns,
And wield their little tridents: but this Isle,
The greatest and the best of all the main,
He quarters to his blue-haired deities;
And all this tract that fronts the falling sun
A noble Peer of mickle trust and power
Has in his charge, with tempered awe to guide
An old and haughty nation proud in arms:

Where his fair offspring, nursed in princely lore,
Are coming to attend their father's state,
And new-intrusted sceptre; but their way
Lies through the perplexed paths of this drear wood,
The nodding horror of whose shady brows
Threats the forlorn and wandering passenger;
And here their tender age might suffer peril,
But that by quick command from sovereign Jove
I was despatched for their defence and guard;
And listen why, for I will tell you now
What never yet was heard in tale or song,
From old or modern bard, in hall or bower.
Bacchus, that first from out the purple grape
Crushed the sweet poison of misusèd wine,
After the Tuscan mariners transformed,
Coasting the Tyrrhene shore, as the winds listed,
On Circé's island fell: who knows not Circé,
The daughter of the sun, whose charmèd cup
Whoever tasted, lost his upright shape,
And downward fell into a grovelling swine?
This Nymph that gazed upon his clustering locks
With ivy berries wreathed, and his blithe youth,
Had by him, ere he parted thence, a son
Much like his father, but his mother more,
Whom therefore she brought up, and Comus named
Who ripe, and frolic of his full grown age,
Roving the Celtic and Iberian fields,
At last betakes him to this ominous wood,
And in thick shelter of black shades imbowered,
Excels his mother at her mighty art,
Offering to every weary traveller
His orient liquor in a crystal glass,
To quench the drouth of Phœbus; which as they taste,
(For most do taste through fond intemperate thirst)
Soon as the potion works, their human count'nance,
The express resemblance of the Gods, is changed
Into some brutish form of wolf, or bear,
Or ounce, or tiger, hog, or bearded goat,
All other parts remaining as they were;
And they, so perfect is their misery,
Not once perceive their foul disfigurement,
But boast themselves more comely than before,
And all their friends and native home forget,
To roll with pleasure in a sensual sty.
Therefore, when any favored of high Jove
Chances to pass through this adventurous glade,
Swift as the sparkle of a glancing star
I shoot from heaven, to give him safe convoy,
As now I do: But first I must put off
These my sky robes spun out of Iris' woof,
And take the weeds and likeness of a swain,
That to the service of this house belongs,
Who with his soft pipe, and smooth-dittied song,
Well knows to still the wild winds when they roar,
And hush the waving woods, nor of less faith,
And in this office of his mountain watch,
Likeliest, and nearest to the present aid
Of this occasion. But I hear the tread
Of hateful steps; I must be viewless now.

COMUS *enters with a charming-rod in one hand, his glass in the other; with him a rout of monsters, headed like sundry sorts of wild beasts, but otherwise like men and women, their apparel glistering; they come in making a riotous and unruly noise, with torches in their hands.*

Comus. — The star that bids the shepherd fold,
Now the top of heaven doth hold;
And the gilded car of day
His glowing axle doth allay
In the steep Atlantic stream;
And the slope sun his upward beam
Shoots against the dusky pole,
Pacing toward the other goal
Of his chamber in the east.
Meanwhile welcome Joy, and Feast,
Midnight Shout and Revelry,
Tipsy Dance and Jollity.
Braid your locks with rosy twine,
Dropping odors, dropping wine.
Rigor now has gone to bed.
And Advice with scrupulous head,
Strict Age, and sour Severity,
With their grave saws in slumber lie.
We that are of purer fire
Imitate the starry quire,
Who in their nightly watchful spheres
Lead in swift round the months and years.
The sounds and seas, with all their finny drove,
Now to the moon in wavering morrice move;
And on the tawny sands and shelves
Trip the pert fairies and the dapper elves.
By dimpled brook, and fountain brim,
The wood-nymphs decked with daisies trim,
Their merry wakes and pastimes keep;
What hath night to do with sleep?
Night hath better sweets to prove,
Venus now wakes, and wakens Love.
Come, let us our rites begin,
'Tis only daylight that makes sin,
Which these dun shades will ne'er report.
Hail, Goddess of nocturnal sport,
Dark-veil'd Cotytto! t'whom the secret flame
Of midnight torches burns; mysterious dame,
That ne'er art called, but when the dragon womb
Of Stygian darkness spets her thickest gloom,
And makes one blot of all the air;
Stay thy cloudy ebon chair,
Wherein thou rid'st with Hecate, and befriend
Us thy vowed priests, till utmost end
Of all thy dues be done, and none left out,
Ere the babbling eastern scout,
The nice Morn, on the Indian steep
From her cabined loophole peep,
And to the telltale sun descry
Our concealed solemnity.
Come, knit hands, and beat the ground
In a light fantastic round.

THE MEASURE.

Break off, break off, I feel the different pace
Of some chaste footing near about this ground.
Run to your shrouds, within these brakes and trees;
Our number may affright: Some virgin sure
(For so I can distinguish by mine art)
Benighted in these woods. Now to my charms,
And to my wily trains; I shall ere long
Be well stocked with as fair a herd as grazed
About my mother Circé. Thus I hurl
My dazzling spells into the spungy air,
Of power to cheat the eye with blear illusion,
And give it false presentments, lest the place
And my quaint habits breed astonishment,
And put the damsel to suspicious flight,
Which must not be, for that's against my course:
I, under fair pretence of friendly ends,
And well-placed words of glozing courtesy
Baited with reasons not unplausible,
Wind me into the easy-hearted man,

And hug him into snares. When once her eye
Hath met the virtue of this magic dust,
I shall appear some harmless villager,
Whom thrift keeps up about his country gear.
But here she comes; I fairly step aside,
And hearken, if I may, her business here.

THE LADY ENTERS.

This way the noise was, if mine ear be true,
My best guide now; methought it was the sound
Of riot and ill-managed merriment,
Such as the jocund flute, or gamesome pipe
Stirs up among the loose unlettered hinds,
When for their teeming flocks, and granges full,
In wanton dance, they praise the bounteous Pan,
And thank the Gods amiss. I should be loath
To meet the rudeness, and swilled insolence
Of such late wassailers; yet O! where else
Shall I inform my unacquainted feet
In the blind mazes of this tangled wood?
My brothers, when they saw me wearied out
With this long way, resolving here to lodge
Under the spreading favor of these pines,
Stepped, as they said, to the next thicket side
To bring me berries, or such cooling fruit
As the kind, hospitable woods provide.
They left me then, when the gray-hooded Even,
Like a sad votarist in palmer's weed,
Rose from the hindmost wheels of Phœbus' wain.
But where they are, and why they came not back,
Is now the labor of my thoughts; 'tis likeliest
They had engaged their wandering steps too far;
And envious darkness, ere they could return,
Had stole them from me: else, O thievish Night,
Why shouldst thou, but for some felonious end,
In thy dark lantern thus close up the stars,
That Nature hung in heaven, and filled their lamps
With everlasting oil, to give due light
To the misled and lonely traveller?
This is the place, as well as I may guess,
Whence even now the tumult of loud mirth
Was rife, and perfect in my listening ear,
Yet nought but single darkness do I find.
What might this be? A thousand fantasies
Begin to throng into my memory,
Of calling shapes, and beckoning shadows dire,
And airy tongues, that syllable men's names
On sands, and shores, and desert wildernesses.
These thoughts may startle well, but not astound
The virtuous mind, that ever walks attended
By a strong-siding champion, Conscience. —
O welcome, pure-eyed Faith, white-handed Hope,
Thou hovering Angel, girt with golden wings,
And thou, unblemished form of Chastity!
I see ye visibly, and now believe
That he, the Supreme Good, t'whom all things ill
Are but as slavish officers of vengeance,
Would send a glistering guardian, if need were,
To keep my life and honor unassailed.
Was I deceived, or did a sable cloud
Turn forth her silver lining on the night?
I did not err, there does a sable cloud

Turn forth her silver lining on the night,
And casts a gleam over this tufted grove:
I cannot halloo to my brothers, but
Such noise as I can make to be heard farthest
I'll venture, for my new enlivened spirits
Prompt me; and they perhaps are not far off.

SONG.

Sweet Echo, sweetest nymph, that liv'st unseen
Within thy airy shell,
By slow Meander's margent green,
And in the violet-embroidered vale,
Where the love-lorn nightingale
Nightly to thee her sad song mourneth well;
Canst thou not tell me of a gentle pair
That likest thy Narcissus are?
O, if thou have
Hid them in some flowery cave,
Tell me but where.
Sweet queen of parley, daughter of the sphere!
So mayst thou be translated to the skies,
And give resounding grace to all heaven harmonies.

Enter COMUS.

Com. — Can any mortal mixture of earth's mould
Breathe such divine enchanting ravishment?
Sure something holy lodges in that breast,
And with these raptures moves the vocal air
To testify his hidden residence:
How sweetly did they float upon the wings
Of silence, through the empty-vaulted night,
At every fall smoothing the raven down
Of darkness till it smiled! I have oft heard
My mother Circé with the Sirens three,
Amidst the flowery-kirtled Naiades,
Culling their potent herbs, and baleful drugs,
Who, as they sung, would take the prisoned soul,
And lap it in Elysium; Scylla wept,
And chid her barking waves into attention,
And fell Charybdis murmured soft applause:
Yet they in pleasing slumber lulled the sense,
And in sweet madness robbed it of itself;
But such a sacred and homefelt delight,
Such sober certainty of waking bliss,
I never heard till now. I'll speak to her,
And she shall be my queen. Hail, foreign wonder!
Whom certain these rough shades did never breed,
Unless the goddess that in rural shrine
Dwell'st here with Pan, or Silvan, by blest song
Forbidding every bleak unkindly fog
To touch the prosperous growth of this tall wood.
Lady. — Nay, gentle Shepherd, ill is lost that praise
That is addressed to unattending ears;
Not any boast of skill, but extreme shift
How to regain my severed company,
Compelled me to awake the courteous Echo
To give me answer from her mossy couch.
Com. — What chance, good Lady, hath bereft you thus?
Lady. — Dim darkness, and this leafy labyrinth.
Com. — Could that divide you from near-ushering guides?
Lady. — They left me weary on a grassy turf.
Com. — By falsehood, or discourtesy, or why?
Lady. — To seek i' the valley some cool friendly spring.
Com. — And left your fair side all unguarded, Lady?
Lady. — They were but twain, and purposed quick return.
Com. — Perhaps forestalling night prevented them.
Lady. — How easy my misfortune is to hit!

Com. — Imports their loss beside the present need?
Lady. — No less than if I should my brothers lose.
Com. Were they of manly prime, or youthful bloom?
Lady. — As smooth as Hebe's their unrazored lips.
Com. — Two such I saw, what time the labored ox
In his loose traces from the furrow came,
And the swinked hedger at his supper sat;
I saw them under a green mantling vine
That crawls along the side of yon small hill,
Plucking ripe clusters from the tender shoots;
Their port was more than human, as they stood:
I took it for a faery vision
Of some gay creatures of the element,
That in the colors of the rainbow live,
And play i' the plighted clouds. I was awestruck,
And as I passed, I worshipped: if those you seek,
It were a journey like the path to heaven
To help you find them.
Lady. — Gentle Villager,
What readiest way would bring me to that place?
Com. — Due west it rises from this shrubby point.
Lady. — To find that out, good shepherd, I suppose
In such a scant allowance of starlight,
Would overtask the best land-pilot's art,
Without the sure guess of well-practised feet.
Com. — I know each lane, and every alley green,
Dingle or bushy dell, of this wild wood,
And every bosky bourn from side to side,
My daily walks and ancient neighborhood;
And if your stray attendants be yet lodged
Or shroud within these limits, I shall know
Ere morrow wake, or the low-roosted lark
From her thatched pallet rouse: if otherwise,
I can conduct you, Lady, to a low
But loyal cottage, where you may be safe
Till further quest.
Lady. — Shepherd, I take thy word,
And trust thy honest offered courtesy,
Which oft is sooner found in lowly sheds
With smoky rafters, than in tap'stry halls
And courts of princes, where it first was named,
And yet is most pretended: in a place
Less warranted than this, or less secure,
I cannot be, that I should fear to change it.
Eye me, blest Providence, and square my trial
To my proportioned strength. Shepherd, lead on.

Enter the TWO BROTHERS.

1 *Br.* — Unmuffle, ye faint stars, and thou, fair moon,
That wont'st to love the traveller's benison,
Stoop thy pale visage through an amber cloud,
And disinherit Chaos, that reigns here
In double night of darkness and of shades;
Or if your influence be quite dammed up
With black usurping mists, some gentle taper,
Through a rush candle, from the wicker-hole
Of some clay habitation, visit us
With thy long-levelled rule of streaming light;
And thou shalt be our star of Arcady,
Or Tyrian Cynosure.
2 *Br.* — Or if our eyes
Be barred that happiness, might we but hear
The folded flocks penned in their wattled cotes,
Or sound of pastoral reed with oaten stops,

Or whistle from the lodge, or village cock
Count the night watches to his feathery dames,
'Twould be some solace yet, some little cheering
In this close dungeon of innumerous boughs.
But O that hapless virgin, our lost sister!
Where may she wander now, whither betake her
From the chill dew, among rude burrs and thistles?
Perhaps some cold bank is her bolster now,
Or 'gainst the rugged bark of some broad elm
Leans her unpillowed head, fraught with sad fears.
What, if in wild amazement and affright,
Or, while we speak, within the direful grasp
Of savage hunger, or of savage heat?
1 *Br.* — Peace, brother, be not over-exquisite
To cast the fashion of uncertain evils;
For grant they be so, while they rest unknown,
What need a man forestall his date of grief,
And run to meet what he would most avoid?
Or if they be but false alarms of fear,
How bitter is such self-delusion!
I do not think my sister so to seek,
Or so unprincipled in virtue's book,
And the sweet peace that goodness bosoms ever,
As that the single want of light and noise
(Not being in danger, as I trust she is not)
Could stir the constant mood of her calm thoughts,
And put them into misbecoming plight.
Virtue could see to do what virtue would
By her own radiant light, though sun and moon
Were in the flat sea sunk. And Wisdom's self
Oft seeks to sweet retired solitude,
Where, with her best nurse, Contemplation,
She plumes her feathers, and lets grow her wings,
That in the various bustle of resort
Were all too ruffled, and sometimes impaired.
He that has light within his own clear breast,
May sit i' the centre, and enjoy bright day:
But he that hides a dark soul, and foul thoughts,
Benighted walks under the mid-day sun;
Himself is his own dungeon.
2 *Br.* — 'Tis most true,
That musing meditation most affects
The pensive secrecy of desert cell,
Far from the cheerful haunt of men and herds,
And sits as safe as in a senate house;
For who would rob a hermit of his weeds,
His few books, or his beads, or maple dish,
Or do his gray hairs any violence?
But beauty, like the fair Hesperian tree
Laden with blooming gold, had need the guard
Of dragon watch with unenchanted eye,
To save her blossoms, and defend her fruit
From the rash hand of bold incontinence.
You may as well spread out the unsunned heaps
Of miser's treasure by an outlaw's den,
And tell me it is safe, as bid me hope
Danger will wink on opportunity,
And let a single helpless maiden pass
Uninjured in this wild surrounding waste.
Of night, or loneliness, it recks me not;
I fear the dread events that dog them both,
Lest some ill-greeting touch attempt the person
Of our unowned sister.
1 *Br.* — I do not, brother,
Infer, as if I thought my sister's state
Secure without all doubt or controversy;
Yet where an equal poise of hope and fear

Does arbitrate the event, my nature is
That I incline to hope rather than fear,
And gladly banish squint suspicion.
My sister is not so defenceless left,
As you imagine; she has a hidden strength
Which you remember not.

2 *Br.* — What hidden strength,
Unless the strength of Heaven, if you mean that?

1 *Br.* — I mean that too, but yet a hidden strength
Which, if Heaven gave it, may be termed her own;
'Tis chastity, my brother, chastity.
She that has that is clad in complete steel,
And like a quivered Nymph with arrows keen
May trace huge forests, and unharbored heaths,
Infamous hills, and sandy perilous wilds,
Where through the sacred rays of chastity,
No savage fierce, bandite, or mountaineer
Will dare to soil her virgin purity:
Yea there, where very desolation dwells,
By grots, and caverns shagged with horrid shades,
She may pass on with unblenched majesty,
Be it not done in pride, or in presumption.
Some say no evil thing that walks by night,
In fog, or fire, by lake, or moorish fen,
Blue meagre hag, or stubborn unlaid ghost,
That breaks his magic chains at curfew time,
No goblin, or swart faery of the mine,
Hath hurtful power o'er true virginity.
Do ye believe me yet, or shall I call
Antiquity from the old schools of Greece
To testify the arms of chastity?
Hence had the huntress Dian her dread bow,
Fair silver-shafted queen, forever chaste,
Wherewith she tamed the brinded lioness
And spotted mountain pard, but set at nought
The frivolous bolt of Cupid; gods and men
Feared her stern frown, and she was queen o' the woods.
What was that snaky-headed Gorgon shield,
That wise Minerva wore, unconquered virgin,
Wherewith she freezed her foes to congealed stone,
But rigid looks of chaste austerity,
And noble grace that dashed brute violence
With sudden adoration and blank awe?
So dear to heaven is saintly chastity,
That when a soul is found sincerely so,
A thousand liveried angels lackey her,
Driving far off each thing of sin and guilt,
And in clear dream, and solemn vision,
Tell her of things that no gross ear can hear,
Till oft converse with heavenly habitants
Begin to cast a beam on the outward shape,
The unpolluted temple of the mind,
And turns it by degrees to the soul's essence,
Till all be made immortal: but when lust,
By unchaste looks, loose gestures, and foul talk,
But most by lewd and lavish act of sin,
Lets in defilement to the inward parts,
The soul grows clotted by contagion,
Imbodies, and imbrutes, till she quite lose
The divine property of her first being.
Such are those thick and gloomy shadows damp
Oft seen in charnel vaults, and sepulchres,
Lingering and sitting by a new-made grave,
As loath to leave the body that it loved,

And linked itself by carnal sensualty
To a degenerate and degraded state,
  2 *Br.* — How charming is divine philosophy!
Not harsh and crabbed, as dull fools suppose,
But musical as is Apollo's lute,
And a perpetual feast of nectared sweets,
Where no crude surfeit reigns,
  1 *Br.* — List, list, I hear
Some far off halloo break the silent air.
  2 *Br.* — Methought so too: what should it be?
  1 *Br.* — For certain
Either some one like us night-foundered here,
Or else some neighbor woodman, or, at worst,
Some roving robber calling to his fellows.
  2 *Br.* — Heaven keep my sister. Again, again, and near!
Best draw, and stand upon our guard.
  1 *Br.* — I'll halloo:
If he be friendly, he comes well; if not,
Defence is a good cause, and Heaven be for us.

Enter the ATTENDANT SPIRIT, *habited like a shepherd.*

That halloo I should know: what are you? speak;
Come not too near, you fall on iron stakes else.
  Spir. — What voice is that? my young Lord? speak again.
  2 *Br.* — O brother, 'tis my father's shepherd, sure.
  1 *Br.* — Thyrsis? Whose artful strains have oft delayed
The huddling brook to hear his madrigal,
And sweetened every muskrose of the dale.
How cam'st thou here, good swain? hath any ram
Slipt from the fold, or young kid lost his dam,
Or straggling wether the pent flock forsook?
How couldst thou find this dark sequestered nook?
  Spir. — O my loved master's heir, and his next joy,
I came not here on such a trivial toy
As a strayed ewe, or to pursue the stealth
Of pilfering wolf; not all the fleecy wealth
That doth enrich these downs is worth a thought
To this my errand, and the care it brought.
But, O my virgin Lady, where is she?
How chance she is not in your company?
  1 *Br.* — To tell thee sadly, Shepherd, without blame,
Or our neglect, we lost her as we came.
  Spir. — Aye me unhappy! then my fears are true.
  1 *Br.* — What fears, good Thyrsis? Prithee briefly show.
  Spir. — I'll tell ye; 'tis not vain or fabulous,
Though so esteemed by shallow ignorance,
What the sage poets, taught by the heavenly Muse,
Storied of old in high immortal verse,
Of dire chimeras, and enchanted isles,
And rifted rocks whose entrance leads to Hell;
For such there be, but unbelief is blind.
  Within the navel of this hideous wood,
Immured in cypress shades a sorcerer dwells,
Of Bacchus and of Circé born, great Comus,
Deep skilled in all his mother's witcheries;
And here to every thirsty wanderer
By sly enticement gives his baneful cup,
With many murmurs mixed, whose pleasing poison
The visage quite transforms of him that drinks,
And the inglorious likeness of a beast
Fixes instead, unmoulding reason's mintage
Charáctered in the face: this I have learnt

Tending my flocks hard by i' the hilly crofts,
That brow this bottom-glade, whence night by night,
He and his monstrous rout are heard to howl,
Like stabled wolves, or tigers at their prey,
Doing abhorred rites to Hecate
In their obscured haunts of inmost bowers.
Yet have they many baits, and guileful spells,
T'inveigle and invite the unwary sense
Of them that pass unweeting by the way.
This evening late, by then the chewing flocks
Had ta'en their supper on the savory herb
Of knot-grass dew-besprent, and were in fold,
I sat me down to watch upon a bank
With ivy canopied, and interwove
With flaunting honey-suckle, and began,
Wrapt in a pleasing fit of melancholy,
To meditate my rural minstrelsy,
Till fancy had her fill, but ere a close,
The wonted roar was up amidst the woods,
And filled the air with barbarous dissonance;
At which I ceased, and listened them a while,
Till an unusual stop of sudden silence
Gave respite to the drowsy frighted steeds,
That draw the litter of close-curtained sleep;
At last a soft and solemn-breathing sound
Rose like a stream of rich distilled perfumes,
And stole upon the air, that even Silence
Was took ere she was ware, and wished she might
Deny her nature, and be never more,
Still to be so displaced. I was all ear,
And took in strains that might create a soul
Under the ribs of death: but O ere long
Too well I did perceive it was the voice
Of my most honored Lady, your dear sister.
Amazed I stood, harrowed with grief and fear,
And O poor hapless nightingale thought I,
How sweet thou sing'st, how near the deadly snare!
Then down the lawns I ran with headlong haste,
Through paths and turnings often trod by day,
Till guided by mine ear I found the place,
Where that damned wizard, hid in sly disguise,
(For so by certain signs I knew) had met
Already, ere my best speed could prevent,
The aidless innocent Lady his wished prey;
Who gently asked if he had seen such two,
Supposing him some neighbor villager.
Longer I durst not stay, but soon I guessed
Ye were the two she meant: with that I sprung
Into swift flight, till I had found you here,
But further know I not.

2 *Br.* — O night and shades,
How are ye joined with Hell in triple knot,
Against the unarmed weakness of one virgin,
Alone and helpless! Is this the confidence
You gave me, brother?

1 *Br.* — Yes, and keep it still,
Lean on it safely; not a period
Shall be unsaid for me: against the threats
Of malice or of sorcery, or that power
Which erring men call Chance, this I hold firm,
Virtue may be assailed, but never hurt,
Surprised by unjust force, but not inthralled;
Yea even that which mischief meant most harm,
Shall in the happy trial prove most glory:

But evil on itself shall back recoil,
And mix no more with goodness, when at last
Gathered like scum, and settled to itself,
It shall be in eternal restless change
Self-fed, and self-consumed: if this fail,
The pillared firmament is rottenness,
And earth's base built on stubble. But come, let's on.
Against the opposing will and arm of heaven
May never this just sword be lifted up;
But for that damned magician, let him be girt
With all the grisly legions that troop
Under the sooty flag of Acheron,
Harpies and Hydras, or all the monstrous forms
'Twixt Africa and Ind, I'll find him out,
And force him to return his purchase back,
Or drag him by the curls to a foul death,
Cursed as his life.
Spir. — Alas! good vent'rous Youth,
I love thy courage yet, and bold emprise;
But here thy sword can do thee little stead;
Far other arms and other weapons must
Be those that quell the might of hellish charms:
He with his bare wand can unthread thy joints,
And crumble all thy sinews.
1 *Br.* — Why prithee, Shepherd,
How durst thou then thyself approach so near,
As to make this relation?
Spir. — Care and utmost shifts
How to secure the Lady from surprisal,
Brought to my mind a certain shepherd lad,
Of small regard to see to, yet well skilled
In every virtuous plant and healing herb,
That spreads her verdant leaf to the morning ray:
He loved me well, and oft would beg me sing,
Which when I did, he on the tender grass
Would sit, and hearken e'en to ecstasy,
And in requital ope his leathern scrip,
And show me simples of a thousand names,
Telling their strange and vigorous faculties:
Amongst the rest a small unsightly root,
But of divine effect, he culled me out:
The leaf was darkish, and had prickles on it,
But in another country, as he said,
Bore a bright golden flower, but not in this soil:
Unknown, and like esteemed, and the dull swain
Treads on it daily with his clouted shoon:
And yet more med'cinal is it than that moly
That Hermes once to wise Ulysses gave;
He called it hæmony, and gave it me,
And bade me keep it as of sovereign use
'Gainst all enchantments, mildew, blast, or damp,
Or ghastly furies' apparition.
I pursed it up, but little reck'ning made,
Till now that this extremity compelled:
But now I find it true; for by this means
I knew the foul enchanter though disguised,
Entered the very lime-twigs of his spells,
And yet came off: if you have this about you,
(As I will give you when we go) you may
Boldly assault the necromancer's hall;
Where if he be, with dauntless hardihood,
And brandished blade rush on him, break his glass,
And shed the luscious liquor on the ground,
But seize his wand; though he and his cursed crew
Fierce sign of battle make, and menace high,

Or like the sons of Vulcan vomit smoke,
Yet will they soon retire, if he but shrink.
1 *Br.* — Thyrsis, lead on apace, I'll follow thee,
And some good Angel bear a shield before us.

The Scene changes to a stately palace, set out with all manner of deliciousness; soft music, tables spread with all dainties. COMUS *appears with his rabble, and the* LADY *set in an enchanted chair, to whom he offers his glass, which she puts by, and goes about to rise.*

Com. — Nay, Lady, sit; if I but wave this wand,
Your nerves are all chained up in alabaster,
And you a statue, or as Daphne was
Root-bound, that fled Apollo.
Lady. — Fool, do not boast.
Thou canst not touch the freedom of my mind
With all thy charms, although this corporal rind
Thou hast immanacled, while heaven sees good.
Com. — Why are you vext, Lady? why do you frown?
Here dwell no frowns, nor anger; from these gates
Sorrow flies far: See, here be all the pleasures
That fancy can beget on youthful thoughts,
When the fresh blood grows lively, and returns
Brisk as the April buds in primrose-season.
And first behold this cordial julep here,
That flames, and dances in his crystal bounds,
With spirits of balm, and fragrant syrups mixed.
Not that Nepenthes, which the wife of Thone
In Egypt gave to Jove-born Helena,
Is of such power to stir up joy as this,
To life so friendly, or so cool to thirst.
Why should you be so cruel to yourself,
And to those dainty limbs which nature lent
For gentle usage, and soft delicacy?
But you invert the covenants of her trust,
And harshly deal, like an ill borrower,
With that which you received on other terms;
Scorning the unexempt condition
By which all mortal frailty must subsist,
Refreshment after toil, ease after pain,
That have been tired all day without repast,
And timely rest have wanted; but, fair Virgin,
This will restore all soon.
Lady. — 'Twill not, false traitor,
'Twill not restore the truth and honesty
That thou hast banished from thy tongue with lies.
Was this the cottage, and the safe abode
Thou told'st me of? What grim aspects are these,
These ugly-headed monsters? Mercy guard me!
Hence with thy brewed enchantments, foul deceiver;
Hast thou betrayed my credulous innocence
With visored falsehood and base forgery?
And wouldst thou seek again to trap me here
With liquorish baits fit to insnare a brute?
Were it a draught for Juno when she banquets,
I would not taste thy treasonous offer; none
But such as are good men can give good things,
And that which is not good is not delicious
To a well-governed and wise appetite.
Com. — O foolishness of men! that lend their ears
To those budge doctors of the Stoic fur,
And fetch their precepts from the Cynic tub,
Praising the lean and sallow Abstinence.
Wherefore did Nature pour her bounties forth

With such a full and unwithdrawing hand,
Covering the earth with odors, fruits, and flocks,
Thronging the seas with spawn innumerable,
But all to please, and sate the curious taste?
And set to work millions of spinning worms,
That in their green shops weave the smooth-haired silk
To deck her sons; and that no corner might
Be vacant of her plenty, in her own loins
She hutched the all worshipped ore, and precious gems,
To store her children with: if all the world
Should in a pet of temperance feed on pulse,
Drink the clear stream, and nothing wear but frieze,
The All-giver would be unthanked, would be unpraised,
Not half his riches known, and yet despised;
And we should serve him as a grudging master,
As a penurious niggard of his wealth;
And live like Nature's bastards, not her sons,
Who would be quite surcharged with her own weight,
And strangled with her waste fertility;
The earth cumbered, and the winged air darked with plumes,
The herds would over-multitude their lords,
The sea o'erfraught would swell, and the unsought diamonds
Would so emblaze the forehead of the deep,
And so bestud with stars, that they below
Would grow inured to light, and come at last
To gaze upon the sun with shameless brows.
List, Lady, be not coy, and be not cozened
With that same vaunted name Virginity.
Beauty is Nature's coin, must not be hoarded,
But must be current, and the good thereof
Consists in mutual and partaken bliss,
Unsavory in the enjoyment of itself;
If you let slip time, like a neglected rose
It withers on the stalk with languished head.
Beauty is Nature's brag, and must be shown
In courts, at feasts, and high solemnities,
Where most may wonder at the workmanship;
It is for homely features to keep home,
They had their name thence; coarse complexions,
And cheeks of sorry grain, will serve to ply
The sampler, and to tease the housewife's wool.
What need a vermeil-tinctured lip for that,
Love-darting eyes, or tresses like the morn?
There was another meaning in these gifts,
Think what, and be advised, you are but young yet.

Lady. — I had not thought to have unlockt my lips
In this unhallowed air, but that this juggler
Would think to charm my judgment, as mine eyes,
Obtruding false rules pranked in reason's garb.
I hate when Vice can bolt her arguments,
And Virtue has no tongue to check her pride.
Impostor, do not charge most innocent Nature,
As if she would her children should be riotous
With her abundance; she, good cateress,
Means her provision only to the good,
That live according to her sober laws,
And holy dictate of spare temperance:
If every just man, that now pines with want,

Had but a moderate and beseeming share
Of that which lewdly-pampered luxury
Now heaps upon some few with vast excess,
Nature's full blessings would be well dispensed
In unsuperfluous even proportion,
And she no wit encumbered with her store;
And then the Giver would be better thanked,
His praise due paid; for swinish gluttony
Ne'er looks to heaven amidst his gorgeous feast,
But with besotted base ingratitude
Crams, and blasphemes his feeder. Shall I go on?
Or have I said enough? To him that dares
Arm his profane tongue with contemptuous words
Against the sun-clad power of Chastity,
Fain would I something say, yet to what end?
Thou hast not ear, nor soul to apprehend
The sublime notion, and high mystery,
That must be uttered to unfold the sage
And serious doctrine of Virginity,
And thou art worthy that thou shouldst not know
More happiness than this thy present lot.
Enjoy your dear wit, and gay rhetoric,
That hath so well been taught her dazzling fence,
Thou art not fit to hear thyself convinced;
Yet should I try, the uncontrolled worth
Of this pure cause would kindle my rapt spirits
To such a flame of sacred vehemence,
That dumb things would be moved to sympathize,
And the brute earth would lend her nerves, and shake,
Till all thy magic structures reared so high,
Were shattered into heaps o'er thy false head.

Com. — She fables not; I feel that I do fear
Her words set off by some superior power:
And though not mortal, yet a cold shuddering dew
Dips me all o'er, as when the wrath of Jove
Speaks thunder, and the chains of Erebus,
To some of Saturn's crew. I must dissemble,
And try her yet more strongly. Come, no more.
This is mere moral babble, and direct
Against the canon laws of our foundation;
I must not suffer this, yet 'tis but the lees
And settlings of a melancholy blood:
But this will cure all straight; one sip of this
Will bathe the drooping spirits in delight,
Beyond the bliss of dreams. Be wise, and taste. —

The BROTHERS *rush in with swords drawn, wrest his glass out of his hand, and break it against the ground: his rout make sign of resistance, but are all driven in. The* ATTENDANT SPIRIT *comes in.*

Spir. — What, have you let the false enchanter 'scape?
O ye mistook, ye should have snatched his wand,
And bound him fast: without his rod reversed,
And backword mutters of dissevering power,
We cannot free the Lady that sits here
In stony fetters fixed, and motionless:
Yet stay, be not disturbed: now I bethink me,
Some other means I have which may be used,
Which once of Melibœus old I learnt,
The soothest shepherd that e'er piped on plains.
There is a gentle nymph not far from hence,
That with moist curb sways the smooth Severn stream,

Sabrina is her name, a virgin pure;
Whilom she was the daughter of Locrine,
That had the sceptre from his father Brute.
She, guiltless damsel, flying the mad pursuit
Of her enraged stepdame Guendolen,
Commended her fair innocence to the flood,
They stayed her flight with his cross-flowing course.
The water-nymphs that in the bottom played,
Held up their pearlèd wrists, and took her in,
Bearing her straight to aged Nereus' hall,
Who, piteous of her woes, reared her lank head,
And gave her to his daughters to imbathe
In nectared lavers strewed with asphodel,
And through the porch and inlet of each sense
Dropped in ambrosial oils, till she revived,
And underwent a quick immortal change,
Made Goddess of the river: still she retains
Her maiden gentleness, and oft at eve
Visits the herds along the twilight meadows,
Helping all urchin blasts, and ill-luck signs
That the shrewd meddling elf delights to make,
Which she with precious vialled liquors heals;
For which the shepherds at their festivals
Carol her goodness loud in rustic lays,
And throw sweet garland wreaths into her stream
Of pansies, pinks, and gaudy daffodils,
And, as the old swain said, she can unlock
The clasping charm, and thaw the numbing spell,
If she be right invoked in warbled song;
For maidenhood she loves, and will be swift
To aid a virgin, such as was herself,
In hard-besetting need; this will I try,
And add the power of some adjuring verse.

SONG.

Sabrina fair,
Listen where thou art sitting
Under the glassy, cool, translucent wave,
In twisted braids of lilies knitting
The loose train of thy amber-dropping hair;
Listen for dear honor's sake,
Goddess of the silver lake,
Listen and save.
Listen and appear to us
In name of great Oceanus,
By the earth-shaking Neptune's mace,
And Tethys' grave majestic pace,
By hoary Nereus' wrinkled look,
And the Carpathian wizard's hook,
By scaly Triton's winding shell,
And old soothsaying Glaucus' spell,
By Leucothea's lovely hands,
And her son that rules the strands,
By Thetis' tinsel-slippered feet,
And the songs of Sirens sweet,
By dead Parthenope's dear tomb,
And fair Ligea's golden comb,
Wherewith she sits on diamond rocks,
Sleeking her soft alluring locks,
By all the nymphs that nightly dance
Upon thy streams with wily glance,
Rise, rise, and heave thy rosy head
From thy coral-paven bed,
And bridle in thy headlong wave,
Till thou our summons answered have.
Listen and save.

SABRINA *rises, attended by water-nymphs, and sings.*

By the rushy-fringed bank,
Where grow the willow and the osier dank,
My sliding chariot stays,
Thick set with agate, and the azurn sheen
Of turkis blue, and emerald green,
That in the channel strays;
Whilst from off the waters fleet,
Thus I set my printless feet

O'er the cowslip's velvet head,
That bends not as I tread;
Gentle Swain, at thy request
I am here.

Spir. — Goddess dear,
We implore thy powerful hand
To undo the charmèd band
Of true virgin here distressed,
Through the force, and through the wile
Of unblest enchanter vile.

Sabr. — Shepherd, 'tis my office best
To help ensnarèd chastity:
Brightest Lady, look on me;
Thus I sprinkle on thy breast
Drops that from my fountain pure
I have kept of precious cure,
Thrice upon thy finger's tip,
Thrice upon thy rubied lip;
Next this marble venomed seat,
Smeared with gums of glutinous heat,
I touch with chaste palms moist and cold:
Now the spell hath lost his hold;
And I must haste ere morning hour
To wait in Amphitrite's bower.

SABRINA *descends, and the* LADY *rises out of her seat.*

Spir. — Virgin, daughter of Locrine,
Sprung of old Anchises' line,
May thy brimmèd waves for this
Their full tribute never miss
From a thousand petty rills,
That tumble down the snowy hills:
Summer drouth, or singèd air
Never scorch thy tresses fair,
Nor wet October's torrent flood
Thy molten crystal fill with mud;
May thy billows roll ashore
The beryl, and the golden ore;
May thy lofty head be crowned
With many a tower and terrace round,
And here and there thy banks upon
With groves of myrrh and cinnamon.
Come, Lady, while heaven lends us grace,
Let us fly this cursed place,
Lest the sorcerer us entice
With some other new device.
Not a waste, or needless sound,
Till we come to holier ground;
I shall be your faithful guide
Through this gloomy covert wide,
And not many furlongs thence
Is your Father's residence,
Where this night are met in state
Many a friend to gratulate
His wished presence, and beside
All the swains that there abide,
With jigs, and rural dance resort;
We shall catch them at their sport,
And our sudden coming there
Will double all their mirth and cheer;
Come, let us haste, the stars grow high,
But night sits monarch yet in the mid sky.

The Scene changes, presenting Ludlow town and the President's castle; then come in country dancers, after them the ATTENDANT SPIRIT, *with the* TWO BROTHERS, *and the* LADY.

SONG.

Spir. — Back, Shepherds, back, enough your play,
Till next sunshine holiday;
Here be without duck or nod
Other trippings to be trod
Of lighter toes, and such court guise
As Mercury did first devise,
With the mincing Dryades,
On the lawns, and on the leas.

This second Song presents them to their Father and Mother.

Noble Lord, and Lady bright,
I have brought ye new delight,
Here behold so goodly grown
Three fair branches of your own;
Heaven hath timely tried their youth,
Their faith, their patience, and their truth,
And sent them here through hard assays
With a crown of deathless praise,
To triumph in victorious dance
O'er sensual folly, and intemperance.

The dances ended, the SPIRIT *epilogizes.*

Spir. — To the ocean now I fly,
And those happy climes that lie
Where day never shuts his eye,
Up in the broad fields of the sky:

There I suck the liquid air
All amidst the gardens fair
Of Hesperus, and his daughters three
That sing about the golden tree:
Along the crisped shades and bowers
Revels the spruce and jocund Spring,
The Graces, and the rosy-bosomed Hours,
Thither all their bounties bring;
There eternal Summer dwells,
And west-winds, with musky wing,
About the cedarn alleys fling
Nard and cassia's balmy smells.
Iris there with humid bow
Waters the odorous banks, that blow
Flowers of more mingled hue
Than her purfled scarf can show,
And drenches with Elysian dew,
(List mortals, if your ears be true)
Beds of hyacinth and roses,
Where young Adonis oft reposes,
Waxing well of his deep wound
In slumber soft, and on the ground
Sadly sits the Assyrian queen;
But far above in spangled sheen
Celestial Cupid, her famed son, advanced,
Holds his dear Psyche sweet entranced,
After her wandering labors long,
Till free consent the Gods among
Make her his eternal bride,
And from her fair unspotted side
Two blissful twins are to be born,
Youth and Joy; so Jove hath sworn.
But now my task is smoothly done,
I can fly, or I can run
Quickly to the green earth's end,
Where the bowed welkin slow doth bend,
And from thence can soar as soon
To the corners of the moon.
Mortals, that would follow me,
Love Virtue, she alone is free;
She can teach ye how to climb
Higher than the sphery chime:
Or, if Virtue feeble were,
Heaven itself would stoop to her.

MILTON.

MYTHOLOGY.

O NEVER rudely will I blame his faith
In the might of stars and angels! 'Tis not merely
The human being's Pride that peoples space
With life and mystical predominance;
Since likewise for the stricken heart of Love
This visible nature, and this common world,
Is all too narrow: yea, a deeper import
Lurks in the legend told my infant years
Than lies upon that truth we live to learn.
For fable is Love's world, his home, his birthplace:
Delightedly dwells he 'mong fays and talismans,
And spirits; and delightedly believes
Divinities, being himself divine.
The intelligible forms of ancient poets,
The fair humanities of old religion,
The power, the beauty, and the majesty,
That had their haunts in dale, or piny mountain,
Or forest by slow stream, or pebbly spring,
Or chasms and watery depths; all these have vanished;
They live no longer in the faith of reason.
But still the heart doth need a language, still
Doth the old instinct bring back the old names,
And to yon starry world they now are gone,
Spirits or gods, that used to share this earth
With man as with their friend; and to the lover
Yonder they move, from yonder visible sky
Shoot influence down; and even at this day
'Tis Jupiter who brings whate'er is great,
And Venus who brings every thing that's fair!

COLERIDGE: *Wallenstein.*

KILMENY.

BONNY Kilmeny gaed up the glen;
But it was na to meet Duneira's men,
Nor the rosy monk of the isle to see,

For Kilmeny was pure as pure could be.
It was only to hear the yorlin sing,
And pu' the cress flower round the spring —
The scarlet hypp, and the hind berry,
And the nut that hangs frae the hazel tree;
For Kilmeny was pure as pure could be.
But lang may her minny look o'er the wa',
And lang may she seek in the green-wood shaw;
Lang the laird of Duneira blame,
And lang, lang greet ere Kilmeny come hame.

When many a day had come and fled,
When grief grew calm, and hope was dead,
When mass for Kilmeny's soul had been sung,
When the bedesman had prayed, and the dead-bell rung,
Late, late in a gloamin, when all was still,
When the fringe was red on the westlin hill,
The wood was sere, the moon in the wane,
The reek of the cot hung over the plain —
Like a little wee cloud in the world its lane;
When the ingle glowed with an eiry flame,
Late, late in a gloamin, Kilmeny came hame!

"Kilmeny, Kilmeny, where have you been?
Long hae we sought baith holt and den —
By linn, by ford, and greenwood tree;
Yet you are halesome and fair to see.
Where got you that joup o' the lily sheen?
That bonny snood of the birk sae green?
And these roses, the fairest that ever were seen?
Kilmeny, Kilmeny, where have you been?"
Kilmeny looked up with a lovely grace,
But nae smile was seen on Kilmeny's face;
As still was her look, and as still was her ee,
As the stillness that lay on the emerant lea,
Or the mist that sleeps on a waveless sea.
For Kilmeny had been she knew not where,
And Kilmeny had seen what she could not declare;
Kilmeny had been where the cock never crew,
Where the rain never fell, and the wind never blew;
But it seemed as the harp of the sky had rung,
And the airs of heaven played round her tongue,
When she spake of the lovely forms she had seen,
And a land where sin had never been —
A land of love and a land of light,
Withouten sun, or moon, or night;
And lovely beings round were rife,
Who erst had travelled mortal life;
They clasped her waist and her hands sae fair,
They kissed her cheek and they kemed her hair;
And round came many a blooming fere,
Saying, "Bonny Kilmeny, ye're wel-come here!
Oh, bonny Kilmeny, free frae stain,
If ever you seek the world again —
That world of sin, of sorrow, and fear —
O, tell of the joys that are waiting here!
And tell of the signs you shall shortly see,
Of the times that are now, and the times that shall be."

But to sing of the sights Kilmeny saw,
So far surpassing Nature's law,
The singer's voice wad sink away,
And the string of his harp wad cease to play.
But she saw till the sorrows of man were by,
And all was love and harmony;
Till the stars of heaven fell calmly away,
Like the flakes of snaw on a winter's day.

Then Kilmeny begged again to see
The friends she had left in her own countrye;
With distant music soft and deep,
They lulled Kilmeny sound asleep;
And when she awakened, she lay her lane,
All lapped with flowers in the green-wood wene.
When seven long years had come and fled;
When grief was calm, and hope was dead;
When scarce was remembered Kilmeny's name,
Late, late in a gloamin, Kilmeny came hame!
And oh, her beauty was fair to see,
But still and steadfast was her ee!
And oh, the words that fell from her mouth
Were words of wonder and words of truth!

It was na her home, and she could na remain;
She left this world of sorrow and pain,
And returned to the land of thought again.

HOGG.

DREAMS.

AGAIN returned the scenes of youth,
Of confident undoubting truth;
Again his soul he interchanged
With friends whose hearts were long estranged:
They come, in dim procession led,
The cold, the faithful, and the dead;
As warm each hand, each brow as gay,
As if they parted yesterday.

SCOTT.

ROMEO'S PRESAGE.

Romeo. — If I may trust the flattering eye of sleep,
My dreams presage some joyful news at hand:
My bosom's lord sits lightly in his throne;
And all this day an unaccustomed spirit
Lifts me above the ground with cheerful thoughts.
I dreamt my lady came and found me dead;
(Strange dream that gives a dead man leave to think,)
And breathed such life with kisses in my lips,
That I revived and was an emperor.
Ah, me! how sweet is love itself possessed
When but love's shadows are so rich in joy.

SHAKSPEARE: *Romeo and Juliet.* Act v. Sc. 1.

SHIPS AT SEA.

I HAVE ships that went to sea
More than fifty years ago:
None have yet come home to me,
But keep sailing to and fro.
I have seen them, in my sleep,
Plunging through the shoreless deep,
With tattered sails and battered hulls,
While around them screamed the gulls,
Flying low, flying low.

I have wondered why they staid
From me, sailing round the world;
And I've said, "I'm half afraid
That their sails will ne'er be furled."
Great the treasures that they hold, —
Silks and plumes, and bars of gold;
While the spices which they bear
Fill with fragrance all the air,
As they sail, as they sail.

Every sailor in the port
Knows that I have ships at sea,
Of the waves and winds the sport;
And the sailors pity me.
Oft they come and with me walk,
Cheering me with hopeful talk,
Till I put my fears aside,
And contented watch the tide
Rise and fall, rise and fall.

I have waited on the piers,
Gazing for them down the bay,
Days and nights, for many years,
Till I turned heart-sick away.
But the pilots, when they land,
Stop and take me by the hand,

Saying, "You will live to see
Your proud vessels come from sea,
One and all, one and all."

So I never quite despair,
Nor let hope or courage fail;
And some day, when skies are fair,
Up the bay my ships will sail.
I can buy then all I need, —
Prints to look at, books to read,
Horses, wines, and works of art,
Every thing except a heart:
That is lost, that is lost.

Once when I was pure and young,
Poorer, too, than I am now,
Ere a cloud was o'er me flung,
Or a wrinkle creased my brow,
There was one whose heart was mine;
But she's something now divine,
And though come my ships from sea,
They can bring no heart to me,
Evermore, evermore.

R. B. Coffin.

THE WHITE ISLAND.

In this world, the Isle of Dreames,
While we sit by Sorrow's streames,
Teares and terrors are our themes,
Reciting:

But when once from hence we flie,
More and more approaching nigh
Unto young eternitie,
Uniting,

In that Whiter Island, where
Things are evermore sincere;
Candor here and lustre there,
Delighting:

There no monstrous fancies shall
Out of hell an Horror call,
To create, or cause at all,
Affrighting.

There, in calm and cooling sleep,
We our eyes shall never steep,
But eternall watch shall keep,
Attending

Pleasures such as shall pursue
Me immortalized and you;
And fresh joyes, as never to
Have ending.

Herrick.

FANTASY.

Break, Fantasy, from thy cave of cloud,
And spread thy purple wings,
Now all thy figures are allowed,
And various shapes of things;
Create of airy forms a stream,
It must have blood, and nought of phlegm,
And, though it be a waking dream,
Yet let it like an odor rise
To all the senses here,
And fall like sleep upon their eyes,
Or music in their ear.

Ben Jonson.

PHŒNIX AND TURTLE DOVE.

Let the bird of loudest lay,
On the sole Arabian tree,
Herald sad and trumpet be,
To whose sound chaste wings obey.

But thou shrieking harbinger,
Foul pre-currer of the fiend,
Augur of the fever's end,
To this troop come thou not near.

From this session interdict
Every fowl of tyrant wing,
Save the eagle, feathered king;
Keep the obsequy so strict.

Let the priest in surplice white
That defunctive music can,
Be the death-divining swan,
Lest the requiem lack his right.

And thou treble-dated crow,
That thy sable gender mak'st
With the breath thou giv'st and tak'st,
'Mongst our mourners shalt thou go.

So they loved, as love in twain
Had the essence but in one;
Two distincts, division none:
Number there in love was slain.

Hearts remote, yet not asunder;
Distance, and no space was seen
'Twixt the turtle and his queen:
But in them it were a wonder.

So between them love did shine,
That the turtle saw his right

Flaming in the Phœnix' sight:
Either was the other's mine.

Property was thus appalled,
That the self was not the same;
Single nature's double name
Neither two nor one was called.

Reason, in itself confounded,
Saw division grow together;
To themselves yet either-neither,
Simple was so well compounded:

That it cried, How true a twain
Seemeth this concordant one!
Love hath reason, reason none,
If what parts can so remain.

Whereupon it made this threne
To the Phœnix and the dove,
Co-supremes and stars of love;
As chorus to their tragic scene.

THRENOS.

BEAUTY, truth, and rarity,
Grace in all simplicity,
Here enclosed in cinders lie.

Death is now the Phœnix' nest;
And the turtle's loyal breast
To eternity doth rest,

Leaving no posterity: —
'Twas not their infirmity,
It was married chastity.

Truth may seem, but cannot be;
Beauty brag, but 'tis not she;
Truth and beauty buried be.

To this urn let those repair
That are either true or fair;
For these dead birds sigh a prayer.

SHAKSPEARE.

COMPLIMENT TO QUEEN ELIZABETH.

MY gentle Puck, come hither, thou remember'st
Since once I sat upon a promontory,
And heard a mermaid on a dolphin's back,
Uttering such dulcet and harmonious breath,
That the rude sea grew civil at her song;
And certain stars shot madly from their spheres,
To hear the sea-maid's music.
That very time, I saw, but thou couldst not,
Flying between the cold moon and the earth,
Cupid all armed: a certain aim he took
At a fair vestal, throned by the west;
And loosed his love-shaft smartly from his bow,
As it should pierce a hundred thousand hearts:
But I might see young Cupid's fiery shaft
Quenched in the chaste beams of the watery moon,
And the imperial votaress passed on,
In maiden meditation, fancy-free.
Yet marked I where the bolt of Cupid fell;
It fell upon a little western flower, —
Before milk-white, now purple with love's wound, —
And maidens call it Love-in-idleness.
Fetch me that flower; the herb I showed thee once.
The juice of it on sleeping eyelids laid
Will make a man or woman madly dote
Upon the next live creature that it sees.
Fetch me this herb: and be thou here again,
Ere the Leviathan can swim a league.
Puck. — I'll put a girdle round about the earth
In forty minutes.

. . . .

Oberon. — Hast thou the flower there? Welcome, wanderer.
Puck. — Ay, there it is.
Oberon. — I pray thee, give it me.
I know a bank whereon the wild thyme blows,
Where ox-lips and the nodding violet grows,
Quite over-canopied with lush woodbine,
With sweet musk-roses, and with eglantine:

There sleeps Titania, some time of the night,
Lulled in these flowers with dances and delight;
And there the snake throws her enamelled skin,
Weed wide enough to wrap a fairy in:
And with the juice of this I'll streak her eyes,
And make her full of hateful fantasies.

SHAKSPEARE: *Midsummer Night's Dream.*

QUEEN MAB.

O THEN, I see, Queen Mab hath been with you.
She is the fairies' midwife; and she comes
In shape no bigger than an agate-stone
On the fore-finger of an alderman,
Drawn with a team of little atomies
Athwart men's noses as they lie asleep:
Her wagon-spokes made of long spinners' legs;
The cover, of the wings of grasshoppers;
The traces, of the smallest spider's web;
The collars, of the moonshine's watery beams;
Her whip, of cricket's bone; the lash, of film;
Her wagoner, a small gray-coated gnat,
Not half so big as a round little worm
Pricked from the lazy finger of a maid:
Her chariot is an empty hazel-hut,
Made by the joiner squirrel, or old grub,
Time out of mind the fairies' coachmakers.
And in this state she gallops night by night
Through lovers' brains, and then they dream of love;
On courtiers' knees, that dream on court'sies straight;
O'er lawyers' fingers, who straight dream on fees;
O'er ladies' lips, who straight on kisses dream,
Which oft the angry Mab with blisters plagues,
Because their breaths with sweetmeats tainted are:
Sometimes she gallops o'er a courtier's nose,
And then dreams he of smelling out a suit;
And sometimes comes she with a tithe-pig's tail,
Tickling a parson's nose as he lies asleep,
Then dreams he of another benefice:
Sometimes she driveth o'er a soldier's neck,
And then dreams he of cutting foreign throats,
Of breaches, ambuscadoes, Spanish blades,
Of healths five fathom deep; and then anon
Drums in his ear, at which he starts, and wakes,
And, being thus frighted, swears a prayer or two,
And sleeps again. This is that very Mab
That plaits the manes of horses in the night,
And bakes the elf-locks in foul sluttish hairs,
Which once untangled, much misfortune bodes.

SHAKSPEARE: *Romeo and Juliet.*

SONG FROM GYPSIES' METAMORPHOSES.

THE owl is abroad, the bat, the toad,
And so is the cat-a-mountain;
The ant and the mole sit both in a hole;
And frog peeps out o' the fountain;
The dogs they bay, and the timbrels play;
The spindle now is a-turning;
The moon it is red, and the stars are fled;
But all the sky is a-burning.

THE faery beam upon you,
And the stars to glister on you,
A moon of light
In the noon of night,

Till the fire-drake hath o'ergone you,
The wheel of Fortune guide you,
The Boy with the bow beside you
Run aye in the way, till the bird of day,
And the luckier lot betide you.

BEN JONSON.

THE SONG OF FIONNUALA.*

SILENT, O Moyle, be the roar of thy water,
Break not, ye breezes, your chain of repose,
While, murmuring mournfully, Lir's lonely daughter
Tells to the night-star her tale of woes.
When shall the swan, her death-note singing,
Sleep, with wings in darkness furled?
When will heaven its sweet bell ringing,
Call my spirit from this stormy world?

Sadly, O Moyle, to thy winter wave weeping,
Fate bids me languish long ages away;
Yet still in her darkness doth Erin lie sleeping,
Still doth the pure light its dawning delay.
When will that day-star, mildly springing,
Warm our isle with peace and love?
When will heaven, its sweet bell ringing,
Call my spirit to the fields above?

THOMAS MOORE.

* Fionnuala, the daughter of Lir, was, by some supernatural power, transformed into a swan, and condemned to wander over certain lakes and rivers in Ireland, till the coming of Christianity, when the first sound of the mass bell was to be the signal of her release.

FAIRIES.

LITTLE was King Laurin, but from many a precious gem
His wondrous strength and power, and his bold courage came;
Tall at times his stature grew, with spells of gramarye,
Then to the noblest princes fellow might he be.

WARTON: *Little Garden of Roses.*

KUBLA KHAN.

IN Xanadu did Kubla Khan
A stately pleasure-dome decree:
Where Alph, the sacred river, ran,
Through caverns measureless to man,
Down to a sunless sea.
So twice five miles of fertile ground
With walls and towers were girdled round:
And here were gardens bright with sinuous rills,
Where blossomed many an incense-bearing tree;
And here were forests ancient as the hills,
Infolding sunny spots of greenery.

But oh! that deep chasm which slanted
Down the green hill athwart a cedarn cover!
A savage place! as holy and enchanted
As e'er beneath a waning moon was haunted
By woman wailing for her demon-lover!
And from this chasm, with ceaseless turmoil seething,
As if this earth in fast thick pants were breathing,
A mighty fountain momently was forced:
Amid whose swift half-intermitted burst
Huge fragments vaulted like rebounding hail,
Or chaffy grain beneath the thresher's flail:
And 'mid these dancing rocks at once and ever
It flung up momently the sacred river.
Five miles meandering with a mazy motion
Through wood and dale the sacred river ran,
Then reached the caverns measureless to man,
And sank in tumult to a lifeless ocean:

And 'mid this tumult Kubla heard from far
Ancestral voices prophecying war!

The shadow of the dome of pleasure
Floated midway on the waves;
Where was heard the mingled measure
From the fountain and the caves.
It was a miracle of rare device,
A sunny pleasure-dome with caves of ice!

A damsel with a dulcimer
In a vision once I saw:
It was an Abyssinian maid,
And on her dulcimer she played,
Singing of Mount Abora.
Could I revive within me
Her symphony and song,
To such a deep delight 'twould win me,
That with music loud and long,
I would build that dome in air,
That sunny dome! those caves of ice!
And all who heard should see them there,
And all should cry, Beware! Beware!
His flashing eyes, his floating hair,
Weave a circle round him thrice,
And close your eyes with holy dread,
For he on honey-dew hath fed,
And drunk the milk of Paradise.

S. T. Coleridge.

ST. CECILIA'S DAY.

From harmony, from heavenly harmony,
This universal frame began:
From harmony to harmony,
Through all the compass of the notes it ran,
The diapason closing full in man.

What passion cannot Music raise and quell?
When Jubal struck the chorded shell,
His listening brethren stood around,
And, wondering, on their faces fell
To worship that celestial sound.
Less than a God they thought there could not dwell
Within the hollow of that shell,
That spoke so sweetly and so well.
What passion cannot Music raise and quell?

Dryden.

MUSIC.

When whispering strains with creeping wind
Distil soft passions through the heart;
And when at every touch we find
Our pulses beat and bear a part;
When threads can make
A heartstring ache,
Philosophy
Can scarce deny
Our souls are made of harmony.

When unto heavenly joys we faine
Whate'er the soul affecteth most,
Which only thus we can explain
By music of the heavenly host;
Whose lays we think
Make stars to wink,
Philosophy
Can scarce deny
Our souls consist of harmony.

O lull me, lull me, charming air!
My senses rock with wonder sweet;
Like snow on wool thy fallings are;
Soft like a spirit's are thy feet!
Grief who needs fear
That hath an ear?
Down let him lie,
And slumbering die,
And change his soul for harmony.

William Strode.

ORPHEUS WITH HIS LUTE.

Orpheus with his lute made trees,
And the mountain-tops that freeze,
Bow themselves, when he did sing:
To his music, plants and flowers
Ever sprung, as sun and showers,
There had been a lasting spring.

Every thing that heard him play,
Even the billows of the sea,
Hung their heads, and then lay by.

In sweet music is such art;
Killing care and grief of heart,
  Fall asleep, or, hearing, die.

SHAKSPEARE.

MUSIC.

NORTHWARD he turneth through a little door,
And scarce three steps, ere Music's golden tongue
Flattered to tears this aged man and poor.

KEATS.

THE PASSIONS.

AN ODE FOR MUSIC.

WHEN Music, heavenly maid, was young,
While yet in early Greece she sung,
The Passions oft, to hear her shell,
Thronged around her magic cell,
Exulting, trembling, raging, fainting,
Possessed beyond the Muse's painting:
By turns they felt the glowing mind
Disturbed, delighted, raised, refined;
Till once, 'tis said, when all were fired,
Filled with fury, rapt, inspired,
From the supporting myrtles round,
They snatched her instruments of sound;
And as they oft had heard apart,
Sweet lessons of her forceful art,
Each (for Madness ruled the hour)
Would prove his own expressive power.

First Fear his hand, its skill to try,
  Amid the chords bewildered laid,
And back recoiled, he knew not why,
  E'en at the sound himself had made.

Next Anger rushed, his eyes on fire,
  In lightnings owned his secret stings:
In one rude clash he struck the lyre,
  And swept with hurried hand the strings.

With woful measures, wan Despair
  Low, sullen sounds his grief beguiled;
A solemn, strange, and mingled air;
  'Twas sad by fits, by starts 'twas wild.

But thou, O Hope! with eyes so fair,
  What was thy delighted measure?
Still it whispered promised pleasure,
  And bade the lovely scenes at distance hail!
Still would her touch the strain prolong;
  And from the rocks, the woods, the vale,
She called on Echo still, through all the song;
  And, where her sweetest theme she chose,
  A soft responsive voice was heard at every close,
And Hope enchanted smiled, and waved her golden hair.
And longer had she sung;—but with a frown
  Revenge impatient rose:
He threw his blood-stained sword, in thunder down;
  And with a withering look,
The war-denouncing trumpet took,
And blew a blast so loud and dread,
Were ne'er prophetic sounds so full of woe!
  And, ever and anon, he beat
  The doubling drum, with furious heat;
And though sometimes, each dreary pause between,
  Dejected Pity, at his side,
  Her soul-subduing voice applied,
Yet still he kept his wild unaltered mien,
While each strained ball of sight seemed bursting from his head.
Thy numbers, Jealousy, to nought were fixed;
  Sad proof of thy distressful state;
Of differing themes the veering song was mixed;
  And now it called on Love, now raving called on Hate.

With eyes upraised, as one inspired,
Pale Melancholy sate retired;
And from her wild sequestered seat,
In notes by distance made more sweet,

Poured through the mellow horn her pensive soul:
And dashing soft from rocks around,
Bubbling runnels joined the sound;
Through glades and glooms the mingled measure stole,
Or, o'er some haunted stream, with fond delay,
Round a holy calm diffusing,
Love of Peace, and lonely musing,
In hollow murmurs died away.

But O! how altered was its sprightlier tone,
When Cheerfulness, a nymph of healthiest hue,
Her bow across her shoulder flung,
Her buskins gemmed with morning dew,
Blew an inspiring air that dale and thicket rung,
The hunter's call, to Faun and Dryad known;
The oak-crowned Sisters, and their chaste-eyed Queen,
Satyrs and Sylvan Boys, were seen,
Peeping from forth their alleys green:
Brown Exercise rejoiced to hear;
And Sport leaped up, and seized his beechen spear.
Last came Joy's ecstatic trial:
He with viny crown advancing,
First to the lively pipe his hand addrest;
But soon he saw the brisk awakening viol,
Whose sweet entrancing voice he loved the best;
They would have thought, who heard the strain,
They saw in Tempe's vale, her native maids,
Amidst the festal sounding shades,
To some unwearied minstrel dancing,
While, as his flying fingers kissed the strings,
Love framed with Mirth a gay fantastic round:
Loose were her tresses seen, her zone unbound;
And he, amidst his frolic and his play,
As if he would the charming air repay,
Shook thousand odors from his dewy wings.

O Music! sphere-descended maid,
Friend of Pleasure, Wisdom's aid!
Why, goddess! why, to us denied,
Lay'st thou thine ancient lyre aside?
As in that loved Athenian bower,
You learned an all-commanding power,
Thy mimic soul, O Nymph endeared,
Can well recall what then it heard;
Where is thy native simple heart,
Devote to Virtue, Fancy, Art?
Arise, as in that elder time,
Warm, energetic, chaste, sublime!
Thy wonders, in that godlike age,
Fill thy recording Sister's page:—
'Tis said, and I believe the tale,
Thy humblest seed could more prevail,
Had more of strength, diviner rage,
Than all which charms this laggard age;
E'en all at once together found,
Cecilia's mingled world of sound,—
O bid our vain endeavors cease;
Revive the just designs of Greece;
Return in all thy simple state!
Confirm the tales her sons relate!

COLLINS.

A SUPPLICATION.

Awake, awake, my Lyre!
And tell thy silent master's humble tale
In sounds that may prevail;
Sounds that gentle thoughts inspire:
Though so exalted she,
And I so lowly be,
Tell her, such different notes make all thy harmony.

Hark! how the strings awake:
And, though the moving hand approach not near,
Themselves with awful fear
A kind of numerous trembling make.
Now all thy forces try;
Now all thy charms apply;
Revenge upon her ear the conquests of her eye.

Weak Lyre! thy virtue sure
Is useless here, since thou art only found
To cure, but not to wound,
And she to wound, but not to cure.

Too weak, too, wilt thou prove
My passion to remove;
Physic to other ills, thou'rt nourishment to love.

Sleep, sleep again, my Lyre!
For thou canst never tell my humble tale
In sounds that will prevail,
Nor gentle thoughts in her inspire;
All thy vain mirth lay by,
Bid thy strings silent lie,
Sleep, sleep again, my Lyre, and let thy master die.

COWLEY.

TO MUSIC.

EVER a current of sadness deep
Through the streams of thy triumph is heard to sweep.

HEMANS.

TO THE HARP.

THAT instrument ne'er heard
Struck by the skilful bard
It strongly to awake,
But it the Infernals scared
And made Olympus quake.

As those prophetic strings
Whose sounds with fiery wings
Drove fiends from their abode,
Touched by the best of kings,
That sung the holy ode.

So his when women slew
And it in Hebrus threw,
Such sounds yet forth it sent,
The banks to weep that drew
As down the stream it went.

And diversely though strong,
So anciently we sung
To it, that now scarce known
If first it did belong
To Greece, or if our own.

The Druidés imbrued
With gore on altars rude
With sacrifices crowned
In hollow woods bedewed,
Adored the trembling sound.

DRAYTON.

ÆOLIAN HARP.

THE sea rolls vaguely, and the stars are dumb.
The ship is sunk full many a year.
Dream no more of loss or gain:
A ship was never here.
A dawn will never, never come.
Is it all in vain?

ALLINGHAM.

ALEXANDER'S FEAST; OR, THE POWER OF MUSIC.

'TWAS at the royal feast for Persia won
By Philip's warlike son —
Aloft in awful state
The godlike hero sate
On his imperial throne;
His valiant peers were placed around,
Their brows with roses and with myrtles bound
(So should desert in arms be crowned);
The lovely Thais by his side
Sate like a blooming Eastern bride
In flower of youth and beauty's pride: —
Happy, happy, happy pair!
None but the brave
None but the brave
None but the brave deserves the fair!

Timotheus placed on high
Amid the tuneful choir
With flying fingers touched the lyre:
The trembling notes ascend the sky,
And heavenly joys inspire.
The song began from Jove,
Who left his blissful seats above —
Such is the power of mighty love!
A dragon's fiery form belied the god;
Sublime on radiant spheres he rode
When he to fair Olympia prest,
And while he sought her snowy breast;
Then round her slender waist he curled,
And stamped an image of himself, a sovereign of the world.
— The listening crowd admire the lofty sound!
A present deity! they shout around:
A present deity! the vaulted roofs rebound!

With ravished ears
The monarch hears,
Assumes the god;
Affects to nod,
And seems to shake the spheres.

The praise of Bacchus then the sweet musician sung, —
Of Bacchus ever fair and ever young:
The jolly god in triumph comes!
Sound the trumpets, beat the drums!
Flushed with a purple grace
He shows his honest face:
Now give the hautboys breath; he comes, he comes!
Bacchus, ever fair and young,
Drinking joys did first ordain;
Bacchus' blessings are a treasure,
Drinking is the soldier's pleasure:
Rich the treasure,
Sweet the pleasure,
Sweet is pleasure after pain.

Soothed with the sound, the king grew vain;
Fought all his battles o'er again,
And thrice he routed all his foes, and thrice he slew the slain!
The master saw the madness rise,
His glowing cheeks, his ardent eyes;
And while he Heaven and Earth defied
Changed his hand and checked his pride.
He chose a mournful Muse
Soft pity to infuse:
He sung Darius great and good,
By too severe a fate
Fallen, fallen, fallen, fallen,
Fallen from his high estate,
And weltering in his blood;
Deserted, at his utmost need,
By those his former bounty fed;
On the bare earth exposed he lies
With not a friend to close his eyes.
With downcast looks the joyless victor sate,
Revolving in his altered soul
The various turns of Chance below;
And now and then a sigh he stole,
And tears began to flow.

The mighty master smiled to see
That love was in the next degree;
'Twas but a kindred sound to move,
For pity melts the mind to love.
Softly sweet, in Lydian measures
Soon he soothed his soul to pleasures.
War, he sung, is toil and trouble,
Honor but an empty bubble,
Never ending, still beginning;
Fighting still, and still destroying;
If the world be worth thy winning,
Think, O think, it worth enjoying:
Lovely Thais sits beside thee,
Take the good the gods provide thee!
The many rend the skies with loud applause;
So Love was crowned, but Music won the cause.
The prince unable to conceal his pain,
Gazed on the fair
Who caused his care,
And sighed and looked, sighed and looked,
Sighed and looked and sighed again:
At length with love and wine at once opprest
The vanquished victor sunk upon her breast.

Now strike the golden lyre again:
A louder yet, and yet a louder strain!
Break his bands of sleep asunder,
And rouse him like a rattling peal of thunder.
Hark, hark! the horrid sound
Has raised up his head:
As awaked from the dead
And amazed he stares around.
Revenge, revenge, Timotheus cries,
See the Furies arise!
See the snakes that they rear
How they hiss in their hair,
And the sparkles that flash from their eyes!
Behold a ghastly band
Each a torch in his hand!
Those are Grecian ghosts, that in battle were slain
And unburied remain
Inglorious on the plain:
Give the vengeance due
To the valiant crew!
Behold how they toss their torches on high,
How they point to the Persian abodes
And glittering temples of their hostile gods.
The princes applaud with a furious joy:
And the King seized a flambeau with zeal to destroy;

Thais led the way
To light him to his prey,
And like another Helen, fired another Troy!

Thus long ago,
Ere heaving bellows learned to blow,
While organs yet were mute,
Timotheus, to his breathing flute
And sounding lyre
Could swell the soul to rage, or kindle soft desire.
At last divine Cecilia came,
Inventress of the vocal frame;
The sweet enthusiast from her sacred store
Enlarged the former narrow bounds,
And added length to solemn sounds,
With Nature's mother-wit, and arts unknown before.
Let old Timotheus yield the prize,
Or both divide the crown;
He raised a mortal to the skies;
She drew an angel down!

DRYDEN.

ART AND NATURE.

NATURE is made better by no mean,
But Nature makes that mean: so over that Art
Which you say adds to Nature is an Art
That Nature makes. You see, sweet maid, we marry
A gentler scion to the wildest stock,
And make conceive a bark of baser kind
By buds of nobler race. This is an Art
Which does mend Nature, change it rather; but
The Art itself is Nature.

SHAKSPEARE: *Winter's Tale.*

DÆDALUS.

WAIL for Dædalus, all that is fairest!
All that is tuneful in air or wave!
Shapes whose beauty is truest and rarest,
Haunt with your lamps and spells his grave!

Statues, bend your heads in sorrow,
Ye that glance 'mid ruins old,
That know not a past, nor expect a morrow
On many a moonlight Grecian wold!

By sculptured cave and speaking river,
Thee, Dædalus, oft the Nymphs recall;
The leaves with a sound of winter quiver,
Murmur thy name, and withering fall.

Yet are thy visions in soul the grandest
Of all that crowd on the tear-dimmed eye,
Though, Dædalus, thou no more commandest
New stars to that ever-widening sky.

Ever thy phantoms arise before us,
Our loftier brothers, but one in blood;
By bed and table they lord it o'er us,
With looks of beauty and words of good.

Calmly they show us mankind victorious
O'er all that's aimless, blind, and base;
Their presence has made our nature glorious,
Unveiling our night's illumined face.

Wail for Dædalus, Earth and Ocean!
Stars and Sun, lament for him!
Ages quake in strange commotion!
All ye realms of Life be dim!

Wail for Dædalus, awful Voices,
From earth's deep centre Mankind appall!
Seldom ye sound, and then Death rejoices,
For he knows that then the mightiest fall.

JOHN STERLING.

CATHEDRAL.

Almeria. — It was thy fear, or else some transient wind
Whistling through hollows of this vaulted aisle:
No, all is hushed and still as death. 'Tis dreadful!
How reverend is the face of this tall pile,
Whose ancient pillars rear their marble heads
To bear aloft its arched and ponderous roof,
By its own weight made steadfast and immovable,
Looking tranquillity! It strikes an awe
And terror on my aching sight; the tombs
And monumental caves of death look cold,
And shoot a chillness to my trembling heart.
Give me thy hand, and let me hear thy voice;
Nay, quickly speak to me, and let me hear
Thy voice; — my own affrights me with its echoes.

WILLIAM CONGREVE.

SONNET.

OH how much more doth beauty beauteous seem
By that sweet ornament which truth doth give!
The rose looks fair, but fairer we it deem
For that sweet odor which doth in it live.
The canker-blooms have full as deep a dye
As the perfumèd tincture of the roses,
Hang on such thorns, and play as wantonly
When summer's breath their maskèd buds discloses:
But, for their virtue only is their show,
They live unwooed, and unrespected fade;
Die to themselves. Sweet roses do not so;
Of their sweet deaths are sweetest odors made:
And so of you, beauteous and lovely youth,
When that shall fade, by verse distils your truth.

SHAKSPEARE.

SONNET.

FROM you have I been absent in the spring,
When proud-pied April, dressed in all his trim,
Hath put a spirit of Youth in every thing,
That heavy Saturn laughed and leaped with him.
Yet nor the lays of birds, nor the sweet smell
Of different flowers in odor and in hue,
Could make me any summer's story tell,
Or from their proud lap pluck them where they grew:
Nor did I wonder at the lilies white,
Nor praise the deep vermilion in the rose;
They were but sweet, but figures of delight,
Drawn after you, you pattern of all those.
Yet seemed it winter still, and, you away,
As with your shadow I with these did play.

SHAKSPEARE.

TO THE CRITIC.

I.

VEX not thou the poet's mind
With thy shallow wit:
Vex not thou the poet's mind;
For thou canst not fathom it.
. . . .

II.

Dark-browed sophist, come not anear;
. . . .

Hollow smile and frozen sneer
  Come not here.

. . . .

The flowers would faint at your cruel cheer.

. . . .

In the heart of the garden the merry bird chants,
It would fall to the ground if you came in.

TENNYSON.

LOCKSLEY HALL.

COMRADES, leave me here a little, while as yet 'tis early morn:
Leave me here, and when you want me, sound upon the bugle-horn.

'Tis the place, and all around it, as of old, the curlews call.
Dreary gleams about the moorland flying over Locksley Hall;

Locksley Hall, that in the distance overlooks the sandy tracts,
And the hollow ocean-ridges roaring into cataracts.

Many a night from yonder ivied casement, ere I went to rest,
Did I look on great Orion sloping slowly to the West.

Many a night I saw the Pleiads, rising through the mellow shade,
Glitter like a swarm of fire-flies tangled in a silver braid.

Here about the beach I wandered, nourishing a youth sublime
With the fairy tales of science, and the long result of time;

When the centuries behind me like a fruitful land reposed;
When I clung to all the present for the promise that it closed;

When I dipt into the future far as human eye could see;
Saw the Vision of the world, and all the wonder that would be. —

In the Spring a fuller crimson comes upon the robin's breast;
In the Spring the wanton lapwing gets himself another crest;

In the Spring a livelier iris changes on the burnished dove;
In the Spring a young man's fancy lightly turns to thoughts of love.

Then her cheek was pale and thinner than should be for one so young,
And her eyes on all my motions with a mute observance hung.

And I said, "My cousin Amy, speak, and speak the truth to me,
Trust me, cousin, all the current of my being sets to thee."

On her pallid cheek and forehead came a color and a light,
As I have seen the rosy red flushing in the northern night.

And she turned — her bosom shaken with a sudden storm of sighs —
All the spirit deeply dawning in the dark of hazel eyes —

Saying, "I have hid my feelings, fearing they should do me wrong;"
Saying, "Dost thou love me, cousin?" weeping, "I have loved thee long."

Love took up the glass of Time, and turned it in his glowing hands;
Every moment, lightly shaken, ran itself in golden sands.

Love took up the harp of Life, and smote on all the chords with might;
Smote the chord of Self, that, trembling, passed in music out of sight.

Many a morning on the moorland did we hear the copses ring,
And her whisper thronged my pulses with the fulness of the Spring.

Many an evening by the waters did
we watch the stately ships,
And our spirits rushed together at
the touching of the lips.

O my cousin, shallow-hearted! O
my Amy, mine no more!
O the dreary, dreary moorland! O
the barren, barren shore!

Falser than all fancy fathoms, falser
than all songs have sung,
Puppet to a father's threat, and servile to a shrewish tongue!

Is it well to wish thee happy? — having known me — to decline
On a range of lower feelings and a
narrower heart than mine!

Yet it shall be: thou shalt lower to
his level day by day,
What is fine within thee growing
coarse to sympathize with clay.

As the husband is, the wife is: thou
art mated with a clown,
And the grossness of his nature will
have weight to drag thee down.

He will hold thee, when his passion
shall have spent its novel
force,
Something better than his dog, a
little dearer than his horse.

What is this? his eyes are heavy:
think not they are glazed with
wine.
Go to him: it is thy duty: kiss him:
take his hand in thine.

It may be my lord is weary, that
his brain is overwrought:
Soothe him with thy finer fancies,
touch him with thy lighter
thought.

He will answer to the purpose, easy
things to understand —
Better thou wert dead before me,
though I slew thee with my
hand!

Better thou and I were lying, hidden
from the heart's disgrace,
Rolled in one another's arms, and
silent in a last embrace.

Cursed be the social wants that sin
against the strength of youth!
Cursed be the social lies that warp
us from the living truth!

Cursed be the sickly forms that err
from honest Nature's rule!
Cursed be the gold that gilds the
straitened forehead of the
fool!

Well — 'tis well that I should bluster! Hadst thou less unworthy proved —
Would to God — for I had loved thee
more than ever wife was
loved.

Am I mad, that I should cherish
that which bears but bitter
fruit?
I will pluck it from my bosom,
though my heart be at the
root.

Never, though my mortal summers
to such length of years should
come
As the many-wintered crow that
leads the clanging rookery
home.

Where is comfort! in division of the
records of the mind?
Can I part her from herself, and love
her, as I knew her kind?

I remember one that perished:
sweetly did she speak and
move:
Such a one do I remember, whom to
look at was to love.

Can I think of her as dead, and love
her for the love she bore?
No — she never loved me truly:
love is love forevermore.

Comfort? comfort scorned of devils!
this is truth the poet sings,
That a sorrow's crown of sorrow is
remembering happier things.

Drug thy memories, lest thou learn
it, lest thy heart be put to
proof,
In the dead unhappy night, and
when the rain is on the roof.

Like a dog, he hunts in dreams, and thou art staring at the wall,
Where the dying night-lamp flickers, and the shadows rise and fall.

Then a hand shall pass before thee, pointing to his drunken sleep,
To thy widowed marriage-pillows, to the tears that thou wilt weep.

Thou shalt hear the "Never, never," whispered by the phantom years,
And a song from out the distance in the ringing of thine ears;

And an eye shall vex thee, looking ancient kindness on thy pain.
Turn thee, turn thee on thy pillow: get thee to thy rest again.

Nay, but Nature brings thee solace; for a tender voice will cry.
'Tis a purer life than thine; a lip to drain thy trouble dry.

Baby lips will laugh me down: my latest rival brings thee rest.
Baby fingers, waxen touches, press me from the mother's breast.

O, the child, too, clothes the father with a dearness not his due.
Half is thine, and half is his: it will be worthy of the two.

O, I see thee old and formal, fitted to thy petty part,
With a little hoard of maxims preaching down a daughter's heart.

"They were dangerous guides the feelings — she herself was not exempt —
Truly, she herself had suffered" — Perish in thy self-contempt!

Overlive it — lower yet — be happy! wherefore should I care?
I myself must mix with action, lest I wither by despair.

What is that which I should turn to, lighting upon days like these?
Every door is barred with gold, and opens but to golden keys.

Every gate is thronged with suitors, all the markets overflow.
I have but an angry fancy: what is that which I should do?

I had been content to perish, falling on the foeman's ground,
When the ranks are rolled in vapor, and the winds are laid with sound.

But the jingling of the guinea helps the hurt that Honor feels,
And the nations do but murmur, snarling at each other's heels.

Can I but relive in sadness? I will turn that earlier page.
Hide me from my deep emotion, O thou wondrous Mother-Age!

Make me feel the wild pulsation that I felt before the strife,
When I heard my days before me, and the tumult of my life,

Yearning for the large excitement that the coming years would yield,
Eager-hearted as a boy when first he leaves his father's field,

And at night along the dusky highway near and nearer drawn,
Sees in heaven the light of London flaring like a dreary dawn;

And his spirit leaps within him to be gone before him then,
Underneath the light he looks at, in among the throngs of men;

Men, my brothers, men the workers, ever reaping something new:
That which they have done but earnest of the things that they shall do:

For I dipped into the future, far as human eye could see,
Saw the Vision of the world, and all the wonder that would be;

Saw the heavens fill with commerce, argosies of magic sails,
Pilots of the purple twilight, dropping down with costly bales;

Heard the heavens fill with shouting, and there rained a ghastly dew
From the nations' airy navies grappling in the central blue;

Far along the world-wide whisper of the south-wind rushing warm,
With the standards of the peoples plunging through the thunder-storm;

Till the war-drum throbbed no longer, and the battle-flags were furled
In the Parliament of man, the Federation of the world.

There the common sense of most shall hold a fretful realm in awe,
And the kindly earth shall slumber, lapped in universal law.

So I triumphed ere my passion sweeping through me left me dry,
Left me with the palsied heart, and left me with the jaundiced eye;

Eye, to which all order festers, all things here are out of joint:
Science moves, but slowly, slowly, creeping on from point to point:

Slowly comes a hungry people, as a lion, creeping nigher,
Glares at one that nods and winks behind a slowly-dying fire.

Yet I doubt not through the ages one increasing purpose runs,
And the thoughts of men are widened with the process of the suns.

What is that to him that reaps not harvest of his youthful joys,
Though the deep heat of existence beat forever like a boy's?

Knowledge comes, but wisdom lingers, and I linger on the shore,
And the individual withers, and the world is more and more.

Knowledge comes, but wisdom lingers, and he bears a laden breast,
Full of sad experience, moving toward the stillness of his rest.

Hark, my merry comrades call me, sounding on the bugle-horn,
They to whom my foolish passion were a target for their scorn:

Shall it not be scorn to me to harp on such a mouldered string?
I am shamed through all my nature to have loved so slight a thing.

Weakness to be wroth with weakness! woman's pleasure, woman's pain —
Nature made them blinder motions bounded in a shallower brain:

Woman is the lesser man, and all thy passions, matched with mine,
Are as moonlight unto sunlight, and as water unto wine —

Here at least, where nature sickens, nothing. Ah, for some retreat
Deep in yonder shining Orient, where my life began to beat;

Where in wild Mahratta-battle fell my father evil-starred; —
I was left a trampled orphan, and a selfish uncle's ward.

Or to burst all links of habit — there to wander far away,
On from island unto island at the gateways of the day.

Larger constellations burning, mellow moons and happy skies,
Breadths of tropic shade and palms in cluster, knots of Paradise.

Never comes the trader, never floats an European flag,
Slides the bird o'er lustrous woodland, swings the trailer from the crag;

Droops the heavy-blossomed bower, hangs the heavy-fruited tree —
Summer isles of Eden lying in dark-purple spheres of sea.

There methinks would be enjoyment more than in this march of mind,
In the steamship, in the railway, in the thoughts that shake mankind.

There the passions cramped no longer shall have scope and breathing-space;
I will take some savage woman, she shall rear my dusky race.

Iron-jointed, supple-sinewed, they shall dive, and they shall run,
Catch the wild goat by the hair, and hurl their lances in the sun;

Whistle back the parrot's call, and leap the rainbows of the brooks,
Not with blinded eyesight poring over miserable books —

Fool, again the dream, the fancy! but I *know* my words are wild,
But I count the gray barbarian lower than the Christian child.

I to herd with narrow foreheads, vacant of our glorious gains,
Like a beast with lower pleasures, like a beast with lower pains!

Mated with a squalid savage, — what to me were sun or clime?
I the heir of all the ages, in the foremost files of time —

I that rather held it better men should perish one by one,
Than that earth should stand at gaze like Joshua's moon in Ajalon!

Not in vain the distance beacons. Forward, forward let us range,
Let the great world spin forever down the ringing grooves of change.

Through the shadow of the globe we sweep into the younger day:
Better fifty years of Europe than a cycle of Cathay.

Mother-Age (for mine I knew not) help me as when life begun:
Rift the hills, and roll the waters, flash the lightnings, weigh the sun.

O, I see the crescent promise of my spirit hath not set.
Ancient founts of inspiration well through all my fancy yet.

Howsoever these things be, a long farewell to Locksley Hall!
Now for me the woods may wither, now for me the roof-tree fall.

Comes a vapor from the margin, blackening over heath and holt,
Cramming all the blast before it, in its breast a thunderbolt.

Let it fall on Locksley Hall, with rain or hail, or fire or snow;
For the mighty wind arises, roaring seaward, and I go.

TENNYSON.

HURTS OF TIME.

OUT upon Time, who will leave no more
Of the things to come than the things before;
Out upon Time, who forever will leave
But enough of the past for the future to grieve,
Relics of things that have passed away,
Fragments of stone reared by creatures of clay.
For who the fool that doth not know
How bloom and beauty come and go,
And how disease, and pain, and sorrow,
May chance to-day, may chance to-morrow,
Unto the merriest of us all?

BYRON.

POET'S MOOD.

HENCE, all you vain delights,
As short as are the nights
Wherein you spend your folly!
There's nought in this life sweet,
If man were wise to see it,
But only melancholy;

Oh, sweetest melancholy!
Welcome folded arms, and fixed eyes,
A sigh that piercing mortifies,
A look that's fastened to the ground,
A tongue chained up, without a sound!
Fountain-head and pathless groves,
Places which pale passion loves!
Moonlight walks, when all the fowls
Are warmly housed, save bats and owls!
A midnight bell, a parting groan!
These are the sounds we feed upon;
Then stretch our bones in a still gloomy valley:
Nothing's so dainty sweet as lovely melancholy.

BEAUMONT AND FLETCHER.

MOODS.

OUT upon it. I have loved
Three whole days together;
And am like to love three more,
If it prove fair weather.

Time shall moult away his wings
Ere he shall discover
In the whole wide world again
Such a constant lover.

But the spite on't is, no praise
Is due at all to me:
Love with me had made no stays,
Had it any been but she.

Had it any been but she,
And that very face,
There had been at least ere this
A dozen dozen in her place.

SIR JOHN SUCKLING.

THE SOUL'S ERRAND.

Go, Soul, the body's guest,
Upon a thankless errand;
Fear not to touch the best;
The truth shall be thy warrant:
Go, since I needs must die,
And give them all the lie.

Go tell the Court it glows
And shines like rotten wood;
Go tell the Church it shows
What's good, but does no good:
If Court and Church reply,
Give Court and Church the lie.

Tell Potentates they live
Acting, but oh! their actions;
Not loved, unless they give,
Nor strong but by their factions;
If Potentates reply,
Give Potentates the lie.

Tell men of high condition,
That rule affairs of state,
Their purpose is ambition;
Their practice only hate:
And if they do reply,
Then give them all the lie.

Tell those that brave it most
They beg for more by spending,
Who in their greatest cost
Seek nothing but commending:
And if they make reply,
Spare not to give the lie.

Tell Zeal it lacks devotion;
Tell Love it is but lust;
Tell Time it is but motion;
Tell Flesh it is but dust:
And wish them not reply,
For thou must give the lie.

Tell Age it daily wasteth;
Tell Honor how it alters;
Tell Beauty that it blasteth;
Tell Favor that she falters:
And as they do reply,
Give every one the lie.

Tell Wit how much it wrangles
In fickle points of niceness;
Tell Wisdom she entangles
Herself in over wiseness:
And if they do reply,
Then give them both the lie.

Tell Physic of her boldness;
Tell Skill it is pretension;
Tell Charity of coldness;
Tell Law it is contention:
And if they yield reply,
Then give them all the lie.

Tell Fortune of her blindness;
Tell Nature of decay;
Tell Friendship of unkindness;
Tell Justice of delay:
And if they do reply,
Then give them still the lie.

Tell Arts they have no soundness,
But vary by esteeming;
Tell Schools they lack profoundness,
And stand too much on seeming:
If Arts and Schools reply,
Give Arts and Schools the lie.

Tell Faith it's fled the city;
Tell how the country erreth;
Tell, Manhood shakes off pity;
Tell, Virtue least preferreth:
And if they do reply,
Spare not to give the lie.

So when thou hast, as I
Commanded thee, done blabbing;
Although to give the lie
Deserves no less than stabbing:
Yet stab at thee who will,
No stab the Soul can kill!

Sir Walter Raleigh.

RABIA.

Rabia, sick upon her bed,
By two saints was visited,—
Holy Malik, Hassan wise —
Men of mark in Moslem eyes.

Hassan says, "Whose prayer is pure,
Will God's chastisement endure."

Malik, from a deeper sense
Uttered his experience:

"He who loves his Master's choice
Will in chastisement rejoice."

Rabia saw some selfish will
In their maxims lingering still,

And replied, "O men of grace!
He who sees his Master's face

Will not, in his prayer, recall
That he is chastised at all."

Trans. by J. F. Clarke.

IV.

CONTEMPLATIVE.—MORAL. RELIGIOUS.

MAN.—VIRTUE.—HONOR.—TIME.—CHANGE. FATE.—DEATH.—IMMORTALITY. HYMNS.—HOLYDAYS.

"Eyes which the beam celestial view,
Which evermore makes all things new."—KEBLE.

CONTEMPLATIVE.—MORAL.—RELIGIOUS.

FROM HYPERION.

As Heaven and Earth are fairer, fairer far
Than Chaos and blank Darkness, though once chiefs;
And as we show beyond that Heaven and Earth
In form and shape compact and beautiful,
In will, in action free, companionship,
And thousand other signs of purer life;
So on our heels a fresh perfection treads,
A power more strong in beauty, born of us,
And fated to excel us, as we pass
In glory that old Darkness.

KEATS.

MAN.

My God, I heard this day
That none doth build a stately habitation
But he that means to dwell therein.
What house more stately hath there been,
Or can be, than is Man? to whose creation
All things are in decay.

For man is every thing,
And more. He is a tree, yet bears no fruit;
A beast, yet is or should be more.
Reason and speech we only bring.
Parrots may thank us, if they are not mute,
They go upon the score.

Man is all symmetry,
Full of proportions, one limb to another,
And all to all the world besides;
Each part may call the farthest, brother;
For head with foot hath private amity,
And both with moons and tides.

Nothing hath got so far,
But man hath caught and kept it as his prey.
His eyes dismount the highest star:
He is in little all the sphere:
Herbs gladly cure our flesh, because that they
Find their acquaintance there.

For us the winds do blow,
The earth doth rest, heaven move, and fountains flow;
Nothing we see but means our good
As our delight, or as our treasure;
The whole is either our cupboard of food,
Or cabinet of pleasure.

The stars have us to bed;
Night draws the curtain, which the sun withdraws.
Music and light attend our head.
All things unto our flesh are kind
In their descent and being; — to our mind,
In their ascent and cause.

Each thing is full of Duty:
Waters united are our navigation;
Distinguished, our habitation;
Below our drink: above our meat:
Both are our cleanliness. Hath one such beauty?
Then how are all things neat.

More servants wait on Man
Than he'll take notice of. In every path
He treads down that which doth befriend him
When sickness makes him pale and wan.
O mighty Love! Man is one world, and hath
Another to attend him.

Since then, my God, thou hast
So brave a palace built, O dwell in it,
That it may dwell with thee at last!
Till then afford us so much wit,
That as the world serves us, we may serve thee,
And both thy servants be.

HERBERT.

HONOR.

SAY, what is Honor? 'Tis the finest sense
Of *justice* which the human mind can frame,
Intent each lurking frailty to disclaim,
And guard the way of life from all offence
Suffered or done.

. . . .

We know the arduous strife, the eternal laws
To which the triumph of all good is given,
High sacrifice, and labor without pause,
Even to the death: else wherefore should the eye
Of man converse with immortality?

WORDSWORTH.

ENGLISH CHANNEL.

INLAND, within a hollow vale, I stood;
And saw, while sea was calm and air was clear,
The coast of France — the coast of France how near!
Drawn almost into frightful neighborhood.
I shrunk; for verily the barrier flood
Was like a lake, or river bright and fair,
A span of waters; yet what power is there!
What mightiness for evil and for good!
Even so doth God protect us, if we be
Virtuous and wise. Winds blow, and waters roll
Strength to the brave, and Power, and Deity;
Yet in themselves are nothing! One decree
Spake laws to *them*, and said, that by the soul
Only, the Nations shall be great and free.

WORDSWORTH.

THE PULLEY.

WHEN God at first made man,
Having a glass of blessings standing by,
"Let us," said he, "pour on him all we can;
Let the world's riches, which dispersèd lie,
Contract into a span."

So strength first made away;
Then beauty flowed; then wisdom, honor, pleasure.
When almost all was out, God made a stay;
Perceiving that alone of all the treasure
Rest in the bottom lay.

"For if I should," said he,
"Bestow *this* jewel also on my creature,
He would adore my gifts instead of me;
And rest in Nature, not the God of Nature:
So both should losers be.

"Yet let him keep the rest;
But keep them, with repining restlessness.
Let him be rich and weary; that, at least,
If goodness lead him not, yet weariness
May toss him to my breast."

HERBERT.

THE CHURCH PORCH.

THOU whose sweet youth and early hopes enhance
Thy rate and price, and mark thee for a treasure,
Hearken unto a Verser, who may chance
Rhyme thee to good, and make a bait of pleasure:
A verse may find him who a sermon flies
And turn delight into a sacrifice.

When thou dost purpose aught (within thy power),
Be sure to doe it, though it be but small;
Constancie knits the bones, and makes us stowre,
When wanton pleasures beckon us to thrall.
Who breaks his own bond, forfeiteth himself:
What nature made a ship, he makes a shelf.

By all means use sometimes to be alone.
Salute thyself: see what thy soul doth wear.
Dare to look in thy chest; for 'tis thine own:
And tumble up and down what thou find'st there.
Who cannot rest till he good fellows finde,
He breaks up house, turns out of doores his minde.

In clothes, cheap handsomenesse doth bear the bell,
Wisdome's a trimmer thing than shop e'er gave.
Say not then, this with that lace will do well;
But, this with my discretion will be brave.
Much curiousnesse is a perpetual wooing,
Nothing with labor, folly long a doing.

Entice all neatly to what they know best;
For so thou dost thyself and him a pleasure:
(But a proud ignorance will lose his rest,
Rather than show his cards) steal from his treasure
What to ask further. Doubts well raised do lock
The speaker to thee, and preserve thy stock.

When once thy foot enters the church, be bare.
God is more there than thou; for thou art there
Only by his permission. Then beware,
And make thyself all reverence and fear.
Kneeling ne'er spoiled silk stockings; quit thy state;
All equal are within the churches' gate.

Resort to sermons, but to prayers most:
Praying's the end of preaching. O be drest;
Stay not for th' other pin: why thou hast lost
A joy for it worth worlds. Thus hell doth jest
Away thy blessings, and extremely flout thee,
Thy clothes being fast, but thy soul loose about thee.

Judge not the preacher; for he is thy judge:
If thou mislike him, thou conceiv'st him not.
God calleth preaching folly. Do not grudge
To pick out treasures from an earthen pot.
The worst speak something good: if all want sense,
God takes a text, and preacheth patience.

HERBERT.

HUMILITY.

To me men are for what they are,
They wear no masks with me.
I never sickened at the jar
Of ill-tuned flattery;
I never mourned affection lent

In folly or in blindness;—
The kindness that on me is spent
Is pure, unasking kindness.

R. M. Milnes.

THE HAPPY LIFE.

How happy is he born and taught
That serveth not another's will;
Whose armor is his honest thought,
And simple truth his utmost skill!

Whose passions not his masters are;
Whose soul is still prepared for death,
Not tied unto the world with care
Of public fame, or private breath;

Who envies none that chance doth raise,
Or vice; who never understood
How deepest wounds are given by praise;
Nor rules of state, but rules of good:

Who hath his life from rumors freed,
Whose conscience is his strong retreat;
Whose state can neither flatterers feed,
Nor ruin make oppressors great;

Who God doth late and early pray
More of his grace than gifts to lend;
And entertains the harmless day
With a religious book or friend;

This man is freed from servile bands
Of hope to rise, or fear to fall;
Lord of himself, though not of lands;
And having nothing, yet hath all.

Sir H. Wotton.

WISDOM.

Would Wisdom for herself be wooed,
And wake the foolish from his dream,
She must be glad as well as good,
And must not only be, but seem:
Beauty and joy are hers by right;
And knowing this, I wonder less
That she's so scorned, when falsely dight
In misery and ugliness.

What's that which Heaven to man endears,
And that which eyes no sooner see
Than the heart says, with floods of tears,
"Ah, that's the thing which I would be!"

Not childhood, full of frown and fret;
Not youth, impatient to disown
Those visions high, which to forget
Were worse than never to have known;
Not great men, even when they're good:
The good man whom the Lord makes great,
By some disgrace of chance or blood
He fails not to humiliate:
Not these: but souls, found here and there,
Oases in our waste of sin,
Where every thing is well and fair,
And God remits his discipline;
Whose sweet subdual of the world
The worldling scarce can recognize,
And ridicule against it hurled,
Drops with a broken sting, and dies;
Who nobly, if they cannot know
Whether a 'scutcheon's dubious field
Carries a falcon or a crow,
Fancy a falcon on the shield;
Yet ever careful not to hurt
God's honor, who creates success,
Their praise of even the best desert
Is but to have presumed no less;
And should their own life plaudits bring,
They're simply vexed at heart that such
An easy, yea, delightful thing
Should move the minds of men so much.
They live by law, not like the fool,
But like the bard, who freely sings
In strictest bonds of rhyme and rule,
And finds in them not bonds, but wings.
They shine like Moses in the face,
And teach our hearts, without the rod,
That God's grace is the only grace,
And all grace is the grace of God.

Their home is home; their chosen lot
A private place and private name,
But, if the world's want calls, they'll not
Refuse the indignities of fame.

COVENTRY PATMORE.

VIRTUE.

SWEET Day! so cool, so calm, so bright,
The bridal of the earth and sky,
The dew shall weep thy fall to-night,—
For thou must die.

Sweet Rose! whose hue, angry and brave,
Bids the rash gazer wipe his eye,
Thy root is ever in its grave;—
And thou must die.

Sweet Spring! full of sweet days and roses;
A box where sweets compacted lie;
My music shows ye have your closes;—
And all must die.

Only a sweet and virtuous soul,
Like seasoned timber, never gives;
But, though the whole world turn to coal,
Then chiefly lives.

HERBERT.

HONEST POVERTY.

Is there, for honest poverty
Wha hangs his head, and a' that?
The coward-slave, we pass him by,
We dare be poor for a' that.
For a' that, and a' that:
Our toils obscure, and a' that,
The rank is but the guinea stamp,
The man's the gowd for a' that.

What though on hamely fare we dine,
Wear hodden gray, and a' that;
Gie fools their silks, and knaves their wine,
A man's a man for a' that.
For a' that, and a' that,
Their tinsel show and a' that;
The honest man though e'er sae poor,
Is king o' men for a' that.

You see yon birkie ca'd a lord,
Wha struts, and stares, and a' that,
Though hundreds worship at his word,
He's but a coof for a' that.
For a' that, and a' that,
His riband, star, and a' that;
The man of independent mind,
He looks and laughs at a' that.

A prince can mak a belted knight,
A marquis, duke, and a' that;
But an honest man's aboon his might,
Guid faith he mauna fa' that!
For a' that, and a' that,
Their dignities, and a' that,
The pith o' sense, and pride o' worth,
Are higher ranks than a' that.

Then let us pray that come it may,
As come it will for a' that,
That sense and worth, o'er a' the earth,
May bear the gree, and a' that,
For a' that, and a' that,
It's coming yet for a' that.
When man to man, the warld o'er,
Shall brothers be for a' that.

BURNS.

THE QUIP.

THE merry world did on a day
With his train-bands and mates agree
To meet together, where I lay,
And all in sport to jeer at me.

First, Beauty crept into a rose;
Which when I plucked not — "Sir," said she,
"Tell me, I pray, whose hands are those?"
But thou shalt answer, Lord, for me.

Then Money came; and, chinking still —
"What tune is this, poor man?" said he;
"I heard in music you had skill."
But thou shalt answer, Lord, for me.

Then came brave Glory puffing by,
In silks, that whistled — "Who but he?"
He scarce allowed me half an eye.
But thou shalt answer, Lord, for me.

Then came quick Wit and Conversation;
And he would needs a comfort be,
And, to be short, make an oration.
But thou shalt answer, Lord, for me.

Yet, when the hour of thy design
To answer these fine things shall come,
Speak not at large; say I am thine;
And then they have their answer home.

HERBERT.

ETON COLLEGE.

YE distant spires, ye antique towers,
That crown the watery glade,
Where grateful Science still adores
Her Henry's holy shade;
And ye, that from the stately brow
Of Windsor's heights the expanse below
Of grove, of lawn, of mead, survey,
Whose turf, whose shade, whose flowers among
Wanders the hoary Thames along
His silver-winding way:

Ah, happy hills! ah, pleasing shade!
Ah, fields beloved in vain!
Where once my careless childhood strayed,
A stranger yet to pain!
I feel the gales that from ye blow
A momentary bliss bestow,
As waving fresh their gladsome wing,
My weary soul they seem to soothe,
And, redolent of joy and youth,
To breathe a second spring.

Say, father Thames, for thou hast seen
Full many a sprightly race
Disporting on thy margent green,
The paths of pleasure trace;
Who foremost now delight to cleave,
With pliant arm, thy glassy wave?
The captive linnet which inthrall?
What idle progeny succeed
To chase the rolling circle's speed,
Or urge the flying ball?

While some on earnest business bent,
Their murmuring labors ply
'Gainst graver hours that bring constraint
To sweeten liberty:
Some bold adventurers disdain
The limits of their little reign,
And unknown regions dare descry:
Still as they run they look behind,
They hear a voice in every wind,
And snatch a fearful joy.

Gay hope is theirs by fancy fed,
Less pleasing when possest;
The tear forgot as soon as shed,
The sunshine of the breast:
Theirs buxom health of rosy hue,
Wild wit, invention ever new,
And lively cheer, of vigor born;
The thoughtless day, the easy night,
The spirits pure, the slumbers light,
That fly the approach of morn.

Alas! regardless of their doom,
The little victims play;
No sense have they of ills to come,
Nor care beyond to-day:
Yet see, how all around them wait
The ministers of human fate,
And black Misfortune's baleful train!
Ah, show them where in ambush stand,
To seize their prey, the murth'rous band!
Ah, tell them, they are men!

These shall the fury Passions tear,
The vultures of the mind,
Disdainful Anger, pallid Fear,
And Shame that skulks behind;
Or pining Love shall waste their youth,
Or Jealousy, with rankling tooth,

That inly gnaws the secret heart;
And Envy wan, and faded Care,
Grim-visaged comfortless Despair,
And Sorrow's piercing dart.

Ambition this shall tempt to rise,
Then whirl the wretch from high,
To bitter Scorn a sacrifice,
And grinning Infamy.
The stings of Falsehood those shall try,
And hard Unkindness' altered eye,
That mocks the tear it forced to flow;
And keen Remorse with blood defiled,
And moody Madness laughing wild
Amid severest woe.

Lo! in the vale of years beneath
A grisly troop are seen,
The painful family of Death,
More hideous than their queen:
This racks the joints, this fires the veins,
That every laboring sinew strains,
Those in the deeper vitals rage:
Lo! Poverty, to fill the band,
That numbs the soul with icy hand,
And slow-consuming Age.

To each his sufferings: all are men,
Condemned alike to groan;
The tender for another's pain,
The unfeeling for his own.
Yet, ah! why should they know their fate,
Since sorrow never comes too late,
And happiness too swiftly flies?
Thought would destroy their paradise.
No more;—where ignorance is bliss,
'Tis folly to be wise.

GRAY.

LIFE.

ART is long, and time is fleeting;
And our hearts, though stout and brave,
Still like muffled drums are beating
Funeral marches to the grave.

Lives of great men all remind us
We can make our lives sublime,
And departing leave behind us
Footprints on the sands of time.

Footprints that perhaps another,
Sáiling o'er life's solemn main,
A forlorn and shipwrecked brother,
Seeing shall take heart again.

LONGFELLOW.

ODE TO DUTY.

STERN daughter of the voice of God!
O Duty! if that name thou love,
Who art a light to guide, a rod
To check the erring, and reprove;
Thou who art victory and law
When empty terrors overawe;
From vain temptations dost set free;
And calm'st the weary strife of frail humanity!

There are who ask not if thine eye
Be on them; who, in love and truth,
Where no misgiving is, rely
Upon the genial sense of youth:
Glad hearts! without reproach or blot;
Who do thy work, and know it not:
May joy be theirs while life shall last!
And thou, if they should totter, teach them to stand fast!

. . . .

Stern lawgiver! yet thou dost wear
The Godhead's most benignant grace;
Nor know we any thing so fair
As is the smile upon thy face;
Flowers laugh before thee on their beds;
And fragrance in thy footing treads;
Thou dost preserve the stars from wrong,
And the most ancient heavens, through thee, are fresh and strong.

To humbler functions, awful power!
I call thee: I myself commend
Unto thy guidance from this hour;
Oh! let my weakness have an end!
Give unto me, made lowly wise,
The spirit of self-sacrifice;
The confidence of reason give;
And, in the light of truth, thy bondman let me live!

WORDSWORTH.

CONFESSION.

No screw, no piercer can
Into a piece of timber worke and winde,
As God's afflictions into man,
When he a torture hath designed.
They are too subtle for the subtlest hearts;
And fall, like rheumes, upon the tenderest parts.

We are the earth; and they,
Like moles within us, heave, and cast about:
And till they foot and clutch their prey,
They never cool, much less give out.
No smith can make such locks, but they have keys;
Closets are halls to them; and hearts, high-ways.

Only an open breast
Doth shut them out, so that they cannot enter;
Or, if they enter, cannot rest,
But quickly seek some new adventure.
Smooth open hearts no fastening have; but fiction
Doth give a hold and handle to affliction.

HERBERT.

THE SHIELD.

THE old man said, "Take thou this shield, my son,
Long tried in battle, and long tried by age,
Guarded by this thy fathers did engage,
Trusting to this the victory they have won."

Forth from the tower Hope and Desire had built,
In youth's bright morn I gazed upon the plain,—
There struggled countless hosts, while many a stain
Marked where the blood of brave men had been spilt.

With spirit strong I buckled to the fight,
What sudden chill rushes through every vein?
Those fatal arms oppress me — all in vain
My fainting limbs seek their accustomed might.

Forged were those arms for men of other mould;
Our hands they fetter, cramp our spirits free:
I throw them on the ground, and suddenly
Comes back my strength — returns my spirit bold.

I stand alone, unarmed, yet not alone;
Who heeds no law but what within he finds,
Trusts his own vision, not to other minds,
He fights with thee — Father, aid thou thy son.

S. G. W.

THE CONSOLERS.

CONSOLERS of the solitary hours
When I, a pilgrim, on a lonely shore
Sought help, and found none, save in those high powers
That then I prayed might never leave me more!

There was the blue, eternal sky above,
There was the ocean silent at my feet,
There was the universe — but nought to love;
The universe did its old tale repeat.

Then came ye to me, with your healing wings,
And said, "Thus bare and branchless must thou be,
Ere thou couldst feel the wind from heaven that springs."

And now again fresh leaves do bud
for me,—
Yet let me feel that still the spirit
sings
Its quiet song, coming from heaven
free.

S. G. W.

THE SEVEN AGES.

All the world's a stage,
And all the men and women merely
players:
They have their exits and their en-
trances;
And one man in his time plays many
parts,
His acts being seven ages. At first
the infant,
Mewling and puking in the nurse's
arms:
And then the whining schoolboy,
with his satchel,
And shining morning face, creeping
like snail
Unwillingly to school: and then the
lover,
Sighing like furnace, with a woful
ballad
Made to his mistress' eyebrow: then
a soldier,
Full of strange oaths, and bearded
like the pard,
Jealous in honor, sudden and quick
in quarrel,
Seeking the bubble reputation
Even in the cannon's mouth: and
then the justice
In fair round belly, with good capon
lined,
With eyes severe, and beard of for-
mal cut,
Full of wise saws and modern in-
stances.
And so he plays his part: the sixth
age shifts
Into the lean and slippered pantaloon,
With spectacles on nose, and pouch
on side,
His youthful hose well saved, a
world too wide
For his shrunk shank; and his big
manly voice,
Turning again toward childish
treble, pipes
And whistles in his sound: Last
scene of all
That ends this strange eventful
history,
Is second childishness, and mere oblivion;
Sans teeth, sans eyes, sans taste,
sans every thing.

Shakspeare: *As you like it.*

SUN-DIAL.

The shadow on the dial's face,
That steals from day to day,
With slow, unseen, unceasing pace,
Moments and months, and years
away;
This shadow, which, in every clime,
Since light and motion first began,
Hath held its course sublime;
What is it? mortal man!
It is the scythe of Time.
Not only o'er the dial's face,
This silent phantom, day by day,
With slow, unseen, unceasing pace,
Steals moments, months, and years
away;
From hoary rock and aged tree,
From proud Palmyra's mouldering
walls,
From Teneriffe, towering o'er the
sea,
From every blade of grass it falls;
And still where'er a shadow sweeps,
The scythe of time destroys,
And man at every footstep weeps
O'er evanescent joys.

Montgomery.

LIFE.

I made a posie while the day ran
by:
Here will I smell my remnant out,
and tie
My life within this band.
But Time did beckon to the flowers,
and they
By noon most cunningly did steal
away,
And withered in my hand.

My hand was next to them, and then
my heart;
I took, without more thinking, in
good part
Time's gentle admonition;

Who did so sweetly Death's sad taste
convey,
Making my mind to smell my fatal
day,
Yet sugaring the suspicion.

Farewell, dear flowers, sweetly your
time ye spent,
Fit, while you lived, for smell and
ornament,
And after death for cures.
I follow straight without complaints
or grief;
Since, if my scent be good, I care not if
It be as short as yours.

HERBERT.

REVOLUTIONS.

LIKE as the waves make towards the
pebbled shore,
So do our minutes hasten to their
end;
Each changing place with that which
goes before,
In sequent toil all forwards do contend.
Nativity once in the main of light
Crawls to maturity, wherewith being
crowned,
Crooked eclipses 'gainst his glory
fight,
And Time that gave, doth now his
gift confound.
Time doth transfix the flourish set
on youth,
And delves the parallels in beauty's
brow
Feeds on the rarities of Nature's
truth,
And nothing stands but for his
scythe to mow.
And yet, to times in hope, my
verse shall stand
Praising thy worth, despite his
cruel hand.

SHAKSPEARE.

GOOD OMENS.

NOT mine own fears, nor the prophetic soul
Of the wide world dreaming on
things to come,
Can yet the lease of my true love
control,
Supposed as forfeit to a confined
doom.
The mortal moon hath her eclipse
endured,
And the sad augurs mock their own
presage;
Incertainties now crown themselves
assured,
And peace proclaims olives of endless age.
Now with the drops of this most
balmy time
My love looks fresh, and Death to me
subscribes,
Since spite of him, I'll live in this
poor rhyme,
While he insults o'er dull and
speechless tribes.
And thou in this shalt find thy
monument,
When tyrants' crests and tombs
of brass are spent.

SHAKSPEARE.

THE SKEPTIC.

I CALLED on dreams and visions to
disclose
That which is veiled from waking
thought; conjured
Eternity, as men constrain a ghost
To appear and answer. Then my
soul
Turned inward, to examine of what
stuff
Time's fetters are composed; and
life was put
To inquisition, long and profitless.
By pain of heart, — now checked,
and now impelled,
The Intellectual Power, through
words and things,
Went sounding on, a dim and peril-
ous way!

WORDSWORTH.

DESTINY.

THE Destiny, Minister General,
That executeth in the world o'er all
The purveiance that God hath seen
beforne;
So strong it is, that though the
world had sworn

The contrary of a thing by Yea or
Nay,
Yet sometime it shall fallen on a day
That falleth not eft in a thousand
year.
For certainly our appetités here,
Be it of war, or peace, or hate, or
love, —
All this is rulèd by the sight above.

CHAUCER.

FORECAST.

OR if the soul of proper kind,
Be so perfect as men find,
That it wot what is to come,
And that he warneth all and some
Of every of their aventures,
By avisions, or by figures,
But that our flesh hath no might
To understandé it aright,
For it is warnèd too derkely,
But why the cause is, not wot I.

CHAUCER.

FORECAST.

THERE are points from which we
can command our life,
When the soul sweeps the future
like a glass,
And coming things, full-freighted
with our fate,
Jut out dark on the offing of the
mind.

BAILEY: *Festus.*

A POET'S HOPE.

LADY, there is a hope that all men
have,
Some mercy for their faults, a grassy
place
To rest in, and a flower-strewn,
gentle grave;
Another hope which purifies our
race,
That when that fearful bourn forever past,
They may find rest, — and rest *so*
long to last.

I seek it not, I ask no rest forever,
My path is onward to the farthest
shores, —
Upbear me in your arms, unceasing
river,
That from the soul's clear fountain
swiftly pours,
Motionless not, until the end is
won,
Which now I feel hath scarcely felt
the sun.

To feel, to know, to soar unlimited,
'Mid throngs of light-winged angels
sweeping far,
And pore upon the realms unvisited,
That tesselate the unseen unthought
star,
To be the thing that now I feebly
dream
Flashing within my faintest, deepest
gleam.

Ah, caverns of my soul! how thick
your shade,
Where flows that life by which I
faintly see, —
Wave your bright torches, for I
need your aid,
Golden-eyed demons of my ances-
try!
Your son though blinded hath a
light within,
A heavenly fire which ye from suns
did win.

O Time! O Death! I clasp you in
my arms,
For I can soothe an infinite cold
sorrow,
And gaze contented on your icy
charms,
And that wild snow-pile which we
call to-morrow;
Sweep on, O soft, and azure-lidded
sky,
Earth's waters to your gentle gaze
reply.

I am not earth-born, though I here
delay;
Hope's child, I summon infiniter
powers;
And laugh to see the mild and sunny
day
Smile on the shrunk and thin au-
tumnal hours;
I laugh, for hope hath happy place
with me,
If my bark sinks, 'tis to another sea.

W. E. CHANNING.

THE UNDERTAKING.

I HAVE done one braver thing
Than all the Worthies did;
And yet a braver thence doth spring,
Which is, to keep that hid.

It were but madness now to impart
The skill of specular stone;
When he, which can have learned the art
To cut it, can find none.

So, if I now should utter this,
Others (because no more
Such stuff to work upon there is)
Would love but as before.

But he, who loveliness within
Hath found, all outward loathes;
For he who color loves and skin,
Loves but their oldest clothes.

If, as I have, you also do
Virtue in women see,
And dare love that, and say so too,
And forget the he and she;

And if this love, though placèd so,
From profane men you hide,
Who will no faith on this bestow,
Or, if they do, deride:

Then you have done a braver thing
Than all the Worthies did,
And a braver thence will spring,
Which is, to keep that hid.

DONNE.

CHARACTER.

How seldom, friends, a good great man inherits
Honor or wealth with all his worth and pains!
It sounds like stories from the land of spirits,
If any man obtain that which he merits,
Or any merit that which he obtains —
For shame, dear friends, renounce this canting strain;
What wouldst thou have a good great man obtain?
Place, titles, salary, a gilded chain?
Or throne of corses which his sword hath slain?
Greatness and goodness are not *means*, but *ends:*
Hath he not always treasures, always friends,
The good great man? — three treasures, *Love* and *Light*,
And *Calm Thoughts* regular as infants' breath;
And three firm friends, more sure than day and night,
Himself, his *Maker*, and the angel *Death*.

COLERIDGE.

THAT EACH THING IS HURT OF ITSELF.

WHY fearest thou the outward foe,
When thou thyself thy harm dost feed?
Of grief or hurt, of pain or woe,
Within each thing is sown the seed.
So fine was never yet the cloth,
No smith so hard his iron did beat,
But th' one consumèd was with moth,
Th' other with canker all to-freate.

The knotty oak and wainscot old
Within doth eat the silly worm;
Even so a mind in envy rolled
Always within itself doth burn.
Thus every thing that nature wrought,
Within itself his hurt doth bear!
No outward harm need to be sought,
Where enemies be within so near.

ANONYMOUS.

MY MIND TO ME A KINGDOM IS.

MY mind to me a kingdom is;
Such perfect joy therein I find
As far exceeds all earthly blisse
That God or Nature hath assigned;
Though much I want that most would have,
Yet still my mind forbids to crave.

Content I live; this is my stay —
I seek no more than may suffice.
I press to bear no haughty sway;
Look, what I lack my mind supplies.
Lo! thus I triumph like a king,
Content with that my mind doth bring.

I see how plentie surfeits oft,
And hasty climbers soonest fall;
I see that such as sit aloft
Mishap doth threaten most of all.
These get with toil, and keep with fear;
Such cares my mind could never bear.

No princely pomp nor wealthy store,
No force to win the victory,
No wily wit to salve a sore,
No shape to win a lover's eye—
To none of these I yield as thrall;
For why, my mind despiseth all.

Some have too much, yet still they crave;
I little have, yet seek no more.
They are but poor, though much they have;
And I am rich with little store.
They poor, I rich; they beg, I give;
They lack, I lend; they pine, I live.

I laugh not at another's loss,
I grudge not at another's gaine;
No worldly wave my mind can toss;
I brook that is another's bane.
I feare no foe, nor fawn on friend;
I loathe not life, nor dread mine end.

I joy not in no earthly blisse;
I weigh not Crœsus' wealth a straw;
For care, I care not what it is;
I fear not fortune's fatal law;
My mind is such as may not move
For beauty bright, or force of love.

I wish but what I have at will;
I wander not to seek for more;
I like the plain, I climb no hill;
In greatest storms I sit on shore,
And laugh at them that toil in vain
To get what must be lost again.

I kisse not where I wish to kill;
I feign not love where most I hate;
I break no sleep to win my will;
I wait not at the mighty's gate.
I scorn no poor, I fear no rich;
I feel no want, nor have too much.

The court nor cart I like nor loathe;
Extremes are counted worst of all;
The golden mean betwixt them both
Doth surest sit, and fears no fall;
This is my choyce; for why, I find
No wealth is like a quiet mind.

My wealth is health and perfect ease;
My conscience clear my chief defence;
I never seek by bribes to please,
Nor by desert to give offence.
Thus do I live, thus will I die;
Would all did so as well as I!

WILLIAM BYRD.

AN HONEST MAN'S FORTUNE.

You that can look through Heaven, and tell the stars,
Observe their kind conjunctions, and their wars;
Find out new lights, and give them where you please,
To these men honors, pleasures, to those ease;
You that are God's surveyors, and can show
How far, and when, and why the wind doth blow;
Know all the charges of the dreadful thunder,
And when it will shoot over, or fall under:
Tell me, by all your art I conjure ye,
Yes, and by truth, what shall become of me?
Find out my star, if each one, as you say,
Have his peculiar Angel, and his way:
Observe my fate, next fall into your dreams,
Sweep clean your houses, and new line your schemes,
Then say your worst: or have I none at all?
Or is it burnt out lately? or did fall?
Or am I poor, not able, no full flame?
My star, like me, unworthy of a name?
Is it, your art can only work on those
That deale with dangers, dignities, and cloathes?
With love, or new opinions? you all lye,
A fishwife hath a fate, and so have I,

But far above your finding; He
that gives,
Out of his providence, to all that
lives;
He that made all the stars, you daily
read,
And from thence filch a knowledge
how to feed;
Hath hid this from you, your con-
jectures all
Are drunken things, not how, but
when they fall;
Man is his own stàr, and the soul
that can
Render an honest, and a perfect
man
Commands all light, all influence,
all fate,
Nothing to him falls early or too
late.
Our acts our Angels are, or good, or
ill,
Our fatal shadows that walk by us
still,
And when the stars are laboring we
believe
It is not that they govern, but they
grieve
Our stubborn ignorance; all things
that are
Made for our general uses are at war,
Even we among ourselves, and from
the strife
Your first unlike opinions got a life.
O man, thou image of thy Maker's
good,
What canst thou fear, when breathed
into thy blood
His spirit is, that built thee? what
dull sense
Makes thee suspect, in need, that
providence?
Who made the morning, and who
placed the light
Guide to thy labors? who called up
the night,
And bid her fall upon thee, like sweet
showers
In hollow murmurs, to lock up thy
powers?
Who gave thee knowledge? who so
trusted thee,
To let thee grow so near himself, the
Tree?
Must he then be distrusted? shall
his frame
Disçourse with him, why thus, and
thus I am?
He made the Angels thine, thy fel-
lows all,
Nay, even thy servants, when devo-
tions call.
Oh canst thou be so stupid then, so
dim,
To seek a saving influence, and lose
him?
Can Stars protect thee? or can pov-
erty,
Which is the light to Heaven, put
out his eye?
He is my star; in him all truth I
find,
All influence, all fate, and when my
mind
Is furnished with his fullnesse, my
poor story
Shall outlive all their Age, and all
their glory.
The hand of danger cannot fall
amiss,
When I know what, and in whose
power it is.
Nor want, the cause of man, shall
make me groan;
A holy hermit is a mind alone.
Doth not experience teach us all we
can
To work ourselves into a glorious
man?
Love's but an exhalation to best eyes
The matter's spent, and then the
fool's fire dyes?
Were I in love, and could that bright
star bring
Increase to wealth, honor, and every
thing:
Were she as perfect good as we can
aim,—
The first was so, and yet she lost the
Game.
My mistress then be knowledge and
faire truth;
So I enjoy all beauty and all youth,
And though to Time her lights and
laws she lends,
She knows no Age that to corruption
bends.
Friends' promises may lead me to
believe,
But he that is his own friend knows
to live.
Affliction, when I know it, is but
this,
A deep alloy whereby man tougher is
To bear the hammer; and the deeper
still,—

We still arise more image of his will.
Sickness an humorous cloud 'twixt us and light,
And Death, at longest but another night.
Man is his own Star, and that soul that can
Be honest is the only perfect man.

JOHN FLETCHER.

PEACE.

SWEET Peace, where dost thou dwell? I humbly crave,
Let me once know.
I sought thee in a secret cave;
And asked, if Peace were there.
A hollow wind did seem to answer, "No!
Go, seek elsewhere."

I did; and, going, did a rainbow note:
"Surely," thought I,
"This is the lace of Peace's coat.
I will search out the matter."
But, while I looked, the clouds immediately
Did break and scatter.

Then went I to a garden, and did spy
A gallant flower, —
The crown-imperial. "Sure," said I,
"Peace at the root must dwell."
But, when I digged, I saw a worm devour
What showed so well.

At length I met a reverend, good old man;
Whom when for Peace
I did demand, he thus began: —
"There was a prince of old
At Salem dwelt, who lived with good increase
Of flock and fold.

"He sweetly lived; yet sweetness did not save
His life from foes.
But, after death, out of his grave
There sprang twelve stalks of wheat;
Which many wondering at, got some of those
To plant and set.

"It prospered strangely, and did soon disperse
Through all the earth.
For they that taste it do rehearse,
That virtue lies therein, —
A secret virtue, bringing peace and mirth,
By flight of sin.

"Take of this grain, which in my garden grows,
And grows for you:
Make bread of it; and that repose
And peace which everywhere
With so much earnestness you do pursue,
Is only there."

HERBERT.

JOY.

O JOY, hast thou a shape?
Hast thou a breath?
How fillest thou the soundless air?
Tell me the pillars of thy house!
What rest they on? Do they escape
The victory of Death?
And are they fair
Eternally, who enter in thy house?
O Joy, thou viewless spirit, canst thou dare
To tell the pillars of thy house?

On adamant of pain
Before the earth
Was born of sea, before the sea,
Yea, and before the light, my house
Was built. None know what loss, what gain,
Attends each travail birth.
No soul could be
At peace when it had entered in my house,
If the foundations it could touch or see,
Which stay the pillars of my house!

H. H.

ABOU BEN ADHEM.

Abou Ben Adhem, (may his tribe increase!)
Awoke one night from a deep dream of peace,
And saw within the moonlight in the room,
Making it rich and like a lily in bloom,
An angel writing in a book of gold;
Exceeding peace had made Ben Adhem bold,
And to the Presence in the room he said,
"What writest thou?" The vision raised its head,
And with a look made all of sweet accord,
Answered, "The names of those who love the Lord."
"And is mine one?" said Adhem. "Nay, not so,"
Replied the angel. Adhem spoke more low,
But cheerly still, and said, "I pray thee, then,
Write me as one who loves his fellow-men."
The angel wrote and vanished; the next night
He came again with a great wakening light,
And showed their names whom love of God had blest,
And lo! Ben Adhem's name led all the rest.

Leigh Hunt.

ORTHODOXY.

"Nought loves another as itself,
Nor venerates another so;
Nor is it possible to thought,
A greater than itself to know.

"And, Father, how can I love you,
Or any of my brothers more?
I love you like the little bird
That picks up crumbs around the door."

The Priest sat by, and heard the child:
In trembling zeal he seized his hair;
He led him by his little coat,
And all admired the priestly care.

And standing on the altar high,
"Lo, what a fiend is here!" said he,
"One who sets reason up for judge
Of our most holy Mystery."

The weeping child could not be heard;
The weeping parents wept in vain;
They stript him to his little shirt,
And bound him in an iron chain;

And burned him in a holy place,
Where many had been burned before;
The weeping parents wept in vain:
Are such things done on Albion's shore?

William Blake.

THE TOUCHSTONE.

A man there came, whence none could tell,
Bearing a Touchstone in his hand,
And tested all things in the land
By its unerring spell.

A thousand transformations rose
From fair to foul, from foul to fair:
The golden crown he did not spare,
Nor scorn the beggar's clothes.

Of heirloom jewels, prized so much,
Were many changed to chips and clods;
And even statues of the Gods
Crumbled beneath its touch.

Then angrily the people cried,
"The loss outweighs the profit far;
Our goods suffice us as they are:
We will not have them tried."

And, since they could not so avail
To check his unrelenting quest,
They seized him, saying, "Let him test
How real is our jail!"

But though they slew him with the sword,
And in a fire his Touchstone burned,
Its doings could not be o'erturned,
Its undoings restored.

And when, to stop all future harm,
They strewed its ashes on the breeze,
They little guessed each grain of these
Conveyed the perfect charm.

ALLINGHAM.

PRAYERS.

Isabella.—Hark, how I'll bribe you,
Ay, with such gifts that Heaven shall share with you.
Not with fond shekels of the tested gold,
Or stones, whose rates are either rich, or poor,
As fancy values them; but with true prayers,
That shall be up at heaven, and enter there,
Ere sunrise; prayers from preserved souls,
From fasting maids, whose minds are dedicate
To nothing temporal.

SHAKSPEARE: *Measure for Measure.*

SIN.

LORD, with what care hast thou begirt us round!
Parents first season us; then schoolmasters
Deliver us to laws; they send us bound
To rules of reason, holy messengers—

Pulpits and Sundays; sorrow dogging sin;
Afflictions sorted; anguish of all sizes;
Fine nets and stratagems to catch us in;
Bibles laid open; millions of surprises;

Blessings beforehand; ties of gratefulness;
The sound of glory ringing in our ears;
Without, our shame; within, our consciences;
Angels and grace; eternal hopes and fears—

Yet all these fences, and their whole array,
One cunning bosom-sin blows quite away.

HERBERT.

WAYFARERS.

How they go by—those strange and dreamlike men!
One glance on each, one gleam from out each eye,
And that I never looked upon till now,
Has vanished out of sight as instantly.

Yet in it passed there a whole heart and life,
The only key it gave that transient look;
But for this key its great event in time
Of peace or strife to me a sealèd book.

E. S. H.

THE STRANGERS.

EACH care-worn face is but a book
To tell of houses bought or sold;
Or filled with words that men have took
From those who lived and spoke of old.

I see none whom I know, for they
See other things than him they meet;
And though they stop me by the way,
'Tis still some other one to greet.

There are no words that reach my ear;
Those speak who tell of other things
Than what they mean for me to hear,
For in their speech the counter rings.

I would be where each word is true,
Each eye sees what it looks upon;
For here my eye has seen but few
Who in each act that act have done.

JONES VERY.

PILGRIMAGE.

Give me my scallop-shell of Quiet,
My staff of Faith to walk upon,
My scrip of Joy, immortal diet;
My bottle of salvation;
My Gown of Glory, (Hope's true gage)
And thus I'll take my pilgrimage.

Blood must be my body's balmer,
Whilst my soul, like a quiet Palmer,
Travelleth towards the land of Heaven;
No other balm will there be given.
Over the silver mountains
Where spring the nectar fountains,
There will I kiss
The bowl of bliss,
And drink mine everlasting fill,
Upon every milken hill;
My soul will be a-dry before,
But after, it will thirst no more.

Sir Walter Raleigh.

SLEEP.

Tired Nature's sweet restorer, balmy sleep, —
He, like the world, his ready visits pays
Where fortune smiles: the wretched he forsakes,
And lights on lids unsullied by a tear.

Young.

SLEEP.

How many thousands of my poorest subjects
Are at this hour asleep! — O Sleep! O gentle sleep!
Nature's soft nurse, how have I frighted thee,
That thou no more wilt weigh my eyelids down,
And steep my senses in forgetfulness?
Why rather, sleep, liest thou in smoky cribs,
Upon uneasy pallets stretching thee,
And hushed with buzzing night-flies to thy slumber;
Than in the perfumed chambers of the great,
Under the canopies of costly state,
And lulled with sounds of sweetest melody?
O thou dull god, why liest thou with the vile,
In loathsome beds; and leav'st the kingly couch,
A watch-case, or a common 'larum bell?
Wilt thou upon the high and giddy mast
Seal up the ship-boy's eyes, and rock his brains
In cradle of the rude imperious surge;
And in the visitation of the winds,
Who take the ruffian billows by the top,
Curling their monstrous heads, and hanging them
With deafening clamors in the slippery clouds,
That, with the hurly, death itself awakes?
Canst thou, O partial sleep! give thy repose
To the wet sea-boy in an hour so rude;
And, in the calmest and most stillest night,
With all appliances and means to boot,
Deny it to a king? Then, happy low, lie down!
Uneasy lies the head that wears a crown.

Shakspeare: *King Henry IV.*

HAMLET'S SOLILOQUY.

To be, or not to be, that is the question: —
Whether 'tis nobler in the mind, to suffer
The slings and arrows of outrageous fortune;
Or to take arms against a sea of troubles,
And, by opposing, end them? — To die, — to sleep, —
No more; — and, by a sleep, to say we end
The heart-ache, and the thousand natural shocks
That flesh is heir to, — 'tis a consummation
Devoutly to be wished. To die; — to sleep: —

To sleep! perchance to dream;—ay, there's the rub;
For in that sleep of death what dreams may come,
When we have shuffled off this mortal coil,
Must give us pause: there's the respect,
That makes calamity of so long life;
For who would bear the whips and scorns of time,
The oppressor's wrong, the proud man's contumely,
The pangs of despised love, the law's delay,
The insolence of office, and the spurns
That patient merit of the unworthy takes,
When he himself might his quietus make,
With a bare bodkin? Who would fardels bear
To grunt and sweat under a weary life;
But that the dread of something after death,—
The undiscovered country, from whose bourn
No traveller returns,—puzzles the will,
And makes us rather bear those ills we have,
Than fly to others that we know not of?
Thus conscience does make cowards of us all,
And thus the native hue of resolution
Is sicklied o'er with the pale cast of thought;
And enterprises of great pith and moment,
With this regard, their currents turn awry,
And lose the name of action.—Soft you, now!
The fair Ophelia:—Nymph, in thy orisons
Be all my sins remembered.

SHAKSPEARE.

LIFE AND DEATH.

REASON thus with life,—
If I do lose thee, I do lose a thing
That none but fools would keep: a breath thou art,
Servile to all the skyey influences,
That dost this habitation, where thou keep'st,
Hourly afflict. Thou art by no means valiant;
For thou dost fear the soft and tender fork
Of a poor worm: thy best of rest is sleep,
And that thou oft provok'st; yet grossly fear'st
Thy death, which is no more.

SHAKSPEARE: *Measure for Measure.*

LIFE AND DEATH.

AY, but to die, and go we know not where,
To lie in cold obstruction, and to rot:
This sensible warm motion to become
A kneaded clod; and the delighted spirit
To bathe in fiery floods, or to reside
In thrilling regions of thick-ribbèd ice;
To be imprisoned in the viewless winds,
And blown with restless violence round about
The pendent world; or to be worse than worst
Of those, that lawless and incertain thoughts
Imagine howling!—'tis too horrible!
The weariest and most loathed worldly life,
That age, ache, penury, and imprisonment
Can lay on nature, is a paradise
To what we fear of death.

SHAKSPEARE: *Measure for Measure.*

INSCRIPTION ON MELROSE ABBEY.

THE earth goes on the earth glittering in gold,
The earth goes to the earth sooner than it would;
The earth builds on the earth castles and towers,
The earth says to the earth—All this is ours.

INSCRIPTION ON A WALL IN ST. EDMUND'S CHURCH IN LOMBARD STREET, LONDON.

MAN, thee behoveth oft to have this in mind,
That thou givest with thine hand, that thou shalt find;
For widows be slothful, and children be unkind,
Executors be covetous, and keep all that they find
If anybody ask where the dead's goods became?
So God help me and Halidam, he died a poor man.

INSCRIPTION IN MARBLE IN THE PARISH CHURCH OF FAVERSHAM, *IN AGRO CANTIANO.*

WHOSO him bethoft
Inwardly and oft,
How hard it were to flit
From bed unto the pit,
From pit unto pain
That ne'er shall cease again,
He would not do one sin
All the world to win.

LAODAMIA.

"WITH sacrifice, before the rising morn
Performed, my slaughtered lord have I required;
And in thick darkness, amid shades forlorn,
Him of the infernal gods have I desired:
Celestial pity I again implore; —
Restore him to my sight, great Jove, restore!"

So speaking, and by fervent love endowed
With faith, the suppliant heavenward lifts her hands;
While, like the sun emerging from a cloud,
Her countenance brightens — and her eye expands,
Her bosom heaves and spreads, her stature grows,
And she expects the issue in repose.

O terror! what hath she perceived? O joy!
What doth she look on — whom doth she behold?
Her hero slain upon the beach of Troy?
His vital presence — his corporeal mould?
It is — if sense deceive her not — 'tis he!
And a god leads him — wingèd Mercury!

Mild Hermes spake, and touched her with his wand
That calms all fear: "Such grace hath crowned thy prayer,
Laodamia, that at Jove's command
Thy husband walks the paths of upper air:
He comes to tarry with thee three hours' space;
Accept the gift; behold him face to face!"

Forth sprang the impassioned queen her lord to clasp;
Again that consummation she essayed;
But unsubstantial form eludes her grasp
As often as that eager grasp was made.
The phantom parts — but parts to re-unite,
And re-assume his place before her sight.

"Protesilaus, lo! thy guide is gone!
Confirm, I pray, the vision with thy voice:
This is our palace, — yonder is thy throne;
Speak, and the floor thou tread'st on will rejoice.
Not to appall me have the gods bestowed
This precious boon, — and blessed a sad abode."

"Great Jove, Laodamia, doth not leave
His gifts imperfect:— Spectre though I be,

I am not sent to scare thee or deceive,
But in reward of thy fidelity.
And something also did my worth obtain;
For fearless virtue bringeth boundless gain.

"Thou know'st, the Delphic oracle foretold
That the first Greek who touched the Trojan strand
Should die; but me the threat did not withhold:
A generous cause a victim did demand;
And forth I leaped upon the sandy plain;
A self-devoted chief—by Hector slain."

"Supreme of heroes—bravest, noblest, best!
Thy matchless courage I bewail no more,
That then, when tens of thousands were depressed
By doubt, propelled thee to the fatal shore;
Thou found'st—and I forgive thee—here thou art—
A nobler counsellor than my poor heart.

"But thou, though capable of sternest deed,
Wert kind as resolute, and good as brave;
And He, whose power restores thee, hath decreed
That thou shouldst cheat the malice of the grave;
Redundant are thy locks, thy lips as fair
As when their breath enriched Thessalian air.

"No spectre greets me,—no vain shadow this:
Come, blooming hero, place thee by my side!
Give, on this well-known couch, one nuptial kiss
To me, this day a second time thy bride!"
Jove frowned in heaven: the conscious Parcæ threw
Upon those roseate lips a Stygian hue.

"This visage tells thee that my doom is past:
Know, virtue were not virtue if the joys
Of sense were able to return as fast
And surely as they vanish.—Earth destroys
Those raptures duly—Erebus disdains:
Calm pleasures there abide—majestic pains.

"Be taught, O faithful consort, to control
Rebellious passion: for the gods approve
The depth, and not the tumult of the soul;
A fervent, not ungovernable love,
Thy transports moderate; and meekly mourn
When I depart, for brief is my sojourn"—

"Ah, wherefore?—Did not Hercules by force
Wrest from the guardian monster of the tomb
Alcestis, a re-animated corse,
Given back to dwell on earth in vernal bloom?
Medea's spells dispersed the weight of years,
And Æson stood a youth 'mid youthful peers.

"The gods to us are merciful—and they
Yet further may relent: for mightier far
Than strength of nerve and sinew, or the sway
Of magic, potent over sun and star,
Is love—though oft to agony distressed;
And though his favorite seat be feeble woman's breast.

"But if thou goest, I follow"—"Peace!" he said—
She looked upon him, and was calmed and cheered;
The ghastly color from his lips had fled;
In his deportment, shape, and mien, appeared

Elysian beauty, melancholy grace,
Brought from a pensive though a happy place.

He spake of love, such love as spirits feel
In worlds whose course is equable and pure;
No fears to beat away — no strife to heal —
The past unsighed for, and the future sure;
Spake of heroic arts in graver mood
Revived, with finer harmony pursued;

Of all that is most beauteous — imaged there
In happier beauty; more pellucid streams,
An ampler ether, a diviner air,
And fields invested with purpureal gleams;
Climes which the sun, who sheds the brightest day
Earth knows, is all unworthy to survey.

Yet there the soul shall enter which hath earned
That privilege by virtue. — "Ill," said he,
"The end of man's existence I discerned,
Who from ignoble games and revelry
Could draw, when we had parted, vain delight,
While tears were thy best pastime, day and night:

"And while my youthful peers, before my eyes
(Each hero following his peculiar bent),
Prepared themselves for glorious enterprise
By martial sports, — or, seated in the tent,
Chieftains and kings in council were detained;
What time the fleet at Aulis lay enchained.

"The wished-for wind was given: — I then revolved
Our future course, upon the silent sea;
And, if no worthier led the way, resolved
That, of a thousand vessels, mine should be
The foremost prow in pressing to the strand, —
Mine the first blood that tinged the Trojan sand.

"Yet bitter, ofttimes bitter, was the pang
When of thy loss I thought, belovèd wife;
On thee too fondly did my memory hang,
And on the joys we shared in mortal life, —
The paths which we had trod — these fountains — flowers;
My new-planned cities, and unfinished towers.

"But should suspense permit the foe to cry,
'Behold they tremble! haughty their array,
Yet of their number no one dares to die?' —
In soul I swept the indignity away:
Old frailties then recurred: but lofty thought,
In act embodied, my deliverance wrought.

"And thou, though strong in love, art all too weak
In reason, in self-government too slow;
I counsel thee by fortitude to seek
Our blessed re-union in the shades below.
The invisible world with thee hath sympathized;
Be thy affections raised and solemnized.

"Learn by a mortal yearning to ascend,
Seeking a higher object: — Love was given,
Encouraged, sanctioned, chiefly for that end:
For this the passion to excess was driven —
That self might be annulled; her bondage prove
The fetters of a dream, opposed to love."

Aloud she shrieked! for Hermes re-appears!
Round the dear shade she would have clung—'tis vain:
The hours are past—too brief had they been years;
And him no mortal effort can detain:
Swift, toward the realms that know not earthly day,
He through the portal takes his silent way—
And on the palace floor a lifeless corse she lay.

Ah, judge her gently who so deeply loved!
Her, who, in reason's spite, yet without crime,
Was in a trance of passion thus removed;
Delivered from the galling yoke of time,
And these frail elements—to gather flowers
Of blissful quiet 'mid unfading bowers.

Yet tears to human suffering are due;
And mortal hopes defeated and o'erthrown
Are mourned by man, and not by man alone,
As fondly he believes.—Upon the side
Of Hellespont (such faith was entertained)
A knot of spiry trees for ages grew
From out the tomb of him for whom she died;
And ever, when such stature they had gained
That Ilium's walls were subject to their view,
The trees' tall summits withered at the sight;
A constant interchange of growth and blight!

WORDSWORTH.

TITHONUS.

THE woods decay, the woods decay and fall,
The vapors weep their burthen to the ground,
Man comes and tills the field and lies beneath,
And after many a summer dies the swan.
Me only cruel immortality
Consumes: I wither slowly in thine arms,
Here at the quiet limit of the world,
A white-haired shadow roaming like a dream
The ever silent spaces of the East,
Far-folded mists, and gleaming halls of morn.

Alas! for this gray shadow, once a man—
So glorious in his beauty and thy choice,
Who madest him thy chosen, that he seemed
To his great heart none other than a God!
I asked thee, "Give me immortality."
Then didst thou grant mine asking with a smile,
Like wealthy men who care not how they give,
But thy strong Hours indignant worked their wills,

And beat me down and marred and wasted me,
And though they could not end me, left me maimed
To dwell in presence of immortal youth,
Immortal age beside immortal youth,
And all I was, in ashes. Can thy love,
Thy beauty, make amends, though even now,
Close over us, the silver star, thy guide,
Shines in those tremulous eyes that fill with tears
To hear me? Let me go: take back thy gift:
Why should a man desire in any way
To vary from the kindly race of men,
Or pass beyond the goal of ordinance
Where all should pause, as is most meet for all?

A soft air fans the cloud apart; there comes
A glimpse of that dark world where I was born.

Once more the old mysterious glimmer steals
From thy pure brows, and from thy shoulders pure,
And bosom beating with a heart renewed.
Thy cheek begins to redden through the gloom,
Thy sweet eyes brighten slowly close to mine,
Ere yet they blind the stars, and the wild team
Which love thee, yearning for thy yoke, arise,
And shake the darkness from their loosened manes,
And beat the twilight into flakes of fire.

Lo! ever thus thou growest beautiful
In silence, then before thine answer given
Departest, and thy tears are on my cheek.

Why wilt thou ever scare me with thy tears,
And make me tremble lest a saying learnt,
In days far-off, on that dark earth, be true?
"The Gods themselves cannot recall their gifts."

Ay me! ay me! with what another heart
In days far-off, and with what other eyes
I used to watch — if I be he that watched —
The lucid outline forming round thee; saw
The dim curls kindle into sunny rings;
Changed with thy mystic change, and felt my blood
Glow with the glow that slowly crimsoned all
Thy presence and thy portals, while I lay,
Mouth, forehead, eyelids, growing dewy-warm
With kisses balmier than half-opening buds
Of April, and could hear the lips that kissed
Whispering I knew not what of wild and sweet,
Like that strange song I heard Apollo sing,
While Ilion like a mist rose into towers.

Yet hold me not forever in thine East:
How can my nature longer mix with thine?
Coldly thy rosy shadows bathe me, cold
Are all thy lights, and cold my wrinkled feet
Upon thy glimmering thresholds, when the steam
Floats up from those dim fields about the homes
Of happy men that have the power to die,
And grassy barrows of the happier dead.
Release me, and restore me to the ground;
Thou seest all things, thou wilt see my grave:
Thou wilt renew thy beauty morn by morn:
I earth in earth forget these empty courts,
And thee returning on thy silver wheels.

TENNYSON.

COME MORIR.

HE leaves the earth, and says, enough and more
Unto thee have I given, oh Earth. — For all
With hand free and ungrudging gave I up, —
But now I leave thy pale hopes and dear pains,
The rude fields where so many years I've tilled,
And where no other feeling gave me strength,
Save that from them my home was aye in view,
For only transient clouds could hide from me
My spirit's home, whence it came, where should go; —
Enough, more than enough, now let me rest.

THE OLD MAN'S FUNERAL.

Ye sigh not when the sun, his course fulfilled,
His glorious course, rejoicing earth and sky,
In the soft evening, when the winds are stilled,
Sinks where his islands of refreshment lie,
And leaves the smile of his departure spread
O'er the warm-colored heaven and ruddy mountain head.

Why weep ye then for him, who, having won
The bound of man's appointed years, at last,
Life's blessings all enjoyed, life's labors done,
Serenely to his final rest has passed;
While the soft memory of his virtues yet
Lingers like twilight hues, when the bright sun is set?

Bryant.

DEATH'S FINAL CONQUEST.

The garlands wither on your brow,
Then boast no more your mighty deeds;
Upon death's purple altar now,
See where the victor-victim bleeds:
All heads must come
To the cold tomb;
Only the actions of the just
Smell sweet and blossom in the dust.

James Shirley.

STANZAS WRITTEN IN THE CHURCHYARD OF RICHMOND, YORKSHIRE.

"It is good for us to be here: if thou wilt, let us make here three tabernacles, one for thee, one for Moses, and one for Elias." — St. Matthew.

Methinks it is good to be here,
If thou wilt let us build, — but for whom?
Nor Elias nor Moses appear;
But the shadows of eve that encompass with gloom
The abode of the dead and the place of the tomb.

Shall we build to Ambition? Ah, no!
Affrighted, he shrinketh away, —
For see, they would pin him below
In a dark narrow cave, and, begirt with cold clay,
To the meanest of reptiles a fear and a prey.

To Beauty? Ah, no! she forgets
The charms which she wielded before,
Nor knows the foul worm that he frets
The skin that but yesterday fools could adore,
For the smoothness it held, or the tint which it wore.

Shall we build to the purple of Pride,
The trappings which dizen the proud?
Alas! they are all laid aside,
And here's neither dress nor adornment allowed,
Save the long winding-sheet and the fringe of the shroud.

To Riches? Alas, 'tis in vain;
Who hide in their turns have been hid;
The treasures are squandered again;
And here in the grave are all metals forbid,
Save the tinsel that shines on the dark coffin lid.

To the pleasures which Mirth can afford,
The revel, the laugh and the jeer?
Ah! here is a plentiful board!
But the guests are all mute at their pitiful cheer,
And none but the worm is a reveller here.

Shall we build to Affection and Love?
Ah, no! They have withered and died,
Or fled with the spirit above:
Friends, brothers, and sisters, are laid side by side,
Yet none have saluted, and none have replied.

Unto Sorrow? The dead cannot grieve;
Not a sob, not a sigh meets mine ear,
Which Compassion itself could relieve.
Ah, sweetly they slumber, nor love, hope, or fear,
Peace, peace! is the watchword, the only one here.

Unto Death, to whom monarchs must bow?
Ah, no! for his empire is known,
And here there are trophies enow!
Beneath the cold head, and around the dark stone,
Are the signs of a sceptre that none may disown.

The first tabernacle to Hope we will build,
And look for the sleepers around us to rise!
The second to Faith, which insures it fulfilled;
And the third to the Lamb of the great sacrifice,
Who bequeathed us them both when he rose to the skies.

HERBERT KNOWLES.

THANATOPSIS.

. . . YET a few days, and thee
The all-beholding sun shall see no more
In all his course; nor yet in the cold ground,
Where thy pale form was laid, with many tears,
Nor in the embrace of ocean, shall exist
Thy image. Earth, that nourished thee, shall claim
Thy growth, to be resolved to earth again;
And lost each human trace, surrendering up
Thine individual being, shalt thou go
To mix forever with the elements,
To be a brother to the insensible rock,
And to the sluggish clod, which the rude swain
Turns with his share, and treads upon. The oak
Shall send his roots abroad, and pierce thy mould.
Yet not to thy eternal resting-place
Shalt thou retire alone — nor couldst thou wish
Couch more magnificent. Thou shalt lie down
With patriarchs of the infant world, — with kings,
The powerful of the earth, — the wise, the good,
Fair forms, and hoary seers of ages past,
All in one mighty sepulchre. The hills
Rock-ribbed and ancient as the sun, — the vales
Stretching in pensive quietness between;
The venerable woods, — rivers that move
In majesty, and the complaining brooks
That make the meadows green; and poured round all,
Old ocean's gray and melancholy waste, —
Are but the solemn decorations all
Of the great tomb of man. The golden sun,
The planets, all the infinite host of heaven,
Are shining on the sad abodes of death,
Through the still lapse of ages. All that tread
The globe are but a handful to the tribes
That slumber in its bosom. . . .

So live, that when thy summons comes to join
The innumerable caravan, that moves
To that mysterious realm, where each shall take
His chamber in the silent halls of death,
Thou go not, like the quarry-slave at night,

Scourged to his dungeon, but sustained and soothed
By an unfaltering trust, approach thy grave,
Like one who wraps the drapery of his couch
About him, and lies down to pleasant dreams.

BRYANT.

TO BE NO MORE.

To be no more — sad cure; for who would lose
Though full of pain, this intellectual being,
Those thoughts that wander through eternity,
To perish rather, swallowed up and lost
In the wide womb of uncreated night,
Devoid of sense and motion?

MILTON.

LIFE.

LIFE! I know not what thou art,
But know that thou and I must part;
And when, or how, or where we met,
I own to me's a secret yet.

Life! we've been long together,
Through pleasant and through cloudy weather;
'Tis hard to part when friends are dear —
Perhaps 'twill cost a sigh, a tear;
Then steal away, give little warning,
Choose thine own time;
Say not Good-night, — but in some brighter clime
Bid me Good-morning.

BARBAULD.

ELEGY WRITTEN IN A COUNTRY CHURCHYARD.

THE curfew tolls the knell of parting day,
The lowing herd winds slowly o'er the lea,
The ploughman homeward plods his weary way,
And leaves the world to darkness and to me.

Now fades the glimmering landscape on the sight,
And all the air a solemn stillness holds,
Save where the beetle wheels his droning flight,
And drowsy tinklings lull the distant folds:

Save that from yonder ivy-mantled tower,
The moping owl does to the moon complain
Of such as, wandering near her secret bower,
Molest her ancient solitary reign.

Beneath those rugged elms, that yew-tree's shade,
Where heaves the turf in many a mouldering heap,
Each in his narrow cell forever laid,
The rude forefathers of the hamlet sleep.

The breezy call of incense-breathing morn,
The swallow twittering from the straw-built shed,
The cock's shrill clarion, or the echoing horn,
No more shall rouse them from their lowly bed.

For them no more the blazing hearth shall burn,
Or busy housewife ply her evening care;
No children run to lisp their sire's return,
Or climb his knees the envied kiss to share.

Oft did the harvest to their sickle yield,
Their furrow oft the stubborn glebe has broke:
How jocund did they drive their team afield!
How bowed the woods beneath their sturdy stroke!

Let not ambition mock their useful toil,
Their homely joys, and destiny obscure;
Nor grandeur hear with a disdainful smile
The short and simple annals of the poor.

The boast of heraldry, the pomp of power,
And all that beauty, all that wealth, e'er gave,
Await alike the inevitable hour.
The paths of glory lead but to the grave.

Nor you, ye proud, impute to these the fault,
If memory o'er their tomb no trophies raise,
Where through the long-drawn aisle and fretted vault
The pealing anthem swells the note of praise.

Can storied urn, or animated bust,
Back to its mansion call the fleeting breath?
Can honor's voice provoke the silent dust,
Or flattery soothe the dull cold ear of death?

Perhaps in this neglected spot is laid
Some heart once pregnant with celestial fire;
Hands, that the rod of empire might have swayed,
Or waked to ecstasy the living lyre:

But knowledge to their eyes her ample page,
Rich with the spoils of time, did ne'er unroll;
Chill penury repressed their noble rage,
And froze the genial current of the soul.

Full many a gem of purest ray serene
The dark unfathomed caves of ocean bear:
Full many a flower is born to blush unseen,
And waste its sweetness on the desert air.

Some village-Hampden, that, with dauntless breast,
The little tyrant of his fields withstood,
Some mute inglorious Milton here may rest,
Some Cromwell guiltless of his country's blood.

The applause of listening senates to command,
The threats of pain and ruin to despise,
To scatter plenty o'er a smiling land,
And read their history in a nation's eyes,

Their lot forbade: nor circumscribed alone
Their growing virtues, but their crimes confined;
Forbade to wade through slaughter to a throne,
And shut the gates of mercy on mankind,

The struggling pangs of conscious truth to hide,
To quench the blushes of ingenuous shame,
Or heap the shrine of luxury and pride
With incense kindled at the Muse's flame.

Far from the madding crowd's ignoble strife,
Their sober wishes never learned to stray;
Along the cool sequestered vale of life
They kept the noiseless tenor of their way.

Yet even these bones from insult to protect,
Some frail memorial still erected high,
With uncouth rhymes and shapeless sculpture decked,
Implores the passing tribute of a sigh.

Their name, their years, spelt by the unlettered Muse,
The place of fame and elegy supply:
And many a holy text around she strews,
That teach the rustic moralist to die.

For who, to dumb forgetfulness a prey,
  This pleasing anxious being e'er resigned,
Left the warm precincts of the cheerful day,
  Nor cast one longing, lingering look behind?

On some fond breast the parting soul relies,
  Some pious drops the closing eye requires;
E'en from the tomb the voice of Nature cries,
  E'en in our ashes live their wonted fires.

For thee, who, mindful of the unhonored dead,
  Dost in these lines their artless tale relate;
If chance, by lonely contemplation led,
  Some kindred spirit shall inquire thy fate,—

Haply some hoary-headed swain may say,
  "Oft have we seen him at the peep of dawn
Brushing with hasty steps the dews away,
  To meet the sun upon the upland lawn:

"There at the foot of yonder nodding beech,
  That wreathes its old fantastic roots so high,
His listless length at noontide would he stretch,
  And pore upon the brook that babbles by.

"Hard by yon wood, now smiling as in scorn,
  Muttering his wayward fancies he would rove;
Now drooping, woful-wan, like one forlorn,
  Or crazed with care, or crossed in hopeless love.

"One morn I missed him on the accustomed hill,
  Along the heath, and near his favorite tree;
Another came; nor yet beside the rill,
  Nor up the lawn, nor at the wood, was he:

"The next, with dirges due, in sad array,
  Slow through the church-way path we saw him borne:—
Approach and read (for thou canst read) the lay
  Graved on the stone beneath yon aged thorn."

THE EPITAPH.

Here rests his head upon the lap of earth,
  A youth, to fortune and to fame unknown:
Fair Science frowned not on his humble birth,
  And Melancholy marked him for her own.

Large was his bounty, and his soul sincere,
  Heaven did a recompense as largely send;
He gave to misery (all he had) a tear,
  He gained from heaven ('twas all he wished) a friend.

No farther seek his merits to disclose,
  Or draw his frailties from their dread abode,
(There they alike in trembling hope repose,)
  The bosom of his Father and his God.

GRAY.

THE SKULL.

REMOVE yon skull from out the scattered heaps:
Is that a temple where a god may dwell?
Why even the worm at last disdains her shattered cell!

Look on its broken arch, its ruined wall,
Its chambers desolate, and portals foul:

Yes, this was once Ambition's airy hall,
The dome of Thought, the palace of the Soul:
Behold through each lack-lustre, eyeless hole,
The gay recess of Wisdom and of Wit,
And Passion's host, that never brooked control:
Can all saint, sage, or sophist ever writ,
People this lonely tower, this tenement refit?

Yet if, as holiest men have deemed, there be
A land of souls beyond that sable shore,
To shame the doctrine of the Sadducee,
And sophists, madly vain of dubious lore;
How sweet it were in concert to adore
With those who made our mortal labors light!
To hear each voice we feared to hear no more!
Behold each mighty shade revealed to sight,
The Bactrian, Samian sage, and all who taught the right!

BYRON: *Childe Harold.*

THE IMMORTAL MIND.

When coldness wraps this suffering clay,
Ah, whither strays the immortal mind?
It cannot die, it cannot stay,
But leaves its darkened dust behind.
Then, unembodied, doth it trace
By steps each planet's heavenly way?
Or fill at once the realms of space,
A thing of eyes, that all survey?

Eternal, boundless, undecayed,
A thought unseen, but seeing all,
All, all in earth, or skies displayed,
Shall it survey, shall it recall:
Each fainter trace that memory holds,
So darkly of departed years,
In one broad glance the soul beholds,
And all, that was, at once appears.

Before creation peopled earth,
Its eyes shall roll through chaos back;
And where the farthest heaven had birth,
The spirit trace its rising track.
And where the future mars or makes,
Its glance dilate o'er all to be,
While sun is quenched or system breaks,
Fixed in its own eternity.

Above or love, hope, hate, or fear,
It lives all passionless and pure:
An age shall fleet like earthly year;
Its years as moments shall endure.
Away, away, without a wing,
O'er all, through all, its thoughts shall fly;
A nameless and eternal thing,
Forgetting what it was to die.

BYRON.

CELINDA.

Walking thus towards a pleasant grove,
Which did, it seemed, in new delight
The pleasures of the time unite
To give a triumph to their love,—
They staid at last, and on the grass
Reposèd so as o'er his breast
She bowed her gracious head to rest,
Such a weight as no burden was.
Long their fixed eyes to heaven bent,
Unchanged they did never move,
As if so great and pure a love
No glass but it could represent.
"These eyes again thine eyes shall see,
Thy hands again these hands infold,
And all chaste pleasures can be told
Shall with us everlasting be.
Let then no doubt, Celinda, touch,
Much less your fairest mind invade;
Were not our souls immortal made,
Our equal loves can make them such."

LORD EDWARD HERBERT.

EUTHANASIA.

But souls that of his own good life partake,
He loves as his own self; dear as his eye
They are to him: He'll never them forsake:
When they shall die, then God himself shall die;
They live, they live in blest eternity.

Henry More.

THE RETREAT.

Happy those early days when I
Shined in my angel-infancy!
Before I understood this place
Appointed for my second race,
Or taught my soul to fancy aught
But a white, celestial thought;
When yet I had not walked above
A mile or two from my first love,
And looking back, at that short space
Could see a glimpse of his bright face;
When on some gilded cloud or flower
My gazing soul would dwell an hour,
And in those weaker glories spy
Some shadows of eternity:
Before I taught my tongue to wound
My conscience with a sinful sound,
Or had the black art to dispense
A several sin to every sense;
But felt through all this fleshly dress
Bright shoots of everlastingness.
O how I long to travel back,
And tread again that ancient track!
That I might once more reach that plain
Where first I left my glorious train,
From whence the enlightened spirit sees
That shady city of palm-trees.
But ah! my soul with too much stay
Is drunk, and staggers in the way!
Some men a forward motion love,
But I by backward steps would move;
And when this dust falls to the urn,
In that state I came, return.

Henry Vaughan.

IMMORTALITY,

"The child is father of the man;
And I could wish my days to be
Bound each to each by natural piety."

I.

There was a time when meadow, grove, and stream,
The earth, and every common sight,
To me did seem
Apparelled in celestial light,
The glory and the freshness of a dream.
It is not now as it hath been of yore;—
Turn whereso'er I may,
By night or day,
The things which I have seen I now can see no more.

II.

The rainbow comes and goes,
And lovely is the rose;
The moon doth with delight
Look round her when the heavens are bare;
Waters on a starry night
Are beautiful and fair;
The sunshine is a glorious birth;
But yet I know, where'er I go,
That there hath passed away a glory from the earth.

III.

Now, while the birds thus sing a joyous song,
And while the young lambs bound
As to the tabor's sound,
To me alone there came a thought of grief:
A timely utterance gave that thought relief,
And I again am strong:
The cataracts blow their trumpets from the steep;
No more shall grief of mine the season wrong;
I hear the echoes through the mountains throng,
The winds come to me from the fields of sleep,
And all the earth is gay;
Land and sea
Give themselves up to jollity,

And with the heart of May
Doth every beast keep holiday;
Thou child of joy,
Shout round me, let me hear thy shouts, thou happy shepherd-boy!

IV.

Ye blessèd creatures, I have heard the call
Ye to each other make; I see
The heavens laugh with you in your jubilee;
My heart is at your festival,
My head hath its coronal,
The fulness of your bliss, I feel — I feel it all.
Oh evil day! if I were sullen
While the earth herself is adorning,
This sweet May-morning,
And the children are culling
On every side,
In a thousand valleys far and wide,
Fresh flowers; while the sun shines warm,
And the babe leaps up on his mother's arm: —
I hear, I hear, with joy I hear!
— But there's a tree, of many one,
A single field which I have looked upon,
Both of them speak of something that is gone:
The pansy at my feet
Doth the same tale repeat:
Whither is fled the visionary gleam?
Where is it now, the glory and the dream?

V.

Our birth is but a sleep and a forgetting:
The soul that rises with us, our life's star,
Hath had elsewhere its setting,
And cometh from afar:
Not in entire forgetfulness,
And not in utter nakedness,
But trailing clouds of glory do we come
From God, who is our home:
Heaven lies about us in our infancy!
Shades of the prison-house begin to close
Upon the growing boy,
But he beholds the light, and whence it flows,
He sees it in his joy;
The youth, who daily farther from the east
Must travel, still is Nature's priest,
And by the vision splendid
Is on his way attended;
At length the man perceives it die away,
And fade into the light of common day.

VI.

Earth fills her lap with pleasures of her own;
Yearnings she hath in her own natural kind,
And, even with something of a mother's mind,
And no unworthy aim,
The homely nurse doth all she can
To make her foster-child, her inmate man,
Forget the glories he hath known,
And that imperial palace whence he came.

VII.

Behold the child among his new-born blisses,
A six years' darling of a pygmy size!
See, where 'mid work of his own hand he lies,
Fretted by sallies of his mother's kisses,
With light upon him from his father's eyes!
See, at his feet, some little plan or chart,
Some fragment from his dream of human life,
Shaped by himself with newly-learnèd art;
A wedding or a festival,
A mourning or a funeral;
And this hath now his heart,
And unto this he frames his song:
Then will he fit his tongue
To dialogues of business, love, or strife;

But it will not be long
Ere this be thrown aside,
And with new joy and pride
The little actor cons another part;
Filling from time to time his "humorous stage"
With all the persons, down to palsied age,
That Life brings with her in her equipage;
As if his whole vocation
Were endless imitation.

VIII.

Thou, whose exterior semblance doth belie
Thy soul's immensity;
Thou best philosopher, who yet dost keep
Thy heritage; thou eye among the blind,
That, deaf and silent, read'st the eternal deep,
Haunted forever by the eternal mind, —
Mighty Prophet! Seer blest!
On whom those truths do rest,
Which we are toiling all our lives to find;
(In darkness lost, the darkness of the grave;)
Thou, over whom thy immortality
Broods like the day, a master o'er a slave,
A presence which is not to be put by;
Thou little child, yet glorious in the might
Of heaven-born freedom, on thy being's height,
Why with such earnest pains dost thou provoke
The years to bring the inevitable yoke,
Thus blindly with thy blessedness at strife?
Full soon thy soul shall have her earthly freight,
And custom lie upon thee with a weight,
Heavy as frost, and deep almost as life!

IX.

O joy! that in our embers
Is something that doth live,
That Nature yet remembers
What was so fugitive!
The thought of our past years in me doth breed
Perpetual benedictions: not indeed
For that which is most worthy to be blest;
Delight and liberty, the simple creed
Of childhood, whether busy or at rest,
With new-fledged hope still fluttering in his breast: —
Not for these I raise
The song of thanks and praise;
But for those obstinate questionings
Of sense and outward things,
Fallings from us, vanishings;
Blank misgivings of a creature
Moving about in worlds not realized,
High instincts, before which our mortal nature
Did tremble like a guilty thing surprised:
But for those first affections,
Those shadowy recollections,
Which, be they what they may,
Are yet the fountain light of all our day,
Are yet a master light of all our seeing;
Uphold us, cherish, and have power to make
Our noisy years seem moments in the being
Of the eternal silence: truths that wake,
To perish never;
Which neither listlessness, nor mad endeavor,
Nor man nor boy,
Nor all that is at enmity with joy,
Can utterly abolish or destroy!
Hence, in a season of calm weather,
Though inland far we be,
Our souls have sight of that immortal sea
Which brought us hither,
Can in a moment travel thither,
And see the children sport upon the shore,
And hear the mighty waters rolling evermore.

X.

Then sing, ye birds, sing, sing a joyous song!
And let the young lambs bound
As to the tabor's sound!

We in thought will join your throng,
Ye that pipe and ye that play,
Ye that through your hearts to-day
Feel the gladness of the May!
What though the radiance which was once so bright
Be now forever taken from my sight,
Though nothing can bring back the hour
Of splendor in the grass, of glory in the flower;
We will grieve not, rather find
Strength in what remains behind,
In the primal sympathy
Which having been, must ever be;
In the soothing thoughts that spring
Out of human suffering;
In the faith that looks through death,
In years that bring the philosophic mind.

XI.

And O ye fountains, meadows, hills, and groves,
Forebode not any severing of our loves!
Yet in my heart of hearts I feel your might;
I only have relinquished one delight,
To live beneath your more habitual sway.
I love the brooks which down their channels fret,
Even more than when I tripped lightly as they:
The innocent brightness of a new-born day
Is lovely yet;
The clouds that gather round the setting sun
Do take a sober coloring from an eye
That hath kept watch o'er man's mortality;
Another race hath been, and other palms are won.
Thanks to the human heart by which we live;
Thanks to its tenderness, its joys, and fears,
To me the meanest flower that blows can give
Thoughts that do often lie too deep for tears.

WORDSWORTH.

LOVE AND HUMILITY.

FAR have I clambered in my mind,
But nought so great as love I find:
Deep-searching wit, mount-moving might,
Are nought compared to that good sprite.
Life of delight, and soul of bliss!
Sure source of lasting happiness!
Higher than heaven! lower than hell!
What is thy tent? Where mayst thou dwell?

My mansion hight humility,
Heaven's vastest capability.
The further it doth downward bend,
The higher up it doth ascend;
If it go down to utmost nought,
It shall return with what it sought.

Could I demolish with mine eye
Strong towers; stop the fleet stars in sky,
Bring down to earth the pale-faced moon,
Or turn black midnight to bright noon;
Though all things were put in my hand, —
As parched, as dry, as Libyan sand
Would be my life, if Charity
Were wanting. But Humility
Is more than my poor soul durst crave,
That lies entombed in lowly grave.
But if 'twere lawful up to send
My voice to heaven, this should it rend,
Lord, thrust me deeper into dust,
That thou mayst raise me with the just.

HENRY MORE.

MY LEGACY.

THEY told me I was heir: I turned in haste,
And ran to seek my treasure,
And wondered as, I ran, how it was placed, —

If I should find a measure
Of gold, or if the titles of fair lands
And houses would be laid within my hands.

I journeyed many roads; I knocked at gates;
I spoke to each wayfarer
I met, and said, "A heritage awaits
Me. Art not thou the bearer
Of news? some message sent to me whereby
I learn which way my new possessions lie?"

Some asked me in; nought lay beyond their door;
Some smiled, and would not tarry,
But said that men were just behind who bore
More gold than I could carry;
And so the morn, the noon, the day, were spent,
While empty handed up and down I went.

At last one cried, whose face I could not see,
As through the mists he hasted;
"Poor child, what evil ones have hindered thee,
Till this whole day is wasted?
Hath no man told thee that thou art joint heir
With one named Christ, who waits the goods to share?"

The one named Christ I sought for many days,
In many places vainly;
I heard men name his name in many ways;
I saw his temples plainly;
But they who named him most gave me no sign
To find him by, or prove the heirship mine.

And when at last I stood before his face,
I knew him by no token
Save subtle air of joy which filled the place;
Our greeting was not spoken;
In solemn silence I received my share,
Kneeling before my brother and "joint heir."

My share! No deed of house or spreading lands,
As I had dreamed; no measure
Heaped up with gold; my elder brother's hands
Had never held such treasure.
Foxes have holes, and birds in nests are fed:
My brother had not where to lay his head.

My share! The right like him to know all pain
Which hearts are made for knowing;
The right to find in loss the surest gain;
To reap my joy from sowing
In bitter tears; the right with him to keep
A watch by day and night with all who weep.

My share! To-day men call it grief and death;
I see the joy and life to-morrow;
I thank my Father with my every breath,
For this sweet legacy of sorrow;
And through my tears I call to each "joint heir
With Christ, make haste to ask him for thy share."

H. H.

DIVINE LOVE.

Thou hidden love of God! whose height,
Whose depth unfathomed, no man knows —
I see from far thy beauteous light,
Inly I sigh for thy repose.
My heart is pained; nor can it be
At rest till it finds rest in Thee.

Thy secret voice invites me still
The sweetness of Thy yoke to prove;
And fain I would; but though my will
Seem fixed, yet wide my passions rove;
Yet hindrances strew all the way —
I aim at Thee, yet from Thee stray.

'Tis mercy all, that Thou hast brought
My mind to seek her peace in Thee!

Yet while I seek, but find Thee not,
No peace my wandering soul shall see.
O when shall all my wanderings end,
And all my steps to Theeward tend?

Is there a thing beneath the sun
That strives with Thee my heart to share?
Ah, tear it thence, and reign alone —
The Lord of every motion there!
Then shall my heart from earth be free,
When it hath found repose in Thee.

GERHARD TERSTEEGEN:
Trans. by John Wesley.

MORAVIAN HYMN.

O DRAW me, Father, after thee,
So shall I run and never tire:
With gracious words still comfort me;
Be thou my hope, my sole desire:
Free me from every weight; nor fear
Nor sin can come, if thou art here.

From all eternity, with love
Unchangeable thou hast me viewed;
Ere knew this beating heart to move,
Thy tender mercies me pursued;
Ever with me may they abide,
And close me in on every side.

In suffering, be thy love my peace;
In weakness, be thy love my power;
And when the storms of life shall cease,
My God! in that transcendent hour,
In death as life be thou my guide,
And bear me through death's whelming tide.

JOHN WESLEY.

PSALM XCIII.

CLOTHED with state, and girt with might,
Monarch-like Jehovah reigns,
He who earth's foundation pight*—
Pight at first, and yet sustains;

* Pitched.

He whose stable throne disdains
Motion's shock and age's flight;
He who endless one remains
One, the same, in changeless plight.

Rivers, — yea though rivers roar,
Roaring though sea-billows rise,
Vex the deep, and break the shore, —
Stronger art thou, Lord of skies!
Firm and true thy promise lies
Now and still as heretofore:
Holy worship never dies
In thy house where we adore.

SIR PHILIP SIDNEY.

PSALM CXXXIX.

O LORD in me there lieth nought
But to thy search revealèd lies;
For when I sit
Thou markest it;
Nor less thou notest when I rise:
Yea, closest closet of my thought
Hath open windows to thine eyes.

Thou walkest with me when I walk;
When to my bed for rest I go,
I find thee there,
And everywhere;
Not youngest thought in me doth grow,
No, not one word I cast to talk
But, yet unuttered, thou dost know.

If forth I march, thou goest before;
If back I turn, thou com'st behind;
So forth nor back
Thy guard I lack;
Nay, on me too thy hand I find.
Well I thy wisdom may adore,
But never reach with earthly mind.

To shun thy notice, leave thine eye,
O whither might I take my way?
To starry sphere?
Thy throne is there:
To dead men's undelightsome stay?
There is thy walk, and there to lie
Unknown, in vain should I assay.

O sun, whom light nor flight can match!
Suppose thy lightful flightful wings

Thou lend to me,
And I could flee
As far as thee the evening brings:
Even led to west he would me catch,
Nor should I lurk with western things.

Do thou thy best, O secret night!
In sable veil to cover me:
Thy sable veil
Shall vainly fail:
With day unmasked my night shall be,
For night is day, and darkness light,
O Father of all lights, to thee.

SIR PHILIP SIDNEY.

SATAN.

BELOW the bottom of the great Abyss,
There where one centre reconciles all things,
The world's profound heart pants; there placed is
Mischief's old Master! close about him clings
A curled knot of embracing snakes, that kiss
His correspondent cheeks: these loathsome strings
Hold the perverse prince in eternal ties,
Fast bound since first he forfeited the skies.

Heaven's golden-wingèd herald late he saw
To a poor Galilean virgin sent;
How long the bright youth bowed, and with what awe
Immortal flowers to her fair hand present:
He saw the old Hebrew's womb neglect the law
Of age and barrenness; and her Babe prevent
His birth by his devotion, who began
Betimes to be a saint before a man!

Yet, on the other side, fain would he start
Above his fears, and think it cannot be:
He studies Scripture, strives to sound the heart
And feel the pulse of every prophecy,
He knows, but knows not how, or by what art
The heaven-expecting ages hope to see
A mighty Babe, whose pure, unspotted birth
From a chaste virgin womb should bless the earth!

But these vast mysteries his senses smother,
And reason,—for what's faith to him!—devour,
How she that is a maid should prove a mother,
Yet keep inviolate her virgin flower;
How God's eternal Son should be man's brother,
Poseth his proudest intellectual power;
How a pure spirit should incarnate be,
And life itself wear death's frail livery.

That the great angel-blinding light should shrink
His blaze, to shine in a poor shepherd's eye;
That the unmeasured God so low should sink
As prisoner in a few poor rags to lie;
That from his mother's breast He milk should drink,
Who feeds with nectar Heaven's fair family;
That a vile manger his low bed should prove
Who in a throne of stars thunders above.

That He whom the sun serves, should faintly peep
Through clouds of infant flesh: that He the old
Eternal Word would be a child, and weep;
That He who made the fire should feel the cold;
That Heaven's high Majesty his court should keep
In a clay-cottage, by each blast controlled:
That Glory's self should serve our griefs and fears:
And free Eternity submit to years.

RICHARD CRASHAW.

NARAYENA: SPIRIT OF GOD.

Blue crystal vault and elemental fires
That in the aerial fluid blaze and breathe!
Thou tossing sea, whose snaky branches wreath
This pensile orb with intertwisted gyves; —
Mountains whose lofty radiant spires
Presumptuous rear their summits to the skies;
Smooth meads and lawns that glow with vergant dyes
Of dew-bespangled leaves and blossoms bright!
Hence! vanish from my sight:
Delusive pictures! Unsubstantial shows!
My soul absorbed, one only Being knows;
Of all perceptions one abundant source;
Whence every object every moment flows:
Suns hence derive their force;
Hence planets learn their course;
But suns and fading worlds I view no more:
God only I perceive; God only I adore.

Sir William Jones: *Translation.*

PENITENCE.

Great God!
Greater than greatest! better than the best!
Kinder than kindest! with soft pity's eye
Look down—
On a poor breathing particle in dust!
Or, lower, — an immortal in his crimes.
His crimes forgive, forgive his virtues too!
Those smaller faults, half converts to the right.

Young.

AN ODE.

The spacious firmament on high,
With all the blue ethereal sky,
The spangled heavens, a shining frame,
Their great Original proclaim.
The unwearied sun, from day to day,
Does his Creator's power display;
And publishes to every land
The work of an Almighty hand.

Soon as the evening shades prevail,
The moon takes up the wondrous tale,
And nightly, to the listening earth,
Repeats the story of her birth;
Whilst all the stars that round her burn,
And all the planets in their turn,
Confirm the tidings as they roll,
And spread the truth from pole to pole.

What though, in solemn silence, all
Move round this dark, terrestrial ball?
What though nor real voice nor sound
Amidst their radiant orbs be found?
In reason's ear they all rejoice,
And utter forth a glorious voice,
Forever singing as they shine,
"The hand that made us is divine!"

Addison.

TWO WENT UP INTO THE TEMPLE TO PRAY.

Two went to pray? Oh! rather say,
One went to brag, the other to pray.

One stands up close, and treads on high,
Where the other dares not lend his eye.

One nearer to God's altar trod;
The other to the altar's God.

Richard Crashaw.

A HYMN TO CHRIST,

AT THE AUTHOR'S LAST GOING INTO GERMANY.

In what torn ship soever I embark,
That ship shall be my emblem of thy ark;
What sea soever swallow me, that flood
Shall be to me an emblem of thy blood.

Though thou with clouds of anger
do disguise
Thy face, yet through that mask I
know those eyes,
Which, though they turn away sometimes, —
They never will despise.

I sacrifice this island unto thee,
And all whom I love here, and who
love me:
When I have put this flood 'twixt
them and me,
Put thou thy blood betwixt my sins
and thee.
As the tree's sap doth seek the root
below
In winter, in my winter now I go
Where none but thee, the eternal root
Of true love, I may know.

Nor thou, nor thy religion, dost con-
trol
The amorousness of an harmonious
soul;
But thou wouldst have that love
thyself: as thou
Art jealous, Lord, so I am jealous
now.
Thou lov'st not till from loving
more thou free
My soul: who ever gives, takes lib-
erty;
Oh! if thou car'st not whom I love,
Alas, thou lov'st not me!

Seal, then, this bill of my divorce to
all
On whom those fainter beams of
love did fall;
Marry those loves, which in youth
scattered be
On face, wit, hopes (false mistresses),
to thee.
Churches are best for prayer that
have least light;
To see God only, I go out of sight;
And to 'scape stormy days, I choose
An everlasting night.

DONNE.

THE ELIXIR.

TEACH me, my God and King,
In all things thee to see;
And, what I do in any thing,
To do it as for thee:

Not rudely, as a beast,
To run into an action;
But still to make thee prepossessed,
And give it his perfection.

A man that looks on glass
On it may stay his eye;
Or, if he pleaseth, through it pass,
And then the heaven espy.

All may of thee partake:
Nothing can be so mean,
Which with this tincture, *for thy
sake*,
Will not grow bright and clean.

A servant, with this clause,
Makes drudgery divine:
Who sweeps a room, as for thy laws,
Makes that, and the action, fine.

This is the famous stone
That turneth all to gold;
For that which God doth touch and
own
Cannot for less be told.

HERBERT.

SING UNTO THE LORD.

PSALM XCVI.

SING, and let your song be new,
Unto him that never endeth!
Sing all earth, and all in you,
Sing to God, and bless his name.
Of the help, the health he sendeth,
Day by day new ditties frame.

Make each country know his worth:
Of his acts the wondered story
Paint unto each people forth.
For Jehovah great alone,
All the gods for awe and glory,
Far above doth hold his throne,

For but idols, what are they
Whom besides mad earth adoreth?
He the skies in frame did lay;
Grace and honor are his guides;
Majesty his temple storeth;
Might in guard about him bides.

Kindreds come! Jehovah give, —
O give Jehovah all together,
Force and fame whereso you live.
Give his name the glory fit;

Take your offerings, get you thither,
Where he doth enshrinèd sit.

Go, adore him in the place
Where his pomp is most displayed.
Earth, O go with quaking pace,
Go proclaim Jehovah king:
Stayless world shall now be stayed;
Righteous doom his rule shall bring.

Starry roof and earthy floor,
Sea and all thy wideness yieldeth;
Now rejoice, and leap, and roar.
Leafy infants of the wood,
Fields, and all that on you feedeth,
Dance, O dance, at such a good!

For Jehovah cometh, lo!
Lo, to reign Jehovah cometh!
Under whom you all shall go.
He the world shall rightly guide;
Truly, as a king becometh,
For the people's weal provide.

SIR PHILIP SIDNEY.

PSALM XVIII.

THE Lord descended from above,
And bowed the heavens high;
And underneath his feet he cast
The darkness of the sky.

On Cherubim and Seraphim
Full royally he rode;
And on the wings of mighty winds
Came flying all abroad.

He sat serene upon the floods,
Their fury to restrain;
And he as sovereign Lord and King
Forevermore shall reign.

STERNHOLD.

DEPENDENCE.

To keep the lamp alive,
With oil we fill the bowl:
'Tis water makes the willow thrive,
And grace that feeds the soul.

The Lord's unsparing hand
Supplies the living stream:
It is not at our own command,
But still derived from him.

Man's wisdom is to seek
His strength in God alone;
And even an angel would be weak,
Who trusted in his own.

Retreat beneath his wings,
And in his grace confide:
This more exalts the King of kings
Than all your works beside.

In Jesus is our store;
Grace issues from his throne:
Whoever says, "I want no more,"
Confesses he has none.

COWPER.

PROVIDENCE.

GOD moves in a mysterious way
His wonders to perform:
He plants his footsteps in the sea,
And rides upon the storm.

Deep in unfathomable mines
Of never-failing skill,
He treasures up his bright designs,
And works his sovereign will.

Ye fearful saints, fresh courage take:
The clouds ye so much dread
Are big with mercy, and shall break
In blessings on your head.

Judge not the Lord by feeble sense,
But trust him for his grace:
Behind a frowning providence
He hides a smiling face.

His purposes will ripen fast,
Unfolding every hour:
The bud may have a bitter taste;
But sweet will be the flower.

Blind unbelief is sure to err,
And scan his works in vain:
God is his own interpreter;
And he will make it plain.

COWPER.

PROVIDENCE.

O SACRED Providence, who from end to end
Strongly and sweetly movest! shall I write,

And not of thee, through whom my fingers bend
To hold my quill? shall they not do thee right?

Wherefore, most sacred Spirit, I here present,
For me and all my fellows, praise to thee:
And just it is that I should pay the rent,
Because the benefit accrues to me.

Tempests are calm to thee: they know thy hand,
And hold it fast, as children do their fathers,
Which cry and follow. Thou hast made poore sand
Check the proud sea, even when it swells and gathers.

How finely dost thou times and seasons spin,
And make a twist checkered with night and day!
Which as it lengthens, windes and windes us in,
As bowls go on, but turning all the way.

Bees work for man; and yet they never bruise
Their master's flower, but leave it, having done,
As fair as ever, and as fit to use:
So both the flower doth stay, and honey run.

Who hath the virtue to expresse the rare
And curious virtues both of herbs and stones?
Is there an herb for that? O that thy care
Would show a root that gives expressions!

The sea which seems to stop the traveller,
Is by a ship the speedier passage made:
The windes, who think they rule the mariner,
Are ruled by him, and taught to serve his trade.

Rain, do not hurt my flowers, but gently spend
Your honey drops; presse not to smell them here:
When they are ripe, their odor will ascend,
And at your lodging with their thanks appeare.

Sometimes thou dost divide thy gifts to man;
Sometimes unite. The Indian nut alone
Is clothing, meat, and trencher, drink and can,
Boat, cable, sail and needle, all in one.

Each thing that is, although in use and name
It go for one, hath many ways in store
To honor thee; and so each hymn thy fame
Extolleth many ways, yet this one more.

HERBERT.

PRAISE TO GOD.

PRAISE to God, immortal praise,
For the love that crowns our days:
Bounteous source of every joy,
Let thy praise our tongues employ;

For the blessings of the field,
For the stores the gardens yield,
For the vine's exalted juice,
For the generous olive's use;

Flocks that whiten all the plain,
Yellow sheaves of ripened grain;
Clouds that drop their fattening dews,
Suns that temperate warmth diffuse;

All that Spring with bounteous hand
Scatters o'er the smiling land:
All that liberal Autumn pours
From her rich o'erflowing stores:

These to thee, my God, we owe;
Source whence all our blessings flow;
And for these my soul shall raise
Grateful vows and solemn praise.

Yet should rising whirlwinds tear
From its stem the ripening ear;
Should the fig-tree's blasted shoot
Drop her green untimely fruit;

Should the vine put forth no more,
Nor the olive yield her store;
Though the sickening flocks should fall,
And the herds desert the stall;

Should thine altered hand restrain
The early and the latter rain,
Blast each opening bud of joy,
And the rising year destroy:

Yet to thee my soul should raise
Grateful vows and solemn praise;
And, when every blessing's flown,
Love thee — for thyself alone.

BARBAULD.

AFFLICTION.

WHEN first Thou didst entice to Thee my heart,
I thought the service brave;
So many joys I writ down for my part!
Besides what I might have
Out of my stock of natural delights,
Augmented with Thy gracious benefits.

I lookèd on Thy furniture so fine,
And made it fine to me.
Thy glorious household stuff did me intwine,
And 'tice me unto Thee.
Such stars I counted mine: both heaven and earth
Paid me my wages in a world of mirth.

What pleasure could I want, whose King I served?
Where joys my fellows were?
Thus argued into hopes, my thoughts reserved
No place for grief or fear:
Therefore my sudden soul caught at the place,
And made her youth and fierceness seek Thy face.

At first Thou gav'st me milk and sweetnesses;
I had my wish and way:
My days were strewed with flowers and happiness:
There was no month but May:
But with my years sorrow did twist and grow,
And made a party unawares for woe.

Whereas my birth and spirit rather took
The way that takes the town;
Thou didst betray me to a lingering book,
And wrap me in a gown.
I was entangled in a world of strife,
Before I had the power to change my life.

Yet lest perchance I should too happy be
In my unhappiness,
Turning my purge to food, Thou throwest me
Into more sicknesses.
Thus does Thy power cross-bias me, not making
Thine own gift good, yet me from my ways taking.

Now I am here; what Thou wilt do with me,
None of my books will show:
I read, and sigh, and wish I were a tree;
For sure then I should grow
To fruit, or shade; at least some bird would trust
Her household to me, and I should be just.

Yet though Thou troublest me, I must be meek;
In weakness must be stout.
Well, I will change the service, and go seek
Some other master out.
Ah, my dear God! though I am clean forgot,
Let me not love Thee, if I love Thee not.

HERBERT.

GRATEFULNESS.

THOU that hast given so much to me,
Give one thing more, — a grateful heart.
See how Thy beggar works on Thee
By art:

He makes Thy gifts occasion more,
And says—If he in this be crost,
All Thou hast given him heretofore
Is lost.

But Thou didst reckon, when at first
Thy word our hearts and hands did crave,
What it would come to at the worst
To save.

Perpetual knockings at Thy door,
Tears sullying Thy transparent rooms,
Gift upon gift, much would have more,
And comes.

This notwithstanding, thou went'st on,
And didst allow us all our noise;
Nay, Thou hast made a sigh and groan,
Thy joys.

Not that Thou hast not still above
Much better tunes than groans can make,
But that these country airs Thy love
Did take.

Wherefore I cry, and cry again;
And in no quiet canst Thou be,
Till I a thankful heart obtain
Of Thee.

Not thankful when it pleaseth me,—
As if Thy blessings had spare days,—
But such a heart, whose pulse may be
Thy praise.

HERBERT.

MATINS.

WHEN with the virgin morning thou dost rise,
Crossing thyself, come thus to sacrifice;
First wash thy heart in innocence, then bring
Pure hands, pure habits, pure, pure every thing.
Next to the altar humbly kneel, and thence
Give up thy soul in clouds of frankincense.
Thy golden censers filled with odors sweet
Shall make thy actions with their ends to meet.

HERRICK.

BEFORE SLEEP.

THE night is come like to the day,—
Depart not thou, great God, away,
Let not my sins, black as the night,
Eclipse the lustre of thy light.
Keep still in my horizon; for to me
The sun makes not the day, but thee.
Thou, whose nature cannot sleep,
On my temples sentry keep;
Guard me 'gainst those watchful foes
Whose eyes are open while mine close.
Let no dreams my head infest
But such as Jacob's temples blest.
While I do rest, my soul advance,
Make my sleep a holy trance,
That I may, my rest being wrought,
Awake into some holy thought,
And with as active vigor run
My course, as doth the nimble sun,
Sleep is a death; O make me try
By sleeping, what it is to die:
And as gently lay my head
On my grave, as now my bed.
Howe'er I rest, great God, let me
Awake again at least with thee;
And thus assured, behold I lie
Secure, or to awake or die.
These are my drowsy days; in vain
I do now wake to sleep again;—
O come that hour, when I shall never
Sleep again, but wake forever.

SIR THOMAS BROWNE.

HYMN.

LORD, when I quit this earthly stage,
Where shall I fly but to thy breast?
For I have sought no other home,
For I have learned no other rest.

I cannot live contented here,
Without some glimpses of thy face;
And heaven without thy presence there
Would be a dark and tiresome place.

When earthly cares engross the day,
And hold my thoughts aside from thee,
The shining hours of cheerful light
Are long and tedious years to me.

And if no evening visit's paid
Between my Saviour and my soul,
How dull the night! how sad the shade!
How mournfully the minutes roll!

My God! and can a humble child
That loves thee with a flame so high,
Be ever from thy face exiled,
Without the pity of thy eye?

Impossible! for thine own hands
Have tied my heart so fast to thee;
And in thy book the promise stands
That where thou art thy friends must be.

WATTS.

HYMN TO GOD, MY GOD, IN MY SICKNESS.

SINCE I am coming to that holy room,
Where with the choir of saints forevermore
I shall be made thy music, as I come
I tune the instrument here at the door,
And what I must do then, think here before.

We think that Paradise and Calvary,
Christ's cross and Adam's tree, stood in one place:
Look, Lord, and find both Adams met in me;
As the first Adam's sweat surrounds my face,
May the last Adam's blood my soul embrace.

So, in his purple wrapped, receive me, Lord;
By these his thorns give me his other crown;
And as to others' souls I preached thy word,
Be this my text, my sermon to mine own:
Therefore, that he may raise, the Lord throws down.

DONNE.

LITANY TO THE HOLY SPIRIT.

IN the hour of my distress,
When temptations me oppress,
And when I my sins confess,
Sweet Spirit, comfort me!

When I lie within my bed,
Sick at heart, and sick in head,
And with doubts discomforted,
Sweet Spirit, comfort me!

When the house doth sigh and weep,
And the world is drowned in sleep,
Yet mine eyes the watch do keep,
Sweet Spirit, comfort me!

When the artless doctor sees
No one hope, but of his fees,
And his skill runs on the lees,
Sweet Spirit, comfort me!

When his potion and his pill,
Has or none or little skill,
Meet for nothing, but to kill, —
Sweet Spirit, comfort me!

When the passing bell doth toll,
And the Furies, in a shoal,
Come to fright a parting soul,
Sweet Spirit, comfort me!

When the tapers now burn blue,
And the comforters are few,
And that number more than true,
Sweet Spirit, comfort me!

When the priest his last hath prayed,
And I nod to what is said,
Because my speech is now decayed,
Sweet Spirit, comfort me!

When, God knows, I'm tost about
Either with despair or doubt,
Yet before the glass be out,
Sweet Spirit, comfort me!

When the Tempter me pursu'th
With the sins of all my youth,
And half damns me with untruth,
Sweet Spirit, comfort me!

When the flames and hellish cries
Fright mine ears, and fright mine eyes,
And all terrors me surprise,
Sweet Spirit, comfort me!

When the judgment is revealed,
And that opened which was sealed;
When to Thee I have appealed,
Sweet Spirit, comfort me!

HERRICK.

CHRISTMAS HYMN.

I.

It was the winter wild,
While the heaven-born child
All meanly wrapt in the rude manger lies;
Nature in awe to him
Had doff'd her gaudy trim,
With her great Master so to sympathize:
It was no season then for her
To wanton with the sun, her lusty paramour.

II.

Only with speeches fair
She wooes the gentle air
To hide her guilty front with innocent snow,
And on her naked shame,
Pollute with sinful blame,
The saintly veil of maiden white to throw;
Confounded that her Maker's eyes
Should look so near upon her foul deformities.

III.

But He, her fears to cease,
Sent down the meek-eyed Peace;
She, crowned with olive green, came softly sliding
Down through the turning sphere
His ready harbinger,
With turtle wing the amorous clouds dividing;
And waving wide her myrtle wand,
She strikes a universal peace through sea and land.

IV.

No war, or battle's sound,
Was heard the world around:
The idle spear and shield were high uphung,
The hookèd chariot stood
Unstained with hostile blood,
The trumpet spake not to the armèd throng,
And kings sat still with awful eye,
As if they surely knew their sovereign Lord was by.

V.

But peaceful was the night
Wherein the Prince of light
His reign of peace upon the earth began:
The winds, with wonder whist,
Smoothly the waters kist,
Whispering new joys to the mild ocean,
Who now hath quite forgot to rave,
While birds of calm sit brooding on the charmèd wave.

VI.

The stars with deep amaze
Stand fixed in steadfast gaze,
Bending one way their precious influence,
And will not take their flight,
For all the morning light,
Or Lucifer, that often warned them thence;
But in their glimmering orbs did glow,
Until their Lord himself bespake, and bade them go.

VII.

And though the shady gloom
Had given day her room,
The sun himself withheld his wonted speed,
And hid his head for shame,
As his inferior flame
The new enlightened world no more should need;
He saw a greater sun appear
Than his bright throne or burning axletree could bear.

VIII.

The shepherds on the lawn,
Or e'er the point of dawn,
Sat simply chatting in a rustic row;
Full little thought they then
That the mighty Pan
Was kindly come to live with them below;

Perhaps their loves, or else their
sheep,
Was all that did their silly thoughts
so busy keep.

IX.

When such music sweet
Their hearts and ears did greet,
As never was by mortal finger
strook,
Divinely-warbled voice
Answering the stringèd noise,
As all their souls in blissful rap-
ture took:
The air, such pleasure loath to lose,
With thousand echoes still prolongs
each heavenly close.

X.

Nature, that heard such sound,
Beneath the hollow round
Of Cynthia's seat, the airy region
thrilling,
Now was almost won
To think her part was done,
And that her reign had here its
last fulfilling;
She knew such harmony alone
Could hold all heaven and earth in
happier union.

XI.

At last surrounds their sight
A globe of circular light,
That with long beams the shame-
faced night arrayed;
The helmèd Cherubim,
And sworded Seraphim,
Are seen in glittering ranks with
wings displayed,
Harping in loud and solemn quire,
With unexpressive notes, to Heaven's
new-born Heir.

XII.

Such music (as 'tis said)
Before was never made,
But when of old the sons of morn-
ing sung,
While the Creator great
His constellations set,
And the well-balanced world on
hinges hung,
And cast the dark foundations deep,
And bid the weltering waves their
oozy channel keep.

XIII.

Ring out, ye crystal spheres,
Once bless our human ears,
If ye have power to touch our
senses so;
And let your silver chime
Move in melodious time,
And let the base of heaven's deep
organ blow;
And with your ninefold harmony
Make up full consort to the angelic
symphony.

XIV.

For if such holy song
Inwrap our fancy long,
Time will run back, and fetch the
age of gold;
And speckled Vanity
Will sicken soon and die,
And leprous Sin will melt from
earthly mould;
And Hell itself will pass away,
And leave her dolorous mansions to
the peering day.

XV.

Yea, Truth and Justice then
Will down return to men,
Orbed in a rainbow; and, like
glories wearing,
Mercy will sit between,
Throned in celestial sheen,
With radiant feet the tissued
clouds down steering:
And heaven, as at some festival,
Will open wide the gates of her high
palace hall.

XVI.

But wisest Fate says, no,
This must not yet be so,
The babe yet lies in smiling in-
fancy,
That on the bitter cross
Must redeem our loss;
So both himself and us to glorify;
Yet first to those ychained in sleep,
The wakeful trump of doom must
thunder through the deep,

XVII.

With such a horrid clang
As on Mount Sinai rang,
While the red fire, and smoulder-
ing clouds outbrake:

The aged earth aghast,
With terror of that blast,
Shall from the surface to the centre shake;
When at the world's last session,
The dreadful Judge in middle air shall spread his throne.

XVIII.

And then at last our bliss
Full and perfect is,
But now begins; for, from this happy day,
The old Dragon under ground
In straiter limits bound,
Not half so far casts his usurpèd sway,
And, wroth to see his kingdom fail,
Swinges the scaly horror of his folded tail.

XIX.

The oracles are dumb;
No voice or hideous hum
Runs through the archèd roof in words deceiving.
Apollo from his shrine
Can no more divine,
With hollow shriek the steep of Delphos leaving.
No nightly trance or breathèd spell
Inspires the pale-eyed priest from the prophetic cell.

XX.

The lonely mountains o'er,
And the resounding shore,
A voice of weeping heard and loud lament;
From haunted spring, and dale
Edged with poplar pale,
The parting Genius is with sighing sent;
With flower-inwoven tresses torn,
The Nymphs in twilight shade of tangled thickets mourn.

XXI.

In consecrated earth,
And on the holy hearth,
The Lars and Lemures moan with midnight plaint;
In urns and altars round,
A drear and dying sound
Affrights the Flamens at their service quaint;
And the chill marble seems to sweat,
While each peculiar Power foregoes his wonted seat.

XXII.

Peor and Baälim
Forsake their temples dim,
With that twice-battered god of Palestine;
And moonèd Ashtaroth,
Heaven's queen and mother both,
Now sits not girt with tapers' holy shine;
The Lybic Hammon shrinks his horn;
In vain the Tyrian maids their wounded Thammuz mourn.

XXIII.

And sullen Moloch fled,
Hath left in shadows dread
His burning idol all of blackest hue;
In vain with cymbals' ring
They call the grisly king,
In dismal dance about the furnace blue:
The brutish gods of Nile as fast,
Isis and Orus, and the dog Anubis, haste.

XXIV.

Nor is Osiris seen
In Memphian grove or green,
Trampling the unshowered grass with lowings loud:
Nor can he be at rest
Within his sacred chest;
Nought but profoundest hell can be his shroud;
In vain with timbrelled anthems dark
The sable-stolèd sorcerers bear his worshipped ark.

XXV.

He feels from Judah's land
The dreaded Infant's hand;
The rays of Bethlehem blind his dusky eyn;
Nor all the gods beside,
Longer dare abide;
Not Typhon huge ending in snaky twine:
Our babe, to show his Godhead true,
Can in his swaddling bands control the damnèd crew.

XXVI.

So when the sun in bed,
Curtained with cloudy red,
Pillows his chin upon an orient wave,
The flocking shadows pale
Troop to the infernal jail,
Each fettered ghost slips to his several grave:
And the yellow-skirted Fayes
Fly after the night-steeds, leaving their moon-loved maze.

XXVII.

But see the Virgin blest
Hath laid her Babe to rest;
Time is our tedious song should here have ending;
Heaven's youngest-teemèd star
Hath fixed her polished car,
Her sleeping Lord with handmaid lamp attending;
And all about the courtly stable
Bright-harnessed angels sit in order serviceable.

MILTON.

THE SHEPHERDS.

O THAN the fairest day, thrice fairer night!
Night to best days, in which a sun doth rise
Of which that Golden eye which clears the skies
Is but a sparkling ray, a shadow light!
And blessèd ye, in silly pastors' sight,
Wild creátures in whose warm crib now lies
That heaven-sent youngling, holy maid-born wight,
'Midst, end, beginning of our prophecies!
Blest cottage that hath flowers in winter spread!
Though withered,—blessed grass, that hath the grace
To deck and be a carpet to that place!
Thus sang unto the sounds of oaten reed,
Before the Babe, the shepherds bowed on knees;
And springs ran nectar, honey dropped from trees.

DRUMMOND.

THE ANGELS.

RUN, shepherds, run where Bethlehem blest appears.
We bring the best of news; be not dismayed:
A Saviour there is born more old than years,
Amidst heaven's rolling height this earth who stayed.
In a poor cottage inned, a virgin maid
A weakling did him bear, who all upbears;
There is he poorly swaddled, in manger laid,
To whom too narrow swaddlings are our spheres:
Run, shepherds, run, and solemnize his birth.
This is that night—no, day, grown great with bliss,
In which the power of Satan broken is:
In heaven be glory, peace unto the earth!
Thus singing, through the air the angels swarm,
And cope of stars re-echoèd the same.

DRUMMOND.

THE STAR SONG.

TELL us, thou clear and heavenly tongue,
Where is the Babe but lately sprung?
Lies he the lily-banks among?

Or say, if this new Birth of ours
Sleeps, laid within some ark of flowers,
Spangled with dew-light; thou canst clear
All doubts, and manifest the where.

Declare to us, bright star, if we shall seek
Him in the morning's blushing cheek,
Or search the beds of spices through,
To find him out?

Star.—No, this ye need not do;
But only come and see Him rest,
A princely babe, in's mother's breast.

HERRICK.

NEW PRINCE, NEW POMP.

BEHOLD a silly, tender Babe,
In freezing winter night,
In homely manger trembling lies;
Alas! a piteous sight.

The inns are full; no man will yield
This little Pilgrim bed;
But forced he is with silly beasts
In crib to shroud his head.

Despise him not for lying there;
First what he is inquire:
An Orient pearl is often found
In depth of dirty mire.

Weigh not his crib, his wooden dish,
Nor beasts that by him feed;
Weigh not his mother's poor attire,
Nor Joseph's simple weed.

This stable is a Prince's court,
The crib his chair of state;
The beasts are parcel of his pomp,
The wooden dish his plate.

The persons in that poor attire
His royal liveries wear;
The Prince himself is come from heaven:
This pomp is praisèd there.

With joy approach, O Christian wight!
Do homage to thy King;
And highly praise this humble pomp,
Which he from heaven doth bring.

SOUTHWELL.

THE BURNING BABE.

As I in hoary winter's night
Stood shivering in the snow,
Surprised I was by sudden heat
Which made my heart to glow;

And lifting up a fearful eye
To view what fire was near,
A pretty babe all burning bright,
Did in the air appear;

Who, scorchèd with excessive heat,
Such floods of tears did shed,
As though his floods should quench his flames;
Which with his tears were bred:

Alas, quoth he, but newly born,
In fiery heats I fry,
Yet none approach to warm their hearts
Or feel the fire, but I.

My faultless breast the furnace is;
The fuel wounding thorns;
Love is the fire, and sighs the smoke,
The ashes shames and scorns.

The fuel justice layeth on,
And mercy blows the coals;
The metal in this furnace wrought
Are men's defilèd souls —

For which, as now on fire I am,
To work them to their good,
So will I melt into a bath,
To wash them in my blood.

With this he vanished out of sight,
And swiftly shrunk away,
And straight I callèd unto mind
That it was Christmas Day.

SOUTHWELL.

THE CHRISTMAS CAROL.

THE minstrels played their Christmas tune
To-night beneath my cottage-eaves;
While, smitten by a lofty moon,
The encircling laurels, thick with leaves,
Gave back a rich and dazzling sheen,
That overpowered their natural green.

Through hill and valley every breeze
Had sunk to rest with folded wings:
Keen was the air, but could not freeze,
Nor check, the music of the strings;
So stout and hardy were the band
That scraped the chords with strenuous hand!

And who but listened? — till was paid
Respect to every inmate's claim:
The greeting given, the music played,
In honor of each household name,
Duly pronounced with lusty call,
And "Merry Christmas" wished to all!

How touching, when, at midnight, sweep
Snow-muffled winds, and all is dark,
To hear, and sink again to sleep!
Or, at an earlier call, to mark,
By blazing fire, the still suspense
Of self-complacent innocence;

The mutual nod, — the grave disguise
Of hearts with gladness brimming o'er;
And some unbidden tears that rise
For names once heard, and heard no more;
Tears brightened by the serenade
For infant in the cradle laid.

Hail, ancient Manners! sure defence,
Where they survive, of wholesome laws;
Remnants of love whose modest sense
Thus into narrow room withdraws;
Hail, Usages of pristine mould,
And ye that guard them, Mountains old!

WORDSWORTH.

CHRISTMAS.

RING out, wild bells, to the wild sky,
The flying cloud, the frosty light:
The year is dying in the night —
Ring out, wild bells, and let him die.

Ring out the old, ring in the new —
Ring, happy bells, across the snow;
The year is going, let him go;
Ring out the false, ring in the true.

Ring out the grief that saps the mind,
For those that here we see no more;
Ring out the feud of rich and poor,
Ring in redress for all mankind.

Ring out a slowly dying cause,
And ancient forms of party strife;
Ring in the nobler modes of life,
With sweeter manners, purer laws.

Ring out the want, the care, the sin,
The faithless coldness of the times:
Ring out, ring out my mournful rhymes,
But ring the fuller minstrel in.

Ring out false pride in place and blood,
The civic slander and the spite:
Ring in the love of truth and right,
Ring in the common love of good.

Ring out old shapes of foul disease,
Ring out the narrowing lust of gold;
Ring out the thousand wars of old,
Ring in the thousand years of peace.

Ring in the valiant man and free,
The larger heart, the kindlier hand;
Ring out the darkness of the land, —
Ring in the Christ that is to be.

TENNYSON.

EASTER.

I GOT me flowers to strew Thy way;
I got me boughs off many a tree;
But thou wast up by break of day,
And brought'st Thy sweets along with Thee.

The sun arising in the east, —
Though *he* give light, and the east perfume;
If they should offer to contest
With Thy arising, they presume.

Can there be any day but this,
Though many suns to shine endeavor?
We count three hundred, — but we miss:
There is but one, and that one ever.

HERBERT.

V.

HEROIC.

PATRIOTIC. — HISTORIC. — POLITICAL.

"*Pallas.* — See yonder souls set far within the shade,
Who in Elysian bowers the blessèd seats do keep,
That for their living good now semi-gods are made,
And went away from earth, as if but tamed with sleep.
These we must join to wake; for these are of the strain
That Justice dare defend, and will the Age sustain."

BEN JONSON: *Golden Age Restored.*

HEROIC.

ON THE LATE MASSACRE IN PIEMONT.

AVENGE, O Lord, thy slaughtered saints, whose bones
Lie scattered on the Alpine mountains cold;
Even them who kept thy truth so pure of old,
When all our fathers worshipped stocks and stones,
Forget not: in thy book record their groans
Who were thy sheep, and in their ancient fold
Slain by the bloody Piemontese that rolled
Mother with infant down the rocks. Their moans
The vales redoubled to the hills, and they
To Heaven. Their martyred blood and ashes sow
O'er all the Italian fields, where still doth sway
The triple tyrant; that from these may grow
A hundred-fold, who, having learned thy way,
Early may fly the Babylonian woe.

MILTON.

HEROISM.

AT the approach
Of extreme peril, when a hollow image
Is found a hollow image and no more,
Then falls the power into the mighty hands
Of Nature, of the spirit giant-born,
Who listens only to himself, knows nothing
Of stipulations, duties, reverences,
And, like the emancipated force of fire,
Unmastered scorches, ere it reaches them,
Their fine-spun webs.

COLERIDGE'S *Translation of "Wallenstein."*

CONSTANCY.

WHO is the honest man?
He that doth still and strongly good pursue;
To God, his neighbor, and himself, most true.
Whom neither force nor fawning can
Unpin, or wrench from giving all their due.

Whose honesty is not
So loose or easy, that a ruffling wind
Can blow away, or glittering look it blind.
Who rides his sure and even trot,
While the world now rides by, now lags behind.

Who, when great trials come,
Nor seeks, nor shuns them, but doth calmly stay,
Till he the thing and the example weigh.

All being brought into a sum,
What place or person calls for, he doth pay.

Whom none can work or woo,
To use in any thing a trick, or sleight;
For above all things he abhors deceit.
His words and works, and fashion too,
All of a piece; and all are clear and straight.

Who never melts or thaws
At close temptations. When the day is done,
His goodness sets not, but in dark can run.
The sun to others writeth laws,
And is their virtue: virtue is *his* sun.

Who, when he is to treat
With sick folks, women, those whom passions sway,
Allows for that, and keeps his constant way;
Whom others' faults do not defeat;
But, though men fail him, yet his part doth play.

Whom nothing can procure,
When the wide world runs bias, from his will
To writhe his limbs, and share, not mend, the ill.
This is the marksman safe and sure;
Who still is right, and prays to be so still.

HERBERT.

EPISTLE TO A FRIEND, TO PERSUADE HIM TO THE WARS.

TAKE along with thee
Thy true friend's wishes, Colby, which shall be,
That thine be just and honest, that thy deeds
Not wound thy conscience, when thy body bleeds;
That thou dost all things more for truth than glory,
And never but for doing wrong be sorry;
That, by commanding first thyself, thou mak'st
Thy person fit for any charge thou tak'st;
That Fortune never make thee to complain,
But what she gives, thou dar'st give her again!
That, whatsoever face thy Fate puts on,
Thou shrink or start not, but be always one:
That thou think nothing great, but what is good;
And from that thought strive to be understood.
These take, and now go seek thy peace in war:
Who falls for love of God shall rise a star.

BEN JONSON.

THE HAPPY WARRIOR.

WHO is the happy warrior? Who is he
Whom every man in arms should wish to be?
It is the generous spirit, who, when brought
Among the tasks of real life, hath wrought
Upon the plan that pleased his childish thought:
Whose high endeavors are an inward light
That make the path before him always bright;
Who, with a natural instinct to discern
What knowledge can perform, is diligent to learn;
Abides by this resolve, and stops not there,
But makes his moral being his prime care;
Who, doomed to go in company with pain,
And fear, and bloodshed, miserable train!
Turns his necessity to glorious gain;
In face of these doth exercise a power
Which is our human nature's highest dower;

Controls them and subdues, transmutes, bereaves
Of their bad influence, and their good receives;
By objects which might force the soul to abate
Her feeling, rendered more compassionate;
Is placable, — because occasions rise
So often that demand such sacrifice;
More skilful in self-knowledge, even more pure,
As tempted more; more able to endure,
As more exposed to suffering and distress;
Thence, also, more alive to tenderness.
—'Tis he whose law is reason; who depends
Upon that law as on the best of friends;
Whence, in a state where men are tempted still
To evil for a guard against worse ill,
And what in quality or act is best
Doth seldom on a right foundation rest,
He fixes good on good alone, and owes
To virtue every triumph that he knows;
— Who, if he rise to station of command,
Rises by open means; and there will stand
On honorable terms, or else retire,
And in himself possess his own desire;
Who comprehends his trust, and to the same
Keeps faithful with a singleness of aim;
And therefore does not stoop, nor lie in wait
For wealth, or honors, or for worldly state:
Whom they must follow; on whose head must fall,
Like showers of manna, if they come at all;
Whose powers shed round him in the common strife,
Or mild concerns of ordinary life,
A constant influence, a peculiar grace;
But who, if he be called upon to face
Some awful moment to which Heaven has joined
Great issues, good or bad for human kind,
Is happy as a lover; and attired
With sudden brightness like a man inspired;
And, through the heat of conflict, keeps the law
In calmness made, and sees what he foresaw;
Or if an unexpected call succeed,
Come when it will, is equal to the need:
— He who, though thus endued as with a sense
And faculty for storm and turbulence,
Is yet a soul whose master bias leans
To homefelt pleasures and to gentle scenes;
Sweet images! which, wheresoe'er he be,
Are at his heart; and such fidelity
It is his darling passion to approve;
More brave for this, that he hath much to love:
'Tis, finally, the man, who, lifted high,
Conspicuous object in a nation's eye,
Or left unthought of in obscurity, —
Who, with a toward or untoward lot,
Prosperous or adverse, to his wish or not,
Plays, in the many games of life, that one
Where what he most doth value must be won;
Whom neither shape of danger can dismay,
Nor thought of tender happiness betray;
Who, not content that former worth stand fast,
Looks forward persevering to the last,
From well to better, daily self-surpassed:
Who, whether praise of him must walk the earth
Forever, and to noble deeds give birth,
Or he must go to dust without his fame,
And leave a dead, unprofitable name, —

Finds comfort in himself and in his cause;
And, while the mortal mist is gathering, draws
His breath in confidence of Heaven's applause:
This is the happy warrior: this is he
Whom every man in arms should wish to be.

WORDSWORTH.

CHRISTIAN MILITANT.

A MAN prepared against all ills to come,
That dares to dead the fire of martyrdom;
That sleeps at home, and sailing there at ease,
Fears not the fierce sedition of the seas;
That's counterproof against the farm's mishaps;
Undreadful too of courtly thunderclaps;
That wears one face, like heaven, and never shows
A change, when fortune either comes or goes;
That keeps his own strong guard, in the despite
Of what can hurt by day, or harm by night;
That takes and re-delivers every stroke
Of chance, as made up all of rock and oak;
That sighs at other's death, smiles at his own
Most dire and horrid crucifixion;
Who for true glory suffers thus, we grant
Him to be here our Christian militant.

HERRICK.

THE PRAYER.

AH God, for a man with heart, head, hand,
Like some of the simple great ones gone
For ever and ever by,
One still strong man in a blatant land,
Whatever they call him, what care I,
Aristocrat, democrat, autocrat—one
Who can rule, and dare not lie!

TENNYSON.

ROYALTY.

THAT regal soul I reverence, in whose eyes
Suffices not all worth the city knows
To pay that debt which his own heart he owes;
For less than level to his bosom rise
The low crowd's heaven and stars: above their skies
Runneth the road his daily feet have pressed;
A loftier heaven he beareth in his breast,
And o'er the summits of achieving hies
With never a thought of merit or of meed;
Choosing divinest labors through a pride
Of soul, that holdeth appetite to feed
Ever on angel-herbage, nought beside;
Nor praises more himself for hero-deed
Than stones for weight, or open seas for tide.

D. A. WASSON.

THE MASTER SPIRIT.

GIVE me a Spirit that on life's rough sea
Loves to have his sails filled with a lusty wind,
Even till his sailyards tremble, his masts crack,
And his rapt ship run on her side so low
That she drinks water, and her keel ploughs air:
There is no danger to a man that knows

Where life and death is; there's not any law
Exceeds his knowledge, neither is it needful
That he should stoop to any other law;
He goes before them, and commands them all,
That to himself is a law rational.

GEORGE CHAPMAN.

CHIVALRY.

THE house of Chivalry decayed,
Or rather ruined seems, her buildings laid
Flat with the Earth, that were the pride of Time;
Those obelisks and columns broke and down,
That strook the stars, and raised the British Crown
To be a constellation.
When to the structure went more noble names
Than to the Ephesian Temple lost in flames,
When every stone was laid by virtuous hands.

BEN JONSON.

SAMSON AGONISTES.

Samson. — O DARK, dark, dark, amid the blaze of noon,
Irrecoverably dark, total eclipse
Without all hope of day!
O first created beam, and thou great Word,
"Let there be light, and light was over all;"
Why am I thus bereaved thy prime decree?
The sun to me is dark
And silent as the moon,
When she deserts the night,
Hid in her vacant interlunar cave.

. . . .

Chorus. — This, this is he; softly a while,
Let us not break in upon him;
O change beyond report, thought, or belief!
See how he lies at random, carelessly diffused,
With languished head unpropped,
As one past hope, abandoned,
And by himself given over;
In slavish habit, ill-fitted weeds
O'er-worn and soiled;
Or do my eyes misrepresent? can this be he,
That heroic, that renowned,
Irresistible Samson? whom unarmed
No strength of man or fiercest wild beast could withstand;
Who tore the lion, as the lion tears the kid,
Ran on embattled armies clad in iron,
And, weaponless himself,
Made arms ridiculous, useless the forgery
Of brazen shield and spear, the hammered cuirass,
Chalybean tempered steel, and frock of mail
Adamantëan proof;
But safest he who stood aloof,
When insupportably his foot advanced,
In scorn of their proud arms and warlike tools,
Spurned them to death by troops. The bold Ascalonite
Fled from his lion ramp; old warriors turned
Their plated backs under his heel,
Or, grovelling, soiled their crested helmets in the dust.
Then with what trivial weapon came to hand,
The jaw of a dead ass, his sword of bone,
A thousand foreskins fell, the flower of Palestine
In Ramath-lechi, famous to this day:
Then by main force pulled up, and on his shoulders bore
The gates of Azza, post, and massy bar,
Up to the hill by Hebron, seat of giants old,
No journey of a Sabbath day, and loaded so;
Like whom the Gentiles feign to bear up heaven.
Which shall I first bewail,
Thy bondage or lost sight,
Prison within prison
Inseparably dark?

Thou art become, O worst imprisonment!
The dungeon of thyself; thy soul,
Which men enjoying sight oft without cause complain,
Imprisoned now indeed,
In real darkness of the body dwells,
Shut up from outward light,
T' incorporate with gloomy night.

. . . .

Oh, how comely it is, and how reviving
To the spirits of just men long oppressed,
When God into the hands of their deliverer
Puts invincible might
To quell the mighty of the earth, the oppressor,
The brute and boisterous force of violent men,
Hardy and industrious to support
Tyrannic power, but raging to pursue
The righteous, and all such as honor truth!
He all their ammunition
And feats of war defeats,
With plain heroic magnitude of mind
And celestial vigor armed;
Their armories and magazines contemns,
Renders them useless, while
With wingèd expedition,
Swift as the lightning glance, he executes
His errand on the wicked, who surprised
Lose their defence, distracted and amazed.

. . . .

Officer. — Samson, to thee our lords thus bid me say;
This day to Dagon is a solemn feast,
With sacrifices, triumph, pomp, and games;
Thy strength they know surpassing human rate,
And now some public proof thereof require
To honor this great feast and great assembly;
Rise therefore with all speed and come along,
Where I will see thee heartened and fresh clad
T' appear as fits before the illustrious lords.

Sams. — Thou know'st I am an Hebrew, therefore tell them,
Our law forbids at their religious rites
My presence; for that cause I cannot come.

. . . .

Chor. — How thou wilt here come off surmounts my reach.

Sams. — Be of good courage, I begin to feel
Some rousing motions in me, which dispose
To something extraordinary my thoughts.
I with this messenger will go along,
Nothing to do, be sure, that may dishonor
Our law, or stain my vow of Nazarite.
If there be aught of presage in the mind,
This day will be remarkable in my life
By some great act, or of my days the last.

Chor. — In time thou hast resolved; the man returns.

Off. — Samson, this second message from our lords
To thee I am bid say. Art thou our slave,
Our captive, at the public mill our drudge,
And dar'st thou at our sending and command
Dispute thy coming? come without delay;
Or we shall find such engines to assail
And hamper thee, as thou shalt come of force,
Though thou wert firmlier fastened than a rock.

Sams. — I could be well content to try their art,
Which to no few of them would prove pernicious;
Yet knowing their advantages too many,
Because they shall not trail me through their streets
Like a wild beast, I am content to go.

. . . .

Manoah. — O what noise!
Mercy of heaven, what hideous noise was that!

Horribly loud, unlike the former shout.
Chor. — To our wish I see one hither speeding,
An Hebrew, as I guess, and of our tribe.
Messenger. — Gaza yet stands, but all her sons are fallen,
All in a moment overwhelmed and fallen.

. . . .

Occasions drew me early to this city,
And as the gates I entered with sunrise,
The morning trumpets festival proclaimed
Through each high-street. Little I had despatched
When all abroad was rumored, that this day
Samson should be brought forth to show the people
Proof of his mighty strength in feats and games;
I sorrowed at his captive state, but minded
Not to be absent at that spectacle.
The building was a spacious theatre,
Half-round, on two main pillars vaulted high,
With seats, where all the lords and each degree
Of sort might sit in order to behold;
The other side was open, where the throng
On banks and scaffolds under sky might stand;
I among these aloof obscurely stood.
The feast and noon grew high, and sacrifice
Had filled their hearts with mirth, high cheer, and wine,
When to their sports they turned. Immediately
Was Samson as a public servant brought,
In their state livery clad; before him pipes
And timbrels, on each side went armèd guards,
Both horse and foot, before him and behind
Archers, and slingers, cataphracts, and spears.
At sight of him the people with a shout
Rifted the air, clamoring their God with praise,
Who had made their dreadful enemy their thrall.
He patient, but undaunted, where they led him,
Came to the place, and what was set before him,
Which without help of eye might be assayed,
To heave, pull, draw, or break, he still performed
All with incredible stupendous force,
None daring to appear antagonist.
At length for intermission sake they led him
Between the pillars; he his guide requested,
For so from such as nearer stood we heard,
As over-tired to let him lean awhile
With both his arms on those two massy pillars,
That to the archèd roof gave main support.
He unsuspicious led him; which when Samson
Felt in his arms, with head awhile inclined,
And eyes fast fixt he stood, as one who prayed,
Or some great matter in his mind revolved:
At last with head erect thus cried aloud,
"Hitherto, lords, what your commands imposed
I have performed, as reason was, obeying,
Not without wonder or delight beheld:
Now of my own accord such other trial
I mean to show you of my strength, yet greater,
As with amaze shall strike all who behold."
This uttered, straining all his nerves he bowed;
As with the force of winds and waters pent,
When mountains tremble, those two massy pillars
With horrible convulsion to and fro
He tugged, he shook, till down they came, and drew
The whole roof after them, with burst of thunder
Upon the heads of all who sat beneath,

Lords, ladies, captains, counsellors, or priests,
Their choice nobility and flower, not only
Of this, but each Philistian city round,
Met from all parts to solemnize this feast.
Samson, with these immixt, inevitably
Pulled down the same destruction on himself;
The vulgar only 'scaped who stood without.

. . . .

2. *Semi-chorus.* — But he, though blind of sight,
Despised and thought extinguished quite,
With inward eyes illuminated,
His fiery virtue roused
From under ashes into sudden flame,
Not as an evening dragon came,
Assailant on the perchèd roosts
And nests in order ranged
Of tame villatic fowl; but as an eagle
His cloudless thunder bolted on their heads.
So virtue given for lost,
Depressed, and overthrown, as seemed,
Like that self-begotten bird
In the Arabian woods imbost,
That no second knows nor third,
And lay ere while a holocaust,
From out her ashy womb now teemed,
Revives, reflourishes, then vigorous most
When most unactive deemed;
And though her body die, her fame survives,
A secular bird, ages of lives.
Man. — Come, come, no time for lamentation now,
Nor much more cause: Samson hath quit himself
Like Samson, and heroically hath finished
A life heroic, on his enemies
Fully revenged.

MILTON.

ARIADNE'S FAREWELL.

THE daughter of a king, how should I know
That there were tinsels wearing face of gold,
And worthless glass, which in the sunlight's hold
Could shameless answer back my diamond's glow
With cheat of kindred fire? The currents slow,
And deep, and strong, and stainless, which had rolled
Through royal veins for ages, what had told
To them that hasty heat and lie could show
As quick and warm a red as theirs? Go free!
The sun is breaking on the sea's blue shield
Its golden lances; by their gleam I see
Thy ship's white sails. Go free, if scorn can yield
Thee freedom!
Then, alone, my love and I, —
We both are royal; we know how to die.

H. H.

CORONATION.

AT the king's gate the subtle noon
Wove filmy yellow nets of sun;
Into the drowsy snare too soon
The guards fell one by one.

Through the king's gate, unquestioned then,
A beggar went, and laughed, "This brings
Me chance, at last, to see if men
Fare better, being kings."

The king sat bowed beneath his crown,
Propping his face with listless hand;
Watching the hour-glass sifting down
Too slow its shining sand.

"Poor man, what wouldst thou have of me?"
The beggar turned, and pitying,
Replied, like one in dream, "Of thee,
Nothing. I want the king."

Uprose the king, and from his head
Shook off the crown, and threw it by.
"O man! thou must have known," he said.
"A greater king than I."

Through all the gates, unquestioned then,
Went king and beggar hand in hand.
Whispered the king, "Shall I know when
Before *his* throne I stand?"

The beggar laughed. Free winds in haste
Were wiping from the king's hot brow
The crimson lines the crown had traced.
"This is his presence now."

At the king's gate, the crafty noon
Unwove its yellow nets of sun;
Out of their sleep in terror soon
The guards waked one by one.

"Ho here! Ho there! Has no man seen
The king?" The cry ran to and fro;
Beggar and king, they laughed, I ween,
The laugh that free men know.

On the king's gate the moss grew gray;
The king came not. They called him dead;
And made his eldest son one day
Slave in his father's stead.

H. H.

JEPHTHAH'S DAUGHTER.

SINCE our country, our God—Oh! my sire!
Demand that thy daughter expire;
Since thy triumph was bought by thy vow,
Strike the bosom that's bared for thee now!

And the voice of my mourning is o'er,
And the mountains behold me no more:
If the hand that I love lay me low,
There cannot be pain in the blow!

And of this, oh, my father! be sure,
That the blood of thy child is as pure
As the blessing I beg ere it flow,
And the last thought that soothes me below.

Though the virgins of Salem lament,
Be the judge and the hero unbent!
I have won the great battle for thee,
And my father and country are free!

When this blood of thy giving hath gushed,
When the voice that thou lovest is hushed,
Let my memory still be thy pride,
And forget not I smiled as I died!

BYRON.

SONG OF SAUL BEFORE HIS LAST BATTLE.

WARRIORS and chiefs! should the shaft or sword
Pierce me in leading the host of the Lord,
Heed not the corse, though a king's, in your path:
Bury your steel in the bosoms of Gath!

Thou who art bearing my buckler and bow,
Should the soldiers of Saul look away from the foe,
Stretch me that moment in blood at thy feet!
Mine be the doom which they dared not to meet.

Farewell to others, but never we part,
Heir to my royalty, son of my heart:
Bright is the diadem, boundless the sway,
Or kingly the death, which awaits us to-day!

BYRON.

CASSIUS.

WELL, honor is the subject of my story.—
I cannot tell, what you and other men

Think of this life; but, for my single self
I had as lief not be, as live to be
In awe of such a thing as I myself.
I was born free as Cæsar; so were you:
We both have fed as well; and we can both
Endure the winter's cold, as well as he.
For once upon a raw and gusty day,
The troubled Tiber chafing with her shores,
Cæsar said to me, "*Dar'st thou, Cassius, now*
Leap in with me into this angry flood,
And swim to yonder point?" Upon the word,
Accoutred as I was, I plungèd in,
And bade him follow: so, indeed, he did.
The torrent roared, and we did buffet it
With lusty sinews; throwing it aside,
And stemming it with hearts of controversy.
But ere we could arrive the point proposed,
Cæsar cried, "*Help me, Cassius, or I sink.*"
I, as Æneas, our great ancestor,
Did from the flames of Troy upon his shoulders
The old Anchises bear, so, from the waves of Tiber
Did I the tired Cæsar: and this man
Is now become a god; and Cassius is
A wretched creature, and must bend his body,
If Cæsar carelessly but nod on him.
He had a fever when he was in Spain;
And when the fit was on him, I did mark
How he did shake: 'tis true, this god did shake:
His coward lips did from their color fly;
And that same eye, whose bend doth awe the world,
Did lose his lustre; I did hear him groan:
Ay, and that tongue of his, that bade the Romans
Mark him, and write his speeches in their books,
Alas! it cried, "*Give me some drink, Titinius,*"
As a sick girl. Ye gods, it doth amaze me,
A man of such a feeble temper should
So get the start of the majestic world,
And bear the palm alone.
Why, man, he doth bestride the narrow world,
Like a Colossus; and we petty men
Walk under his huge legs, and peep about
To find ourselves dishonorable graves.
Men at some time are masters of their fates;
The fault, dear Brutus, is not in our stars
But in ourselves, that we are underlings.
Brutus and Cæsar: What should be in that Cæsar?
Why should that name be sounded more than yours?
Write them together, yours is as fair a name;
Sound them, it doth become the mouth as well;
Weigh them, it is as heavy; conjure with them,
Brutus will start a spirit as soon as Cæsar.
Now in the names of all the gods at once,
Upon what meat doth this our Cæsar feed,
That he is grown so great? Age, thou art shamed:
Rome, thou hast lost the breed of noble bloods!
When went there by an age, since the great flood,
But it was famed with more than with one man?
When could they say, till now, that talked of Rome,
That her wide walls encompassed but one man?
Now is it Rome indeed, and room enough,
When there is in it but one only man,
O! you and I have heard our fathers say,
There was a Brutus once, that would have brooked
The eternal devil to keep his state in Rome,
As easily as a king.

SHAKSPEARE.

ANTONY OVER THE DEAD BODY OF CÆSAR.

Antony. — FRIENDS, Romans, countrymen, lend me your ears:
I come to bury Cæsar, not to praise him.
The evil that men do lives after them;
The good is oft interred with their bones;
So let it be with Cæsar. The noble Brutus
Hath told you Cæsar was ambitious;
If it were so, it was a grievous fault,
And grievously hath Cæsar answered it.
Here, under leave of Brutus, and the rest,
(For Brutus is an honorable man;
So are they all, all honorable men;)
Come I to speak in Cæsar's funeral.
He was my friend, faithful and just to me:
But Brutus says he was ambitious;
And Brutus is an honorable man.
He hath brought many captives home to Rome,
Whose ransoms did the general coffers fill:
Did this in Cæsar seem ambitious?
When that the poor have cried, Cæsar hath wept:
Ambition should be made of sterner stuff:
Yet Brutus says he was ambitious,
And Brutus is an honorable man.
You all did see, that on the Lupercal;
I thrice presented him a kingly crown,
Which he did thrice refuse. Was this ambition?
Yet Brutus says he was ambitious;
And, sure, he is an honorable man.
I speak not to disprove what Brutus spoke;
But here I am to speak what I do know.
You all did love him once, not without cause;
What cause withholds you, then, to mourn for him?
O judgment, thou art fled to brutish beasts,
And men have lost their reason! — bear with me;
My heart is in the coffin there with Cæsar,
And I must pause till it come back to me.
But yesterday, the word of Cæsar might
Have stood against the world: now lies he there,
And none so poor to do him reverence.
O masters! if I were disposed to stir
Your hearts and minds to mutiny and rage,
I should do Brutus wrong, and Cassius wrong,
Who, you all know, are honorable men:
I will not do them wrong; I rather choose
To wrong the dead, to wrong myself, and you,
Than I will wrong such honorable men.
But here's a parchment, with the seal of Cæsar,
I found it in his closet, 'tis his will:
Let but the commons hear this testament,
(Which, pardon me, I do not mean to read,)
And they would go and kiss dead Cæsar's wounds,
And dip their napkins in his sacred blood:
Yea, beg a hair of him for memory,
And, dying, mention it within their wills,
Bequeathing it, as a rich legacy,
Unto their issue.

Citizen. — We'll hear the will; Read it, Mark Antony.

Citizen. — The will, the will; we will hear Cæsar's will.

Antony. — Have patience, gentle friends, I must not read it;
It is not meet you know how Cæsar loved you.
You are not wood, you are not stones, but men;
And being men, hearing the will of Cæsar,
It will inflame you, it will make you mad:
'Tis good you know not that you are his heirs,
For if you should, O, what would come of it!

Cit. — Read the will; we will hear it, Antony,

You shall read us the will; Cæsar's will.

Antony. — Will you be patient? Will you stay awhile?
I have o'ershot myself, to tell you of it.
I fear I wrong the honorable men,
Whose daggers have stabbed Cæsar: I do fear it.

Cit. — They were traitors: Honorable men!

Cit. — The will! the testament!

Cit. — They were villains, murderers: the will! read the will!

Ant. — You will compel me then to read the will,
Then make a ring about the corse of Cæsar,
And let me show you him that made the will.
Shall I descend? And will you give me leave?

Cit. — Come down.

Ant. — Nay, press not so upon me; stand far off.

Cit. — Stand back! room! bear back!

Ant. — If you have tears, prepare to shed them now.
You all do know this mantle: I remember
The first time ever Cæsar put it on;
'Twas on a summer's evening in his tent;
That day he overcame the Nervii: —
Look! in this place ran Cassius' dagger through:
See what a rent the envious Casca made:
Through this, the well-beloved Brutus stabbed;
And, as he plucked his cursèd steel away,
Mark how the blood of Cæsar followed it;
As rushing out of doors, to be resolved
If Brutus so unkindly knocked, or no;
For Brutus, as you know, was Cæsar's angel:
Judge, O you gods, how dearly Cæsar loved him!
This was the most unkindest cut of all.
For when the noble Cæsar saw him stab,
Ingratitude, more strong than traitors' arms,
Quite vanquished him: then burst his mighty heart;
And, in his mantle muffling up his face,
Even at the base of Pompey's statue,
Which all the while ran blood, great Cæsar fell.
O, what a fall was there, my countrymen!
Then I, and you, and all of us, fell down,
Whilst bloody treason flourished over us.
O, now you weep! and I perceive you feel
The dint of pity: these are gracious drops.
Kind souls, what, weep you when you but behold
Our Cæsar's vesture wounded? Look you here,
Here is himself, marred, as you see, with traitors.

. . . .

Good friends, sweet friends, let me not stir you up
To such a sudden flood of mutiny.
They that have done this deed are honorable;
What private griefs they have, alas, I know not,
That made them do it; they are wise and honorable,
And will, no doubt, with reasons answer you.
I come not, friends, to steal away your hearts:
I am no orator, as Brutus is,
But as you know me all, a plain blunt man,
That love my friend: and that they know full well
That gave me public leave to speak of him.
For I have neither wit, nor words, nor worth,
Action, nor utterance, nor the power of speech,
To stir men's blood: I only speak right on;
I tell you that which you yourselves do know;
Show you sweet Cæsar's wounds, poor, poor dumb mouths,
And bid them speak for me: But were I Brutus,

And Brutus Antony, there were an Antony
Would ruffle up your spirits, and put a tongue
In every wound of Cæsar, that should move
The stones of Rome to rise and mutiny.

SHAKSPEARE.

SPEECH OF THE DAUPHIN.

Dauphin. — Your grace shall pardon me, I will not back;
I am too high-born to be propertied,
To be a secondary at control,
Or useful serving-man and instrument,
To any sovereign state throughout the world.
Your breath first kindled the dead coal of wars,
Between this chástised kingdom and myself,
And brought in matter that should feed this fire;
And now 'tis far too huge to be blown out
With that same weak wind which enkindled it.
You taught me how to know the face of right,
Acquainted me with interest to this land,
Yea, thrust this enterprise into my heart;
And come you now to tell me, John hath made
His peace with Rome? What is that peace to me?
I, by the honor of mẏ marriage-bed,
After young Arthur, claim this land for mine;
And, now it is half conquered, must I back,
Because that John hath made his peace with Rome?
Am I Rome's slave? What penny hath Rome borne,
What men provided, what munition sent,
To underprop this action? Is't not I,
That undergo this charge? Who else but I,
And such as to my claim are liable,
Sweat in this business, and maintain this war?
Have I not heard these islanders shout out,
Vive le roy! as I have banked their towns?
Have I not here the best cards for the game,
To win this easy match played for a crown?
And shall I now give o'er the yielded set?
No, on my soul, it never shall be said.
Outside or inside, I will not return
Till my attempt so much be glorified
As to my ample hope was promisèd
Before I drew this gallant head of war,
And culled these fiery spirits from the world,
To outlook conquest, and to win renown
Even in the jaws of danger and of death.

SHAKSPEARE: *King John.*

HOTSPUR'S QUARREL WITH HENRY IV.

Hotspur. — The king is kind; and well we know, the king
Knows at what time to promise, when to pay.
My father, and my uncle, and myself,
Did give him that same royalty he wears:
And, — when he was not six and twenty strong,
Sick in the world's regard, wretched and low,
A poor unminded outlaw sneaking home, —
My father gave him welcome to the shore:
And, — when he heard him swear, and vow to God,
He came but to be Duke of Lancaster,
To sue his livery, and beg his peace;
With tears of innocency, and terms of zeal, —
My father in kind heart and pity moved,
Swore him assistance, and performed it too.

Now when the lords and barons of the realm
Perceived Northumberland did lean to him,
The more and less came in with cap and knee,
Met him in boroughs, cities, villages;
Attended him on bridges, stood in lanes,
Laid gifts before him, proffered him their oaths,
Gave him their heirs as pages; followed him,
Even at the heels, in golden multitudes.
He presently, — as greatness knows itself, —
Steps me a little higher than his vow
Made to my father, while his blood was poor,
Upon the naked shore at Ravenspurg;
And now, forsooth, takes on him to reform
Some certain edicts, and some strait decrees,
That lie too heavy on the commonwealth:
Cries out upon abuses, seems to weep
Over his country's wrongs; and by this face,
This seeming brow of justice, did he win
The hearts of all that he did angle for.
Proceeded farther; cut me off the heads
Of all the favorites, that the absent king
In deputation left behind him here,
When he was personal in the Irish war.
Then to the point. —
In short time after, he deposed the king;
Soon after that, deprived him of his life:
And, in the neck of that, tasked the whole state;
To make that worse, suffered his kinsman, March,
(Who is, if every owner were well placed,
Indeed his king), to be incaged in Wales,
There without ransom to lie forfeited:
Disgraced me in my happy victories;
Sought to entrap me by intelligence;
Rated my uncle from the council-board;
In rage dismissed my father from the court;
Broke oath on oath, committed wrong on wrong,
And, in conclusion, drove us to seek out
This head of safety; and, withal, to pry
Into his title, the which we find
Too indirect for long continuance.

SHAKSPEARE: *King Henry IV.*

HOTSPUR.

King Henry. — Send us your prisoners, or you'll hear of it. [*Exit.*

Hotspur. — And if the devil come and roar for them,
I will not send them: — I will after straight,
And tell him so: for I will ease my heart,
Although it be with hazard of my head.
Not speak of Mortimer?
Zounds, I will speak of him; and let my soul
Want mercy, if I do not join with him:
Yea, on his part, I'll empty all these veins,
And shed my dear blood drop by drop in the dust
But I will lift the down-trod Mortimer
As high in the air as this unthankful king,
As this ingrate and cankered Bolingbroke.
He will, forsooth, have all my prisoners,
And when I urged the ransom once again,
Of my wife's brother, then his cheek looked pale;
And on my face he turned an eye of death,
Trembling even at the name of Mortimer.
. . . I cannot blame his cousin king,

That wished him on the barren mountains starved,
But shall it be, that you, — that set the crown
Upon the head of this forgetful man,
And, for his sake, wear the detested blot
Of murderous subornation, — shall it be,
That you a world of curses undergo,
Being the agents, or base second means,
The cords, the ladder, or the hangman rather? —
(O, pardon me, that I descend so low,
To show the line, and the predicament,
Wherein you range under this subtle king, —)
Shall it, for shame, be spoken in these days,
Or fill up chronicles in time to come,
That men of your nobility and power,
Did gage them both in an unjust behalf, —
As both of you, God pardon it! have done, —
To put down Richard, that sweet lovely rose,
And plant this thorn, this canker, Bolingbroke?

. . . .

Send danger from the east unto the west,
So honor cross it from the north to south,
And let them grapple; O! the blood more stirs
To rouse a lion than to start a hare.
By heaven, methinks, it were an easy leap,
To pluck bright Honor from the pale-faced moon;
Or dive into the bottom of the deep,
Where fathom-line could never touch the ground,
And pluck up drownèd honor by the locks;
So he that doth redeem her thence, might wear,
Without corrival, all her dignities:
But out upon this half-faced fellowship!

Worcester. — Those same noble Scots,
That are your prisoners, —

Hot. — I'll keep them all;
By heaven, he shall not have a Scot of them:
No, if a Scot would save his soul, he shall not:
I'll keep them, by this hand.
I will; that's flat: —
He said he would not ransom Mortimer;
Forbade my tongue to speak of Mortimer;
But I will find him when he lies asleep,
And in his ear I'll holla — "Mortimer!"
Nay,
I'll have a starling shall be taught to speak
Nothing but Mortimer, and give it him,
To keep his anger still in motion.
All studies here I solemnly defy,
Save how to gall and pinch this Bolingbroke:
And that same sword-and-buckler Prince of Wales, —
But that I think his father loves him not,
And would be glad he met with some mischance,
I'd have him poisoned with a pot of ale.
Why, look you, I am whipped and scourged with rods,
Nettled, and stung with pismires, when I hear
Of this vile politician, Bolingbroke.
In Richard's time, — What do you call the place?
A plague upon't! it is in Gloucestershire; —
'Twas where the madcap duke his uncle kept;
His uncle York; — where I first bowed my knee
Unto this king of smiles, this Bolingbroke,
When you and he came back from Ravenspurg.
Why, what a candy deal of courtesy
This fawning greyhound then did proffer me!
Look, — *when his infant fortune came to age*,
And, — *gentle Harry Percy*, — and *kind cousin*, —
The devil take such cozeners! — Heaven forgive me! —
Good uncle, tell your tale, for I have done.

SHAKSPEARE: *King Henry IV.*

HENRY V.'S AUDIENCE OF FRENCH AMBASSADORS.

Henry V. — Call in the messengers sent from the Dauphin.
[*Exit an* Attendant. *The* King *ascends his throne.*]
Now are we well resolved: and, — by God's help,
And yours, the noble sinews of our power, —
France being ours, we'll bend it to our awe,
Or break it all to pieces: or there we'll sit,
Ruling in large and ample empery,
O'er France, and all her almost kingly dukedoms,
Or lay these bones in an unworthy urn,
Tombless, with no remembrance over them:
Either our history shall, with full mouth,
Speak freely of our acts; or else our grave,
Like Turkish mute, shall have a tongueless mouth,
Not worshipped with a waxen epitaph.
Enter Ambassadors of France.
Now are we well prepared to know the pleasure
Of our fair cousin Dauphin; for we hear
Your greeting is from him, not from the king.
[And as the Dauphin sends us tennis-balls,]
We are glad the Dauphin is so pleasant with us:
His present, and your pains, we thank you for:
When we have matched our rackets to these balls,
We will, in France, by God's grace, play a set,
Shall strike his father's crown into the hazard:
Tell him, he hath made a match with such a wrangler,
That all the courts of France will be disturbed
With chaces. And we understand him well,
How he comes o'er us with our wilder days,
Not measuring what use we made of them.
We never valued this poor seat of England;
And therefore, living hence, did give ourself
To barbarous license; as 'tis ever common,
That men are merriest when they are from home.
But tell the Dauphin, — I will keep my state;
Be like a king, and show my sail of greatness,
When I do rouse me in my throne of France:
For that I have laid by my majesty,
And plodded like a man for working-days;
But I will rise there with so full a glory,
That I will dazzle all the eyes of France,
Yea, strike the Dauphin blind to look on us.
And tell the pleasant prince, — this mock of his
Hath turned his balls to gun-stones; and his soul
Shall stand sore chargèd for the wasteful vengeance
That shall fly with them: for many a thousand widows
Shall this his mock mock out of their dear husbands:
Mock mothers from their sons, mock castles down;
And some are yet ungotten, and unborn,
That shall have cause to curse the Dauphin's scorn.
But this lies all within the will of God,
To whom I do appeal; and in whose name,
Tell you the Dauphin, I am coming on,
To venge me as I may, and to put forth
My rightful hand in a well-hallowed cause.
So get you hence in peace; and tell the Dauphin,
His jest will savor but of shallow wit,
When thousands weep, more than did laugh at it. —
Convey them with safe conduct. — Fare you well.

Shakspeare.

BATTLE ON ST. CRISPIAN'S DAY.

Westmoreland. — O that we now had here
(*Enter* King Henry)
But one ten thousand of those men in England
That do no work to-day!
K. Henry. — What's he that wishes so?
My cousin Westmoreland? — No, my fair cousin:
If we are marked to die, we are enough
To do our country loss; and if to live,
The fewer men, the greater share of honor.
God's will! I pray thee, wish not one man more.
By Jove, I am not covetous for gold;
Nor care I who doth feed upon my cost;
It yearns me not, if men my garments wear:
Such outer things dwell not in my desires:
But, if it be a sin to covet honor,
I am the most offending soul alive.
No, 'faith, my coz, wish not a man from England:
God's peace! I would not lose so great an honor,
As one man more, methinks, would share from me,
For the best hope I have. O, do not wish one more:
Rather proclaim it, Westmoreland, through my host,
That he who hath no stomach to this fight,
Let him depart; his passport shall be made,
And crowns for convoy put into his purse:
We would not die in that man's company,
That fears his fellowship to die with us.
This day is called — the feast of Crispian:
He that outlives this day, and comes safe home,
Will stand on tip-toe when this day is named,
And rouse him at the name of Crispian:
He that shall live this day, and see old age,
Will yearly on the vigil feast his friends,
And say — To-morrow is Saint Crispian:
Then will he strip his sleeves, and show his scars,
And say, these wounds I had on Crispian's day.
Old men forget; yet all shall be forgot,
But he'll remember, with advantages,
What feats he did that day: then shall our names,
Familiar in their mouths as household words, —
Harry the king, Bedford, and Exeter,
Warwick and Talbot, Salisbury and Gloster, —
Be in their flowing cups freshly remembered:
This story shall the good man teach his son;
And Crispin Crispian shall ne'er go by,
From this day to the ending of the world,
But we in it shall be rememberèd:
We few, we happy few, we band of brothers;
For he, to-day, that sheds his blood with me,
Shall be my brother; be he ne'er so vile,
This day shall gentle his condition:
And gentlemen in England, now abed,
Shall think themselves accursed they were not here,
And hold their manhood cheap, while any speaks
That fought with us upon Saint Crispin's day.

Shakspeare.

KING RICHARD'S SOLILOQUY.

Richard III. — Now is the winter of our discontent
Made glorious summer by this son of York;
And all the clouds, that lowered upon our house,
In the deep bosom of the ocean buried.

Now are our brows bound with victorious wreaths;
Our bruisèd arms hung up for monuments;
Our stern alarums changed to merry meetings,
Our dreadful marches to delightful measures.
Grim-visaged war hath smoothed his wrinkled front;
And now, — instead of mounting barbèd steeds,
To fright the souls of fearful adversaries, —
He capers nimbly in a lady's chamber,
To the lascivious pleasing of a lute.
But I, — that am not shaped for sportive tricks,
Nor made to court an amorous looking-glass;
I, that am rudely stamped, and want love's majesty,
To strut before a wanton ambling nymph,
I, that am curtailed of this fair proportion,
Cheated of feature by dissembling nature,
Deformed, unfinished, sent before my time
Into this breathing world, scarce half made up,
And that so lamely and unfashionable
That dogs bark at me as I halt by them; —
Why I, in this weak piping time of peace,
Have no delight to pass away the time;
Unless to spy my shadow in the sun,
And descant on mine own deformity;
And therefore, since I cannot prove a lover,
To entertain these fair well-spoken days, —
I am determined to prove a villain,
And hate the idle pleasures of these days, —
Plots have I laid, inductions dangerous,
By drunken prophecies, libels, and dreams,
To set my brother Clarence, and the king
In deadly hate the one against the other:
And, if King Edward be as true and just
As I am subtle, false, and treacherous,
This day should Clarence closely be mewed up;
About a prophecy, which says — that G
Of Edward's heirs the murderer shall be.
Dive, thoughts, down to my soul: here Clarence comes.

SHAKSPEARE.

BOADICEA.

When the British warrior queen,
Bleeding from the Roman rods,
Sought, with an indignant mien,
Counsel of her country's gods,

Sage beneath the spreading oak
Sat the Druid, hoary chief;
Every burning word he spoke
Full of rage and full of grief.

"Princess! if our aged eyes
Weep upon thy matchless wrongs,
'Tis because resentment ties
All the terrors of our tongues.

Rome shall perish: write that word
In the blood that she has spilt, —
Perish, hopeless and abhorred,
Deep in ruin as in guilt.

Rome, for empire far renowned,
Tramples on a thousand states;
Soon her pride shall kiss the ground:
Hark! the Gaul is at her gates!

Other Romans shall arise,
Heedless of a soldier's name;
Sounds, not arms, shall win the prize,
Harmony the path to fame.

Then the progeny that springs
From the forests of our land,
Armed with thunder, clad with wings,
Shall a wider world command.

Regions Cæsar never knew
Thy posterity shall sway;
Where his eagles never flew,
None invincible as they."

Such the bard's prophetic words,
Pregnant with celestial fire,
Bending as he swept the chords
Of his sweet but awful lyre.

She, with all a monarch's pride,
Felt them in her bosom glow:
Rushed to battle, fought, and died;
Dying, hurled them at the foe.

Ruffians! pitiless as proud,
Heaven awards the vengeance due;
Empire is on us bestowed,
Shame and ruin wait for you.

COWPER.

BONDUCA.

[Bonduca the British queen, taking occasion from a defeat of the Romans to impeach their valor, is rebuked by Caratac.]

QUEEN BONDUCA, I do not grieve your fortune.
If I grieve, 'tis at the bearing of your fortunes;
You put too much wind to your sail: discretion
And hardy valor are the twins of honor,
And nursed together, make a conqueror;
Divided, but a talker. 'Tis a truth,
That Rome has fled before us twice, and routed; —
A truth we ought to crown the gods for, lady,
And not our tongues.
You call the Romans fearful, fleeing Romans,
And Roman girls: —
Does this become a doer? are they such?
Where is your conquest then?
Why are your altars crowned with wreaths of flowers,
The beast with gilt horns waiting for the fire?
The holy Druidés composing songs
Of everlasting life to Victory?
Why are these triumphs, lady? for a May-game?
For hunting a poor herd of wretched Romans?
Is it no more? shut up your temples, Britons,
And let the husbandman redeem his heifers;
Put out our holy fires; no timbrel ring;
Let's home and sleep; for such great overthrows
A candle burns too bright a sacrifice;
A glow-worm's tail too full a flame.
You say, I doat upon these Romans; —
Witness these wounds, I do; they were fairly given:
I love an enemy, I was born a soldier;
And he that in the head of 's troop defies me,
Rending my manly body with his sword,
I make a mistress. Yellow-tressèd Hymen
Ne'er tied a longing virgin with more joy,
Than I am married to that man that wounds me:
And are not all these Romans? Ten struck battles
I sucked these honored scars from, and all Roman.
Ten years of bitter nights and heavy marches,
When many a frozen storm sung through my cuirass,
And made it doubtful whether that or I
Were the more stubborn metal, have I wrought through,
And all to try these Romans. Ten times a night
I have swum the rivers, when the stars of Rome
Shot at me as I floated, and the billows
Tumbled their watery ruins on my shoulders,
Charging my battered sides with troops of agues,
And still to try these Romans; whom I found
As ready, and as full of that I brought,
(Which was not fear nor flight,) as valiant,
As vigilant, as wise, to do and suffer,
Ever advanced as forward as the Britons;
Have I not seen these Britons
Run, run, Bonduca? — not the quick rack swifter;
The virgin from the hated ravisher

Not half so fearful; — not a flight drawn home,
A round stone from a sling, a lover's wish,
E'er made that haste they have. By heavens!
I have seen these Britons that you magnify,
Run as they would have out-run time, and roaring, —
Basely for mercy, roaring; the light shadows,
That in a thought scour o'er the fields of corn,
Halted on crutches to them. Yes, Bonduca,
I have seen thee run too, and thee, Nennius;
Yea, run apace, both; then when Penyus,
The Roman girl, cut through your armèd carts,
And drove them headlong on ye down the hill; —
Then when he hunted ye like Britain foxes,
More by the scent than sight: then did I see
These valiant and approvèd men of Britain,
Like boding owls, creep into tods of ivy,
And hoot their fears to one another nightly.
I fled too,
But not so fast; your jewel had been lost then,
Young Hengo there; he trasht me, Nennius:
For when your fears outrun him, then stept I,
And in the head of all the Romans' fury
Took him, and, with my tough belt to my back,
I buckled him; — behind him, my sure shield; —
And then I followed. If I say I fought
Five times in bringing off this bud of Britain,
I lie not, Nennius. Neither had ye heard
Me speak this, or ever seen the child more,
But that the son of Virtue, Penyus,
Seeing me steer through all these storms of danger,
My helm still on my head, my sword my prow,
Turned to my foe my face, he cried out nobly,
"Go, Briton, bear thy lion's whelp off safely;
Thy manly sword has ransomed thee: grow strong,
And let me meet thee once again in arms:
Then if thou stand'st, thou art mine." I took his offer,
And here I am to honor him.

There's not a blow we gave since Julius landed,
That was of strength and worth, but like records
They file to after-ages. Our Registers
The Romans are, for noble deeds of honor;
And shall we burn their mentions with upbraidings?
Had we a difference with some petty Isle,
Or with our neighbors, lady, for our landmarks,
The taking in of some rebellious Lord,
Or making a head against commotions,
After a day of blood, peace might be argued:
But where we grapple for the ground we live on,
The Liberty we hold as dear as life,
The gods we worship, and next those, our honors,
And with those swords that know no end of battle:
Those men beside themselves allow no neighbor;
Those minds that, where the day is, claim inheritance;
And where the sun makes ripe the fruits, their harvest;
And where they march, but measure out more ground
To add to *Rome*, and here in the bowels on us;
It must not be; no, as they are our foes,
And those that must be so until we tire 'em,
Let's use the peace of Honor, that's fair dealing;
But in our ends, our swords.

Beaumont and Fletcher.

THE BARD.

I. 1.

"Ruin seize thee, ruthless king!
Confusion on thy banners wait;
Though fanned by Conquest's crimson wing,
They mock the air with idle state.
Helm, nor hauberk's twisted mail,
Nor e'en thy virtues, Tyrant, shall avail
To save thy secret soul from nightly fears,
From Cambria's curse, from Cambria's tears!"
Such were the sounds that o'er the crested pride
Of the first Edward scattered wild dismay,
As down the steep of Snowdon's shaggy side
He wound with toilsome march his long array.
Stout Glo'ster stood aghast in speechless trance:
"To arms!" cried Mortimer, and couched his quivering lance.

I. 2.

On a rock, whose haughty brow
Frowns o'er old Conway's foaming flood,
Robed in the sable garb of woe,
With haggard eyes the poet stood;
(Loose his beard, and hoary hair
Streamed, like a meteor, to the troubled air),
And with a master's hand, and prophet's fire,
Struck the deep sorrows of his lyre.
"Hark, how each giant-oak, and desert cave,
Sighs to the torrent's awful voice beneath!
O'er thee, oh King! their hundred arms they wave,
Revenge on thee in hoarser murmurs breathe;
Vocal no more, since Cambria's fatal day,
To high-born Hoel's harp, or soft Llewellyn's lay.

I. 3.

"Cold is Cadwallo's tongue,
That hushed the stormy main:
Brave Urien sleeps upon his craggy bed:
Mountains! ye mourn in vain
Modred, whose magic song
Made huge Plinlimmon bow his cloud-topped head.
On dreary Arvon's shore they lie,
Smeared with gore, and ghastly pale:
Far, far aloof the affrighted ravens sail;
The famished eagle screams, and passes by.
Dear lost companions of my tuneful art,
Dear as the light that visits these sad eyes,
Dear as the ruddy drops that warm my heart,
Ye died amidst your dying country's cries —
No more I weep. They do not sleep.
On yonder cliffs, a grisly band,
I see them sit, they linger yet,
Avengers of their native land:
With me in dreadful harmony they join,
And weave with bloody hands the tissue of thy line.

II. 1.

"Weave the warp, and weave the woof,
The winding sheet of Edward's race.
Give ample room, and verge enough
The characters of hell to trace.
Mark the year, and mark the night,
When Severn shall re-echo with affright
The shrieks of death, through Berkley's roof that ring,
Shrieks of an agonizing king!
She-wolf of France, with unrelenting fangs,
That tear'st the bowels of thy mangled mate,
From thee be born, who o'er thy country hangs
The scourge of heaven. What terrors round him wait!
Amazement in his van, with flight combined,
And sorrow's faded form, and solitude behind.

II. 2.

"Mighty victor, mighty lord!
Low on his funeral couch he lies!
No pitying heart, no eye, afford
A tear to grace his obsequies.
Is the sable warrior fled?
Thy son is gone. He rests among the dead.
The swarm, that in thy noontide beam were born?
Gone to salute the rising morn.
Fair laughs the morn, and soft the zephyr blows,
While proudly riding o'er the azure realm
In gallant trim the gilded vessel goes;
Youth on the prow, and Pleasure at the helm;
Regardless of the sweeping whirlwind's sway,
That, hushed in grim repose, expects his evening prey.

II. 3.

"Fill high the sparkling bowl,
The rich repast prepare;
Reft of a crown, he yet may share the feast:
Close by the regal chair
Fell Thirst and Famine scowl
A baleful smile upon their baffled guest.
Heard ye the din of battle bray,
Lance to lance, and horse to horse?
Long years of havoc urge their destined course,
And through the kindred squadrons mow their way.
Ye towers of Julius, London's lasting shame,
With many a foul and midnight murder fed,
Revere his consort's faith, his father's fame,
And spare the meek usurper's holy head.
Above, below, the rose of snow,
Twined with her blushing foe, we spread:
The bristled boar in infant-gore
Wallows beneath the thorny shade.
Now, brothers, bending o'er the accursed loom,
Stamp we our vengeance deep, and ratify his doom.

III. 1.

"Edward, lo! to sudden fate
(Weave we the woof. The thread is spun.)
Half of thy heart we consecrate.
(The web is wove. The work is done.)
Stay, oh stay! nor thus forlorn
Leave me unblessed, unpitied, here to mourn:
In yon bright track, that fires the western skies,
They melt, they vanish from my eyes.
But oh! what solemn scenes on Snowdon's height
Descending slow their glittering skirts unroll?
Visions of glory, spare my aching sight!
Ye unborn ages, crowd not on my soul!
No more our long-lost Arthur we bewail.
All hail, ye genuine kings, Britannia's issue, hail!

III. 2.

"Girt with many a baron bold,
Sublime their starry fronts they rear;
And gorgeous dames, and statesmen old
In bearded majesty, appear.
In the midst a form divine!
Her eye proclaims her of the Briton-line;
Her lion-port, her awe-commanding face,
Attempered sweet to virgin-grace.
What strings symphonious tremble in the air,
What strains of vocal transport round her play
Hear from the grave, great Taliessin, hear;
They breathe a soul to animate thy clay.
Bright Rapture calls, and soaring as she sings,
Waves in the eye of heaven her many-colored wings.

III. 3.

"The verse adorn again
Fierce war, and faithful love,
And truth severe, by fairy fiction drest.

In buskined measures move
Pale grief, and pleasing pain,
With horror, tyrant of the throbbing breast.
A voice, as of the cherub-choir,
Gales from blooming Eden bear;
And distant warblings lessen on my ear,
That lost in long futurity expire.
Fond impious man, think'st thou yon sanguine cloud,
Raised by thy breath, has quenched the orb of day?
To-morrow he repairs the golden flood,
And warms the nations with redoubled ray.
Enough for me; with joy I see
The different doom our fates assign.
Be thine despair, and sceptred care;
To triumph, and to die, are mine."
He spoke, and headlong from the mountain's height
Deep in the roaring tide he plunged to endless night.

GRAY.

LOCHIEL'S WARNING.

WIZARD. — LOCHIEL.

Wizard. — Lochiel! Lochiel, beware of the day
When the Lowlands shall meet thee in battle array!
For a field of the dead rushes red on my sight,
And the clans of Culloden are scattered in fight:
They rally, they bleed, for their kingdom and crown;
Woe, woe to the riders that trample them down!
Proud Cumberland prances, insulting the slain,
And their hoof-beaten bosoms are trod to the plain.
But hark! through the fast-flashing lightning of war,
What steed to the desert flies frantic and far?
'Tis thine, Oh Glenullin! whose bride shall await,
Like a love-lighted watch-fire, all night at the gate.
A steed comes at morning: no rider is there;
But its bridle is red with the sign of despair.
Weep, Albin! to death and captivity led!
Oh weep! but thy tears cannot number the dead:
For a merciless sword on Culloden shall wave,
Culloden! that reeks with the blood of the brave.

Lochiel. — Go, preach to the coward, thou death-telling seer!
Or, if gory Culloden so dreadful appear,
Draw, dotard, around thy old wavering sight!
This mantle, to cover the phantoms of fright.

Wizard. — Ha! laugh'st thou, Lochiel, my vision to scorn?
Proud bird of the mountain, thy plume shall be torn!
Say, rushed the bold eagle exultingly forth,
From his home, in the dark rolling clouds of the north?
Lo! the death-shot of foemen outspeeding, he rode
Companionless, bearing destruction abroad;
But down let him stoop from his havoc on high!
Ah! home let him speed — for the spoiler is nigh.
Why flames the far summit? Why shoot to the blast
Those embers, like stars from the firmament cast?
'Tis the fire-shower of ruin, all dreadfully driven
From his eyry, that beacons the darkness of heaven.
Oh, crested Lochiel! the peerless in might,
Whose banners arise on the battlement's height,
Heaven's fire is around thee, to blast and to burn;
Return to thy dwelling! all lonely return!
For the blackness of ashes shall mark where it stood,
And a wild mother scream o'er her famishing brood.

Lochiel. — False wizard, avaunt! I have marshalled my clan:
Their swords are a thousand, their bosoms are one!
They are true to the last of their blood and their breath,
And like reapers descend to the harvest of death.
Then welcome be Cumberland's steed to the shock!
Let him dash his proud foam like a wave on the rock!
But woe to his kindred, and woe to his cause,
When Albin her claymore indignantly draws;
When her bonnetted chieftains to victory crowd,
Clanranald the dauntless, and Moray the proud;
All plaided and plumed in their tartan array —

Wizard. — Lochiel, Lochiel, beware of the day!
For, dark and despairing, my sight I may seal,
But man cannot cover what God would reveal:
'Tis the sunset of life gives me mystical lore,
And coming events cast their shadow before.
I tell thee, Culloden's dread echoes shall ring
With the bloodhounds, that bark for thy fugitive king.
Lo! anointed by Heaven with the vials of wrath,
Behold; where he flies on his desolate path!
Now, in darkness and billows, he sweeps from my sight:
Rise! rise! ye wild tempests, and cover his flight!
'Tis finished. Their thunders are hushed on the moors;
Culloden is lost, and my country deplores;
But where is the iron-bound prisoner? Where?
For the red eye of battle is shut in despair.
Say, mounts he the ocean-wave, banished, forlorn,
Like a limb from his country cast bleeding and torn?
Ah, no! for a darker departure is near;
The war-drum is muffled, and black is the bier;
His death-bell is tolling; oh! mercy, dispel
Yon sight, that it freezes my spirit to tell!
Life flutters convulsed in his quivering limbs,
And his blood-streaming nostril in agony swims.
Accursed be the fagots that blaze at his feet,
Where his heart shall be thrown, ere it ceases to beat,
With the smoke of its ashes to poison the gale —

Lochiel. — Down, soothless insulter! I trust not the tale:
Though my perishing ranks should be strewed in their gore,
Like ocean-weeds heaped on the surf-beaten shore,
Lochiel, untainted by flight or by chains,
While the kindling of life in his bosom remains,
Shall victor exult, or in death be laid low,
With his back to the field, and his feet to the foe!
And leaving in battle no blot on his name,
Look proudly to heaven from the death-bed of fame.

CAMPBELL.

DEFIANCE.

THE unearthly voices ceased,
And the heavy sound was still;
It died on the river's breast,
And it died on the side of the hill;
But round Lord David's tower
The sound still floated near,
For it rung in the Lady's bower,
And it rung in the Lady's ear;
She raised her stately head,
And her heart throbbed high with pride, —
"Your mountains shall bend,
And your streams shall ascend,
Ere Margaret be our foeman's bride."

SIR WALTER SCOTT: *Lay of Last Minstrel.*

BANNOCKBURN.

ROBERT BRUCE'S ADDRESS TO HIS ARMY.

SCOTS, wha hae wi' Wallace bled;
Scots, wham Bruce has aften led;
Welcome to your gory bed,
Or to victorie.

Now's the day, and now's the hour;
See the front o' battle lower;
See approach proud Edward's power:
Chains and slaverie!

Wha will be a traitor knave?
Wha can fill a coward's grave?
Wha sae base as be a slave?
Let him turn and flee!

Wha for Scotland's king and law
Freedom's sword will strongly draw,
Freeman stand, or freeman fa'?
Let him follow me!

By oppression's woes and pains!
By your sons in servile chains!
We will drain our dearest veins,
But they shall be free!

Lay the proud usurpers low!
Tyrants fall in every foe!
Liberty's in every blow!
Let us do, or die!

BURNS.

CROMWELL AND KING CHARLES.

'TIS madness to resist or blame
The force of angry heaven's flame;
And if we would speak true,
Much to the man is due,
Who from his private gardens, where
He lived reservèd and austere,
As if his highest plot
To plant the bergamot,
Could by industrious valor climb
To ruin the great work of Time,
And cast the kingdoms old,
Into another mould.
What field of all the civil war,
Where his were not the deepest scar?
And Hampton shows what part
He had of wiser art;
Where, twining subtile fears with hope,
He wove a net of such a scope,
That Charles himself might chase
To Carisbrook's narrow case;
That thence the royal actor borne,
The tragic scaffold might adorn.
While round the armèd bands,
Did clap their bloody hands,
He nothing common did, or mean,
Upon that memorable scene,
But with his keener eye
The axe's edge did try;
Nor called the gods, with vulgar spite,
To vindicate his helpless right;
But bowed his comely head
Down, as upon a bed.

MARVELL.

THE VISION.

As I stood by yon roofless tower,
Where the wa'-flower scents the dewy air,
Where the howlet mourns in her ivy bower,
And tells the midnight moon her care:

The winds were laid, the air was still,
The stars they shot alang the sky;
The fox was howling on the hill,
And the distant-echoing glens reply.

The stream, adown its hazelly path,
Was rushing by the ruined wa's,
Hasting to join the sweeping Nith,
Whose distant roaring swells and fa's.

The cauld blue north was streaming forth
Her lights, wi' hissing eerie din;
Athort the lift they start and shift,
Like fortune's favors, tint as win.

By heedless chance I turned mine eyes,
And by the moonbeam shook to see
A stern and stalwart ghaist arise,
Attired as minstrels wont to be.

Had I a statue been o' stane,
His daurin' look had daunted me;
And on his bonnet graved was plain,
The sacred posy — *Libertie!*

BURNS.

SCOTLAND.

I MIND it weel, in early date,
When I was beardless, young, and blate,
And first could thresh the barn;
Or haud a yokin' at the pleugh;
An' though forfoughten sair eneugh,
Yet unco proud to learn!

Even then, a wish (I mind its power),
A wish that to my latest hour
Shall strongly heave my breast —
That I for poor auld Scotland's sake
Some usefu' plan or book could make,
Or sing a sang at least.
The rough burr-thistle spreading wide
Amang the bearded bear,
I turned the weedin'-heuk aside,
An' spared the symbol dear.

BURNS.

BATTLE OF THE BALTIC.

OF Nelson and the North,
Sing the glorious day's renown,
When to battle fierce came forth
All the might of Denmark's crown,
And her arms along the deep proudly shone;
By each gun the lighted brand,
In a bold determined hand,
And the Prince of all the land
Led them on, —

Like leviathans afloat,
Lay their bulwarks on the brine;
While the sign of battle flew
On the lofty British line;
It was ten of April morn by the chime:
As they drifted on their path,
There was silence deep as death;
And the boldest held his breath,
For a time. —

But the might of England flushed
To anticipate the scene;
And her van the fleeter rushed
O'er the deadly space between.
"Hearts of oak," our captains cried; when each gun
From its adamantine lips
Spread a death-shade round the ships,
Like the hurricane eclipse
Of the sun. —

Again! again! again!
And the havoc did not slack,
Till a feeble cheer the Dane
To our cheering sent us back; —
Their shots along the deep slowly boom: —
Then ceased — and all is wail,
As they strike the shattered sail;
Or, in conflagration pale,
Light the gloom. —

Outspoke the victor then,
As he hailed them o'er the wave,
"Ye are brothers! ye are men!
And we conquer but to save: —
So peace instead of death let us bring.
But yield, proud foe, thy fleet,
With the crews, at England's feet,
And make submission meet
To our king." —

Then Denmark blest our chief,
That he gave her wounds repose;
And the sounds of joy and grief,
From her people wildly rose,
As death withdrew his shades from the day;
While the sun looked smiling bright
O'er a wide and woful sight,
Where the fires of funeral light
Died away. —

Now joy, old England, raise!
For the tidings of thy might,
By the festal cities' blaze,
While the wine cup shines in light;
And yet amidst that joy and uproar,
Let us think of them that sleep,
Full many a fathom deep,
By thy wild and stormy steep
Elsinore! —

Brave hearts! to Britain's pride
Once so faithful and so true,
On the deck of fame that died, —
With the gallant good Riou:
Soft sigh the winds of heaven o'er their grave!
While the billow mournful rolls,
And the mermaid's song condoles,
Singing glory to the souls
Of the brave! —

CAMPBELL.

YE MARINERS OF ENGLAND.

Ye mariners of England!
That guard our native seas;
Whose flag has braved a thousand years
The battle and the breeze:
Your glorious standard launch again,
To match another foe!
And sweep through the deep,
While the stormy tempests blow;
While the battle rages loud and long,
And the stormy tempests blow.

The spirit of your fathers
Shall start from every wave!
For the deck it was their field of fame,
And ocean was their grave;
Where Blake and mighty Nelson fell,
Your manly hearts shall glow,
As ye sweep through the deep,
While the stormy tempests blow;
While the battle rages loud and long,
And the stormy tempests blow.

Britannia needs no bulwark,
No towers along the steep;
Her march is o'er the mountain waves,
Her home is on the deep.
With thunders from her native oak
She quells the flood below,—
As they roar on the shore,
When the stormy tempests blow;
When the battle rages loud and long,
And the stormy tempests blow.

The meteor flag of England
Shall yet terrific burn,
Till danger's troubled night depart,
And the star of peace return.
Then, then, ye ocean warriors,
Our song and feast shall flow
To the fame of your name,
When the storm has ceased to blow;
When the fiery fight is heard no more,
And the storm has ceased to blow.

CAMPBELL.

THOUGHT OF A BRITON ON THE SUBJUGATION OF SWITZERLAND.

Two voices are there,—one is of the sea,
One of the mountains,—each a mighty voice;
In both from age to age, thou didst rejoice,
They were thy chosen music, Liberty!
There came a tyrant, and with holy glee
Thou foughtst against him, but hast vainly striven;
Thou from thy Alpine holds at length art driven,
Where not a torrent murmurs heard by thee.
Of one deep bliss thine ear hath been bereft:
Then cleave, O cleave to that which still is left;
For, high-souled maid, what sorrow would it be
That mountain floods should thunder as before,
And ocean bellow from his rocky shore,
And neither awful voice be heard by thee!

WORDSWORTH.

SONNET.

Alas! what boots the long, laborious quest
Of moral prudence, sought through good and ill;
Or pains abstruse, to elevate the will,
And lead us on to that transcendent rest
Where every passion shall the sway attest
Of Reason, seated on her sovereign hill?
What is it but a vain and curious skill,
If sapient Germany must lie depressed
Beneath the brutal sword? Her haughty schools
Shall blush; and may not we with sorrow say,
A few strong instincts and a few plain rules,
Among the herdsmen of the Alps, have wrought
More for mankind at this unhappy day,
Than all the pride of intellect and thought.

WORDSWORTH.

SCHILL.

Brave Schill! by death delivered, take thy flight
From Prussia's timid region. Go, and rest
With heroes, 'mid the Islands of the Blest,
Or in the fields of empyrean light.
A meteor wert thou crossing a dark night;
Yet shall thy name, conspicuous and sublime,
Stand in the spacious firmament of time,
Fixed as a star: such glory is thy right.
Alas! it may not be: for earthly fame
Is fortune's frail dependent; yet there lives
A Judge, who, as man claims by merit, gives;
To whose all-pondering mind a noble aim,
Faithfully kept, is as a noble deed;
In whose pure sight all virtue doth succeed.

Wordsworth.

WATERLOO.

There was a sound of revelry by night,
And Belgium's capital had gathered then
Her beauty and her chivalry, and bright
The lamps shone o'er fair women and brave men:
A thousand hearts beat happily; and when
Music arose with its voluptuous swell,
Soft eyes looked love to eyes which spake again,
And all went merry as a marriage bell;
But hush! hark! a deep sound strikes like a rising knell!

Did ye not hear it?—No; 'twas but the wind,
Or the car rattling o'er the stony street:
On with the dance! let joy be unconfined;
No sleep till morn, when youth and pleasure meet
To chase the glowing hours with flying feet.
But, hark!—that heavy sound breaks in once more,
As if the clouds its echo would repeat,
And nearer, clearer, deadlier than before!
Arm! arm! it is—it is—the cannon's opening roar!

Within a windowed niche of that high hall
Sate Brunswick's fated chieftain: he did hear
That sound the first amidst the festival,
And caught its tone with death's prophetic ear;
And when they smiled because he deemed it near,
His heart more truly knew that peal too well
Which stretched his father on a bloody bier,
And roused the vengeance blood alone could quell:
He rushed into the field, and, foremost fighting, fell.

Ah! then and there was hurrying to and fro,
And gathering tears, and tremblings of distress,
And cheeks all pale, which, but an hour ago,
Blushed at the praise of their own loveliness;
And there were sudden partings, such as press
The life from out young hearts, and choking sighs
Which ne'er might be repeated: who could guess
If ever more should meet those mutual eyes,
Since upon night so sweet such awful morn could rise?

And there was mounting in hot haste: the steed,
The mustering squadron, and the clattering car,
Went pouring forward with impetuous speed,

And swiftly forming in the ranks of war;
And the deep thunder peal on peal afar;
And near, the beat of the alarming drum
Roused up the soldier ere the morning star;
While thronged the citizens with terror dumb,
Or whispering, with white lips, "The foe! They come! they come!"

BYRON.

IN THE FIGHT.

Thy voice is heard through rolling drums
That beat to battle where he stands;
Thy face across his fancy comes,
And gives the battle to his hands:
A moment, while the trumpets blow,
He sees his brood about thy knee;
The next, like fire he meets the foe,
And strikes him dead for thine and thee.

TENNYSON.

MURAT.

There, where death's brief pang was quickest,
And the battle's wreck lay thickest,
Strewed beneath the advancing banner
Of the eagles' burning crest —
There with thunder-clouds to fan her
Victory beaming from her breast!
While the broken line enlarging
Fell, or fled along the plain: —
There be sure *Murat* was charging!
There he ne'er shall charge again!

BYRON.

HOHENLINDEN.

On Linden, when the sun was low,
All bloodless lay the untrodden snow,
And dark as winter was the flow
Of Iser, rolling rapidly.

But Linden saw another sight
When the drum beat, at dead of night,
Commanding fires of death to light
The darkness of her scenery.

By torch and trumpet fast arrayed,
Each horseman drew his battle blade,
And furious every charger neighed,
To join the dreadful revelry.

Then shook the hills with thunder riven,
Then rushed the steed to battle driven,
And louder than the bolts of heaven
Far flashed the red artillery.

But redder yet that light shall glow
On Linden's hills of stainèd snow,
And bloodier yet the torrent flow
Of Iser, rolling rapidly.

'Tis morn, but scarce yon lurid sun
Can pierce the war-clouds, rolling dun,
Where furious Frank and fiery Hun
Shout in their sulphurous canopy.

The combat deepens. On, ye brave,
Who rush to glory, or the grave!
Wave, Munich, all thy banners wave!
And charge with all thy chivalry!

Ah! few shall part where many meet!
The snow shall be their winding-sheet,
And every turf beneath their feet
Shall be a soldier's sepulchre.

CAMPBELL.

SONNET.

It is not to be thought of that the flood
Of British freedom, which, to the open sea
Of the world's praise, from dark antiquity
Hath flowed, "with pomp of waters unwithstood,"
Roused though it be full often to a mood
Which spurns the check of salutary bands,
That this most famous stream in bogs and sands
Should perish, and to evil and to good

Be lost forever. In our halls is hung
Armory of the invincible knights of old:
We must be free or die, who speak the tongue
That Shakspeare spake — the faith and morals hold
Which Milton held. In every thing we are sprung
Of Earth's first blood, have titles manifold.

WORDSWORTH.

THE WARDEN OF THE CINQUE PORTS.

A MIST was driving down the British Channel;
The day was just begun;
And through the window-panes, on floor and panel,
Streamed the red autumn sun.

It glanced on flowing flag and rippling pennon,
And the white sails of ships;
And, from the frowning rampart, the black cannon
Hailed it with feverish lips.

Sandwich and Romney, Hastings, Hithe, and Dover,
Were all alert that day,
To see the French war-steamers speeding over
When the fog cleared away.

Sullen and silent, and like couchant lions,
Their cannon, through the night,
Holding their breath, had watched in grim defiance
The seacoast opposite;

And now they roared, at drum-beat, from their stations
On every citadel;
Each answering each, with morning salutations,
That all was well!

And down the coast, all taking up the burden,
Replied the distant forts —
As if to summon from his sleep the warden
And lord of the Cinque Ports.

Him shall no sunshine from the fields of azure,
No drum-beat from the wall,
No morning gun from the black forts' embrasure,
Awaken with their call!

No more, surveying with an eye impartial
The long line of the coast,
Shall the gaunt figure of the old field-marshal
Be seen upon his post!

For in the night, unseen, a single warrior,
In sombre harness mailed,
Dreaded of man, and surnamed the Destroyer,
The rampart wall has scaled!

He passed into the chamber of the sleeper, —
The dark and silent room;
And, as he entered, darker grew, and deeper
The silence and the gloom.

He did not pause to parley, or dissemble,
But smote the warden hoar —
Ah! what a blow! that made all England tremble
And groan from shore to shore.

Meanwhile, without, the surly cannon waited,
The sun rose bright o'erhead, —
Nothing in Nature's aspect intimated
That a great man was dead!

LONGFELLOW.

THE LOST LEADER.

I.

JUST for a handful of silver he left us;
Just for a ribbon to stick in his coat;
Found the one gift of which fortune bereft us,
Lost all the others she lets us devote.
They, with the gold to give, doled him out silver,

So much was theirs who so little allowed.
How all our copper had gone for his service!
Rags — were they purple, his heart had been proud:
We that had loved him so, followed him, honored him,
Lived in his mild and magnificent eye,
Learned his great language, caught his clear accents,
Made him our pattern to live and to die!
Shakspeare was of us, Milton was for us,
Burns, Shelley, were with us, — they watch from their graves!
He alone breaks from the van and the freemen;
He alone sinks to the rear and the slaves!

II.

We shall march prospering, — not through his presence;
Songs may inspirit us, — not from his lyre;
Deeds will be done — while he boasts his quiescence,
Still bidding crouch whom the rest bade aspire.
Blot out his name, then, — record one lost soul more,
One task more declined, one more foot-path untrod,
One more triumph for devils, and sorrow for angels,
One wrong more to man, one more insult to God!
Life's night begins; let him never come back to us!
There would be doubt, hesitation, and pain,
Forced praise on our part, — the glimmer of twilight,
Never glad confident morning again!
Best fight on well, for we taught him, — strike gallantly,
Aim at our heart ere we pierce through his own;
Then let him receive the new knowledge and wait us,
Pardoned in Heaven, the first by the throne!

ROBERT BROWNING.

WESTWARD the course of Empire takes its way.
The four first acts already past,
A fifth shall close the drama with the day:
Time's noblest offspring is his last.

BISHOP GEORGE BERKELEY.

ENTRANCE OF COLUMBUS INTO BARCELONA.

LO! on his far-resounding path
Sink crucifix and crown,
And from high tower and balcony
The light of Spain looks down, —
For Beauty's dark, dark virgin eyes
Gleam ceaseless round him now,
As stars from still upheaving skies
Would new-born from the waves arise
On his advancing prow.

GRENVILLE MELLEN.

INDIANS.

ALAS! for them, their day is o'er,
Their fires are out on hill and shore;
No more for them the wild deer bounds,
The plough is on their hunting grounds;
The pale man's axe rings through their woods,
The pale man's sail skims o'er their floods;
Their pleasant springs are dry;
Their children, — look, by power opprest,
Beyond the mountains of the west,
Their children go to die.

CHARLES SPRAGUE.

THE LANDING OF THE PILGRIM FATHERS IN NEW ENGLAND.

THE breaking waves dashed high
On a stern and rockbound coast,
And the woods against a stormy sky
Their giant branches tossed.

And the heavy night hung dark
The hills and waters o'er,
When a band of exiles moored their bark
On the wild New England shore.

Not as the conqueror comes,
They, the true-hearted, came;
Not with the roll of the stirring drums,
And the trumpet that sings of fame.

Not as the flying come,
In silence and in fear;—
They shook the depths of the desert gloom
With their hymns of lofty cheer.

Amidst the storm they sang,
And the stars heard, and the sea:
And the sounding aisles of the dim woods rang
To the anthem of the free!

The ocean eagle soared
From his nest by the white wave's foam:
And the rocking pines of the forest roared,—
This was their welcome home!

There were men with hoary hair
Amidst that pilgrim band:—
Why had *they* come to wither there,
Away from their childhood's land?

There was woman's fearless eye,
Lit by her deep love's truth;
There was manhood's brow serenely high,
And the fiery heart of youth.

What sought they thus afar?
Bright jewels of the mine?
The wealth of seas, the spoils of war?—
They sought a faith's pure shrine!

Ay, call it holy ground,
The soil where first they trod:
They have left unstained what there they found,—
Freedom to worship God.

HEMANS.

GEORGE WASHINGTON.

By broad Potomac's silent shore
Better than Trajan lowly lies,
Gilding her green declivities
With glory now and evermore;
Art to his fame no aid hath lent;
His country is his monument.

BUNKER HILL.

Now deeper roll the maddening drums,
The mingling host like Ocean heaves,
While from the midst a horrid wailing comes,
And high above the fight the lonely bugle grieves.

GRENVILLE MELLEN.

OLD IRONSIDES.

Ay, tear her tattered ensign down!
Long has it waved on high,
And many an eye has danced to see
That banner in the sky;
Beneath it rung the battle-shout,
And burst the cannon's roar:
The meteor of the ocean air
Shall sweep the clouds no more!

Her deck, once red with heroes' blood,
Where knelt the vanquished foe,
When winds were hurrying o'er the flood,
And waves were white below,
No more shall feel the victor's tread,
Or know the conquered knee:
The harpies of the shore shall pluck
The eagle of the sea!

O better that her shattered hulk
Should sink beneath the wave!
Her thunders shook the mighty deep,
And there should be her grave:
Nail to the mast her holy flag,
Set every threadbare sail,
And give her to the god of storms,
The lightning and the gale!

O. W. HOLMES.

ICHABOD!

So fallen! so lost! the light with-
drawn
Which once he wore!
The glory from his gray hairs gone
Forevermore!

Revile him not, — the tempter hath
A snare for all;
And pitying tears, not scorn and
wrath,
Befit his fall!

Oh! dumb be passion, stormy rage,
When he who might
Have lighted up and led his age,
Falls back in night.

Scorn! would the angels laugh, to
mark
A bright soul driven,
Fiend-goaded, down the endless
dark,
From hope and heaven!

Let not the land, once proud of him,
Insult him now,
Nor brand with deeper shame his
dim
Dishonored brow.

But let its humbled sons, instead,
From sea to lake,
A long lament, as for the dead,
In sadness make.

Of all we loved and honored, nought
Save power remains, —
A fallen angel's pride of thought,
Still strong in chains.

All else is gone; from those great
eyes
The soul has fled:
When faith is lost, when honor dies,
The man is dead!

Then pay the reverence of old days
To his dead fame;
Walk backward, with averted gaze,
And hide the shame!

WHITTIER.

GREETING TO "THE GEORGE GRISWOLD."

[The ship which bore to the Mersey the contribution of the United States to the relief of Lancashire.]

BEFORE thy stem smooth seas were
curled,
Soft winds thy sails did move,
Good ship, that from the Western
world
Bore freight of brothers' love.

'Twixt starving here and thriving
there,
When wrath flies to and fro,
Till all seems hatred everywhere,
How fair thy white wings show!

O'er the great seas thy keel ploughed
through
Good ships have borne the chain
That should have knit old world and
new
Across the weltering main.

The chain was borne, — one kindly
wave
Of speech pulsed through its coil;
Then dumb and dead in ocean's
grave
Lay hope and cost and toil.

But thou, good ship, again hast
brought
O'er these wide waves of blue,
The chain of kindly word and
thought
To link those worlds anew.

PUNCH.

JOHN BROWN OF OSAWATOMIE.

A BALLAD OF THE TIMES.

[Containing ye True History of ye Great Virginia Fright.]

JOHN BROWN in Kansas settled, like
a steadfast Yankee farmer,
Brave and godly, with four sons —
all stalwart men of might.
There he spoke aloud for Freedom,
and the Border-strife grew
warmer,
Till the Rangers fired his dwelling,
in his absence, in the night;

And Old Brown,
Osawatomie Brown,
Came homeward in the morning — to find his house burned down.

Then he grasped his trusty rifle, and boldly fought for Freedom;
Smote from border unto border the fierce, invading band;
And he and his brave boys vowed — so might Heaven help and speed 'em! —
They would save those grand old prairies from the curse that blights the land;
And Old Brown,
Osawatomie Brown,
Said, "Boys, the Lord will aid us!" and he shoved his ramrod down.

And the Lord *did* aid these men; and they labored day and even,
Saving Kansas from its peril, and their very lives seemed charmed;
Till the ruffians killed one son, in the blessèd light of Heaven —
In cold blood the fellows slew him, as he journeyed all unarmed;
Then Old Brown,
Osawatomie Brown,
Shed not a tear, but shut his teeth, and frowned a terrible frown!

Then they seized another brave boy, — not amid the heat of battle,
But in peace, behind his plough-share, — and they loaded him with chains,
And with pikes, before their horses, even as they goad their cattle,
Drove him, cruelly, for their sport, and at last blew out his brains;
Then Old Brown,
Osawatomie Brown,
Raised his right hand up to Heaven, calling Heaven's vengeance down.

And he swore a fearful oath, by the name of the Almighty,
He would hunt this ravening evil that had scathed and torn him so; —
He would seize it by the vitals; he would crush it day and night; he
Would so pursue its footsteps, — so return it blow for blow —
That Old Brown,
Osawatomie Brown,
Should be a name to swear by, in backwoods or in town!

Then his beard became more grizzled, and his wild blue eye grew wilder,
And more sharply curved his hawk's-nose, snuffing battle from afar;
And he and the two boys left, though the Kansas strife waxed milder,
Grew more sullen, till was over the bloody Border War,
And Old Brown,
Osawatomie Brown,
Had gone crazy, as they reckoned by his fearful glare and frown.

So he left the plains of Kansas and their bitter woes behind him,
Slipt off into Virginia, where the statesmen all are born,
Hired a farm by Harper's Ferry, and no one knew where to find him,
Or whether he'd turned parson, or was jacketed and shorn;
For Old Brown,
Osawatomie Brown,
Mad as he was, knew texts enough to wear a parson's gown.

He bought no ploughs and harrows, spades and shovels, or such trifles;
But quietly to his rancho there came, by every train,
Boxes full of pikes and pistols, and his well-beloved Sharpe's rifles;
And eighteen other madmen joined their leader there again.
Says Old Brown,
Osawatomie Brown,
"Boys, we've got an army large enough to march and whip the town!

"Take the town, and seize the muskets, free the negroes, and then arm them;
Carry the County and the State, ay, and all the potent South;

On their own heads be the slaughter, if their victims rise to harm them —
These Virginians! who believed not, nor would heed the warning mouth."
Says Old Brown,
Osawatomie Brown,
"The world shall see a Republic, or my name is not John Brown!"

'Twas the sixteenth of October, on the evening of a Sunday:
"This good work," declared the captain, "shall be on a holy night!"
It was on a Sunday evening, and, before the noon of Monday,
With two sons, and Captain Stephens, fifteen privates — black and white,
Captain Brown,
Osawatomie Brown,
Marched across the bridged Potomac, and knocked the sentry down;

Took the guarded armory-building, and the muskets and the cannon;
Captured all the county majors and the colonels, one by one;
Scared to death each gallant scion of Virginia they ran on,
And before the noon of Monday, I say, the deed was done.
Mad Old Brown,
Osawatomie Brown,
With his eighteen other crazy men, went in and took the town.

Very little noise and bluster, little smell of powder, made he;
It was all done in the midnight, like the emperor's *coup d'état*;
"Cut the wires! stop the rail-cars! hold the streets and bridges!" said he,
Then declared the new Republic, with himself for guiding star, —
This Old Brown,
Osawatomie Brown;
And the bold two thousand citizens ran off and left the town.

Then was riding and railroading and expressing here and thither;
And the Martinsburg Sharpshooters and the Charlestown Volunteers,
And the Shepherdstown and Winchester Militia hastened whither
Old Brown was said to muster his ten thousand grenadiers!
General Brown,
Osawatomie Brown!
Behind whose rampant banner all the North was pouring down.

But at last, 'tis said, some prisoners escaped from Old Brown's durance,
And the effervescent valor of the Chivalry broke out,
When they learned that nineteen madmen had the marvellous assurance —
Only nineteen — thus to seize the place and drive them straight about;
And Old Brown,
Osawatomie Brown,
Found an army come to take him, encamped around the town.

But to storm with all the forces we have mentioned, was too risky;
So they hurried off to Richmond for the Government Marines —
Tore them from their weeping matrons, fired their souls with Bourbon whiskey,
Till they battered down Brown's castle with their ladders and machines;
And Old Brown,
Osawatomie Brown,
Received three bayonet stabs, and a cut on his brave old crown.

Tallyho! the old Virginia gentry gather to the baying!
In they rushed and killed the game, shooting lustily away;
And whene'er they slew a rebel, those who came too late for slaying,

Not to lose a share of glory, fixed their bullets in his clay;
And Old Brown,
Osawatomie Brown,
Saw his sons fall dead beside him, and between them laid him down.

How the conquerors wore their laurels; how they hastened on the trial;
How Old Brown was placed, half-dying, on the Charlestown court-house floor;
How he spoke his grand oration, in the scorn of all denial;
What the brave old madman told them — these are known the country o'er.
"Hang Old Brown,
Osawatomie Brown,"
Said the judge, "and all such rebels!" with his most judicial frown.

But, Virginians, don't do it! for I tell you that the flagon,
Filled with blood of Old Brown's offspring, was first poured by Southern hands;
And each drop from Old Brown's life-veins, like the red gore of the dragon,
May spring up a vengeful Fury, hissing through your slave-worn lands!
And Old Brown,
Osawatomie Brown,
May trouble you more than ever, when you've nailed his coffin down!

E. C. Stedman.

November, 1859.

BATTLE HYMN OF THE REPUBLIC.

Mine eyes have seen the glory of the coming of the Lord;
He is trampling out the vintage where the grapes of wrath are stored!
He hath loosed the fateful lightning of his terrible swift sword;
His truth is marching on.

I have seen him in the watch-fires of a hundred circling camps;
They have builded him an altar in the evening dews and damps:
I have read his righteous sentence by the dim and flaring lamps:
His day is marching on.

I have read a fiery gospel writ in burnished rows of steel:
"As ye deal with my contemners, so with you my grace shall deal:
Let the Hero, born of woman, crush the serpent with his heel,
Since God is marching on."

He has sounded forth the trumpet that shall never call retreat;
He is sifting out the hearts of men before his judgment-seat;
Oh be swift my soul, to answer him! be jubilant, my feet!
Our God is marching on.

In the beauty of the lilies Christ was born across the sea,
With a glory in his bosom that transfigures you and me:
As he died to make men holy, let us die to make men free,
While God is marching on.

Julia Ward Howe.

MARYLAND.

The despot's heel is on thy shore,
Maryland!
His torch is at thy temple door,
Maryland!
Avenge the patriotic gore
That flecked the streets of Baltimore,
And be the battle-queen of yore,
Maryland! My Maryland!

Hark to thy wandering son's appeal,
Maryland!
My mother State! to thee I kneel,
Maryland!
For life and death, for woe and weal,
Thy peerless chivalry reveal,
And gird thy beauteous limbs with steel,
Maryland! My Maryland!

Thou wilt not cower in the dust,
Maryland!
Thy beaming sword shall never rust,
Maryland!
Remember Carroll's sacred trust;
Remember Howard's warlike thrust;
And all thy slumberers with the just,
Maryland! My Maryland!

Come! 'tis the red dawn of the day,
Maryland!
Come! with thy panoplied array,
Maryland!
With Ringgold's spirit for the fray,
With Watson's blood, at Monterey,
With fearless Lowe, and dashing May,
Maryland! My Maryland!

Come! for thy shield is bright and strong,
Maryland!
Come! for thy dalliance does thee wrong,
Maryland!
Come! to thine own heroic throng,
That stalks with Liberty along,
And give a new key to thy song,*
Maryland! My Maryland!

Dear Mother! burst the tyrant's chain,
Maryland!
Virginia should not call in vain,
Maryland!
She meets her sisters on the plain:
"*Sic semper*" 'tis the proud refrain,
That baffles minions back amain,
Maryland!
Arise in majesty again,
Maryland! My Maryland!

I see the blush upon thy cheek,
Maryland!
But thou wast ever bravely meek,
Maryland!
But lo! there surges forth a shriek
From hill to hill, from creek to creek:
Potomac calls to Chesapeake,
Maryland! My Maryland!

Thou wilt not yield the Vandal toll,
Maryland!
Thou wilt not crook to his control,
Maryland!

Better the fire upon thee roll,
Better the blade, the shot, the bowl,
Than crucifixion of the soul,
Maryland! My Maryland!

I hear the distant thunder hum,
Maryland!
The old Line's bugle, fife and drum,
Maryland!
She is not dead, nor deaf, nor dumb:
Huzza! she spurns the Northern scum!
She breathes — she burns! she'll come! she'll come!
Maryland! My Maryland!

JAMES R. RANDALL.

POINTE COUPÉE,
April 26, 1861.

* The Star-Spangled Banner was written during the war of 1812 by Francis Key of Maryland.

AT PORT ROYAL.

THE tent-lights glimmer on the land,
The ship-lights on the sea;
The night-wind smooths with drifting sand
Our track on lone Tybee.

At last our grating keels outslide,
Our good boats forward swing;
And while we ride the land-locked tide,
Our negroes row and sing.

For dear the bondman holds his gifts
Of music and of song:
The gold that kindly Nature sifts
Among his sands of wrong;

The power to make his toiling days
And poor home-comforts please;
The quaint relief of mirth that plays
With sorrow's minor keys.

Another glow than sunset's fire
Has filled the West with light,
Where field and garner, barn, and byre
Are blazing through the night.

The land is wild with fear and hate,
The rout runs mad and fast;
From hand to hand, from gate to gate,
The flaming brand is passed.

The lurid glow falls strong across
Dark faces broad with smiles:
Not theirs the terror, hate, and loss
That fire yon blazing piles.

With oar-strokes timing to their song,
They weave in simple lays
The pathos of remembered wrong,
The hope of better days, —

The triumph-note that Miriam sung,
The joy of uncaged birds:
Softening with Afric's mellow tongue
Their broken Saxon words.

SONG OF THE NEGRO BOATMEN.

O, praise an' tanks! De Lord he come
To set de people free;
An' massa tink it day ob doom,
An' we ob jubilee.
De Lord dat heap de Red Sea waves
He jus' as 'trong as den;
He say de word: we las' night slaves;
To-day, de Lord's freemen.
De yam will grow, de cotton blow,
We'll hab de rice an' corn;
O nebber you fear, if nebber you hear
De driver blow his horn!

Ole massa on he trabbels gone;
He leaf de land behind:
De Lord's breff blow him furder on,
Like corn-shuck in de wind.
We own de hoe, we own de plough,
We own de hands dat hold;
We sell de pig, we sell de cow,
But nebber chile be sold.
De yam will grow, de cotton blow,
We'll hab de rice an' corn:
O nebber you fear, if nebber you hear
De driver blow his horn!

We pray de Lord: he gib us signs
Dat some day we be free;
De norf-wind tell it to de pines,
De wild-duck to de sea;
We tink it when de church-bell ring,
We dream it in de dream;
De rice-bird mean it when he sing,
De eagle when he scream.
De yam will grow, de cotton blow,
We'll hab de rice an' corn:
O nebber you fear, if nebber you hear
De driver blow his horn!

We know de promise nebber fail,
An' nebber lie de word;
So like de 'postles in de jail,
We waited for de Lord:
An' now he open ebery door,
An' trow away de key;
He tink we lub him so before,
We lub him better free.
De yam will grow, de cotton blow,
He'll gib de rice an' corn:
O nebber you fear, if nebber you hear
De driver blow his horn!

So sing our dusky gondoliers;
And with a secret pain,
And smiles that seem akin to tears,
We hear the wild refrain.

We dare not share the negro's trust,
Nor yet his hope deny:
We only know that God is just,
And every wrong shall die.

Rude seems the song; each swarthy face,
Flame-lighted, ruder still:
We start to think that hapless race
Must shape our good or ill;

That laws of changeless justice bind
Oppressor with oppressed;
And, close as sin and suffering joined,
We march to Fate abreast.

Sing on, poor hearts! your chant shall be
Our sign of blight or bloom, —
The Vala-song of Liberty,
Or death-rune of our doom!

WHITTIER.

NEVER OR NOW.

In vain the common theme my tongue would shun,
All tongues, all thoughts, all hearts can find but one.
Our alcoves, where the noisy world was dumb,
Throb with dull drum-beats, and the echoes come
Laden with sounds of battle and wild cries,
That mingle their discordant symphonies.

Old books from yonder shelves are whispering, "Peace!
This is the realm of letters, not of strife."
Old graves in yonder field are saying, "Cease!
Hic jacet ends the noisiest mortal's life."
—Shut your old books! What says the telegraph?
We want an Extra, not an epitaph.
Old Classmates, (Time's unconscious almanacs,
Counting the years we leave behind our backs,
And wearing them in wrinkles on the brow
Of friendship with his kind "How are you *now?*")
Take us by the hand, and speak of times that were.—
Then comes a moment's pause: "Pray tell me where
Your boy is now! Wounded, as I am told."—
"Twenty?" "What—bless me! twenty-one years old!"
"Yes,—time moves fast." "That's so. Old classmate, say,
Do you remember *our* Commencement Day?
Were we such boys as these at twenty?" Nay,
God called them to a nobler task than ours,
And gave them holier thoughts and manlier powers,—
This is the day of fruits and not of flowers!
These "boys" we talk about like ancient sages
Are the same *men* we read of in old pages,—
The bronze recast of dead heroic ages!
We grudge them not,—our dearest, bravest, best,—
Let but the quarrel's issue stand confest:
'Tis Earth's old slave-God battling for his crown,
And Freedom fighting with her visor down!

Better the jagged shells their flesh should mangle,—
Better their bones from Rahab-necks should dangle,
Better the fairest flower of all our culture
Should cram the black maw of the Southern vulture,
Than Cain act o'er the murder of his brother
Unum on our side—*pluribus* on the other!
Each of us owes the rest his best endeavor;
Take these few lines,—we call them

NOW OR NEVER.

Listen, young heroes! your country is calling!
Time strikes the hour for the brave and the true!
Now, while the foremost are fighting and falling,
Fill up the ranks that have opened for you!

You whom the fathers made free and defended,
Stain not the scroll that emblazons their fame!
You whose fair heritage spotless descended,
Leave not your children a birthright of shame!

Stay not for questions while Freedom stands gasping!
Wait not till Honor lies wrapped in his pall!
Brief the lips' meeting be, swift the hands' clasping.—
"Off for the wars" is enough for them all!

Break from the arms that would fondly caress you!
Hark! 'tis the bugle blast! sabres are drawn!
Mothers shall pray for you, fathers shall bless you,
Maidens shall weep for you when you are gone!

Never or now! cries the blood of a nation
Poured on the turf where the red rose should bloom;
Now is the day and the hour of salvation;
Never or now! peals the trumpet of doom!

Never or now! roars the hoarse-throated cannon
Through the black canopy blotting the skies;
Never or now! flaps the shell-blasted pennon
O'er the deep ooze where the Cumberland lies!

From the foul dens where our brothers are dying,
Aliens and foes in the land of their birth,
From the rank swamps where our martyrs are lying
Pleading in vain for a handful of earth;

From the hot plains where they perish outnumbered,
Furrowed and ridged by the battle-field's plough,
Comes the loud summons; too long you have slumbered,
Hear the last Angel-trump — Never or Now!

O. W. Holmes.

MASON AND SLIDELL: A YANKEE IDYLL.

CONCORD BRIDGE.

. . . .

Hearken in your ear, —
I'm older'n you, — Peace wun't keep house with Fear:
Ef you want peace, the thing you've gut to du
Is jes' to show you're up to fightin', tu.
I recollect how sailors' rights was won
Yard locked in yard, hot gun-lip kissin' gun:
Why, afore thet, John Bull sot up thet he
Hed gut a kind o' mortgage on the sea;
You'd thought he held by Gran'ther Adam's will,
An' ef you knuckle down, *he*'ll think so still.
Better thet all our ships an' all their crews
Should sink to rot in ocean's dreamless ooze,
Each torn flag wavin' chellenge ez it went,
An' each dumb gun a brave man's moniment,
Than seek sech peace ez only cowards crave:
Give *me* the peace of dead men or of brave!

THE MONIMENT.

I say, ole boy, it ain't the Glorious Fourth:
You'd oughto larned 'fore this wut talk wuz worth.
It ain't *our* nose thet gits put out o' jint;
It's England thet gives up her dearest pint.
We've gut, I tell ye now, enough to du
In our own fem'ly fight, afore we're thru.
I hoped, las' spring, jest arter Sumter's shame,
When every flagstaff flapped its tethered flame,
An' all the people, startled from their doubt,
Come must'rin' to the flag with sech a shout, —
I hoped to see things settled 'fore this fall,
The Rebbles licked, Jeff Davis hanged, an' all;
Then come Bull Run, an' *sence* then I've ben waitin'
Like boys in Jennooary thaw for skatin',
Nothin' to du but watch my shadder's trace
Swing, like a ship at anchor, roun' my base,
With daylight's flood an' ebb: it's gitting slow,
An' I 'most think we'd better let 'em go.
I tell ye wut, this war's agoin to cost —

THE BRIDGE.

An' I tell *you* it wun't be money lost;
We wun't give up afore the ship goes down:
It's a stiff gale, but Providence wun't drown;

An' God wun't leave us yit to sink or swim,
Ef we don't fail to du wut's right by him.
This land o' ourn, I tell ye, 's gut to be
A better country than man ever see.
I feel my sperit swellin' with a cry
Thet seems to say, "Break forth an' prophesy!"
O strange New World, thet yit wast never young,
Whose youth from thee by gripin' need was wrung,
Brown foundlin' o' the woods, whose baby-bed
Was prowled roun' by the Injuns' cracklin' tread,
An' who grew'st strong thru shifts an' wants an' pains,
Nussed by stern men with empires in their brains,
Who saw in vision their young Ishmel strain
With each hard hand a vassal ocean's mane,
Thou, skilled by Freedom an' by gret events
To pitch new States ez Old-World men pitch tents,
Thou, taught by Fate to know Jehovah's plan,
Thet man's devices can't unmake a man,
An' whose free latch-string never was drawed in
Against the poorest child of Adam's kin, —
The grave's not dug where traitor hands shall lay
In fearful haste thy murdered corse away!
I see —
Jest here some dogs begun to bark,
So thet I lost old Concord's last remark:
I listened long; but all I seemed to hear
Was dead leaves goss'pin' on some birch-trees near;
But ez they hedn't no gret things to say,
An' sed 'em often, I come right away,
An', walkin' home'ards, jest to pass the time,
I put some thoughts thet bothered me in rhyme:
I hain't hed time to fairly try 'em on,
But here they be — it's —

JONATHAN TO JOHN.

It don't seem hardly right, John,
When both my hands was full,
To stump me to a fight, John,
Your cousin, tu, John Bull!
Ole Uncle S. sez he, "I guess
We know it now," sez he,
"The lion's paw is all the law,
Accordin' to J. B.,
Thet's fit for you an' me!"

Blood ain't so cool as ink, John;
It's likely you'd ha' wrote,
An' stopped a spell to think, John,
Arter they'd cut your throat?
Ole Uncle S. sez he, "I guess
He'd skurce ha' stopped," sez he,
"To mind his p's an' q's ef thet weasan'
He'd b'longed to ole J. B.,
Instid o' you an' me!"

Ef *I* turned mad dogs loose, John,
On *your* front-parlor stairs,
Would it jest meet your views, John,
To wait an' sue their heirs?
Ole Uncle S. sez he, "I guess,
I on'y guess," sez he,
"Thet, ef Vattell on *his* toes fell,
'Twould kind o' rile J. B.,
Ez wal ez you and me!"

Who made the law thet hurts, John,
Heads I win — ditto, tails?
"*J. B.*" was on his shirts, John,
Onless my memory fails.
Ole Uncle S. sez he, "I guess,
(I'm good at thet,") sez he,
"Thet sauce for goose ain't *jest* the juice
For ganders with J. B.,
No more than you or me!"

When your rights was our wrong, John,
You didn't stop for fuss, —
Britanny's trident-prongs, John,
Was good 'nough law for us.
Ole Uncle S. sez he, "I guess,
Though physic's good," sez he,

"It doesn't foller thet he can swaller
Prescriptions signed '*J. B.*'
Put up by you an' me!"

We own the ocean, tu, John:
You mus'n' take it hard,
Ef we can't think with you, John,
It's jest your own back-yard.
Ole Uncle S. sez he, "I guess,
Ef *thet's* his claim," sez he,
"The fencin'-stuff'll cost enough
To bust up friend J. B.,
Ez wal ez you an' me!"

Why talk so dreffle big, John,
Of honor, when it meant
You didn't care a fig, John,
But jest for *ten per cent?*
Ole Uncle S. sez he, "I guess,
He's like the rest," sez he:
"When all is done, it's number one
Thet's nearest to J. B.,
Ez wal ez you an' me!"

We give the critters back, John,
Coz Abra'm thought 'twas right;
It warn't your bullyin' clack, John,
Provokin' us to fight.
Ole Uncle S. sez he, "I guess
We've a hard row," sez he,
"To hoe just now: but thet, somehow,
May happen to J. B.,
Ez wal ez you an' me!"

We ain't so weak an' poor, John,
With twenty million people,
An' close to every door, John,
A school-house an' a steeple.
Ole Uncle S. sez he, "I guess
It is a fact," sez he,
"The surest plan to make a Man
Is, Think him so, J. B.,
Ez much ez you or me!"

Our folks believe in Law, John:
An' it's for her sake, now,
They've left the axe an' saw, John,
The anvil an' the plough.
Ole Uncle S. sez he, "I guess,
Ef't warn't for law," sez he,
"There'd be one shindy from here to Indy;
An' thet don't suit J. B.,
(When 'tain't 'twixt you an' me!")

We know we've gut a cause, John,
Thet's honest, just, an' true;
We thought 'twould win applause, John,
Ef nowheres else, from you.
Ole Uncle S. sez he, "I guess
His love of right," sez he,
"Hangs by a rotten fibre o'cotton:
There's natur' in J. B.,
Ez wal ez you an' me!"

The South says, "*Poor folks down!*" John,
An' "*All men up!*" say we,—
White, yaller, black, an' brown, John:
Now which is your idee?
Ole Uncle S. sez he, "I guess,
John preaches wal," sez he:
"But, sermon thru, an' come to *du*,
Why, there's the ole J. B.
A-crowdin' you an' me!"

Shall it be love or hate, John?
It's you thet's to decide:
Ain't *your* bonds held by Fate, John,
Like all the world's beside?
Ole Uncle S. sez he, "I guess
Wise men forgive," sez he,
"But not forget; an' sometime yet
The truth may strike J. B.,
Ez wal ez you an' me!"

God means to make this land, John,
Clear thru, from sea to sea,
Believe an' understand, John,
The *wuth* o' bein' free.
Ole Uncle S, sez he, "I guess,
God's price is high," sez he:
"But nothin' else than wut he sells
Wears long, an' thet J. B.
May larn like you an' me!"

J. R. LOWELL: *Mason and Slidell.*

THE FLAG.

THERE'S a flag hangs over my threshold, whose folds are more dear to me
Than the blood that thrills in my bosom its earnest of liberty;
And dear are the stars it harbors in its sunny field of blue
As the hope of a further heaven that lights all our dim lives through.

But now should my guests be merry,
the house is in holiday guise,
Looking out, through its burnished
windows like a score of welcoming eyes.
Come hither, my brothers who wander in saintliness and in sin!
Come hither, ye pilgrims of Nature!
my heart doth invite you in.

My wine is not of the choicest, yet
bears it an honest brand;
And the bread that I bid you lighten
I break with no sparing hand;
But pause, ere you pass to taste it,
one act must accomplished be:
Salute the flag in its virtue, before
ye sit down with me.

The flag of our stately battles, not
struggles of wrath and greed:
Its stripes were a holy lesson, its
spangles a deathless creed;
'Twas red with the blood of freemen, and white with the fear
of the foe,
And the stars that fight in their
courses 'gainst tyrants its
symbols know.

Come hither, thou son of my mother! we were reared in the
selfsame arms;
Thou hast many a pleasant gesture,
thy mind hath its gifts and
charms,
But my heart is as stern to question
as mine eyes are of sorrows
full:
Salute the flag in its virtue, or pass
on where others rule.

Thou lord of a thousand acres, with
heaps of uncounted gold,
The steeds of thy stall are haughty,
thy lackeys cunning and bold:
I envy no jot of thy splendor, I rail
at thy follies none:
Salute the flag in its virtue, or leave
my poor house alone.

Fair lady with silken trappings, high
waving thy stainless plume,
We welcome thee to our numbers, a
flower of costliest bloom:
Let a hundred maids live widowed
to furnish thy bridal bed;
But pause where the flag doth question, and bend thy triumphant
head.

Take down now your flaunting banner, for a scout comes breathless and pale,
With the terror of death upon him;
of failure is all his tale:
"They have fled while the flag
waved o'er them! they have
turned to the foe their back!
They are scattered, pursued, and
slaughtered! the fields are all
rout and wrack!"

Pass hence, then, the friends I gathered, a goodly company!
All ye that have manhood in you,
go, perish for Liberty!
But I and the babes God gave
me will wait with uplifted
hearts,
With the firm smile ready to kindle,
and the will to perform our
parts.

When the last true heart lies bloodless, when the fierce and the
false have won,
I'll press in turn to my bosom each
daughter and either son;
Bid them loose the flag from its
bearings, and we'll lay us
down to rest
With the glory of home about us,
and its freedom locked in our
breast.

JULIA WARD HOWE.

THE WASHERS OF THE SHROUD.

ALONG a river-side, I know not
where,
I walked one night in mystery of
dream;
A chill creeps curdling yet beneath
my hair,
To think what chanced me by the pallid gleam
Of a moor-wraith that waned through
haunted air.

Pale fire-flies pulsed within the meadow mist
Their halos, wavering thistle-downs
of light;
The loon, that seemed to mock some
goblin tryst,

Laughed; and the echoes, huddling in affright,
Like Odin's hounds, fled baying down the night.

Then all was silent, till there smote my ear
A movement in the stream that checked my breath:
Was it the slow plash of a wading deer?
But something said, "This water is of Death!
The Sisters wash a Shroud, — ill thing to hear!"

I, looking then, beheld the ancient Three,
Known to the Greek's and to the Norseman's creed,
That sit in shadow of the mystic Tree,
Still crooning, as they weave their endless brede,
One song: "Time was, Time is, and Time shall be."

No wrinkled crones were they, as I had deemed,
But fair as yesterday, to-day, to-morrow,
To mourner, lover, poet, ever seemed:
Something too high for joy, too deep for sorrow,
Thrilled in their tones, and from their faces gleamed.

"Still men and nations reap as they have strawn;"
So sang they, working at their task the while;
"The fatal raiment must be cleansed ere dawn;
For Austria? Italy? the Sea-Queen's Isle?
O'er what quenched grandeur must our shroud be drawn?

"Or is it for a younger, fairer corse,
That gathered States for children round his knees,
That tamed the wave to be his posting-horse,
Feller of forests, linker of the seas,
Bridge-builder, hammerer, youngest son of Thor's?

"What make we, murmur'st thou, and what are we?
When empires must be wound, we bring the shroud,
The time-old web of the implacable Three:
Is it too coarse for him, the young and proud?
Earth's mightiest deigned to wear it; why not he?"

"Is there no hope?" I moaned. "So strong, so fair!
Our Fowler, whose proud bird would brook erewhile
No rival's swoop in all our western air!
Gather the ravens, then, in funeral file
For him, life's morn-gold bright yet in his hair!

"Leave me not hopeless, ye unpitying dames!
I see, half seeing. Tell me, ye who scanned
The stars, Earth's elders, still must noblest aims
Be traced upon oblivious ocean-sands?
Must Hesper join the wailing ghosts of names?"

"When grass-blades stiffen with red battle-dew,
Ye deem we choose the victor and the slain:
Say, choose we them that shall be leal and true
To the heart's longing, the high faith of brain?
Yet there the victory lies, if ye but knew.

"Three roots bear up dominion: Knowledge, Will;
These twain are strong, but stronger yet the third —
Obedience, 'tis the great tap-root, that still,
Knit round the rock of Duty, is not stirred,
Though Heaven-loosed tempests spend their utmost skill.

"Is the doom sealed for Hesper? 'Tis not we
Denounce it, but the Law before all time:

The brave makes danger opportunity;
The waverer, paltering with the chance sublime,
Dwarfs it to peril: which shall Hesper be?

"Hath he let vultures climb his eagle's seat,
To make Jove's bolts purveyors of their maw?
Hath he the Many's plaudits found more sweet
Than Wisdom? held Opinion's wind for Law?
Then let him hearken for the doomster's feet!

"Rough are the steps, slow-hewn in flintiest rock,
States climb to power by; slippery those with gold,
Down which they stumble to eternal mock;
No chafferer's hand shall long the sceptre hold,
Who, given a Fate to shape, would sell the block.

"We sing old sagas, songs of weal and woe,
Mystic because too cheaply understood;
Dark sayings are not ours; men hear and know,
See Evil weak; see strength alone in Good,
Yet hope to stem God's fire with walls of tow.

"Time Was unlocks the riddle of Time Is,
That offers choice of glory or of gloom;
The solver makes Time Shall Be surely his.
But hasten, Sisters! for even now the tomb
Grates its slow hinge, and calls from the abyss."

"But not for him," I cried, "not yet for him,
Whose large horizon, westering, star by star
Wins from the void to where on Ocean's rim
The sunset shuts the world with golden bar—
Not yet his thews shall fail, his eye grow dim!

"His shall be larger manhood, saved for those
That walk unblenching through the trial-fires;
Not suffering, but faint heart, is worst of woes,
And he no base-born son of craven sires,
Whose eye need blench, confronted with his foes.

"Tears may be ours, but proud, for those who win
Death's royal purple in the foeman's lines:
Peace, too, brings tears, and 'mid the battle-din,
The wiser ear some text of God divines;
For the sheathed blade may rust with darker sin.

"God, give us peace! not such as lulls to sleep,
But sword on thigh, and brow with purpose knit!
And let our Ship of State to harbor sweep,
Her ports all up, her battle-lanterns lit,
And her leashed thunders gathering for their leap!"

So cried I, with clinched hands and passionate pain,
Thinking of dear ones by Potomac's side:
Again the loon laughed, mocking; and again
The echoes bayed far down the night, and died,
While waking, I recalled my wandering brain.

J. R. LOWELL.

THE CUMBERLAND.

AT anchor in Hampton Roads we lay,
  On board of the Cumberland, sloop-of-war;
And at times from the fortress across the bay

The alarum of drums swept past,
Or a bugle blast
From the camp on the shore.

Then far away to the south uprose
A little feather of snow-white smoke,
And we knew that the iron ship of our foes
Was steadily steering its course
To try the force
Of our ribs of oak.

Down upon us heavily runs,
Silent and sullen, the floating fort;
Then comes a puff of smoke from her guns,
And leaps the terrible death,
With fiery breath,
From each open port.

We are not idle, but send her straight
Defiance back in a full broadside!
As hail rebounds from a roof of slate,
Rebounds our heavier hail
From each iron scale
Of the monster's hide.

"Strike your flag!" the rebel cries,
In his arrogant old plantation strain.
"Never!" our gallant Morris replies:
"It is better to sink than to yield!"
And the whole air pealed
With the cheers of our men.

Then, like a kraken huge and black,
She crushed our ribs in her iron grasp!
Down went the Cumberland all a wrack,
With a sudden shudder of death,
And the cannon's breath
For her dying gasp.

Next morn, as the sun rose over the bay,
Still floated our flag at the main-mast-head.
Lord, how beautiful was thy day!
Every waft of the air
Was a whisper of prayer,
Or a dirge for the dead.

Ho! brave hearts that went down in the seas!
Ye are at peace in the troubled stream.
Ho! brave land! with hearts like these,
Thy flag, that is rent in twain,
Shall be one again,
And without a seam!

LONGFELLOW.

SUNTHIN IN A PASTORAL LINE.

ONCE git a smell o' musk into a draw,
An' it clings hold like precerdents in law:
Your gra'ma'am put it there, — when, goodness knows, —
To jes' this-worldify her Sunday-clo'es;
But the old chist wun't sarve her gran'son's wife,
(For, 'thout new funnitoor, wut good in life?)
An' so ole clawfoot, from the precinks dread
O' the spare chamber, slinks into the shed,
Where, dim with dust, it fust or last subsides
To holdin' seeds, an' fifty things besides;
But better days stick fast in heart an' husk,
An' all you keep in't gits a scent o' musk.

Jes' so with poets: wut they've airly read
Gits kind o' worked into their heart an' head,
So's't they can't seem to write but jest on sheers
With furrin countries or played-out ideers,
Nor hev a feelin', ef it doosn't smack
O' wut some critter chose to feel 'way back:
This makes 'em talk o' daises, larks, an' things,
Ez though we'd nothin' here that blows an' sings, —
(Why, I'd give more for one live bobolink

Than a square mile o' larks in printer's ink,) —
This makes 'em think our fust 'o May is May,
Which't ain't, for all the almanicks can say.

O little city-gals! don't never go it
Blind on the word o' noospaper or poet!
They're apt to puff, an' May-day seldom looks
Up in the country ez it doos in books;
They're no more like than hornets' nests an' hives,
Or printed sarmons be to holy lives.
I, with my trouses perched on cowhide boots,
Tuggin' my foundered feet out by the roots,
Hev seen ye come to fling on April's hearse
Your muslin nosegays from the milliner's,
Puzzlin' to find dry ground your queen to choose,
An' dance your throats sore in morocker shoes:
I've seen ye, an' felt proud, thet, come wut would,
Our Pilgrim stock wuz pithed with hardihood.
Pleasure doos make us Yankees kind o' winch,
Ez though 'twuz sunthin' paid for by the inch;
But yit we du contrive to worry thru,
Ef Dooty tells us thet the thing's to du,
An' kerry a hollerday, ef we set out,
Ez stiddily ez though 'twuz a redoubt.

I, country-born an' bred, know where to find
Some blooms thet make the season suit the mind,
An' seem to metch the doubtin' bluebird's notes, —
Half-vent'rin' liverworts in furry coats,
Bloodroots, whose rolled-up leaves ef you oncurl,
Each on 'em's cradle to a baby-pearl, —
But these are jes' Spring's pickets; sure ez sin,
The rebble frosts'll try to drive 'em in;
For half our May's so awfully like Mayn't,
'Twould rile a Shaker or an evrige saint;
Though I own up I like our back'ard springs
Thet kind o' haggle with their greens an' things,
An' when you 'most give up, 'ithout more words
Toss the fields full o' blossoms, leaves, an' birds:
Thet's Northun natur', slow, an' apt to doubt,
But when it *doos* git stirred, ther's no gin-out!

Fust come the blackbirds clatt'rin' in tall trees,
An' settlin' things in windy Congresses, —
Queer politicians, though, for I'll be skinned
Ef all on 'em don't head against the wind.
'Fore long the trees begin to show belief, —
The maple crimsons to a coral-reef,
Then saffern swarms swing off from all the willers
So plump they look like yaller caterpillars,
Then gray hoss-ches'nuts leetle hands unfold
Softer'n a baby's be at three days old:
Thet's robin-redbreast's almanick; he knows
Thet arter this ther's only blossom-snows;
So, choosin' out a handy crotch an' spouse,
He goes to plast'rin' his adobë house.

Then seems to come a hitch, — things lag behind,
Till some fine mornin' Spring makes up her mind,
An' ez, when snow-swelled rivers cresh their dams
Heaped-up with ice thet dovetails in an' jams,
A leak comes spirtin' thru some pin-hole cleft,

Grows stronger, fercer, tears out right an' left,
Then all the waters bow themselves an' come,
Suddin, in one great slope o' shedderin' foam,
Jes' so our Spring gits every thin' in tune,
An' gives one leap from April into June:
Then all comes crowdin' in; afore you think,
Young oak-leaves mist the side-hill woods with pink;
The cat-bird in the laylock-bush is loud;
The orchards turn to heaps o' rosy cloud;
Red-cedars blossom tu, though few folks know it,
An' look all dipt in sunshine like a poet;
The lime-trees pile their solid stacks o' shade,
An' drows'ly simmer with the bees' sweet trade;
In ellum-shrouds the flashin' hang-bird clings
An' for the summer vy'ge his hammock slings:
All down the loose-walled lanes in archin' bowers
The barb'ry droops its strings o' golden flowers,
Whose shrinkin' hearts the school-gals love to try
With pins, — they'll worry yourn so, boys, bimeby!
But I don't love your cat'logue style, — do you? —
Ez ef to sell off Natur' by vendoo;
One word with blood in't's ez twice ez good ez two:
'Nuff sed, June's bridesman, poet o' the year,
Gladness on wings, the bobolink, is here;
Half-hid in tip-top apple-blooms he swings,
Or climbs aginst the breeze with quiverin' wings,
Or, givin' way to't in a mock despair,
Runs down, a brook o' laughter, thru the air.
I ollus feel the sap start in my veins
In Spring, with curus heats an' prickly pains,
Thet drive me, when I git a chance, to walk
Off by myself to hev a privit talk
With a queer critter thet can't seem to 'gree
Along o' me like most folks, — Mister Me.
Ther' is times when I'm unsoshle ez a stone,
An' sort o' suffocate to be alone, —
I'm crowded jes' to think thet folks are nigh,
An' can't bear nothin' closer than the sky;
Now the wind's full ez shifty in the mind
Ez wut it is ou'-doors, ef I ain't blind,
An, sometimes, in the fairest sou'-west weather,
My inward vane pints east for weeks together,
My natur' gits all goose-flesh, an' my sins
Come drizzlin' on my conscience sharp ez pins:
Wal, et sech times I jes' slip out o' sight,
An' take it out in a fair stan' up fight
With the one cuss I can't lay on the shelf,
The crook'dest stick in all the heap, — myself.

'Twuz so las' Sabbath arter meetin'-time:
Findin' my feelin's wouldn't noways rhyme
With nobody's, but off the hendle flew
An' took things from an east-wind pint o' view,
I started off to lose me in the hills
Where the pines be, up back o' Siah's Mills:
Pines, ef you're blue, are the best friends I know,
They mope an' sigh an' sheer your feelin's so, —
They hesh the ground beneath so, tu, I swan,
You half-forgit you've gut a body on.
Ther's a small skool'us' there where four roads meet,
The door-steps hollered out by little feet,
An' side-post carved with names whose owners grew

To gret men, some on 'em an' deacons, tu;
'Tain't used no longer, coz the town hez gut
A high-school, where they teach the Lord knows wut:
Three-story larnin's pop'lar now; I guess
We thriv' ez wal on jes' two stories less,
For it strikes me ther's sech a thing ez sinnin'
By overloadin' children's underpinnin':
Wal, here it wuz I larned my A, B, C,
An' it's a kind o' favorite spot with me.

We're curus critters: Now ain't jes' the minute
That ever fits us easy while we're in it;
Long ez 'twuz futur', 'twould be perfect bliss,—
Soon ez it's past, *thet* time's wuth ten o' this;
An' yit there ain't a man thet need be told
Thet Now's the only bird lays eggs o' gold.
A knee-high lad, I used to plot an' plan
An' think 'twuz life's cap-sheaf to be a man;
Now, gittin' gray, there's nothin' I enjoy
Like dreamin' back along into a boy:
So the ole school'us' is a place I choose
Afore all others, ef I want to muse;
I set down where I used to set, an' git
My boyhood back, an' better things with it,—
Faith, Hope, an' sunthin', ef it isn't Cherrity,
It's want o' guile, an' thet's ez gret a rerrity.

Now, 'fore I knowed, thet Sabbath arternoon
Thet I sot out to tramp myself in tune,
I found me in the school'us' on my seat,
Drummin' the march to No-wheres with my feet.
Thinkin' o' nothin', I've heerd ole folks say,
Is a hard kind o' dooty in its way:
It's thinkin' every thin' you ever knew,
Or ever hearn, to make your feelins blue.
I sot there tryin' thet on for a spell:
I thought o' the Rebellion, then o' Hell,
Which some folks tell ye now is jes' a metterfor,
(A the'ry, p'raps, it wun't *feel* none the better for);
I thought o' Reconstruction, wut we'd win
Patchin' our patent self-blow-up agin:
I thought ef this 'ere milkin' o' the wits,
So much a month, warn't givin' Natur' fits,—
Ef folks warn't druv, findin' their own milk fail,
To work the cow thet hes an iron tail,
An' ef idees 'thout ripenin' in the pan
Would send up cream to humor ary man:
From this to thet I let my worryin' creep,
Till finally I must ha' fell asleep.

Our lives in sleep are some like streams thet glide
'Twixt flesh an' sperrit boundin' on each side,
Where both shores' shadders kind o' mix an' mingle
In sunthin' thet ain't jes' like either single;
An' when you cast off moorin's from To-day,
An' down towards To-morrer drift away,
The imiges thet tengle on the stream
Make a new upside-down'ard world o' dream:
Sometimes they seem like sunrise-streaks an' warnin's
O' wut'll be in Heaven on Sabbath-mornin's,
An', mixed right in ez ef jest out o' spite,
Sunthin' thet says your supper ain't gone right.
I'm gret on dreams, an' often, when I wake,

I've lived so much it makes my mem'ry ache,
An' can't skurce take a cat-nap in my cheer
'Thout hevin' 'em, some good, some bad, all queer.

Now I wuz settin' where I'd ben, it seemed,
An' ain't sure yit whether I r'ally dreamed,
Nor, ef I did, how long I might ha' slep',
When I hearn some un stompin' up the step,
An' lookin' round, ef two an' two make four,
I see a Pilgrim Father in the door.
He wore a steeple-hat, tall boots, an' spurs
With rowels to 'em big ez ches'nut-burrs,
An' his gret sword behind him sloped away
Long'z a man's speech thet dunno wut to say. —
"Ef your name's Biglow, an' your given-name
Hosee," sez he, "it's arter you I came;
I'm your gret-gran'ther multiplied by three." —
"My *wut?*" sez I. — "Your gret-gret-gret," sez he:
"You wouldn't ha' never ben here but for me.
Two hundred an' three year ago this May
The ship I come in sailed up Boston Bay;
I'd been a cunnle in our Civil War, —
But wut on airth hev *you* gut up one for?
Coz we du things in England, 'tain't for you
To git a notion you can du 'em tu:
I'm told you write in public prints: ef true,
It's nateral you should know a thing or two." —
'Thet air's an argymunt I can't endorse, —
'Twould prove, coz you wear spurs, you kep' a horse:
For brains," sez I, "wutever you may think,
Ain't boun' to cash the drafs o' pen-an'-ink, —
Though mos' folks write ez ef they hoped jes' quickenin'
The churn would argoo skim-milk into thickenin';
But skim-milk ain't a thing to change its view
O' wut it's meant for more'n a smoky flue.
But du pray tell me, 'fore we furder go,
How in all Natur' did you come to know
'Bout our affairs," sez I, "in Kingdom Come?" —
"Wal, I worked round at sperrit-rappin' some,
An' danced the tables till their legs wuz gone,
In hopes o' larnin' wut wuz goin' on,"
Sez he, "but mejums lie so like all-split
Thet I concluded it wuz best to quit.
But, come now, ef you wun't confess to knowin',
You've some conjectures how the thing's a-goin'." —
"Gran'ther," sez I, "a vane warn't never known
Nor asked to hev a jedgment of its own;
An' yit, ef 'tain't gut rusty in the jints,
It's safe to trust its say on certin pints:
It knows the wind's opinions to a T,
An' the wind settles wut the weather'll be."
"I never thought a scion of our stock
Could grow the wood to make a weathercock;
When I wuz younger'n you, skurce more'n a shaver,
No airthly wind," sez he, "could make me waver!"
(Ez he said this, he clinched his jaw an' forehead,
Hitchin' his belt to bring his sword-hilt forrard.) —
"Jes' so it wuz with me," sez I, "I swow,
When *I* wuz younger'n what you see me now, —
Nothin' from Adam's fall to Huldy's bonnet,
Thet I warn't full-cocked with my jedgment on it;

But now I'm gittin' on in life, I find
It's a sight harder to make up my mind, —
Nor I don't often try tu, when events
Will du it for me free of all expense.
The moral question's ollus plain enough, —
It's jes' the human-natur' side thet's tough;
Wut's best to think mayn't puzzle me nor you, —
The pinch comes in decidin' wut to *du;*
Ef you *read* History, all runs smooth ez grease,
Coz there the men ain't nothin' more'n idees, —
But come to *make* it, ez we must to-day,
Th' idees hev arms an' legs, an' stop the way:
It's easy fixin' things in facts an' figgers, —
They can't resist, nor warn't brought up with niggers;
But come to try your the'ry on,— why, then
Your facts an' figgers change to ign'ant men
Actin' ez ugly" — "Smite 'em hip an' thigh!"
Sez gran'ther, "an' let every man-child die!
Oh for three weeks o' Crommle an' the Lord!
Up, Isr'el, to your tents an' grind the sword!" —
"Thet kind o' thing worked wal in ole Judee,
But you forgit how long it's ben A.D.;
You think thet's ellerkence, — I call it shoddy,
A thing," sez I, "wun't cover soul nor body;
I like the plain all-wool o' common-sense,
Thet warms ye now, an' will a twelvemonth hence.
You took to follerin' where the Prophets beckoned,
An,' fust you knowed on, back come Charles the Second;
Now wut I want's to hev all *we* gain stick,
An' not to start Millennium too quick;
We hain't to punish only, but to keep,
An' the cure's gut to go a cent'ry deep."
"Wal, milk-an'-water ain't the best o' glue,"
Sez he, "an' so you'll find before you're thru;
Ef reshness venters sunthin', shilly-shally
Lozes ez often wut's ten times the vally.
Thet exe of ourn, when Charles's neck gut split,
Opened a gap thet ain't bridged over yit:
Slav'ry's your Charles, the Lord hez gin the exe" —
"Our Charles," sez I, "hez gut eight million necks.
The hardest question ain't the black man's right,
The trouble is to 'mancipate the white;
One's chained in body an' can be sot free,
But t'other's chained in soul to an idee:
It's a long job, but we shall worry thru it;
Ef bag'nets fail, the spellin'-book must du it."
"Hosee," sez he, "I think you're goin' to fail:
The rettlesnake ain't dangerous in the tail;
This 'ere rebellion's nothin' but the rettle, —
You'll stomp on thet an' think you've won the bettle;
It's Slavery thet's the fangs an' thinkin' head,
An' ef you want selvation, cresh it dead, —
An' cresh it suddin, or you'll larn by waitin'
Thet Chance wun't stop to listen to debatin'!—
"God's truth!" sez I, — "an' ef *I* held the club,
An' knowed jes' where to strike, — but there's the rub!" —
"Strike soon," sez he, "or you'll be deadly ailin', —
Folks thet's afeared to fail are sure o' failin';
God hates your sneakin' creturs thet believe

He'll settle things they run away an' leave!"
He brought his foot down fercely, ez he spoke,
An' give me sech a startle thet I woke.

J. R. Lowell: *Biglow Papers.*

WHAT THE BIRDS SAID.

The birds, against the April wind,
Flew northward, singing as they flew;
They sang, "The land we leave behind
Has swords for corn-blades, blood for dew."

"O wild-birds, flying from the South,
What saw and heard ye, gazing down?"
"We saw the mortar's upturned mouth,
The sickened camp, the blazing town!

"Beneath the bivouac's starry lamps,
We saw your march-worn children die;
In shrouds of moss, in cypress swamps,
We saw your dead uncoffined lie.

"We heard the starving prisoner's sighs;
And saw, from line and trench, your sons
Follow our flight with home-sick eyes
Beyond the battery's smoking guns."

"And heard and saw ye only wrong
And pain," I cried, "O wing-worn flocks?"
"We heard," they sang, "the Freedman's song,
The crash of Slavery's broken locks!

"We saw from new, uprising States
The treason-nursing mischief spurned,
As, crowding Freedom's ample gates,
The long-estranged and lost returned.

"O'er dusky faces, seamed and old,
And hands horn-hard with unpaid toil,
With hope in every rustling fold,
We saw your star-dropt flag uncoil.

"And, struggling up through sounds accursed,
A grateful murmur clomb the air,
A whisper scarcely heard at first,
It filled the listening heavens with prayer.

"And sweet and far, as from a star,
Replied a voice which shall not cease,
Till, drowning all the noise of war,
It sings the blessed song of peace!"

So to me, in a doubtful day
Of chill and slowly-greening spring,
Low stooping from the cloudy gray,
The wild-birds sang or seemed to sing.

They vanished in the misty air,
The song went with them in their flight;
But lo! they left the sunset fair,
And in the evening there was light.

Whittier.

A LOYAL WOMAN'S NO.

No! is my answer from this cold bleak ridge
Down to your valley: you may rest you there:
The gulf is wide, and none can build a bridge
That your gross weight would safely hither bear.

Pity me, if you will. I look at you
With something that is kinder far than scorn,
And think, "Ah well! I might have grovelled too;
I might have walked there, fettered and forsworn."

I am of nature weak as others are;
I might have chosen comfortable ways;

Once from these heights I shrank, beheld afar,
In the soft lap of quiet, easy days.

I might — (I will not hide it) — once I might
Have lost, in the warm whirlpools of your voice,
The sense of Evil, the stern cry of Right;
But truth has steered me free, and I rejoice:

Not with the triumph that looks back to jeer
At the poor herd that call their misery bliss;
But as a mortal speaks when God is near,
I drop you down my answer; it is this: —

I am not yours, because you seek in me
What is the lowest in my own esteem:
Only my flowery levels can you see,
Nor of my heaven-smit summits do you dream.

I am not yours, because you love yourself:
Your heart has scarcely room for me beside.
I could not be shut in with name and pelf;
I spurn the shelter of your narrow pride!

Not yours; because you are not man enough
To grasp your country's measure of a man!
If such as you, when Freedom's ways are rough,
Cannot walk in them, learn that women can!

Not yours, because, in this the nation's need,
You stoop to bend her losses to your gain,
And do not feel the meanness of your deed;
I touch no palm defiled with such a stain!

Whether man's thought can find too lofty steeps
For woman's scaling, care not I to know;
But when he falters by her side, or creeps,
She must not clog her soul with him to go.

Who weds me must at least with equal pace
Sometimes move with me at my being's height:
To follow him to his more glorious place,
His purer atmosphere, were keen delight.

You lure me to the valley: men should call
Up to the mountains, where the air is clear.
Win me and help me climbing, if at all!
Beyond these peaks rich harmonies I hear, —

The morning chant of Liberty and Law!
The dawn pours in, to wash out Slavery's blot:
Fairer than aught the bright sun ever saw
Rises a nation without stain or spot.

The men and women mated for that time
Tread not the soothing mosses of the plain;
Their hands are joined in sacrifice sublime;
Their feet firm set in upward paths of pain.

Sleep your thick sleep, and go your drowsy way!
You cannot hear the voices in the air!
Ignoble souls will shrivel in that day:
The brightness of its coming can you bear?

For me, I do not walk these hills alone:
Heroes who poured their blood out for the Truth,

Women whose hearts bled, martyrs all unknown,
Here catch the sunrise of immortal youth
On their pale cheeks and consecrated brows!
It charms me not, — your call to rest below:
I press their hands, my lips pronounce their vows:
Take my life's silence for your answer: No.

LUCY LARCOM.

THE BAY FIGHT.*

"On the forecastle, Ulf the Red
Watched the lashing of the ships —
'If the Serpent lies so far ahead,
We shall have hard work of it here,'
Said he."

THREE days through sapphire seas we sailed,
The steady Trade blew strong and free,
The Northern Light his banners paled,
The Ocean Stream our channels wet,
We rounded low Canaveral's lee,
And passed the isles of emerald set
In blue Bahama's turquoise sea.

By reef and shoal obscurely mapped,
And hauntings of the gray sea-wolf,
The palmy Western Key lay lapped
In the warm washing of the Gulf.

But weary to the hearts of all
The burning glare, the barren reach
Of Santa Rosa's withered beach,
And Pensacola's ruined wall.

And weary was the long patrol,
The thousand miles of shapeless strand,
From Brazos to San Blas that roll
Their drifting dunes of desert sand.

Yet coast-wise as we cruised or lay,
The land-breeze still at nightfall bore,
By beach and fortress-guarded bay,
Sweet odors from the enemy's shore,

Fresh from the forest solitudes,
Unchallenged of his sentry lines, —
The bursting of his cypress buds,
And the warm fragrance of his pines.

Ah, never braver bark and crew,
Nor bolder Flag a foe to dare,
Had left a wake on ocean blue
Since Lion-Heart sailed Trenc-le-mer!*

But little gain by that dark ground
Was ours, save, sometime, freer breath
For friend or brother strangely found,
'Scaped from the drear domain of death.

And little venture for the bold,
Or laurel for our valiant Chief,
Save some blockaded British thief,
Full fraught with murder in his hold,

Caught unawares at ebb or flood,
Or dull bombardment, day by day,
With fort and earth-work, far away,
Low couched in sullen leagues of mud.

A weary time, — but to the strong
The day at last, as ever, came;
And the volcano, laid so long,
Leaped forth in thunder and in flame!

"Man your starboard battery!"
Kimberly shouted; —
The ship, with her hearts of oak,
Was going, 'mid roar and smoke,
On to victory!
None of us doubted,
No, not our dying, —
Farragut's Flag was flying!

Gaines growled low on our left,
Morgan roared on our right; —
Before us, gloomy and fell,
With breath like the fume of hell,
Lay the Dragon of iron shell,
Driven at last to the fight!

Ha, old ship! do they thrill,
The brave two hundred scars

* Mobile Bay, Aug. 5, 1864.

* The flag-ship of Richard I.

You got in the River-Wars?
That were leeched with clamorous skill,
(Surgery savage and hard,)
Splinted with bolt and beam,
Probed in scarfing and seam,
Rudely linted and tarred
With oakum and boiling pitch,
And sutured with splice and hitch,
At the Brooklyn Navy-Yard!

Our lofty spars were down,
To bide the battle's frown,
(Wont of old renown) —
But every ship was drest
In her bravest and her best,
As if for a July day;
Sixty flags and three,
As we floated up the bay —
At every peak and mast-head flew
The brave Red, White, and Blue, —
We were eighteen ships that day.

With hawsers strong and taut,
The weaker lashed to port,
On we sailed two by two —
That if either a bolt should feel
Crash through caldron or wheel,
Fin of bronze, or sinew of steel,
Her mate might bear her through.

Forging boldly ahead,
The great Flag-Ship led,
Grandest of sights!
On her lofty mizzen flew
Our Leader's dauntless Blue,
That had waved o'er twenty fights;
So we went, with the first of the tide,
Slowly, 'mid the roar
Of the rebel guns ashore
And the thunder of each full broadside.

Ah, how poor the prate
Of statute and state
We once held with these fellows!
Here, on the flood's pale-green,
Hark how he bellows,
Each bluff old Sea-Lawyer!
Talk to them Dahlgren,
Parrott, and Sawyer!

On, in the whirling shade
Of the cannon's sulphury breath,
We drew to the Line of Death
That our devilish Foe had laid, —
Meshed in a horrible net,
And baited villanous well,
Right in our path were set
Three hundred traps of hell!

And there, O sight forlorn!
There, while the cannon
Hurtled and thundered, —
(Ah, what ill raven
Flapped o'er the ship that morn!) —
Caught by the under-death,
In the drawing of a breath
Down went dauntless Craven,
He and his hundred!

A moment we saw her turret,
A little heel she gave,
And a thin white spray went o'er her,
Like the crest of a breaking wave; —
In that great iron coffin,
The channel for their grave,
The fort their monument,
(Seen afar in the offing,)
Ten fathom deep lie Craven
And the bravest of our brave.

Then, in that deadly track,
A little the ships held back,
Closing up in their stations; —
There are minutes that fix the fate
Of battles and of nations,
(Christening the generations)
When valor were all too late,
If a moment's doubt be harbored; —
From the main-top, bold and brief,
Came the word of our grand old chief, —
"Go on!" — 'twas all he said, —
Our helm was put to starboard,
And the Hartford passed ahead.

Ahead lay the Tennessee,
On our starboard bow he lay,
With his mail-clad consorts three,
(The rest had run up the Bay,) —
There he was, belching flame from his bow,
And the steam from his throat's abyss
Was a Dragon's maddened hiss; —
In sooth a most cursed craft! —
In a sullen ring, at bay,
By the Middle Ground they lay,
Raking us, fore and aft.

Trust me, our berth was hot,
Ah, wickedly well they shot —
How their death-bolts howled and stung!
And the water-batteries played
With their deadly cannonade
Till the air around us rung;
So the battle raged and roared; —
Ah, had you been aboard
To have seen the fight we made!

How they leaped, the tongues of flame,
From the cannon's fiery lip!
How the broadsides, deck and frame,
Shook the great ship!

And how the enemy's shell
Came crashing, heavy and oft,
Clouds of splinters flying aloft
And falling in oaken showers; —
But ah, the pluck of the crew!
Had you stood on that deck of ours,
You had seen what men may do.

Still, as the fray grew louder,
Boldly they worked and well —
Steadily came the powder,
Steadily came the shell.
And if tackle or truck found hurt,
Quickly they cleared the wreck —
And the dead were laid to port,
All a-row, on our deck.

Never a nerve that failed,
Never a cheek that paled,
Not a tinge of gloom or pallor; —
There was bold Kentucky's grit,
And the old Virginian valor,
And the daring Yankee wit.

There were blue eyes from turfy Shannon,
There were black orbs from palmy Niger, —
But there, alongside the cannon,
Each man fought like a tiger!

A little, once, it looked ill,
Our consort began to burn —
They quenched the flames with a will,
But our men were falling still,
And still the fleet was astern.

Right abreast of the Fort
In an awful shroud they lay,
Broadsides thundering away,
And lightning from every port;
Scene of glory and dread!
A storm-cloud all aglow
With flashes of fiery red,
The thunder raging below,
And the forest of flags o'erhead!

So grand the hurly and roar,
So fiercely their broadsides blazed,
The regiments fighting ashore
Forgot to fire as they gazed.

There, to silence the Foe,
Moving grimly and slow,
They loomed in that deadly wreath,
Where the darkest batteries frowned, —
Death in the air all round,
And the black torpedoes beneath!

And now, as we looked ahead,
All for'ard, the long white deck,
Was growing a strange dull red —
But soon, as once and again
Fore and aft we sped,
(The firing to guide or check,)
You could hardly choose but tread
On the ghastly human wreck,
(Dreadful gobbet and shred
That a minute ago were men!)

Red, from main-mast to bitts!
Red, on bulwark and wale,
Red, by combing and hatch,
Red, o'er netting and vail!

And ever, with steady con,
The ship forged slowly by, —
And ever the crew fought on,
And their cheers rang loud and high.

Grand was the sight to see
How by their guns they stood,
Right in front of our dead,
Fighting square abreast, —
Each brawny arm and chest
All spotted with black and red,
Chrism of fire and blood!

Worth our watch, dull and sterile,
Worth all the weary time,
Worth the woe and the peril,
To stand in that strait sublime!

Fear? A forgotten form!
Death? A dream of the eyes!
We were atoms in God's great storm
That roared through the angry skies.

One only doubt was ours,
One only dread we knew, —
Could the day that dawned so well
Go down for the Darker Powers?
Would the fleet get through?
And ever the shot and shell
Came with the howl of hell,
The splinter-clouds rose and fell,
And the long line of corpses grew, —
Would the fleet win through?

They are men that never will fail,
(How aforetime they've fought!)
But Murder may yet prevail, —
They may sink as Craven sank.
Therewith one hard fierce thought,
Burning on heart and lip,
Ran like fire through the ship, —
Fight her, to the last plank!

A dimmer renown might strike
If Death lay square alongside, —
But the Old Flag has no like,
She must fight, whatever betide; —
When the War is a tale of old,
And this day's story is told,
They shall hear how the Hartford died!

But as we ranged ahead,
And the leading ships worked in,
Losing their hope to win,
The enemy turned and fled —
And one seeks a shallow reach;
And another, winged in her flight,
Our mate, brave Jouett, brings in; —
And one, all torn in the fight,
Runs for a wreck on the beach,
Where her flames soon fire the night.

And the Ram, when well up the Bay,
And we looked that our stems should meet,
(He had us fair for a prey,)
Shifting his helm midway,
Sheered off, and ran for the fleet;
There, without skulking or sham,
He fought them, gun for gun.
And ever he sought to ram,
But could finish never a one.

From the first of the iron shower
Till we sent our parting shell,
'Twas just one savage hour
Of the roar and the rage of hell.

With the lessening smoke and thunder,
Our glasses around we aim, —
What is that burning yonder?
Our Philippi — aground and in flame!

Below, 'twas still all a-roar,
As the ships went by the shore,
But the fire of the Fort had slacked,
(So fierce their volleys had been) —
And now, with a mighty din,
The whole fleet came grandly in,
Though sorely battered and wracked.

So, up the Bay we ran,
The Flag to port and ahead —
And a pitying rain began
To wash the lips of our dead.

A league from the Fort we lay,
And deemed that the end must lag, —
When lo! looking down the Bay,
There flaunted the Rebel Rag; —
The Ram is again under way
And heading dead for the Flag!

Steering up with the stream,
Boldly his course he lay,
Though the fleet all answered his fire,
And, as he still drew nigher,
Ever on bow and beam
Our Monitors pounded away; —
How the Chickasaw hammered away!

Quickly breasting the wave,
Eager the prize to win,
First of us all the brave
Monongahela went in
Under full head of steam; —
Twice she struck him abeam,
Till her stem was a sorry work,
(She might have run on a crag!)
The Lackawana hit fair,
He flung her aside like cork,
And still he held for the Flag.

High in the mizzen shroud,
(Lest the smoke his sight o'erwhelm,)
Our Admiral's voice rang loud,
"Hard-a-starboard your helm!
Starboard! and run him down!"

Starboard it was, — and so,
Like a black squall's lifting frown,
Our mighty bow bore down
On the iron beak of the Foe.

We stood on the deck together,
Men that had looked on death
In battle and stormy weather, —
Yet a little we held our breath,
When, with the hush of death,
The great ships drew together.

Our Captain strode to the bow,
Drayton, courtly and wise,
Kindly cynic, and wise,
(You hardly had known him now,
The flame of fight in his eyes!) —
His brave heart eager to feel
How the oak would tell on the steel!

But, as the space grew short,
A little he seemed to shun us,
Out peered a form grim and lanky,
And a voice yelled — "Hard-a-port!
Hard-a-port! — here's the damned Yankee
Coming right down on us!"

He sheered, but the ships ran foul
With a gnarring shudder and growl:
He gave us a deadly gun;
But, as he passed in his pride,
(Rasping right alongside!)
The Old Flag, in thunder-tones,
Poured in her port broadside,
Rattling his iron hide,
And cracking his timber bones!

Just then, at speed on the Foe,
With her bow all weathered and brown,
The great Lackawana came down
Full tilt, for another blow; —
We were forging ahead,
She reversed — but, for all our pains,
Rammed the old Hartford, instead,
Just for'ard the mizzen chains!

Ah! how the masts did buckle and bend,
And the stout hull ring and reel,
As she took us right on end!
(Vain were engine and wheel,
She was under full steam) —
With the roar of a thunder-stroke
Her two thousand tons of oak
Brought up on us, right abeam!

A wreck, as it looked, we lay, —
(Rib and plank shear gave way
To the stroke of that giant wedge!)
Here, after all, we go —
The old ship is gone! — ah, no,
But cut to the water's edge.

Never mind then, — at him again!
His flurry now can't last long;
He'll never again see land, —
Try that on *him*, Marchand!
On him again, brave Strong!

Heading square at the hulk,
Full on his beam we bore;
But the spine of the huge Sea-Hog
Lay on the tide like a log,
He vomited flame no more.

By this, he had found it hot; —
Half the fleet, in an angry ring,
Closed round the hideous Thing,
Hammering with solid shot,
And bearing down, bow on bow, —
He has but a minute to choose;
Life or renown? — which now
Will the Rebel Admiral lose?

Cruel, haughty, and cold,
He ever was strong and bold; —
Shall he shrink from a wooden stem?
He will think of that brave band
He sank in the Cumberland; —
Ay, he will sink like them.

Nothing left but to fight
Boldly his last sea-fight!
Can he strike? By Heaven, 'tis true!
Down comes the traitor Blue,
And up goes the captive White!

Up went the White! Ah, then
The hurrahs that, once and again,
Rang from three thousand men
All flushed and savage with fight!
Our dead lay cold and stark,
But our dying, down in the dark,
Answered as best they might,
Lifting their poor lost arms,
And cheering for God and Right!

Ended the mighty noise,
Thunder of forts and ships.
Down we went to the hold, —
Oh, our dear dying boys!

How we pressed their poor brave lips,
(Ah, so pallid and cold!)
And held their hands to the last
(Those that had hands to hold.)

Still thee, O woman heart!
(So strong an hour ago) —
If the idle tears must start,
'Tis not in vain they flow.

They died, our children dear,
On the drear berth-deck they died, —
Do not think of them here —
Even now their footsteps near
The immortal, tender sphere —
(Land of love and cheer!
Home of the Crucified!)

And the glorious deed survives.
Our threescore, quiet and cold,
Lie thus, for a myriad lives
And treasure-millions untold, —
(Labor of poor men's lives,
Hunger of weans and wives,
Such is war-wasted gold.)

Our ship and her fame to-day
Shall float on the storied Stream
When mast and shroud have crumbled away,
And her long white deck is a dream.

One daring leap in the dark,
Three mortal hours, at the most, —
And hell lies stiff and stark
On a hundred leagues of coast.

For the mighty Gulf is ours, —
The bay is lost and won,
An Empire is lost and won!
Land, if thou yet hast flowers,
Twine them in one more wreath
Of tenderest white and red,
(Twin buds of glory and death!)
For the brows of our brave dead, —
For thy Navy's noblest Son.

Joy, O Land, for thy sons,
Victors by flood and field!
The traitor walls and guns
Have nothing left but to yield; —
(Even now they surrender!)

And the ships shall sail once more,
And the cloud of war sweep on
To break on the cruel shore; —
But Craven is gone,
He and his hundred are gone.

The flags flutter up and down
At sunrise and twilight dim,
The cannons menace and frown, —
But never again for him,
Him and the hundred.

The Dahlgrens are dumb,
Dumb are the mortars;
Never more shall the drum
Beat to colors and quarters, —
The great guns are silent.

O brave heart and loyal!
Let all your colors dip; —
Mourn him, proud ship!
From main deck to royal.
God rest our Captain,
Rest our lost hundred!

Droop, flag and pennant!
What is your pride for?
Heaven, that he died for,
Rest our Lieutenant.
Rest our brave threescore!

O Mother Land! this weary life
We led, we lead, is 'long of thee;
Thine the strong agony of strife,
And thine the lonely sea.

Thine the long decks all slaughter-sprent,
The weary rows of cots that lie
With wrecks of strong men, marred and rent,
'Neath Pensacola's sky.

And thine the iron caves and dens
Wherein the flame our war-fleet drives;
The fiery vaults, whose breath is men's
Most dear and precious lives!

Ah, ever, when with storm sublime
Dread Nature clears our murky air,
Thus in the crash of falling crime
Some lesser guilt must share.

Full red the furnace fires must glow
That melt the ore of mortal kind:
The Mills of God are grinding slow,
But ah, how close they grind!

To-Day the Dahlgren and the drum
  Are dread Apostles of His Name;
His Kingdom here can only come
  By chrism of blood and flame.

Be strong: already slants the gold
  Athwart these wild and stormy skies;
From out this blackened waste, behold
  What happy homes shall rise!

But see thou well no traitor gloze,
  No striking hands with Death and Shame,
Betray the sacred blood that flows
  So freely for thy name.

And never fear a victor foe: —
  Thy children's hearts are strong and high;
Nor mourn too fondly; — well they know
  On deck or field to die.

Nor shalt thou want one willing breath,
  Though, ever smiling round the brave,
The blue sea bear us on to death,
  The green were one wide grave.

U. S. Flag-ship Hartford, Mobile Bay,
August, 1864.

BROWNELL.

ABRAHAM LINCOLN.

FOULLY ASSASSINATED APRIL 14, 1865.

You lay a wreath on murdered Lincoln's bier,
  You, who with mocking pencil wont to trace,
Broad for the self-complacent British sneer,
  His length of shambling limb, his furrowed face,

His gaunt, gnarled hands, his unkempt, bristling hair,
  His garb uncouth, his bearing ill at ease,
His lack of all we prize as debonair,
  Of power or will to shine, of art to please;

You, whose smart pen backed up the pencil's laugh,
  Judging each step as though the way were plain;
Reckless, so it could point its paragraph
  Of chief's perplexity, or people's pain:

Beside this corpse, that bears for winding-sheet
  The Stars and Stripes he lived to rear anew,
Between the mourners at his head and feet,
  Say, scurrile jester, is there room for *you*?

Yes: he had lived to shame me from my sneer,
  To lame my pencil, and confute my pen; —
To make me own this hind of princes peer,
  This rail-splitter a true-born king of men.

My shallow judgment I had learned to rue,
  Noting how to occasion's height he rose;
How his quaint wit made home-truth seem more true;
  How, iron-like, his temper grew by blows.

How humble, yet how hopeful he could be:
  How in good fortune and in ill, the same:
Nor bitter in success, nor boastful he,
  Thirsty for gold, nor feverish for fame.

He went about his work,— such work as few
  Ever had laid on head and heart and hand, —
As one who knows, where there's a task to do,
  Man's honest will must Heaven's good grace command;

Who trusts the strength will with the burden grow,
  That God makes instruments to work his will,

If but that will we can arrive to know,
Nor tamper with the weights of good and ill.

So he went forth to battle, on the side
That he felt clear was Liberty's and Right's,
As in his peasant boyhood he had plied
His warfare with rude Nature's thwarting mights, —

The uncleared forest, the unbroken soil,
The iron-bark, that turns the lumberer's axe,
The rapid, that o'erbears the boatman's toil,
The prairie, hiding the mazed wanderer's tracks,

The ambushed Indian, and the prowling bear; —
Such were the deeds that helped his youth to train:
Rough culture, — but such trees large fruit may bear,
If but their stocks be of right girth and grain.

So he grew up, a destined work to do,
And lived to do it: four long-suffering years'
Ill-fate, ill-feeling, ill-report, lived through,
And then he heard the hisses change to cheers,

The taunts to tribute, the abuse to praise,
And took both with the same unwavering mood:
Till, as he came on light, from darkling days,
And seemed to touch the goal from where he stood,

A felon hand, between the goal and him,
Reached from behind his back, a trigger prest, —
And those perplexed and patient eyes were dim,
Those gaunt, long-laboring limbs were laid to rest!

The words of mercy were upon his lips,
Forgiveness in his heart and on his pen,
When this vile murderer brought swift eclipse
To thoughts of peace on earth, good-will to men.

The Old World and the New, from sea to sea,
Utter one voice of sympathy and shame!
Sore heart, so stopped when it at last beat high;
Sad life, cut short just as its triumph came.

A deed accurst! Strokes have been struck before
By the assassin's hand, whereof men doubt
If more of horror or disgrace they bore;
But thy foul crime, like Cain's, stands darkly out.

Vile hand, that brandest murder on a strife,
Whate'er its grounds, stoutly and nobly striven;
And with the martyr's crown crownest a life
With much to praise, little to be forgiven.

TOM TAYLOR *in Punch.*

IN STATE.

I.

O KEEPER of the Sacred Key,
And the Great Seal of Destiny,
Whose eye is the blue canopy,
Look down upon the warring world, and tell us what the end will be.

"Lo, through the wintry atmosphere,
On the white bosom of the sphere,
A cluster of five lakes appear;
And all the land looks like a couch, or warrior's shield, or sheeted bier.

"And on that vast and hollow field,
With both lips closed and both eyes sealed,
A mighty Figure is revealed,—
Stretched at full length, and stiff and stark, as in the hollow of a shield.

"The winds have tied the drifted snow
Around the face and chin; and lo,
The sceptred Giants come and go,
And shake their shadowy crowns and say: 'We always feared it would be so!'

"She came of an heroic race:
A giant's strength, a maiden's grace,
Like two in one seem to embrace,
And match, and blend, and thorough-blend, in her colossal form and face.

"Where can her dazzling falchion be?
One hand is fallen in the sea;
The Gulf-Stream drifts it far and free;
And in that hand her shining brand gleams from the depths resplendently.

"And by the other, in its rest,
The starry banner of the West
Is clasped forever to her breast;
And of her silver helmet, lo, a soaring eagle is the crest.

"And on her brow, a softened light,
As of a star concealed from sight
By some thin veil of fleecy white,
Or of the rising moon behind the raining vapors of the night.

"The Sisterhood that was so sweet,
The Starry System sphered complete,
Which the mazed Orient used to greet,
The Four and Thirty fallen Stars glimmer and glitter at her feet.

"And over her,—and over all,
For panoply and coronal,—
The mighty Immemorial,
And everlasting Canopy and Starry Arch and Shield of All."

II.

"Three cold, bright moons have marched and wheeled;
And the white cerement that revealed
A Figure stretched upon a Shield,
Is turned to verdure; and the Land is now one mighty Battle-field.

"And lo, the children which she bred,
And more than all else cherishèd,
To make them true in heart and head,
Stand face to face, as mortal foes, with their swords crossed above the dead.

"Each hath a mighty stroke and stride:
One true,—the more that he is tried;
The other dark and evil-eyed;—
And by the hand of one of them, his own dear mother surely died!

"A stealthy step, a gleam of hell,—
It is the simple truth to tell,—
The Son stabbed and the Mother fell:
And so she lies, all mute and pale, and pure and irreproachable!

"And then the battle-trumpet blew;
And the true brother sprang and drew
His blade to smite the traitor through;
And so they clashed above the bier, and the Night sweated bloody dew.

"And all their children, far and wide,
That are so greatly multiplied,
Rise up in frenzy and divide;
And choosing, each whom he will serve, unsheathe the sword and take their side.

"And in the low sun's bloodshot rays,
Portentous of the coming days,
The Two great Oceans blush and blaze,
With the emergent continent between them, wrapt in crimson haze.

"Now whichsoever stand or fall,
As God is great, and man is small,
The Truth shall triumph over all:
Forever and forevermore, the Truth shall triumph over all!"

III.

"I see the champion sword-strokes flash;
I see them fall and hear them clash;
I hear the murderous engines crash;
I see a brother stoop to loose a foeman-brother's bloody sash.

"I see the torn and mangled corse,
The dead and dying heaped in scores,
The headless rider by his horse,
The wounded captive bayoneted through and through without remorse.

"I hear the dying sufferer cry,
With his crushed face turned to the sky,
I see him crawl in agony
To the foul pool, and bow his head into its bloody slime, and die.

"I see the assassin crouch and fire,
I see his victim fall, — expire;
I see the murderer creeping nigher
To strip the dead. He turns the head, — the face! The son beholds his sire!

"I hear the curses and the thanks;
I see the mad charge on the flanks,
The rents, the gaps, the broken ranks,
The vanquished squadrons driven headlong down the river's bridgeless banks.

"I see the death-gripe on the plain,
The grappling monsters on the main,
The tens of thousands that are slain,
And all the speechless suffering and agony of heart and brain.

"I see the dark and bloody spots,
The crowded rooms and crowded cots,
The bleaching bones, the battle blots, —
And writ on many a nameless grave, a legend of forget-me-nots.

"I see the gorgèd prison-den,
The dead line and the pent-up pen,
The thousands quartered in the fen,
The living-deaths of skin and bone that were the goodly shapes of men.

"And still the bloody Dew must fall!
And His great Darkness with the Pall
Of His dread Judgment cover all,
Till the Dead Nation rise Transformed by Truth to triumph over all!"

"And Last — and Last I see — The Deed."
Thus saith the Keeper of the Key,
And the Great Seal of Destiny,
Whose eye is the blue canopy,
And leaves the Pall of His great Darkness over all the Land and Sea.

FORCEYTHE WILSON.

REQUIEM.

BREATHE, trumpets, breathe slow notes of saddest wailing;
Sadly responsive peal, ye muffled drums.
Comrades, with downcast eyes and muskets trailing,
Attend him home: the youthful warrior comes,

Upon his shield, upon his shield returning,
Borne from the field of battle where he fell.
Glory and grief together clasped in mourning,
His fame, his fate, with sobs exulting tell.

Wrap round his breast the flag his breast defended, —
His country's flag, in battle's front unrolled:
For it he died, — on earth forever ended,
His brave young life lives in each sacred fold.

With proud, proud tears, by tinge of shame untainted,
Bear him, and lay him gently in his grave.
Above the hero write, the young, half-sainted,
"His country asked his life, his life he gave."

GEORGE LUNT.

ODE.

[Sung on the occasion of decorating the graves of the Confederate dead, at Magnolia Cemetery, Charleston, S.C.]

SLEEP sweetly in your humble graves, —
Sleep, martyrs of a fallen cause!
Though yet no marble column craves
The pilgrim here to pause,

In seeds of laurel in the earth
The blossom of your fame is blown,
And somewhere, waiting for its birth,
The shaft is in the stone!

Meanwhile, behalf the tardy years
Which keep in trust your storied tombs,
Behold! your sisters bring their tears,
And these memorial blooms.

Small tributes! but your shades will smile
More proudly on these wreaths to-day,
Than when some cannon-mouldered pile
Shall overlook this bay.

Stoop, angels, hither from the skies!
There is no holier spot of ground
Than where defeated valor lies,
By mourning beauty crowned!

HENRY TIMROD.

COMMEMORATION ODE.

HARVARD UNIVERSITY, JULY 21, 1865.

. . . . . .

LIFE may be given in many ways,
And loyalty to Truth be sealed
As bravely in the closet as the field,
So generous is Fate;
But then to stand beside her,
When craven churls deride her,
To front a lie in arms, and not to yield, —
This shows, methinks, God's plan
And measure of a stalwart man,
Limbed like the old heroic breeds,
Who stand self-poised on manhood's solid earth,
Not forced to frame excuses for his birth,
Fed from within with all the strength he needs.

Such was he, our Martyr-Chief,
Whom late the Nation he had led,
With ashes on her head,
Wept with the passion of an angry grief:
Forgive me, if from present things I turn
To speak what in my heart will beat and burn,
And hang my wreath on his world-honored urn.
Nature, they say, doth dote,
And cannot make a man
Save on some worn-out plan,
Repeating us by rote:
For him her Old-World moulds aside she threw,
And, choosing sweet clay from the breast
Of the unexhausted West,
With stuff untainted shaped a hero new,
Wise, steadfast in the strength of God, and true.
How beautiful to see
Once more a shepherd of mankind indeed,
Who loved his charge, but never loved to lead;
One whose meek flock the people joyed to be,

Not lured by any cheat of birth,
But by his clear-grained human worth,
And brave old wisdom of sincerity!
They knew that outward grace is dust;
They could not choose but trust
In that sure-footed mind's unfaltering skill,
And supple-tempered will
That bent like perfect steel to spring again and thrust.
His was no lonely mountain-peak of mind,
Thrusting to thin air o'er our cloudy bars,
A seamark now, now lost in vapors blind;
Broad prairie rather, genial, level-lined,
Fruitful and friendly for all human kind,
Yet also nigh to Heaven and loved of loftiest stars.
Nothing of Europe here,
Or, then, of Europe fronting mornward still,
Ere any names of Serf and Peer
Could Nature's equal scheme deface;
Here was a type of the true elder race,
And one of Plutarch's men talked with us face to face.
I praise him not; it were too late;
And some innative weakness there must be
In him who condescends to victory
Such as the Present gives, and cannot wait,
Safe in himself as in a fate.
So always firmly he:
He knew to bide his time,
And can his fame abide,
Still patient in his simple faith sublime,
Till the wise years decide.
Great captains, with their guns and drums,
Disturb our judgment for the hour,
But at last silence comes:
These all are gone, and, standing like a tower,
Our children shall behold his fame,
The kindly-earnest, brave, foreseeing man,
Sagacious, patient, dreading praise, not blame,
New birth of our new soil, the first American.

. . . .

We sit here in the Promised Land
That flows with Freedom's honey and milk;
But 'twas they won it, sword in hand,
Making the nettle danger soft for us as silk.
We welcome back our bravest and our best;—
Ah, me! not all! some come not with the rest,
Who went forth brave and bright as any here!
I strive to mix some gladness with my strain,
But the sad strings complain,
And will not please the ear;
I sweep them for a pæan, but they wane
Again and yet again
Into a dirge, and die away in pain.
In these brave ranks I only see the gaps,
Thinking of dear ones whom the dumb turf wraps,
Dark to the triumph which they died to gain:
Fitlier may others greet the living,
For me the past is unforgiving;
I with uncovered head
Salute the sacred dead,
Who went, and who return not.—Say not so!
'Tis not the grapes of Canaan that repay,
But the high faith that failed not by the way;
Virtue treads paths that end not in the grave;
No bar of endless night exiles the brave;
And to the saner mind
We rather seem the dead that staid behind.

Blow, trumpets, all your exultations blow!
For never shall their aureoled presence lack:
I see them muster in a gleaming row,
With ever-youthful brows that nobler show;
We find in our dull road their shining track;
In every nobler mood
We feel the orient of their spirit glow,
Part of our life's unalterable good,
Of all our saintlier aspiration;
They come transfigured back,
Secure from change in their high-hearted ways,
Beautiful evermore, and with the rays
Of morn on their white Shields of Expectation!

. . . .

Not in anger, not in pride,
Pure from passion's mixture rude
Ever to base earth allied,
But with far-heard gratitude,
Still with heart and voice renewed,
To heroes living and dear martyrs dead,
The strain should close that consecrates our brave.
Lift the heart and lift the head!
Lofty be its mood and grave,
Not without a martial ring,
Not without a prouder tread
And a peal of exultation:
Little right has he to sing
Through whose heart in such an hour
Beats no march of conscious power,
Sweeps no tumult of elation!
'Tis no Man we celebrate,
By his country's victories great,
A hero half, and half the whim of Fate,
But the pith and marrow of a Nation
Drawing force from all her men,
Highest, humblest, weakest, all,
For her day of need, and then
Pulsing it again through them,
Till the basest can no longer cower
Feeling his soul spring up divinely tall,
Touched but in passing by her mantle-hem.
Come back, then, noble pride, for 'tis her dower!
How could poet ever tower,
If his passions, hopes, and fears,
If his triumphs and his tears,
Kept not measure with his people?
Boom, cannon, boom to all the winds and waves!
Clash out, glad bells, from every rocking steeple!
Banners, adance with triumph, bend your staves!
And from every mountain-peak
Let beacon-fire to answering beacon speak,
Katahdin tell Monadnock, Whiteface he,
And so leap on in light from sea to sea,
Till the glad news be sent
Across a kindling continent,
Making earth feel more firm and air breathe braver: —
"Be proud! for she is saved, and all have helped to save her!
She that lifts up the manhood of the poor,
She of the open soul and open door,
With room about her hearth for all mankind!
The fire is dreadful in her eyes no more;
From her bold front the helm she doth unbind,
Send all her handmaid armies back to spin,
And bid her navies that so lately hurled
Their crashing battle, hold their thunders in,
Swimming like birds of calm along the unharmful shore.
No challenge sends she to the elder world,
That looked askance and hated; a light scorn
Plays on her mouth, as round her mighty knees
She calls her children back, and waits the morn
Of nobler day, enthroned between her subject seas."

Bow down, dear Land, for thou hast found release!
Thy God, in these distempered days,
Hath taught thee the sure wisdom of his ways,
And through thine enemies hath wrought thy peace!
Bow down in prayer and praise!
O Beautiful! my Country! ours once more!
Smoothing thy gold of war-dishevelled hair
O'er such sweet brows as never other wore,
And letting thy set lips,
Freed from wrath's pale eclipse,
The rosy edges of their smile lay bare,
What words divine of lover or of poet
Could tell our love and make thee know it,
Among the Nations bright beyond compare?
What were our lives without thee?
What all our lives to save thee?
We reck not what we gave thee;
We will not dare to doubt thee,
But ask whatever else, and we will dare!

J. R. LOWELL.

CHICAGO.

OCT. 10, 1871.

BLACKENED and bleeding, helpless, panting, prone,
On the charred fragments of her shattered throne
Lies she who stood but yesterday alone.

Queen of the West! by some enchanter taught
To lift the glory of Aladdin's court,
Then lose the spell that all that wonder wrought.

Like her own prairies by some chance seed sown,
Like her own prairies in one brief day grown,
Like her own prairies in one fierce night mown.

She lifts her voice, and in her pleading call
We hear the cry of Macedon to Paul,
The cry for help that makes her kin to all.

But haply with wan fingers may she feel
The silver cup hid in the proffered meal,
The gifts her kinship and our loves reveal.

BRET HARTE.

VI.

PORTRAITS.—PERSONAL. PICTURES.

"Who will not honor noble numbers, when
Verses outlive the bravest deeds of men?"—HERRICK.

PORTRAITS.—PERSONAL.—PICTURES.

NEBUCHADNEZZAR.

There was a king that much might,
Who Nabugodonosor hight.
To his empire and to his laws,
As who saith, all in thilke dawes
Were obeisant, and tribute bear,
As tho' God of earth he were:
Till that the high king of kings
Which seeth and knoweth all things,
Whose eye may nothing asterte,
The privates of man's heart
They speken and sound in his ear
As though they loud winds were,—
He took vengeance of his pride.

Gower: *Confessio Amantis.*

NESTOR TO HECTOR.

Nestor.—I have, thou gallant Trojan, seen thee oft,
Laboring for destiny, make cruel way
Through ranks of Greekish youth: and I have seen thee,
As hot as Perseus, spur thy Phrygian steed,
Despising many forfeits and subduements,
When thou hast hung thy advanced sword i' the air,
Not letting it decline on the declined:
That I have said to some my standers-by,
Lo, Jupiter is yonder, dealing life!
And I have seen thee pause, and take thy breath
When that a ring of Greeks have hemmed thee in,
Like an Olympian wrestling: This have I seen
But this thy countenance, still locked in steel,
I never saw till now.
Let an old man embrace thee:
And, worthy warrior, welcome to our tents.

Shakspeare.

CORIOLANUS.

Cominius.—I shall lack voice; the deeds of Coriolanus
Should not be uttered feebly.—It is held,
That valor is the chiefest virtue, and
Most dignifies the haver: if it be,
The man I speak of cannot in the world
Be singly counterpoised. At sixteen years,
When Tarquin made a head for Rome, he fought
Beyond the mark of others: our then dictator,
Whom with all praise I point at, saw him fight
When with his Amazonian chin he drove
The bristled lips before him: he bestrid
An o'erpressed Roman, and in the consul's view
Slew three opposers: Tarquin's self he met,
And struck him on his knee: in that day's feats,
When he might act the woman in the scene,
He proved best man of the field, and for his meed
Was brow-bound with the oak. His pupil age

Man-entered thus, he waxèd like a sea;
And, in the brunt of seventeen battles since,
He lurched all swords o' the garland.
For this last,
Before and in Corioli, let me say,
I cannot speak him home. He stopped the fliers;
And, by his rare example, made the coward
Turn terror into sport: as waves before
A vessel under sail, so men obeyed,
And fell below his stem: his sword (death's stamp),
Where it did mark it took; from face to foot
He was a thing of blood, whose every motion
Was timed with dying cries; alone he entered
The mortal gate o' the city, which he painted
With shunless destiny, aidless came off,
And with a sudden re-enforcement struck
Corioli, like a planet: now all's his:
When by and by the din of war 'gan pierce
His ready sense: then straight his doubled spirit
Re-quickened what in flesh was fatigate,
And to the battle came he; where he did
Run reeking o'er the lives of men, as if
'Twere a perpetual spoil; and till we called
Both field and city ours, he never stood
To ease his breast with panting.
Our spoils he kicked at,
And looked upon things precious, as they were
The common muck o' the world; he covets less
Than misery itself would give; rewards
His deeds with doing them; and is content
To spend the time to end it.
His nature is too noble for the world:
He would not flatter Neptune for his trident,
Or Jove for his power to thunder.
His heart's his mouth:
What his breast forges, that his tongue must vent;
And, being angry, does forget that ever
He heard the name of death.

CORIOLANUS AT ANTIUM.

Coriolanus. — Hear'st thou, Mars!
Aufidius. — Name not the god, thou boy of tears —
Cor. — Ha!
Auf. — No more.
Cor. — Measureless liar, thou hast made my heart
Too great for what contains it. Boy! O slave! —
Pardon me, lords, 'tis the first time that ever
I was forced to scold. Your judgments, my grave lords,
Must give this cur the lie: and his own notion
(Who wears my stripes impressed on him; that must bear
My beating to his grave) shall join to thrust
The lie unto him.
Cut me to pieces, Volsces; men and lads,
Stain all your edges on me. — Boy! False hound!
If you have writ your annals true, 'tis there,
That like an eagle in a dove-cote, I
Fluttered your Volsces in Corioli:
Alone I did it. — Boy!

SHAKSPEARE.

THE BLACK PRINCE.

French King. — Think we King Harry strong;
And, princes, look you strongly arm to meet him.
The kindred of him hath been fleshed upon us;
And he is bred out of that bloody strain,
That haunted us in our familiar paths:
Witness our too much memorable shame,
When Cressy battle fatally was struck,
And all our princes captived, by the hand

Of that black name, Edward, black prince of Wales;
Whiles that his mountain sire, — on mountain standing,
Up in the air, crowned with a golden sun, —
Saw his heroical seed, and smiled to see him
Mangle the work of nature, and deface
The patterns that by God and by French fathers
Had twenty years been made. This is a stem
Of that victorious stock; and let us fear
The native mightiness and fate of him.

SHAKSPEARE.

HENRY V.

Canterbury. — The king is full of grace and fair regard.
Ely. — And a true lover of the holy church.
Cant. — The courses of his youth promised it not.
The breath no sooner left his father's body,
But that his wildness, mortified in him,
Seemed to die too; yea, at that very moment,
Consideration like an angel came,
And whipped the offending Adam out of him;
Leaving his body as a paradise,
To envelop and contain celestial spirits.
Never was such a sudden scholar made:
Never came reformation in a flood,
With such a heady current, scouring faults;
Nor never hydra-headed wilfulness
So soon did lose his seat, and all at once,
As in this king.
Hear him but reason in divinity,
And, all-admiring, with an inward wish
You would desire, the king were made a prelate;
Hear him debate of commonwealth affairs,
You would say, — it hath been all-in-all his study:
List his discourse of war, and you shall hear
A fearful battle rendered you in music:
Turn him to any cause of policy,
The Gordian knot of it he will unloose,
Familiar as his garter; that, when he speaks,
The air, a chartered libertine, is still,
And the mute wonder lurketh in men's ears,
To steal his sweet and honeyed sentences;
So that the air and practic part of life
Must be the mistress to this theoric:
Which is a wonder, how his grace should glean it,
Since his addiction was to courses vain:
His companies unlettered, rude, and shallow;
His hours filled up with riots, banquets, sports,
And never noted in him any study,
Any retirement, any sequestration
From open haunts and popularity.

SHAKSPEARE.

SPENSER AT COURT.

FULL little knowest thou, that hast not tried,
What hell it is, in suing long to bide:
To loose good dayes that might be better spent;
To waste long nights in pensive discontent;
To speed to-day, to be put back to-morrow;
To feed on hope, to pine with feare and sorrow;
To have thy prince's grace, yet want her peers;
To have thy asking, yet waite many yeares;
To fret thy soule with crosses and with cares;
To eate thy heart through comfortless despairs;
To fawn, to crouch, to wait, to ride, to run,
To spend, to give, to want, to be undone.

SPENSER.

ON LUCY, COUNTESS OF BEDFORD.

This morning, timely rapt with holy fire,
I thought to form unto my zealous Muse
What kind of creature I could most desire
To honor, serve, and love, as poets use.
I meant to make her fair, and free, and wise,
Of greatest blood, and yet more good than great;
I meant the Day-Star should not brighter rise,
Nor lend like influence from his lucent seat.
I meant she should be courteous, facile, sweet,
Hating that solemn vice of greatness, pride;
I meant each softest virtue there should meet
Fit in that softer bosom to reside.
Only a learnèd and a manly soul
I purposed her, that should, with even powers,
The rock, the spindle, and the shears control
Of Destiny, and spin her own free hours.
Such when I meant to feign, and wished to see,
My Muse bade *Bedford* write, and that was she.

Ben Jonson.

SIR PHILIP SIDNEY.

A sweet, attractive kind of grace,
A full assurance given by looks,
Continual comfort in a face,
The lineaments of Gospel books!
I trow, that countenance cannot lie
Whose thoughts are legible in the eye.

Was ever eye did see that face,
Was ever ear did hear that tongue,
Was ever mind did mind his grace
That ever thought the travel long?
But eyes and ears, and every thought,
Were with his sweet perfections caught.

Matthew Royden.

EPITAPH ON SHAKSPEARE.

What needs my Shakspeare for his honored bones,
The labor of an age in pilèd stones?
Or that his hallowed relics should be hid
Under a star-y-pointing pyramid?
Dear son of Memory, great heir of fame,
What need'st thou such weak witness of thy name?
Thou in our wonder and astonishment
Hast built thyself a live long monument.
For whilst, to the shame of slow-endeavoring art
Thy easy numbers flow, and that each heart
Hath from the leaves of thy unvalued book
Those Delphic lines with deep impression took,
Then thou, our fancy of itself bereaving,
Dost make us marble with too much conceiving;
And so sepùlchred in such pomp dost lie,
That kings for such a tomb would wish to die.

Milton.

EPITAPH.

Underneath this stone doth lye
As much beauty as could dye;
Which in life did harbor give
To more virtue than doth live.
If at all she had a fault,
Leave it buried in this vault.
One name was Elizabeth —
The other, let it sleep with death:
Fitter, where it dyed to tell,
Than that it lived at all. Farewell!

Ben Jonson.

TRANSLATION OF COWLEY'S EPIGRAM ON FRANCIS DRAKE.

The stars above will make thee known,
If man were silent here;
The sun himself cannot forget
His fellow-traveller.

Ben Jonson.

EPITAPH.

UNDERNEATH this sable hearse
Lies the subject of all verse, —
Sidney's sister, Pembroke's mother.
Death! ere thou hast killed another
Fair, and learned, and good as she,
Time shall throw a dart at thee.

BEN JONSON.

EPIGRAM.

UVEDALE, thou piece of the first times, a man
Made for what Nature could, or Virtue can;
Both whose dimensions lost, the world might find
Restorèd in thy body, and thy mind!
Who sees a soul in such a body set,
Might love the treasure for the cabinet.
But I, no child, no fool, respect the kind
The full, the glowing graces there enshrined,
Which, (would the world not miscall it flattery,)
I could adore, almost to idolatry.

BEN JONSON.

TO THE COUNTESS OF RUTLAND.

THERE, like a rich and golden pyramid,
Borne up by statues, shall I rear your head
Above your under-carvèd ornaments,
And show how to the life my soul presents
Your form imprest there, not with tickling rhymes
Or common-places filched, that take these times,
But high and noble matter, such as flies
From brains entranced, and filled with ecstasies,
Moods which the god-like Sidney oft did prove,
And your brave friend and mine so well did love.

BEN JONSON.

TO WILLIAM SIDNEY, ON HIS BIRTHDAY.

GIVE me my cup, but from the Thespian well,
That I may tell to Sidney, what
This day doth say,
And he may think on that
Which I do tell
When all the noise
Of these forced joys
Are fled and gone,
And he with his best genius left alone,

. . . .

'Twill be exacted of your name whose son,
Whose nephew, whose grandchild you are;
And men will then
Say you have followed far,
When well begun:
Which must be now: they teach you how;
And he that stays
To live until to-morrow, hath lost two days.
Then
The birthday shines, when logs not burn, but men.

BEN JONSON.

PRAYER TO BEN JONSON.

WHEN I a verse shall make,
Know I have prayed thee,
For old religion's sake,
Saint Ben, to aid me.

Make the way smooth for me,
When I, thy Herrick,
Honoring thee, on my knee
Offer my lyric.

Candles I'll give to thee,
And a new altar;
And thou, Saint Ben, shalt be
Writ in my psalter.

HERRICK.

TO LIVE MERRILY, AND TO TRUST TO GOOD VERSES.

Now is the time for mirth,
Nor cheek or tongue be dumb;
For the flowry earth,
The golden pomp is come.

The golden pomp is come;
  For now each tree does wear,
Made of her pap and gum,
  Rich beads of amber here.

Now reigns the Rose, and now
  The Arabian dew besmears
My uncontrollèd brow,
  And my retorted hairs.

Homer! this health to thee,
  In sack of such a kind,
That it would make thee see,
  Though thou wert ne'er so blind.

Next, Virgil I'll call forth,
  To pledge this second health
In wine, whose each cup's worth
  An Indian commonwealth.

A goblet next I'll drink
  To Ovid; and suppose
Made he the pledge, he'd think
  The world had all one nose.

Then this immensive cup
  Of aromatic wine,
Catullus, I quaff up
  To that terse muse of thine.

Wild I am now with heat,
  O Bacchus! cool thy rays;
Or frantic I shall eat
  Thy Thyrse, and bite the Bays.

Round, round, the roof does run;
  And being ravisht thus,
Come, I will drink a tun
  To my Propertius.

Now, to Tibullus next,
  This flood I drink to thee;
But stay, I see a text,
  That this presents to me.

Behold! Tibullus lies
  Here burnt, whose small return
Of ashes scarce suffice
  To fill a little urn.

Trust to good verses then;
  They only will aspire,
When pyramids, as men,
  Are lost in the funeral fire.

And when all bodies meet
  In Lethe, to be drowned;
Then only numbers sweet,
  With endless life are crowned.

HERRICK.

SONNET.

ON HIS BEING ARRIVED TO THE AGE OF TWENTY-THREE.

How soon hath Time, the subtle thief of youth,
Stolen on his wing my three and twentieth year!
  My hasting days fly on with full career,
  But my late spring no bud or blossom show'th.
Perhaps my semblance might deceive the truth,
  That I to manhood am arrived so near,
  And inward ripeness doth much less appear,
  That some more timely-happy spirits indu'th.
Yet be it less or more, or soon or slow,
  It shall be still in strictest measure even
  To that same lot, however mean or high,
Toward which Time leads me, and the will of Heaven:
  All is, if I have grace to use it so,
  As ever in my great Task-master's eye.

MILTON.

ODE TO BEN JONSON.

    AH Ben!
  Say how or when
  Shall we, thy guests,
  Meet at those lyric feasts,
    Made at the Sun,
  The Dog, the Triple Tun;
  Where we such clusters had
  As made us nobly wild, not mad;
    And yet each verse of thine
Outdid the meat, outdid the frolic wine.

    My Ben!
  Or come again,
    Or send to us
Thy wit's great overplus;
  But teach us yet
Wisely to husband it,
Lest we that talent spend:
And having once brought to an end
  That precious stock, the store
Of such a wit, the world should have no more.

HERRICK.

TO SIR HENRY VANE.

VANE, young in years, but in sage counsel old,
Than whom a better senator ne'er held
The helm of Rome, when gowns, not arms, repelled
The fierce Epirot, and the African bold,
Whether to settle peace, or to unfold
The drift of hollow states, hard to be spelled;
Then to advise how War may, best upheld,
Move by her two main nerves, iron and gold,
In all her equipage: besides to know
Both spiritual power and civil, what each means,
What severs each, thou hast learned, which few have done:
The bounds of either sword to thee we owe:
Therefore on thy firm hand Religion leans
In peace, and reckons thee her eldest son.

MILTON.

ON HIS BLINDNESS.

WHEN I consider how my light is spent,
Ere half my days, in this dark world and wide,
And that one talent which is death to hide,
Lodged with me useless, though my soul more bent
To serve therewith my Maker, and present
My true account, lest he returning chide;
"Doth God exact day-labor, light denied?"
I fondly ask: But Patience, to prevent
That murmur, soon replies, "God doth not need
Either man's work, or his own gifts; who best
Bear his mild yoke, they serve him best: his state
Is kingly; thousands at his bidding speed,
And post o'er land and ocean without rest;
They also serve who only stand and wait."

MILTON.

SONNET.

O, FOR my sake do you with Fortune chide,
The guilty goddess of my harmful deeds,
That did not better for my life provide,
Than public means, which public manners breeds.
Thence comes it that my name receives a brand,
And almost thence my nature is subdued
To what it works in, like the dyer's hand:
Pity me then, and wish I were renewed;
Whilst, like a willing patient, I will drink
Potions of eyesell, 'gainst my strong infection:
No bitterness that I will bitter think,
Nor double penance, to correct correction.
Pity me then, dear friend, and I assure ye,
Even that your pity is enough to cure me.

SHAKSPEARE.

PORTRAIT OF ADDISON.

PEACE to all such! but were there one whose fires
True genius kindles, and fair fame inspires;
Blest with each talent and each art to please,
And born to write, converse, and live with ease;
Should such a man, too fond to rule alone,
Bear, like the Turk, no brother near the throne,
View him with scornful, yet with jealous eyes,
And hate for arts that caused himself to rise;
Damn with faint praise, assent with civil leer,

And, without sneering, teach the rest to sneer;
Willing to wound, and yet afraid to strike,
Just hint a fault, and hesitate dislike;
Alike reserved to blame, or to commend,
A timorous foe, and a suspicious friend;
Dreading even fools, by flatterers besieged,
And so obliging that he ne'er obliged;
Like Cato, give his little senate laws,
And sit attentive to his own applause;
Whilst wits and Templars every sentence raise,
And wonder with a foolish face of praise:—
Who but must laugh, if such a one there be?
Who would not weep, if Atticus were he?

POPE.

LINES TO ALEXANDER POPE.

WHILE malice, Pope, denies thy page
Its own celestial fires;
While critics, and while bards in rage,
Admiring, won't admire:

While wayward pens thy worth assail,
And envious tongues decry;
These times, though many a friend bewail,
These times bewail not I.

But when the world's loud praise is thine,
And spleen no more shall blame:
When with thy Homer thou shalt shine
In one unclouded fame:

When none shall rail, and every lay
Devote a wreath to thee;
That day, (for come it will,) that day
Shall I lament to see.

DAVID LEWIS.

THE MAN OF ROSS.

BUT all our praises why should lords engross?
Rise, honest muse! and sing the Man of Ross:
Pleased Vaga echoes through her winding bounds,
And rapid Severn hoarse applause resounds.
Who hung with woods yon mountain's sultry brow?
From the dry rock who bade the waters flow?
Not to the skies in useless columns tost,
Or in proud falls magnificently lost,
But clear and artless, pouring through the plain
Health to the sick, and solace to the swain.
Whose causeway parts the vale with shady rows?
Whose seats the weary traveller repose?
Who taught that heaven-directed spire to rise?
"The Man of Ross," each lisping babe replies.
Behold the market-place with poor o'erspread!
The Man of Ross divides the weekly bread:
He feeds yon almshouse, neat, but void of state,
Where age and want sit smiling at the gate:
Him portioned maids, apprenticed orphans blest,
The young who labor, and the old who rest.
Is any sick? The Man of Ross relieves,
Prescribes, attends, the medicine makes and gives.
Is there a variance? enter but his door,
Balked are the courts, and contest is no more:
Despairing quacks with curses fled the place,
And vile attorneys, now a useless race.
Thrice happy man! enabled to pursue
What all so wish but want the power to do!
Oh say, what sums that generous hand supply?
What mines to swell that boundless charity?
Of debts and taxes, wife and children clear,
This man possessed — five hundred pounds a year.

Blush grandeur, blush! proud courts, withdraw your blaze;
Ye little stars! hide your diminished rays.
And what? no monument, inscription, stone,
His race, his form, his name almost unknown?
Who builds a church to God, and not to fame
Will never mark the marble with his name.

POPE.

ELEGY ON MISTRESS ELIZABETH DRURY.

SHE, of whose soul, if we may say, 'twas gold,
Her body was the Electrum, and did hold
Many degrees of that; we understood
Her by her sight; her pure and eloquent blood
Spoke in her cheeks, and so distinctly wrought,
That one might almost say, her body thought.
She, she thus richly, largely housed, is gone,
And chides us slow-paced snails who crawl upon
Our prison's prison, Earth, nor think us well
Longer than whilst we bear our little shell.

. . . .

What hope have we to know ourselves, when we
Know not the least things which for our use be?
What Cæsar did, yea, and what Cicero said,
Why grass is green, or why our blood is red,
Are mysteries which none have reached unto;
In this low form, poor soul, what wilt thou do?
O when wilt thou shake off this pedantry
Of being caught by sense and fantasy?
Thou look'st through spectacles; small things seem great
Below; but up into the watch-tower get,
And see all things despoiled of fallacies;
Thou shalt not peep through lattices of eyes,
Nor hear through labyrinths of ears, nor learn
By circuit or collections to discern;
In heaven then straight know'st all concerning it,
And what concerns it not, shall straight forget.
There thou but in no other school mayst be
Perchance as learned and as full as she;
She, who all libraries had thoroughly read
At home in her own thoughts, and practisèd
So much good as would make as many more.

. . . .

Up, up, my drowsy soul! where thy new ear
Shall in the angels' songs no discord hear;
Where thou shalt see the blessed Mother-maid
Joy in not being that which men have said;
Where she's exalted more for being good,
Than for her interest of Motherhood:
Up to those Patriarchs, who did longer sit
Expecting Christ, than they've enjoyed him yet:
Up to those Prophets, who now gladly see
Their prophecies grown to be history:
Up to the Apostles, who did bravely run
All the sun's course, with more light than the sun:
Up to those Martyrs, who did calmly bleed
Oil to the Apostles' lamps, dew to their seed:
Up to those Virgins, who thought that almost
They made joint-tenants with the Holy Ghost,
If they to any should his Temple give:
Up, up, for in that squadron there doth live
She who hath carried thither new degrees,

(As to their number,) to their dignities.

. . . .

She whom we celebrate is gone before:
She who had here so much essential joy,
As no chance could distract, much less destroy;
Who with God's presence was acquainted so,
(Hearing and speaking to him,) as to know
His face in any natural stone or tree
Better than when in images they be:
Who kept by diligent devotion
God's image in such reparation
Within her heart, that what decay was grown
Was her first Parent's fault, and not her own:
Who, being solicited to any act,
Still heard God pleading his safe pre-contract:
Who, by a faithful confidence was here
Betrothed to God, and now is married there:
Whose twilights were more clear than our mid-day;
Who dreamed devoutlier than most use to pray:
Who being here filled with grace, yet strove to be
Both where more grace and more capacity
At once is given. She to Heaven is gone,
Who made this world in some proportion
A Heaven, and here became unto us all
Joy, (as our joys admit,) essential.

DONNE.

TO MILTON.

MILTON! thou shouldst be living at this hour:
England hath need of thee: she is a fen
Of stagnant waters: altar, sword, and pen,
Fireside, the heroic wealth of hall and bower,
Have forfeited their ancient English dower
Of inward happiness. We are selfish men;
Oh! raise us up, return to us again;
And give us manners, virtue, freedom, power.
Thy soul was like a star, and dwelt apart:
Thou hadst a voice whose sound was like the sea:
Pure as the naked heavens, majestic, free,
So didst thou travel on life's common way,
In cheerful godliness; and yet thy heart
The lowliest duties on herself did lay.

WORDSWORTH.

WHEN THE ASSAULT WAS INTENDED TO THE CITY.

CAPTAIN or Colonel, or Knight in arms,
Whose chance on these defenceless doors may seize,
If deed of honor did thee ever please,
Guard them, and him within protect from harms.
He can requite thee, for he knows the charms
That call fame on such gentle acts as these,
And he can spread thy name o'er lands and seas,
Whatever clime the sun's bright circle warms.
Lift not thy spear against the Muses' bower:
The great Emathian conqueror bid spare
The house of Pindarus, when temple and tower
Went to the ground; and the repeated air
Of sad Electra's poet had the power
To save the Athenian walls from ruin bare.

MILTON.

ROB ROY'S GRAVE.

A FAMOUS man is Robin Hood,
The English ballad-singer's joy!
And Scotland has a thief as good,
An outlaw of as daring mood;
She has her brave Rob Roy!

Then clear the weeds from off his grave,
And let us chant a passing stave
In honor of that hero brave!

Heaven gave Rob Roy a dauntless heart,
And wondrous length and strength of arm:
Nor craved he more to quell his foes,
Or keep his friends from harm.

Yet was Rob Roy as *wise* as brave;
Forgive me if the phrase be strong;—
A poet worthy of Rob Roy
Must scorn a timid song.

Say, then, that he was wise as brave;
As wise in thought as bold in deed:
For in the principle of things
He sought his moral creed.

Said generous Rob, "What need of books?
Burn all the statutes and their shelves;
They stir us up against our kind;
And worse, against ourselves.

"We have a passion, make a law,
Too false to guide us or control!
And for the law itself we fight
In bitterness of soul.

"And, puzzled, blinded thus, we lose
Distinctions that are plain and few:
These find I graven on my heart:
That tells me what to do.

"The creatures see of flood and field,
And those that travel on the wind!
With them no strife can last: they live
In peace, and peace of mind.

"For why?—because the good old rule
Sufficeth them, the simple plan,
That they should take who have the power,
And they should keep who can.

"A lesson which is quickly learned;
A signal this which all can see!
Thus nothing here provokes the strong
To wanton cruelty.

"All freakishness of mind is checked;
He tamed, who foolishly aspires:
While to the measure of his might
Each fashions his desires.

"All kinds, and creatures, stand and fall
By strength of prowess or of wit:
'Tis God's appointment who must sway,
And who is to submit.

"Since, then, the rule of right is plain,
And longest life is but a day;
To have my ends, maintain my rights,
I'll take the shortest way."

And thus among the rocks he lived,
Through summer's heat and winter's snow:
The eagle, he was lord above,
And Rob was lord below.

So was it—*would*, at least, have been,
But through untowardness of fate;
For polity was then too strong;
He came an age too late.

Or shall we say, an age too soon?
For, were the bold man living *now*,
How might he flourish in his pride,
With buds on every bough!

Then rents and factors, rights of chase,
Sheriffs, and lairds and their domains,
Would all have seemed but paltry things,
Not worth a moment's pains.

Rob Roy had never lingered here,
To these few meagre vales confined;
But thought how wide the world, the times
How fairly to his mind.

And to his sword he would have said,
"Do thou my sovereign will enact
From land to land through half the earth!
Judge thou of law and fact!

"'Tis fit that we should do our part;
Becoming, that mankind should learn
That we are not to be surpassed
In fatherly concern.

"Of old things all are over old,
Of good things none are good
enough: —
We'll show that we can help to frame
A world of other stuff.

"I, too, will have my kings that take
From me the sign of life and death;
Kingdoms shall shift about like
clouds,
Obedient to my breath."

And, if the word had been fulfilled,
As *might* have been, then, thought
of joy!
France would have had her present
boast,
And we our brave Rob Roy!

Oh! say not so; compare them not;
I would not wrong thee, champion
brave!
Would wrong thee nowhere; least
of all
Here standing by thy grave.

For thou, although with some wild
thoughts,
Wild chieftain of a savage clan!
Hadst this to boast of; thou didst love
The *liberty* of man.

And, had it been thy lot to live
With us who now behold the light,
Thou wouldst have nobly stirred thy-
self,
And battled for the right.

For thou wert still the poor man's
stay,
The poor man's heart, the poor man's
hand!
And all the oppressed who wanted
strength
Had thine at their command.

Bear witness many a pensive sigh
Of thoughtful herdsman when he
strays
Alone upon Loch Veol's heights,
And by Loch Lomond's braes!

And far and near, through vale and
hill,
Are faces that attest the same,
And kindle, like a fire new stirred,
At sound of Rob Roy's name.

WORDSWORTH.

TO CAMPBELL.

TRUE bard and simple, — as the race
Of heaven-born poets always are,
When stooping from their starry
place
They're children near, though gods
afar.

MOORE.

STANZAS TO * * *

THOUGH the day of my destiny's
over,
And the star of my fate hath declined,
Thy soft heart refused to discover
The faults which so many could
find.

Though human, thou didst not deceive me;
Though woman, thou didst not
forsake;
Though loved, thou foreborest to
grieve me;
Though slandered, thou never
couldst shake.

Though trusted, thou didst not disclaim me;
Though parted, it was not to fly;
Though watchful, 'twas not to de-
fame me,
Nor mute that the world might
belie.

In the desert a fountain is spring-
ing,
In the wild waste there still is a
tree,
And a bird in the solitude singing,
Which speaks to my spirit of *thee*.

BYRON.

OUTWARD BOUND.

Is thy face like thy mother's, my
fair child!
Ada! sole daughter of my house
and heart?
When last I saw thy young blue
eyes, they smiled,
And then we parted, — not as now
we part,
But with a hope. —

Awaking with a start,
The waters heave around me; and on high
The winds lift up their voices: I depart,
Whither I know not; but the hour's gone by,
When Albion's lessening shores could grieve or glad mine eye.

Once more upon the waters! yet once more!
And the waves bound beneath me as a steed
That knows his rider. Welcome to their roar!
Swift be their guidance, wheresoe'er it lead!
Though the strained mast should quiver as a reed,
And the rent canvas fluttering, strew the gale,
Still must I on; for I am as a weed,
Flung from the rock, on ocean's foam, to sail
Where'er the surge may sweep, the tempest's breath prevail.

BYRON.

LOVE OF ENGLAND.

I've taught me other tongues, — and in strange eyes
Have made me not a stranger; to the mind
Which is itself, no changes bring surprise;
Nor is it harsh to make, nor hard to find
A country with, — ay, or without mankind;
Yet was I born where men are proud to be,
Not without cause; and should I leave behind
The inviolate island of the sage and free,
And seek me out a home by a remoter sea, —

Perhaps I loved it well; and should I lay
My ashes in a soil which is not mine,
My spirit shall resume it, — if we may
Unbodied choose a sanctuary. I twine
My hopes of being remembered in my line
With my land's language; if too fond and far
These aspirations in their scope incline, —
If my fame should be as my fortunes are,
Of hasty growth and blight, and dull Oblivion bar

My name from out the temple where the dead
Are honored by the nations — let it be, —
And light the laurels on a loftier head!
And be the Spartan's epitaph on me, —
"Sparta hath many a worthier son than he."

BYRON.

FARE THEE WELL.

Fare thee well! and if forever,
Still forever, fare *thee well!*
Even though unforgiving, never
'Gainst thee shall my heart rebel.
Would that breast were bared before thee
Where thy head so oft has lain,
While that placid sleep came o'er thee
Which thou ne'er canst know again:
Would that breast, by thee glanced over,
Every inmost thought could show!
Then thou wouldst at last discover
'Twas not well to spurn it so.
Though the world for this commend thee, —
Though it smile upon the blow,
Even its praises must offend thee,
Founded on another's woe.
Though my many faults defaced me,
Could no other arm be found
Than the one which once embraced me,
To inflict a cureless wound?
Yet, oh yet, thyself deceive not;
Love may sink by slow decay,
But by sudden wrench, believe not
Hearts can thus be torn away:

Still thine own its life retaineth;
Still must mine, though bleeding, beat;
And the undying thought which paineth,
Is — that we no more may meet.
These are words of deeper sorrow
Than the wail above the dead;
Both shall live, but every morrow
Wake us from a widowed bed.
And when thou wouldst solace gather,
When our child's first accents flow,
Wilt thou teach her to say "Father!"
Though his care she must forego?
When her little hands shall press thee,
When her lip to thine is pressed,
Think of him whose prayer shall bless thee,
Think of him thy love had blessed!
Should her lineaments resemble
Those thou never more mayst see,
Then thy heart will softly tremble
With a pulse yet true to me.
All my faults perchance thou knowest,
All my madness none can know;
All my hopes, where'er thou goest,
Whither, — yet with *thee* they go.
Every feeling hath been shaken;
Pride, which not a world could bow,
Bows to thee, — by thee forsaken,
Even my soul forsakes me now;
But 'tis done, — all words are idle, —
Words from me are vainer still;
But the thoughts we cannot bridle
Force their way without the will.
Fare thee well! thus disunited,
Torn from every nearer tie,
Seared in heart, and love, and blighted, —
More than this I scarce can die.

BYRON.

NO MORE.

No more — no more — Oh! never more on me
The freshness of the heart can fall like dew,
Which out of all the lovely things we see,
Extracts emotions beautiful and new,
Hived in our bosoms like the bag o' the bee.
Think'st thou the honey with those objects grew?
Alas! 'twas not in them, but in thy power,
To double even the sweetness of a flower.

No more — no more — Oh! never more, my heart,
Canst thou be my sole world, my universe!
Once all in all, but now a thing apart,
Thou canst not be my blessing, or my curse:
The illusion's gone forever.

BYRON.

TO A MOUSE.

ON TURNING HER UP IN HER NEST, WITH THE PLOUGH, NOVEMBER, 1785.

WEE, sleekit, cowrin, tim'rous beastie,
O, what a panic's in thy breastie!
Thou need na start awa sae hasty,
Wi' bickering brattle!
I wad be laith to rin an' chase thee,
Wi' murd'ring pattle!

I'm truly sorry man's dominion
Has broken Nature's social union,
An' justifies that ill opinion,
Which makes thee startle
At me, thy poor, earth-born companion,
An' fellow-mortal!

I doubt na, whyles, but thou may thieve;
What then? poor beastie, thou maun live!
A daimen icker in a thrave
'S a sma' request:
I'll get a blessin wi' the lave,
And never miss't!

Thy wee bit housie, too, in ruin!
Its silly wa's the win's are strewin!
An' naething, now, to big a new ane,
O' foggage green!
An' bleak December's winds ensuin,
Baith snell an' keen!

Thou saw the fields laid bare an' waste,
An' weary winter comin' fast,
An' cozie here, beneath the blast,
Thou thought to dwell,
Till, crash! the cruel coulter past
Out thro' thy cell.

That wee bit heap o' leaves an' stibble
Has cost thee mony a weary nibble!
Now thou's turned out, for a' thy trouble,
But house or hald,
To thole the winter's sleety dribble,
An' cranreuch cauld!

But, Mousie, thou art no thy lane,
In proving foresight may be vain:
The best-laid schemes o' mice an' men,
Gang aft a-gley,
An' lea'e us nought but grief and pain,
For promised joy.

Still thou art blest, compared wi' me!
The present only toucheth thee:
But, Och! I backward cast my e'e
On prospects drear!
An' forward, tho' I canna see,
I guess an' fear!

BURNS.

TO A MOUNTAIN DAISY.

ON TURNING ONE DOWN WITH THE PLOUGH, IN APRIL, 1786.

WEE, modest, crimson-tippèd flower,
Thou's met me in an evil hour;
For I maun crush amang the stoure
Thy slender stem:
To spare thee now is past my power,
Thou bonnie gem.

Alas! it's no thy neebor sweet,
The bonnie lark, companion meet!
Bending thee 'mang the dewy weet!
Wi' spreckled breast,
When upward-springing, blythe, to greet
The purpling east.

Cauld blew the bitter-biting north
Upon thy early, humble birth;
Yet cheerfully thou glinted forth
Amid the storm,
Scarce reared above the parent-earth
Thy tender form.

The flaunting flowers our gardens yield
High sheltering woods and wa's maun shield;
But thou, beneath the random bield
O' clod, or stane,
Adorns the histie stibble-field,
Unseen, alane.

There, in thy scanty mantle clad,
Thy snawy bosom sunward spread,
Thou lifts thy unassuming head
In humble guise;
But now the share uptears thy bed,
And low thou lies!

Such is the fate of artless Maid,
Sweet floweret of the rural shade!
By love's simplicity betrayed,
And guileless trust,
Till she, like thee, all soiled, is laid
Low in the dust.

Such is the fate of simple Bard,
On life's rough ocean luckless starred!
Unskilful he to note the card
Of prudent lore,
Till billows rage, and gales blow hard,
And whelm him o'er!

Such fate to suffering worth is given,
Who long with wants and woes has striven,
By human pride or cunning driven
To misery's brink,
Till, wrenched of every stay but Heaven,
He, ruined, sink!

Even thou who mourn'st the daisy's fate,
That fate is thine — no distant date;
Stern Ruin's ploughshare drives, elate,
Full on thy bloom,
Till crushed beneath the furrow's weight
Shall be thy doom!

BURNS.

SANTA FILOMENA.

Whene'er a noble deed is wrought,
Whene'er is spoken a noble thought,
Our hearts, in glad surprise,
To higher levels rise.

The tidal wave of deeper souls
Into our inmost being rolls,
And lifts us unawares
Out of all meaner cares.

Honor to those whose words and deeds
Thus help us in our daily needs,
And by their overflow
Raise us from what is low.

Thus thought I, as by night I read
Of the great army of the dead,
The trenches cold and damp,
The starved and frozen camp, —

The wounded from the battle-plain,
In dreary hospitals of pain,
The cheerless corridors,
The cold and stony floors.

Lo! in that house of misery
A lady with a lamp I see
Pass through the glimmering gloom,
And flit from room to room.

And slow, as in a dream of bliss,
The speechless sufferer turns to kiss
Her shadow as it falls
Upon the darkened walls.

As if a door in heaven should be
Opened, and then closed suddenly,
The vision came and went,
The light shone, and was spent.

On England's annals, through the long
Hereafter of her speech and song,
That light its rays shall cast
From portals of the past.

The lady with a lamp shall stand
In the great history of the land,
A noble type of good
Heroic womanhood.

Nor even shall be wanting here
The palm, the lily, and the spear, —
The symbols that of yore
Saint Filomena bore.

Longfellow.

THE FIFTIETH BIRTHDAY OF AGASSIZ.

MAY 28, 1857.

It was fifty years ago,
In the pleasant month of May,
In the beautiful Pays de Vaud,
A child in its cradle lay.

And Nature, the old nurse, took
The child upon her knee,
Saying, "Here is a story-book
Thy Father has written for thee."

"Come, wander with me," she said,
"Into regions yet untrod,
And read what is still unread
In the manuscripts of God."

And he wandered away and away,
With Nature, the dear old nurse,
Who sang to him night and day
The rhymes of the universe.

And whenever the way seemed long,
Or his heart began to fail,
She would sing a more wonderful song,
Or tell a more marvellous tale.

So she keeps him still a child,
And will not let him go,
Though at times his heart beats wild
For the beautiful Pays de Vaud;

Though at times he hears in his dreams
The Ranz des Vaches of old,
And the rush of mountain streams
From glaciers clear and cold;

And the mother at home says, "Hark!
For his voice I listen and yearn:
It is growing late and dark,
And my boy does not return!"

Longfellow.

THE WANTS OF MAN.

"Man wants but little here below,
Nor wants that little long."
'Tis not with *me* exactly so;
But 'tis so in the song.

My wants are many, and, if told,
Would muster many a score;
And were each wish a mint of gold,
I still should long for more.

What first I want is daily bread —
And canvas-backs — and wine —
And all the realms of nature spread
Before me, when I dine.
Four courses scarcely can provide
My appetite to quell;
With four choice cooks from France beside
To dress my dinner well.

What next I want at princely cost,
Is elegant attire:
Black sable furs for winter's frost,
And silks for summer's fire.
And Cashmere shawls, and Brussels lace
My bosom's front to deck, —
And diamond rings my hands to grace,
And rubies for my neck.

I want (who does not want) a wife —
Affectionate and fair;
To solace all the woes of life,
And all its joys to share.
Of temper sweet, of yielding will,
Of firm yet placid mind, —
With all my faults to love me still
With sentiment refined.

And as Time's car incessant runs,
And fortune fills my store,
I want of daughters and of sons
From eight to half a score.
I want (alas! can mortal dare
Such bliss on earth to crave?)
That all the girls be chaste and fair,
The boys all wise and brave.

I want a warm and faithful friend,
To cheer the adverse hour;
Who ne'er to flattery will descend,
Nor bend the knee to power, —
A friend to chide me when I'm wrong,
My inmost soul to see;
And that my friendship prove as strong
For him as his for me.

I want the seals of power and place,
The ensigns of command;
Charged by the People's unbought grace
To rule my native land.

Nor crown nor sceptre would I ask,
But from my country's will,
By day, by night, to ply the task
Her cup of bliss to fill.

I want the voice of honest praise
To follow me behind,
And to be thought in future days
The friend of human kind,
That after ages, as they rise,
Exulting may proclaim
In choral union to the skies
Their blessings on my name.

These are the *wants* of mortal *man*,
I cannot want them long;
For life itself is but a span,
And earthly bliss — a song.
My last great *want*, absorbing all —
Is, when beneath the sod,
And summoned to my final call,
The "mercy of my God."

JOHN QUINCY ADAMS.

WASHINGTON, Aug. 31, 1841.

LINES WRITTEN IN A LADY'S ALBUM BELOW THE AUTOGRAPH OF JOHN ADAMS.

DEAR lady, I a little fear
'Tis dangerous to be writing here.
His hand who bade our eagle fly,
Trust his young wings, and mount the sky, —
Who bade across the Atlantic tide
New thunders sweep, new navies ride,
Has traced in lines of trembling age
His autograph upon this page.
Higher than that eagle soars,
Wider than that thunder roars,
His fame shall through the world be sounding,
And o'er the waves of time be bounding.
Though thousands as obscure as I,
Cling to his skirts, he still will fly
And leap to immortality.
If by his name I write my own,
He'll take me where I am not known,
The cold salute will meet my ear,
"Pray, stranger, how did you come here?"

DANIEL WEBSTER.

TO GEORGE PEABODY.

"BANKRUPT — our pockets inside out!
Empty of words to speak his praises!
Worcester and Webster up the spout!
Dead broke of laudatory phrases!
But why with flowery speeches tease,
With vain superlatives distress him?
Has language better words than these?
The friend of all his race, God bless him!

A simple prayer — but words more sweet
By human lips were never uttered,
Since Adam left the country seat
Where angel wings around him fluttered.
The old look on with tear-dimmed eyes,
The children cluster to caress him,
And every voice unbidden cries,
The friend of all his race, God bless him!

O. W. HOLMES.

A KING.

A KING lived long ago,
In the morning of the world,
When Earth was nigher Heaven than now:
And the King's locks curled
Disparting o'er a forehead full
As the milk-white space 'twixt horn and horn
Of some sacrificial bull.
Only calm as a babe new-born:
For he was got to a sleepy mood,
So safe from all decrepitude,
Age with its bane so sure gone by,
(The gods so loved him while he dreamed,)
That, having lived thus long, there seemed
No need the King should ever die.

Among the rocks his city was;
Before his palace, in the sun,
He sat to see his people pass,
And judge them every one
From its threshold of smooth stone

ROBERT BROWNING.

THE DESTRUCTION OF SENNACHERIB.

THE Assyrian came down like the wolf on the fold,
And his cohorts were gleaming in purple and gold;
And the sheen of their spears was like stars on the sea,
When the blue wave rolls nightly on deep Galilee.

Like the leaves of the forest when summer is green,
That host with their banners at sunset were seen:
Like the leaves of the forest when autumn hath blown,
That host on the morrow lay withered and strewn.

For the Angel of Death spread his wing on the blast,
And breathed in the face of the foe as he passed;
And the eyes of the sleepers waxed deadly and chill,
And their hearts but once heaved, and forever grew still.

And there lay the steed with his nostril all wide,
But through it there rolled not the breath of his pride;
And the foam of his gasping lay white on the turf,
And cold as the spray of the rock-beating surf.

And there lay the rider distorted and pale,
With the dew on his brow, and the rust on his mail;
And the tents were all silent, the banners alone,
The lances unlifted, the trumpet unblown.

And the widows of Ashur are loud in their wail,
And the idols are broke in the temple of Baal;
And the might of the Gentile, unsmote by the sword,
Hath melted like snow in the glance of the Lord!

BYRON.

CLEOPATRA.

THE barge she sat in, like a burnished throne,
Burned on the water: the poop was beaten gold,
Purple the sails, and so perfumèd, that
The winds were love-sick with them: the oars were silver;
Which to the tune of flutes kept stroke, and made
The water, which they beat, to follow faster,
As amorous of their strokes. For her own person,
It beggared all description: she did lie
In her pavilion, (cloth-of-gold, of tissue,)
O'er-picturing that Venus, where we see,
The fancy out-work nature: on each side her,
Stood pretty boys, like smiling Cupids,
With diverse-colored fans, whose wind did seem
To glow the delicate cheeks which they did cool
And what they undid, did.
Her gentlewomen, like the Nereides,
So many mermaids, tended her i' the eyes,
And made their bends adornings: at the helm
A seeming mermaid steers; the silken tackles
Swell with the touches of those flower-soft hands,
That yarely frame the office. From the barge
A strange invisible perfume hits the sense
Of the adjacent wharfs. The city cast
Her people out upon her; and Antony,
Enthronèd in the market-place, did sit alone,
Whistling to the air; which, but for vacancy,
Had gone to gaze on Cleopatra too,
And made a gap in nature.

SHAKSPEARE.

THE GLADIATOR.

I SEE before me the gladiator lie:
He leans upon his hand; — his manly brow
Consents to death, but conquers agony,
And his drooped head sinks gradually low —
And through his side the last drops, ebbing slow
From the red gash, fall heavy, one by one,
Like the first of a thunder-shower; and now
The arena swims around him — he is gone,
Ere ceased the inhuman shout which hailed the wretch who won.

He heard it, but he heeded not, — his eyes
Were with his heart, and that was far away;
He recked not of the life he lost, nor prize,
But where his rude hut by the Danube lay,
There were his young barbarians all at play,
There was their Dacian mother, — he, their sire,
Butchered to make a Roman holiday; —
All this rushed with his blood; — Shall he expire,
And unavenged? — Arise! ye Goths, and glut your ire!

BYRON.

THE PRISONER OF CHILLON.

I MADE a footing in the wall,
It was not therefrom to escape,
For I had buried one and all,
Who loved me in a human shape;
And the whole earth would henceforth be
A wider prison unto me:
But I was curious to ascend
To my barred windows, and to bend
Once more upon the mountains high,
The quiet of a loving eye.

I saw them — and they were the same;
They were not changed like me in frame;

I saw their thousand years of snow
On high, — their wide long lake below,
And the blue Rhone in fullest flow;
I heard the torrents leap and gush
O'er channelled rock and broken bush;
I saw the white-walled distant town,
And whiter sails go skimming down;
And then there was a little isle,
Which in my very face did smile,
The only one in view;
A small green isle, it seemed no more,
Scarce broader than my dungeon floor,
But in it there were three tall trees,
And o'er it blew the mountain breeze,
And by it there were waters flowing,
And on it there were young flowers growing,
Of gentle breath and hue.
The fish swam by the castle-wall,
And they seemed joyous each and all;
The eagle rode the rising blast;
Methought he never flew so fast
As then to me he seemed to fly, —
And then new tears came in my eye,
And I felt troubled, — and would fain
I had not left my recent chain.

BYRON.

FROM PARISINA.

EXECUTION.

THE convent-bells are ringing,
But mournfully and slow;
In the gray square turret swinging,
With a deep sound, to and fro.
Heavily to the heart they go!
Hark! the hymn is singing —
The song for the dead below,
Or the living, who shortly shall be so!
For a departing being's soul
The death-hymn peals, and the hollow bells knoll:
He is near his mortal goal;
Kneeling at the friar's knee;
Sad to hear, — and piteous to see, —
Kneeling on the bare cold ground,
With the block before and the guards around; —
And the headsman with his bare arm ready,
That the blow may be both swift and steady,
Feels if the axe be sharp and true —
Since he set its edge anew:
While the crowd in a speechless circle gather,
To see the son fall by the doom of the father.

It is a lovely hour as yet
Before the summer sun shall set,
And his evening beams are shed
Full on Hugo's fated head,
As, his last confession pouring,
To the monk his doom deploring,
In penitential holiness,
He bends to hear his accents bless
With absolution such as may
Wipe our mortal stains away.

. . . .

He died, as erring man should die,
Without display, without parade;
Meekly had he bowed and prayed,
As not disdaining priestly aid,
Nor desperate of all hope on high.

BYRON.

FROM THE SIEGE OF CORINTH.

THE night is past, and shines the sun
As if that morn were a jocund one.
Lightly and brightly breaks away
The morning from her mantle gray,
And the moon will look on a sultry day.
Hark to the trump, and the drum,
And the mournful sound of the barbarous horn,
And the flap of the banners, that flit as they're borne,
And the neigh of the steed, and the multitude's hum,
And the clash, and the shout, "They come, they come!"
The horse-tails are plucked from the ground, and the sword
From its sheath; and they form, and but wait for the word.

Tartar, and Spahi, and Turcoman,
Strike your tents, and throng to the van;
Mount ye, spur ye, skim the plain,
That the fugitive may flee in vain,
When he breaks from the town; and none escape,
Aged or young, in the Christian shape;
While your fellows on foot, in fiery mass,
Bloodstain the breach through which they pass.
The steeds are all bridled, and snort to the rein;
Curved is each neck, and flowing each mane;
White is the foam of their champ on the bit:
The spears are uplifted; the matches are lit;
The cannon are pointed and ready to roar,
And crush the wall they have crumbled before:
Forms in his phalanx each Janizar;
Alp at their head; his right arm is bare,
So is the blade of his scimitar;
The Khan and his pachas are all at their post:
The vizier himself at the head of the host.
When the culverin's signal is fired, then On!
Leave not in Corinth a living one—
A priest at her altars, a chief in her halls,
A hearth in her mansions, a stone on her walls.
God and the prophet—Alla Hu!
Up to the skies with that wild halloo!
"There the breach lies for passage, the ladder to scale;
And your hands on your sabres, and how should ye fail?
He who first downs with the red cross may crave
His heart's dearest wish; let him ask it, and have!"
Thus uttered Coumourgi, the dauntless vizier;
The reply was the brandish of sabre and spear,
And the shout of fierce thousands in joyous ire:—
Silence—hark to the signal—fire!

BYRON.

ENTRANCE OF BOLINGBROKE INTO LONDON.

Duchess. — My lord, you told me you would tell the rest,
When weeping made you break the story off,
Of our two cousins coming into London.
York. — Where did I leave?
Duch. — At that sad stop, my lord,
Where rude misgoverned hands, from windows' tops,
Threw dust and rubbish on King Richard's head,
York. — Then as I said, the duke, great Bolingbroke, —
Mounted upon a hot and fiery steed,
Which his aspiring rider seemed to know, —
With slow but stately pace, kept on his course,
While all tongues cried, "God save thee, Bolingbroke!"
You would have thought the very windows spake,
So many greedy looks of young and old
Through casements darted their desiring eyes
Upon his visage, and that all the walls,
With painted imagery, had said at once, —
"Jesu preserve thee! welcome, Bolingbroke!"
Whilst he, from one side to the other turning,
Bareheaded, lower than his proud steed's neck,
Bespake them thus, — "I thank you, countrymen:"
And thus still doing, thus he passed along.
Duch. — Alas, poor Richard, where rides he the while?
York. — As in a theatre, the eyes of men,
After a well-graced actor leaves the stage,
Are idly bent on him that enters next,
Thinking his prattle to be tedious:
Even so, or with much more contempt, men's eyes
Did scowl on Richard; no man cried, God save him!
No joyful tongue gave him his welcome home:

But dust was thrown upon his sacred head,
Which with such gentle sorrow he shook off, —
His face still combating with tears and smiles,
The badges of his grief and patience, —
That, had not God, for some strong purpose, steeled
The hearts of men, they must perforce have melted,
And barbarism itself have pitied him.

SHAKSPEARE: *King Richard II.*

THE CALIPH'S ENCAMPMENT.

WHOSE are the gilded tents that crowd the way,
Where all was waste and silent yesterday?
This City of War, which, in a few short hours,
Hath sprung up here, as if the magic powers
Of Him who, in the twinkling of a star,
Built the high-pillared walls of Chilminar,
Had conjured up, far as the eye can see,
This world of tents, and domes, and sun-bright armory: —
Princely pavilions, screened by many a fold
Of crimson cloth, and topped with balls of gold: —
Steeds, with their housings of rich silver spun,
Their chains and poitrels glittering in the sun;
And camels, tufted o'er with Temen's shells
Shaking in every breeze their light-toned bells!

MOORE.

FOP.

Hotspur. — My liege, I did deny no prisoners.
But I remember, when the fight was done,
When I was dry with rage, and extreme toil,
Breathless and faint, leaning upon my sword,
Came there a certain lord, neat, trimly dressed,
Fresh as a bridegroom; and his chin, new reaped,
Showed like a stubble-land at harvest-home;
He was perfumèd like a milliner;
And 'twixt his finger and his thumb he held
A pouncet-box, which ever and anon
He gave his nose, and took't away again; —
Who therewith angry, when it next came there,
Took it in snuff: — and still he smiled and talked;
And, as the soldiers bore dead bodies by,
He called them untaught knaves, unmannerly,
To bring a slovenly unhandsome corse
Betwixt the wind and his nobility.
With many holiday and lady terms
He questioned me; among the rest demanded
My prisoners, in your majesty's behalf.
I then, all smarting, with my wounds being cold,
To be so pestered with a popinjay,
Out of my grief and my impatience,
Answered neglectingly, I know not what;
He should, or he should not; — for he made me mad
To see him shine so brisk, and smell so sweet,
And talk so like a waiting-gentlewoman,
Of guns, and drums, and wounds, (God save the mark!)
And telling me, the sovereign'st thing on earth
Was parmaceti, for an inward bruise;
And that it was great pity, so it was,
That villanous saltpetre should be digged
Out of the bowels of the harmless earth,
Which many a good tall fellow had destroyed
So cowardly; and but for these vile guns,

He would himself have been a soldier.
This bald unjointed chat of his, my lord,
I answered indirectly, as I said;
And I beseech you, let not his report
Come current for an accusation,
Betwixt my love and your high majesty.

SHAKSPEARE.

THE FORGING OF THE ANCHOR.

COME, see the Dolphin's anchor forged, —'tis at a white-heat now:
The bellows ceased, the flames decreased, though on the forge's brow
The little flames still fitfully play through the sable mound,
And fitfully you still may see the grim smiths ranking round,
All clad in leather panoply, their broad hands only bare, —
Some rest upon their sledges here, some work the windlass there.

The windlass strains the tackle chains, the black mound heaves below,
And red and deep a hundred veins burst out at every throe:
It rises, roars, rends all outright, — O Vulcan, what a glow!

'Tis blinding white, 'tis blasting bright, — the high sun shines not sō!
The high sun sees not, on the earth, such a fiery fearful show;
The roof-ribs swarth, the candent hearth, the ruddy lurid row
Of smiths that stand, an ardent band, like men before the foe.
As, quivering through his fleece of flame, the sailing monster, slow
Sinks on the anvil; — all about the faces fiery grow.
"Hurrah!" they shout, "leap out — leap out;" bang, bang, the sledges go;
Hurrah! the jetted lightnings are hissing high and low; —
A hailing fount of fire is struck at every squashing blow,
The leathern mail rebounds the hail, the rattling cinders strew
The ground around; at every bound the sweltering fountains flow,
And thick and loud the swinking crowd at every stroke pant "Ho!"

Leap out, leap out, my masters; leap out, and lay on load!
Let's forge a goodly anchor; — a bower thick and broad;
For a heart of oak is hanging on every blow, I bode,
And I see the good ship riding, all in a perilous road, —
The low reef roaring on her lee, — the roll of ocean poured
From stem to stern, sea after sea; the mainmast by the board;
The bulwarks down, the rudder gone, the boats stove at the chains!
But courage still, brave mariners! the bower yet remains,
And not an inch to flinch he deigns, save when ye pitch sky high;
Then moves his head, as though he said, "Fear nothing — here am I."

Swing in your strokes in order, let foot and hand keep time:
Your blows make music sweeter far than any steeple's chime.
But while you sling your sledges, sing, — and let the burthen be,
The anchor is the anvil king, and royal craftsmen we!
Strike in, strike in — the sparks begin to dull their rustling red;
Our hammers ring with sharper din, our work will soon be sped.
Our anchor soon must change his bed of fiery rich array,
For a hammock at the roaring bows, or an oozy couch of clay;
Our anchor soon must change the lay of merry craftsmen here,
For the yeo-heave-o', and the heave-away, and the sighing seaman's cheer;
When, weighing slow, at eve they go — far, far from love and home;
And sobbing sweethearts, in a row, wail o'er the ocean foam.

In livid and obdurate gloom he darkens down at last;
A shapely one he is, and strong, as e'er from cat was cast.
O trusted and trustworthy guard, if thou hadst life like me,
What pleasures would thy toils reward beneath the deep green sea!
O deep sea-diver, who might then behold such sights as thou?
The hoary monster's palaces! methinks what joy 'twere now
To go plumb plunging down amid the assembly of the whales,
And feel the churned sea round me boil beneath their scourging tails!
Then deep in tangle-woods to fight the fierce sea-unicorn,
And send him foiled and bellowing back, for all his ivory horn;
To leave the subtile sworder-fish of bony blade forlorn;
And for the ghastly-grinning shark to laugh his jaws to scorn;
To leap down on the kraken's back, where 'mid Norwegian isles
He lies, a lubber anchorage for sudden shallowed miles;
Till snorting, like an under-sea volcano, off he rolls;
Meanwhile to swing, a-buffeting the far astonished shoals
Of his back-browsing ocean-calves; or, haply in a cove,
Shell-strewn, and consecrate of old to some Undiné's love,
To find the long-haired maidens; or, hard by icy lands,
To wrestle with the sea-serpent, upon cerulean sands.

O broad-armed fisher of the deep, whose sports can equal thine?
The Dolphin weighs a thousand tons, that tugs thy cable line;
And night by night, 'tis thy delight, thy glory day by day,
Through sable sea and breaker white, the giant game to play, —
But shamer of our little sports! forgive the name I gave, —
A fisher's joy is to destroy, — thine office is to save.

O lodger in the sea-king's halls! couldst thou but understand
Whose be the white bones by thy side, — or who that dripping band,
Slow swaying in the heaving wave, that round about thee bend,
With sounds like breakers in a dream, blessing their ancient friend; —
O, couldst thou know what heroes glide with larger steps round thee,
Thine iron side would swell with pride, — thou'dst leap within the sea!

Give honor to their memories who left the pleasant strand
To shed their blood so freely for the love of father-land, —
Who left their chance of quiet age and grassy churchyard grave
So freely, for a restless bed amid the tossing wave!
O, though our anchor may not be all I have fondly sung,
Honor him for their memory whose bones he goes among!

SAMUEL FERGUSSON.

THE ICE PALACE.

LESS worthy of applause, though more admired,
Because a novelty, the work of man,
Imperial mistress of the fur-clad Russ,
Thy most magnificent and mighty freak,
The wonder of the North. No forest fell
When thou wouldst build; no quarry sent its stores
To enrich thy walls; but thou didst hew the floods,
And make thy marble of the glassy wave.
Silently as a dream the fabric rose;
No sound of hammer or of saw was there:
Ice upon ice, the well-adjusted parts
Were soon conjoined, nor other cement asked
Than water interfused to make them one.
Lamps gracefully disposed, and of all hues,

Illumined every side: a watery light
Gleamed through the clear transparency, that seemed
Another moon new risen, or meteor fallen
From Heaven to Earth, of lambent flame serene.
So stood the brittle prodigy: though smooth
And slippery the materials, yet frost-bound
Firm as a rock. Nor wanted aught within,
That royal residence might well befit,
For grandeur or for use. Long wavy wreaths
Of flowers, that feared no enemy but warmth,
Blushed on the panels. Mirror needed none
Where all was vitreous; but in order due
Convivial table and commodious seat,
(What seemed at least commodious seat,) were there;
Sofa and couch and high-built throne august.
The same lubricity was found in all,
And all was moist to the warm touch; a scene
Of evanescent glory, once a stream,
And soon to slide into a stream again.

COWPER.

THE SOLDIER'S DREAM.

OUR bugles sang truce; for the night-cloud had lowered,
And the sentinel stars set their watch in the sky;
And thousands had sunk on the ground overpowered,
The weary to sleep, and the wounded to die.

When reposing that night on my pallet of straw,
By the wolf-scaring fagot that guarded the slain,
At the dead of the night a sweet vision I saw,
And thrice ere the morning I dreamt it again.

Methought from the battle-field's dreadful array
Far, far I had roamed on a desolate track:
'Twas autumn; and sunshine arose on the way
To the home of my fathers, that welcomed me back.

I flew to the pleasant fields traversed so oft
In life's morning march, when my bosom was young:
I heard my own mountain-goats bleating aloft,
And knew the sweet strains that the corn-reapers sung.

Then pledged we the wine-cup, and fondly I swore
From my home and my weeping friends never to part:
My little ones kissed me a thousand times o'er,
And my wife sobbed aloud in her fulness of heart.

"Stay, stay with us — rest, thou art weary and worn:"
And fain was their war-broken soldier to stay;
But sorrow returned with the dawning of morn,
And the voice in my dreaming ear melted away.

CAMPBELL.

THE PALM AND THE PINE.

BENEATH an Indian palm a girl
Of other blood reposes;
Her cheek is clear and pale as pearl,
Amid that wild of roses.

Beside a northern pine a boy
Is leaning fancy-bound,
Nor listens where with noisy joy
Awaits the impatient hound.

Cool grows the sick and feverish calm, —
Relaxed the frosty twine, —
The pine-tree dreameth of the palm,
The palm-tree of the pine.

As soon shall nature interlace
Those dimly visioned boughs,
As these young lovers face to face
Renew their early vows!

MILNES.

BURIAL OF MOSES.

"And he buried him in a valley in the land of Moab, over against Beth-peor; but no man knoweth of his sepulchre unto this day." — DEUT. xxxiv. 6.

By Nebo's lonely mountain,
On this side Jordan's wave,
In a vale in the land of Moab,
There lies a lonely grave;
But no man built that sepulchre,
And no man saw it e'er;
For the angels of God upturned the sod,
And laid the dead man there.

That was the grandest funeral
That ever passed on earth;
Yet no man heard the trampling,
Or saw the train go forth:
Noiselessly as the daylight
Comes when the night is done,
And the crimson streak on ocean's cheek
Grows into the great sun;

Noiselessly as the spring-time
Her crown of verdure weaves,
And all the trees on all the hills
Unfold their thousand leaves:
So without sound of music
Or voice of them that wept,
Silently down from the mountain's crown
The great procession swept.

Perchance the bald old eagle
On gray Beth-peor's height
Out of his rocky eyry
Looked on the wondrous sight;
Perchance the lion stalking
Still shuns that hallowed spot;
For beast and bird have seen and heard
That which man knoweth not.

But, when the warrior dieth,
His comrades of the war,
With arms reversed and muffled drums,
Follow the funeral car:
They show the banners taken;
They tell his battles won,
And after him lead his masterless steed,
While peals the minute-gun.

Amid the noblest of the land
Men lay the sage to rest,
And give the bard an honored place,
With costly marbles drest,
In the great minster transept
Where lights like glories fall,
And the sweet choir sings, and the organ rings
Along the emblazoned hall.

This was the bravest warrior
That ever buckled sword;
This the most gifted poet
That ever breathed a word;
And never earth's philosopher
Traced with his golden pen,
On the deathless page, truths half so sage
As he wrote down for men.

And had he not high honor?
The hillside for his pall!
To lie in state while angels wait
With stars for tapers tall!
And the dark rock pines like tossing plumes
Over his bier to wave,
And God's own hand, in that lonely land,
To lay him in his grave! —

In that deep grave without a name,
Whence his uncoffined clay
Shall break again, — O wondrous thought!
Before the judgment-day,
And stand, with glory wrapped around,
On the hills he never trod,
And speak of the strife that won our life
With the incarnate Son of God.

Oh lonely tomb in Moab's land!
Oh dark Beth-peor's hill!
Speak to these curious hearts of ours,
And teach them to be still:
God hath his mysteries of grace,
Ways that we cannot tell,
He hides them deep, like the secret sleep
Of him he loved so well.

MRS. ALEXANDER.

VII.

NARRATIVE POEMS

AND

BALLADS.

Fragments of the lofty strain
Float down the tide of years,
As buoyant on the stormy main
A parted wreck appears."—SCOTT.

NARRATIVE POEMS AND BALLADS.

HOUSE OF BUSYRANE.

KINGS, queens, lords, ladies, knights, and damsels great
Were heaped together with the vulgar sort,
And mingled with the rascal rabblement
Without respect of person or of port,
To show Dan Cupid's power and great effort:
And round about a border was entrailed
Of broken bows and arrows shivered short,
And a long bloody river through them rayled
So lively and so like that living scene it failed.

And at the upper end of that fair room
There was an altar built of precious stone
Of passing value and of great renown,
On which there stood an image all alone,
Of massy gold, which with his own light shone;
And wings it had with sundry colors dight, —
More sundry colors than the proud pavone
Bears in his boasted fan, or Iris bright
When her discolored bow she spreads through heaven bright.

Blindfold he was; and in his cruel fist
A mortal bow of arrows keen did hold,
With which he shot at random when him list;
Some headed with sad lead, some with pure gold;
(Ah! man, beware how thou those darts behold!)
A wounded dragon under him did lie,
Whose hideous tail did his left foot infold,
And with a shaft was shot through either eye
That no man forth might draw, nor no man remedy.

And underneath his feet was written thus:
"*Unto the Victor of the gods this be;*"
And all the people in that ample house
Did to that image bow their humble knee,
And oft committed foul idolatry.
That wondrous sight fair Britomart amazed,
Nor seeing could her wonder satisfy,
But evermore and more upon it gazed
The while the passing brightness her frail senses dazed.

Though as she backward cast her busy eye,
To search each secret of that goodly stead,
Over the door thus written she did spy,
"*Be bold:*" she oft and oft it over-read,
Yet could not find what sense it figured;
But whatso were therein, or writ, or meant,
She was thereby no whit discouraged
From prosecuting of her first intent,
But forward with bold steps into the next room went.

Much fairer than the former was that room,
And richlier by many parts arrayed;

For not with arras, made in painful loom,
But with pure gold, it all was overlaid,
Wrought with wild antics, which their follies played
In the rich metal as they living were:
A thousand monstrous forms therein were made,
Such as false Love doth oft upon him wear;
For love in thousand monstrous forms doth oft appear.

And all about the glistering walls were hung
With warlike spoils and with victorious prayes
Of mighty conquerors and captains strong,
Which were whilom captived in their days
To cruel love, and wrought their own decays.
Their swords and spears were broke, and hauberks rent,
And their proud garlands of triumphant bays
Trodden to dust with fury insolent,
To show the victor's might and merciless intent.

The warlike maid, beholding earnestly
The goodly ordinance of this rich place,
Did greatly wonder, nor did satisfy
Her greedy eyes by gazing a long space.
But more she marvelled that no footing's trace
Nor wight appeared, but wasteful emptiness
And solemn silence over all that space:
Strange thing it seemed that none was to possess
So rich purveyance, nor them keep with carefulness.

And as she looked about, she did behold
How over that same door was likewise writ,
"*Be bold, be bold,*" and everywhere, "*Be bold;*"
That much she mused, yet could not construe it
By any riddling skill, nor common wit.
At last she spied at that room's upper end
Another iron door, on which was writ,
"*Be not too bold;*" whereto though she did bend
Her earnest mind, yet wist not what it might intend.

SPENSER.

THE GATE OF CAMELOT.

So, when their feet were planted on the plain
That broadened toward the base of Camelot,
Far off they saw the silver-misty morn
Rolling her smoke about the Royal mount,
That rose between the forest and the field.
At times the summit of the high city flashed;
At times the spires and turrets half-way down
Pricked through the mist: at times the great gate shone
Only, that opened on the field below:
Anon, the whole fair city had disappeared.

Then those who went with Gareth were amazed,
One crying, "Let us go no further, lord.
Here is a city of Enchanters, built
By fairy Kings." The second echoed him,
"Lord, we have heard from our wise men at home
To Northward, that this King is not the King,
But only changeling out of Fairyland,
Who drave the heathen hence by sorcery
And Merlin's glamour." Then the first again,
"Lord, there is no such city anywhere,
But all a vision."

Gareth answered them
With laughter, swearing he had glamour enow

In his own blood, his princedom, youth and hopes,
To plunge old Merlin in the Arabian sea;
So pushed them all unwilling toward the gate.
And there was no gate like it under heaven.
For barefoot on the keystone, which was lined
And rippled like an ever-fleeting wave,
The Lady of the Lake stood: all her dress
Wept from her sides as water flowing away;
But like the cross her great and goodly arms
Stretched under all the cornice, and upheld:
And drops of water fell from either hand;
And down from one a sword was hung, from one
A censer, either worn with wind and storm;
And o'er her breast floated the sacred fish;
And in the space to left of her and right,
Were Arthur's wars in weird devices done,
New things and old co-twisted, as if Time
Were nothing, so inveterately, that men
Were giddy gazing there; and over all
High on the top were those three Queens, the friends
Of Arthur, who should help him at his need.

Then those with Gareth for so long a space
Stared at the figures, that at last it seemed
The dragon-boughts and elvish emblemings
Began to move, seethe, twine and curl: they called
To Gareth, "Lord, the gateway is alive."

And Gareth likewise on them fixt his eyes
So long, that even to him they seemed to move.
Out of the city a blast of music pealed.
Back from the gate started the three, to whom
From out thereunder came an ancient man,
Long-bearded, saying, "Who be ye, my sons?"

Then Gareth, "We be tillers of the soil,
Who leaving share in furrow, come to see
The glories of our King: but these, my men
(Your city moved so weirdly in the mist),
Doubt if the King be King at all, or come
From fairyland; and whether this be built
By magic, and by fairy Kings and Queens;
Or whether there be any city at all,
Or all a vision: and this music now
Hath scared them both; but tell thou these the truth."

Then that old Seer made answer playing on him
And saying, "Son, I have seen the good ship sail
Keel upward and mast downward in the heavens,
And solid turrets topsy-turvy in air:
And here is truth; but an it please thee not,
Take thou the truth as thou hast told it me.
For truly, as thou sayest, a Fairy King
And Fairy Queens have built the city, son;
They came from out a sacred mountain-cleft
Toward the sunrise, each with harp in hand,
And built it to the music of their harps.
And as thou sayest it is enchanted, son,
For there is nothing in it as it seems,
Saving the King; though some there be that hold
The King a shadow, and the city real:
Yet take thou heed of him, for so thou pass
Beneath this archway, then wilt thou become

A thrall to his enchantments, for the King
Will bind thee by such vows, as is a shame
A man should not be bound by, yet the which
No man can keep; but, so thou dread to swear,
Pass not beneath this gateway, but abide
Without, among the cattle of the field,
For, an ye heard a music, like enow
They are building still, seeing the city is built
To music, therefore never built at all,
And therefore built forever."

Gareth spake
Angered, "Old Master, reverence thine own beard
That looks as white as utter truth, and seems
Well-nigh as long as thou art statured tall!
Why mockest thou the stranger that hath been
To thee fair-spoken?"

But the Seer replied,
"Know ye not then the Riddling of the Bards?
'Confusion, and illusion, and relation,
Elusion, and occasion, and evasion'?
I mock thee not but as thou mockest me,
And all that see thee, for thou art not who
Thou seemest, but I know thee who thou art.
And now thou goest up to mock the King,
Who cannot brook the shadow of any lie."

Unmockingly the mocker ending here
Turned to the right, and past along the plain;
Whom Gareth looking after, said, "My men,
Our one white lie sits like a little ghost
Here on the threshold of our enterprise.
Let love be blamed for it, not she, nor I:
Well, we will make amends."

With all good cheer
He spake and laughed, then entered with his twain
Camelot, a city of shadowy palaces
And stately, rich in emblem and the work
Of ancient kings who did their days in stone;
Which Merlin's hand, the Mage at Arthur's court,
Knowing all arts, had touched, and everywhere
At Arthur's ordinance, tipt with lessening peak
And pinnacle, and had made it spire to heaven.
And ever and anon a knight would pass
Outward, or inward to the hall: his arms
Clashed; and the sound was good to Gareth's ear.
And out of bower and casement shyly glanced
Eyes of pure women, wholesome stars of love;
And all about a healthful people stept
As in the presence of a gracious king.

TENNYSON.

THE CROWNING OF ARTHUR.

THERE came to Cameliard,
With Gawin and young Modred, her two sons,
Lot's wife, the Queen of Orkney, Bellicent;
Whom as he could, not as he would, the King
Made feast for, saying, as they sat at meat,

"A doubtful throne is ice on summer seas.
Ye come from Arthur's court. Victor his men
Report him! Yea, but ye, — think ye this king, —
So many those that hate him, and so strong,
So few his knights, however brave they be, —
Hath body enow to hold his foemen down?"

"O King," she cried, "and I will tell thee: few,
Few, but all brave, all of one mind with him;
For I was near him when the savage yells
Of Uther's peerage died, and Arthur sat
Crowned on the dais, and his warriors cried,
'Be thou the king, and we will work thy will
Who love thee.' Then the King in low deep tones,
And simple words of great authority,
Bound them by so strait vows to his own self,
That when they rose, knighted from kneeling, some
Were pale as at the passing of a ghost,
Some flushed, and others dazed, as one who wakes
Half-blinded at the coming of a light.

"But when he spake and cheered his Table Round
With large, divine and comfortable words
Beyond my tongue to tell thee,—I beheld
From eye to eye through all their Order flash
A momentary likeness of the King:
And ere it left their faces, through the cross
And those around it and the Crucified,
Down from the casement over Arthur, smote
Flame-color, vert and azure, in three rays,
One falling upon each of three fair queens,
Who stood in silence near his throne, the friends
Of Arthur, gazing on him, tall, with bright
Sweet faces, who will help him at his need.

"And there I saw mage Merlin, whose vast wit
And hundred winters are but as the hands
Of loyal vassals toiling for their liege.
"And near him stood the Lady of the Lake,
Who knows a subtler magic than his own,—
Clothed in white samite, mystic, wonderful.
She gave the King his huge cross-hilted sword,
Whereby to drive the heathen out: a mist
Of incense curled about her, and her face
Well-nigh was hidden in the minster gloom;
But there was heard among the holy hymns
A voice as of the waters, for she dwells
Down in a deep, calm, whatsoever storms
May shake the world, and when the surface rolls,
Hath power to walk the waters like our Lord.

"There likewise I beheld Excalibur
Before him at his crowning borne, the sword
That rose from out the bosom of the lake,
And Arthur rowed across and took it,—rich
With jewels, elfin Urim, on the hilt,
Bewildering heart and eye,—the blade so bright
That men are blinded by it;—on one side,
Graven in the oldest tongue of all this world,
'Take me;' but turn the blade and ye shall see,
And written in the speech ye speak yourself,
'Cast me away!' And sad was Arthur's face
Taking it, but old Merlin counselled him,
'Take thou and strike! the time to cast away
Is yet far-off.' So this great brand the king
Took, and by this will beat his foemen down."

TENNYSON.

ALFRED THE HARPER.

Dark fell the night, the watch was set,
The host was idly spread,
The Danes around their watchfires met,
Caroused, and fiercely fed.

The chiefs beneath a tent of leaves,
And Guthrum, king of all,
Devoured the flesh of England's beeves,
And laughed at England's fall.
Each warrior proud, each Danish earl,
In mail and wolf-skin clad,
Their bracelets white with plundered pearl,
Their eyes with triumph mad.

From Humber-land to Severn-land,
And on to Tamar stream,
Where Thames makes green the towery strand,
Where Medway's waters gleam, —
With hands of steel and mouths of flame
They raged the kingdom through;
And where the Norseman sickle came,
No crop but hunger grew.

They loaded many an English horse
With wealth of cities fair;
They dragged from many a father's corse
The daughter by her hair.
And English slaves, and gems and gold,
Were gathered round the feast;
Till midnight in their woodland hold,
Oh! never that riot ceased.

In stalked a warrior tall and rude
Before the strong sea-kings;
"Ye Lords and Earls of Odin's brood,
Without a harper sings.
He seems a simple man and poor,
But well he sounds the lay;
And well, ye Norseman chiefs, be sure,
Will ye the song repay."

In trod the bard with keen cold look,
And glanced along the board,
That with the shout and war-cry shook
Of many a Danish lord.
But thirty brows, inflamed and stern,
Soon bent on him their gaze,
While calm he gazed, as if to learn
Who chief deserved his praise.

Loud Guthrum spake, — "Nay, gaze not thus,
Thou Harper weak and poor!
By Thor! who bandy looks with us
Must worse than looks endure.
Sing high the praise of Denmark's host,
High praise each dauntless Earl;
The brave who stun this English coast
With war's unceasing whirl."

The Harper slowly bent his head,
And touched aloud the string;
Then raised his face, and boldly said,
"Hear thou my lay, O king!
High praise from every mouth of man
To all who boldly strive,
Who fall where first the fight began,
And ne'er go back alive.

"Fill high your cups, and swell the shout,
At famous Regnar's name!
Who sank his host in bloody rout,
When he to Humber came.
His men were chased, his sons were slain,
And he was left alone.
They bound him in an iron chain
Upon a dungeon stone.

"With iron links they bound him fast;
With snakes they filled the hole,
That made his flesh their long repast,
And bit into his soul.

"Great chiefs, why sink in gloom your eyes?
Why champ your teeth in pain?
Still lives the song though Regnar dies!
Fill high your cups again.
Ye too, perchance, O Norsemen lords!
Who fought and swayed so long,
Shall soon but live in minstrel words,
And owe your names to song.

"This land has graves by thousands more
Than that where Regnar lies.
When conquests fade, and rule is o'er,
The sod must close your eyes.
How soon, who knows? Not chief, nor bard;
And yet to me 'tis given,
To see your foreheads deeply scarred,
And guess the doom of Heaven.

"I may not read or when or how,
But, Earls and Kings, be sure
I see a blade o'er every brow,
Where pride now sits secure.
Fill high the cups, raise loud the strain!
When chief and monarch fall,
Their names in song shall breathe again,
And thrill the feastful hall."

Grim sat the chiefs; one heaved a groan,
And one grew pale with dread,
His iron mace was grasped by one,
By one his wine was shed.
And Guthrum cried, "Nay, bard, no more
We hear thy boding lay;
Make drunk the song with spoil and gore!
Light up the joyous fray!"

"Quick throbs my brain," — so burst the song, —
"To hear the strife once more.
The mace, the axe, they rest too long;
Earth cries, My thirst is sore.
More blithely twang the strings of bows
Than strings of harps in glee;
Red wounds are lovelier than the rose,
Or rosy lips to me.

"Oh! fairer than a field of flowers,
When flowers in England grew,
Would be the battle's marshalled powers,
The plain of carnage new.
With all its deaths before my soul
The vision rises fair;
Raise loud the song, and drain the bowl!
I would that I were there!"

Loud rang the harp, the minstrel's eye
Rolled fiercely round the throng;
It seemed two crashing hosts were nigh,
Whose shock aroused the song.
A golden cup King Guthrum gave
To him who strongly played;
And said, "I won it from the slave
Who once o'er England swayed."

King Guthrum cried, "'Twas Alfred's own;
Thy song befits the brave:
The King who cannot guard his throne
Nor wine nor song shall have."
The minstrel took the goblet bright,
And said, "I drink the wine
To him who owns by justest right
The cup thou bid'st be mine.

"To him, your Lord, Oh shout ye all!
His meed be deathless praise!
The King who dares not nobly fall,
Dies basely all his days."

"The praise thou speakest," Guthrum said,
"With sweetness fills mine ear;
For Alfred swift before me fled,
And left me monarch here.
The royal coward never dared
Beneath mine eye to stand.
Oh, would that now this feast he shared,
And saw me rule his land!"

Then stern the minstrel rose, and spake,
And gazed upon the King, —
"Not now the golden cup I take,
Nor more to thee I sing.
Another day, a happier hour,
Shall bring me here again:
The cup shall stay in Guthrum's power
Till I demand it then."

The Harper turned and left the shed,
Nor bent to Guthrum's crown;
And one who marked his visage said
It wore a ghastly frown.
The Danes ne'er saw that Harper more,
For soon as morning rose,
Upon their camp King Alfred bore,
And slew ten thousand foes.

JOHN STERLING.

GARCI PEREZ DE VARGAS.

KING Ferdinand alone did stand one day upon the hill,
Surveying all his leaguer, and the ramparts of Seville;
The sight was grand when Ferdinand by proud Seville was lying,
O'er tower and tree far off to see the Christian banners flying.

Down chanced the king his eye to fling, where far the camp below
Two gentlemen along the glen were riding soft and slow;
As void of fear each cavalier seemed to be riding there,
As some strong hound may pace around the roebuck's thicket lair.

It was Don Garci Perez; and he would breathe the air,
And he had ta'en a knight with him that as lief had been elsewhere:
For soon this knight to Garci said, "Ride, ride, or we are lost!
I see the glance of helm and lance, — it is the Moorish host!"

The Lord of Vargas turned him round, his trusty squire was near;
The helmet on his brow he bound, his gauntlet grasped the spear;
With that upon his saddle-tree he planted him right steady, —
"Now come," quoth he, "whoe'er they be, I trow they'll find us ready."

By this the knight that rode with him had turned his horse's head,
And up the glen in fearful trim unto the camp had fled.
"Ha! gone?" quoth Garci Perez: he smiled, and said no more,
But slowly on with his esquire rode as he rode before.

It was the Count Lorenzo, just then it happened so,
He took his stand by Ferdinand, and with him gazed below;
"My liege," quoth he, "seven Moors I see a-coming from the wood,
Now bring they all the blows they may, I trow they'll find as good;
For it is Don Garci Perez, — if his cognizance they know,
I guess it will be little pain to give them blow for blow."

The Moors from forth the greenwood came riding one by one,
A gallant troop with armor resplendent in the sun;
Full haughty was their bearing, as o'er the sward they came;
But the calm Lord of Vargas, his march was still the same.

They stood drawn up in order, while past them all rode he;
But when upon his shield they saw the sable blazonry,
And the wings of the Black Eagle, that o'er his crest were spread,
They knew Don Garci Perez, and never word they said.

He took the casque from off his brow, and gave it to the squire;
"My friend," quoth he, "no need I see why I my brows should tire."
But as he doffed the helmet he saw his scarf was gone,
"I've dropped it, sure," quoth Garci, "when I put my helmet on."

He looked around and saw the scarf, for still the Moors were near,
And they had picked it from the sward, and looped it on a spear.
"These Moors," quoth Garci Perez, "uncourteous Moors they be,—
Now, by my soul, the scarf they stole, yet durst not question me!

Now reach once more my helmet." The esquire said him nay,
"For a silken string why should ye fling perchance your life away?"
"I had it from my lady," quoth Garci, "long ago,
And never Moor that scarf, be sure, in proud Seville shall show."

But when the Moslem saw him, they stood in firm array:
He rode among their armèd throng, he rode right furiously;
"Stand, stand, ye thieves and robbers, lay down my lady's pledge!"
He cried; and ever as he cried they felt his falchion's edge.

That day the Lord of Vargas came to the camp alone;
The scarf, his lady's largess, around his breast was thrown;
Bare was his head, his sword was red, and from his pommel strung
Seven turbans green, sore hacked I ween, before Don Garci hung.

LOCKHART: *Spanish Ballads.*

BATTLE OF HARLAW.

Now haud your tongue, baith wife and carle,
And listen great and sma',
And I will sing of Glenallan's Earl
That fought on the red Harlaw.

The cronach's cried on Bennachie,
And down the Don and a',
And hieland and lawland may mournfu' be
For the sair field of Harlaw.

They saddled a hundred milk-white steeds,
They hae bridled a hundred black,
With a chafron of steel on each horse's head,
And a good knight upon his back.

They hadna ridden a mile, a mile,
A mile but barely ten,
When Donald came branking down the brae
Wi' twenty thousand men.

Their tartans they were waving wide,
Their glaives were glancing clear,
The pibrochs rung frae side to side,
Would deafen ye to hear.

The great Earl in his stirrups stood,
That Highland host to see:
"Now here a knight that's stout and good
May prove a jeopardie:

"What wouldst thou do, my squire so gay,
That rides beside my reyne, —
Were ye Glenallan's Earl the day,
And I were Roland Cheyne?

"To turn the rein were sin and shame,
To fight were wondrous peril, —
What would ye do now, Roland Cheyne,
Were ye Glenallan's Earl?"

"Were I Glenallan's Earl this tide,
And ye were Roland Cheyne,
The spur should be in my horse's side,
And the bridle upon his mane.

"If they hae twenty thousand blades,
And we twice ten times ten,
Yet they hae but their tartan plaids,
And we are mail-clad men.

"My horse shall ride through ranks sae rude,
As through the moorland fern, —
Then ne'er let the gentle Norman blude
Grow cauld for Highland kerne."

SCOTT.

KINMONT WILLIE.

OH, have ye na heard o' the fause Sakelde?
Oh, have ye na heard o' the keen Lord Scroope?
How they hae ta'en bauld Kinmont Willie,
On Haribee to hang him up?

Had Willie had but twenty men,
But twenty men as stout as he,
Fause Sakelde had never the Kinmont ta'en,
Wi' eightscore in his companie.

They band his legs beneath the steed,
They tied his hands behind his back;
They guarded him, fivesome on each side,
And they brought him ower the Liddel-rack.

They led him through the Liddel-rack,
And also through the Carlisle sands;
They brought him to Carlisle castell,
To be at my Lord Scroope's commands.

"My hands are tied, but my tongue is free,
And whae will dare this deed avow?
Or answer by the Border law?
Or answer to the bauld Buccleuch?"

"Now haud thy tongue, thou rank reiver!
There's never a Scot shall set thee free:
Before ye cross my castle yate,
I trow ye shall take farewell o' me."

"Fear na ye that, my lord," quoth Willie.
"By the faith o' my body, Lord Scroope," he said,
"I never yet lodged in a hostelrie,
But I paid my lawing before I gaed." —

Now word is gane to the bauld Keeper,
In Branksome Ha', wher that he lay,
That Lord Scroope has ta'en the Kinmont Willie,
Between the hours of night and day.

He has ta'en the table wi' his hand,
He garr'd the red wine spring on hie, —
"Now Christ's curse on my head," he said,
"But avenged of Lord Scroope, I'll be!

"O is my basnet a widow's curch?
Or my lance a wand of the willow-tree?
Or my arm a ladye's lilye hand,
That an English lord sets light by me!

"And have they ta'en him, Kinmont Willie,
Against the truce of Border tide?
And forgotten that the bauld Buccleuch
Is keeper here on the Scottish side?

"And have they e'en ta'en him, Kinmont Willie,
Withouten either dread or fear?
And forgotten that the bauld Buccleuch
Can back a steed, or shake a spear?

"O were there war between the lands,
As well I wot that there is none,
I would slight Carlisle castell high,
Though it were builded of marble stone.

"I would set that castell in a low,*
And sloken it with English blood!
There's never a man in Cumberland,
Should ken where Carlisle castell stood.

"But since nae war's between the lands,
And there is peace, and peace should be;
I'll neither harm English lad or lass,
And yet the Kinmont freed shall be!"

He has called him forty Marchmen bauld,
Were kinsmen to the bauld Buccleuch;
With spur on heel, and splent on spauld,
And gleuves of green, and feathers blue.

There were five and five before them a',
Wi' hunting-horns and bugles bright:

* Flame.

And five and five came wi' Buccleuch,
  Like warden's men, arrayed for fight.

And five and five, like a mason gang,
  That carried the ladders lang and hie;
And five and five, like broken men;
  And so they reached the Woodhouselee.

And as we crossed the Bateable Land,
  When to the English side we held,
The first o' men that we met wi',
  Whae sould it be but fause Sakelde?

"Where be ye gaun, ye hunters keen?"
  Quo' fause Sakelde; "come tell to me!" —
"We go to hunt an English stag,
  Has trespassed on the Scots countrie."

"Where be ye gaun, ye marshal men?"
  Quo' fause Sakelde; "come tell me true!"
"We go to catch a rank reiver,
  Has broken faith wi' the bauld Buccleuch."

"Where are ye gaun, ye mason lads,
  Wi' a' your ladders, lang and hie?"
"We gang to herry a corbie's nest,
  That wons not far frae Woodhouselee."

"Where be ye gaun, ye broken men?"
  Quo' fause Sakelde; "come tell to me!" —
Now Dickie of Dryhope led that band,
  And the nevir a word of lore had he.

"Why trespass ye on the English side?
  Row-footed outlaws, stand!" quo' he;
The nevir a word had Dickie to say,
  Sae he thrust the lance through his fause bodie.

Then on we held for Carlisle toun,
  And at Staneshaw-bank the Eden we crossed;
The water was great and meikle of spait,
  But the nevir a horse nor man we lost.

And when we reached the Staneshaw-bank,
  The wind was rising loud and hie;
And there the laird garr'd leave our steeds,
  For fear that they should stamp and nie.

And when we left the Staneshaw-bank,
  The wind began full loud to blaw;
But 'twas wind and weet, and fire and sleet,
  When we came beneath the castle wa'.

We crept on knees, and held our breath,
  Till we placed the ladders against the wa';
And sae ready was Buccleuch himsell
  To mount the first before us a'.

He has ta'en the watchman by the throat,
  He flung him down upon the lead —
"Had there not been peace between our lands,
  Upon the other side thou hadst gaed!

"Now sound out, trumpets!" quo' Buccleuch;
  "Let's waken Lord Scroope right merrilie!"
Then loud the warden's trumpet blew —
  O wha dare meddle wi' me?

Then speedilie to wark we gaed,
  And raised the slogan ane and a',
And cut a hole through a sheet of lead,
  And so we wan to the castle ha'.

They thought King James and a' his men
  Had won the house wi' bow and spear;
It was but twenty Scots and ten,
  That put a thousand in sic a stear!

Wi' coulters, and wi' forehammers,
We garr'd the bars bang merrilie,
Untill we came to the inner prison,
Where Willie o' Kinmont he did lie.

And when we cam to the lower prison,
Where Willie o' Kinmont he did lie, —
"O sleep ye, wake ye, Kinmont Willie,
Upon the morn that thou's to die?"

"O I sleep saft, and I wake aft;
It's lang since sleeping was fley'd frae me!
Gie my service back to my wife and bairns,
And a' gude fellows that spier for me."

Then red Rowan has hente him up,
The starkest man in Teviotdale —
"Abide, abide now, Red Rowan,
Till of my Lord Scroope I take farewell.

"Farewell, farewell, my gude Lord Scroope!
My gude Lord Scroope, farewell!" he cried —
"I'll pay you for my lodging maill,
When first we meet on the Border side."

Then shoulder high, with shout and cry,
We bore him down the ladder lang;
At every stride Red Rowan made,
I wot the Kinmont's airns played clang!

"O mony a time," quo' Kinmont Willie,
"I've ridden horse baith wild and wood;
But a rougher beast than Red Rowan
I ween my legs have ne'er bestrode.

"And mony a time," quo' Kinmont Willie,
"I've pricked a horse out oure the furs;
But since the day I backed a steed,
I never wore sic cumbrous spurs!"

We scarce had won the Staneshaw-bank,
When a' the Carlisle bells were rung,
And a thousand men on horse and foot,
Cam wi' the keen Lord Scroope along.

Buccleuch has turned to Eden Water,
Even where it flowed frae bank to brim,
And he has plunged in wi' a' his band,
And safely swam them through the stream.

He turned him on the other side,
And at Lord Scroope his glove flung he —
"If ye like na my visit in merry England,
In fair Scotland come visit me!"

All sore astonished stood Lord Scroope,
He stood as still as rock of stane;
He scarcely dared to trust his eyes,
When through the water they had gane.

"He is either himsell a devil frae hell,
Or else his mother a witch maun be;
I wadna have ridden that wan water
For a' the gowd in Christentie."

SCOTT'S BORDER MINSTRELSY.

SKIPPER IRESON'S RIDE.

Of all the rides since the birth of time,
Told in story or sung in rhyme, —
On Apuleius's Golden Ass,
Or one-eyed Calendar's horse of brass,
Witch astride of a human back,
Islam's prophet on Al-Borák, —
The strangest ride that ever was sped
Was Ireson's, out from Marblehead!
Old Floyd Ireson, for his hard heart,
Tarred and feathered and carried in a cart
By the women of Marblehead!

Body of turkey, head of owl,
Wings a-droop like a rained-on fowl,
Feathered and ruffled in every part,
Skipper Ireson stood in the cart.
Scores of women, old and young,
Strong of muscle, and glib of tongue,
Pushed and pulled up the rocky lane,
Shouting and singing the shrill refrain:
"Here's Flud Oirson, fur his horrd horrt,
Torr'd an' futherr'd an corr'd in a corrt
By the women o' Morble'ead!"

Wrinkled scolds with hands on hips,
Girls in bloom of cheek and lips,
Wild-eyed, free-limbed, such as chase
Bacchus round some antique vase,
Brief of skirt, with ankles bare,
Loose of kerchief and loose of hair,
With conch-shells blowing and fish-horns' twang,
Over and over the Mænads sang:
"Here's Flud Oirson, fur his horrd horrt,
Torr'd an' futherr'd an' corr'd in a corrt
By the women o' Morble'ead!"

Small pity for him! — He sailed away
From a leaking ship, in Chaleur Bay, —
Sailed away from a sinking wreck,
With his own town's-people on her deck!
"Lay by! lay by!" they called to him.
Back he answered, "Sink or swim!
Brag of your catch of fish again!"
And off he sailed through the fog and rain!
Old Floyd Ireson, for his hard heart,
Tarred and feathered and carried in a cart
By the women of Marblehead!

Fathoms deep in dark Chaleur
That wreck shall lie forevermore.
Mother and sister, wife and maid,
Looked from the rocks of Marblehead
Over the moaning and rainy sea, —
Looked for the coming that might not be!
What did the winds and the sea-birds say
Of the cruel captain who sailed away? —
Old Floyd Ireson for his hard heart,
Tarred and feathered and carried in a cart
By the women of Marblehead!

Through the street, on either side,
Up flew windows, doors swung wide;
Sharp-tongued spinsters, old wives gray,
Treble lent the fish-horn's bray.
Sea-worn grandsires, cripple-bound,
Hulks of old sailors run aground,
Shook head, and fist, and hat, and cane,
And cracked with curses the hoarse refrain:
"Here's Flud Oirson fur his horrd horrt,
Torr'd an' futherr'd an' corr'd in a corrt
By the women o' Morble'ead!"

Sweetly along the Salem road
Bloom of orchard and lilac showed.
Little the wicked skipper knew
Of the fields so green and the sky so blue.
Riding there in his sorry trim,
Like an Indian idol glum and grim,
Scarcely he seemed the sound to hear
Of voices shouting, far and near:
"Here's Flud Oirson, fur his horrd horrt,
Torr'd an' futherr'd an' corr'd in a corrt
By the women o' Morble'ead!"

"Hear me, neighbors!" at last he cried, —
"What to me is this noisy ride?
What is the shame that clothes the skin
To the nameless horror that lives within?
Waking or sleeping, I see a wreck,
And hear a cry from a reeling deck!
Hate me and curse me, — I only dread
The hand of God and the face of the dead!"
Said old Floyd Ireson, for his hard heart,
Tarred and feathered and carried in a cart
By the women of Marblehead!

Then the wife of the skipper lost at sea
Said, "God has touched him! — why should we?"
Said an old wife mourning her only son,
"Cut the rogue's tether and let him run!"
So with soft relentings and rude excuse,
Half scorn, half pity, they cut him loose,
And gave him a cloak to hide him in,
And left him alone with his shame and sin.
Poor Floyd Ireson, for his hard heart,
Tarred and feathered and carried in a cart
By the women of Marblehead!

WHITTIER.

WILLIAM OF CLOUDESLÉ.

THE king called his best archers
To the buttes with him to go,
"I will see these fellows shoot," he said,
"In the north have wrought this wo."

The king's bowmen busk them blyve,
And the queen's archers alsoe,
So did these three wight yeomen
With them they thought to go.

There twice or thrice they shoot about
For to assay their hand,
There was no shot these yeomen shot
That any prick might them stand.

Then spake William of Cloudeslé,
"By him that for me died,
I hold him never no good archer
That shooteth at buttes so wide."

"Whereat?" then said our king,
"I pray thee tell me:"
"At such a bυtte, sir," he said,
"As men use in my countree."

William went into a field,
And his two brethren with him,
There they set up hazle rods,
Twenty score paces between.

"I hold him an archer," said Cloudeslé,
"That yonder wande cleaveth in two."
"Here is none such," said the king,
"Nor none that can so do."

"I shall assay, sir," said Cloudeslé,
"Or that I farther go."
Cloudeslé with a bearing arrow
Clave the wand in two.

"Thou art the best archer," then said the king,
"Forsooth that ever I see;" —
"And yet for your love," said William,
"I will do more mastery.

"I have a son is seven years old,
He is to me full dear;
I will him tie to a stake
All shall see that be here.

"And lay an apple upon his head,
And go six score paces him fro,
And I myself with a broad arrow
Shall cleave the apple in two."

"Now haste thee then," said the king,
"By him that died on a tree;
But if thou do not as thou hast said,
Hangèd shalt thou be.

"And thou touch his head or gown,
In sight that men may see,
By all the saints that be in Heaven,
I shall hang you all three!"

"That I have promised," said William,
"I will it never forsake;"
And there even before the king,
In the earth he drove a stake,

And bound thereto his eldest son,
And bade him stand still thereat,
And turned the child's head from him,
Because he should not start.

An apple upon his head he set,
And then his bow he bent;
Six score paces were out-met,
And thither Cloudeslé went.

There he drew out a fair broad arrow,
His bow was great and long,
He set that arrow in his bow,
That was both stiff and strong.

He prayed the people that was there,
That they would still stand,
"For he that shooteth for such a wager,
Behoveth a steadfast hand."

Much people prayed for Cloudeslé,
That his life saved might be,
And when he made him ready to shoot
There was many a weeping eye.

Thus Cloudeslé cleft the apple in two
That many a man might see;
"Over-gods forbode," then said the king,
"That thou should shoot at me!

"I give thee eighteen pence a day,
And my bow shalt thou bear,
And over all the north country
I make thee chief rider."

THE HEIR OF LINNE.

PART THE FIRST.

Lithe and listen, gentlemen,
To sing a song I will beginne:
It is of a lord of faire Scotlánd,
Which was the unthrifty heire of Linne.

His father was a right good lord,
His mother a lady of high degree;
But they, alas! were dead him froe,
And he lov'd keeping companie.

To spend the day with merry cheer,
To drink and revell every night,
To card and dice from eve to morn,
It was, I ween, his heart's delight.

To ride, to run, to rant, to roar,
To alway spend and never spare,
I wott, an' it were the king himself,
Of gold and fee he mote be bare.

So fares the unthrifty lord of Linne,
Till all his gold is gone and spent:
And he maun sell his landes so broad,
His house, and landes, and all his rent.

His father had a keen stewárde,
And John o' the Scales was callèd he:
But John is become a gentel-man,
And John has gott both gold and fee.

Sayes "Welcome, welcome, Lord of Linne,
Let nought disturb thy merry cheer:
If thou wilt sell thy landes so broad,
Good store of gold I'll give thee here."

"My gold is gone, my money is spent;
My lande nowe take it unto thee:
Give me the golde, good John o' the Scales,
And thine for aye my lande shall be."

Then John he did him to record draw,
And John he cast him a gods-pennie;
But for every pound that John agreed,
The lande, I wis, was well worth three.

He told him the gold upon the borde,
He was right glad his land to winne;
"The gold is thine, the land is mine,
And now I'll be the lord of Linne."

Thus he hath sold his land so broad,
Both hill and holt, and moor and fen,
All but a poor and lonesome lodge,
That stood far off in a lonely glen.

For so he to his father hight.
"My son, when I am gone," said he,
"Then thou wilt spend thy land so broad,
And thou wilt spend thy gold so free.

"But swear me now upon the rood,
That lonesome lodge thou'lt never spend;
For when all the world doth frown on thee,
Thou there shalt find a faithful friend."

The heir of Linne is full of gold:
"And come with me, my friends," said he,

"Let's drink, and rant, and merry make,
And he that spares, ne'er mote be thee."

They ranted, drank, and merry made,
Till all his gold it waxèd thin;
And then his friends they slunk away;
They left the unthrifty heir of Linne.

He had never a penny left in his purse,
Never a penny left but three,
And one was brass, another was lead,
And another it was white monéy.

"Now well-a-day" said the heir of Linne,
"Now well-a-day, and woe is me,
For when I was the lord of Linne,
I never wanted gold nor fee.

"But many a trusty friend have I,
And why should I feel dole or care?
I'll borrow of them all by turns,
So need I not be never bare."

But one I wis, was not at home;
Another had paid his gold away;
Another called him thriftless loon,
And bade him sharply wend his way.

"Now well-a-day," said the heir of Linne,
"Now well-a-day, and woe is me;
For when I had my landes so broad,
On me they lived right merrily.

"To beg my bread from door to door,
I wis, it were a burning shame;
To rob and steal it were a sin;
To work, my limbs I cannot frame.

"Now I'll away to the lonesome lodge,
For there my father bade me wend:
When all the world should frown on me
I there should find a trusty friend."

PART THE SECOND.

Away then hied the heir of Linne,
O'er hill and holt, and moor and fen,
Until he came to the lonesome lodge,
That stood so low in a lonely glen.

He lookèd up, he lookèd down,
In hope some comfort for to win;
But bare and lothly were the walls;
"Here's sorry cheer," quo' the heir of Linne.

The little window, dim and dark,
Was hung with ivy, brere and yew;
No shimmering sun here ever shone,
No halesome breeze here ever blew.

No chair, ne table he mote spy,
No cheerful hearth, ne welcome bed,
Nought save a rope with renning noose,
That dangling hung up o'er his head.

And over it in broad letters
These words were written so plain to see:
"Ah! gracelesse wretch, hast spent thine all,
And brought thyself to penurie?

"All this my boding mind misgave,
I therefore left this trusty friend:
Let it now shield thy foul disgrace,
And all thy shame and sorrows end."

Sorely shent wi' this rebuke,
Sorely shent was the heire of Linne:
His heart I wis, was near to brast
With guilt and sorrow, shame and sin.

Never a word spake the heir of Linne,
Never a word he spake but three:
"This is a trusty friend indeed,
And is right welcome unto me."

Then round his neck the cord he drew,
And sprang aloft with his bodie,
When lo! the ceiling burst in twain,
And to the ground came tumbling he.

Astonyed lay the heir of Linne,
He knew if he were live or dead:
At length he looked, and sawe a bille,
And in it a key of gold so red.

He took the bill, and lookt it on,
Straight good comfort found he there:
It told him of a hole in the wall,
In which there stood three chests in-fere.

Two were full of the beaten golde,
The third was full of white monéy;
And over them in broad lettérs
These words were written so plain to see.

"Once more, my sonne, I set thee clere;
Amend thy life and follies past;
For but thou amend thee of thy life,
That rope must be thy end at last."

"And let it be" said the heire of Linne,
"And let it be, but if I amend:
For here I will make mine avow,
This reade shall guide me to the end."

Away then went with a merry cheare,
Away then went the heire of Linne;
I wis, he neither ceased ne blanne,
Till John o' the Scales house he did winne.

And when he came to John o' the Scales,
Up at the speere then lookèd he:
There sate three lords upon a rowe,
Were drinking of the wine so free.

And John himself sate at the bord-head,
Because now lord of Linne was he;
"I pray thee" he said, "good John o' the Scales,
One forty pence for to lend me."

"Away, away, thou thriftless loone;
Away, away, this may not be:
For Christ's curse on my head" he said,
"If ever I trust thee one pennie."

Then bespake the heir of Linne,
To John o' the Scales' wife then spake he:
"Madame, some almes on me bestowe,
I pray for sweet saint Charitie."

"Away, away, thou thriftless loone,
I sweare thou gettest no almes of me;
For if we should hang any losel here,
The first we wold begin with thee."

Then bespake a good fellówe,
Which sat at John o' the Scales his bord;
Said, "Turn again, thou heir of Linne;
Some time thou wast a well good lord.

"Some time a good fellow thou hast been,
And sparedst not thy gold and fee;
Therefore I'll lend thee forty pence,
And other forty if need be.

"And ever I pray thee, John o' the Scales,
To let him sit in thy companie:
For well I wot thou hadst his land,
And a good bargain it was to thee."

Up then spake him John o' the Scales,
All wood he answered him againe:
"Now Christ's curse on my head" he said,
"But I did lose by that bargáine.

And here I proffer thee, heir of Linne,
Before these lords so faire and free,
Thou shalt have it backe again better cheape
By a hundred markes than I had it of thee."

"I draw you to record, lords," he said,
With that he cast him a gods-pennie:
"Now by my fay" said the heire of Linne,
"And here, good John, is thy monéy."

And he pulled forth three bagges of gold,
And laid them down upon the bord;
All woe begone was John o' the Scales,
So shent he could say never a word.

He told him forth the good red gold.
He told it forth with mickle dinne.
"The gold is thine, the land is mine,
And now Ime againe the lord of Linne."

Says, "Have thou here, thou good fellówe,
Forty pence thou didst lend me:
Now I am again the lord of Linne,
And forty pounds I will give thee.

"Ile make thee keeper of my forrest,
Both of the wild deere and the tame;
For but I reward thy bounteous heart,
I wis, good fellowe, I were to blame."

"Now welladay!" sayth Joan o' the Scales;
"Now welladay, and woe is my life!
Yesterday I was lady of Linne,
Now Ime but John o' the Scales his wife."

"Now fare thee well" said the heire of Linne,
"Farewell now, John o' the Scales," said he:
"Christ's curse light on me, if ever again
I bring my lands in jeopardy."

PERCY'S RELIQUES.

SIEGE AND CONQUEST OF ALHAMA.

THE Moorish king rides up and down
Through Granada's royal town;
From Elvira's gates to those
Of Bivarambla on he goes.
Woe is me, Alhama!

Letters to the monarch tell
How Alhama's city fell;
In the fire the scroll he threw,
And the messenger he slew.
Woe is me, Alhama!

He quits his mule, and mounts his horse,
And through the street directs his course;
Through the street of Zacatin
To the Alhambra spurring in.
Woe is me, Alhama!

When the Alhambra walls he gained,
On the moment he ordained
That the trumpet straight should sound,
With the silver clarion round.
Woe is me, Alhama!

Out then spake an aged Moor
In these words the king before,
"Wherefore call on us, O king?
What may mean this gathering?"
Woe is me, Alhama!

"Friends! ye have, alas! to know
Of a most disastrous blow,
That the Christians, stern and bold,
Have obtained Alhama's hold."
Woe is me, Alhama!

Out then spake old Alfaqui,
With his beard so white to see,
"Good king, thou art justly served,
Good king, this thou hast deserved.
Woe is me, Alhama!

"By thee were slain, in evil hour,
The Abencerrage, Granada's flower;
And strangers were received by thee
Of Cordova the chivalry.
Woe is me, Alhama!

"And for this, O king! is sent
On thee a double chastisement,
Thee and thine, thy crown and realm,
One last wreck shall overwhelm.
Woe is me, Alhama!"

Fire flashed from out the old Moor's eyes,
The monarch's wrath began to rise,
Because he answered, and because
He spake exceeding well of laws.
Woe is me, Alhama!

"There is no law to say such things
As may disgust the ear of kings:" —
Thus, snorting with his choler, said
The Moorish king, and doomed him dead.
Woe is me, Almaha!

Moor Alfaqui! Moor Alfaqui!
Though thy beard so hoary be,
The king hath sent to have thee seized,
For Alhama's loss displeased.
Woe is me, Alhama!

And to fix thy head upon
High Alhambra's loftiest stone;
That this for thee should be the law,
And others tremble when they saw.
Woe is me, Alhama!

"Cavalier! and man of worth!
Let these words of mine go forth;
Let the Moorish monarch know,
That to him I nothing owe.
Woe is me, Alhama!

"But on my soul Alhama weighs,
And on my inmost spirit preys;
And if the king his land hath lost,
Yet others may have lost the most."
Woe is me, Alhama!

And as these things the old Moor said,
They severed from the trunk his head;
And to Alhambra's wall with speed
'Twas carried as the king decreed.
Woe is me, Alhama!

And from the windows o'er the walls
The sable web of mourning falls!
The king weeps as a woman o'er
His loss, for it is much and sore.
Woe is me, Alhama!

BYRON.

THE RELIEF OF LUCKNOW.

OH, that last day in Lucknow fort!
We knew that it was the last;
That the enemy's lines crept surely on,
And the end was coming fast.

To yield to that foe meant worse than death;
And the men and we all worked on;
It was one day more of smoke and roar,
And then it would all be done.

There was one of us, a corporal's wife,
A fair, young, gentle thing,
Wasted with fever in the siege,
And her mind was wandering.

She lay on the ground, in her Scottish plaid,
And I took her head on my knee;
"When my father comes hame frae the pleugh," she said,
"Oh! then please wauken me."

She slept like a child on her father's floor,
In the flecking of woodbine-shade,
When the house-dog sprawls by the open door,
And the mother's wheel is stayed.

It was smoke and roar and powder-stench,
And hopeless waiting for death;
And the soldier's wife, like a full-tired child,
Seemed scarce to draw her breath.

I sank to sleep; and I had my dream
Of an English village-lane,
And wall and garden;—but one wild scream
Brought me back to the roar again.

There Jessie Brown stood listening
Till a sudden gladness broke
All over her face; and she caught my hand
And drew me near as she spoke:—

"The Hielanders! O! dinna ye hear
The slogan far awa?
The McGregor's. O! I ken it weel;
It's the grandest o' them a'!

"God bless the bonny Hielanders!
We're saved! we're saved!" she cried;
And fell on her knees; and thanks to God
Flowed forth like a full flood-tide.

Along the battery-line her cry
Had fallen among the men,
And they started back;—they were there to die;
But was life so near them, then?

They listened for life; the rattling fire
Far off, and the far-off roar,
Were all; and the colonel shook his head,
And they turned to their guns once more.

But Jessie said, "The slogan's done;
But winna ye hear it noo.
The Campbells are comin'? It's no a dream;
Our succors hae broken through!"

We heard the roar and the rattle afar,
But the pipes we could not hear;
So the men plied their work of hopeless war,
And knew that the end was near.

It was not long ere it made its way, —
A thriling, ceaseless sound:
It was no noise from the strife afar,
Or the sappers under ground.

It *was* the pipes of the Highlanders!
And now they played *Auld Lang Syne.*
It came to our men like the voice of God,
And they shouted along the line.

And they wept, and shook one another's hands,
And the women sobbed in a crowd;
And every one knelt down where he stood,
And we all thanked God aloud.

That happy time, when we welcomed them,
Our men put Jessie first;
And the general gave her his hand, and cheers
Like a storm from the soldiers burst.

And the pipers' ribbons and tartan streamed,
Marching round and round our line;
And our joyful cheers were broken with tears,
As the pipes played *Auld Lang Syne.*

ROBERT LOWELL.

SIR ANDREW BARTON.

THE FIRST PART.

WHEN Flora with her fragrant flowers
Bedeckt the earth so trim and gaye,
And Neptune with his dainty showers
Came to present the month of Maye,
King Henry rode to take the air,
Over the River Thames past he;
When eighty merchants of London came,
And down they knelt upon their knee.

"O ye are welcome, rich merchants,
Good saylors, welcome unto me:"
They swore by the rood, they were saylors good,
But rich merchants they could not be.
"To France nor Flanders dare we pass,
Nor Bordeaux voyage dare we fare,
And all for a robber that lyes on the seas,
Who robs us of our merchant ware."

King Henry frowned, and turned him round,
And swore by the Lord that was mickle of might,
"I thought he had not been in the world,
Durst have wrought England such unright."
The merchants sighed and said, "Alas!"
And thus they did their answer frame;
"He is a proud Scot that robs on the seas,
And Sir Andrew Barton is his name."

The king looked over his left shoulder,
And an angry look then lookèd he;
"Have I never a lord in all my realm
Will fetch yond traitor unto me?"
"Yea, that dare I," Lord Charles Howard says;
"Yea, that dare I with heart and hand;
If it please your grace to give me leave,
Myself will be the only man."

"Thou art but young," the king replied,
"Yond Scot hath numbered many a year:"
"Trust me, my liege, I'll make him quail,
Or before my prince I'll never appear."
"Then bowmen and gunners thou shalt have,
And chuse them over my realm so free;
Besides mariners and good sea-boys
To guide the great ship on the sea."

The first man that Lord Howard chose,
  Was the ablest gunner in all the realm,
Though he was threescore years and ten;
  Good Peter Simon was his name.
"Peter," says he, "I must to the sea
  To bring home a traitor live or dead;
Before all others I have chosen thee,
  Of a hundred gunners to be the head."

"If you, my lord, have chosen me
  Of a hundred gunners to be the head,
Then hang me up on your main-mast tree,
  If I miss my mark one shilling bread." *
My lord then chose a bowman rare,
  Whose active hands had gainèd fame;
In Yorkshire was this gentleman born,
  And William Horseley was his name.

"Horseley," said he, "I must with speed
  Go seek a traitor on the sea,
And now of a hundred bowmen brave
  To be the head I have chosen thee."
"If you," quoth he, "have chosen me
  Of a hundred bowmen to be the head,
On your mainmast I'll hangèd be,
  If I miss twelvescore one penny bread."

With pikes, and guns, and bowmen bold,
  This noble Howard is gone to the sea;
With a valiant heart and a pleasant cheer,
  Out at Thamés mouth sailed he.
And days he scant had sailèd three,
  Upon the journey he took in hand,
But there he met with a noble ship,
  And stoutly made it stay and stand.

* Broad.

"Thou must tell me," Lord Howard said,
  "Now who thou art, and what's thy name;
And show me where thy dwelling is,
  And whither bound, and whence thou came."
"My name is Henry Hunt," quoth he,
  With a heavy heart and a careful mind;
"I and my ship do both belong
  To the Newcastle that stands upon Tyne."

"Hast thou not heard, now, Henry Hunt,
  As thou hast sailed by day and by night,
Of a Scottish robber on the seas;
  Men call him Sir Andrew Barton, knight?"
Then ever he sighed, and said, "Alas!"
  With a grievèd mind and well-away,
"But over-well I know that wight;
  I was his prisoner yesterday.

"As I was sailing upon the sea,
  A Bordeaux voyage for to fare,
To his hachborde he claspèd me,
  And robbed me of all my merchant ware.
And mickle debts, God wot, I owe,
  And every man will have his own,
And I am now to London bound,
  Of our gracious king to beg a boon."

"Thou shalt not need," Lord Howard says;
  "Let me but once that robber see,
For every penny tane thee fro
  It shall be doubled shillings three."
"Now God forfend," the merchant said,
  "That you should seek so far amiss!
God keep you out of that traitor's hands!
  Full little ye wot what a man he is.

"He is brass within, and steel without,
  With beams on his topcastle strong;
And eighteen pieces of ordinance
  He carries on each side along.

"And he hath a pinnace dearly dight,
St. Andrew's cross, that is his guide;
His pinnace beareth ninescore men,
And fifteen cannons on each side.

"Were ye twenty ships, and he but one,
I swear by kirk, and bower, and hall,
He would overcome them every one,
If once his beams they do downfall."
"This is cold comfort," said my lord,
"To welcome a stranger thus to the sea:
Yet I'll bring him and his ship to the shore,
Or to Scotland he shall carry me."

"Then a noble gunner you must have,
And he must aim well with his ee,
And sink his pinnace into the sea,
Or else he never overcome will be.
And if you chance his ship to board,
This counsell I must give withal,
Let no man to his topcastle go
To strive to let his beams downfall.

"And seven pieces of ordinance,
I pray your honor lend to me,
On each side of my ship along,
And I will lead you on the sea.
A glass I'll get, that may be seen,
Whether you sail by day or night,
And to-morrow, I swear, by nine of the clock,
You shall meet with Sir Andrew Barton, knight."

THE SECOND PART.

The merchant sette my lord a glass,
So well apparent in his sight,
And on the morrow, by nine of the clock,
He showed him Sir Andrew Barton, knight.
His hacheborde it was hached with gold,
So dearly dight it dazzled the ee;
"Now, by my faith," Lord Howard said,
"This is a gallant sight to see.

"Take in your ancients, standards eke,
To close that no man may them see;
And put me forth a white willow wand,
As merchants use to sail the sea."
But they stirred neither top nor mast;
Stoutly they passed Sir Andrew by;
"What English churls are yonder," he said,
"That can so little curtesie?

"Now by the rood, three years and more
I have been admiral over the sea,
And never an English or Portugal,
Without my leave can pass this way."
Then called he forth his stout pinnace;
"Fetch back yon peddlers now to me:
I swear by the mass, yon English churls
Shall all hang at my mainmast tree."

With that the pinnace it shot off;
Full well Lord Howard might it ken;
For it stroke down my lord's foremast,
And killed fourteen of his men.
"Come hither, Simon," says my lord,
"Look that thy word be true, thou said:
For at the mainmast shalt thou hang,
If thou miss thy mark one shilling bread."

Simon was old, but his heart was bold:
His ordinance he laid right low:
He put in chain full nine yards long,
With other great shot less and moe,
And he let go his great gun's shott;
So well he settled it with his ee,
The first sight that Sir Andrew saw,
He saw his pinnace sunk in the sea.

And when he saw his pinnace sunk,
Lord, how his heart with rage did swell!
"Now, cut my ropes, it is time to be gone;

I'll fetch you peddlers back mysell."
When my lord saw Sir Andrew loose,
Within his heart he was full fain;
"Now spread your ancients, strike up drums,
Sound all your trumpets out amain."

"Fight on, my men," Sir Andrew says,
"Weale, howsoever this gear will sway:
It is my lord admiral of England,
Is come to seek me on the sea."
Simon had a son who shot right well,
That did Sir Andrew mickle scare;
In at his deck he gave a shot,
Killed threescore of his men of war.

Then Henry Hunt, with vigor hot,
Came bravely on the other side;
Soon he drove down his foremast tree,
And killed fourscore men beside.
"Now, out alas!" Sir Andrew cried,
"What may a man now think or say?
Yonder merchant thief that pierceth me,
He was my prisoner yesterday.

"Come hither to me, thou Gordon good,
That aye was ready at my call;
I will give thee three hundred pounds
If thou wilt let my beams downfall."
Lord Howard he then called in haste,
"Horsely, see thou be true in stead;
For thou shalt at the mainmast hang,
If thou miss twelvescore one penny bread."

Then Gordon swarved the mainmast tree,
He swarvèd it with might and main;
But Horsely with a bearing arrow
Stroke the Gordon through the brain;
And he fell unto the haches again,
And sore his deadly wound did bleed:
Then word went through Sir Andrew's men,
How that the Gordon he was dead.

"Come hither to me, James Hambilton,
Thou art my only sister's son;
If thou wilt let my beams downfall,
Six hundred nobles thou hast won."
With that he swarved the mainmast tree,
He swarvèd it with nimble art;
But Horsely with a broad arrow
Pierced the Hambilton through the heart;

And down he fell upon the deck,
That with his blood did stream amain:
Then every Scot cried, "Walaway!
Alas, a comely youth is slain!"
All wo begone was Sir Andrew then,
With grief and rage his heart did swell;
"Go fetch me forth my armor of proof,
For I will to the topcastle mysell.

"Go fetch me forth my armor of proof,
That gilded is with gold so clear;
God be with my brother, John of Barton!
Against the Portugalls he it ware.
And when he had on this armor of proof,
He was a gallant sight to see;
Ah! ne'er didst thou meet with living wight,
My dear brother, could cope with thee."

"Come hither, Horsely," says my lord,
"And look your shaft that it go right;
Shoot a good shot in time of need,
And for it thou shalt be made a knight."
"I'll shoot my best," quoth Horsely then,
"Your honor shall see, with might and main;
But if I were hanged at your mainmast,
I have now left but arrows twain."

Sir Andrew he did swarve the tree,
With right goodwill he swarved it then,
Upon his breast did Horsely hitt,
But the arrow bounded back again.

Then Horsely spied a private place,
With a perfect eye, in a secret part;
Under the spole of his right arm
He smote Sir Andrew to the heart.

"Fight on, my men," Sir Andrew says,
"A little I'm hurt, but yet not slain;
I'll but lie down and bleed awhile,
And then I'll rise and fight again.
Fight on, my men," Sir Andrew says,
"And never flinch before the foe;
And stand fast by St. Andrew's cross,
Until you hear my whistle blow."

They never heard his whistle blow,
Which made their hearts wax sore adread:
Then Horsely said, "Aboard, my lord,
For well I wot Sir Andrew's dead."
They boarded then his noble ship,
They boarded it with might and main;
Eighteen score Scots alive they found,
The rest were either maimed or slain.

Lord Howard took a sword in hand,
And off he smote Sir Andrew's head;
"I must have left England many a day,
If thou wert alive as thou art dead."
He caused his body to be cast
Over the hatchbord into the sea,
And about his middle three hundred crowns:
"Wherever thou land, this will bury thee."

Thus from the wars Lord Howard came,
And back he sailèd o'er the main;
With mickle joy and triumphing
Into Thames' mouth he came again.
Lord Howard then a letter wrote,
And sealed it with seal and ring:
"Such a noble prize have I brought to your grace
As never did subject to a king.

"Sir Andrew's ship I bring with me,
A braver ship was never none;
Now hath your grace two ships of war,
Before in England was but one."
King Henry's grace with royal cheer
Welcomed the noble Howard home;
"And where," said he, "is this rover stout,
That I myself may give the doom?"

"The rover, he is safe, my liege,
Full many a fathom in the sea;
If he were alive as he is dead,
I must have left England many a day.
And your grace may thank four men in the ship,
For the victory we have won;
These are William Horsely, Henry Hunt,
And Peter Simon, and his son."

"To Henry Hunt," the king then said,
"In lieu of what was from thee taen,
A noble a day now thou shalt have,
Sir Andrew's jewels and his chain.
And Horsely thou shalt be a knight,
And lands and livings shalt have store;
Howard shall be Earl Surry hight.
As Howards erst have been before.

"Now Peter Simon, thou art old,
I will maintain thee and thy son;
And the men shall have five hundred marks
For the good service they have done."
Then in came the queen with ladies fair,
To see Sir Andrew Barton, knight;
They weened that he were brought on shore,
And thought to have seen a gallant sight.

But when they see his deadly face,
And eyes so hollow in his head,
"I would give," quoth the king, "a thousand marks,
This man were alive as he is dead.

Yet for the manful part he played,
  Which fought so well with heart and hand,
His men shall have twelvepence a day,
  Till they come to my brother king's high land."

SIR PATRICK SPENS.

THE king sits in Dunfermline town,
  Drinking the blude-red wine:
"O where will I get a skeely skipper
  To sail this new ship of mine?"

O up and spake an eldern knight,
  Sat at the king's right knee:
"Sir Patrick Spens is the best sailor
  That ever sailed the sea."

Our king has written a braid letter,
  And sealed it with his hand,
And sent it to Sir Patrick Spens,
  Was walking on the strand.

"To Noroway, to Noroway,
  To Noroway o'er the faem;
The king's daughter of Noroway,
  'Tis thou maun bring her hame!"

The first word that Sir Patrick read,
  Sae loud, loud laughed he;
The neist word that Sir Patrick read,
  The tear blindit his e'e.

"O wha is this has done this deed,
  And tauld the king o' me,
To send us out at this time of the year,
  To sail upon the sea?

"Be it wind, be it weet, be it hail, be it sleet,
  Our ship must sail the faem;
The king's daughter of Noroway,
  'Tis we must fetch her hame."

They hoysed their sails on Monenday morn
  Wi' a' the speed they may;
They hae landed in Noroway
  Upon a Wodensday.

They hadna been a week, a week
  In Noroway, but twae,
When that the lords o' Noroway
  Began aloud to say:

"Ye Scottishmen spend a' our king's gowd
  And a' our queené's fee."
"Ye lie, ye lie, ye liars loud!
  Fu' loud I hear ye lie!

"For I hae brought as much white monie
  As gane my men and me,
And I hae brought a half-fou o' gude red gowd
  Out owre the sea wi' me.

"Make ready, make ready, my merry men a'!
  Our gude ship sails the morn."
"Now, ever alake! my master dear,
  I fear a deadly storm!

"I saw the new moon, late yestreen,
  Wi' the auld moon in her arm;
And if we gang to sea, master,
  I fear we'll come to harm."

They hadna sailed a league, a league,
  A league, but barely three,
When the lift grew dark, and the wind blew loud,
  And gurly grew the sea.

The ankers brak, and the topmasts lap,
  It was sic a deadly storm;
And the waves came o'er the broken ship
  Till a' her sides were torn.

"O where will I get a gude sailor
  To take my helm in hand,
Till I get up to the tall topmast
  To see if I can spy land?"

"O here am I, a sailor gude,
  To take the helm in hand,
Till you go up to the tall topmast,—
  But I fear you'll ne'er spy land."

He hadna gane a step, a step,
  A step, but barely ane,
When a boult flew out of our goodly ship,
  And the salt sea it came in.

"Gae fetch a web o' the silken claith,
  Another o' the twine,
And wap them into our ship's side
  And let na the sea come in."

They fetched a web o' the silken claith,
Another o' the twine,
And they wapped them roun' that gude ship's side,
But still the sea came in.

O laith, laith were our gude Scots lords
To weet their cork-heeled shoon!
But lang or a' the play was played,
They wat their hats aboon.

And mony was the feather-bed
That floated on the faem;
And mony was the gude lord's son
That never mair came hame.

The ladyes wrange their fingers white,
The maidens tore their hair;
A' for the sake of their true loves, —
For them they'll see na mair.

O lang, lang, may the ladyes sit,
Wi' their fans into their hand,
Before they see Sir Patrick Spens
Come sailing to the strand!

And lang lang may the maidens sit,
Wi' their gowd kaims in their hair,
A' waiting for their ain dear loves,
For them they'll see na mair.

O forty miles off Aberdeen
'Tis fifty fathoms deep,
And there lies gude Sir Patrick Spens
Wi' the Scots lords at his feet.

ANONYMOUS.

THE EARL O' QUARTERDECK.

A NEW OLD BALLAD.

THE wind it blew, and the ship it flew;
And it was "Hey for hame!
And ho for hame!" But the skipper cried,
"Haud her oot o'er the saut sea faem."

Then up and spoke the king himsel':
"Haud on for Dumferline!"
Quo he skipper, "Ye're king upo' the land —
I'm king upo' the brine."

And he took the helm intil his hand,
And he steered the ship sae free;
Wi' the wind astarn, he crowded sail,
And stood right out to sea.

Quo the king, "There's treason in this, I vow;
This is something underhand!
'Bout ship!" Quo the skipper, "Yer grace forgets
Ye are king but o' the land!"

And still he held to the open sea;
And the east wind sank behind;
And the west had a bitter word to say,
Wi' a white-sea roarin' wind.

And he turned her head into the north.
Said the king: "Gar fling him o'er."
Quo the fearless skipper: "It's a' ye're worth!
Ye'll ne'er see Scotland more."

The king crept down the cabin-stair,
To drink the gude French wine.
And up she came, his daughter fair,
And luikit ower the brine.

She turned her face to the drivin' hail,
To the hail but and the weet;
Her snood it brak, and, as lang 's hersel',
Her hair drave out i' the sleet.

She turned her face frae the drivin' win' —
"What's that ahead?" quo she.
The skipper he threw himsel' frae the win',
And he drove the helm a-lee.

"Put to yer hand, my lady fair!
Put to yer hand," quoth he;
"Gin she dinna face the win' the mair,
It's the waur for you and me."

For the skipper kenned that strength is strength,
Whether woman's or man's at last.
To the tiller the lady she laid her han',
And the ship laid her cheek to the blast.

For that slender body was full o' soul,
And the will is mair than shape;
As the skipper saw when they cleared the berg,
And he heard her quarter scrape.

Quo the skipper: "Ye are a lady fair,
And a princess grand to see;
But ye are a woman, and a man wad sail
To hell in yer company."

She liftit a pale and a queenly face;
Her een flashed, and syne they swam.
"And what for no to heaven?" she says,
And she turned awa' frae him.

But she took na her han' frae the good ship's helm,
Until the day did daw;
And the skipper he spak, but what he said
It was said atween them twa.

And then the good ship, she lay to,
With the land far on the lee;
And up came the king upo' the deck,
Wi' wan face and bluidshot ee.

The skipper he louted to the king:
"Gae wa', gae wa'," said the king.
Said the king, like a prince, "I was a' wrang,
Put on this ruby ring."

And the wind blew lowne, and the stars cam oot,
And the ship turned to the shore;
And, afore the sun was up again,
They saw Scotland ance more.

That day the ship hung at the pier-heid,
And the king he stept on the land.
"Skipper, kneel down," the king he said,
"Hoo daur ye afore me stand?"

The skipper he louted on his knee,
The king his blade he drew:
Said the king, "How daured ye contre me?
I'm aboard my ain ship noo.

"I canna mak ye a king," said he,
"For the Lord alone can do that;
And besides ye took it intil yer ain han',
And crooned yersel' sae pat!

"But wi' what ye will I redeem my ring;
For ance I am at your beck.
And first, as ye loutit Skipper o' Doon,
Rise up Yerl o' Quarterdeck."

The skipper he rose and looked at the king
In his een for all his croon;
Said the skipper, "Here is yer grace's ring,
And yer daughter is my boon."

The reid blude sprang into the king's face, —
A wrathful man to see:
"The rascal loon abuses our grace;
Gae hang him upon yon tree."

But the skipper he sprang aboard his ship,
And he drew his biting blade;
And he struck the chain that held her fast,
But the iron was ower weel made.

And the king he blew a whistle loud;
And tramp, tramp, down the pier,
Cam' twenty riders on twenty steeds,
Clankin' wi' spur and spear.

"He saved your life!" cried the lady fair;
"His life ye daurna spill!"
"Will ye come atween me and my hate?"
Quo the lady, "And that I will!"

And on cam the knights wi' spur and spear,
For they heard the iron ring.
"Gin ye care na for yer father's grace,
Mind ye that I am the king."

"I kneel to my father for his grace,
Right lowly on my knee;
But I stand and look the king in the face,
For the skipper is king o' me."

She turned and she sprang upo' the deck,
And the cable splashed in the sea.
The good ship spread her wings sae white,
And away with the skipper goes she.

Now was not this a king's daughter,
And a brave lady beside?
And a woman with whom a man might sail
Into the heaven wi' pride?

GEORGE MACDONALD.

WRECK OF "THE GRACE OF SUNDERLAND."

"HE's a rare man,
Our parson; half a head above us all."

"That's a great gift, and notable," said I.

"Ay, Sir; and when he was a younger man
He went out in the life-boat very oft,
Before 'The Grace of Sunderland' was wrecked.
He's never been his own man since that hour;
For there were thirty men aboard of her,
Anigh as close as you are now to me,
And ne'er a one was saved.
They're lying now,
With two small children, in a row: the church
And yard are full of seamen's graves, and few
Have any names.

She bumped upon the reef;
Our parson, my young son, and several more
Were lashed together with a two-inch rope,
And crept along to her; their mates ashore
Ready to haul them in. The gale was high,
The sea was all a boiling seething froth,
And God Almighty's guns were going off,
And the land trembled.

"When she took the ground,
She went to pieces like a lock of hay
Tossed from a pitchfork. Ere it came to that,
The captain reeled on deck with two small things,
One in each arm — his little lad and lass.
Their hair was long and blew before his face,
Or else we thought he had been saved; he fell,
But held them fast. The crew, poor luckless souls!
The breakers licked them off; and some were crushed,
Some swallowed in the yeast, some flung up dead,
The dear breath beaten out of them: not one
Jumped from the wreck upon the reef to catch
The hands that strained to reach, but tumbled back
With eyes wide open. But the captain lay
And clung — the only man alive.
They prayed —
'For God's sake, captain, throw the children here!'
'Throw them!' our parson cried; and then she struck:
And he threw one, a pretty two years' child,
But the gale dashed him on the slippery verge,
And down he went. They say they heard him cry.

"Then he rose up and took the other one,
And all our men reached out their hungry arms,
And cried out, 'Throw her, throw her!' and he did.
He threw her right against the parson's breast,
And all at once a sea broke over them,
And they that saw it from the shore have said
It struck the wreck, and piecemeal scattered it,
Just as a woman might the lump of salt
That 'twixt her hands into the kneading-pan
She breaks and crumbles on her rising bread.

"We hauled our men in: two of them were dead —
The sea had beaten them, their heads hung down;
Our parson's arms were empty, for the wave
Had torn away the pretty, pretty lamb;
We often see him stand beside her grave:
But 'twas no fault of his, no fault of his."

JEAN INGELOW.

THE DROWNED LOVERS.

WILLIE stands in his stable door,
And clapping at his steed;
And looking o'er his white fingers,
His nose began to bleed.

"Gie corn to my horse, mother;
And meat to my young man:
And I'll awa' to Meggie's bower,
I'll win ere she lie down."

"O bide this night wi' me, Willie,
O bide this night wi' me;
The best an' cock o' a' the reest,
At your supper shall be."

"A' your cocks, and a' your reests,
I value not a prin;
For I'll awa' to Meggie's bower,
I'll win ere she lie down."

"Stay this night wi' me, Willie,
O stay this night wi' me;
The best an' sheep in a' the flock
At your supper shall be."

"A' your sheep, and a' your flocks,
I value not a prin;
For I'll awa' to Meggie's bower,
I'll win ere she lie down."

"O an' ye gang to Meggie's bower,
Sae sair against my will,
The deepest pot in Clyde's water,
My malison ye's feel."

"The guid steed that I ride upon
Cost me thrice thretty pound;
And I'll put trust in his swift feet,
To hae me safe to land."

As he rade ower yon high, high hill,
And down yon dowie den,
The noise that was in Clyde's water
Wou'd fear'd five hunder men.

"Ye're roaring loud, Clyde water,
Your waves seem ower strang;
Make me your wreck as I come back,
But spare me as I gang."

Then he is on to Meggie's bower,
And tirlèd at the pin;
"O sleep ye, wake ye, Meggie," he said,
"Ye'll open, lat me come in."

"O wha is this at my bower door,
That calls me by my name?"
"It is your first love, sweet Willie,
This night newly come hame."

"I hae few lovers thereout, thereout,
As few hae I therein;
The best an' love that ever I had,
Was here just late yestreen."

"The warstan stable in a' your stables,
For my puir steed to stand;
The warstan bower in a' your bowers,
For me to lie therein:
My boots are fu' o' Clyde's water,
I'm shivering at the chin."

"My barns are fu' o' corn, Willie,
My stables are fu' o' hay;
My bowers are fu' o' gentlemen; —
They'll nae remove till day."

"O fare-ye-well, my fause Meggie,
O farewell, and adieu;
I've gotten my mither's malison,
This night coming to you."

As he rode ower yon high, high hill,
And down yon dowie den;
The rushing that was in Clyde's water
Took Willie's cane fra him.

He lean'd him ower his saddle bow,
To catch his cane again;
The rushing that was in Clyde's water
Took Willie's hat frae him.

He lean'd him ower his saddle bow,
To catch his hat thro' force;
The rushing that was in Clyde's water
Took Willie frae his horse.

His brither stood upo' the bank,
Says, "Fye, man, will ye drown?
Ye'll turn ye to your high horse head,
And learn how to sowm."

"How can I turn to my horse head,
And learn how to sowm?
I've gotten my mither's malison,
It's here that I maun drown!"

The very hour this young man sank
Into the pot sae deep,
Up it waken'd his love, Meggie,
Out o' her drowsy sleep.

"Come here, come here, my mither dear,
And read this dreary dream;
I dream'd my love was at our gates,
And nane wad let him in."

"Lye still, lye still now, my Meggie,
Lye still and tak your rest;
Sin' your true love was at your gates,
It's but twa quarters past."

Nimbly, nimbly raise she up,
And nimbly pat she on;
And the higher that the lady cried,
The louder blew the win'.

The first an' step that she stepp'd in,
She stepped to the queet;
"Ohon, alas!" said that lady,
"This water's wondrous deep."

The next an' step that she wade in,
She wadit to the knee;
Says she, "I cou'd wade farther in,
If I my love cou'd see."

The next an' step that she wade in,
She wadit to the chin;
The deepest pot in Clyde's water,
She got sweet Willie in.

"You've had a cruel mither, Willie,
And I have had anither;
But we shall sleep in Clyde's water,
Like sister an' like brither."

WINSTANLEY.

Winstanley's deed, you kindly folk,
With it I fill my lay,
And a nobler man ne'er walked the world,
Let his name be what it may.

The good ship "Snowdrop" tarried long,
Up at the vane looked he;
"Belike," he said, for the wind had dropped,
"She lieth becalmed at sea."

The lovely ladies flocked within,
And still would each one say,
"Good mercer, be the ships come up?"
But still he answered, "Nay."

Then stepped two mariners down the street,
With looks of grief and fear:
"Now, if Winstanley be your name,
We bring you evil cheer!

"For the good ship 'Snowdrop' struck, — she struck
On the rock, — the Eddystone,
And down she went with threescore men,
We two being left alone.

"Down in the deep, with freight and crew,
Past any help she lies,
And never a bale has come to shore
Of all thy merchandise."

"For cloth o' gold and comely frieze,"
Winstanley said, and sighed,
"For velvet coif, or costly coat,
They fathoms deep may bide.

"O thou brave skipper, blithe and kind,
O mariners, bold and true,
Sorry at heart, right sorry am I,
A-thinking of yours and you.

"Many long days Winstanley's breast
Shall feel a weight within,
For a waft of wind he shall be 'feared,
And trading count but sin.

"To him no more it shall be joy
  To pace the cheerful town,
And see the lovely ladies gay
  Step on in velvet gown."

The "Snowdrop" sank at Lammas tide,
  All under the yeasty spray;
On Christmas Eve the brig "Content"
  Was also cast away.

He little thought o' New Year's night,
  So jolly as he sat then,
While drank the toast and praised the roast
  The round-faced Aldermen, —

While serving lads ran to and fro,
  Pouring the ruby wine,
And jellies trembled on the board,
  And towering pasties fine, —

While loud huzzas ran up the roof
  Till the lamps did rock o'erhead,
And holly-boughs from rafters hung
  Dropped down their berries red, —

He little thought on Plymouth Hoe,
  With every rising tide,
How the wave washed in his sailor lads,
  And laid them side by side.

There stepped a stranger to the board:
  "Now, stranger, who be ye?"
He looked to right, he looked to left,
  And "Rest you merry," quoth he;

"For you did not see the brig go down,
  Or ever a storm had blown;
For you did not see the white wave rear
  At the rock, — the Eddystone.

"She drave at the rock with stern-sails set;
  Crash went the masts in twain;
She staggered back with her mortal blow,
  Then leaped at it again.

"There rose a great cry, bitter and strong;
  The misty moon looked out!
And the water swarmed with seamen's heads,
  And the wreck was strewed about.

"I saw her mainsail lash the sea
  As I clung to the rock alone;
Then she heeled over, and down she went,
  And sank like any stone.

"She was a fair ship, but all's one!
  For naught could bide the shock."
"I will take horse," Winstanley said,
  "And see this deadly rock.

"For never again shall bark o' mine
  Sail over the windy sea,
Unless, by the blessing of God, for this
  Be found a remedy."

Winstanley rode to Plymouth town
  All in the sleet and the snow;
And he looked around on shore and sound,
  As he stood on Plymouth Hoe.

Till a pillar of spray rose far away,
  And shot up its stately head,
Reared, and fell over, and reared again:
  "Tis the rock! the rock!" he said.

Straight to the Mayor he took his way:
  "Good Master Mayor," quoth he,
"I am a mercer of London town,
  And owner of vessels three, —

"But for your rock of dark renown,
  I had five to track the main."
"You are one of many," the old Mayor said,
"That on the rock complain.

"An ill rock, mercer! your words ring right,
  Well with my thoughts they chime,
For my two sons to the world to come
  It sent before their time."

"Lend me a lighter, good Master Mayor,
  And a score of shipwrights free,
For I think to raise a lantern tower
  On this rock o' destiny."

The old Mayor laughed, but sighed alsó:
  "Ah, youth," quoth he, "is rash;
Sooner, young man, thou'lt root it out
  From the sea that doth it lash.

"Who sails too near its jagged teeth,
He shall have evil lot;
For the calmest seas that tumble there
Froth like a boiling pot.

"And the heavier seas few look on nigh,
But straight they lay him dead;
A seventy-gun-ship, sir! — they'll shoot
Higher than her masthead.

"Oh, beacons sighted in the dark,
They are right welcome things,
And pitchpots flaming on the shore
Show fair as angel wings.

"Hast gold in hand? then light the land,
It 'longs to thee and me;
But let alone the deadly rock
In God Almighty's sea."

Yet said he, "Nay, — I must away,
On the rock to set my feet;
My debts are paid, my will I made,
Or ever I did thee greet.

"If I must die, then let me die
By the rock, and not elswhere;
If I may live, O let me live
To mount my lighthouse stair."

The old Mayor looked him in the face,
And answered, "Have thy way;
Thy heart is stout, as if round about
It was braced with an iron stay:

"Have thy will, mercer! choose thy men,
Put off from the storm-rid shore;
God with thee be, or I shall see
Thy face and theirs no more."

Heavily plunged the breaking wave,
And foam flew up the lea,
Morning and even the drifted snow
Fell into the dark gray sea.

Winstanley chose him men and gear;
He said, "My time I waste,"
For the seas ran seething up the shore,
And the wrack drave on in haste.

But twenty days he waited and more,
Pacing the strand alone,
Or ever he sat his manly foot
On the rock, — the Eddystone.

Then he and the sea began their strife,
And worked with power and might:
Whatever the man reared up by day
The sea broke down by night.

He wrought at ebb with bar and beam,
He sailed to shore at flow;
And at his side, by that same tide,
Came bar and beam alsó.

"Give in, give in," the old Mayor cried,
"Or thou wilt rue the day."
"Yonder he goes," the townsfolk sighed,
But the rock will have its way.

"For all his looks that are so stout,
And his speeches brave and fair,
He may wait on the wind, wait on the wave,
But he'll build no lighthouse there."

In fine weather and foul weather
The rock his arts did flout,
Through the long days and the short days,
Till all that year ran out.

With fine weather and foul weather
Another year came in;
"To take his wage," the workmen said,
"We almost count a sin."

Now March was gone, came April in,
And a sea-fog settled down,
And forth sailed he on a glassy sea,
He sailed from Plymouth town.

With men and stores he put to sea,
As he was wont to do:
They showed in the fog like ghosts full faint, —
A ghostly craft and crew.

And the sea-fog lay and waxed alway,
For a long eight days and more;
"God help our men," quoth the women then;
"For they bide long from shore."

They paced the Hoe in doubt and dread:
"Where may our mariners be?"
But the brooding fog lay soft as down
Over the quiet sea.

A Scottish schooner made the port,
The thirteenth day at e'en;
"As I am a man," the captain cried,
"A strange sight I have seen:

"And a strange sound heard, my masters all,
At sea, in the fog and the rain,
Like shipwrights' hammers tapping low,
Then loud, then low again.

"And a stately house one instant showed,
Through a rift, on the vessel's lee;
What manner of creatures may be those
That built upon the sea?"

Then sighed the folk, "The Lord be praised!"
And they flocked to the shore amain:
All over the Hoe that livelong night,
Many stood out in the rain.

It ceased; and the red sun reared his head,
And the rolling fog did flee;
And, lo! in the offing faint and far
Winstanley's house at sea!

In fair weather with mirth and cheer
The stately tower uprose;
In foul weather, with hunger and cold,
They were content to close;

Till up the stair Winstanley went,
To fire the wick afar;
And Plymouth in the silent night
Looked out, and saw her star.

Winstanley set his foot ashore:
Said he, "My work is done;
I hold it strong to last as long
As aught beneath the sun.

"But if it fail, as fail it may,
Borne down with ruin and rout,
Another than I shall rear it high,
And brace the girders stout.

"A better than I shall rear it high,
For now the way is plain;
And though I were dead," Winstanley said,
"The light would shine again.

"Yet were I fain still to remain,
Watch in my tower to keep,
And tend my light in the stormiest night
That ever did move the deep;

"And if it stood, why then 'twere good,
Amid their tremulous stirs,
To count each stroke when the mad waves broke,
For cheers of mariners.

"But if it fell, then this were well,
That I should with it fall;
Since, for my part, I have built my heart
In the courses of its wall.

"Ay! I were fain, long to remain,
Watch in my tower to keep,
And tend my light in the stormiest night
That ever did move the deep."

With that Winstanley went his way,
And left the rock renowned,
And summer and winter his pilot star
Hung bright o'er Plymouth Sound.

But it fell out, fell out at last,
That he would put to sea,
To scan once more his lighthouse tower
On the rock o' destiny.

And the winds broke, and the storm broke,
And wrecks came plunging in;
None in the town that night lay down
Or sleep or rest to win.

The great mad waves were rolling graves,
And each flung up its dead;
The seething flow was white below,
And black the sky o'erhead.

And when the dawn, the dull, gray dawn, —
Broke on the trembling town,
And men looked south to the harbor mouth,
The lighthouse tower was down.

Down in the deep where he doth sleep,
Who made it shine afar,

And then in the night that drowned its light,
Set, with his pilot star.

Many fair tombs in the glorious glooms
At Westminster they show;
The brave and the great lie there in state:
Winstanley lieth low.

JEAN INGELOW.

FIDELITY.

A BARKING sound the shepherd hears,
A cry as of a dog or fox;
He halts, and searches with his eyes
Among the scattered rocks:
And now at distance can discern
A stirring in a brake of fern;
And instantly a dog is seen
Glancing from that covert green.

The dog is not of mountain breed;
Its motions, too, are wild and shy;
With something, as the shepherd thinks,
Unusual in its cry:
Nor is there any one in sight
All round, in hollow or on height;
Nor shout, nor whistle strikes his ear:
What is the creature doing here?

It was a cove, a huge recess,
That keeps till June December's snow;
A lofty precipice in front,
A silent tarn below!
Far in the bosom of Helvellyn,
Remote from public road or dwelling,
Pathway, or cultivated land,
From trace of human foot or hand.

There sometimes doth a leaping fish
Send through the tarn a lonely cheer;
The crags repeat the ravens' croak
In symphony austere;
Thither the rainbow comes — the cloud —
And mists that spread the flying shroud;
And sunbeams: and the sounding blast,
That, if it could, would hurry past,
But that enormous barrier binds it fast.

Not free from boding thoughts, a while
The shepherd stood; then makes his way
Towards the dog, o'er rocks and stones,
As quickly as he may;
Nor far had gone before he found
A human skeleton on the ground;
The appalled discoverer with a sigh
Looks round, to learn the history.

From those abrupt and perilous rocks
The man had fallen, that place of fear!
At length upon the shepherd's mind
It breaks, and all is clear:
He instantly recalled the name,
And who he was, and whence he came;
Remembered, too, the very day
On which the traveller passed this way.

But hear a wonder, for whose sake
This lamentable tale I tell!
A lasting monument of words
This wonder merits well.
The dog, which still was hovering nigh,
Repeating the same timid cry,
This dog had been through three months' space
A dweller in that savage place.

Yes, proof was plain that since the day
On which the traveller thus had died
The dog had watched about the spot,
Or by his master's side:
How nourished here through such long time
He knows, who gave that love sublime,
And gave that strength of feeling, great
Above all human estimate.

WORDSWORTH.

HELVELLYN.

I CLIMBED the dark brow of the mighty Helvellyn,
Lakes and mountains beneath me gleamed misty and wide;
All was still, save by fits, when the eagle was yelling,
And starting around me the echoes replied.

On the right, Striden-edge round the Red-tarn was bending,
And Catchedicam its left verge was defending,
One huge nameless rock in the front was ascending,
When I marked the sad spot where the wanderer had died.

Dark green was that spot 'mid the brown mountain heather,
Where the Pilgrim of Nature lay stretched in decay,
Like the corpse of an outcast abandoned to weather,
Till the mountain-winds wasted the tenantless clay.
Nor yet quite deserted, though lonely extended,
For, faithful in death, his mute favorite attended,
The much-loved remains of her master defended,
And chased the hill-fox and the raven away.

How long didst thou think that his silence was slumber?
When the wind waved his garment, how oft didst thou start?
How many long days and long weeks didst thou number,
Ere he faded before thee, the friend of thy heart?
And, oh, was it meet, that, no requiem read o'er him, —
No mother to weep, and no friend to deplore him,
And thou, little guardian, alone stretched before him, —
Unhonored the Pilgrim from life should depart?

When a Prince to the fate of the Peasant has yielded,
The tapestry waves dark round the dim-lighted hall;
With scutcheons of silver the coffin is shielded,
And pages stand mute by the canopied pall:
Through the courts, at deep midnight, the torches are gleaming;
In the proudly-arched chapel the banners are beaming;
Far adown the long aisle sacred music is streaming,
Lamenting a Chief of the People should fall.

But meeter for thee, gentle lover of nature,
To lay down thy head like the meek mountain lamb,
When, wildered, he drops from some cliff huge in stature,
And draws his last sob by the side of his dam.
And more stately thy couch by this desert lake lying,
Thy obsequies sung by the gray plover flying,
With one faithful friend but to witness thy dying,
In the arms of Helvellyn and Catchedicam.

SCOTT.

GEORGE NIDIVER.

MEN have done brave deeds,
And bards have sung them well:
I of good George Nidiver
Now the tale will tell.

In Californian mountains
A hunter bold was he:
Keen his eye and sure his aim
As any you should see.

A little Indian boy
Followed him everywhere,
Eager to share the hunter's joy,
The hunter's meal to share.

And when the bird or deer
Fell by the hunter's skill,
The boy was always near
To help with right good-will.

One day as through the cleft
Between two mountains steep,
Shut in both right and left,
Their questing way they keep,

They see two grizzly bears,
With hunger fierce and fell,
Rush at them unawares
Right down the narrow dell.

The boy turned round with screams,
And ran with terror wild:
One of the pair of savage beasts
Pursued the shrieking child.

The hunter raised his gun,—
He knew *one* charge was all,—
And through the boy's pursuing foe
He sent his only ball.

The other on George Nidiver
Came on with dreadful pace:
The hunter stood unarmed,
And met him face to face.

I say *unarmed* he stood:
Against those frightful paws
The rifle butt, or club of wood,
Could stand no more than straws.

George Nidiver stood still,
And looked him in the face:
The wild beast stopped amazed,
Then came with slackening pace.

Still firm the hunter stood,
Although his heart beat high:
Again the creature stopped,
And gazed with wondering eye.

The hunter met his gaze,
Nor yet an inch gave way;
The bear turned slowly round,
And slowly moved away.

What thoughts were in his mind
It would be hard to spell:
What thoughts were in George Nidiver
I rather guess than tell.

But sure that rifle's aim,
Swift choice of generous part,
Showed in its passing gleam
The depths of a brave heart.

SVEND VONVED.

[From the old Danish.]

SVEND VONVED binds his sword to his side;
He fain will battle with knights of pride.
"When may I look for thee once more here?
When roast the heifer, and spice the beer?"
Look out, look out, Svend Vonved.

"When stones shall take, of themselves, a flight,
And ravens' feathers are woxen white,
Then expect Svend Vonved home:
In all my days, I will never come."
Look out, look out, Svend Vonved.

His mother took that in evil part:
"I hear, young gallant, that mad thou art;
Wherever thou goest, on land or sea,
Disgrace and shame shall attend on thee."
Look out, look out, Svend Vonved.

He kissed her thrice with his lips of fire:
"Appease, O mother, appease thine ire!
Ne'er wish me any mischance to know,
For thou canst not tell how far I may go."
Look out, look out, Svend Vonved.

"Then I will bless thee, this very day;
Thou never shalt perish in any fray;
Success shall be in thy courser tall,
Success in thyself which is best of all.
Look out, look out, Svend Vonved.

"Success in thy hand, success in thy foot,
In struggle with man, in battle with brute;
The Holy God and Saint Drotten dear
Shall guide and watch thee through thy career."
Look out, look out, Svend Vonved.

Svend Vonved took up the word again—
"I'll range the mountain, and rove the plain,
Peasant and noble I'll wound and slay;
All, all, for my father's wrong shall pay."
Look out, look out, Svend Vonved.

His helm was blinking against the sun,
His spurs were clinking his heels upon,
His horse was springing, with bridle ringing,
While sat the warrior wildly singing,
Look out, look out, Svend Vonved.

He rode and lilted, he rode and sang,
Then met he by chance Sir Thulé Vang;
Sir Thulé Vang, with his twelve sons bold,
All cased in iron, the bright and cold.
Look out, look out, Svend Vonved.

Svend Vonved took his sword from his side,
He fain would battle with knights so tried;
The proud Sir Thulé he first ran through,
And then, in succession, his sons he slew.
Look out, look out, Svend Vonved.

Svend Vonved binds his sword to his side,
It lists him farther to ride, to ride;
He rode along by the grené shaw,
The Brute-carl there with surprise he saw.
Look out, look out, Svend Vonved.

A wild swine sat on his shoulders broad,
Upon his bosom a black bear snored;
And about his fingers with hair o'er-hung,
The squirrel sported and weasel clung.
Look out, look out, Svend Vonved.

"Now, Brute-carl, yield thy booty to me,
Or I will take it by force from thee.
Say, wilt thou quickly thy beasts forego,
Or venture with me to bandy a blow?"
Look out, look out, Svend Vonved.

"Much rather, much rather, I'll fight with thee,
Than thou my booty should get from me:
I never was bidden the like to do,
Since good King Esmer in fight I slew."
Look out, look out, Svend Vonved.

"And didst thou slay King Esmer fine?
Why, then thou slewest dear father mine;
And soon, full soon, shalt thou pay for him,
With the flesh hackt off from thy every limb!"
Look out, look out, Svend Vonved.

They drew a circle upon the sward;
They both were dour, as the rocks are hard;
Forsooth, I tell you, their hearts were steeled, —
The one to the other no jot would yield.
Look out, look out, Svend Vonved.

They fought for a day, — they fought for two, —
And so on the third they were fain to do;
But ere the fourth day reached the night,
The Brute-carl fell, and was slain outright.
Look out, look out, Svend Vonved.

Svend Vonved binds his sword to his side,
Farther and farther he lists to ride;
He rode at the foot of a hill so steep,
There saw he a herd as he drove the sheep.
Look out, look out, Svend Vonved.

"Now listen, Herd, with the fleecy care;
Listen, and give me answers fair.
Look out, look out, Svend Vonved.

"What is rounder than a wheel?
Where do they eat the holiest meal?
Where does the sun go down to his seat?
And where do they lay the dead man's feet?
Look out, look out, Svend Vonved.

"What fills the valleys one and all?
What is clothed best in the monarch's hall?
What cries more loud than cranes can cry?
And what in whiteness the swan outvie?
Look out, look out, Svend Vonved.

"Who on his back his beard doth wear?
Who 'neath his chin his nose doth bear?

What's more black than the blackest sloe?
And what is swifter than a roe?
Look out, look out, Svend Vonved.

"Where is the bridge that is most broad?
What is, by man, the most abhorred?
Where leads, where leads, the highest road up?
And say where the hottest of drink they sup?"
Look out, look out, Svend Vonved.

"The sun is rounder than a wheel.
They eat at the altar the holiest meal.
The sun in the West goes down to his seat:
And they lay to the East the dead man's feet.
Look out, look out, Svend Vonved.

"Snow fills the valleys, one and all.
Man is clothed best in the monarch's hall.
Thunder cries louder than cranes can cry.
Angels in whiteness the swan outvie.
Look out, look out, Svend Vonved.

"His beard on his back the lapwing wears.
His nose 'neath his chin the elfin bears.
More black is sin than the blackest sloe:
And thought is swifter than any roe.
Look out, look out, Svend Vonved.

"Ice is of bridges the bridge most broad.
The toad is, of all things, the most abhorred.
To paradise leads the highest road up:
And in hell the hottest of drink they sup."
Look out, look out, Svend Vonved.

Svend Vonved binds his sword to his side,
It lists him farther to ride, to ride:
He found upon the desolate wold
A burly knight, of aspect bold.
Look out, look out, Svend Vonved.

"Now tell me, Rider, noble and good,
Where does the fish stand up in the flood?
Where do they mingle the best, best wine?
And where with his knights does Vidrick dine?
Look out, look out, Svend Vonved."

"The fish in the East stands up in the flood.
They drink in the North the wine so good.
In Halland's hall does Vidrick dine,
With his swains around, and his warriors fine."
Look out, look out, Svend Vonved.

From his breast Svend Vonved a gold ring drew,
At the foot of the knight the gold ring he threw;
"Go! say thou wert the very last man
Who gold from the hand of Svend Vonved wan."
Look out, look out, Svend Vonved.

. . . .

Then in he went to his lonely bower,
There drank he the wine, the wine of power;
His much-loved harp he played upon
Till the strings were broken every one.
Look out, look out, Svend Vonved.

Translated from the old Danish by
GEORGE BORROW.

THE WILD HUNTSMAN.

THE Wildgrave winds his bugle-horn,
To horse, to horse! halloo, halloo!
His fiery courser snuffs the morn,
And thronging serfs their lord pursue.

The eager pack, from couples freed,
Dash through the bush, the brier, the brake;
While answering hound, and horn, and steed,
The mountain echoes startling wake.

The beams of God's own hallowed
day
Had painted yonder spire with
gold,
And, calling sinful man to pray,
Loud, long, and deep the bell had
tolled:

But still the Wildgrave onward rides;
Halloo, halloo! and, hark again!
When, spurring from opposing sides,
Two Stranger Horsemen join the
train.

Who was each Stranger, left and right,
Well may I guess, but dare not tell;
The right-hand steed was silver
white,
The left, the swarthy hue of hell.

The right-hand Horseman, young
and fair,
His smile was like the morn of
May;
The left, from eye of tawny glare,
Shot midnight lightning's lurid
ray.

He waved his huntsman's cap on
high,
Cried, "Welcome, welcome, noble
lord!
What sport can earth, or sea, or sky,
To match the princely chase, afford?"

"Cease thy loud bugle's clanging
knell,"
Cried the fair youth, with silver
voice;
"And for devotion's choral swell,
Exchange the rude unhallowed
noise.

"To-day the ill-omened chase for-
bear,
Yon bell yet summons to the fane;
To-day the Warning Spirit hear,
To-morrow thou mayst mourn in
vain." —

"Away, and sweep the glades
along!"
The Sable Hunter hoarse replies;
"To muttering monks leave matin-
song,
And bells, and books, and mysteries."

The Wildgrave spurred his ardent
steed,
And, launching forward with a
bound,
"Who, for thy drowsy priestlike
rede,
Would leave the jovial horn and
hound?

"Hence, if our manly sport offend!
With pious fools go chant and
pray! —
Well hast thou spoke, my dark-
browed friend;
Halloo, halloo! and, hark away!"

The Wildgrave spurred his courser
light,
O'er moss and moor, o'er holt and
hill;
And on the left, and on the right,
Each Stranger Horseman followed
still.

Up springs, from yonder tangled
thorn,
A stag more white than mountain
snow;
And louder rung the Wildgrave's
horn,
"Hark forward, forward! holla,
ho!"

A heedless wretch has crossed the
way;
He gasps, the thundering hoofs
below; —
But, live who can, or die who may,
Still, "Forward, forward!" on
they go.

See, where yon simple fences meet,
A field with autumn's blessings
crowned;
See, prostrate at the Wildgrave's feet,
A husbandman with toil em-
browned:

"O mercy, mercy, noble lord!
Spare the poor's pittance," was
his cry,
"Earned by the sweat these brows
have poured
In scorching hour of fierce July."

Earnest the right-hand Stranger
pleads,
The left still cheering to the prey;

The impetuous Earl no warning heeds,
But furious holds the onward way.

"Away, thou hound! so basely born,
Or dread the scourge's echoing blow!" —
Then loudly rung his bugle-horn,
"Hark forward, forward! holla, ho!"

So said, so done: — A single bound
Clears the poor laborer's humble pale;
Wild follows man, and horse, and hound,
Like dark December's stormy gale.

And man and horse, and hound and horn,
Destructive sweep the field along;
While, joying o'er the wasted corn,
Fell Famine marks the maddening throng.

Again uproused, the timorous prey
Scours moss and moor, and holt and hill;
Hard run, he feels his strength decay,
And trusts for life his simple skill.

Too dangerous solitude appeared;
He seeks the shelter of the crowd:
Amid the flock's domestic herd
His harmless head he hopes to shroud.

O'er moss and moor, and holt and hill,
His track the steady bloodhounds trace;
O'er moss and moor, unwearied still,
The furious Earl pursues the chase.

Full lowly did the herdsman fall; —
"O spare, thou noble Baron, spare
These herds, a widow's little all;
These flocks, an orphan's fleecy care!" —

Earnest the right-hand Stranger pleads,
The left still cheering to the prey;
The Earl nor prayer nor pity heeds,
But furious keeps the onward way.

"Unmannered dog! To stop my sport,
Vain were thy cant and beggar whine,
Though human spirits, of thy sort,
Were tenants of these carrion kine!" —

Again he winds his bugle-horn,
"Hark forward, forward, holla, ho!"
And through the herd, in ruthless scorn,
He cheers his furious hounds to go.

In heaps the throttled victims fall;
Down sinks their mangled herdsman near;
The murderous cries the stag appal, —
Again he starts, new-nerved by fear.

With blood besmeared, and white with foam,
While big the tears of anguish pour,
He seeks, amid the forest's gloom,
The humble hermit's hallowed bower.

But man and horse, and horn and hound,
Fast rattling on his traces go;
The sacred chapel rung around
With, "Hark away! and, holla, ho!"

All mild, amid the rout profane,
The holy hermit poured his prayer:
"Forbear with blood God's house to stain;
Revere his altar, and forbear!

"The meanest brute has rights to plead,
Which, wronged by cruelty, or pride,
Draw vengeance on the ruthless head: —
Be warned at length, and turn aside." —

Still the Fair Horseman anxious pleads;
The Black, wild whooping, points the prey:
Alas! the Earl no warning heeds,
But frantic keeps the forward way.

"Holy or not, or right or wrong,
Thy altar, and its rites, I spurn;
Not sainted martyrs' sacred song,
Not God himself, shall make me turn!"

He spurs his horse, he winds his horn,
"Hark forward, forward! holla, ho!"
But off, on whirlwind's pinions borne,
The stag, the hut, the hermit, go.

And horse and man, and horn and hound,
And clamor of the chase, were gone;
For hoofs, and howls, and bugle sound,
A deadly silence reigned alone.

Wild gazed the affrighted Earl around;
He strove in vain to wake his horn,
In vain to call: for not a sound
Could from his anxious lips be borne.

He listens for his trusty hounds;
No distant baying reached his ears;
His courser, rooted to the ground,
The quickening spur unmindful bears.

Still dark and darker frown the shades,
Dark as the darkness of the grave;
And not a sound the still invades,
Save what a distant torrent gave.

High o'er the sinner's humbled head
At length the solemn silence broke;
And from a cloud of swarthy red,
The awful voice of thunder spoke.

"Oppressor of creation fair!
Apostate Spirit's hardened tool!
Scorner of God! Scourge of the poor!
The measure of thy cup is full.

"Be chased forever through the wood;
Forever roam the affrighted wild;
And let thy fate instruct the proud,
God's meanest creature is his child."

"'Twas hushed: one flash, of sombre glare,
With yellow tinged the forests brown;
Up rose the Wildgrave's bristling hair,
And horror chilled each nerve and bone.

Cold poured the sweat in freezing rill;
A rising wind began to sing;
And louder, louder, louder still,
Brought storm and tempest on its wing.

Earth heard the call; — her entrails rend;
From yawning rifts, with many a yell,
Mixed with sulphureous flames, ascend
The misbegotten dogs of hell.

What ghastly Huntsman next arose,
Well may I guess, but dare not tell:
His eye like midnight lightning glows,
His steed the swarthy hue of hell.

The Wildgrave flies o'er bush and thorn,
With many a shriek of helpless woe;
Behind him hound, and horse, and horn,
And, "Hark away, and holla, ho!"

With wild Despair's reverted eye,
Close, close behind, he marks the throng,
With bloody fangs, and eager cry;
In frantic fear he scours along. —

Still, still shall last the dreadful chase,
Till time itself shall have an end:
By day, they scour earth's caverned space,
At midnight's witching hour, ascend.

This is the horn, and hound, and horse,
That oft the lated peasant hears;
Appalled he signs the frequent cross,
When the wild din invades his ears.

The wakeful priest oft drops a tear
  For human pride, for human woe,
When, at his midnight mass, he hears
  The infernal cry of, "Holla, ho!"

SCOTT: *trans. from* BÜRGER.

ALICE BRAND.

MERRY it is in the good greenwood,
  When the mavis and merle are singing,
When the deer sweeps by, and the hounds are in cry,
  And the hunter's horn is ringing.

"O Alice Brand, my native land
  Is lost for love of you;
And we must hold by wood and wold,
  As outlaws wont to do.

"O Alice, 'twas all for thy locks so bright,
  And 'twas all for thine eyes so blue,
That on the night of our luckless flight,
  Thy brother bold I slew.

"Now must I teach to hew the beech
  The hand that held the glaive,
For leaves to spread our lowly bed,
  And stakes to fence our cave.

"And for vest of pall, thy fingers small,
  That wont on harp to stray,
A cloak must shear from the slaughtered deer,
  To keep the cold away." —

"O Richard! if my brother died,
  'Twas but a fatal chance;
For darkling was the battle tried,
  And fortune sped the lance.

"If pall and vair no more I wear,
  Nor thou the crimson sheen,
As warm, we'll say, is the russet gray,
  As gay the forest green.

"And, Richard, if our lot be hard,
  And lost thy native land,
Still Alice has her own Richard,
  And he his Alice Brand."

'Tis merry, 'tis merry, in good greenwood,
  So blithe Lady Alice is singing;
On the beech's pride, and oak's brown side,
  Lord Richard's axe is ringing.

Up spoke the moody Elfin King,
  Who woned within the hill, —
Like wind in the porch of a ruined church,
  His voice was ghostly shrill.
"Why sounds yon stroke on beech and oak,
  Our moonlight circle's screen?
Or who comes here to chase the deer,
  Beloved of our Elfin Queen?
Or who may dare on wold to wear
  The fairies' fatal green?

"Up, Urgan, up! to yon mortal hie,
  For thou wert christened man;
For cross or sign thou wilt not fly,
  For muttered word or ban."

'Tis merry, 'tis merry, in good greenwood,
  Though the birds have stilled their singing;
The evening blaze doth Alice raise,
  And Richard is fagots bringing.

Up Urgan starts, that hideous dwarf,
  Before Lord Richard stands,
And, as he crossed and blessed himself,
"I fear not sign," quoth the grisly elf,
  "That is made with bloody hands."

But out then spoke she, Alice Brand,
  That woman void of fear, —
"And if there's blood upon his hand,
  'Tis but the blood of deer." —

"Now loud thou liest, thou bold of mood!
  It cleaves unto his hand,
The stain of thine own kindly blood,
  The blood of Ethert Brand."

Then forward stepped she, Alice Brand,
  And made the holy sign, —
"And if there's blood on Richard's hand,
  A spotless hand is mine.

"And I conjure thee, Demon elf,
By Him whom Demons fear,
To show us whence thou art thyself,
And what thine errand here?" —

"It was between the night and day,
When the Fairy King has power,
That I sunk down in a sinful fray,
And, 'twixt life and death, was snatched away
To the joyless Elfin bower.

"But wist I of a woman bold,
Who thrice my brow durst sign,
I might regain my mortal mould,
As fair a form as thine."

She crossed him once — she crossed him twice —
That lady was so brave;
The fouler grew his goblin hue,
The darker grew the cave.

She crossed him thrice, that lady bold;
He rose beneath her hand
The fairest knight on Scottish mould,
Her brother, Ethert Brand!

Merry it is in good greenwood,
When the mavis and merle are singing,
But merrier were they in Dunfermline gray,
When all the bells were ringing.

SCOTT.

THE LAKE OF THE DISMAL SWAMP.

"THEY made her a grave too cold and damp
For a soul so warm and true;
And she's gone to the Lake of the Dismal Swamp,
Where all night long, by a firefly lamp,
She paddles her white canoe.

And her firefly lamp I soon shall see,
And her paddle I soon shall hear;
Long and loving our life shall be,
And I'll hide the maid in a cypress-tree,
When the footstep of death is near!"

Away to the Dismal Swamp he speeds, —
His path was rugged and sore,
Through tangled juniper, beds of reeds,
Through many a fen where the serpent feeds,
And man never trod before!

And when on the earth he sunk to sleep,
If slumber his eyelids knew,
He lay where the deadly vine doth weep
Its venomous tear, and nightly steep
The flesh with blistering dew!

And near him the she-wolf stirred the brake,
And the copper-snake breathed in his ear,
Till he starting cried, from his dream awake,
"O when shall I see the dusky Lake,
And the white canoe of my dear?"

He saw the Lake, and a meteor bright
Quick over its surface played, —
"Welcome," he said "my dear one's light!"
And the dim shore echoed for many a night
The name of the death-cold maid!

Till he hollowed a boat of the birchen bark,
Which carried him off from shore;
Far he followed the meteor spark,
The wind was high and the clouds were dark,
And the boat returned no more.

But oft, from the Indian hunter's camp,
This lover and maid so true
Are seen, at the hour of midnight damp,
To cross the Lake by a firefly lamp,
And paddle their white canoe!

MOORE.

CHILD DYRING.

CHILD DYRING has ridden him up under öe,
(And O gin I were young!)
There wedded he him sae fair a may.
(I' the greenwood it lists me to ride.)

Thegither they lived for seven lang year,
(And O, &c.)
And they seven bairnes hae gotten in fere.
(I' the greenwood, &c.)

Sae Death's come there intill that stead,
And that winsome lily flower is dead.

That swain he has ridden him up under öe,
And syne he has married anither may.

He's married a may, and he's fessen her hame;
But she was a grim and a laidly dame.

When into the castell court drave she,
The seven bairnes stood wi' the tear in their ee.

The bairnes they stood wi' dule and doubt;—
She up wi' her foot, and she kicked them out.

Nor ale nor mead to the bairnes she gave:
"But hunger and hate frae me ye's have."

She took frae them the bowster blae,
And said, "Ye sall ligg i' the bare strae!"

She took frae them the groff wax-light:
Says, "Now ye sall ligg i' the mirk a' night!"

'Twas lang i' the night, and the bairnies grat:
Their mither she under the mools heard that;

That heard the wife under the eard that lay:
"For sooth maun I to my bairnies gae!"

That wife can stand up at our Lord's knee,
And "May I gang and my bairnies see?"

She prigged sae sair, and she prigged sae lang,
That he at the last gae her leave to gang.

"And thou sall come back when the cock does craw;
For thou nae langer sall bide awa."

Wi' her banes sae stark a bowt she gae;
She's riven baith wa' and marble gray.

When near to the dwalling she can gang,
The dogs they wow'd till the lift it rang.

When she came till the castell yett,
Her eldest dochter stood thereat.

"Why stand ye here, dear dochter mine?
How are sma brithers and sisters thine?"—

"For sooth ye're a woman baith fair and fine;
But ye are nae dear mither of mine."—

"Och! how should I be fine or fair?
My cheek is pale, and the ground's my lair."—

"My mither was white, wi' cheek sae red,
But thou art wan, and liker ane dead?"

"Och, how should I be white and red;
Sae lang as I've been cauld and dead?"

When she came till the chalmer in,
Down the bairns' cheeks the tears did rin.

She buskit the tane, and she brushed it there;
She kem'd and plaited the tither's hair.

Till her eldest dochter syne said she,
"Ye bid Child Dyring come here to me."

When he cam till the chalmer in,
Wi' angry mood she said to him;

"I left you routh o' ale and bread;
My bairnes quail for hunger and need.

"I left ahind me braw bowsters blae;
My bairnes are ligging i' the bare strae.

"I left ye sae mony a groff wax-light;
My bairnes ligg i' the mirk a' night.

"Gin aft I come back to visit thee,
Wae, dowy, and weary thy luck shall be."

Up spak little Kirstin in bed that lay:
"To thy bairnies I'll do the best I may."

Aye when they heard the dog nirr and bell,
Sae gae they the bairnies bread and ale.

Aye when the dog did mow, in haste,
They cross'd and sain'd themselves frae the ghaist.

Aye whan the little dog yowl'd, with fear
They shook at the thought that the dead was near.

SCOTT.

CHILDREN IN THE WOOD.

Being a true relation of the inhuman murder of two children of a deceased gentleman in Norfolk, England, whom he left to the care of his brother; but the wicked uncle, in order to get the children's estate, contrived to have them destroyed by two ruffians whom he hired for that purpose; with an account of the heavy judgments of God, which befell him, for this inhuman deed, and of the untimely end of the two bloody ruffians. To which is added a word of advice to executors, &c.

Now ponder well, you parents dear,
These words which I do write;
A doleful story you shall hear,
In time, brought forth to light.

A gentleman of good account
In Norfolk lived of late,
Whose fame and credit did surmount
Most men of his estate.

So sick he was, and like to die,
No help he then could have;
His wife by him as sick did lie,
And both possess one grave.

No love between these two was lost,
Each was to other kind;
In love they lived, in love they died,
And left two babes behind;—

The one a fine and pretty boy,
Not passing three years old;
The other a girl more young than he,
And made of beauteous mould.

The father left his little son,
As plainly doth appear,
When he to perfect age should come,
Three hundreds pounds a year.

And to his little daughter Jane
Two hundred pounds in gold,
For to be paid on marriage day,
Which might not be controlled.

But, if these children chanced to die
Ere they to age did come,
The uncle should possess the wealth;
For so the will did run.

"Now, brother," said the dying man,
"Look to my children dear,
Be good unto my boy and girl:
No friend else have I here.

"To God and you I do commend
  My children night and day:
A little while be sure we have
  Within this world to stay.

"You must be father, mother both,
  "And uncle, all in one;
God knows what will become of them
  When I am dead and gone."

With that bespoke the mother dear,
  "O brother kind!" quoth she,
"You are the man must bring my babes
  To wealth or misery.

"If you do keep them carefully,
  Then God will you reward:
If otherwise you seem to deal,
  God will your deeds regard."

With lips as cold as any stone,
  She kissed her children small;
"God bless you both, my children dear!"
  With that the tears did fall.

These speeches then the brother spoke
  To the sick couple there;
"The keeping of your children dear,
  Sweet sister, never fear.

"God never prosper me nor mine,
  Nor aught else that I have,
If I do wrong your children dear,
  When you're laid in the grave."

The parents being dead and gone,
  The children home he takes,
And brings them home unto his house,
  And much of them he makes.

He had not kept these pretty babes
  A twelvemonth and a day,
But for their wealth he did devise
  To make them both away.

He bargained with two ruffians rude,
  Who were of furious mood,
That they should take these children young,
  And slay them in a wood;

And told his wife and all he had,
  He did those children send,
To be brought up in fair London,
  With one that was his friend.

Away then went these pretty babes,
  Rejoicing at the tide,
And smiling with a merry mind,
  They on cock-horse should ride.

They prate and prattle pleasantly
  As they rode on the way,
To them that should their butchers be,
  And work their lives' decay.

So that the pretty speech they had
  Made murderers' hearts relent;
And they that took the deed to do,
  Full sore they did repent.

Yet one of them, more hard of heart,
  Did vow to do his charge,
Because the wretch that hired him
  Had paid him very large.

The other would not agree thereto,
  So here they fell in strife:
With one another they did fight
  About the children's life.

And he that was of mildest mood
  Did slay the other there,
Within an unfrequented wood,
  Where babes do quake for fear.

He took the children by the hand,
  When tears stood in their eye,
And bid them come, and go with him,
  And see they did not cry.

And two long miles he led them thus,
  While they for bread complain;
"Stay here," quoth he: "I'll bring you bread
  When I do come again."

These pretty babes, with hand in hand,
  Went wandering up and down;
But never more they saw the man
  Approaching from the town.

Their pretty lips with blackberries
  Were all besmeared and dyed;
But, when they saw the darksome night,
  They sat them down and cried.

Thus wandered these two little babes,
  Till death did end their grief:
In one another's arms they died,
  As babes wanting relief.

No burial these pretty babes
  Of any man receives;
But robin red-breast painfully
  Did cover them with leaves.

And now the heavy wrath of God
  Upon the uncle fell;
Yea, fearful fiends did haunt his house,
  His conscience felt a hell.

His barns were fired, his goods consumed,
  His lands were barren made;
His cattle died within the field,
  And nothing with him staid.

And in a voyage to Portugal,
  Two of his sons did die;
And to conclude, himself was brought
  Unto much misery.

He pawned and mortgaged all his lands
  Ere seven years came about;
And now at length, this wicked act
  By this means did come out:

The fellow that did take in hand
  These children for to kill
Was for a robbery judged to die,
  As was God's blessed will.

Who did confess the very truth
  That is herein expressed:
The uncle died, where he, for debt,
  Did in the prison rest.

A WORD OF ADVICE TO EXECUTORS.

All ye who be executors made,
  And overseërs eke,
Of children that be fatherless,
  And infants mild and meek,

Take you example by this thing,
  And yield to each his right;
Lest God, by such like misery,
  Your wicked deeds requite.

THE CHIMNEY-SWEEP.

Sweep ho! Sweep ho!
He trudges on through sleet and snow.

Tired and hungry both is he,
And he whistles vacantly.

Sooty black his rags and skin,
But the child is fair within.

Ice and cold are better far
Than his master's curses are.

Mother of this little one,
Could'st thou see thy little son!

Sweep ho! Sweep ho!
He trudges on through sleet and snow.

At the great man's door he knocks,
Which the servant maid unlocks.

Now let in with laugh and jeer,
In his eye there stands a tear.

He is young, but soon will know
How to bear both word and blow.

Sweep ho! Sweep ho!
In the chimney sleet and snow.

Gladly should his task be done,
Were't the last beneath the sun.

Faithfully it now shall be,
But, soon spent, down droppeth he.

Gazes round as in a dream,
Very strange, but true, things seem.

Led by a fantastic power
Which sets by the present hour,

Creeps he to a little bed,
Pillows there his aching head,

And, poor thing! he does not know
There he lay long years ago!

E. S. H.

THE BOY OF EGREMOND.

"*What is good for a bootless bené?*"
With these dark words begins my tale;
And their meaning is, "Whence can comfort spring,
When prayer is of no avail?"

"*What is good for a bootless bené?*"
The falconer to the lady said;
And she made answer, "Endless sorrow!"
For she knew that her son was dead.

She knew it by the falconer's words,
And from the look of the falconer's eye;
And from the love which was in her soul
For her youthful Romilly.

— Young Romilly through Barden Woods
Is ranging high and low;
And holds a greyhound in a leash,
To let slip up on buck or doe.

The pair have reached that fearful chasm,
How tempting to bestride!
For lordly Wharf is there pent in
With rocks on either side.

This striding-place is called "the Strid,"
A name which it took of yore:
A thousand years hath it borne that name,
And shall, a thousand more.

And hither is young Romilly come,
And what may now forbid
That he, perhaps for the hundredth time,
Shall bound across "the Strid"?

He sprang in glee, — for what cared he
That the river was strong, and the rocks were steep!
— But the greyhound in the leash hung back,
And checked him in his leap.

The boy is in the arms of Wharf,
And strangled by a merciless force;
For never more was young Romilly seen
Till he rose a lifeless corse.

Now there is stillness in the vale,
And long unspeaking sorrow:
Wharf shall be, to pitying hearts,
A name more sad than Yarrow.

If for a lover the lady wept,
A solace she might borrow
From death, and from the passion of death;
Old Wharf might heal her sorrow.

She weeps not for the wedding-day
Which was to be to-morrow:
Her hope was a farther-looking hope,
And hers is a mother's sorrow.

He was a tree that stood alone,
And proudly did its branches wave:
And the root of this delightful tree
Was in her husband's grave!

Long, long in darkness did she sit,
And her first words were, "Let there be
In Bolton, on the field of Wharf,
A stately Priory!"

The stately Priory was reared;
And Wharf, as he moved along,
To matins joined a mournful voice,
Nor failed at evensong.

And the lady prayed in heaviness
That looked not for relief!
But slowly did her succor come,
And a patience to her grief.

Oh! there is never sorrow of heart
That shall lack a timely end,
If but to God we turn and ask
Of Him to be our friend!

WORDSWORTH.

THE HIGH TIDE ON THE COAST OF LINCOLNSHIRE.

(1571.)

THE old mayor climbed the belfry tower,
The ringers ran by two, by three;
"Pull, if ye never pulled before;
Good ringers, pull your best," quoth he.
"Play uppe, play uppe, O Boston bells!
Ply all your changes, all your swells,
Play uppe 'The Brides of Enderby!'"

Men say it was a stolen tyde, —
The Lord that sent it, He knows all;
But in myne ears doth still abide
The message that the bells let fall:
And there was nought of strange, beside

The flights of mews and peewits pied,
By millions crouched on the old sea wall.

I sat and spun within the doore,
My thread brake off, I raised myne eyes;
The level sun, like ruddy ore,
Lay sinking in the barren skies;
And dark against day's golden death
She moved where Lindis wandereth, —
My sonne's faire wife, Elizabeth.

"Cusha! Cusha! Cusha!" calling,
Ere the early dews were falling,
Farre away I heard her song.
"Cusha! Cusha!" all along;
Where the reedy Lindis floweth,
Floweth, floweth,
From the meads where melick groweth
Faintly came her milking song. —

"Cusha! Cusha! Cusha!" calling,
"For the dews will soone be falling;
Leave your meadow grasses mellow,
Mellow, mellow;
Quit your cowslips, cowslips yellow;
Come uppe Whitefoot, come uppe Lightfoot,
Quit the stalks of parsley hollow,
Hollow, hollow;
Come uppe Jetty, rise and follow,
From the clovers lift your head;
Come uppe Whitefoot, come uppe Lightfoot,
Come uppe Jetty, rise and follow,
Jetty, to the milking shed."

If it be long, aye, long ago,
When I beginne to think howe long,
Againe I hear the Lindis flow,
Swift as an arrowe, sharpe and strong;
And all the aire it seemeth mee
Bin full of floating bells (sayth shee),
That ring the tune of Enderby.

Alle fresh the level pasture lay,
And not a shadowe mote be seene,
Save where full fyve good miles away
The steeple towered from out the greene;
And lo! the great bell farre and wide
Was heard in all the country side
That Saturday at eventide.

The swannerds where their sedges are
Moved on in sunset's golden breath,
The shepherde lads I heard afarre,
And my sonne's wife, Elizabeth;
Till floating o'er the grassy sea
Came downe that kyndly message free,
The "Brides of Mavis Enderby."

Then some looked uppe into the sky,
And all along where Lindis flows
To where the goodly vessels lie,
And where the lordly steeple shows.
They sayde, "And why should this thing be,
What danger lowers by land or sea?
They ring the tune of Enderby!

"For evil news from Màblethorpe,
Of pyrate galleys warping down;
For shippes ashore beyond the scorpe,
They have not spared to wake the towne;
But while the west bin red to see,
And storms be none, and pyrates flee,
Why ring 'The Brides of Enderby?'"

I looked without, and lo! my sonne
Came riding downe with might and main.
He raised a shout as he drew on,
Till all the welkin rang again,
"Elizabeth! Elizabeth!"
(A sweeter woman ne'er drew breath
Than my sonne's wife, Elizabeth.)

"The olde sea wall (he cried) is downe,
The rising tide comes on apace,
And boats adrift in yonder towne
Go sailing uppe the market-place."
He shook as one that looks on death:
"God save you, mother!" straight he saith;
"Where is my wife, Elizabeth?"

"Good sonne, where Lindis winds away
With her two bairns I marked her long;
And ere yon bells beganne to play,
Afar I heard her milking song."

He looked across the grassy sea,
To right, to left, "Ho Enderby!"
They rang "The Brides of Enderby!"

With that he cried and beat his breast;
For lo! along the river's bed
A mighty eygre reared his crest,
And uppe the Lindis raging sped.
It swept with thunderous noises loud;
Shaped like a curling snow-white cloud,
Or like a demon in a shroud.

And rearing Lindis backward pressed,
Shook all her trembling bankes amaine;
Then madly at the eygre's breast
Flung uppe her weltering walls again.
Then bankes came downe with ruin and rout, —
Then beaten foam flew round about, —
Then all the mighty floods were out.

So farre, so fast the eygre drave,
The heart had hardly time to beat,
Before a shallow seething wave
Sobbed in the grasses at our feet:
The feet had hardly time to flee
Before it brake against the knee,
And all the world was in the sea.

Upon the roofe we sate that night,
The noise of bells went sweeping by:
I marked the lofty beacon light
Stream from the church tower, red and high, —
A lurid mark and dread to see;
And awsome bells they were to mee,
That in the dark rang "Enderby."

They rang the sailor lads to guide
From roofe to roofe who fearless rowed;
And I, — my sonne was at my side,
And yet the ruddy beacon glowed:
And yet he moaned beneath his breath,
"O come in life, or come in death!
O lost! my love, Elizabeth."

And didst thou visit him no more?
Thou didst, thou didst my daughter deare!
The waters laid thee at his doore,
Ere yet the early dawn was clear.
Thy pretty bairns in fast embrace,
The lifted sun shone on thy face,
Downe drifted to thy dwelling-place.

That flow strewed wrecks about the grass;
That ebbe swept out the flocks to sea;
A fatal ebbe and flow, alas!
To manye more than myne and me:
But each will mourn his own, (she saith).
And sweeter woman ne'er drew breath
Than my sonne's wife, Elizabeth.

I shall never hear her more
By the reedy Lindis' shore,
"Cusha, Cusha, Cusha!" calling,
Ere the early dews be falling;
I shall never hear her song,
"Cusha, Cusha!" all along,
Where the sunny Lindis floweth,
Goeth, floweth;
From the meads where melick groweth,
When the water winding down,
Onward floweth to the town.

I shall never see her more
Where the reeds and rushes quiver,
Shiver, quiver:
Stand beside the sobbing river,
Sobbing, throbbing, in its falling,
To the sandy lonesome shore;
I shall never hear her calling,
"Leave your meadow grasses mellow,
Mellow, mellow;
Quit your cowslips, cowslips yellow;
Come uppe Whitefoot, come uppe Lightfoot;
Quit your pipes of parsley hollow,
Hollow, hollow;
Come uppe Lightfoot, rise and follow;
Lightfoot, Whitefoot,
From your clovers lift the head;
Come uppe Jetty, follow, follow,
Jetty, to the milking shed."

JEAN INGELOW.

BRISTOWE TRAGEDY; OR, THE DEATH OF SIR CHARLES BAWDIN.

I.

The feathered songster chanticleer
Had wound his bugle horn,
And told the early villager
The coming of the morn.

II.

King Edward sawe the ruddy streaks
Of light eclipse the grey;
And heard the raven's croaking throat
Proclaim the fated day.

III.

"Thou'rt right," quoth he, "for, by the God
That sits enthroned on high!
Charles Bawdin, and his fellows twain,
To-day shall surely die."

IV.

Then with a jug of nappy ale
His knights did on him wait.
"Go tell the traitor, that to-day
He leaves this mortal state."

V.

Sir Canterlone then bended low,
With heart brimful of woe;
He journeyed to the castle-gate,
And to Sir Charles did go.

VI.

But when he came, his children twain,
And eke his loving wife,
With briny tears did wet the floor,
For good Sir Charles's life.

VII.

"O good Sir Charles!" said Canterlone,
"Bad tidings do I bring."
"Speak boldly, man," said brave Sir Charles,
"What says thy traitor king?"

VIII.

"I grieve to tell, before yon sun
Does from the welkin fly,
He hath upon his honor sworn,
That thou shalt surely die."

IX.

"We all must die," quoth brave Sir Charles,
"Of that I'm not affeared;
What boots to live a little space?
Thank Jesu, I'm prepared;

X.

"But tell thy king, for mine he's not,
I'd sooner die to-day
Than live his slave, as many are,
Though I should live for aye."

XI.

Then Canterlone he did go out,
To tell the mayor straight
To get all things in readiness
For good Sir Charles's fate.

XII.

Then Master Canning sought the king,
And fell down on his knee:
"I'm come," quoth he, "unto your grace
To move your clemency."

XIII.

Then quoth the king, "Your tale speak out,
You have been much our friend;
Whatever your request may be,
We will to it attend."

XIV.

"My noble liege! all my request
Is for a noble knight,
Who, though mayhap he has done wrong,
He thought it still was right:

XV.

"He has a spouse and children twain,
All ruined are for aye,
If that you are resolved to let
Charles Bawdin die to-day."

XVI.

"Speak not of such a traitor vile,"
The king in fury said;
"Before the evening star doth shine,
Bawdin shall loose his head;

XVII.

"Justice does loudly for him call,
And he shall have his meed;
Speak, Master Canning! What thing else
At present do you need?"

XVIII.

"My noble liege," good Canning said,
"Leave justice to our God,
And lay the iron rule aside;
Be thine the olive rod.

XIX.

"Was God to search our hearts and reins,
The best were sinners great;
Christ's vicar only knows no sin,
In all this mortal state.

XX.

"Let mercy rule thine infant reign,
'Twill fast thy crown full sure;
From race to race thy family
All sovereigns shall endure:

XXI.

"But if with blood and slaughter thou
Begin thy infant reign,
Thy crown upon thy children's brows
Will never long remain."

XXII.

"Canning, away! this traitor vile
Has scorned my power and me;
How canst thou then for such a man
Intreat my clemency?"

XXIII.

"My noble liege! the truly brave
Will val'rous actions prize,
Respect a brave and noble mind,
Although in enemies."

XXIV.

"Canning, away! By God in Heaven,
That did my being give,
I will not taste a bit of bread
Whilst this Sir Charles doth live.

XXV.

"By Mary and all Saints in Heaven,
This sun shall be his last;"
Then Canning dropped a briny tear,
And from the presence passed.

XXVI.

With heart brimful of gnawing grief,
He to Sir Charles did go,
And sat him down upon a stool,
And teares began to flow.

XXVII.

"We all must die," quoth brave Sir Charles;
"What boots it how or when;
Death is the sure, the certain fate
Of all we mortal men.

XXVIII.

"Say, why, my friend, thy honest soul
Runs over at thine eye;
Is it for my most welcome doom
That thou dost child-like cry?"

XXIX.

Quoth godly Canning, "I do weep,
That thou so soon must die,
And leave thy sons and helpless wife;
'Tis this that wets mine eye."

XXX.

"Then dry the tears that out thine eye
From godly fountains spring;
Death I despise, and all the power
Of Edward, traitor king.

XXXI.

"When through the tyrant's welcome means
I shall resign my life,
The God I serve will soon provide
For both my sons and wife.

XXXII.

"Before I saw the lightsome sun,
This was appointed me;
Shall mortal man repine or grudge
What God ordains to be?

XXXIII.

"How oft in battle have I stood,
When thousands died around;
When smoking streams of crimson blood
Imbrued the fattened ground:

XXXIV.

"How did I know that every dart
That cut the airy way,
Might not find passage to my heart,
And close mine eyes for aye?

XXXV.

"And shall I now, for fear of death,
Look wan and be dismayed?
No! from my heart fly childish fear,
Be all the man displayed.

XXXVI.

"Ah! Godlike Henry! God forfend,
And guard thee and thy son,
If 'tis His will; but if 'tis not,
Why then His will be done.

XXXVII.

"My honest friend, my fault has been
To serve God and my prince;
And that I no time-server am,
My death will soon convince.

XXXVIII.

"In London city was I born,
Of parents of great note;
My father did a noble arms
Emblazon on his coat:

XXXIX.

"I make no doubt but he is gone
Where soon I hope to go;
Where we forever shall be blest,
From out the reach of woe:

XL.

"He taught me justice and the laws
With pity to unite;
And eke he taught me how to know
The wrong cause from the right:

XLI.

"He taught me with a prudent hand,
To feed the hungry poor,
Nor let my servant drive away
The hungry from my door:

XLII.

"And none can say but all my life
I have his wordys kept;
And summed the actions of the day
Each night before I slept.

XLIII.

"I have a spouse, go ask of her,
If I defiled her bed?
I have a king, and none can lay
Black treason on my head.

XLIV.

"In Lent, and on the holy eve,
From flesh I did refrain;
Why should I then appear dismayed
To leave this world of pain?

XLV.

"No! hapless Henry! I rejoice,
I shall not see thy death;
Most willingly in thy just cause
Do I resign my breath.

XLVI.

"Oh, fickle people! ruined land!
Thou wilt ken peace nae moe;
While Richard's sons exalt themselves,
Thy brooks with blood will flow.

XLVII.

"Say, were ye tired of godly peace,
And godly Henry's reign,
That you did chop your easy days
For those of blood and pain?

XLVIII.

"What though I on a sled be drawn,
And mangled by a hind?
I do defy the traitor's power,
He can not harm my mind;

XLIX.

"What though, uphoisted on a pole,
My limbs shall rot in air,
And no rich monument of brass
Charles Bawdin's name shall bear;

L.

"Yet in the holy book above,
Which time can't eat away,
There with the servants of the Lord
My name shall live for aye.

LI.

"Then welcome death! for life eterne
I leave this mortal life:
Farewell, vain world, and all that's dear,
My sons and loving wife!

LII.

"Now death as welcome to me comes,
As e'er the month of May;
Nor would I even wish to live,
With my dear wife to stay."

LIII.

Quoth Canning, "'Tis a goodly thing
To be prepared to die;
And from this world of pain and grief
To God in Heaven to fly."

LIV.

And now the bell began to toll,
And clarions to sound;
Sir Charles he heard the horses' feet
A prancing on the ground:

LV.

And just before the officers
His loving wife came in,
Weeping unfeignèd tears of woe,
With loud and dismal din.

LVI.

"Sweet Florence! now I pray, forbear, —
In quiet let me die;
Pray God that every Christian soul
May look on death as I.

LVII.

"Sweet Florence! why these briny tears?
They wash my soul away,
And almost make me wish for life,
With thee, sweet dame, to stay.

LVIII.

"'Tis but a journey I shall go
Unto the land of bliss;
Now, as a proof of husband's love,
Receive this holy kiss."

LIX.

Then Florence, faltering in her say,
Trembling these wordys spoke,
"Ah, cruel Edward! bloody king!
My heart is well nigh broke:

LX.

"Ah, sweet Sir Charles! why wilt thou go,
Without thy loving wife!
The cruel axe that cuts thy neck,
It eke shall end my life."

LXI.

And now the officers came in
To bring Sir Charles away,
Who turnèd to his loving wife,
And thus to her did say:

LXII.

"I go to life, and not to death;
Trust thou in God above,
And teach thy sons to fear the Lord,
And in their hearts Him love:

LXIII.

"Teach them to run the noble race
That I their father run:
Florence! should death thee take, — adieu!
Ye officers, lead on."

LXIV.

Then Florence raved as any mad,
And did her tresses tear;
"Oh! stay, my husband! lord! and life!" —
Sir Charles then dropped a tear.

LXV.

Till tired out with raving loud,
She fellen on the floor;
Sir Charles exerted all his might,
And marched from out the door.

LXVI.

Upon a sled he mounted then,
With looks full brave and sweet;
Looks that enshone ne more concern
Than any in the street.

LXVII.

Before him went the council-men,
In scarlet robes and gold,
And tassels spangling in the sun,
Much glorious to behold:

LXVIII.

The friars of Saint Augustine next
Appearèd to the sight,
All clad in homely russet weeds,
Of godly monkish plight:

LXIX.

In different parts a godly psalm
Most sweetly did they chant;
Behind their backs six minstrels came,
Who tuned the strung bataunt.

LXX.

Then five and twenty archers came;
Each one the bow did bend,
From rescue of King Henry's friends
Sir Charles for to defend.

LXXI.

Bold as a lion came Sir Charles,
Drawn on a cloth-laid sled,
By two black steeds in trappings white,
With plumes upon their head:

LXXII.

Behind him five and twenty more
Of archers strong and stout,
With bended bow each one in hand,
Marchèd in goodly rout:

LXXIII.

Saint James's Friars marchèd next,
Each one his part did chant;
Behind their backs six minstrels came,
Who tuned the strung bataunt:

LXXIV.

Then came the mayor and aldermen,
In cloth of scarlet decked;
And their attending-men each one,
Like Eastern princes trickt.

LXXV.

And after them a multitude
Of citizens did throng:
The windows were all full of heads,
As he did pass along.

LXXVI.

And when he came to the high cross,
Sir Charles did turn and say,
"O Thou, that savest man from sin,
Wash my soul clean this day!"

LXXVII.

At the great minster window sat
The king in mickle state,
To see Charles Bawdin go along
To his most welcome fate.

LXXVIII.

Soon as the sled drew nigh enough,
That Edward he might hear,
The brave Sir Charles he did stand up,
And thus his words declare:

LXXIX.

"Thou seest me, Edward! traitor vile!
Exposed to infamy;
But be assured, disloyal man!
I'm greater now than thee.

LXXX.

"By foul proceedings, murder, blood,
Thou wearest now a crown;
And hast appointed me to die,
By power not thine own.

LXXXI.

"Thou thinkest I shall die to-day;
I have been dead till now,
And soon shall live to wear a crown
For aye upon my brow;

LXXXII.

"Whilst thou, perhaps, for some few years,
Shall rule this fickle land,
To let them know how wide the rule
'Twixt king and tyrant hand:

LXXXIII.

"Thy power unjust, thou traitor slave!
Shall fall on thy own head" —
From out of hearing of the king
Departed then the sled.

LXXXIV.

King Edward's soule rushed to his face,
He turned his head away,
And to his brother Gloucester
He thus did speak and say:

LXXXV.

"To him that so-much-dreaded death
No ghastly terrors bring;
Behold the man! he spake the truth,
He's greater than a king!"

LXXXVI.

"So let him die!" Duke Richard said;
"And may each one our foes
Bend down their necks to bloody axe,
And feed the carrion crows."

LXXXVII.

And now the horses gently drew
Sir Charles up the high hill;
The axe did glister in the sun,
His precious blood to spill.

LXXXVIII.

Sir Charles did up the scaffold go,
As up a gilded car
Of victory, by val'rous chiefs
Gained in the bloody war:

LXXXIX.

And to the people he did say,
"Behold you see me die,
For serving loyally my king,
My king most rightfully.

XC.

"As long as Edward rules this land,
No quiet will you know;
Your sons and husbands shall be slain,
And brooks with blood shall flow.

XCI.

"You leave your good and lawful king,
When in adversity;
Like me, unto the true cause stick,
And for the true cause die."

XCII.

Then he, with priests, upon his knees,
A prayer to God did make,
Beseeching Him unto Himself
His parting soul to take.

XCIII.

Then, kneeling down, he laid his head
Most seemly on the block;
Which from his body fair at once
The able headsman stroke;

XCIV.

And out the blood began to flow,
And round the scaffold twine;
And tears, enough to wash't away,
Did flow from each man's eyne.

XCV.

The bloody axe his body fair
Into four partés cut;
And every part and eke his head,
Upon a pole was put.

XCVI.

One part did rot on Kynwulft-hill,
One on the minster tower,
And one from off the castle-gate
The crowen did devour;

XCVII.

The other on St. Powle's good gate,
A dreary spectacle;
His head was placed on the high cross,
In high-street most nobel.

XCVIII.

Thus was the end of Bawdin's fate:
God prosper long our king,
And grant he may, with Bawdin's soul,
In heaven God's mercy sing!

THOMAS CHATTERTON.

THE MASS.

WITH naked foot, and sackcloth vest,
And arms infolded on his breast,
Did every pilgrim go;
The standers-by might hear uneath,
Footstep, or voice, or high-drawn breath,
Through all the lengthened row:
No lordly look, nor martial stride,
Gone was their glory, sunk their pride,
Forgotten their renown;
Silent and slow, like ghosts, they glide
To the high altar's hallowed side,
And there they knelt them down:
Above the suppliant chieftains wave
The banners of departed brave;
Beneath the lettered stones were laid
The ashes of their fathers dead;
From many a garnished niche around,
Stern saints and tortured martyrs frowned.

And slow up the dim aisle afar,
With sable cowl and scapular,
And snow-white stoles, in order due,
The holy Fathers, two and two,
In long procession came:
Taper, and host, and book they bare,
And holy banner, flourished fair
With the Redeemer's name.
Above the prostrate pilgrim band
The mitred Abbot stretched his hand,
And blessed them as they kneeled;
With holy cross he signed them all,
And prayed they might be sage in hall,
And fortunate in field.
Then mass was sung, and prayers were said,
And solemn requiem for the dead;
And bells tolled out their mighty peal,
For the departed spirit's weal;
And ever in the office close
The hymn of intercession rose;
And far the echoing aisles prolong
The awful burden of the song, —
DIES IRÆ, DIES ILLA
SOLVET SÆCLUM IN FAVILLA;
While the pealing organ rung;
Were it meet with sacred strain
To close my lay, so light and vain,
Thus the holy Fathers sung: —

HYMN FOR THE DEAD.

That day of wrath, that dreadful day,
When heaven and earth shall pass away,
What power shall be the sinner's stay?
How shall he meet that dreadful day?

When, shrivelling like a parchèd scroll,
The flaming heavens together roll;
When louder yet, and yet more dread,
Swells the high trump that wakes the dead!

Oh! on that day, that wrathful day,
When man to judgment wakes from clay,
Be THOU the trembling sinner's stay,
Though heaven and earth shall pass away!

SCOTT.

FRIAR OF ORDERS GRAY.

"AND whither would you lead me then?"
Quoth the Friar of orders gray;
And the ruffians twain replied again,
"By a dying woman to pray." —

"I see," he said, "a lovely sight,
A sight bodes little harm,
A lady as a lily bright,
With an infant on her arm." —

"Then do thine office, Friar gray,
And see thou shrive her free!
Else shall the sprite that parts to-night,
Fling all its guilt on thee.

"Let mass be said, and trentals read,
When thou'rt to convent gone,
And bid the bell of St. Benedict
Toll out its deepest tone."

The shrift is done, the Friar is gone,
Blindfolded as he came; —
Next morning all, in Littlecot Hall
Were weeping for their dame.

Wild Darrell is an altered man,
The village crones can tell;
He looks pale as clay, and strives to pray,
If he hears the convent bell.

If prince or peer cross Darrell's way,
He'll beard him in his pride; —
If he meet a Friar of orders gray,
He droops and turns aside.

SCOTT.

GRÆME AND BEWICK.

GUDE Lord Græme is to Carlisle gane:
Sir Robert Bewick there met he;
And arm in arm to the wine they did go,
And they drank till they were baith merrie.

Gude Lord Græme has ta'en up the cup,
"Sir Robert Bewick, and here's to thee!
And here's to our twae sons at hame!
For they like us best in our ain countrie." —

"O were your son a lad like mine,
And learned some books that he could read,
They might hae been twae brethren bauld,
And they might hae bragged the Border side.

"But your son's a lad, and he is but bad,
And billie to my son he canna be:

. . . .

"Ye sent him to school, and he wadna learn:
Ye bought him books, and he wadna read." —
"But my blessing shall he never earn,
Till I see how his arm can defend his head." —

Gude Lord Græme has a reckoning called;
A reckoning then called he;
And he paid a crown, and it went roun';
It was all for the gude wine and free.

And he has to the stable gane,
Where there stude thirty steeds and three;
He's ta'en his ain horse amang them a',
And hame he rade sae manfullie.

"Welcome, my auld father!" said Christie Græme,
"But where sae lang frae hame were ye?" —
"It's I hae been at Carlisle town,
And a baffled man by thee I be.

"I hae been at Carlisle town,
Where Sir Robert Bewick he met me;
He says ye're a lad, and ye are but bad,
And billie to his son ye canna be.

"I sent ye to school, and ye wadna learn;
I bought ye books, and ye wadna read;
Wherefore my blessing ye shall never earn,
Till I see with Bewick thou save thy head."

"Now, God forbid, my auld father;
That ever sic a thing suld be!
Billie Bewick was my master, and I was his scholar,
And aye sae weel as he learned me." —

"O hald thy tongue, thou limmer loon,
And of thy talking let me be!
If thou does na end me this quarrel soon,
There is my glove, I'll fight wi' thee." —

Then Christie Græme he stoopèd low
Unto the ground, you shall understand; —
"O father, put on your glove again,
The wind has blown it from your hand?" —

"What's that thou says, thou limmer loon?
How dares thou stand to speak to me?
If thou do not end this quarrel soon,
There's my right hand, thou shalt fight with me." —

Then Christie Græme's to his chamber gane,
To consider weel what then should be;
Whether he should fight with his auld father,
Or with his billie Bewick, he.

"If I suld kill my billie dear,
God's blessing I shall never win;
But if I strike at my auld father,
I think 'twald be a mortal sin.

"But if I kill my billie dear,
It is God's will, so let it be;
But I make a vow, ere I gang frae hame,
That I shall be the next man's die." —

Then he's put on's back a gude auld jack,
And on his head a cap of steel,
And sword and buckler by his side;
O gin he did not become them weel!

We'll leave off talking of Christie Græme,
And talk of him again belive;
And we will talk of bonny Bewick,
Where he was teaching his scholars five.

When he had taught them well to fence,
And handle swords without any doubt,
He took his sword under his arm,
And he walked his father's close about.

He looked atween him and the sun,
And a' to see what there might be,
Till he spied a man in armour bright,
Was riding that way most hastilie.

"O wha is yon that came this way,
Sae hastilie that hither came?
I think it be my brother dear!
I think it be young Christie Græme. —

"Ye're welcome here, my billie dear,
And thrice ye're welcome unto me!" —
"But I'm wae to say, I've seen the day,
When I am come to fight wi' thee.

"My father's gane to Carlisle town,
Wi' your father Bewick there met he:
He says I'm a lad, and I am but bad,
And a baffled man I trow I be.

"He sent me to school, and I wadna learn;
He gae me books, and I wadna read;
Sae my father's blessing I'll never earn,
Till he see how my arm can guard my head." —

"O God forbid, my billie dear,
That ever such a thing suld be!
We'll take three men on either side,
And see if we can our fathers agree." —

"O hald thy tongue, now, billie Bewick,
And of thy talking let me be!
But if thou'rt a man, as I'm sure thou art,
Come o'er the dyke, and fight wi' me." —

"But I hae nae harness, billie, on my back,
As weel I see there is on thine." —
"But as little harness as is on thy back,
As little, billie, shall be on mine." —

Then he's thrown aff his coat o' mail
His cap of steel away flung he;
He stuck his spear into the ground,
And he tied his horse unto a tree.

Then Bewick has thrown aff his cloak,
And's psalter-book frae's hand flung he;
He laid his hand upon the dyke,
And ower he lap most manfullie.

O they hae fought for twae lang hours;
When twae lang hours were come and gane,
The sweat drapped fast frae aff them baith,
But a drap of blude could not be seen.

Till Græme gae Bewick an ackward stroke,
Ane ackward stroke strucken sickerlie;
He has hit him under the left breast,
And dead-wounded to the ground fell he.

"Rise up, rise up, now, billie dear!
Arise and speak three words to me! —
Whether thou's gotten thy deadly wound,
Or if God and good leeching may succour thee?" —

"O horse, O horse, now, billie Græme,
And get thee far from hence with speed:
And get thee out of this country,
That none may know who has done the deed." —

"O I hae slain thee, billie Bewick,
If this be true thou tellest to me;
But I made a vow, ere I came frae hame,
That aye the next man I wad be."

He has pitched his sword in a moodie-hill,
And he has leaped twenty lang feet and three,
And on his ain sword's point he lap,
And dead upon the ground fell he.

'Twas then came up Sir Robert Bewick,
And his brave son alive saw he;
"Rise up, rise up, my son," he said,
"For I think ye hae gotten the victorie." —

"O hald your tongue, my father dear!
Of your prideful talking let me be!
Ye might hae drunken your wine in peace,
And let me and my billie be.

"Gae dig a grave, baith wide and deep,
And a grave to hald baith him and me;
But lay Christie Græme on the sunny side,
"For I'm sure he wan the victorie."

"Alack! a wae!" auld Bewick cried.
"Alack! was I not much to blame?
I'm sure I've lost the liveliest lad
That e'er was born unto my name."

"Alack! a wae!" quo' gude Lord Græme,
"I'm sure I hae lost the deeper lack!
I durst hae ridden the Border through,
Had Christie Græme been at my back.

"Had I been led through Liddesdale,
And thirty horseman guarding me,
And Christie Græme been at my back,
Sae soon as he had set me free!

"I've lost my hopes, I've lost my joy,
I've lost the key but and the lock:
I durst hae ridden the world round,
Had Christie Græme been at my back."

SCOTT'S BORDER MINSTRELSY.

KING JOHN AND THE ABBOT OF CANTERBURY.

AN ancient story I'll tell you anon
Of a notable prince that was called King John;
And he ruled England with main and with might,
For he did great wrong, and maintained little right.

And I'll tell you a story, a story so merry
Concerning the Abbot of Canterbúry;
How for his house-keeping and high renown,
They rode poste for him to fair London towne.

An hundred men the king did heare say,
The abbot kept in his house every day;
And fifty golde chaynes without any doubt,
In velvet coates waited the abbot about.

"How now, father abbot, I heare it of thee,
Thou keepest a farre better house than mee;
And for thy house-keeping and high renowne,
I feare thou work'st treason against my crown."

"My liege" quo' the abbot, "I would it were knowne
I never spend nothing, but what is my owne;
And I trust your grace will doe me no deere,
For spending of my owne true-gotten geere."

"Yes, yes, father abbot, thy fault it is highe,
And now for the same thou needest must dye;
For except thou canst answer me questions three,
Thy head shall be smitten from thy bodie.

"And first," quo' the king, "when I'm in this stead,
With my crowne of golde so faire on my head,
Among all my liege-men so noble of birthe,
Thou must tell me to one penny what I am worthe.

"Secondly, tell me, without any doubt,
How soone I may ride the whole world about;
And at the third question thou must not shrink,
But tell me here truly what I do think."

"O these are hard questions for my shallow witt.
Nor I cannot answer your grace as yet:
But if you will give me but three weeks space,
Ile do my endeavour to answer your grace."

"Now three weeks space to thee will I give,
And that is the longest time thou hast to live;
For if thou dost not answer my questions three,
Thy lands and thy livings are forfeit to mee."

Away rode the abbot all sad at that word,
And he rode to Cambridge, and Oxenford;
But never a doctor there was so wise,
That could with his learning an answer devise.

Then home rode the abbot of comfort so cold,
And he met his shepheard a-going to fold:
"How now, my lord abbot, you are welcome home;
What newes do you bring us from good King John?"

"Sad news, sad news, shepheard, I must give,
That I have but three days more to live;
For if I do not answer him questions three,
My head will be smitten from my body.

"The first is to tell him, there in that stead,
With his crowne of golde so fair on his head,
Among all his liege-men so noble of birth,
To within one penny of what he is worth.

"The seconde, to tell him without any doubt,
How soone he may ride this whole world about;
And at the third question I must not shrinke,
But tell him there truly what he does thinke."

"Now cheare up, sire abbot, did you never hear yet,
That a fool he may learne a wise man witt?
Lend me horse, and serving men, and your apparel,
And Ile ride to London to answere your quarrel.

"Nay frowne not, if it hath bin told unto me,
I am like your lordship, as ever may be;
And if you will but lend me your gowne,
There is none shall know us at fair London towne."

"Now horses and serving-men thou shalt have,
With sumptuous array most gallant and brave,
With crozier, and miter, and rochet, and cope,
Fit to appear 'fore our fader the pope."

"Now welcome, sire abbot," the king he did say,
"Tis well thou'rt come back to keepe thy day:
For and if thou canst answer my questions three,
Thy life and thy living both savèd shall be.

"And first, when thou seest me here in this stead,
With my crowne of golde so fair on my head,
Among all my liege-men so noble of birthe,
Tell me to one penny what I am worth."

"For thirty pence our Saviour was sold
Among the false Jewes, as I have bin told:
And twenty-nine is the worth of thee,
For I thinke thou art one penny worser than he."

The king he laughed, and swore by St. Bittel,
"I did not think I had been worth so littel!
—Now secondly tell me, without any doubt,
How soone I may ride this whole world about."

"You must rise with the sun, and ride with the same
Until the next morning he riseth againe;
And then your grace need not make any doubt
But in twenty-four hours you'll ride it about."

The king he laughed, and swore by St. Jone,
"I did not think it could be gone so soone!
—Now from the third question thou must not shrinke,
But tell me here truly what I do thinke."

"Yea, that shall I do, and make your grace merry;
You thinke I'm the abbot of Canterbúry;
But I'm his poor shepheard, as plain you may see,
That am come to beg pardon for him and for me."

The king he laughed, and swore by the Masse,
"Ile make thee lord abbot this day in his place!"
"Now naye, my liege, be not in such speede,
For alacke I can neither write ne reade."

"Four nobles a week, then I will give thee,
For this merry jest thou hast showne unto me;
And tell the old abbot when thou comest home,
Thou hast brought him a pardon from good King John."

Percy's Reliques.

THE SALLY FROM COVENTRY.

"Passion o' me!" cried Sir Richard Tyrone,
Spurning the sparks from the broad paving-stone,
"Better turn nurse and rock children to sleep,
Than yield to a rebel old Coventry Keep.
No, by my halidom, no one shall say,
Sir Richard Tyrone gave a city away."

Passion o' me! how he pulled at his beard!
Fretting and chafing if any one sneered,
Clapping his breastplate and shaking his fist,
Giving his grizzly moustachios a twist,
Running the protocol through with his steel,
Grinding the letter to mud with his heel.

Then he roared out for a pottle of sack,
Clapped the old trumpeter twice on the back,
Leaped on his bay with a dash and a swing,
Bade all the bells in the city to ring,
And when the red flag from the steeple went down,
Open they flung every gate in the town.

To boot! and to horse! and away like a flood,
A fire in their eyes, and a sting in their blood;
Hurrying out with a flash and a flare,
A roar of hot guns, a loud trumpeter's blare,
And first, sitting proud as a king on his throne,
At the head of them all dashed Sir Richard Tyrone.

Crimson, and yellow, and purple and dun,
Fluttering scarf, flowing bright in the sun,
Steel like a mirror on brow and on breast,
Scarlet and white on their feather and crest,
Banner that blew in a torrent of red,
Borne by Sir Richard, who rode at their head.

The "trumpet" went down—with a gash on his poll,
Struck by the parters of body and soul.
Forty saddles were empty; the horses ran red
With foul Puritan blood from the slashes that bled.

Curses and cries and a gnashing of teeth,
A grapple and stab on the slippery heath,
And Sir Richard leaped up on the fool that went down,
Proud as a conqueror donning his crown.
They broke them away through a flooding of fire,
Trampling the best blood of London to mire,
When suddenly rising a smoke and a blaze.
Made all "the dragon's sons" stare in amaze:
"O ho!" quoth Sir Richard, "my city grows hot,
I've left it rent-paid to the villainous Scot."

ANONYMOUS.

HOW THEY BROUGHT THE GOOD NEWS FROM GHENT TO AIX.

I SPRANG to the stirrup, and Joris and he;
I galloped, Dirck galloped, we galloped all three;
"Good speed!" cried the watch as the gate-bolts undrew,
"Speed!" echoed the wall to us galloping through;
Behind shut the postern, the lights sank to rest,
And into the midnight we galloped abreast.

Not a word to each other: we kept the great pace
Neck and neck, stride by stride, never changing our place.
I turned in my saddle and made its girths tight,
Then shortened each stirrup and set the pique right,
Re-buckled the check-strap, chained slacker the bit;
Nor galloped less steadily Roland a whit.

'Twas moonset at starting, but while we drew near
Lokeren, the cocks crew, and twilight dawned clear;
At Boom, a great yellow star came out to see,

At Duffield, 'twas morning as plain as could be;
And from Mecheln church-steeple we heard the half chime;
So Joris broke silence with "Yet there is time."

At Aerschot, up leaped of a sudden the sun,
And against him the cattle stood black every one
To stare through the mist at us galloping past,
And I saw my stout galloper, Roland, at last,
With resolute shoulders each butting away
The haze, as some bluff river headland its spray.

And his low head and crest, just one sharp ear bent back
For my voice, and the other pricked out on his track;
And one eye's black intelligence, — ever that glance
O'er its white edge at me, its own master, askance!
And the thick heavy spume-flakes, which aye and anon
His fierce lips shook upwards in galloping on.

By Hasselt, Dirck groaned; and cried Joris, "Stay spur!
Your Roos galloped bravely, the fault's not in her,
We'll remember at Aix;" — for one heard the quick wheeze
Of her chest, saw the stretched neck and staggering knees,
And sunk tail, and horrible heave of the flank,
As down on her haunches she shuddered and sank.

So we were left galloping, Joris and I,
Past Looz and past Tongres, no cloud in the sky;
The broad sun above laughed a pitiless laugh,
'Neath our feet broke the brittle bright stubble like chaff;
Till over by Dalhelm a dome-spire sprang white,
And "Gallop," gasped Joris, "for Aix is in sight!"

"How they'll greet us!" — and all in a moment his roan
Rolled neck and croup over, lay dead as a stone,
And there was my Roland to bear the whole weight
Of the news, which alone could save Aix from her fate,
With his nostrils like pits full of blood to the brim,
And with circles of red for his eye-socket's rim.

Then I cast loose my buff coat, each holster let fall,
Shook off both my jack-boots, let go belt and all,
Stood up in the stirrup, leaned, patted his ear,
Called my Roland his pet name, my horse without peer;
Clapped my hands, laughed and sang, any noise bad or good,
Till at length into Aix Roland galloped and stood.

And all I remember is friends flocking round,
As I sate with his head 'twixt my knees on the ground,
And no voice but was praising this Roland of mine,
As I poured down his throat our last measure of wine,
Which, (the burgesses voted by common consent,)
Was no more than his due who brought good news from Ghent.

ROBERT BROWNING.

LOCHINVAR.

O, YOUNG Lochinvar is come out of the west,
Through all the wide Border his steed was the best;
And save his good broadsword, he weapon had none,
He rode all unarmed, and he rode all alone.
So faithful in love, and so dauntless in war,
There never was knight like the young Lochinvar.

He staid not for brake, and he stopped not for stone,
He swam the Eske river where ford there was none;
But ere he alighted at Netherby gate,
The bride had consented, the gallant came late;
For a laggard in love, and a dastard in war,
Was to wed the fair Ellen of brave Lochinvar.

So boldly he entered the Netherby Hall,
Among bridesmen, and kinsmen, and brothers and all:
Then spoke the bride's father, his hand on his sword,
(For the poor craven bridegroom said never a word,)
"O come ye in peace here, or come ye in war,
Or to dance at our bridal, young Lord Lochinvar?"—

"I long wooed your daughter, my suit you denied;—
Love swells like the Solway, but ebbs like its tide—
And now am I come, with this lost love of mine,
To lead but one measure, drink one cup of wine.
There are maidens in Scotland more lovely by far,
That would gladly be bride to the young Lochinvar."

The bride kissed the goblet: the knight took it up,
He quaffed off the wine, and he threw down the cup.
She looked down to blush, and she looked up to sigh,
With a smile on her lips, and a tear in her eye.
He took her soft hand, ere her mother could bar,—
"Now tread we a measure!" said young Lochinvar.

So stately his form, and so lovely her face,
That never a hall such a galliard did grace;
While her mother did fret, and her father did fume,
And the bridegroom stood dangling his bonnet and plume;
And the bride-maidens whispered, "'Twere better by far,
To have matched our fair cousin with young Lochinvar."

One touch to her hand, and one word in her ear,
When they reached the hall-door, and the charger stood near;
So light to the croupe the fair lady he swung,
So light to the saddle before her he sprung!
"She is won! we are gone, over bank, bush, and scaur;
They'll have fleet steeds that follow," quoth young Lochinvar.

There was mounting 'mong Græmes of the Netherby clan;
Forsters, Fenwicks, and Musgraves, they rode and they ran:
There was racing and chasing on Cannobie Lee,
But the lost bride of Netherby ne'er did they see.
So daring in love, and so dauntless in war,
Have ye e'er heard of gallant like young Lochinvar?

SCOTT.

RHOTRUDA.

IN the golden reign of Charlemagne the king,
The three and thirtieth year, or thereabout,
Young Eginardus, bred about the court,
(Left mother-naked at a postern-door,)
Had thence by slow degrees ascended up;—
First page, then pensioner, lastly the king's knight
And secretary; yet held these steps for naught
Save as they led him to the Princess' feet,
Eldest and loveliest of the regal three,
Most gracious too, and liable to love:
For Bertha was betrothed; and she, the third,

Giselia, would not look upon a man.
So, bending his whole heart unto this end,
He watched and waited, trusting to stir to fire
The indolent interest in those large eyes,
And feel the languid hands beat in his own,
Ere the new spring. And well he played his part;
Slipping no chance to bribe, or brush aside,
All that would stand between him and the light;
Making fast foes in sooth, but feeble friends.
But what cared he, who had read of ladies' love,
And how young Launcelot gained his Guinevere;
A foundling too, or of uncertain strain?
And when one morning, coming from the bath,
He crossed the Princess on the palace-stair,
And kissed her there in her sweet disarray,
Nor met the death he dreamed of, in her eyes, —
He knew himself a hero of (old) romance;
Not seconding, but surpassing, what had been.

And so they loved; if that tumultuous pain
Be love, — disquietude of deep delight,
And sharpest sadness: nor though he knew her heart
His very own, — gained on the instant too,
And like a waterfall that at one leap
Plunges from pines to palms, — shattered at once
To wreaths of mist, and broken spray-bows bright,
He loved not less, nor wearied of her smile;
But through the daytime held aloof and strange
His walk; mingling with knightly mirth and game;
Solicitous but to avoid alone
Aught that might make against him in her mind;
Yet strong in this, — that, let the world have end,
He had pledged his own, and held Rhotruda's troth.

But Love, who had led these lovers thus along,
Played them a trick one windy night and cold:
For Eginardus, as his wont had been,
Crossing the quadrangle, and under dark, —
No faint moonshine, nor sign of any star, —
Seeking the Princess' door, such welcome found,
The knight forgot his prudence in his love;
For lying at her feet, her hands in his,
And telling tales of knightship and emprise,
And ringing war; while up the smooth white arm
His fingers slid insatiable of touch,
The night grew old: still of the hero-deeds
That he had seen, he spoke; and bitter blows
Where all the land seemed driven into dust!
Beneath fair Pavia's wall, where Loup beat down
The Longobard, and Charlemagne laid on,
Cleaving horse and rider; then, for dusty drought
Of the fierce tale, he drew her lips to his,
And silence locked the lovers fast and long,
Till the great bell crashed One into their dream.

The castle-bell! and Eginard not away!
With tremulous haste she led him to the door,
When, lo! the courtyard white with fallen snow,
While clear the night hung over it with stars.
A dozen steps, scarce that, to his own door:
A dozen steps? a gulf impassable!
What to be done? Their secret must not lie

Bare to the sneering eye with the first light;
She could not have his footsteps at her door!
Discovery and destruction were at hand:
And, with the thought, they kissed, and kissed again;
When suddenly the lady, bending, drew
Her lover towards her half-unwillingly,
And on her shoulders fairly took him there, —
Who held his breath to lighten all his weight, —
And lightly carried him the court-yard's length
To his own door; then, like a frightened hare,
Fled back in her own tracks unto her bower,
To pant awhile, and rest, that all was safe.

But Charlemagne the king, who had risen by night
To look upon memorials, or at ease
To read and sign an ordinance of the realm, —
The Fanolehen, or Cunigosteura
For tithing corn, so to confirm the same,
And stamp it with the pommel of his sword, —
Hearing their voices in the court below,
Looked from his window, and beheld the pair.

Angry, the king; yet laughing-half to view
The strangeness and vagary of the feat;
Laughing indeed! with twenty minds to call
From his inner bed-chamber the Forty forth,
Who watched all night beside their monarch's bed,
With naked swords and torches in their hands,
And test this lover's-knot with steel and fire;
But with a thought, "To-morrow yet will serve
To greet these mummers," softly the window closed,
And so went back to his corn-tax again.

But, with the morn, the king a meeting called
Of all his lords, courtiers and kindred too,
And squire and dame, — in the great Audience Hall
Gathered; where sat the king, with the high crown
Upon his brow; beneath a drapery
That fell around him like a cataract,
With flecks of colour crossed and cancellate;
And over this, like trees about a stream,
Rich carven-work, heavy with wreath and rose,
Palm and palmirah, fruit and frondage, hung.

And more the high Hall held of rare and strange;
For on the king's right hand Leæna bowed
In cloudlike marble, and beside her crouched
The tongueless lioness; on the other side,
And poising this, the second Sappho stood, —
Young Erexcéa, with her head discrowned,
The anadema on the horn of her lyre;
And by the walls there hung in sequence long
Merlin himself, and Uterpendragon,
With all their mighty deeds; down to the day
When all the world seemed lost in wreck and rout, —
A wrath of crashing steeds and men; and, in
The broken battle fighting hopelessly,
King Arthur, with the ten wounds on his head!

But not to gaze on these, appeared the peers.
Stern looked the king, and, when the court was met, —
The lady and her lover in the midst, —

Spoke to his lords, demanding them of this:
"What merits he, the servant of the king,
Forgetful of his place, his trust, his oath,
Who, for his own bad end, to hide his fault,
Makes use of her, a Princess of the realm,
As of a mule; — a beast of burthen! — borne
Upon her shoulders through the winter's night,
And wind and snow?" — "Death!" said the angry lords;
And knight and squire and minion murmured, "Death!"
Not one discordant voice. But Charlemagne,
Though to his foes a circulating sword,
Yet, as a king, mild, gracious, exorable,
Blest in his children too, with but one born
To vex his flesh like an ingrowing nail, —
Looked kindly on the trembling pair, and said:
"Yes, Eginardus, well hast thou deserved
Death for this thing; for, hadst thou loved her so,
Thou shouldst have sought her Father's will in this, —
Protector and disposer of his child, —
And asked her hand of him, her lord and thine.
Thy life is forfeit here; but take it, thou! —
Take even two lives for this forfeit one;
And thy fair portress — wed her; honour God,
Love one another, and obey the king."

Thus far the legend; but of Rhotrude's smile,
Or of the lords' applause, as truly they
Would have applauded their first judgment too,
We nothing learn: yet still the story lives;
Shines like a light across those dark old days,
Wonderful glimpse of woman's wit and love;
And worthy to be chronicled with hers
Who to her lover dear threw down her hair,
When all the garden glanced with angry blades!
Or like a picture framed in battle-pikes
And bristling swords, it hangs before our view; —
The palace-court white with the fallen snow,
The good king leaning out into the night
And Rhotrude bearing Eginard on her back.

TUCKERMAN.

GLENLOGIE.

THREE score o' nobles rade up the king's ha',
But bonnie Glenlogie's the flower o' them a',
Wi' his milk-white steed and his bonnie black e'e,
"Glenlogie, dear mither, Glenlogie for me!"

"O haud your tongue, daughter, ye'll get better than he;"
"O say nae sae, mither, for that canna be;
Though Doumlie is richer, and greater than he,
Yet if I maun tak him, I'll certainly dee.

"Where will I get a bonnie boy, to win hose and shoon,
Will gae to Glenlogie, and come again soon?"
"O here am I a bonnie boy, to win hose and shoon,
Will gae to Glenlogie and come again soon."

When he gaed to Glenlogie, 'twas "wash and go dine;"
'Twas "wash ye, my pretty boy, wash and go dine,"
"O 'twas ne'er my father's fashion, and it ne'er shall be mine
To gar a lady's hasty errand wait till I dine."

"But there is, Glenlogie, a letter for thee;"
The first line that he read, a low smile gave he,
The next line that he read, the tear blindit his e'e;
But the last line that he read, he gart the table flee.

"Gar saddle the black horse, gar saddle the brown;
Gar saddle the swiftest steed e'er rade frae a town;"
But lang ere the horse was drawn and brought to the green,
O bonnie Glenlogie was twa mile his lane.

When he came to Glenfeldy's door, little mirth was there;
Bonnie Jean's mother was tearing her hair;
"Ye're welcome, Glenlogie, ye're welcome," said she,
"Ye're welcome, Glenlogie, your Jeanie to see."

Pale and wan was she, when Glenlogie gaed ben,
But red and rosy grew she, whene'er he sat down;
She turned awa' her head, but the smile was in her e'e,
"O binna feared, mither, I'll maybe no dee."

SMITH'S SCOTTISH MINSTREL.

THE GAY GOSS-HAWK.

"O WALY, waly, my gay goss-hawk,
Gin your feathering be sheen!"
"And waly, waly, my master dear,
Gin ye look pale and lean!"

"O have ye tint, at tournament,
Your sword, or yet your spear?
Or mourn ye for the southern lass,
Whom ye may not win near?"

"I have not tint, at tournament,
My sword nor yet my spear;
But sair I mourn for my true love,
Wi' mony a bitter tear.

"But weel's me on ye, my gay goss-hawk,
Ye can baith speak and flee;
Ye sall carry a letter to my love,
Bring an answer back to me."

"But how sall I your true love find,
Or how suld I her know?
I bear a tongue ne'er wi' her spake,
An eye that ne'er her saw."

"O weel sall ye my true love ken,
Sae sune as ye her see;
For, of a' the flowers of fair England,
The fairest flower is she.

"The red, that's on my true love's cheek,
Is like blood-drops on the snaw;
The white, that is on her breast bare,
Like the down o' the white sea-maw.

"And even at my love's bouer-door
There grows a flowering birk;
And ye maun sit and sing thereon
As she gangs to the kirk.

"And four and twenty fair ladyes
Will to the mass repair;
But weel may ye my ladye ken,
The fairest ladye there."

Lord William has written a love-letter,
Put it under his pinion gray;
And he is awa to southern land
As fast as wings can gae.

And even at the ladye's bouer
There grew a flowering birk;
And he sat down and sung thereon
As she gaed to the kirk.

And weel he kent that ladye fair
Amang her maidens free;
For the flower that springs in May morning
Was not sae sweet as she.

He lighted at the ladye's gate,
And sat him on a pin;
And sang fu' sweet the notes o' love,
Till a' was cosh within.

And first he sang a low, low note,
And syne he sang a clear;
And aye the o'erword o' the sang
Was—"Your love can no win here."—

"Feast on, feast on, my maidens a',
The wine flows you amang,
While I gang to my shot-window,
And hear yon bonny bird's sang.

"Sing on, sing on, my bonny bird,
The sang ye sung yestreen;
For weel I ken, by your sweet singing,
Ye are frae my true love sen."

O first he sang a merry sang,
And syne he sang a grave;
And syne he picked his feathers gray,
To her the letter gave.

"Have there a letter from Lord William;
He says he's sent ye three;
He canna wait your love langer,
But for your sake he'll die." —

"Gae bid him bake his bridal bread,
And brew his bridal ale;
And I shall meet him at Mary's kirk,
Lang, lang ere it be stale."

The lady's gane to her chamber,
And a moanfu' woman was she;
As gin she had ta'en a sudden brash,
And were about to die.

"A boon, a boon, my father deir,
A boon I beg of thee!" —
"Ask not that haughty Scottish lord,
For him you ne'er shall see:

"But, for your honest asking else,
Weel granted it shall be." —
"Then gin I die in Southern land,
In Scotland gar bury me.

"And the first kirk that ye come to,
Ye's gar the mass be sung;
And the next kirk that ye come to,
Ye's gar the bells be rung.

"And when you come to St. Mary's kirk,
Ye's tarry there till night."
And so her father pledged his word,
And so his promise plight.

She has ta'en her to her bigly bouer
As fast as she could fare;
And she has drank a sleepy draught,
That she had mixed wi' care.

And pale, pale, grew her rosy cheek,
That was sae bright of blee,
And she seemed to be as surely dead
As any one could be.

Then spake her cruel step-minnie,
"Tak ye the burning lead,
And drap a drap on her bosome,
To try if she be dead."

They took a drap o' boiling lead,
They drapped it on her breast;
"Alas! alas!" her father cried,
She's dead without the priest."

She neither chattered with her teeth,
Nor shivered with her chin;
"Alas! alas!" her father cried,
"There is nae breath within."

Then up arose her seven brethren,
And hewed to her a bier;
They hewed it frae the solid aik,
Laid it o'er wi' silver clear.

Then up and gat her seven sisters,
And sewed to her a kell;
And every stitch that they put in
Sewed to a siller bell.

The first Scots kirk that they cam to,
They garr'd the bells be rung;
The next Scots kirk that they cam to,
They garr'd the mass be sung.

But when they cam to St. Mary's kirk,
There stude spearmen all in a raw;
And up and started Lord William,
The chieftane amang them a'.

"Set down, set down the bier," he said,
"Let me look her upon:"
But as soon as Lord William touched her hand,
Her colour began to come.

She brightened like the lily flower,
Till her pale colour was gone;
With rosy cheek, and ruby lip,
She smiled her love upon.

"A morsel of your bread, my lord,
And one glass of your wine;
For I hae fasted these three lang days,
All for your sake and mine. —

"Gae hame, gae hame, my seven bauld brothers,
Gae hame and blaw your horn!
I trow ye wad hae gi'en me the skaith,
But I've gi'en you the scorn.

"Commend me to my grey father,
That wished my saul gude rest;
But wae to my cruel step-dame,
Garr'd burn me on the breast."—

"Ah! woe to you, you light woman!
An ill death may ye die!
For we left father and sisters at hame
Breaking their hearts for thee."

SCOTT'S BORDER MINSTRELSY.

ALLEN-A-DALE.

ALLEN-A-DALE has no fagot for burning,
Allen-a-Dale has no furrow for turning,
Allen-a-Dale has no fleece for the spinning,
Yet Allen-a-Dale has red gold for the winning.
Come, read me my riddle! come, hearken my tale!
And tell me the craft of bold Allen-a-Dale.

The Baron of Ravensworth prances in pride,
And he views his domains upon Arkindale side.
The mere for his net, and the land for his game,
The chase for the wild, and the park for the tame;
Yet the fish of the lake, and the deer of the vale,
Are less free to Lord Dacre than Allen-a-Dale!

Allen-a-Dale was ne'er belted a knight,
Though his spur be as sharp, and his blade be as bright;
Allen-a-Dale is no baron or lord,
Yet twenty tall yeomen will draw at his word;
And the best of our nobles his bonnet will vail,
Who at Rere-cross on Stanmore meets Allen-a-Dale.

Allen-a-Dale to his wooing is come;
The mother, she asked of his household and home:
"Though the castle of Richmond stand fair on the hill,
My hall," quoth bold Allen, "shows gallanter still;
'Tis the blue vault of heaven, with its crescent so pale,
And with all its bright spangles!" said Allen-a-Dale.

The father was steel, and the mother was stone;
They lifted the latch, and they bade him be gone;
But loud, on the morrow, their wail and their cry:
He had laughed on the lass with his bonny black eye,
And she fled to the forest to hear a love-tale,
And the youth it was told by was Allen-a-Dale!

SCOTT.

GLENARA.

O, HEARD ye yon pibroch sound sad in the gale,
Where a band cometh slowly with weeping and wail?
'Tis the chief of Glenara laments for his dear;
And her sire and her people are called to her bier.

Glenara came first, with the mourners and shroud;
Her kinsmen they followed, but mourned not aloud;
Their plaids all their bosoms were folded around;
They marched all in silence,—they looked on the ground.

In silence they reached, over mountain and moor,
To a heath where the oak-tree grew lonely and hoar;
"Now here let us place the gray stone of her cairn;—
Why speak ye no word?" said Glenara the stern.

"And tell me, I charge ye, ye clan of my spouse,
Why fold ye your mantles, why cloud ye your brows?"

So spake the rude chieftain; no answer is made,
But each mantle, unfolding, a dagger displayed.

"I dreamt of my lady, I dreamt of her shroud,"
Cried a voice from the kinsmen, all wrathful and loud;
"And empty that shroud and that coffin did seem;
Glenara! Glenara! now read me my dream!"

O, pale grew the cheek of that chieftain, I ween,
When the shroud was unclosed and no lady was seen;
When a voice from the kinsmen spoke louder in scorn, —
'Twas the youth who had loved the fair Ellen of Lorn,

"I dreamt of my lady, I dreamt of her grief,
I dreamt that her lord was a barbarous chief;
On a rock of the ocean fair Ellen did seem;
Glenara! Glenara! now read me my dream!"

In dust low the traitor has knelt to the ground,
And the desert revealed where his lady was found;
From a rock of the ocean that beauty is borne;
Now joy to the house of fair Ellen of Lorn.

CAMPBELL.

FITZ TRAVER'S SONG.

'Twas All-soul's eve, and Surrey's heart beat high;
He heard the midnight bell with anxious start,
Which told the mystic hour, approaching nigh,
When wise Cornelius promised, by his art,
To show to him the ladye of his heart,
Albeit betwixt them roared the ocean grim;
Yet so the sage had hight to play his part,
That he should see her form in life and limb,
And mark, if still she loved, and still she thought of him.

Dark was the vaulted room of gramarye,
To which the wizard led the gallant knight,
Save that before a mirror, huge and high,
A hallowed taper shed a glimmering light
On mystic implements of magic might;
On cross, and character, and talisman,
And almagest, and altar, nothing bright:
For fitful was the lustre, pale and wan,
As watchlight by the bed of some departing man.

But soon, within that mirror huge and high,
Was seen a self-emitted light to gleam;
And forms upon its breast the earl 'gan spy,
Cloudy and indistinct, as feverish dream;
Till, slow arranging, and defined, they seem
To form a lordly and a lofty room,
Part lighted by a lamp with silver beam,
Placed by a couch of Agra's silken loom,
And part by moonshine pale, and part was hid in gloom.

Fair all the pageant, — but how passing fair
The slender form which lay on couch of Ind!
O'er her white bosom strayed her hazel hair,
Pale her dear cheek, as if for love she pined;
All in her night-robe loose she lay reclined,
And, pensive, read from tablet eburnine,
Some strain that seemed her inmost soul to find: —

That favored strain was Surrey's raptured line,
That fair and lovely form, the Lady Geraldine.

Slow rolled the clouds upon the lovely form,
And swept the goodly vision all away; —
So royal envy rolled the murky storm
O'er my beloved Master's glorious day.
Thou jealous, ruthless tyrant! Heaven repay
On thee, and on thy children's latest line,
The wild caprice of thy despotic sway,
The gory bridal bed, the plundered shrine,
The murdered Surrey's blood, the tears of Geraldine!

SCOTT.

LADY CLARA VERE DE VERE.

LADY Clara Vere de Vere,
Of me you shall not win renown:
You thought to break a country heart
For pastime, ere you went to town.
At me you smiled, but unbeguiled
I saw the snare, and I retired:
The daughter of a hundred Earls,
You are not one to be desired.

Lady Clara Vere de Vere,
I know you proud to bear your name,
Your pride is yet no mate for mine,
Too proud to care from whence I came.
Nor would I break for your sweet sake
A heart that dotes on truer charms.
A simple maiden in her flower
Is worth a hundred coats-of-arms.

Lady Clara Vere de Vere,
Some meeker pupil you must find,
For were you queen of all that is,
I could not stoop to such a mind.
You sought to prove how I could love,
And my disdain is my reply.
The lion on your old stone gates
Is not more cold to you than I.

Lady Clara Vere de Vere,
You put strange memories in my head.
Not thrice your branching limes have blown
Since I beheld young Laurence dead.
Oh your sweet eyes, your low replies:
A great enchantress you may be;
But there was that across his throat
Which you had hardly cared to see.

Lady Clara Vere de Vere,
When thus he met his mother's view,
She had the passions of her kind,
She spake some certain truths of you.
Indeed I heard one bitter word
That scarce is fit for you to hear;
Her manners had not that repose
Which stamps the caste of Vere de Vere.

Lady Clara Vere de Vere,
There stands a spectre in your hall:
The guilt of blood is at your door:
You changed a wholesome heart to gall.
You held your course without remorse,
To make him trust his modest worth,
And, last, you fixed a vacant stare,
And slew him with your noble birth.

Trust me, Clara Vere de Vere,
From yon blue heavens above us bent,
The gardener Adam and his wife
Smile at the claims of long descent.
Howe'er it be, it seems to me,
'Tis only noble to be good.
Kind hearts are more than coronets,
And simple faith than Norman blood.

I know you, Clara Vere de Vere;
You pine among your halls and towers:
The languid light of your proud eyes
Is wearied of the rolling hours.
In glowing health, with boundless wealth,
But sickening of a vague disease,
You know so ill to deal with time,
You needs must play such pranks as these.

Clara, Clara Vere de Vere,
  If Time be heavy on your hands,
Are there no beggars at your gate,
  Nor any poor about your lands?
Oh! teach the orphan-boy to read,
  Or teach the orphan-girl to sew,
Pray Heaven for a human heart,
  And let the foolish yeoman go.

TENNYSON.

LADY GERALDINE'S COURTSHIP.

A poet writes to his friend.—Place, a room in Wycombe Hall.—Time, late in the evening.

DEAR my friend and fellow-student,
    I would lean my spirit o'er you:
Down the purple of this chamber,
    tears should scarcely run at will:
I am humbled who was humble!
    Friend,—I bow my head before you!
You should lead me to my peasants!
    —but their faces are too still.

There's a lady,—an earl's daughter;
    she is proud and she is noble:
And she treads the crimson carpet,
    and she breathes the perfumed air;
And a kingly blood sends glances up
    her princely eye to trouble,
And the shadow of a monarch's
    crown is softened in her hair.

She has halls among the woodlands,
    she has castles by the breakers,
She has farms and she has manors,
    she can threaten and command,
And the palpitating engines snort in
    steam across her acres,
As they mark upon the blasted heaven
    the measure of her land.

There are none of England's daughters
    who can show a prouder presence;
Upon princely suitors praying, she
    has looked in her disdain:
She has sprung of English nobles, I
    was born of English peasants;
What was *I* that I should love her,—
    save for competence to pain!

I was only a poor poet, made for
    singing at her casement,
As the finches or the thrushes, while
    she thought of other things.
Oh, she walked so high above me,
    she appeared to my abasement,
In her lovely silken murmur, like an
    angel clad in wings!

Many vassals bow before her as her
    carriage sweeps their doorways;
She has blest their little children,—
    as a priest or queen were she.
Far too tender, or too cruel far, her
    smile upon the poor was,
For I thought it was the same smile
    which she used to smile on me.

She has voters in the commons, she
    has lovers in the palace,—
And of all the fair court-ladies, few
    have jewels half as fine:
Oft the prince has named her beauty,
    'twixt the red wine and the chalice:
Oh, and what was *I* to love her? my
    Beloved, my Geraldine!

Yet I could not choose but love her,—
    I was born to poet uses,—
To love all things set above me, all
    of good and all of fair:
Nymphs of mountain, not of valley,
    we are wont to call the Muses,
And in nympholeptic climbing, poets
    pass from mount to star.

And because I was a poet, and because
    the people praised me,
With their critical deduction for the
    modern writer's fault;
I could sit at rich men's tables,—
    though the courtesies that raised me,
Still suggested clear between us the
    pale spectrum of the salt.

And they praised me in her presence:—"Will
    your book appear this summer?"
Then returning to each other, "Yes,
    our plans are for the moors;"
Then with whisper dropped behind
    me,—"There he is! the latest comer!
Oh, she only likes his verses! what
    is over, she endures.

"Quite low born! self-educated! somewhat gifted though by nature, —
And we make a point by asking him, of being very kind; —
You may speak, he does not hear you; and besides, he writes no satire, —
All these serpents kept by charmers, leave their natural sting behind."

I grew scornfuller, grew colder, as I stood up there among them,
Till, as frost intense will burn you, the cold scorning scorched my brow;
When a sudden silver speaking, gravely cadenced, overrung them,
And a sudden silken stirring touched my inner nature through.

I looked upward and beheld her! With a calm and regnant spirit,
Slowly round she swept her eyelids, and said clear before them all,
"Have you such superfluous honor, sir, that able to confer it,
You will come down, Mr. Bertram, as my guest to Wycombe Hall?"

Here she paused, — she had been paler at the first word of her speaking;
But because a silence followed it, blushed somewhat as for shame;
Then, as scorning her own feeling, resumed calmly — "I am seeking
More distinction than these gentlemen think worthy of my claim.

"Nevertheless, you see, I seek it — not because I am a woman,"
(Here her smile sprang like a fountain, and, so overflowed her mouth,)
"But because my woods in Sussex have some purple shades at gloaming
Which are worthy of a king in state, or poet in his youth.

"I invite you, Mr. Bertram, to no scene for worldly speeches, —
Sir, I scarce should dare, — but only where God asked the thrushes first, —
And if *you* will sing beside them, in the covert of my beeches,
I will thank you for the woodlands, . . . for the human world at worst."

Then she smiled around right childly, then she gazed around right queenly;
And I bowed, — I could not answer! Alternate light and gloom, —
While as one who quells the lions, with a steady eye serenely,
She, with level fronting eyelids, passed out stately from the room.

Oh, the blessed woods of Sussex, I can hear them still around me,
With their leafy tide of greenery still rippling up the wind!
Oh, the cursed woods of Sussex! where the hunter's arrow found me,
When a fair face and a tender voice had made me mad and blind!

In that ancient hall of Wycombe, thronged the numerous guests invited,
And the lovely London ladies trod the floors with gliding feet;
And their voices low with fashion, not with feeling, softly freighted
All the air about the windows, with elastic laughters sweet.

For at eve, the open windows flung their light out on the terrace,
Which the floating orbs of curtains did with gradual shadow sweep:
While the swans upon the river, fed at morning by the heiress,
Trembled downward through their snowy wings at music in their sleep.

And there evermore was music, both of instrument and singing;
Till the finches of the shrubberies grew restless in the dark;

But the cedars stood up motionless, each in a moonlight ringing,
And the deer, half in the glimmer, strewed the hollows of the park.

And though sometimes she would bind me with her silver-corded speeches,
To commix my words and laughter with the converse and the jest,
Oft I sat apart, and gazing on the river through the beeches,
Heard, as pure the swans swam down it, her pure voice o'er-float the rest.

In the morning, horn of huntsman, hoof of steed, and laugh of rider
Spread out cheery from the court-yard till we lost them in the hills;
While herself and other ladies, and her suitors left beside her,
Went a-wandering up the gardens through the laurels and abeles.

Thus, her foot upon the new-mown grass,—bareheaded,—with the flowing
Of the virginal white vesture gathered closely to her throat;
With the golden ringlets in her neck just quickened by her going,
And appearing to breathe sun for air, and doubting if to float,—

With a branch of dewy maple, which her right hand held above her,
And which trembled a green shadow in betwixt her and the skies,
As she turned her face in going, thus, she drew me on to love her,
And to worship the divineness of the smile hid in her eyes.

For her eyes alone smile constantly: her lips have serious sweetness,
And her front is calm, — the dimple rarely ripples on her cheek:
But her deep blue eyes smile constantly, — as if they in discreetness
Kept the secret of a happy dream she did not care to speak.

Thus she drew me the first morning, out across into the garden:
And I walked among her noble friends, and could not keep behind:
Spake she unto all and unto me, — "Behold, I am the warden
Of the song-birds in these lindens, which are cages to their mind.

"But within this swarded circle, into which the lime-walk brings us, —
Whence the beeches rounded greenly, stand away in reverent fear;
I will let no music enter, saving what the fountain sings us,
Which the lilies round the basin may seem pure enough to hear.

"The live air that waves the lilies waves this slender jet of water,
Like a holy thought sent feebly up from soul of fasting saint!
Whereby lies a marble Silence, sleeping! (Lough the sculptor wrought her,)
So asleep she is forgetting to say *Hush!* — a fancy quaint!

"Mark how heavy white her eyelids! not a dream between them lingers!
And the left hand's index droppeth from the lips upon the cheek:
And the right hand, — with the symbol rose held slack within the fingers, —
Has fallen back within the basin, — yet this Silence will not speak!

"That the essential meaning growing may exceed the special symbol,
Is the thought as I conceive it: it applies more high and low.
Our true noblemen will often through right nobleness grow humble,
And assert an inward honor by denying outward show."

"Nay, your Silence," said I, "truly holds her symbol rose but slackly,
Yet *she holds it* — or would scarcely be a Silence to our ken!

And your nobles wear their ermine on the outside, or walk blackly
In the presence of the social law, as most ignoble men.

"Let the poets dream such dreaming! Madam, in these British Islands,
'Tis the substance that wanes ever, 'tis the symbol that exceeds;
Soon we shall have nought but symbol! and for statues like this Silence,
Shall accept the rose's image, — in another case, the weed's."

"Not so quickly!" she retorted, — "I confess where'er you go, you
Find for things, names; — shows for actions, and pure gold for honor clear;
But when all is run to symbol in the Social, I will throw you
The world's book which now reads dryly, and sit down with Silence here."

Half in playfulness she spoke, I thought, and half in indignation;
Friends who listened laughed her words off while her lovers deemed her fair;
A fair woman — flushed with feeling, in her noble-lighted station
Near the statue's white reposing, — and both bathed in sunny air!

With the trees round, not so distant but you heard their vernal murmur,
And beheld in light and shadow the leaves in and outward move;
And the little fountain leaping toward the sun-heart to be warmer,
And recoiling in a tremble from the too much light above.

'Tis a picture for remembrance! and thus, morning after morning,
Did I follow as she drew me by the spirit to her feet, —
Why, her greyhound followed also! dogs — we both were dogs for scorning, —
To be sent back when she pleased it, and her path lay through the wheat.

And thus, morning after morning, spite of vows and spite of sorrow,
Did I follow at her drawing, while the week-days passed along;
Just to feed the swans this noontide, or to see the fawns to-morrow,
Or to teach the hill-side echo some sweet Tuscan in a song.

Ay, for sometimes on the hill-side, while we sat down in the gowans,
With the forest green behind us, and its shadow cast before;
And the river running under; and across it from the rowans
A brown partridge whirring near us, till we felt the air it bore, —

There, obedient to her praying, did I read aloud the poems
Made by Tuscan flutes, or instruments more various of our own;
Read the pastoral parts of Spenser, — or the subtle interflowings
Found in Petrarch's sonnets, — here's the book — the leaf is folded down! —

Or at times a modern volume, — Wordsworth's solemn-thoughted idyl,
Howitt's ballad-verse, or Tennyson's enchanted revery, —
Or from Browning some "Pomegranate," which, if cut deep down the middle,
Shows a heart within blood-tinctured, of a veined humanity.

Or at times I read there, hoarsely, some new poem of my making, —
Poets ever fail in reading their own verses to their worth, —
For the echo in you breaks upon the words which you are speaking,
And the chariot-wheels jar in the gate through which you drive them forth.

After, when we were grown tired of books, the silence round us flinging
A slow arm of sweet compression, felt with beatings at the breast,

She would break out on a sudden,
in a gush of woodland singing,
Like a child's emotion in a god, — a
naiad tired of rest.

Oh, to see or hear her singing! scarce
I know which is divinest, —
For her looks sing too, — she modulates
her gestures on the tune;
And her mouth stirs with the song,
like song; and when the notes
are finest,
'Tis the eyes that shoot out vocal
light, and seem to swell them
on.

Then we talked, — oh, how we talked!
her voice, so cadenced in the
talking,
Made another singing — of the soul!
a music without bars, —
While the leafy sounds of woodlands,
humming round where
we were walking,
Brought interposition worthy sweet,
— as skies about the stars.

And she spake such good thoughts
natural, as if she always
thought them, —
And had sympathies so rapid, open,
free as bird on branch,
Just as ready to fly east as west,
whichever way besought them,
In the birchen wood a chirrup, or a
cock-crow in the grange.

In her utmost rightness there is truth,
— and often she speaks lightly,
Has a grace in being gay, which even
mournful souls approve,
For the root of some grave earnest
thought is under-struck so
rightly,
As to justify the foliage and the
waving flowers above.

And she talked on, — *we* talked, rather!
upon all things — substance
— shadow —
Of the sheep that browsed the
grasses, — of the reapers in the
corn, —
Of the little children from the
schools, seen winding through
the meadow, —
Of the poor rich world beyond them,
still kept poorer by its scorn.

So of men, and so of letters, — books
are men of higher stature,
And the only men that speak aloud
for future times to hear:
So, of mankind in the abstract, which
grows slowly into nature,
Yet will lift the cry of "progress," as
it trod from sphere to sphere.

And her custom was to praise me
when I said, — "The Age culls
simples,
With a broad clown's back turned
broadly to the glory of the
stars —
We are gods by our own reck'ning, —
and may well shut up the
temples,
And wield on, amid the incense-steam,
the thunder of our cars.

"For we throw out acclamations of
self-thanking, self-admiring,
With, at every mile run faster, —
'O the wondrous, wondrous
age!'
Little thinking if we work our SOULS
as nobly as our iron,
Or if angels will commend us at the
goal of pilgrimage.

"Why, what *is* this patient entrance
into nature's deep resources,
But the child's most gradual learning
to walk upright without
bane?
When we drive out from the cloud
of steam, majestical white
horses,
Are we greater than the first men
who led black ones by the
mane?

"If we trod the deeps of ocean, if
we struck the stars in rising,
If we wrapped the globe intensely
with one hot electric breath,
'Twere but power within our *tether*, —
no new spirit-power comprising,
And in life we were not greater men,
nor bolder men in death."

She was patient with my talking;
and I loved her, loved her
certes,
As I loved all Heavenly objects,
with uplifted eyes and hands!

As I loved pure inspirations, — loved the graces, loved the virtues,
In a Love content with writing his own name on desert sands.

Or at least I thought so purely! — thought no idiot Hope was raising
Any crown to crown Love's silence,— silent Love that sat alone, —
Out, alas! the stag is like me, — he, that tries to go on grazing
With the great deep gun-wound in his neck, then reels with sudden moan.

It was thus I reeled! I told you that her hand had many suitors —
But she smiles them down imperially, as Venus did the waves; —
And with such a gracious coldness, that they cannot press their futures
On the present of her courtesy, which yieldingly enslaves.

And this morning, as I sat alone within the inner chamber,
With the great saloon beyond it lost in pleasant thought serene, —
For I had been reading Camoens — that poem you remember,
Which his lady's eyes are praised in, as the sweetest ever seen;

And the book lay open, and my thought flew from it, taking from it
A vibration and impulsion to an end beyond its own,
As the branch of a green osier, when a child would overcome it,
Springs up freely from his clasping and goes swinging in the sun.

As I mused I heard a murmur, — it grew deep as it grew longer —
Speakers using earnest language, — "Lady Geraldine, you *would!*"
And I heard a voice that pleaded ever on, in accents stronger,
As a sense of reason gave it power to make its rhetoric good.

Well I knew that voice, — it was an earl's, of soul that matched his station —
Soul completed into lordship,—might and right read on his brow:
Very finely courteous,—far too proud to doubt his domination
Of the common people, — he atones for grandeur by a bow.

High, straight forehead, nose of eagle, cold blue eyes, of less expression
Than resistance, coldly casting off the looks of other men,
As steel, arrows, — unelastic lips, which seem to taste possession,
And be cautious lest the common air should injure or distrain.

For the rest, accomplished, upright,— ay, and standing by his order
With a bearing not ungraceful; fond of art, and letters too;
Just a good man made a proud man, as the sandy rocks that border
A wild coast, by circumstances, in a regnant ebb and flow.

Thus I knew that voice, — I heard it — and I could not help the hearkening:
In the room I stood up blindly, and my burning heart within
Seemed to seethe and fuse my senses, till they ran on all sides darkening,
And scorchèd, weighed like melted metal round my feet that stood therein.

And that voice, I heard it pleading, for love's sake, — for wealth, position,
For the sake of liberal uses, and great actions to be done, —
And she interrupted gently, "Nay, my lord, the old tradition
Of your Normans, by some worthier hand than mine is, should be won."

"Ah, that white hand," he said quickly, — and in his he either drew it
Or attempted — for with gravity and instance she replied, —
"Nay, indeed, my lord, this talk is vain, and we had best eschew it,
And pass on like friends, to other points less easy to decide."

What he said again, I know not. It is likely that his trouble
Worked his pride up to the surface, for she answered in slow scorn, —
"And your lordship judges rightly. Whom I marry, shall be noble,
Ay, and wealthy. I shall never blush to think how he was born."

There, I maddened! her words stung me! Life swept through me into fever,
And my soul sprang up astonished; sprang full-statured in an hour:
Know you what it is when anguish, with apocalyptic NEVER,
To a Pythian height dilates you, — and despair sublimes to power?

From my brain the soul-wings budded! — waved a flame about my body,
Whence conventions coiled to ashes: I felt self-drawn out, as man,
From amalgamate false natures; and I saw the skies grow ruddy
With the deepening feet of angels, and I knew what spirits can.

I was mad, — inspired, — say either! anguish worketh inspiration,—
Was a man or beast — perhaps so; for the tiger roars when speared;
And I walked on, step by step, along the level of my passion —
Oh my soul! and passed the doorway to her face, and never feared.

He had left her, — peradventure, when my footstep proved my coming, —
But for *her*, — she half arose, then sat — grew scarlet and grew pale:
Oh she trembled! — 'tis so always with a worldly man or woman
In the presence of true spirits,— what else *can* they do but quail?

Oh, she fluttered like a tame bird, in among its forest brothers
Far too strong for it! then drooping, bowed her face upon her hands, —
And I spake out wildly, fiercely, brutal truths of her and others!
I, she planted in the desert, swathed her, windlike, with my sands.

I plucked up her social fictions, bloody-rooted though leaf-verdant,
Trod them down with words of shaming, — all the purple and the gold,
All the "landed stakes" and lordships, — all that spirits pure and ardent
Are cast out of love and honor because chancing not to hold.

"For myself I do not argue," said I, "though I love you, madam;
But for better souls that nearer to the height of yours have trod.
And this age shows to my thinking, still more infidels to Adam,
Than directly, by profession, simple infidels to God.

"Yet, O God," I said, "O grave," I said, "O mother's heart and bosom,
With whom first and last are equal, saint and corpse and little child!
We are fools to your deductions, in these figments of heart-closing!
We are traitors to your causes, in these sympathies defiled!

"Learn more reverence, madam, not for rank or wealth, — *that* needs no learning;
That comes quickly — quick as sin does, ay, and culminates to sin;
But for Adam's seed, MAN! Trust me, 'tis a clay above your scorning,
With God's image stamped upon it, and God's kindling breath within.

"What right have you, madam, gazing in your palace-mirror daily,
Getting so by heart your beauty, which all others must adore,
While you draw the golden ringlets down your fingers, to vow gayly
You will wed no man that's only good to God, — and nothing more?

"Why, what right have you, made fair by that same God, — the sweetest woman
Of all women He has fashioned, — with your lovely spirit-face,
Which would seem too near to vanish if its smile were not so human,
And your voice of holy sweetness, turning common words to grace,

"What right *can* you have, God's other works to scorn, despise, revile them
In the gross, as mere men, broadly, — not as *noble* men, forsooth, —
As mere Pariahs of the outer world, forbidden to assoil them
In the hope of living, dying, near that sweetness of your mouth?

"Have you any answer, madam? If my spirit were less earthly,
If its instrument were gifted with a better silver string,
I would kneel down where I stand, and say, — Behold me! I am worthy
Of thy loving, for I love thee! I am worthy as a king.

"As it is, — your ermined pride, I swear, shall feel this stain upon her, —
That *I*, poor, weak, tost with passion, scorned by me and you again,
Love you, Madam, — dare to love you, — to my grief and your dishonor, —
To my endless desolation, and your impotent disdain!"

More mad words like these, — more madness! friend, I need not write them fuller;
And I hear my hot soul dropping on the lines in showers of tears —
Oh, a woman! friend, a woman! Why, a beast had scarce been duller
Than roar bestial loud complaints against the shining of the spheres.

But at last there came a pause. I stood all vibrating with thunder
Which my soul had used. The silence drew her face up like a call.
Could you guess what word she uttered? She looked up, as if in wonder,
With tears beaded on her lashes, and said "Bertram!" it was all.

If she had cursed me, — and she might have, — or if even, with queenly bearing
Which at needs is used by women, she had risen up and said,
"Sir, you are my guest, and therefore I have given you a full hearing, —
Now, beseech you, choose a name exacting somewhat less instead," —

I had borne it! — but that "Bertram" — why it lies there on the paper,
A mere word, without her accent, — and you cannot judge the weight
Of the calm which crushed my passion! I seemed drowning in a vapor, —
And her gentleness destroyed me whom her scorn made desolate.

So, struck backward and exhausted by that inward flow of passion
Which had rushed on, sparing nothing, into forms of abstract truth,
With a logic agonizing through unseemly demonstration,
And with youth's own anguish turning grimly gray the hairs of youth, —

By the sense accursed and instant, that if even I spake wisely,
I spake basely, — using truth, — if what I spake indeed was true, —
To avenge wrong on a woman, — *her*, who sat there weighing nicely
A full manhood's worth, found guilty of such deeds as I could do! —

With such wrong and woe exhausted — what I suffered and occasioned, —
As a wild horse through a city runs with lightning in his eyes,
And then dashing at a church's cold and passive wall, impassioned,
Strikes the death into his burning brain, and blindly drops and dies, —

So I fell, struck down before her! Do you blame me friend, for weakness?
'Twas my strength of passion slew me! — fell before her like a stone;
Fast the dreadful world rolled from me, on its roaring wheels of blackness!
When the light came I was lying in this chamber — and alone.

Oh, of course, she charged her lackeys to bear out the sickly burden,
And to cast it from her scornful sight, — but not *beyond* the gate —
She was too kind to be cruel, and too haughty not to pardon
Such a man as I, — 'twere something to be level to her hate.

But for *me*, — you now are conscious why, my friend, I write this letter,
How my life is read all backward, and the charm of life undone!
I shall leave her house at dawn; — I would to-night, if I were better; —
And I charge my soul to hold my body strengthened for the sun.

When the sun has dyed the oriel, I depart with no last gazes,
No weak moanings — one word only left in writing for her hands,
Out of reach of all derision, and some unavailing praises,
To make front against this anguish in the far and foreign lands.

Blame me not, I would not squander life in grief; — I am abstemious:
I but nurse my spirit's falcon, that its wings may soar again:
There's no room for tears of weakness in the blind eyes of a Phemius:
Into work the poet kneads them, — and he does not die *till then*.

CONCLUSION.

Bertram finished the last pages, while along the silence ever
Still in hot and heavy splashes, fell the tears on every leaf:
Having ended, he leans backward in his chair, with lips that quiver
From the deep unspoken, ay, and deep unwritten thoughts of grief.

Soh! how still the lady standeth! 'tis a dream! — a dream of mercies!
'Twixt the purple lattice-curtains, how she standeth still and pale!
'Tis a vision, sure, of mercies, sent to soften his self-curses —
Sent to sweep a patient quiet o'er the tossing of his wail.

"Eyes," he said, "now throbbing through me! are ye eyes that did undo me?
Shining eyes, like antique jewels set in Parian statue-stone!
Underneath that calm white forehead, are ye ever burning torrid
O'er the desolate sand-desert of my heart and life undone?"

With a murmurous stir uncertain, in the air, the purple curtain
Swelleth in and swelleth out around her motionless pale brows;
While the gliding of the river sends a rippling noise forever
Through the open casement whitened by the moonlight's slant repose.

Said he — "Vision of a lady! stand there silent, stand there steady!
Now I see it plainly, plainly; now I cannot hope or doubt —
There, the brows of mild repression, — there, the lips of silent passion,
Curved like an archer's bow to send the bitter arrows out."

Ever, evermore the while in a slow silence she kept smiling,
And approached him slowly, slowly, in a gliding measured pace;
With her two white hands extended, as if praying one offended,
And a look of supplication, gazing earnest in his face.

Said he, — "Wake me by no gesture, — sound of breath, or stir of vesture;
Let the blessèd apparition melt not yet to its divine!
No approaching, — hush! no breathing! or my heart must swoon to death in
That too utter life thou bringest — O thou dream of Geraldine!"

Ever, evermore the while in a slow silence she kept smiling —
But the tears ran over lightly from her eyes, and tenderly;
"Dost thou, Bertram, truly love me? Is no woman far above me
Found more worthy of thy poet-heart than such a one as *I?*"

Said he — "I would dream so ever, like the flowing of that river,
Flowing ever in a shadow greenly onward to the sea;
So, thou vision of all sweetness — princely to a full completeness, —
Would my heart and life flow onward — deathward — through this dream of THEE!"

Ever, evermore the while in slow silence she kept smiling,
While the silver tears ran faster down the blushing of her cheeks;
Then with both her hands enfolding both of his, she softly told him,
"Bertram, if I say I love thee, . . . 'tis the vision only speaks."

Softened, quickened to adore her, on his knee he fell before her, —
And she whispered low in triumph, — "It shall be as I have sworn!
Very rich he is in virtues, — very noble — noble, certes;
And I shall not blush in knowing that men call him lowly born!"

MRS. BROWNING.

ŒNONE, OR THE CHOICE OF PARIS.

. . . .

"DEAR mother Ida, harken ere I die.
He smiled, and opening out his milk-white palm
Disclosed a fruit of true Hesperian gold,
That smelt ambrosially, and while I looked
And listened, the full-flowing river of speech
Came down upon my heart.
"'My own Œnone,
Beautiful-browed Œnone, my own soul,
Behold this fruit, whose gleaming rind ingraven
"For the most fair," would seem to award it thine,
As lovelier than whatever Oread haunt
The knolls of Ida, loveliest in all grace
Of movement, and the charm of married brows.'

"Dear mother Ida, harken ere I die.
He prest the blossom of his lips to mine,
And added, 'This was cast upon the board,
When all the full-faced presence of the Gods
Ranged in the halls of Peleus; whereupon
Rose feud, with question unto whom 'twere due:
But light-foot Iris brought it yester-eve,
Delivering, that to me, by common voice,
Elected umpire, Heré comes to-day,
Pallas and Aphrodité, claiming each
This meed of fairest. Thou, within the cave
Behind yon whispering tuft of oldest pine,
Mayst well behold them unbeheld, unheard
Hear all, and see thy Paris judge of Gods.'

"Dear mother Ida, harken ere I die.
It was the deep midnoon: one silvery cloud

Had lost his way between the piney sides
Of this long glen. Then to the bower they came,
Naked they came to that smooth-swarded bower,
And at their feet the crocus brake like fire,
Violet, amaracus, and asphodel,
Lotos and lilies: and a wind arose,
And overhead the wandering ivy and vine,
This way and that, in many a wild festoon
Ran riot, garlanding the gnarled boughs
With bunch and berry and flower through and through.

"O mother Ida, harken ere I die.
On the tree-tops a crested peacock lit,
And o'er him flowed a golden cloud, and leaned
Upon him, slowly dropping fragrant dew.
Then first I heard the voice of her, to whom
Coming through Heaven, like a light that grows
Larger and clearer, with one mind the Gods
Rise up for reverence. She to Paris made
Proffer of royal power, ample rule
Unquestioned, overflowing revenue
Wherewith to embellish state, 'from many a vale
And river-sundered champaign clothed with corn,
Or labored mines undrainable of ore.
Honor,' she said, 'and homage, tax and toll,
From many an inland town and haven large,
Mast-thronged beneath her shadowing citadel
In glassy bays among her tallest towers.'

"O mother Ida, harken ere I die.
Still she spake on and still she spake of power,
'Which in all action is the end of all;
Power fitted to the season; wisdom-bred
And throned of wisdom — from all neighbor crowns
Alliance and allegiance, till thy hand
Fail from the sceptre-staff. Such boon from me,
From me, Heaven's Queen, Paris, to thee king-born,
A shepherd all thy life, but yet king-born,
Should come most welcome, seeing men, in power,
Only, are likest gods, who have attained
Rest in a happy place and quiet seats
Above the thunder, with undying bliss
In knowledge of their own supremacy.'

"Dear mother Ida, harken ere I die.
She ceased, and Paris held the costly fruit
Out at arm's-length, so much the thought of power
Flattered his spirit; but Pallas where she stood
Somewhat apart, her clear and bared limbs
O'erthwarted with the brazen-headed spear
Upon her pearly shoulder leaning cold,
The while, above, her full and earnest eye
Over her snow-cold breast and angry cheek
Kept watch, waiting decision, made reply.

"'Self-reverence, self-knowledge, self-control,
These three alone lead life to sovereign power.
Yet not for power (power of herself
Would come uncalled for), but to live by law,
Acting the law we live by without fear;
And, because right is right, to follow right
Were wisdom in the scorn of consequence.'

"Dear mother Ida, harken ere I die.
Again she said: 'I woo thee not with gifts.
Sequel of guerdon could not alter me
To fairer. Judge thou me by what I am,
So shalt thou find me fairest.

Yet, indeed,
If gazing on divinity disrobed
Thy mortal eyes are frail to judge of fair,
Unbiased by self-profit, oh! rest thee sure
That I shall love thee well and cleave to thee,
So that my vigor, wedded to thy blood,
Shall strike within thy pulses, like a God's,
To push thee forward through a life of shocks,
Dangers, and deeds, until endurance grow
Sinewed with action, and the full-grown will,
Circled through all experiences, pure law,
Commeasure perfect freedom.'
"Here she ceased,
And Paris pondered, and I cried, 'O Paris,
Give it to Pallas!' but he heard me not,
Or hearing would not hear me, woe is me!

"O mother Ida, many-fountained Ida,
Dear mother Ida, harken ere I die.
Idalian Aphroditè beautiful,
Fresh as the foam, new-bathed in Paphian wells,
With rosy slender fingers backward drew
From her warm brows and bosom her deep hair
Ambrosial, golden round her lucid throat
And shoulder: from the violets her light foot
Shone rosy-white, and o'er her rounded form
Between the shadows of the vine-bunches
Floated the glowing sunlights, as she moved.

"Dear mother Ida, harken ere I die.
She with a subtle smile in her mild eyes,
The herald of her triumph, drawing nigh
Half-whispered in his ear, 'I promise thee
The fairest and most loving wife in Greece,'
She spoke and laughed: I shut my sight for fear:
But when I looked, Paris had raised his arm,
And I beheld great Herè's angry eyes,
As she withdrew into the golden cloud,
And I was left alone within the bower,
And from that time to this I am alone,
And I shall be alone until I die."

. . . .

TENNYSON.

THE ISLAND.

How pleasant were the songs of Toobonai,
When summer's sun went down the coral bay!
Come let us to the islet's softest shade,
And hear the warbling birds! the damsels said:
The wood-dove from the forest depth shall coo,
Like voices of the gods from Bolotoo;
We'll cull the flowers that grow above the dead,
For these most bloom where rests the warrior's head;
And we will sit in twilight's face, and see
The sweet moon dancing through the tooa-tree,
The lofty accents of whose sighing bough
Shall sadly please us as we lean below;
Or climb the steep, and view the surf in vain
Wrestle with rocky giants o'er the main,
Which spurn in columns back the baffled spray.
How beautiful are these, how happy they,
Who, from the toil and tumult of their lives,
Steal to look down where nought but ocean strives!

Even he too loves at times the blue
lagoon,
And smooths his ruffled mane beneath the moon.

Yes — from the sepulchre we'll gather flowers,
Then feast like spirits in their
promised bowers,
Then plunge and revel in the rolling
surf,
Then lay our limbs along the tender
turf,
And wet and shining from the sportive toil,
Anoint our bodies with the fragrant
oil,
And plait our garlands gathered
from the grave,
And wear the wreaths that sprung
from out the brave.
But lo! night comes, the Mooa
wooes us back,
The sound of mats is heard along
our track;
Anon the torchlight-dance shall fling
its sheen
In flashings mazes o'er the Marly's
green;
And we too will be there; we too recall
The memory bright with many a
festival,
Ere Fiji blew the shell of war, when
foes
For the first time were wafted in
canoes.
Strike up the dance, the cava bowl
fill high,
Drain every drop! — to-morrow we
may die.
In summer garments be our limbs
arrayed;
Around our waist the Tappa's white
displayed;
Thick wreaths shall form our coronal, like spring's,
And round our necks shall glance
the Hooni strings;
So shall their brighter hues contrast
the glow
Of the dusk bosoms that beat high
below.

Thus rose a song, — the harmony of
times
Before the winds blew Europe o'er
these climes.
True, they had vices, — such are
nature's growth, —
But only the barbarians' — we have
both;
The sordor of civilization, mixed
With all the savage which man's fall
hath fixed.
Who hath not seen dissimulation's
reign,
The prayers of Abel linked to deeds
of Cain?
Who such would see, may from his
lattice view
The old world more degraded than
the new, —
Now *new* no more, save where
Columbia rears
Twin giants, born by freedom to
her spheres,
Where Chimborazo, over air, earth,
wave,
Glares with his Titan eye, and sees
no slave.

BYRON.

THE SEA-CAVE.

YOUNG Neuha plunged into the deep,
and he
Followed: her track beneath her
native sea
Was as a native's of the element,
So smoothly, bravely, brilliantly she
went,
Leaving a streak of light behind her
heel,
Which struck and flashed like an
amphibious steel.
Closely, and scarcely less expert to
trace
The depths where divers hold the
pearl in chase,
Torquil, the nursling of the Northern seas,
Pursued her liquid steps with art
and ease.
Deep — deeper for an instant Neuha
led
The way — then upward soared —
and, as she spread
Her arms, and flung the foam from
off her locks,
Laughed, and the sound was answered by the rocks.
They had gained a central realm of
earth again,
But looked for tree, and field, and
sky, in vain.

Around she pointed to a spacious cave,
Whose only portal was the keyless wave,
(A hollow archway by the sun unseen,
Save through the billows' glassy veil of green,
In some transparent ocean holiday,
When all the finny people are at play),
Wiped with her hair the brine from Torquil's eyes,
And clapped her hands with joy at his surprise.
Forth from her bosom the young savage drew
A pine torch, strongly girded with gnatoo;
A plantain leaf o'er all, the more to keep
Its latent sparkle from the sapping deep.
This mantle kept it dry; then from a nook
Of the same plantain leaf, a flint she took,
A few shrunk withered twigs, and from the blade
Of Torquil's knife struck fire, and thus arrayed
The grot with torchlight. Wide it was and high,
And showed a self-born Gothic canopy;
The arch upreared by Nature's architect,
The architrave some earthquake might erect;
The buttress from some mountain's bosom hurled,
When the poles crashed and water was the world;
There, with a little tinge of phantasy,
Fantastic faces moped and mowed on high,
And then a mitre or a shrine would fix
The eye upon its seeming crucifix.
Then Nature played with the stalactites,
And built herself a chapel of the seas.

And Neuha took her Torquil by the hand,
And waved along the vault her kindled brand,
And led him into each recess, and showed
The secret places of their new abode.
Nor these alone, for all had been prepared
Before, to soothe the lover's lot she shared;
The mat for rest; for dress the fresh gnatoo,
The sandal-oil to fence against the dew;
For food the cocoa-nut, the yam, the bread
Born of the fruit; for board the plantain spread
With its broad leaf, or turtle-shell which bore
A banquet in the flesh if covered o'er;
The gourd with water recent from the rill,
The ripe banana from the mellow hill;
A pine torch pile to keep undying light;
And she herself as beautiful as night,
To fling her shadowy spirit o'er the scene,
And make their subterranean world serene.
She had foreseen, since first the stranger's sail
Drew to their isle, that force or flight might fail,
And formed a refuge of the rocky den
For Torquil's safety from his countrymen.
Each dawn had wafted there her light canoe,
Laden with all the golden fruits that grew;
Each eve had seen her gliding through the hour
With all could cheer or deck their sparry bower;
And now she spread her little store with smiles,
The happiest daughter of the loving isles.

'Twas morn; and Neuha, who by dawn of day
Swam smoothly forth to catch the rising ray,
And watch if aught approached the amphibious lair
Where lay her lover, saw a sail in air:

It flapped, it filled, then to the growing gale
Bent its broad arch: her breath began to fail
With fluttering fear, her heart beat thick and high,
While yet a doubt sprung where its course might lie:
But no! it came not; fast and far away,
The shadow lessened as it cleared the bay.
She gazed, and flung the sea-foam from her eyes,
To watch as for a rainbow in the skies.
On the horizon verged the distant deck,
Diminished, dwindled to a very speck —
Then vanished. All was ocean, all was joy!

BYRON.

SONG OF THE TONGA-ISLANDERS.

COME to Licoö! the sun is riding
Down hills of gold to his coral bowers;
Come where the wood-pigeon's moan is chiding
The song of the wind, while we gather flowers.

Let us plait the garland, and weave the chi,
While the wild waves dance on our iron strand;
To-morrow these waves may wash our graves,
And the moon look down on a ruined land.

Let us light the torches, and dip our hair
In the fragrant oil of the sandal-tree;
Strike the bonjoo, and the oola share,
Ere the death-gods hear our jubilee.

Who are they that in floating towers
Come with their skins of curdled snows?
They shall see our maidens dress our bowers,
While the hooni shines on their sunny brows.

Who shall mourn when red with slaughter,
Finow sits on the funeral stone?
Who shall weep for his dying daughter?
Who shall answer the red chief's moan?

He shall cry unheard by the funeral stone,
He shall sink unseen by the split canoe,
Though the plantain-bird be his alone,
And the thundering gods of Fanfonnoo.

Let us not think 'tis but an hour
Ere the wreath shall drop from the warrior's waist;
Let us not think 'tis but an hour
We have on our perfumed mats to waste.

Shall we not banquet, though Tonga's king
To-morrow may hurl the battle-spear?
Let us whirl our torches, and tread the ring, —
He only shall find our foot-prints here.

We will dive, — and the turtle's track shall guide
Our way to the cave where Hoonga dwells,
Where under the tide he hides his bride,
And lives by the light of its starry shells.

Come to Licoö! in yellow skies
The sun shines bright, and the wild waves play;
To-morrow for us may never rise; —
Come to Licoö, to-day, to-day.

ANONYMOUS.

AMY WENTWORTH.

HER fingers shame the ivory keys
They dance so light along;
The bloom upon her parted lips
Is sweeter than the song.

O perfumed suitor, spare thy smiles!
  Her thoughts are not of thee:
She better loves the salted wind,
  The voices of the sea.

Her heart is like an outbound ship
  That at its anchor swings;
The murmur of the stranded shell
  Is in the song she sings.

She sings, and, smiling, hears her praise,
  But dreams the while of one
Who watches from his sea-blown deck
  The icebergs in the sun.

She questions all the winds that blow,
  And every fog-wreath dim,
And bids the sea-birds flying north
  Bear messages to him.

She speeds them with the thanks of men
  He perilled life to save,
And grateful prayers like holy oil
  To smooth for him the wave.

Brown Viking of the fishing-smack!
  Fair toast of all the town!—
The skipper's jerkin ill beseems
  The lady's silken gown!

But ne'er shall Amy Wentworth wear
  For him the blush of shame
Who dares to set his manly gifts
  Against her ancient name.

The stream is brightest at its spring,
  And blood is not like wine;
Nor honored less than he who heirs
  Is he who founds a line.

Full lightly shall the prize be won,
  If love be Fortune's spur;
And never maiden stoops to him
  Who lifts himself to her.

Her home is brave in Jaffrey Street,
  With stately stairways worn
By feet of old Colonial knights
  And ladies gentle-born.

Still green about its ample porch
  The English ivy twines,
Trained back to show in English oak
  The herald's carven signs.

And on her, from the wainscot old,
  Ancestral faces frown,—
And this has worn the soldier's sword,
  And that the judge's gown.

But, strong of will and proud as they,
  She walks the gallery-floor
As if she trod her sailor's deck
  By stormy Labrador!

The sweet-brier blooms on Kittery-side,
  And green are Elliot's bowers;
Her garden is the pebbled beach,
  The mosses are her flowers.

She looks across the harbor-bar
  To see the white gulls fly;
His greeting from the Northern sea
  Is in their clanging cry.

She hums a song, and dreams that he,
  As in its romance old,
Shall homeward ride with silken sails
  And masts of beaten gold!

O, rank is good, and gold is fair,
  And high and low mate ill;
But love has never known a law
  Beyond its own sweet will!

WHITTIER.

LADY CLARE.

It was the time when lilies blow,
  And clouds are highest up in air,
Lord Ronald brought a lily-white doe
  To give his cousin, Lady Clare.

I trow they did not part in scorn:
  Lovers long-betrothed were they:
They two will wed the morrow morn:
  God's blessing on the day!

"He does not love me for my birth,
  Nor for my lands so broad and fair;
He loves me for my own true worth,
  And that is well," said Lady Clare.

In there came old Alice the nurse,
  Said, "Who was this that went from thee?"
"It was my cousin," said Lady Clare,
  "To-morrow he weds with me."

"O God be thanked!" said Alice the nurse,
"That all comes round so just and fair:
Lord Ronald is heir of all your lands,
And you are not the Lady Clare."

"Are ye out of your mind, my nurse, my nurse?"
Said Lady Clare, "that ye speak so wild?"
"As God's above," said Alice the nurse,
"I speak the truth: you are my child.

"The old Earl's daughter died at my breast;
I speak the truth, as I live by bread!
I buried her like my own sweet child,
And put my child in her stead."

"Falsely, falsely have ye done,
O mother," she said, "if this be true,
To keep the best man under the sun
So many years from his due."

"Nay now, my child," said Alice the nurse,
"But keep the secret for your life,
And all you have will be Lord Ronald's,
When you are man and wife."

"If I'm a beggar born," she said,
"I will speak out, for I dare not lie.
Pull off, pull off, the brooch of gold,
And fling the diamond necklace by."

"Nay now, my child," said Alice the nurse,
"But keep the secret all ye can."
She said, "Not so: but I will know
If there be any faith in man."

"Nay now, what faith?" said Alice the nurse,
"The man will cleave unto his right."
"And he shall have it," the lady replied,
"Though I should die to-night."

"Yet give one kiss to your mother dear!
Alas, my child, I sinned for thee."
"O mother, mother, mother," she said,
"So strange it seems to me.

"Yet here's a kiss for my mother dear,
My mother dear, if this be so,
And lay your hand upon my head,
And bless me, mother, ere I go."

She clad herself in a russet gown,
She was no longer Lady Clare:
She went by dale, and she went by down,
With a single rose in her hair.

The lily-white doe Lord Ronald had brought
Leapt up from where she lay,
Dropt her head in the maiden's hand,
And followed her all the way.

Down stept Lord Ronald from his tower:
"O Lady Clare, you shame your worth!
Why come you drest like a village maid,
That are the flower of the earth?"

"If I come drest like a village maid,
I am but as my fortunes are:
I am a beggar born," she said,
"And not the Lady Clare."

"Play me no tricks," said Lord Ronald,
"For I am yours in word and in deed.
Play me no tricks," said Lord Ronald,
"Your riddle is hard to read."

O and proudly stood she up!
Her heart within her did not fail;
She looked into Lord Ronald's eyes,
And told him all her nurse's tale.

He laughed a laugh of merry scorn:
He turned and kissed her where she stood:
"If you are not the heiress born,
And I," said he, "the next in blood —

"If you are not the heiress born,
And I," said he, "the lawful heir,
We two will wed to-morrow morn,
And you shall still be Lady Clare."

TENNYSON.

AULD ROBIN GRAY.

YOUNG Jamie lo'ed me weel, and he sought me for his bride,
But saving a crown he had naething else beside;
To make that crown a pound, my Jamie gaed to sea,
And the crown and the pound were baith for me.
He had na been awa a week but only twa,
When my mither she fell sick, and the cow was stown awa,
My father brak his arm, and my Jamie at the sea,
And auld Robin Gray cam' a-courting to me.

My father cou'dna work, and my mither cou'dna spin;
I toiled baith day and night, but their bread I cou'dna win;
Auld Rob maintained them baith, and wi' tears in his ee
Said, Jenny, for their sakes, oh, will you marry me?
My heart it said nay; I looked for Jamie back;
But the wind it blew high, and the ship it proved a wrack,
The ship it proved a wrack, — why didna Jenny dee?
And why do I live to say, Oh, waes me!

Auld Robin argued sair, though my mither didna speak.
She looked in my face till my heart was like to break;
So they gied him my hand, though my heart was at the sea,
And auld Robin Gray is a gudeman to me.
I hadna been a wife a week but only four,
When sitting sae mournfully ae day at the door,
I saw my Jamie's wraith, for I cou'dna think it he,
Until he said, Jenny, I'm come to marry thee.

Oh, sair did we greet, and muckle did we say,
We took but ae kiss, and tore ourselves away:
I wish I were dead, but I'm nae like to dee;
And why do I live to say, Oh, waes me!
I gang like a ghaist, I carena to spin,
I darena think on Jamie, for that wad be a sin;
But I'll do my best a gude wife for to be,
For auld Robin Gray is kind unto me.

LADY ANNE LINDSAY.

WALY, WALY, BUT LOVE BE BONNY.

O, WALY, waly up the bank,
And waly, waly down the brae,
And waly, waly yon burn-side,
Where I and my love wont to gae.

I leaned my back unto an aik,
I thought it was a trusty tree;
But first it bowed, and syne it brak, —
Sae my true love did light by me!

O, waly, waly, but love be bonny,
A little time while it is new;
But when 'tis auld it waxeth cauld,
And fades away like the morning dew.

O, wherefore should I busk my head?
Or wherefore should I kame my hair?
For my true love has me forsook,
And says he'll never love me mair.

Now Arthur-Seat shall be my bed;
The sheets shall ne'er be fyled by me;
St. Anton's well shall be my drink,
Since my true love has forsaken me.

Martinmas wind, when wilt thou blaw,
And shake the green leaves off the tree?
O gentle death, when wilt thou come?
For of my life I'm weary.

'Tis not the frost that freezes fell,
Nor blawing thaw's inclemency;
'Tis not sic cauld that makes me cry,
But my love's heart grown cauld to me.

When we came in by Glasgow town,
We were a comely sight to see;
My love was clad in the black velvet,
And I mysel in cramasie.

But had I wist before I kissed,
That love had been sae ill to win,
I'd locked my heart in a case of gold,
And pinned it with a silver pin.

O, O, if my young babe were born,
And set upon the nurse's knee,
And I mysel were dead and gane
And the green grass growin' ower me!

ANONYMOUS.

FAIR ANNIE.

"It's narrow, narrow, make your bed,
And learn to lie your lane;
For I'm gaun o'er the sea, Fair Annie,
A braw bride to bring hame.
Wi' her I will get gowd and gear;
Wi' you I ne'er got nane.

"But wha will bake my bridal bread,
Or brew my bridal ale?
And wha will welcome my brisk bride,
That I bring o'er the dale?" —

"It's I will bake your bridal bread,
And brew your bridal ale;
And I will welcome your brisk bride,
That you bring o'er the dale." —

"But she that welcomes my brisk bride
Maun gang like maiden fair;
She maun lace on her robe sae jimp,
And braid her yellow hair." —

"But how can I gang maiden-like,
When maiden I am nane?
Have I not born seven sons to thee,
And am with child again?" —

She's ta'en her young son in her arms,
Another in her hand;
And she's up to the highest tower,
To see him come to land.

"Come up, come up, my eldest son,
And look o'er yon sea-strand,
And see your father's new-come bride,
Before she come to land." —

"Come down, come down, my mother dear,
Come frae the castle wa'!
I fear, if langer ye stand there,
Ye'll let yoursell down fa'." —

And she gaed down, and farther down,
Her love's ship for to see;
And the topmast and the mainmast
Shone like the silver free.

And she's gane down, and farther down,
The bride's ship to behold;
And the topmast and the mainmast
They shone just like the gold.

She's ta'en her seven sons in her hand;
I wot she did'na fail!
She met Lord Thomas and his bride,
As they came o'er the dale.

"You're welcome to your house, Lord Thomas;
You're welcome to your land;
You're welcome, with your fair ladye,
That you lead by the hand.

"You're welcome to your ha's ladye,
You're welcome to your bowers;
You're welcome to your hame, ladye,
For a' that's here is yours." —

"I thank thee, Annie; I thank thee, Annie;
Sae dearly as I thank thee;
You're the likest to my sister Annie,
That ever I did see.

"There came a knight out o'er the sea,
And stealed my sister away;
The shame scoup in his company
And land where'er he gae!" —

She hang ae napkin at the door,
Another in the ha';
And a' to wipe the trickling tears,
Sae fast as they did fa'.

And aye she served the lang tables
With white bread and with wine;
And aye she drank the wan water,
To haud her colour fine.

And aye she served the lang tables,
With white bread and with brown;
And ay she turned her round about,
Sae fast the tears fell down.

And he's ta'en down the silk napkin,
Hung on a silver pin;
And aye he wipes the tear trickling
Adown her cheek and chin.

And aye he turned him round about,
And smiled amang his men,
Says — "Like ye best the old ladye,
Or her that's new come hame?" —

When bells were rung, and mass was
sung,
And a' men bound to bed,
Lord Thomas and his new-come bride,
To their chamber they were gaed.

Annie made her bed a little forbye,
To hear what they might say;
"And ever alas!" fair Annie cried,
"That I should see this day!

"Gin my seven sons were seven
young rats,
Running on the castle wa',
And I were a grey cat mysell,
I soon would worry them a'.

"Gin my seven sons were seven
young hares,
Running o'er yon lilly lee,
And I were a grew hound mysell,
Soon worried they a' should be." —

And wae and sad fair Annie sat,
And drearie was her sang;
And ever, as she sobbed and grat,
"Wae to the man that did the
wrang!" —

"My gown is on," said the new-come
bride,
"My shoes are on my feet,
And I will to fair Annie's chamber,
And see what gars her greet.

"What ails ye, what ails ye, Fair
Annie,
That ye make sic a moan?
Has your wine barrells cast the girds,
Or is your white bread gone?

"O wha was't was your father, Annie,
Or wha was't was your mother?
And had you ony sister, Annie,
Or had you ony brother?" —

"The Earl of Wemyss was my father,
The Countess of Wemyss my mother;
And a' the folk about the house,
To me were sister and brother." —

"If the Earl of Wemyss was your
father,
I wot sae was he mine;
And it shall not be for lack o'gowd,
That ye your love sall tyne.

"Come to your bed, my sister dear,
It ne'er was wranged for me,
But an ae kiss of his merry mouth,
As we cam owre the sea."

"Awa, awa, ye forenoon bride,
Awa, awa frae me:
I wudna hear my Annie greet,
For a' the gold I got wi' thee."

"O I have seven ships o' mine ain,
A' loaded to the brim;
And I will gie them a' to thee,
Wi' four to thine eldest son,
But thanks to a' the powers in heaven
That I gae maiden hame!"

SCOTT'S VERSION.

GRISELDA.

THE CLERKES TALE.

Ther is right at the West side of
Itaille
Doun at the rote of Vesulus the cold,
A lusty plain, abundant of vitaille,
Ther many a toun and tour thou
maist behold,
That founded were in time of fa-
thers old,
And many another delitable sighte.
And Saluces this noble contree
highte.

A markis whilom lord was of that
land,
As were his worthy elders him before,
And obeysant, ay redy to his hand,

Were all his lieges, bothe lesse and more:
Thus in delit he liveth, and hath done yore,
Beloved and drad, thurgh favour of fortune,
Both of his lordes, and of his commune.

Therwith he was, to speken of linage,
The gentilest yborne of Lombardie,
A faire person, and strong, and yong of age,
And ful of honour and of curtesie:
Discret ynough, his contree for to gie,
Save in som thingés that he was to blame,
And Walter was this yongé lordés name.

I blame him thus, that he considered nought
In time coming what might him betide,
But on his lust present was all his thought,
And for to hauke and hunt on every side:
Wel neigh all other curés let he slide,
And eke he n'old (and that was worst of all)
Wedden no wif for ought that might befall.

Only that point his peple bare so sore,
That flockmel on a day to him they went.
And one of them, that wisest was of lore,
(Or ellés that the lord wold best assent
That he shuld tell him what the peple ment,
Or ellés coud he wel shew suich matere)
He to the markis said as ye shall here.

"O noble markis, your humanitee
Assureth us and yeveth us hardinesse,
As oft as time is of necessitee,
That we to you may tell our hevinesse:
Accepteth, lord, then of your gentillesse,
That we with pitous herte unto you plaine,
And let your erés not my vois disdaine.

Al have I not to don in this matere
More than another man hath in this place,
Yet for as moch as ye, my lord so dere
Han alway shewèd me favour and grace,
I dare the better aske of you a space
Of audience, to shewen our request,
And ye, my lord, to don right as you lest.

For certes, lord, so wel us liketh you
And all your werke, and ever have don, that we
Ne couden not ourself devisen how
We mighten live in more felicitee:
Save one thing, lord, if it your willé be,
That for to be a wedded man you lest,
Then were your peple in soverain hertés rest.

Boweth your nekke under the blisful yok
Of soveraintee, and not of servise,
Which that men clepen spousalile or wedlok:
And thinketh, lord, among your thoughtés wise,
How that our dayes passe in sondry wise;
For though we slepe, or wake, or rome, or ride,
Ay fleth the time, it wol no man abide.

And though your grené youthe floure as yet,
In crepeth age alway as still as stone,
And deth menaceth every age, and smit
In eche estat, for ther escapeth none:
And al so certain, as we knowe eche one
That we shul die, as uncertain we all
Ben of that day whan deth shal on us fall.

Accepteth then of us the trewe entent,
That never yet refuséden your hest,
And we wol, lord, if that ye wol assent,
Chese you a wife in short time at the mest,

Borne of the gentillest and of the best
Of all this lond, so that it oughté seme
Honour to God and you, as we can deme.

Deliver us out of all this besy drede,
And take a wif, for highé Goddés sake:
For if it so befell, as God forbede,
That thurgh your deth your linage shulde slake,
And that a strange successour shuld take
Your heritage, o! wo were us on live:
Wherfore we pray you hastily to wive."

Hir meké praiére and hir pitous chere
Made the markis for to han pitee.
"Ye wol," quod he, "min owen peple dere,
To that I never ere thought constrainen me.
I me rejoycèd of my libertee,
That selden time is found in mariage:
Ther I was free, I moste ben in servage.

"But natheles I see your trewe entent,
And trust upon your wit, and have don ay:
Wherfore of my free will I wol assent
To wedden me, as sone as ever I may.
But ther as ye han profred me today
To chesen me a wife, I you relese
That chois, and pray you of that profer cese.

"For God it wot, that children often ben
Unlike hir worthy eldres them before,
Bountee cometh al of God, not of the stren,
Of which they ben ygendred and ybore:
I trust in Goddés bountee, and therfore
My mariage, and min estat, and rest
I him betake, he may do as him lest.

"Let me alone in chosing of my wife,
That charge upon my bak I wol endure:
But I you pray, and charge upon your life,
That what wif that I take, ye me assure
To worship her while that her life may dure,
In word and work both here and elles where,
As she an emperourés daughter were.

"And forthermore this shuln ye swere, that ye
Again my chois shal never grutch ne strive.
For sith I shal forgo my libertee
At your request, as ever mote I thrive,
Where as min herte is set, ther wol I wive:
And but ye wol assent in such manere,
I pray you speke no more of this matere."

With hertly will they sworen and assenten
To all this thing, ther saide not one wight nay.
Beseching him of grace, or that they wenten,
That he wold granten them a certain day
Of his spousaile, as soon as ever he may,
For yet alway the peple somwhat dred,
Lest that this markis wolde no wif wed.

He granted hem a day, such as him lest,
On which he wold be wedded sikerly,
And said he did all this at hir request.
And they with humble herte ful buxumly
Kneling upon their knees ful reverently

Him thankèd all, and thus they had
an end
Of their entente, and home agen they
wend.

And hereupon he to his officeres
Commandeth for the festé to purvay.
And to his priveé knightes and
squieres
Such charge he gave, as him list on
them lay:
And they to his commandément obey,
And eche of them doth all his dili-
gence
To do unto the feste all reverence.

PARS SECUNDA.

Nought far fro thilke paleis honourable,
Wher as this markis shope his mariage,
Ther stood a thorpe, of sighte delitable,
In which that pouré folk of that
village
Hadden their bestês and their her-
bergage,
And of hir labour toke hir suste-
tenance,
After that the erthe gave them
abundance.

Among this pouré folk ther dwelt
a man,
Which that was holden poorest of
them all:
But highé God somtimé senden can
His grace unto a litel oxes stall:
Janicola men of that thorpe him call.
A doughter had he, faire enough to
sight,
And Grisildis this yongé maiden
hight.

But for to speke of vertuous beautee,
Then was she one the fairest under
sonne:
Ful pourléy yfostred up was she:
No likerous lust was in hire herte
yronne;
Wel ofter of the well than of the
tonne
She dranke, and for she woldé vertue
plese,
She knew wel labour, but none idel
ese.

But though this mayden tendre
were of age,
Yet in the brest of her virginitee
Ther was enclosèd sad and ripe
corage :
And in great reverence and charitee
Her oldé pouré father fostred she:
A few sheep spinning on the feld she
kept,
She wolde not ben idel til she slept.

And whan she homeward came,
she wolde bring
Wortes and other herbés times oft,
The which she shred and sethe for
her living,
And made her bed ful hard, and
nothing soft:
And ay she kept her fadres life on
loft
With every obeisance and diligence,
That child may don to fadres rever-
ence.

Upon Grisilde, this pouré creature,
Ful often sithe this markis sette his
eye,
As he on hunting rode paraventure:
And whan it fell that he might hire
espie,
He not with wanton loking of folie
His eyen cast on her, but in sad
wise
Upon her chere he wold him oft
avise,

Commending in his herte her
womanhede,
And eke her vertue, passing any
wight
Of so yong age, as wel in chere as
dede.
For though the peple have no great
insight
In virtue, he considerèd ful right
Her bountee, and disposèd that he
wold
Wedde her only, if ever he wedden
shold.

The day of wedding came, but no
wight can
Tellen what woman that it shuldé
be,
For which mervaillé wondred many
a man,
And saiden, whan they were in pri-
vetee,

Wol not our lord yet leve his vanitee?
Wol he not wedde? alas, alas the while!
Why wol he thus himself and us begile?

But natheles this markis hath do make
Of gemmes, sette in gold and in asure,
Broches and ringes, for Grisildes sake,
And of her clothing toke he the mesure
Of a maiden like unto her stature,
And eke of other ornamentés all,
That unto swiche a wedding shuldé fall.

The time of underne of the same day
Approcheth, that this wedding shuldé be,
And all the paleis put was in array,
Both halle and chambres, eche in his degree,
Houses of office stuffèd with plentee
Ther mayst thou see of dainteous vitaillé,
That may be found, as far as lasteth Itaille.

This real markis richély arraide,
Lordes and ladies in his compagnie,
The which unto the festé weren praide,
And of his retenue the bachelerie,
With many a sound of sondry melodie,
Unto the village, of the which I told,
In this array the righté way they hold.

Grisilde of this (God wot) ful innocent,
That for her shapen was all this array,
To fetchen water at a welle is went,
And cometh home as sone as ever she may.
For wel she had herd say, that thilké day
The markis shuldé wedde, and, if she might,
She woldé fayn han seen some of that sight.

She thought, "I wol with other maidens stond,
That ben my felawes, in our dore, and see
The markisesse, and therto wol I fond
To don at home, as soon as it may be,
The labour which that longeth unto me,
And than I may at leiser her behold,
If she this way unto the castel hold."

And as she wolde over the threswold gon,
The markis came and gan her for to call,
And she set doun her water-pot anon
Beside the threswold in an oxes stall,
And doun upon her knees she gan to fall,
And with sad countenancé kneleth still,
Til she had herd what was the lordés will.

This thoughtful markis spake unto this maid
Ful soberly, and said in this manere:
"Wher is your fader, Grisildis?" he said.
And she with reverence in humble chere
Answered, "Lord, he is al redy here."
And in she goth withouten lenger lette,
And to the markis she hire fader fette.

He by the hand than toke this poure man,
And saide thus, whan he him had aside:
"Janicola, I neither may nor can
Longer the plesance of mine herté hide,
If that thou vouchesauf, what so betide,
Thy doughter wol I take or that I wend
As for my wif, unto her livés end.

"Thou lovest me, that wot I wel certain,
And art my faithful liegéman ybore,
And all that liketh me, I dare wel sain
It liketh thee, and specially therfore
Tell me that point, that I have said before,

If that thou wolt unto this purpos drawe,
To taken me as for thy son in lawe."

This soden cas this man astoned so,
That red he wex, abaist, and al quaking
He stood, unnethès said he wordés mo,
But only thus; "Lord," quod he, "my willing
Is as ye wol, ne ageins your liking
I wol no thing, min owen lord so dere,
Right as you list, governeth this matere."

"Than wol I," quod this markis softely,
"That in thy chambre, I, and thou, and she,
Have a collation, and wost thou why?
For I wol ask her, if it her wille be
To be my wif, and rule her after me:
And all this shal be done in thy presence,
I wol not speke out of thine audience."

And in the chambre, while they were about
The tretee, which as ye shul after here,
The peple came into the hous without,
And wondred them, in how honest manere
Ententifly she kept hire fader dere:
But utterly Grisildis wonder might,
For never erst ne saw she swiche a sight.

No wonder is though that she be astoned,
To see so gret a gest come in that place,
She never was to non such gestes woned,
For which she loked with ful pale face.
But shortly forth this matere for to chace,
These are the wordés that the markis said
To this benigné, veray, faithful maid.

"Grisilde," he said, "ye shuln wel understond,
It liketh to your fader and to me,
That I you wedde, and eke it may so stond
As I suppose, ye wol that it so be:
But thise demaundés aske I first (quod he)
That sin it shal be don in hasty wise,
Wol ye assent, or elles you avise?

"I say this, be ye redy with good herte
To all my lust, and that I freely may
As me best thinketh do you laugh or smerte,
And never ye to grutchen, night ne day,
And eke whan I say yea, ye say not nay,
Neither by word, ne frouning countenance?
Swere this, and here I swere our alliance."

Wondring upon this thing, quaking for drede,
She saide, "Lord, indigne and unworthy
Am I, to thilke honour, that ye me bede,
But as ye wol yourself, right so wol I:
And here I swere, that never willingly
In werk, ne thought, I n'ill you disobeie
For to be ded, though me were loth to deie."

"This is ynough, Grisilde min," quod he.
And forth he goth with a ful sobre chere,
Out at the dore, and after then came she,
And to the peple he said in this manere:
"This is my wif," quod he, "that stondeth here.
Honoureth her, and loveth her, I pray,
Who so me loveth, ther n'is no more to say."

And for that nothing of her oldé gere
She shulde bring into his hous, he bad

That women shuld despoilen her right there,
Of which thise ladies weren nothing glad
To handle her clothes wherin she was clad:
But natheles this maiden bright of hew
Fro foot to hed they clothed han all new.

Her heres han they kempt, that lay untressed
Ful rudély, and with her fingres smal
A coroune on her hed they han ydressed,
And sette her ful of nouches gret and smal:
Of her array what shuld I make a tale?
Unneth the peple her knew for her fairnesse,
Whan she transmewèd was in swiche richesse.

This markis hath her spousèd with a ring
Brought for the same cause, and than her sette
Upon an hors snow-white, and wel ambling,
And to his paleis, or he lenger lette,
(With joyful peple, that her lad and mette)
Conveyèd her, and thus the day they spende
In revel, til the sonné gan descende.

And shortly forth this tale for to chace,
I say, that to this newé markisesse
God hath swiche favour sent her of his grace,
That it ne semeth not by likelinesse
That she was borne and fed in rudenesse,
As in a cote, or in an oxes stall,
But nourished in an emperoures hall.

To every wight she waxen is so dere,
And worshipful, that folk ther she was bore
And fro her birthé knew her yere by yere,
Unnethes trowed they, but dorst han swore,
That to Janicle, of which I spake before,
She doughter n'as, for as by conjecture
Hem thoughte she was another creáture.

For though that ever vertuous was she,
She was encresèd in swiche excellence
Of thewés good, yset in high bountee,
And so discrete, and faire of eloquence,
So benigne, and so digne of reverence,
And coudé so the peples herte embrace,
That eche her loveth that loketh on her face.

Nor only of Saluces in the toun
Publishèd was the bountee of her name,
But eke beside in many a regioun,
If one saith wel, another saith the same:
So spredeth of her hie bountee the fame,
That men and women, yong as wel as old,
Gon to Saluces upon her to behold.

Thus Walter lowly, nay but rëally,
Wedded with fortunat honestetee,
In Goddés peace liveth ful esily
At home, and grace ynough outward had he:
And for he saw that under low degree
Was honest vertue hid, the peple him held
A prudent man, and that is seen ful seld.

Not only this Grisildis thurgh her wit
Coude all the fete of wifly homlinesse,
But eke whan that the cas required it,
The comuné profit coude she redresse:
Ther n'as discord, rancour, ne hevinesse
In all the lond, that she ne coude appese,
And wisely bring hem all in hertés ese.

Though that her husbond absent were or non,
If gentilmen, or other of that contree
Were wroth, she wolde bringen them at one,
So wise and ripe wordes hadde she,
And jugement of so gret equitee,
That she from heven sent was, as men wend,
Peple to save, and every wrong to amend.

Not longe time after that this Grisilde
Was wedded, she a doughter hath ybore,
All had hire lever han borne a knave child:
Glad was the markis and his folk therfore,
For though a maiden childe come all before,
She may unto a knave child atteine
By likelyhed, sin she n'is not barreine.

PARS TERTIA.

Ther fell, as it befalleth timés mo,
Whan that this childe had soukèd but a throwe,
This markis in his herté longèd so
To tempt his wif, her sadnesse for to knowe,
That he ne might out of his herte throwe
This marveillous desir his wif to assay,
Needles, God wot, he thought hire to affray.

He had assaied her enough before,
And found her ever good, what nedeth it
Her for to tempt, and alway more and more?
Though some men praise it for a subtil wit,
But as for me, I say that evil it sit
To assay a wife when that it is no nede,
And putten her in anguish and in drede.

For which this markis wrought in this manere;
He came a-night alone ther as she lay
With sterné face, and with ful trouble chere,
And sayde thus: "Grisilde" (quod he) "that day
That I you toke out of your poure array,
And put you in estat of high noblesse,
Ye han it not forgotten, as I gesse.

"I say, Grisilde, this present dignitee,
In which that I have put you, as I trow,
Maketh you not forgetful for to be
That I you toke in poure estat ful low,
For ony wele ye mote yourselven know.
Take hede of every word that I you say,
Ther is no wight that hereth it but we tway.

"Ye wote yourself wel how that ye came here
Into this hous, it is not long ago,
And though to me ye be right lefe and dere,
Unto my gentils ye be nothing so:
They say, to hem it is gret shame and wo
For to be suggetes, and ben in servage
To thee, that borne art of a smal linage.

"And namely since thy doughter was ybore,
These wordes han they spoken douteles,
But I desire, as I have don before,
To live my lif with them in rest and peace:
I may not in this case be reccheles;
I mote do with thy doughter for the best,
Not as I wold, but as my gentils lest.

"And yet, God wote, this is ful loth to me:
But natheles withouten youre weting
I wol nought do, but thus wol I (quod he)
That ye to me assenten in this thing.
Shew now youre patience in youre werking
That ye me hight and swore in youre village
The day that makèd was our mariage."

Whan she had herd all this, she not ameved
Neyther in word, in chere, ne countenance,
(For as it semed, she was not agreved)
She sayde: "Lord, all lith in your plesance,
My child and I, with hertely obeisance
Ben youres all, and ye may save or spill,
Your owen thing: werketh after your will.

Ther may no thing, so God my soule save,
Like unto you, that may displesen me:
Ne I desire nothing for to have,
Ne drede for to lese, sauf only ye:
This will is in myn herte, and ay shal be,
No length of time, or deth may this deface,
Ne change my corage to an other place."

Glad was this markis for her answering,
But yet he feined as he were not so,
Al drery was his chere and his loking,
Whan that he shuld out of the chambre go.
Sone after this, a furlong way or two,
He prively hath told all his entent
Unto a man, and to his wif him sent.

A maner sergeant was this privé man,
The which he faithful often founden had
In thinges gret, and eke swiche folk wel can
Don execution on thinges bad:
The lord knew wel, that he him loved and drad.
And whan this sergeant wist his lordes will,
Into the chambre he stalked him ful still.

"Madame," he sayd, "ye mote forgive it me,
Though I do thing, to which I am constreined:
Ye ben so wise, that right wel knowen ye,
That lordés hestés may not ben yfeined,
They may wel be bewailed and complained,
But men mote nedes to their lust obey,
And so wol I, ther n'is no more to say.

"This child I am commanded for to take."
And spake no more, but out the child he hent
Despiteously, and gan a chere to make,
As though he wold have slain it, or he went.
Grisildis must al suffer and al consent:
And as a lambe, she sitteth meke and still,
And let this cruel sergeant do his will.

Suspecious was the diffame of this man,
Suspect his face, suspect his word also,
Suspect the time in which he this began:
Alas! her doughter, that she lovèd so,
She wende he wold han slaién it right tho,
But natheles she neither wept ne siked,
Conforming her to that the markis liked.

But at the last to speken she began,
And mekely she to the sergeant praid
(So as he was a worthy gentil man)
That she might kiss her child, or that it deid:
And in her barme this litel child she leid,
With ful sad face, and gan the child to blisse,
And lulled it, and after gan it kisse.

And thus she sayd in her benigne vois:
"Farewel, my child, I shal thee never see,
But sin I have thee marked with the crois,
Of thilke fader yblessed mote thou be,

That for us died upon a crois of tree:
Thy soule, litel child, I him betake,
For this night shalt thou dien for my sake."

I trow that to a norice in this case
It had ben hard this routhe for to see:
Wel might a moder than han cried alas,
But natheles so sad stedfast was she,
That she endured all adversitee,
And to the sergeant mekely she sayde,
"Have here agen your litel yonge mayde.

"Goth now" (quod she) "and doth my lordés hest:
And one thing wold I pray you of your grace,
But if my lord forbade you at the lest,
Burieth this litel body in some place,
That bestes ne no birdies it to-race."
But he no word to that purpos wold say,
But toke the child and went upon his way.

This sergeant came unto his lord again,
And of Grisildés wordés and her chere
He told him point for point, in short and plain,
And him presented with his doughter dere.
Somwhat this lord hath routhe in his manere,
But natheles his purpos held he still,
As lordes don, whan they wol han hir will.

And bad this sergeant that he prively
Shulde this child ful softe wind and wrappe,
With alle circumstances tendrely,
And carry it in a coffer, or in a lappe;
But upon peine his hed off for to swappe
That no man shulde know of his entent,
Ne whence he came, ne whither that he went;

But at Boloigne, unto his sister dere,
That thilke time of Pavie was countesse,
He shuld it take, and shew hire this matere,
Beseching hire to don her besinesse
This child to fostren in all gentillesse,
And whos child that it was he bade her hide
From every wight, for ought that may betide.

This sergeant goth, and hath fulfilde this thing.
But to this marquis now retorné we;
For now goth he ful fast imagining,
If by his wivés chere he mighté see,
Or by her wordés apperceive, that she
Were changed, but he never coud hire finde,
But ever in one ylike sad and kinde.

As glad, as humble, as besy in service
And eke in love, as she was wont to be,
Was she to him, in every manner wise;
Ne of her doughter not a word spake she:
Non accident for non adversitee
Was seen in her, ne never her doughter's name
Ne nevened she, for ernest ne for game.

PARS QUARTA.

In this estat ther passèd ben foure yere
Er she with childe was, but, as God wold,
A knave childe she bare by this Waltere
Ful gracious, and fair for to behold:
And whan that folk it to his fader told,
Not only he, but all his contree mery
Was for this childe, and God they thonke and hery.

Whan it was two yere old, and from the brest
Departed of his norice, on a day
This markis caughte yet another lest
To tempte his wif yet ofter, if he may.
O! nedeles was she tempted in assay.
But wedded men ne connen no mesure,
Whan that they finde a patient creature.

"Wif," quod this markis, "ye han herd or this
My peple sikely beren our mariage,
And namely sin my son yboren is,
Now is it worse than ever in all our age:
The murmur sleth myn herte and my corage,
For to mine eres cometh the vois so smerte,
That it wel nie destroyed hath my herte.

"Now say they thus, whan Walter is agon,
Than shal the blood of Janicle succede,
And ben our lord, for other han we none:
Swiche wordes sayn my peple, it is no drede,
Wel ought I of swiche murmur taken hede,
For certainly I drede al swiche sentence,
Though they not plainen in myn audience.

"I wolde live in pees, if that I might:
Wherfore I am disposed utterly,
As I his suster served er by night,
Right so thinke I to serve him prively.
This warne I you, that ye not sodenly
Out of yourself for no wo shuld outraie,
Beth patient, and thereof I you praie."

"I have," quod she, "sayd thus and ever shal,
I wol no thing, ne n'ill no thing certain,
But as you list: not greveth me at al,
Though that my doughter and my sone be slain
At your commandement: that is to sain,
I have not had no part of children twein,
But first sikenesse, and after wo and peine.

"Ye ben my lord, doth with your owen thing
Right as you list, asketh no rede of me:
For as I left at home al my clothing
Whan I came first to you, right so (quod she)
Left I my will and al my libertee,
And toke your clothing: wherfore I you prey,
Doth your plesance, I wol youre lust obey.

"And certes, if I hadde prescience
Your will to know, er ye your lust me told,
I wold it do withouten negligence:
But now I wote your lust, and what ye wold,
All your plesance ferme and stable I hold,
For wist I that my deth might do you ese,
Right gladly wold I dien, you to plese.

"Deth may not maken no comparisoun
Unto your love." And whan this markis say
The constance of his wif, he cast adoun
His eyen two, and wondreth how she may
In patience suffer al this array:
And forth he goth with drery contenance,
But to his herte it was ful gret plesance.

This ugly sergeant in the same wise
That he her doughter caughte, right so he
(Or werse, if men can any werse devise)
Hath hent her son, that ful was of beautee:
And ever in on so patient was she,
That she no chere made of hevinesse,
But kist her sone and after gan it blesse.

Save this she praied him, if that he might,
Her litel sone he wold in erthé grave,
His tendre limmés, delicat to sight,
Fro foules and fro bestes for to save.
But she non answer of him mighte have,

He went his way, as him no thing ne rought,
But to Boloigne he tendrely it brought.

This markis wondreth ever lenger the more
Upon her patience, and if that he
Ne hadde sothly knowen therbefore,
That parfitly her children lovèd she,
He wold han wend that of som subtiltee
And of malice, or for cruel corage,
That she had suffred this with sad visage.

But wel he knew, that next himself, certain
She loved her children best in every wise.
But now of women wold I asken fayn,
If thise assaies mighten not suffise;
What coud a sturdy husbond more devise
To preve her wifhood, and her stedfastnesse,
And he continuing ever in sturdinesse?

But ther be folk of such condition,
That, whan they han a certain purpos take,
They can not stint of their intention,
But, right as they were bounden to a stake,
They wol not of their firste purpose slake:
Right so this markis fully hath purposed
To tempt his wif, as he was first disposed.

He waiteth, if by word or contenance
That she to him was changed of corage:
But never coud he finden variance,
She was ay one in herte and in visage,
And ay the further that she was in age,
The more trewe (if that were possible)
She was to him in love, and more penible.

For which it semed thus, that of them two
Ther was but one will; for as Walter lest,
The same lust was hire plesance also;
And God be thanked, all fell for the best.
She shewed wel, for no worldly unrest
A wif, as of hirself, no thing ne sholde
Wille in effect, but as her husbond wolde.

The sclandre of Walter wonder wide spradde,
That of a cruel herte he wikkedly,
For he a poure woman wedded hadde,
Hath murdred both his children prively:
Such murmur was among them comunly.
No wonder is: for to the peples' ere
Ther came no word, but that they murdred were.

For which ther as his people therbefore
Had loved him wel, the sclandre of his diffame
Made them that they him hateden therfore:
To ben a murdrour is an hateful name.
But natheles, for ernest ne for game,
He of his cruel purpos n'olde stente,
To tempt his wif was sette all his entente.

Whan that his doughter twelf yere was of age,
He to the court of Rome, in subtil wise
Enformed of his will, sent his message,
Commanding him, swiche billes to devise,
As to his cruel purpos may suffise,
How that the pope, as for his peples rest,
Bade him to wed another, if him lest.

I say he bade, they shulden contrefete
The popes bulles, making mention
That he hath leve his firste wif to lete,
As by the popes dispensation,

To stinten rancour and dissension
Betwix his peple and him: thus spake the bull,
The which they han publishèd at the full.

The rude peple, as no wonder is,
Wenden ful wel, that it had ben right so:
But whan thise tidings came to Grisildis,
I deme that her herte was ful of wo;
But she ylike sad for evermo
Disposed was, this humble creature,
The adversitee of fortune al to endure;

Abiding ever his lust and his plesance,
To whom that she was yeven, herte and al,
As to hire veray worldly suffisance.
But shortly if this storie tell I shal,
This markis writen hath in special
A lettre, in which he sheweth his entente,
And secretly he to Bologne it sente,

To the erl of Pavie, which that hadde tho
Wedded his suster, prayed he specially
To bringen home agein his children two
In honourable estat al openly:
But one thing he him prayèd utterly,
That he to no wight, though men wold enquere,
Shulde not tell whos children that they were,

But say, the maiden shuld ywedded be
Unto the markis of Saluces anon.
And as this erl was prayed, so did he,
For at day sette he on his way is gon
Toward Saluces, and lordes many on
In rich arraie, this maiden for to gide,
Her yonge brother riding hire beside.

Arraied was toward her mariage
This fresshe maiden, ful of gemmes clere,
Her brother, which that seven yere was of age,
Arraied eke ful fresh in his manere:
And thus in gret noblesse and with glade chere
Toward Saluces shaping their journay
Fro day to day they riden in their way.

PARS QUINTA.

Among al this, after his wicked usage,
This markis yet his wif to tempten more
To the uttereste proof of hire corage,
Fully to have experience and lore,
If that she were as stedefast as before,
He on a day in open audience
Ful boistously hath said her this sentence:

"Certes, Grisilde, I had ynough plesance
To han you to my wif, for your goodnesse,
And for your trouthe, and for your obeysance,
Not for your linage, ne for your richesse,
But now know I in veray sothfastnesse,
That in gret lordship, if I me wel avise,
Ther is gret servitude in sondry wise.

"I may not do, as every ploughman may:
My peple me constreineth for to take
Another wif, and crien day by day;
And eke the pope rancour for to slake
Consenteth it, that dare I undertake:
And trewely, thus moche I wol you say,
My newe wif is coming by the way.

"Be strong of herte, and voide anon hire place,
And thilke dower that ye broughten me
Take it agen, I grant it of my grace,
Returneth to your fadres hous, (quod he)
No man may alway have prosperitee.
With even herte I rede you to endure
The stroke of fortune, or of aventure."

And she agen answerd in patience:
"My lord," quod she, "I wote, and wist alway,
How that betwixen your magnificence
And my poverte no wight ne can ne may
Maken comparison, it is no nay;
I ne held me never digne in no manere
To be your wif, ne yet your chamberere.

"And in this hous, ther ye me lady made,
(The highe God take I for my witnesse,
And all so wisly he my soule glad)
I never held me lady ne maistresse,
But humble servant to your worthinesse,
And ever shal, while that my lif may dure,
Aboven every worldly creature.

"That ye so longe of your benignitee
Han holden me in honour and nobley,
Wheras I was not worthy for to be,
That thanke I God and you, to whom I prey
Foryelde it you, ther is no more to sey:
Unto my fader gladly wol I wende,
And with him dwell unto my livés ende;

"Ther I was fostred of a childe ful smal,
Till I be dead my life there will I lead,
A widew clene in body, herte and al.
For sith I gave to you my maidenhede,
And am your trewe wif, it is no drede,
God shilde such a lordés wif to take
Another man to husbond or to make.

"And of your newe wif, God of his grace
So graunte you wele and prosperite:
For I wol gladly yelden her my place,
In which that I was blisful wont to be.
For sith it liketh you, my lord, (quod she)
That whilom weren all myn hertés rest,
That I shal gon, I wot go whan you lest.

"But ther as ye me profer swiche dowaire
As I first brought, it is wel in my mind,
It were my wretched clothés, nothing faire,
The which to me were hard now for to find.
O goode God! how gentil and how kind
Ye semed by your speche and your visage,
The day that maked was oure marriage!

"But soth is said, algate I find it trewe,
For in effect it preved is on me,
Love is not old, as whan that it is newe.
But certes, lord, for non adversitee
To dien in this cas, it shal not be
That ever in word or werke I shal repent,
That I you yave min herte in whole entent.

"My lord, ye wot, that in my father's place
Ye did me stripe out of my poure wede.
And richely ye clad me of your grace;
To you brought I nought elles out of drede,
But faith and nakednesse, and maidenhede;
And here agen your clothing I restore,
And eke your wedding ring for evermore.

"The remenant of your jeweles redy be
Within your chambre, I dare it safly sain;
Naked out of my father's hous (quod she)
I came, and naked I mote turne again.
All your plesance wolde I folwe fain:
But yet I hope it be not your entent,
That I smockless out of your paleis went.

"Ye coude not do so dishonest a thing,
That thilke wombe, in which your children lay,
Shulde before the peple, in my walking,
Be seen al bare: wherfore I you pray
Let me not like a worme go by the way:
Remembre you, min owen lord so dere,
I was your wif, though I unworthy were.

"Wherfore in guerdon of my maidenhede,
Which that I brought and not agen I bere,
As vouchesauf to yeve me to my mede
But swiche a smok as I was wont to were,
That I therwith may wrie the wombe of her
That was your wif: and here I take my leve
Of you, min owen lord, lest I you greve."

"The smok," quod he, "that thou hast on thy bake,
Let it be still, and bere it forth with thee."
But wel unnethes thilke word he spake,
But went his way for routhe and for pitee.
Before the folk hireselven stripeth she,
And in her smok, with foot and hed al bare,
Toward her fadres hous forth is she fare.

The folk her folwen weping in hir wey,
And fortune ay they cursen as they gon:
But she fro weping kept her eyen drey,
Ne in this time word ne spake she non.
Her fader, that this tiding herd anon,
Curseth the day and time, that nature
Shope him to ben a lives creature.

For out of doute this olde poure man
Was ever in suspect of her mariage:
For ever he demed, sin it first began,
That whan the lord fulfilled had his corage,
Him wolde thinke it were a disparage
To his estat, so lowe for to alight,
And voiden her as sone as ever he might.

Agein his doughter hastily goth he,
(For he by noise of folk knew her coming)
And with her olde cote, as it might be,
He covereth her ful sorwefully weping:
But on her body might he it not bring,
For rude was the cloth, and more of age
By daies fele than at her mariage.

Thus with her fader for a certain space
Dwelleth this flour of wifly patience,
That nother by her wordes ne her face,
Beforn the folk, ne eke in her absence,
Ne shewed she that her was don offence,
Ne of her high estat no remembrance
Ne hadde she, as by hire contenance.

No wonder is, for in her gret estat
Her gost was ever in pleine humilitee;
No tendre mouth, no herte delicat,
No pompe, no semblant of realtee;
But ful of patient benignitee,
Discrete, and prideles, ay honourable,
And to her husbond ever meke and stable.

Men speke of Job, and most for his humblesse,
As clerkes, whan hem list, can wel endite,
Namely of men, but as in sothfastnesse,
Though clerkes preisen women but a lite,
Ther can no man in humblesse him acquite

As woman can, ne can be half so trewe
As women ben, but it be falle of newe.

PARS SEXTA.

Fro Boloigne is this erl of Pavie come,
Of which the fame up sprang to more and lesse:
And to the peples eres all and some
Was couth eke, that a newe markisesse
He with him brought, in swiche pomp and richesse,
That never was ther seen with mannes eye
So noble array in al West Lumbardie.

The markis, which that shope and knew all this,
Er that this erl was come, sent his message
For thilke poure sely Grisildis;
And she with humble herte and glad visage,
Not with no swollen thought in her corage,
Came at his hest, and on her knees her sette,
And reverently and wisely she him grette.

"Grisilde," (quod he) "my will is utterly,
This maiden, that shal wedded be to me,
Received be to-morwe as really
As it possible is in myn hous to be:
And eke that every wight in his degree
Have his estat in sitting and service,
And high plesance, as I can best devise.

"I have no woman suffisant certain
The chambres for to array in ordinance
After my lust, and therfore wolde I fain,
That thin were all swiche manere governance:
Thou knowest eke of old all my plesance;
Though thin array be bad, and evil besey,
Do thou thy devoir at the leste wey.

Not only, lord, that I am glad (quod she)
To don your lust, but I desire also
You for to serve and plese in my degree,
Withouten fainting, and shal evermo:
Ne never for no wele, ne for no wo,
Ne shal the gost within myn herte stente
To love you best with all my trewe entente."

And with that word she gan the hous to dight,
And tables for to sette, and beddes make,
And peined hire to don all that she might,
Praying the chambereres for Goddés' sake
To hasten hem, and faste swepe and shake,
And she the moste serviceable of all
Hath every chambre arraied, and his hall.

Abouten undern gan this erl alight,
That with him brought thise noble children twey;
For which the peple ran to see the sight
Of hir arrayed, so richely besey:
And than at erst amonges them they sey,
That Walter was no fool, though that him lest
To change his wif; for it was for the best.

For she is fairer, as they demen all,
Than is Grisilde, and more tendre of age,
And fairer fruit betwene hem shulde fall,
And more plesant for hire high linage:
Hire brother eke so faire was of visage,
That hem to seen the peple hath caught plesance,
Commending now the markis governance.

O stormy peple; unsad and ever untrewe,
And undiscrete, and changing as a fane,

Delighting ever in rombel that is newe,
For like the mone waxen ye and wane:
Ay ful of clapping, dere ynough a jane,
Your dome is fals, your constance evil preveth,
A ful gret fool is he that on you leveth.

Thus saiden sade folk in that citee,
Whan that the peple gased up and doun:
For they were glad, right for the noveltee,
To have a newe lady of hir toun.
No more of this make I now mentioun,
But to Grisilde agen I wol me dresse,
And telle hire constance, and hire besinesse.

Ful besy was Grisilde in every thing,
That to the feste was appertinent;
Right naught was she abaist of hire clothing,
Though it were rude, and somdel eke to-rent,
But with glad chere to the yate is went
With other folk, to grete the markisesse,
And after that doth forth hire besinesse.

With so glad chere his gestes she receiveth,
And conningly everich in his degree,
That no defaute no man apperceiveth,
But ay they wondren what she mighte be,
That in so poure array was for to see,
And coude swiche honour and reverence,
And worthily they preisen hire prudence.

In all this mene while she ne stent
This maide and eke hire brother to commend
With all hire herte in ful benigne entent,
So wel, that no man coud hire preise amend:
But at the last whan that thise lordes wend
To sitten doun to mete, he gan to call
Grisilde, as she was besy in the hall.

"Grisilde, (quod he, as it were in his play)
How liketh thee my wif, and hire beautee?"
"Right wel, my lord, (quod she,) for in good fay,
A fairer saw I never non than she:
I pray to God yeve you prosperitee;
And so I hope, that he wol to you send
Plesance ynough unto your lives end."

"O thing beseche I you and warne also,
That ye ne prikke with no turmenting
This tendre maiden as ye han do mo:
For she is fostred in her norishing
More tendrely, and to my supposing
She mighte not adversitee endure,
As coude a poure fostred creature."

And when this Walter saw her patience,
Her glade chere, and no malice at all,
And he so often hadde her don offence,
And she ay sade and constant as a wall,
Continuing ever her innocence over all,
This sturdy markis gan his herte dresse
To rewe upon her wifly stedefastnesse.

"This is ynough, Grisilde min, (quod he;)
Be now no more agast, ne evil apaid,
I have thy faith and thy benignitee,
As wel as ever woman was, assaid
I gret estat, and pourelich arraied:
Now know I, dere wif, thy stedefastnesse,
And her in armes toke, and gan to kesse.

And she for wonder toke of it no kepe,
She herde not what thing he to her said:

She ferde as she had stert out of a slepe,
Til she out of her masednesse abraid.
"Grisilde, (quod he,) by God that for us deid,
Thou art my wif, non other I ne have,
Ne never had, as God my soule save.

"This is thy doughter, which thou hast supposed
To be my wif; that other faithfully
Shal be min heir, as I have ay disposed;
Thou bare hem of thy body trewely:
At Bologne have I kept hem prively:
Take hem agen, for now maist thou not say,
That thou hast lorn non of thy children tway.

"And folk, that otherwise han said of me,
I warne hem wel, that I have don this dede
For no malice, ne for no crueltee,
But for to assay in thee thy womanhede:
And not to slee my children (God forbede)
But for to kepe hem prively and still,
Til I thy purpos knew, and all thy will."

Whan she this herd aswoune doun she falleth
For pitous joye, and after her swouning
She both her yonge children to her calleth,
And in her armes pitously weping
Embraceth hem, and tendrely kissing
Ful like a moder with her salte teres
She bathed both her visage and her heres.

O, which a pitous thing it was to see
Her swouning, and her humble vois to here!
"*Grand mercy*, lord, God thank it you (quod she)
That ye han saved me my children dere:
Now rekke I never to be ded right here,
Sin I stond in your love, and in your grace,
No force of deth, ne whan my spirit pace.

"O tendre, o dere, o yonge children mine,
Your woful mother wened stedfastly,
That cruel houndes, or some foul vermine
Had eten you; but God of his mercy,
And your benigne fader tendrely
Hath don you kepe:" and in that same stound
Al sodenly she swapt adoun to ground.

And in her swough so sadly holdeth she
Her children two, whan she gan hem embrace,
That with gret sleight and gret difficultee
The children from her arm they gan arrace;
O! many a tere on many a pitous face
Doun ran of hem that stoden her beside,
Unnethe abouten her might they abide.

Walter her gladeth, and her sorwe slaketh,
She riseth up abashed from her trance,
And every wight her joye and feste maketh,
Til she hath caught agen her contenance.
Walter hire doth so faithfully plesance,
Thet it was deintee for to seen the chere
Betwix hem two, sin they ben met in fere.

Thise ladies, whan that they her time sey,
Han taken her, and into chambre gon,
And stripen her out of her rude arrey,
And in a cloth of gold that brighte shone,
With a coroune of many a riche stone
Upon her hed, they into hall her broughte:
And ther she was honoured as her ought.

Thus hath this pitous day a blisful end;
For every man, and woman, doth his might

This day in mirth and revel to dispend,
Til on the welkin shone the sterres bright:
For more solempne in every mannes sight
This festé was, and greter of costage,
Than was the revel of her mariage.

Ful many a yere in high prosperitee
Liven thise two in concord and in rest,
And richely his doughter maried he
Unto a lord, on of the worthiest
Of all Itaille, and than in pees and rest
His wivês fader in his court he kepeth,
Til that the soule out of his body crepeth.

His sone succedeth in his heritage,
In rest and pees, after his fadres day:
And fortunat was eke in mariage,
Al put he not his wif in gret assay:
This world is not so strong, it is no nay,
As it hath ben in olde times yore,
And herkneth, what this auctour saith therfore.

This story is said, not for that wives shuld
Folwe Grisilde, as in humilitee,
For it were importable, tho they wold;
But for that every wight in his degree
Shulde be constant in adversitee,
As was Grisilde, therfore Petrark writeth
This storie, which with high stile he enditeth.

For sith a woman was so patient
Unto a mortal man, wel more we ought
Receiven all in gree that God us sent.
For gret skill is he preve that he wrought
But he ne tempteth no man that he bought
As saith seint Jame, if ye his pistell rede;
He preveth folk al day, it is no drede:

And suffreth us, as for our exercise,
With sharpe scourges of adversitee
Ful often to be bete in sondry wise;
Not for to know our will, for certes he
Or we were borne, knew all our freeletee;
And for our best is all his governance;
Let us than live in vertuous suffrance.

But one word, lordings, herkeneth, ere I go:
It were ful hard to finden now adayes
In all a toun Grisildes three or two:
For if that they were put to swiche assayes,
The gold of hem hath now so bad alayes
With bras, that though the coine be faire at eye,
It wolde rather brast atwo than plie.

For which here, for the wives love of Bathe,
Whos lif and al hire secte God maintene
In high maistrie, and elles were it scathe,
I wol with lusty herte fresshe and grene,
Say you a song to gladen you, I wene:
And let us stint of ernestful matere.
Herkneth my song, that saith in this manere.

Grisilde is ded, and eke her patience,
And both at ones buried in Itaille:
For which I crie in open audience,
No wedded man so hardy be to assaille
His wives patience, in trust to find
Grisildes, for in certain he shal faille.

O noble wives, ful of high prudence,
Let non humilitee your tonges naile:
Ne let no clerk have cause or diligence
To write of you a storie of swiche mervaille,
As of Grisildis patient and kinde,
Lest Chichevache you swalwe in her entraille.

Folweth ecco, that holdeth no silence,
But ever answereth at the countretaille:
Beth not bedaffed for your innocence,
But sharply taketh on you the governaille:
Emprenteth wel this lesson in your minde,
For comun profit, sith it may availle.

Ye archewives, stondeth ay at defence,
Sin ye be strong, as is a gret camaille,
Ne suffreth not, that men do you offence.
And sclendre wives, feble as in bataille,
Beth egre as is a tigre yond in Inde;
Ay clappeth as a mill, I you counsaille

Ne drede hem not, doth hem no reverence,
For though thin husbond armèd be in maille,
The arwes of thy crabbed eloquence
Shal perce his brest, and eke his aventaille:
In jalousie I rede eke thou him binde,
And thou shalt make him couche as doth a quaille.

If thou be faire, ther folk ben in presence
Shew thou thy visage, and thin apparaille:
If thou be foule, be free of thy dispence,
To get the frendes ay do thy travaille:
Be ay of chere as light as lefe on linde,
And let him care, and wepe, and wringe, and waille.

CHAUCER.

RHYME OF THE DUCHESS MAY.

To the belfry, one by one, went the ringers from the sun,
Toll slowly.
And the oldest ringer said, "Ours is music for the Dead,
When the rebecks are all done."

Six abeles i' the churchyard grow on the northside in a row,
Toll slowly.
And the shadows of their tops rock across the little slopes
Of the grassy graves below.

On the south side and the west, a small river runs in haste,
Toll slowly.
And between the river flowing and the fair green trees a-growing
Do the dead lie at their rest.

On the east I sate that day, up against a willow gray:
Toll slowly,
Through the rain of willow-branches,
I could see the low hill-ranges,
And the river on its way.

There I sate beneath the tree, and the bell tolled solemnly,
Toll slowly.
While the trees' and river's voices flowed between the solemn noises, —
Yet death seemed more loud to me.

There I read this ancient rhyme, while the bell did all the time
Toll slowly.
And the solemn knell fell in with the tale of life and sin,
Like a rhythmic fate sublime.

THE RHYME.

Broad the forest stood (I read) on the hills of Linteged —
Toll slowly.
And three hundred years had stood mute adown each hoary wood,
Like a full heart having prayed.

And the little birds sang east, and the little birds sang west,
Toll slowly.
And but little thought was theirs, of the silent antique years,
In the building of their nest.

Down the sun dropped large and red, on the towers of Linteged, —
Toll slowly.
Lance and spear upon the height, bristling strange in fiery light,
While the castle stood in shade.

There, the castle stood up black, with the red sun at its back, —
Toll slowly.
Like a sullen smouldering pyre, with a top that flickers fire,
When the wind is on its track.

And five hundred archers tall did besiege the castle wall,
Toll slowly.
And the castle, seethed in blood, fourteen days and nights had stood,
And to-night was near its fall.

Yet thereunto, blind to doom, three months since, a bride did come, — *Toll slowly.*
One who proudly trod the floors, and softly whispered in the doors,
"May good angels bless our home."

Oh, a bride of queenly eyes, with a front of constancies, —
Toll slowly.
Oh, a bride of cordial mouth, — where the untired smile of youth
Did light outward its own sighs.

'Twas a Duke's fair orphan-girl, and her uncle's ward, the Earl
Toll slowly.
Who betrothed her, twelve years old, for the sake of dowry gold,
To his son Lord Leigh, the churl.

But what time she had made good all her years of womanhood,
Toll slowly.
Unto both those Lords of Leigh, spake she out right sovranly,
"My will runneth as my blood.

"And while this same blood makes red this same right hand's veins," she said, —
Toll slowly.
"'Tis my will as lady free, not to wed a Lord of Leigh,
But Sir Guy of Linteged."

The old Earl he smilèd smooth, then he sighed for wilful youth. —
Toll slowly.
"Good my niece, that hand withal looketh somewhat soft and small,
For so large a will, in sooth."

She, too, smiled by that same sign, — but her smile was cold and fine. — *Toll slowly.*
"Little hand clasps muckle gold; or it were not worth the hold
Of thy son, good uncle mine!"

Then the young lord jerked his breath, and sware thickly in his teeth, *Toll slowly.*
"He would wed his own betrothed, an she loved him, and she loathed,
Let the life come or the death."

Up she rose with scornful eyes, as her father's child might rise,
Toll slowly.
"Thy hound's blood, my Lord of Leigh, stains thy knightly heel," quoth she,
"And he moans not where he lies,

'But a woman's will dies hard, in the hall or on the sward! —
Toll slowly.
By that grave, my lords, which made me orphaned girl and dowered lady,
I deny you wife and ward."

Unto each she bowed her head, and swept past with lofty tread.
Toll slowly.
Ere the midnight-bell had ceased, in the chapel had the priest
Blessed her, bride of Linteged.

Fast and fain the bridal train along the night-storm rode amain:
Toll slowly.
Hard the steeds of lord and serf struck their hoofs out on the turf,
In the pauses of the rain.

Fast and fain the kinsmen's train along the storm pursued amain — *Toll slowly.*
Steed on steed-track, dashing off — thickening, doubling hoof on hoof,
In the pauses of the rain.

And the bridegroom led the flight on his red-roan steed of might,
Toll slowly.
And the bride lay on his arm, still as if she feared no harm,
Smiling out into the night.

"Dost thou fear?" he said at last;—"Nay!" she answered him in haste, — *Toll slowly.*
"Not such death as we could find — only life with one behind —
Ride on fast as fear — ride fast!"

Up the mountain wheeled the steed — girth to ground, and fetlocks spread, — *Toll slowly.*
Headlong bounds, and rocking flanks, — down he staggered — down the banks,
To the towers of Linteged.

High and low the serfs looked out, red the flambeaus tossed about, — *Toll slowly.*
In the courtyard rose the cry — "Live the Duchess and Sir Guy!"
But she never heard them shout.

On the steed she dropped her cheek, kissed his mane and kissed his neck, — *Toll slowly.*
"I had happier died by thee, than lived on a Lady Leigh,"
Were the first words she did speak.

But a three months' joyaunce lay 'twixt that moment and to-day, *Toll slowly.*
When five hundred archers tall stand beside the castle wall
To recapture Duchess May.

And the castle standeth black, with the red sun at its back, —
Toll slowly.
And a fortnight's siege is done — and, except the Duchess, none
Can misdoubt the coming wrack.

Then the captain, young Lord Leigh, with his eyes so gray of blee,
Toll slowly.
And thin lips that scarcely sheath the cold white gnashing of his teeth
Gnashed in smiling, absently,

Cried aloud — "So goes the day, bridegroom fair of Duchess May! — *Toll slowly.*
Look thy last upon that sun. If thou seest to-morrow's one,
'Twill be through a foot of clay.

"Ha, fair bride! Dost hear no sound, save that moaning of the hound? — *Toll slowly.*
Thou and I have parted troth, — yet I keep my vengeance-oath,
And the other may come round.

"Ha! thy will is brave to dare, and thy new love past compare, —
Toll slowly.
Yet thine old love's falchion brave is as strong a thing to have,
As the will of lady fair.

"Peck on blindly, netted dove!—if a wife's name thee behove,
Toll slowly.
Thou shalt wear the same to-morrow, ere the grave has hid the sorrow
Of thy last ill-mated love.

"O'er his fixed and silent mouth, thou and I will call back troth,
Toll slowly.
He shall altar be and priest, — and he will not cry at least
'I forbid you, — I am loath!'

"I will wring my fingers pale in the gauntlet of my mail,
Toll slowly.
'Little hand and muckle gold' close shall lie within my hold,
As the sword did, to prevail."

Oh the little birds sang east, and the little birds sang west,
Toll slowly.
Oh, and laughed the Duchess May, and her soul did put away
All his boasting, for a jest.

In her chamber did she sit, laughing low to think of it, —
Toll slowly.
"Tower is strong and will is free — thou canst boast, my Lord of Leigh,
But thou boasteth little wit."

In her tire-glass gazèd she, and she blushed right womanly.
Toll slowly.
She blushed half from her disdain — half, her beauty was so plain,
— "Oath for oath, my Lord of Leigh!"

Straight she called her maidens in — "Since ye gave me blame herein, *Toll slowly.*
That a bridal such as mine should lack gauds to make it fine,
Come and shrive me from that sin.

"It is three months gone to-day, since I gave mine hand away.
Toll slowly.
Bring the gold and bring the gem, we will keep bride-state in them,
While we keep the foe at bay.

"On your arms I loose my hair; — comb it smooth and crown it fair, *Toll slowly.*
I would look in purple pall from this lattice down the wall,
And throw scorn to one that's there!"

Oh, the little birds sang east, and the little birds sang west,
Toll slowly.
On the tower the castle's lord leant in silence on his sword,
With an anguish in his breast.

With a spirit-laden weight, did he lean down passionate.
Toll slowly.
They have almost sapped the wall, — they will enter there withal,
With no knocking at the gate.

Then the sword he leant upon, shivered — snapped upon the stone, — *Toll slowly.*
"Sword," he thought, with inward laugh, "ill thou servest for a staff
When thy nobler use is done!

"Sword, thy nobler use is done! — tower is lost, and shame begun; *Toll slowly.*
If we met them in the breach, hilt to hilt, or speech to speech,
We should die there, each for one.

"If we met them at the wall, we should singly, vainly fall, —
Toll slowly.
But if *I* die here alone, — then I die, who am but one,
And die nobly for them all.

"Five true friends lie for my sake, in the moat and in the brake,—
Toll slowly.
Thirteen warriors lie at rest, with a black wound in the breast,
And not one of these will wake.

"So no more of this shall be! — heart-blood weighs too heavily — *Toll slowly.*
And I could not sleep in grave, with the faithful and the brave
Heaped around and over me.

"Since young Clare a mother hath, and young Ralph a plighted faith, *Toll slowly.*
Since my pale young sister's cheeks blush like rose when Ronald speaks,
Albeit never a word she saith —

"These shall never die for me — life-blood falls too heavily:
Toll slowly.
And if *I* die here apart, — o'er my dead and silent heart
They shall pass out safe and free.

"When the foe hath heard it said — 'Death holds Guy of Linteged,' — *Toll slowly.*
That new corse new peace shall bring; and a blessèd, blessèd thing,
Shall the stone be at its head.

"Then my friends shall pass out free, and shall bear my memory, —
Toll slowly.
Then my foes shall sleek their pride, soothing fair my widowed bride
Whose sole sin was love of me.

"With their words all smooth and sweet, they will front her and entreat *Toll slowly.*
And their purple pall will spread underneath her fainting head
While her tears drop over it.

"She will weep her woman's tears,
she will pray her woman's
prayers, — *Toll slowly.*
But her heart is young in pain, and
her hopes will spring again
By the suntime of her years.

"Ah, sweet May! — ah, sweetest
grief! — once I vowed thee my
belief, *Toll slowly.*
That thy name expressed thy sweetness, — May of poets, in completeness!
Now my May-day seemeth brief."

All these silent thoughts did swim
o'er his eyes grown strange
and dim, — *Toll slowly.*
Till his true men in the place, wished
they stood there face to face
With the foe instead of him.

"One last oath, my friends that wear
faithful hearts to do and
dare! — *Toll slowly.*
Tower must fall, and bride be lost!
— swear me service worth the
cost,"
— Bold they stood around to
swear.

"Each man clasp my hand and swear,
by the deed we failed in there,
Toll slowly.
Not for vengeance, not for right, will
ye strike one blow to-night!"
— Pale they stood around — to
swear.

"One last boon, young Ralph and
Clare! faithful hearts to do
and dare! *Toll slowly.*
Bring that steed up from his stall,
which she kissed before you
all,
Guide him up the turret-stair.

"Ye shall harness him aright, and
lead upward to this height!
Toll slowly.
Once in love and twice in war, hath
he borne me strong and far,
He shall bear me far to-night."

Then his men looked to and fro,
when they heard him speaking
so. *Toll slowly.*
— "'Las! the noble heart," they
thought, — "he in sooth is
grief-distraught.
Would we stood here with the
foe!"

But a fire flashed from his eye, 'twixt
their thought and their re-
ply, — *Toll slowly.*
"Have ye so much time to waste!
We who ride here, must ride
fast,
As we wish our foes to fly."

They have fetched the steed with
care, in the harness he did
wear, *Toll slowly.*
Past the court and through the
doors, across the rushes of the
floors;
But they goad him up the stair.

Then from out her bower chambère,
did the Duchess May repair.
Toll slowly.
"Tell me now what is your need,"
said the lady, "of this steed,
That ye goad him up the stair?"

Calm she stood; unbodkined through,
fell her dark hair to her
shoe, — *Toll slowly.*
And the smile upon her face, ere she
left the tiring-glass,
Had not time enough to go.

"Get thee back, sweet Duchess May!
hope is gone like yesterday, —
Toll slowly.
One half-hour completes the breach;
and thy lord grows wild of
speech,
Get thee in, sweet lady, and pray.

"In the east tower, high'st of all, —
loud he cries for steed from
stall. *Toll slowly.*
He would ride as far," quoth he, "as
for love and victory,
Though he rides the castle wall.

"And we fetch the steed from stall,
up where never a hoof did
fall. — *Toll slowly.*
Wifely prayer meets deathly need!
may the sweet Heavens hear
thee plead,
If he rides the castle-wall."

Low she dropped her head, and lower, till her hair coiled on the floor, — *Toll slowly.*
And tear after tear you heard fall distinct as any word
Which you might be listening for.

"Get thee in, thou soft ladie! — here is never a place for thee! — *Toll slowly.*
Braid thy hair and clasp thy gown, that thy beauty in its moan
May find grace with Leigh of Leigh."

She stood up in bitter case, with a pale yet stately face, *Toll slowly.*
Like a statue thunderstruck, which, though quivering, seems to look
Right against the thunder-place.

And her foot trod in, with pride, her own tears i' the stone beside, — *Toll slowly.*
"Go to, faithful friends, go to! — Judge no more what ladies do, —
No, nor how their lords may ride!"

Then the good steed's rein she took, and his neck did kiss and stroke: *Toll slowly.*
Soft he neighed to answer her; and then followed up the stair,
For the love of her sweet look.

Oh, and steeply, steeply wound up the narrow stair around, — *Toll slowly.*
Oh, and closely speeding, step by step beside her treading,
Did he follow, meek as hound.

On the east tower, high'st of all, — there, where never a hoof did fall, — *Toll slowly.*
Out they swept, a vision steady, — noble steed and lovely lady,
Calm as if in bower or stall!

Down she knelt at her lord's knee, and she looked up silently, — *Toll slowly.*
And he kissed her twice and thrice, for that look within her eyes
Which he could not bear to see.

Quoth he, "Get thee from this strife, — and the sweet saints bless thy life! — *Toll slowly.*
In this hour, I stand in need of my noble red-roan steed —
But no more of my noble wife."

Quoth she, "Meekly have I done all thy biddings under sun: *Toll slowly.*
But by all my womanhood, — which is proved so true and good,
I will never do this one.

"Now by womanhood's degree, and by wifehood's verity, *Toll slowly.*
In this hour if thou hast need of thy noble red-roan steed,
Thou hast also need of *me.*

"By this golden ring ye see on this lifted hand pardie, *Toll slowly.*
If this hour, on castle-wall, can be room for steed from stall,
Shall be also room for *me.*

"So the sweet saints with me be" (did she utter solemnly,) *Toll slowly.*
"If a man, this eventide, on this castle-wall will ride,
He shall ride the same with *me.*"

Oh, he sprang up in the selle, and he laughed out bitter well, — *Toll slowly.*
"Wouldst thou ride among the leaves, as we used on other eves,
To hear chime a vesper-bell?"

She clang closer to his knee — "Ay, beneath the cypress-tree! — *Toll slowly.*
Mock me not; for otherwhere than along the greenwood fair,
Have I ridden fast with thee!

"Fast I rode with new-made vows, from my angry kinsman's house! *Toll slowly.*
What! and would you men should reck that I dared more for love's sake
As a bride than as a spouse?

"What, and would you it should fall, as a proverb, before all,
Toll slowly.
That a bride may keep your side while through castlegate you ride,
Yet eschew the castle-wall?"

Ho! the breach yawns into ruin, and roars up against her suing, —
Toll slowly.
With the inarticulate din, and the dreadful falling in —
Shrieks of doing and undoing!

Twice he wrung her hands in twain; but the small hands closed again. *Toll slowly.*
Back he reined the steed — back, back! but she trailed along his track
With a frantic clasp and strain!

Evermore the foemen pour through the crash of window and door, — *Toll slowly.*
And the shouts of Leigh and Leigh, and the shrieks of "kill!" and "flee!"
Strike up clear amid the roar.

Thrice he wrung her hands in twain, — but they closed and clung again, — *Toll slowly.*
Wild she clung, as one, withstood, clasps a Christ upon the rood,
In a spasm of deathly pain.

She clung wild and she clung mute, — with her shuddering lips half-shut. *Toll slowly.*
Her head fallen as half in swound, — hair and knee swept on the ground,
She clung wild to stirrup and foot.

Back he reined his steed back-thrown on the slippery coping-stone.
Toll slowly.
Back the iron hoofs did grind on the battlement behind,
Whence a hundred feet went down.

And his heel did press and goad on the quivering flank bestrode,
Toll slowly.
"Friends and brothers, save my wife! — Pardon, sweet, in change for life, —
But I ride alone to God."

Straight as if the Holy name had upbreathed her like a flame,
Toll slowly.
She upsprang, she rose upright, — in his selle she sat in sight;
By her love she overcame.

And her head was on his breast, where she smiled as one at rest, — *Toll slowly.*
"Ring," she cried, "O vesper-bell, in the beech-wood's old chapelle!
But the passing-bell rings best."

They have caught out at the rein, which Sir Guy threw loose — in vain, *Toll slowly.*
For the horse in stark despair, with his front hoofs poised in air,
On the last verge rears amain.

Now he hangs, he rocks between — and his nostrils curdle in, —
Toll slowly.
And he shivers head and hoof — and the flakes of foam fall off;
And his face grows fierce and thin!

And a look of human woe from his staring eyes did go,
Toll slowly.
And a sharp cry uttered he, in a foretold agony
Of the headlong death below, —

And "Ring, ring, — thou passing-bell," still she cried, i' the old chapelle! —
Toll slowly.
Then back-toppling, crushing back, a dead weight flung out to wrack,
Horse and riders overfell!

Oh, the little birds sang east, and the little birds sang west, —
Toll slowly.
And I read this ancient Rhyme in the churchyard, while the chime.
Slowly tolled for one at rest.

The abeles moved in the sun, and the river smooth did run,
Toll slowly.
And the ancient Rhyme rang strange, with its passion and its change,
Here, where all done lay undone.

And beneath a willow tree, I a little grave did see,
Toll slowly.
Where was graved, — HERE UNDEFILED, LIETH MAUD, A THREE-YEAR CHILD,
EIGHTEEN HUNDRED FORTY-THREE.

Then, O Spirits — did I say — ye who rode so fast that day, —
Toll slowly.
Did star-wheels and angel-wings, with their holy winnowings,
Keep beside you all the way?

Though in passion ye would dash, with a blind and heavy crash.
Toll slowly.
Up against the thick-bossed shield of God's judgment in the field, —
Though your heart and brain were rash, —

Now, your will is all unwilled — now your pulses are all stilled, —
Toll slowly.
Now, ye lie as meek and mild (whereso laid) as Maud the child,
Whose small grave was lately filled.

Beating heart and burning brow, ye are very patient now,
Toll slowly.
And the children might be bold to pluck the kingcups from your mould
Ere a month had let them grow.

And you let the goldfinch sing in the alder near in spring,
Toll slowly
Let her build her nest and sit all the three weeks out on it,
Murmuring not at any thing.

In your patience ye are strong; cold and heat ye take not wrong:
Toll slowly.
When the trumpet of the angel blows eternity's evangel,
Time will seem to you not long.

Oh, the little birds sang east, and the little birds sang west,
Toll slowly.
And I said in underbreath, — all our life is mixed with death,
And who knoweth which is best?

Oh, the little birds sang east, and the little birds sang west,
Toll slowly.
And I smiled to think God's greatness flowed around our incompleteness, —
Round our restlessness, his rest.

MRS. BROWNING.

FAIR HELEN.

I WISH I were where Helen lies:
Night and day on me she cries;
O that I were where Helen lies
On fair Kirconnell lea!

Curst be the heart that thought the thought,
And curst the hand that fired the shot,
When in my arms burd Helen dropt,
And died to succor me!

O think na but my heart was sair
When my love dropt down and spake nae mair!
I laid her down wi' meikle care
On fair Kirconnell lea;

As I went down to the water-side,
None but my foe to be my guide,
None but my foe to be my guide,
On fair Kirconnell lea;

I lighted doun my sword to draw,
I hackèd him in pieces sma',
I hackèd him in pieces sma',
For her sake that died for me.

O Helen fair, beyond compare!
I'll make a garland of thy hair
Shall bind my heart forevermair
Until the day I die.

O that I were where Helen lies!
Night and day on me she cries;
Out of my bed she bids me rise,
Says, 'Haste and come to me!'

O Helen fair! O Helen chaste!
If I were with thee, I were blest,
Where thou lies low and takes thy rest
On fair Kirconnell lea.

SCOTT.

THE BRAES OF YARROW.

"BUSK ye, busk ye, my bonnie, bonnie bride!
Busk ye, busk ye, my winsome marrow!
Busk ye, busk ye, my bonnie, bonnie bride,
And think nae mair of the Braes of Yarrow."

"Where gat ye that bonnie, bonnie bride,
Where gat ye that winsome marrow?"
"I gat her where I daurna weel be seen,
Pu'ing the birks on the Braes of Yarrow.

"Weep not, weep not, my bonnie, bonnie bride,
Weep not, weep not, my winsome marrow!
Nor let thy heart lament to leave
Pu'ing the birks on the Braes of Yarrow."

"Why does she weep, thy bonnie, bonnie bride?
Why does she weep, thy winsome marrow?
And why daur ye nae mair weel be seen
Pu'ing the birks on the Braes of Yarrow?"

"Lang maun she weep, lang maun she, maun she weep—
Lang maun she weep wi' dule and sorrow;
And lang maun I nae mair weel be seen
Pu'ing the birks on the Braes of Yarrow.

"For she has tint her lover, lover dear,
Her lover dear, the cause of sorrow;
And I hae slain the comeliest swain
That e'er pu'd birks on the Braes of Yarrow.

"Why runs thy stream, O Yarrow, Yarrow, red?
Why on thy braes heard the voice of sorrow?
And why yon melancholious weeds
Hung on the bonnie birks of Yarrow?

"What's yonder floats on the rueful, rueful flood?
What's yonder floats? O, dule and sorrow!
'Tis he, the comely swain I slew
Upon the dulefu' Braes of Yarrow.

"Wash, O wash his wounds, his wounds in tears,
His wounds in tears o' dule and sorrow;
And wrap his limbs in mourning weeds,
And lay him on the banks of Yarrow.

"Then build, then build, ye sisters, sisters sad,
Ye sisters sad, his tomb wi' sorrow;
And weep around, in waeful wise,
His hapless fate on the Braes of Yarrow!

"Curse ye, curse ye, his useless, useless shield,
The arm that wrought the deed of sorrow,
The fatal spear that pierced his breast,
His comely breast, on the Braes of Yarrow!

"Did I not warn thee not to, not to love,
And warn from fight? But, to my sorrow,
Too rashly bold, a stronger arm thou met'st,
Thou met'st, and fell on the Braes of Yarrow.

"Sweet smell the birk; green grows, green grows the grass;
Yellow on Yarrow's braes the gowan;
Fair hangs the apple frae the rock;
Sweet the wave of Yarrow flowan!

"Flows Yarrow sweet? As sweet, as sweet flows Tweed;
As green its grass; its gowan as yellow;
As sweet smells on its braes the birk;
The apple frae its rock as mellow!

"Fair was thy love! fair, fair indeed thy love!
In flowery bands thou didst him fetter;
Though he was fair, and well-beloved again,
Than I he never loved thee better.

"Busk ye, then, busk, my bonnie, bonnie bride!
Busk ye, busk ye, my winsome marrow!
Busk ye, and lo'e me on the banks of Tweed
And think nae mair on the Braes of Yarrow."

"How can I busk a bonnie, bonnie bride?
How can I busk a winsome marrow?
How love him on the banks of Tweed,
That slew my love on the Braes of Yarrow?

"O Yarrow fields, may never, never rain,
Nor dew, thy tender blossoms cover!
For there was basely slain my love,
My love, as he had not been a lover!

"The boy put on his robes, his robes of green,
His purple vest, — 'twas my ain sewing;
Ah, wretched me! I little, little kenned
He was, in these, to meet his ruin.

"The boy took out his milk-white, milk-white steed,
Unmindful of my dule and sorrow;
But ere the too fa' of the night,
He lay a corpse on the banks of Yarrow!

"Much I rejoiced that waefu', waefu' day;
I sang, my voice the woods returning;
But lang ere night the spear was flown,
That slew my love, and left me mourning.

"What can my barbarous, barbarous father do,
But with his cruel rage pursue me?
My lover's blood is on thy spear, —
How canst thou, barbarous man, then woo me?

"My happy sisters may be, may be proud;
With cruel and ungentle scoffin,
May bid me seek, on Yarrow Braes,
My lover nailèd in his coffin.

"My brother Douglas may upbraid,
And strive, with threatening words, to move me;
My lover's blood is on thy spear, —
How can thou ever bid me love thee?

"Yes, yes, prepare the bed, the bed of love!
With bridal-sheets my body cover!
Unbar, ye bridal-maids, the door!
Let in the expected husband-lover!

"But who the expected husband, husband is?
His hands, methinks, are bathed in slaughter!
Ah me! what ghastly spectre's yon
Comes in his pale shroud, bleeding after?

"Pale as he is, here lay him, lay him down;
Oh lay his cold head on my pillow!
Take off, take off these bridal weeds,
And crown my careful head with willow.

"Pale though thou art, yet best, yet best belovèd,
Oh could my warmth to life restore thee!
Yet lie all night within my arms —
No youth lay ever there before thee!

"Pale, pale indeed, O lovely, lovely youth!
Forgive, forgive so foul a slaughter,
And lie all night within my arms,
No youth shall ever lie there after!"

"Return, return, O mournful, mournful bride!
Return, and dry thy useless sorrow!
Thy lover heeds nought of thy sighs;
He lies a corpse on the Braes of Yarrow."

WILLIAM HAMILTON.

ROSABELLE.

OH listen, listen, ladies gay!
No haughty feat of arms I tell;
Soft is the note, and sad the lay,
That mourns the lovely Rosabelle.

"Moor, moor the barge, ye gallant crew,
And, gentle lady, deign to stay!
Rest thee in Castle Ravensheuch,
Nor tempt the stormy firth to-day.

"The blackening wave is edged with white;
To inch and rock the sea-mews fly:
The fishers have heard the Water-Sprite,
Whose screams forebode that wreck is nigh.

"Last night the gifted Seer did view
A wet shroud swathed round lady gay;
Then stay thee, Fair, in Ravensheuch;
Why cross the gloomy firth to-day?"

"'Tis not because Lord Lindesay's heir
To-night at Roslin leads the ball,
But that my lady-mother there
Sits lonely in her castle-hall.

"'Tis not because the ring they ride,
And Lindesay at the ring rides well,
But that my sire the wine will chide
If 'tis not filled by Rosabelle."

O'er Roslin all that dreary night
A wondrous blaze was seen to gleam;
'Twas broader than the watch-fire's light,
And redder than the bright moonbeam.

It glared on Roslin's castled rock,
It ruddied all the copse-wood glen;
'Twas seen from Dryden's groves of oak,
And seen from caverned Hawthornden.

Seemed all on fire that chapel proud
Where Roslin's chiefs uncoffined lie,
Each baron, for a sable shroud,
Sheathed in his iron panoply.

Blazed battlement and pinnet high,
Blazed every rose-carved buttress fair, —
So still they blaze when fate is nigh
The lordly line of high Saint Clair.

There are twenty of Roslin's barons bold
Lie buried within that proud chapelle;
Each one the holy vault doth hold,
But the sea holds lovely Rosabelle!

And each Saint Clair was buried there
With candle, with book, and with knell;
But the sea-caves rung, and the wild winds sung
The dirge of lovely Rosabelle.

SCOTT.

TELLING THE BEES.

HERE is the place; right over the hill
Runs the path I took;
You can see the gap in the old wall still,
And the stepping-stones in the shallow brook.

There is the house, with the gate red-barred,
And the poplars tall;
And the barn's brown length, and the cattle-yard,
And the white horns tossing above the wall.

There are the beehives ranged in the sun;
And down by the brink
Of the brook are her poor flowers, weed-o'errun,
Pansy and daffodil, rose and pink.

A year has gone, as the tortoise goes,
Heavy and slow;
And the same rose blows, and the same sun glows,
And the same brook sings of a year ago.

There's the same sweet clover-smell in the breeze;
And the June sun warm
Tangles his wings of fire in the trees,
Setting, as then, over Fernside farm.

I mind me how with a lover's care
From my Sunday coat
I brushed off the burrs, and smoothed my hair,
And cooled at the brookside my brow and throat.

Since we parted, a month had passed, —
To love, a year;
Down through the beeches I looked at last
On the little red gate and the well-sweep near.

I can see it all now, — the slantwise rain
Of light through the leaves,
The sundown's blaze on her window-pane,
The bloom of her roses under the eves.

Just the same as a month before, —
The house and the trees,
The barn's brown gable, the vine by the door, —
Nothing changed but the hive of bees.

Before them, under the garden wall,
Forward and back,
Went drearily singing the chore-girl small,
Draping each hive with a shred of black.

Trembling, I listened: the summer sun
Had the chill of snow;
For I knew she was telling the bees of one
Gone on the journey we all must go!

Then I said to myself, "My Mary weeps
For the dead to-day:
Haply her blind old grandsire sleeps
The fret and the pain of his age away."

But her dog whined low; on the doorway sill,
With his cane to his chin,
The old man sat; and the chore-girl still
Sung to the bees stealing out and in.

And the song she was singing ever since
In my ear sounds on: —
"Stay at home, pretty bees, fly not hence!
Mistress Mary is dead and gone!"

WHITTIER.

BRUCE AND THE ABBOT.

THE Abbot on the threshold stood,
And in his hand the holy rood:
Then, cloaking hate with fiery zeal,
Proud Lorn first answered the appeal; —
"Thou comest, O holy man,
True sons of blessèd church to greet,
But little deeming here to meet
A wretch, beneath the ban
Of Pope and Church, for murder done
Even on the sacred altar-stone! —
Well mayst thou wonder we should know
Such miscreant here, nor lay him low,

Or dream of greeting, peace, or truce,
With excommunicated Bruce!
Yet will I grant to end debate,
Thy sainted voice decide his fate."

The Abbot seemed with eye severe
The hardy chieftain's speech to hear;
Then on King Robert turned the Monk, —
But twice his courage came and sunk,
Confronted with the hero's look;
Twice fell his eye, his accents shook;
Like man by prodigy amazed,
Upon the King the Abbot gazed;
Then o'er his pallid features glance
Convulsions of ecstatic trance;
His breathing came more thick and fast,
And from his pale blue eyes were cast
Strange rays of wild and wandering light;
Uprise his locks of silver white,
Flushed is his brow; through every vein
In azure tide the currents strain,
And undistinguished accents broke
The awful silence ere he spoke.

"De Bruce! I rose with purpose dread
To speak my curse upon thy head,
And give thee as an outcast o'er
To him who burns to shed thy gore; —
But, like the Midianite of old,
Who stood on Zophim, heaven-controlled,
I feel within mine aged breast
A power that will not be repressed.
It prompts my voice, it swells my veins,
It burns, it maddens, it constrains! —
De Bruce, thy sacrilegious blow
Hath at God's altar slain thy foe:
O'ermastered yet by high behest,
I bless thee, and thou shalt be blessed!"
He spoke, and o'er the astonished throng
Was silence, awful, deep, and long.

Again that light has fired his eye,
Again his form swells bold and high,
The broken voice of age is gone,
'Tis vigorous manhood's lofty tone: —
"Thrice vanquished on the battle plain, —
Thy followers slaughtered, fled, or ta'en, —
A hunted wanderer on the wild,
On foreign shores a man exiled,
Disowned, deserted, and distressed, —
I bless thee, and thou shalt be blessed!
Blessed in the hall and in the field,
Under the mantle as the shield.
Avenger of thy country's shame,
Restorer of her injured fame,
Blessed in thy sceptre and thy sword, —
De Bruce, fair Scotland's rightful Lord,
Blessed in thy deeds and in thy fame,
What lengthened honors wait thy name!
In distant ages, sire to son
Shall tell thy tale of freedom won,
And teach his infants, in the use
Of earliest speech, to falter Bruce.
Go, then, triumphant! sweep along
Thy course, the theme of many a song!
The Power, whose dictates swell my breast,
Hath blessed thee, and thou shalt be blessed!"

SCOTT.

VISION OF BELSHAZZAR.

THE king was on his throne,
The satraps thronged the hall;
A thousand bright lamps shone
O'er that high festival.
A thousand cups of gold,
In Judah deemed divine, —
Jehovah's vessels hold
The godless heathen's wine!

In that same hour and hall,
The fingers of a hand
Came forth against the wall,
And wrote as if on sand:
The fingers of a man; —
A solitary hand
Along the letters ran,
And traced them like a wand.

The monarch saw, and shook,
And bade no more rejoice:
All bloodless waxed his look,
And tremulous his voice.

"Let the men of lore appear,
  The wisest of the earth,
And expound the words of fear,
  Which mar our royal mirth."

Chaldæa's seers are good,
  But here they have no skill;
And the unknown letters stood,
  Untold and awful still.
And Babel's men of age
  Are wise and deep in lore;
But now they were not sage,
  They saw, — but knew no more.

A captive in the land,
  A stranger and a youth, —
He heard the king's command,
  He saw that writing's truth.
The lamps around were bright,
  The prophecy in view:
He read it on that night, —
  The morrow proved it true.

"Belshazzar's grave is made,
  His kingdom passed away,
He in the balance weighed,
  Is light and worthless clay.
The shroud, his robe of state;
  His canopy, the stone;
The Mede is at his gate!
  The Persian on his throne!"

BYRON.

SIR PAVON AND ST. PAVON.

PART I.

ST. MARK'S hushed abbey heard,
  Through prayers, a roar and din;
A brawling voice did shout,
  "Knave shaveling, let me in!"

The cagèd porter peeped,
  All fluttering, through the grate,
Like birds that hear a mew.
  A knight was at the gate.

His left hand reined his steed,
  Still smoking from the ford;
His crimson right, that dangled, clutched
  Half of his broken sword.

His broken plume flapped low;
  His charger's mane with mud
Was clogged; he wavered in his seat;
  His mail dropped drops of blood.

"Who cometh in such haste?"
  "Sir Pavon, late, I hight,
Of all the land around
  The stanchest, mightiest knight.

"My foes — they dared not face —
  Beset me at my back
In ambush. Fast and hard
  They follow on my track.

"Now wilt thou let me in,
  Or shall I burst the door?"
The grating bolts ground back; the knight
  Lay swooning in his gore.

As children, half afraid,
  Draw near a crushèd wasp,
Look, touch, and twitch away
  Their hands, then lightly grasp, —

Him to their spital soon
  The summoned brethren bore,
And searched his wounds. He woke,
  And roundly cursed and swore.

The younger friar stopped his ears;
  The elder chid. He flung
His gummy plasters at his mouth,
  And bade him hold his tongue.

But, faint and weak, when, left
  Upon his couch alone,
He viewed the valley, framed within
  His window's carven stone,

He learned anew to weep,
  All as he lay along,
To see the smoke-wreaths from his towers
  Climb up the clouds among.

The abbot came to bring
  A balsam to his guest,
On soft feet tutored long
  To break no sufferer's rest,

And heard his sobbing heart
  Drink deep in draughts of woe;
Then "Benedicite, my son,"
  He breathed, in murmurs low.

Right sharply turned the knight
  Upon the unwelcome spy;
But changed his shaggy face, as when,
  Down through a stormy sky,

The quiet autumn sun
  Looks on a landscape grim.
He crossed himself before the priest,
  And speechless gazed on him.

His brow was large and grand,
  And meet for governing;
The beauty of his holiness
  Did crown him like a king.

His mien was high, yet mild;
  His deep and reverent eye
Seemed o'er a peaceful past to gaze, —
  A blest futurity.

His stainless earthy shell
  Was worn so pure and thin,
That through the callow angel showed,
  Half-hatched that stirred within.

The cloisters when he paced
  At eve, the brethren said,
E'en then a shimmering halo dawned
  Around his saintly head.

If forth he went, the street
  Became a hallowed aisle.
Men knelt; and children ran to seek
  The blessing of his smile;

And mothers on each side came out,
  And stood at every door,
And held their babies up, and put
  The weanlings forth before.

As pure white lambs unto
  Men sickening unto death
Their sweet infectious health give out,
  And heal them with their breath,

His white and thriving soul,
  In heavenly pastures fed,
Still somewhat of its innocence
  On all around him shed.

Sir Pavon's scarce-stanched wounds
  He bound with fearless skill,
Who lay and watched him, meek and mute,
  And let him work his will,

While in his fevered brain
  Thus mused his fancy quaint:
"My grandam told me once of saints,
  And this is, sure, a saint!

"(I was a new-breeched boy,
  And sat upon her knee,
Less mindful of the story than
  Of catęs she gave to me.)

"But then I thought a flood
  Came down to drown them all,
And that they only now in stone
  Stood on the minster wall,

"Or painted in the glass
  Upon the window high,
Where, swelled with spring-tides, breaks the sea
  Beneath, and leaves them dry,

"Quite out of danger's way,
  And breathed and walked no more
Upon the muddy earth, to do
  The deeds they did of yore,

"When still the sick were healed
  Where e'en their shadows fell;
But here is one that's living yet,
  And he shall make me well."

The patient priest benign
  His watch beside him kept,
Until he dropped his burning lids,
  And like an infant slept.

PART II.

Some weary weeks were spent
  In tossing and in pain,
Before the knight's huge frame was braced
  With strength and steel again.

(He had his armor brought
  The day he left his bed,
And fitted on by novice hands,
  "To prop him up," he said.)

Soon jangling then he stamped,
  Amazed with all he saw,
Through cell and through refectory,
  With little grace or awe.

Unbidden at the board
  He sat, a mouthful took,
And shot it spattering through his beard,
  Sprang up, and cursed the cook.

If some bowed friar passèd by,
  He chucked him 'neath the chin,
And cried, "What cheer?" or, "Dost thou find
  That hair-cloth pricks the skin?"

Or if he came on one
  In meditation meet,
Or penance, mute, he kindly vowed
  To cheer his lone retreat.

"Poor palsied sire," he cried,
  "How fares thy stiffened tongue?
Let mine suffice for both," — and trolled
  A lusty drinking-song.

One softly in his cell
  Did scourge his meagre hide,
When Pavon on his rounds came in,
  And stood, well pleased, beside:

"What, man! Lay on! lay on!
  Nay, hast thou tired thine arm?
Give me thy hempen bunch of cords,
  And I will make thee warm."

With doubtful thanks agreed
  The monk. Him Pavon whipped
Right deftly, through the cloister, till
  For aid he cried and skipped.

In brief, within the house
  Of holy Quiet, all
Where'er Sir Pavon went or came
  Was outcry, noise, and brawl;

Until the abbot said,
  "Anon this coil must cease.
To-morrow is the Truce of God;
  Then let him go in peace.

"But call him hither first,
  To render thanks to-night
For life restored; for now we go
  To do our vesper rite."

With tamèd mien abashed,
  The wild, unruly guest
His hest obeyed, and mutely moved
  Beside the solemn priest.

Unto a noiseless pace
  He strove to curb his stride,
And blushed to hear his jack-boots' clang
  Amid the sandals' slide.

The censer waved around
  Its misty, sweet perfume,
As over him the minster great
  Came with its awful gloom.

Through shadowy aisle, 'neath vaulted roof,
  His faltering steps were led;
Beside him was the living saint,
  Beneath, the sainted dead.

Bespread with nun-wrought tapestry,
  The holy altar stood;
Above it, carved by martyr hands,
  Arose the Holy Rood;

Burned round it, tipped with tongues of flame,
  Vowed candles white and tall;
And frosted cup and patine, clear,
  In silver, painted all.

The prisoned giant Music in
  The rumbling organ rolled,
And roared sweet thunders up to heaven,
  Through all its pipes of gold.

He started. 'Mid the prostrate throng
  Upright, he heard the hymn
With fallen chin and lifted eye
  That searched the arches dim;

For in the lurking echoes there
  Responding, tone and word,
A choir of answering seraphim
  Above he deemed he heard.

They saw him thus when all was done,
  Still rapt and pale as death;
So passed he through the banging gate,
  Then drew a long-drawn breath,

As to the priest he turned:
  "I cannot 'go in peace,'
Nor find elsewhere a man like thee,
  Nor hear such strains as these!"

"This is no place for knights."
  "Then I a monk will be."*
"Kneel down upon thy knee, fair son,
  And tell thy sins to me."

* "Henry de Joyeuse, Comte du Bouchage, Frère puîné du Duc de Joyeuse, tué à Coutras. 'Un jour qu'il passoit à Paris à quatre heures du matin, près du Couvent des Capucins, après avoir passé la nuit en débauche, il s'imagina que les Anges chantoient Matines dans le Couvent. Frappé de cette idée, il se fit Capucin, sous le nom de Frère-Ange.' . . . Cette anecdote est tirée des Notes sur l'Henriade." — *Mémoires de Sully*, Livre Dixième, Note 67.

"My knee is stiff with steel,
And will not bend it well.
'My sins!' A peerless knight like me,
What should he have to tell?

"I never turned in fight
Till treason wrought my harm,
Nor then, before my shattered sword
Weighed down my shattered arm.

"I never broke mine oath,
Forgot my friend or foe,
Nor left a benefit unpaid
With weal, or wrong with woe.

"'Keep thee from me!' * I said,
Still, ere my blows began,
Nor gashed mine unarmed enemy, †
Nor smote a fellèd man,

"Observing every rule
Of generous chivalry;
And maid and matron ever found
A champion leal in me.

"What gallantly I won
In war, I did not hoard,
But spent as gallantly in peace,
With neighbors round my board."

"Thy neighbors, son? The serfs
For miles who tilled thy ground?"
"Tush, father, nay! The high-born knights
For many a league around.

"They were my brethren sworn,
In battle and in sport.
'Twere wondrous shame, should one like me
With beggar kernes consort!

"Clean have I made my shrift,"
He said; and so he ceased,
And bore a blithe and guileless cheer,
That sore perplexed the priest.

With words both soft and keen,
He searched his breast within.
Still said he, "So I sinnèd not,"
Or, "That is, sure, no sin."

The abbot beat his breast:
"Alack, the man is lost!
Erewhile he must have grieved away
The warning Holy Ghost!

"His guardian angel he
Hath scared from him to heaven!
Who cannot mourn, nor see, his sin,
How can he be forgiven?

"E'en Patmos' gentle seer,
Doth he not say, in sooth,
He lies who saith, I have no sin,
Quite empty of the truth!

"Search thou this sacred tome."
"'Sblood!—Saints!—A knight to read!"
The abbot read. The novice strove,
With duteous face, to heed,

But heard a hunt sweep by,
And to the door did leap,
Cried, "Holla, ho!" and then, abashed,
Sat down and dropped asleep.

"Such novice ne'er I saw!
Sweet Mary be my speed!
For sure the sorer is my task,
The sorer is his need."

He gazed upon him long,
With pondering, pitying eyes,
As the leech on the sick whose hidden ail
All herbs and drugs defies;

And, "Hath thy heart might," at last, "to-night,"
He to Sir Pavon said,
"When all men sleep, thy vigil to keep,
In the crypt among the dead?

"Night hath many a tongue, her black hours among,
Less false than the tongues of Day,
While Mercy the prayer hath full leisure to hear,
Of all who wake to pray.

"The mute swart queen hides many a sin,
But oft to the sinner's heart
Remorse, with the tale, she sends to wail,
And thus atones in part."

* The regular form of announcement that a single combat had begun between knights.

† "To smyte a wounded man that may not stonde, God deffende me from such a shame." "Wyt thou well, Syr Gawayn, I wyl neuer smyte a fellyd knight." — *Prose Romance of King Arthur.*

Well-nigh laughed the knight, "Ay, and many a night,
Good father, do not spare.
Ne'er yet have I found, on or under the ground,
The venture I could not dare.

"Ten years I've quelled in war lively warriors, near and far;
Shall I shun a dead clerk's bones to see?
Ne'er till now I pledged my hand to serve in the band
Of captain I lovèd like thee."

PART III.

Sir Pavon sat upon his shield,
And breathed the earthy damp,
And strained his empty ear to hear
The simmering of his lamp.

It made a little tent of light,
Hung round with shadows dim,
That drooped as if the low-groined roof
Did crouch to fall on him.

The stunted columns, thick and short,
Like sentry gnomes stood round;
And lettered slabs, that roofed the dead,
Lay thickly on the ground.

He watched to hear the midnight lauds,
But heard them not until
He deemed it dawn. They swelled at last,
And ceased; and all was still.

The Future towards him marched no more;
The Past was dead and gone;
Time dwindled to a single point;
The convent-clock tolled One.

Then the door was oped and closed,
But by no human hand;
And there entered in a Cry,
And before him seemed to stand,—

A viewless, bodiless Cry,
That lifted the hair on his head;—
'Twas small as a new-born babe's at first,
But straightway it rose and spread,

Till it knocked against the roof,
And his ears they rang and beat;
The hard walls throbbed around, above,
And the stones crept under his feet;

And when it fell away,
He reeled and almost fell;
And fast for aid he gasped and prayed,
Till he heard the matin-bell.

The monk who came to let him out
Scarce knew him. In that night,
His nut-brown beard and crispèd hair
Had turned to snowy white.

PART IV.

Like to a hunted beast,
To Abbot Urban's cell
He rushed; and with a foamy lip
Down at his feet he fell:

"I heard a voice,—a voice!—
O father, help! It said
That I the Lord of life
Had scourged and buffeted,

"Spit in his face, and mocked,
And sold him to his foes;
Then, through the hollow earth,
In dreary triumph rose

"Up, till the words I snatched,
A fiendish chorus dim,
'*He did it unto one of* HIS!
He did it unto HIM!'"

"My son, what meaneth this?"
"My father, on my word,
In court or camp, abroad, at home,
I never knew the Lord!

"I do remember once
I had a hunchback slave,
Who to the beggars round my door
From his own trencher gave,

"And made them swarm the more,
Despite the porter's blows,
And broke into my banquet-hall,
With tidings of their woes.

"Him I chastised and sold.
But thought no harm, nor knew
The Lord so squalid minions had,
Among his chosen few;

"But if the man was his,
I'll freely give thee thrice,
In broad, bright rounds of ruddy gold,
The pittance of his price."

"Gold buys this world, not heaven.
This cannot make thee whole.
Each stripe that rends the slave's poor flesh,
It hurts his Master's soul;

"And if the slave doth die,"
He said beneath his breath,
"I fear the Master's sprite for aye
Rots in the second death.

"But be of better cheer.
Since thou thy sin canst see,
'Tis plain thy guardian angel back
Hath flown from heaven to thee.

"The soul benumbed by sin,
And limb that's numb with frost,
Are saved by timely aches. If first
They reach the fire, they're lost.

"The Sun of righteousness,
Whose beaming smile on high,
With light, and life, and love doth fill
The mansions of the sky,

"And kindles risen souls
Unto a rapturous glow,
Who duly sought his scattered rays,
To bask in them below,

"Seems but a hideous glare
Of blazing pangs untold,
To those whom death hath made more pale,
But could not make more cold.

"Full many a man like thee,
Unless by devils driven,
Would never turn his laggard steps
To hurry unto heaven.

"Thank God, who oped thine ear
Unto their dreary lay,
Ere came the night that summoned thee
To chant with them for aye!

"That holy text, which through
Their gnashing teeth they laughed
And screamed, I read thee yester eve,
And they with wonted craft

"Told o'er, their fright and pain
That thou shouldst come to share,
As birds by hissing serpents scared
Drop down, through sheer despair.

"But in its two pure hands
Each holy Scripture still
Doth bear a blessing for the good,
A curse unto the ill.

"Heed thou, but do not fear
Too much their threatening voice,
Who tremble and believe. Thou yet
Believing mayst rejoice.

"Take up thy cross with speed.
This penance shalt thou do;
Thyself in sad humility
To seek Christ's servant go,

"Both near and far; and dry
His tears with thine, if still
His limbs the toil-exacting earth
In misery tread and till."

His forehead from his hands
Upraised the haggard guest:
"And even here, and even yet,
For me no heavenly rest!"

The abbot shook his head:
"God help thee now, poor son!
The heavenly rest is but for those
Who heavenly work have done.

"Strife is the bridge o'er hell
'Twixt sin and sin forgiven;
Still purgatory lies between
The wicked world and heaven.

"The priceless pearl is worth
The plunge through whelming floods.
The bitter years man loathes are but
Eternity's green buds.

"Thou hast, in Satan's ranks,
To harm been brisk and brave;
Thou wilt not shrink, when sent by Christ
To suffer and to save."

PART V.

Sir Pavon's gallant steed was dead;
Sir Pavon's sword was broke.
On foot he went; and in his hand
The abbot's staff he took,

And many an hour fared patiently,
  Beneath the parching sun,
That eyed him through his riven wall
  Before the day was done.

The shattered casements gaped and
    stared;
  Black charcoal paved the floor;
Up rose his hunger-maddened hound,
  And bit him in the door.

He climbed the scathed and tottering
    stair
  Unto the sooty tower;
His rifled coffers upside down
  Lay in his secret bower.

With heavy heart and tread he trod
  The banquet-hall below;
The hollow-voicèd echoes chid
  Each other, to and fro.

A jeering face peeped in; he heard
  A titter and a shout;
In rushed his rabble rout of hinds,
  And round him danced about:

"Ho, worthy master, welcome home!
  Where hast thou left thy sword,
Thy kingly port, and lusty blows?
  We serve another lord."

They strove to trip him as he went;
  They drove him from his door:
"Now fare ye well, my fathers' halls!
  We part to meet no more.

"Farewell my pride and pomp and
    power!
  Farewell, my slippery wealth,
That bought my soul's sore malady,
  Nor stayed to buy my health!

"Farewell, my sturdy strength, that
    did
  The Devil's work so well,
All blasted by God's thunderbolts,
  That on my spirit fell!

"And thou, O brave and loyal Christ,
  Who, 'mid the sordid Jews,
By love, not fear, constrainèd couldst
  At Satan's hands refuse

"The crown and sceptre of the world,
  And choose the cross and rod, —
Thy more than earthly manhood in
  Its glory unto God

"Lay down, — accept, and do not
    scorn
  The beaten losel me,
Who, worthless for thy service, come
  For shelter unto thee."

Walked with him flagging Weariness;
  And Famine spun his head:
"I would, of all my feasts, were left
  One little crust of bread."

When maids and stars their tapers lit,
  He reached a wooden hut;
The chinks were gilt by light therein,
  But close the door was shut.

What seemed an aged woman's voice
  Within, with sob and groan,
Entreated Heaven in agony
  To send her back her son:

"The day is night that shows me not
  His face, — the voice of joy
Mere heart-break till his laugh I hear!
  O, send me back my boy!

"In pity send some tidings soon!
  If thus I grieve, I dread
Lest, when he hurries back to me, —
  Poor youth! — he find me dead.

"Let them not tell me he is dead,
  And buried anywhere!
What has the ground or brine to do
  With his dear mouth and hair,

"That I have kissed and stroked so
    oft
  There by his empty chair?
Yon doublet new, I've wrought for
    him,
  He'll soon come back to wear.

"I brushed the very flies away,
  That with his brows did toy,
When tired he slept. How could
    the worms
  Or fishes eat my boy?

"O Father, who thine only Son
  Didst yield to pain and death,
And know'st 'tis deadlier pain to do't,
  Than give the rattling breath,

"If not my boy, let unto me
  His faith and trust be given,
That I may clasp him yet again,
  If not on earth, in heaven."

She ceased. Sir Pavon softly knocked;
The door flew open wide.
"Fear not, good mother," he began.
"O, is it thou?" she cried,

Then turned away and wrung her hands.
"If thou wilt give to me
A morsel, and a cup of wine,
Perchance thy charity,

"When ended is my present quest,
I may full well requite,
If lives thy son, and bring him back.
I am a famous knight, —

"Although of late mine ambushed foe
Despoiled me traitorly, —
And maid and matron ever found
A champion leal in me."

"Alack, I have no wine nor flesh,
Nor yet a crust of bread!
Herbs for my noontide meal I culled,
Untasted still," she said;

"And water from the brook I'll bring, —
Scant fare for hungry guest! —
But sit thee down at least, and feed
Thy weariness with rest.

"Thou hast seen other lands perchance?"
"Good mother, many a one.
I pray you fill my cup once more."
"O, hast thou seen my son?"

"Went he a soldier?" "Nay, but he
Was seized and sold away,
I know not where. No news of him
Has reached me from that day.

"He bade me still with wayfarers
His scanty portion share.
Thou eatest from his platter now,
And sittest in his chair.

"He was so good!" "Who used him so?"
"Sir Pavon was his name."
His platter dropped, and over him
A deadly sickness came.

"I knew not half my guilt!" he shrieked,
And on his brow did strike;
These mothers are like God, then, — love
Ugly and fair alike!

"'Twas I. Thou art avenged on me.
To find him is my quest;
Nor till 'tis done, in life or death,
For me is any rest.

"God's heaviest hand is for his sake
Meanwhile upon me laid.
For his deliverance pray, and mine;
And take me in his stead.

"A duteous son I'll be to thee
Until I give him back.
I've many friends would give us steeds
To bear us on his track."

PART VI.

"Who may yon man be, who on foot
Comes in his iron coat,
And, with an old wife at his side,
Toils towards the castle-moat?

"He looketh as Sir Pavon should
If thirty years were o'er;
But he is dead, they say. We'll know.
Ho, there! The drawbridge lower!

"What, Pavon! Hast thou come to life?
Thou lookest like a ghost."
"Nigh slain was I by treachery:
My sword and all is lost.

"And I was ill, and worse. Alas!
With thee I may not bide,
But day and night, by fiends pursued,
Upon a quest must ride,

"To free my soul, that erst I sold
To bondage with a slave.
My merry life is dead in me!
Myself a haunted grave!

"Of thy dear love, long pledged and sworn,
Some food and drink I pray
For this poor dame, and gold and steeds,
To bear us on our way."

He reeled with weakness: "He is starved.
Lead hence, and feed him well;
And when our feast is done to-night,
His tale we'll hear him tell.

"He's crazed with shame, as erst with pride, —
Perchance 'twill please my guests
To list. My fool is growing old,
And oft repeats his jests."

Scarce were they at the burdened board
Ranged by the seneschal,
When Pavon fed and calmed came in,
And stood before them all,

And clasped each slackened hand, and smiled
In many a well-known face,
And fell upon some cooling hearts
Once more in kind embrace:

"Dear mates, how good it is to stand
Again among you here,
Though 'neath my ruined towers no more
We make our wonted cheer!

"I must not stay; but list a word,
And mark it well, before
I look my last upon you all,
Perchance, forevermore.

"Among the tombs I sat, and heard
Within me or without, —
I know not which, — a horrid voice:
It drives me still about.

"A wondrous thing it told to me,
As terrible as new,
Undreamed of to that hour by me,
To this, I ween, by you.

"Christ 'mid the serfs hath men, whom he
Dear as himself doth hold;
Thus he who sells his Christian slave,
His master, Christ, hath sold,

"For from the very book of peace
The fiends have learned a hymn, —
'Who did it unto one of *his*,
Hath done it unto *him*.'"

Each in his neighbors' faces looked;
And some were pale with fear;

"Out!" roared the host, "ye serving men,
What make ye gaping here,

"To swallow what concerns you not?
Such ravings if they hear,
They'll rave themselves. I saw them all
Prick up each meddling ear.

"Your pardon, noble comrades all;
A very sorry jest
Was this to make you sport withal;
He told me of a quest."

"My quest it is to find and free
The hunchback, whom of old,
When thou wert wassailing with me
At Christmastide, I sold.

"Look not so darkly on me, friends,
I will not mar your feast;
But, Raymond, for the red-roan steeds
I lent thee, give at least

"To me one jennet, mule, or ass,
That I thereon may lead
His blister-footed mother hence,
And make the better speed."

"Poor man, his case is pitiful.
If madman e'er I saw,
He's mad! What say ye? Let him go?
Or give him chains and straw!"

"He was a gallant champion late!"
"He's harmless; let him go."
"Nay, if he stirreth up the serfs
I cannot count him so."

Then rage brought back Sir Pavon's strength:
He dashed the casement through,
Leaped headlong down, and all in steel
He swam the moat below.

Forth swarmed the valets sent, for him,
But soon returned without,
So hotly with the abbot's staff
He 'mongst them laid about.

His comrades from the battlements
Looked wondering down to see
The knight the hobbling crone await,
With pity and with glee.

He paced to meet her courteously;
He propped her with his arm,
And with his staff, and bent as if
To soothe her weak alarm;

But with a bitter laugh he said,
"Sure, he who findeth out
How fickle are the world's sweet smiles,
Can do its smiles without."

PART VII.

Long years of hunger, cold, and heat,
And home-sick toil in vain;—
Long years of wandering up and down,
O'er inland, coast, and main;—

Long years of asking still for one,
And longing day and night,
Who, ever present with the soul,
Hath vanished from the sight!

The freeman like a growing tree
Thrives, rooted in his place;
The bondman, like a withered leaf,
Flits on and leaves no trace.

Sir Pavon's armor rusted off;
He seemed no more a knight;
Yet ever to himself he said,
While raged his inward fight,

"How quickly may a wrong be done,
How slowly done away!
Shall all eternity repair
My trespass of a day?"

While some said, "East," and some said, "West,"
And most, "I cannot tell,"
They ate the stranger's crusts, and drank
At many a stranger's well.

He ever walked, or stood, or sat,
Between her and the blast.
She cheered him with forgiving words,
And begged his scant repast.

In penitent and pardoning woe,
Thus went they hand in hand,
The master and the slave. They trod
The cactus-hatching sand.

They stood beneath the snowy pole,
Where, quenched, the heavenward eye,
Sinks dizzy back to earth, beneath
The crumbling, sinking sky.

PART VIII.

"O, sail-borne trader, hast thou seen,
In lands beneath the sun,
Or in the shadow of the pole,
My Anselm? O my son!"

"A pilgrim, dame?" "A slave."
"A slave!
Ask, have I seen a sheep!
Ay, flocks and flocks, where'er I go.
Yon Moors their hundreds keep,—

"The lazy tawny dogs!—beyond,
Where 'twixt these fronting lands
The writhing sea his pent-up way
Tears 'twixt the rocks and sands."

"He is like no one else. His face
Is wondrous mild and fair;
His eyes are kind and bright; and fine
And silky is his hair."

"Ha, ha! So whines the shepherd lad
Whose petted ewe hath strayed!"
"He bore a hump upon his back,"
Sir Pavon softly said,—

"Was helpful to the poor beyond
The custom of mankind."
Before the statelier questioner
The merchant searched his mind.

"Such slave I saw in Barbary,
A twelvemonth scarce agone.
A fever-smitten sailor there
We left to die alone;—

"It grieved me much. We could not choose.
Our venture had been lost,
Had we not seized the first fair gale
To sweep us from the coast.

"I hurried back. I thought to see
His living face no more,
But haply give him burial.
He met me on the shore,

"Thin as this blade, and white as is
This handle of my knife.
A slave, he said, had ta'en him in
And nursed him like a wife,

"A hunchback, for he showed me him.
How called you yours?" "His name
Was Anselm." "Ay, and so was his,
It is the very same.

"Old Hassan's steward in the sun
Doth beat him to and fro;
He limps with water from the tanks
To make the melons grow.

"See how my Sea-gull flaps her wings,
Impatient for the deep!
Anon shall she to Tripoli
So lightly dart and leap;

"And for that bounteous deed of his
His mother shall he see;—
What costs a good turn now and then?—
Embark and sail with me,

"For nothing,—if ye nothing have.
They'll call for little food,
On landlocked billows, sickened by
The tossing of the flood."

The anchor climbed. The wind blew fair,
But ere they neared the pier
The old wife on death's threshold lay,
Distraught with hope and fear.

"How canst thou free him from his woes?
Thou hast nor friends nor gold.
How may I even crawl to him
His misery to behold?

"O master, trail me through the dust
And leave me at his feet!"
"Nay, thou wert patient all those years.
Here, sheltered from the heat,

"A little longer wait and pray;
It may be but an hour.
Our Lord, who bade to succor him,
I think shall give the power.

"And, merchant, if he fly with me
Wilt bear him hence?" "My head,
And thine, were lost belike! Art mad?
'Twould surely cost my trade.

"I buy and sell, but steal not, slaves!"
"Thou'rt known to Hassan?" "Ay."
"Then lead me to him; and the Lord,
I think, the slave shall buy.

"Then wilt thou bear him hence, and her?"
"Ay, on mine honest word.
Oft as I may, I gladly do
A pleasure to the Lord."

Turbaned and robed old Hassan sat.
An atmosphere of rest
Hung brooding o'er his soft divan,
His beard slept on his breast.

His rolling eyes upon the floor
Did round about him fall,
To thread the mazy arabesques
Paved in his marble hall.

They shone and glimmered moist with dew,
While, robed in spangled spray,
Amidst them high a fountain danced
In whispering, tittering play.

No joy, grief, awe, nor doubt looked through
His features swart and still;
"I ought" had ne'er been written there,
But petrified, "I will."

"What wouldst thou, merchant?" "Nothing, I;
This godly man would speak,
A very godly man!—Methinks
His wits are somewhat weak."

"Good Hassan, for thy hunchback slave
I've sought through dreary years;
Wilt give him up?" "In change for what?"
"Our prayers and grateful tears."

"I want them not." "Thou mayst one day!
When misbelievers stand
Amazed in judgment, he shall plead
For thee at God's right hand;

"His mother, too; — they're dear to Christ;
I know it all too well!
And I up from my lower place
Will cry aloft and tell,

"That thou art he my sinking soul
Who lifted out of hell;
Till all the saints shall join with me,
O blessed infidel!"

"Hast nothing else to offer?" "Ay,
To serve thee faithfully,
Another slave I'll give, — myself, —
As stout a wight as he."

"Nought hast thou of his look; yet sure
He is thy son or brother?"
"My serf of yore." "'Tis strange, if true!
Most Christians hate each other.

"I take thy proffer, false or fair;
But if to me thou liest,
And seek'st to steal thyself away,
E'en in my gates thou diest."

He clapped his hands; and in there rushed
A turbaned menial throng.
Strange words he spake. A dusky Moor
Good Pavon led along,

With bounding heart, and beaded brow,
And paling, glowing cheek,
And trembling lips compressed, that strove
To brace themselves to speak,

Through cool, dank courts, and sultry paths,
Till, 'twixt the twinkling twigs
Of citron, and of orange-trees,
And sun-bathed purple figs,

He saw the fattening melons bask
On beds both long and broad,
And Anselm, staggering forth to them,
Bent 'neath his watery load.

He oped his mouth to call on him;
Amazed, he did but choke;
For with its mighty wrath and joy,
His great heart almost broke.

He darted on his track, and wrenched
His pitcher from his hand.
The slave dropped back his drooping head,
And strove to understand,

With bony fingers interlaced
His dazzled eyes above,
Why came the tall mute man to him,
In enmity or love.

Then muttered he, "This scorching sun
At last hath fired my brain!
I seem to see one far away,
Perchance long dead again, —

"Sir Pavon! 'Tis some fancy, bred
Of famine, wild and weak,
Or fever. Wherefore gaze on it?
If 'twas a man 'twould speak."

Then Pavon in a storm of tears
Fell crying on his breast:
"Forgive me, brother, if thou canst!
I've known no peace nor rest,

"For years or ages, but to right
The wrong I did to thee,
And mine own soul, roamed o'er the earth!
From henceforth thou art free."

"Sir Pavon! Is it thou? — and here?"
"Ay; and I hold thee fast
In verity, as oft in dreams,
When, as my slumber past,

"'Mid fading forms I clutched at thine,
'Mid fading visioned lands,
And shouting woke, with bloody nails
Clenched in mine empty hands."

"God! Heardst thou then my hopeless prayers?
He's saved! — And am I free?"
"Ay, go thy ways in joy, poor friend,
Nor cease to pray for me.

"The merchant Andrew on the shore
Awaits thee, in his bark.
His homeward voyage bears him by
The abbey of St. Mark.

"The monks, for Abbot Urban's sake,
Will house and feed thine age
When thou hast told to them the end
Of Pavon's pilgrimage,

"By him enjoined. Though he be dead,
He must remembered be
By novices he nurtured." "Sir,
Dost thou not come with me?"

"Long wilt thou tarry?" "Be content."
"Not to forsake thee here.
I'll serve thee in this homesick land
For love, as erst from fear."

"Go thou. I stay." A change came o'er
The hunchback's raptured face:
"Why stays he, Selim, know'st?" "To draw
Our water in thy place."

He tore his hair; he turned away;
He spake: "It shall not be!
All blessings bless thee for the thought,
But 'twere not meet for thee!

"Few years are left me on the earth;
And God hath taught to me
That willing bondage borne in Christ
Is loftier liberty."

"Then grudge it not unto thy lord,"
St. Pavon following said.
The slave took up his water-pots,
Moved on, and shook his head.

"This is my penance I must do,
Or be for aye abhorred
Of Heaven." "I'll help thee bear it."
"Nay, stint not mine earned reward!"

St. Pavon's eyes and hands on his
He fixed, and joyously
Cried, "Laggard son, thy mother waits
Among the ships for thee!"

The new slave let the melons thirst
Till, through the twinkling twigs
Of citron, and of orange-flowers,
And sun-bathed purple figs,

He saw the hunchback hurry o'er
The beach, and scale the deck,
Towards outstretched arms, that like a trap
Did spring and catch his neck.

Then out he let his pent-up breath,
Which seemed to blow away,
In one great sigh, his life's great woe,
And to himself did say,

"Howe'er, where'er now, in this world
Or that, my lot may fall,
I bear this scene in memory,
And I can bear it all."

Then to his task he turned, with mien
As eager and as bold
As when his brethren's blood plashed round
His iron march of old.

Joy drained his lees of life nigh-spent
All in one brimming cup, —
One wasteful draught of feverish strength, —
And bade him drink it up.

He dragged the sinking waters out:
He dashed them on the ground;
He panted to and fro; well-nigh
The melons swam or drowned.

Sly women's jet and diamond eyes
Did near the lattice lurk,
And twinkle through its screen, to see
The Christian madman work.

The steward cried, "By Mahmoud's beard,
Some demon toils within
Yon unbeliever, or a troop
Of slaves in one's shrunk skin."

Above him like a vulture came
The noontide sun, and beat
Upon his old bald head, and pricked
Through all his frame with heat;

It set but spurs unto his zeal:
"O Christ, and didst thou see
My brother in this torment gasp,
And through my cruelty!"

His short-lived might sank with the light;
Black turned the red-hot day;
He scarce could drag to Anselm's lair
His heavy limbs away.

He heard a sound; he felt a light;
He deemed it was the dawn.
He oped his eyes; and, lo! the veil
Of glory was withdrawn;

A radiance brighter than the sun,
And sweeter than the moon,
Showed earth a part of heaven! He sighed,
"'Tis a God-granted boon, —

"A vision sent to cheer my soul, —
A glimpse of Paradise!
O, fade not yet! A moment more,
Ere to my toil I rise."

A quivering fanned the air; and shapes
Like wingèd Joys stood round.
"Arise!" they said. He rose and left
His body on the ground,

His weariness and age. Surprised
With sudden buoyancy
And ease, he turned and saw aghast
His ghastly effigy.

"'Tis but a dream!" "'Tis heaven." "For me?
Not yet! not yet!" he said;
"I am a traitor! Give me time!
O, let me not be dead!

"In mercy put me back to toil
And scorch, nor bid me brook,
Ere I've avenged him well on me,
Mine outraged Master's look!"

A tender smile glowed through them all.
"Brave martyr, do not fear.
Our Master calls! He waits for thee
To share his bridal cheer!

"Full many a weary year is told,
As mortals tell their years,
Since loud we struck our harps, and sang
Thy triumph o'er thy tears."

Before him, spreading welcoming arms,
A shining Urban stood:
"God gave thee grace to overcome
Thine evil with thy good.

"My lesson, brother, hast forgot? —
I taught to thee of yore,
That blessings hid, their threats amid,
The awful Scriptures bore."

Then Pavon to his dear embrace
In wildered transports sprang;
And up the sunny morn they soared.
The dwindling earth did hang

Beneath. The air flapped, white with wings
That thickened all about;
And wide a song of triumph pealed
And rang this burden out:

"To wrest him out of Satan's hands
His charity sufficed;
He did it unto one of CHRIST'S,
He did it unto CHRIST!"

E. FOXTON.

VIII.

SONGS.

SONGS.

MASQUE OF PLEASURE AND VIRTUE.

SONG I.

Come on, come on, and where you go
So interweave the curious knot
As even the Observer scarce may know
Which lines are pleasure, and which not:
First figure out the doubtful way
At which awhile the youth should stay
Where she and Virtue did contend
Which should have Hercules to friend.
Then as all actions of mankind
Are but a labyrinth or maze,
So let your dances be entwined,
Yet not perplex men unto gaze:
But measured, and so numerous too,
As men may read each act they do;
And, when they see your graces meet,
Admire the wisdom of your feet:
For dancing is an exercise
Not only shows the mover's wit,
But maketh the beholder wise,
As he hath power to rise to it.

SONG II.

O more and more, this was so well
As praise wants half his voice to tell.
Again yourselves compose,
And now put all the aptness on
Of figure, that proportion
Or color can disclose:
That, if those silent arts were lost,
Design and Picture, they might boast
From you a newer ground
Instructed by the heightening sense
Of dignity and reverence
In their true motions found.
Begin, begin; for look, the pair
Do longing listen to what air
You form your second touch
That they may vent their murmuring hymns
Just to the tune you move your limbs,
And wish their own were such.
Make haste, make haste, for this
The labyrinth of Beauty is.

SONG III.

It follows now you are to prove
The subtlest maze of all, — that's Love,
And, if you stay too long,
The fair will think you do them wrong.
Go choose among them, with a mind
As gentle as the stroking wind
Runs o'er the gentler flowers,
And so let all your actions smile,
As if they meant not to beguile
The ladies, but the hours.
Grace, laughter, and discourse may meet,
And yet the beauty not go less:
For what is noble should be sweet,
But not dissolved in wantonness.
Will you that I give the law
To all your sport, and sum it
It should be such should envy draw,
But overcome it.

Ben Jonson.

SONG.

Shake off your heavy trance,
And leap into a dance,
Such as no mortals use to tread,
Fit only for Apollo —
To play to, for the moon to lead,
And all the stars to follow!
O blessed youth! for Jove doth pause,
Laying aside his graver laws

For this device:
And at the wedding such a pair
Each dance is taken for a prayer,
Each song a sacrifice.
You should stay longer if we durst;
Away! Alas! that he that first
Gave Time wild wings to fly away,
Has now no power to make him stay.

BEAUMONT AND FLETCHER.

MARY DONNELLY.

OH! lovely Mary Donnelly, it's you I love the best!
If fifty girls were round you, I'd hardly see the rest.
Be what it may the time of day, the place be where it will,
Sweet looks of Mary Donnelly, they bloom before me still.

Her eyes like mountain water that's flowing on a rock,
How clear they are, how dark they are! and they give me many a shock.
Red rowans warm in sunshine and wetted in a shower,
Can ne'er express the charming lip that has me in its power.

Her nose is straight and handsome, her eyebrows lifted up;
Her chin is very neat and pert, and smooth like a china cup;
Her hair's the brag of Ireland, so weighty and so fine;
It's rolling down upon her neck, and gathered in a twine.

The dance o' last Whit-Monday night exceeded all before;
No pretty girl for miles about was missing from the floor;
But Mary kept the belt of love, and O but she was gay!
She danced a jig, she sang a song, that took my heart away.

When she stood up for dancing, her steps were so complete,
The music nearly killed itself to listen to her feet;
The fiddler moaned his blindness, he heard her so much praised,
But blessed himself he wasn't deaf when once her voice she raised.

And evermore I'm whistling or lilting what you sung;
Your smile is always in my heart, your name beside my tongue;
But you've as many sweethearts as you'd count on both your hands,
And for myself there's not a thumb or little finger stands.

Oh, you're the flower of womankind in country or in town;
The higher I exalt you, the lower I'm cast down.
If some great lord should come this way, and see your beauty bright,
And you to be his lady, I'd own it was but right.

Oh might we live together in a lofty palace hall,
Where joyful music rises, and where scarlet curtains fall!
Oh might we live together in a cottage mean and small;
With sods of grass the only roof, and mud the only wall!

Oh! lovely Mary Donnelly, your beauty's my distress.
It's far too beauteous to be mine, but I'll never wish it less.
The proudest place would fit your face, and I am poor and low;
But blessings be about you, dear, wherever you may go!

ALLINGHAM.

SONG.

SPRING all the graces of the age,
And all the Loves of time;
Bring all the pleasures of the stage,
And relishes of rhyme:
Add all the softnesses of Courts,
The looks, the laughters, and the sports:
And mingle all their sweets and salts
That none may say the triumph halts.

BEN JONSON: *Neptune's Triumph.*

SONG TO CERES.

THOU that art our Queen again,
And may in the sun be seen again,
Come, Ceres, come,
For the War's gone home,
And the fields are quiet and green again.

The air, dear Goddess, sighs for thee,
The light-heart brooks arise for thee,
And the poppies red
On their wistful bed
Turn up their dark blue eyes for thee.

Laugh out in the loose green jerkin
That's fit for a Goddess to work in,
With shoulders brown,
And the wheaten crown
About thy temples perking.

And with thee came Stout Heart in,
And Toil that sleeps his cart in,
Brown Exercise,
The ruddy and wise,
His bathèd forelocks parting.

And Dancing too, that's lither
Than willow or birch, drop hither,
To thread the place
With a finishing grace,
And carry our smooth eyes with her.

LEIGH HUNT.

ARABY'S DAUGHTER.

FAREWELL — farewell to thee, Araby's daughter!
(Thus warbled a Peri beneath the dark sea,)
No pearl ever lay under Oman's green water,
More pure in its shell than thy spirit in thee.

Oh! fair as the sea-flower close to thee growing,
How light was thy heart till love's witchery came,
Like the wind of the South o'er a summer lute blowing,
And hushed all its music, and withered its frame.

But long upon Araby's green sunny highlands,
Shall maids and their lovers remember the doom
Of her who lies sleeping among the Pearl Islands,
With nought but the sea-star to light up her tomb.

And still when the merry date-season is burning,
And calls to the palm-groves the young and the old,
The happiest there, from their pastime returning,
At sunset, still weep when thy story is told.

The young village maid, when with flowers she dresses
Her dark flowing hair, for some festival day,
Will think of thy fate, till, neglecting her tresses,
She mournfully turns from her mirror away.

Nor shall Iran, beloved of her hero! forget thee;
Though tyrants watch over her tears as they start;
Close, close by the side of that hero she'll set thee,
Embalmed in the innermost shrine of her heart.

Around thee shall glisten the loveliest amber
That ever the sorrowing sea-bird has wept;
With many a shell, in whose hollow wreathed chamber
We, Peris of Ocean, by moonlight have slept.

We'll dive where the gardens of coral lie darkling,
And plant all the rosiest stems at thy head;
We'll seek where the sands of the Caspian are sparkling,
And gather their gold to strew over thy head.

Farewell — farewell — until Pity's sweet fountain
Is lost in the hearts of the fair and the brave,
They'll weep for the chieftain who died on that mountain,
They'll weep for the maiden who sleeps in this wave.

MOORE.

THE HARP THAT ONCE THROUGH TARA'S HALLS.

THE harp that once through Tara's halls
The soul of music shed,
Now hangs as mute on Tara's walls
As if that soul were fled.

So sleeps the pride of former days,
So glory's thrill is o'er,
And hearts that once beat high for praise
Now feel that pulse no more!

No more to chiefs and ladies bright
The harp of Tara swells;
The chord alone that breaks at night
Its tale of ruin tells.
Thus Freedom now so seldom wakes,
The only throb she gives
Is when some heart indignant breaks,
To show that still she lives.

MOORE.

CANADIAN BOAT-SONG.

[Written on the River St. Lawrence]

FAINTLY as tolls the evening chime
Our voices keep tune and our oars keep time.
Soon as the woods on shore look dim,
We'll sing at St. Ann's our parting hymn.
Row, brothers, row, the stream runs fast,
The rapids are near and the daylight's past.

Why should we yet our sail unfurl?
There is not a breath the blue wave to curl.
But, when the wind blows off the shore,
Oh, sweetly we'll rest our weary oar.
Blow, breezes, blow, the stream runs fast,
The rapids are near and the daylight's past.

Utawas' tide! this trembling moon
Shall see us float over thy surges soon.
Saint of this green isle! hear our prayers,
Oh, grant us cool heavens and favoring airs.
Blow, breezes, blow, the stream runs fast.
The rapids are near and the daylight's past.

MOORE.

THE SAILOR.

A ROMAIC BALLAD.

THOU that hast a daughter
For one to woo and wed,
Give her to a husband
With snow upon his head;
Oh, give her to an old man,
Though little joy it be,
Before the best young sailor
That sails upon the sea!

How luckless is the sailor
When sick and like to die;
He sees no tender mother,
No sweetheart standing by.
Only the captain speaks to him, —
Stand up, stand up, young man,
And steer the ship to haven,
As none beside thee can.

Thou says't to me, "Stand, stand up;"
I say to thee, take hold,
Lift me a little from the deck,
My hands and feet are cold.
And let my head, I pray thee,
With handkerchiefs be bound;
There, take my love's gold handkerchief,
And tie it tightly round.

Now bring the chart, the doleful chart;
See, where these mountains meet —
The clouds are thick around their head,
The mists around their feet:
Cast anchor here; 'tis deep and safe
Within the rocky cleft;
The little anchor on the right,
The great one on the left.

And now to thee, O captain,
Most earnestly I pray,
That they may never bury me
In church or cloister gray; —
But on the windy sea-beach,
At the ending of the land,
All on the surfy sea-beach,
Deep down into the sand.

For there will come the sailors,
Their voices I shall hear,
And at casting of the anchor
The yo-ho loud and clear;

And at hauling of the anchor
  The yo-ho and the cheer, —
Farewell, my love, for to thy bay
  I never more may steer!

ALLINGHAM.

THE BOATIE ROWS.

OH, weel may the boatie row,
  And better may she speed;
And liesome may the boatie row
  That wins the bairnies' bread.
The boatie rows, the boatie rows,
  The boatie rows indeed;
And weel may the boatie row
  That wins the bairnies' bread.

I coost my line in Largo Bay,
  And fishes I catched nine;
'Twas three to boil, and three to fry,
  And three to bait the line.
The boatie rows, the boatie rows,
  The boatie rows indeed,
And happy be the lot o' a'
  Wha wishes her to speed.

Oh, weel may the boatie row,
  That fills a heavy creel,
And cleeds us a' frae tap to tae,
  And buys our parritch meal.
The boatie rows, the boatie rows,
  The boatie rows, indeed,
And happy be the lot o' a'
  That wish the boatie speed.

When Jamie vowed he wad be mine,
  And wan frae me my heart,
Oh, muckle lighter grew my creel —
  He swore we'd never part.
The boatie rows, the boatie rows,
  The boatie rows fu' weel;
And muckle lighter is the load
  When love bears up the creel.

My kurtch I put upo' my head,
  And dressed mysel' fu' braw;
I trow my heart was dough and wae,
  When Jamie gade awa'.
But weel may the boatie row,
  And lucky be her part,
And lightsome be the lassie's care
  That yields an honest heart.

ANONYMOUS.

THERE'S NAE LUCK ABOUT THE HOUSE.

BUT are ye sure the news is true?
  And are ye sure he's weel?
Is this a time to think o' wark?
  Ye jauds, fling bye your wheel!
    For there's nae luck about the house,
      There's nae luck at a';
    There's nae luck about the house,
      When our gudeman's awa.

Is this a time to think o' wark,
  When Colin's at the door?
Rax down my cloak — I'll to the quay,
  And see him come ashore.

Rise up and make a clean fireside,
  Put on the muckle pot;
Gie little Kate her cotton gown,
  And Jock his Sunday's coat.

Make their shoon as black as slaes,
  Their stockings white as snaw;
It's a' to pleasure our gudeman —
  He likes to see them braw.

There are twa hens into the crib
  Hae fed this month or mair;
Mak haste and thraw their necks about,
  That Colin weel may fare.

My Turkey slippers I'll put on,
  My stockins pearl-blue, —
It's a' to pleasure our gudeman,
  For he's baith leal and true.

Sae sweet his voice, sae smooth his tongue,
  His breath's like cauler air;
His very foot has music in't,
  As he comes up the stair.

And will I see his face again,
  And will I hear him speak?
I'm downricht dizzy wi' the thought,
  In troth I'm like to greet.
    There's nae luck about the house,
      There's nae luck at a';
    There's nae luck about the house,
      When our gudeman's awa.'

WILLIAM JULIUS MICKLE.

JOHN ANDERSON, MY JO.

John Anderson, my jo, John,
When we were first acquent,
Your locks were like the raven,
Your bonnie brow was brent;
But now your brow is beld, John,
Your locks are like the snaw;
But blessings on your frosty pow,
John Anderson, my jo.

John Anderson, my jo, John,
We clamb the hill thegither;
And mony a canty day, John,
We've had wi' ane anither:
Now we maun totter down, John;
But hand in hand we'll go,
And sleep thegither at the foot,
John Anderson, my jo.

Burns.

OFT IN THE STILLY NIGHT.

Oft in the stilly night,
Ere Slumber's chain has bound me,
Fond Memory brings the light
Of other days around me;
The smiles, the tears,
Of boyhood's years,
The words of love then spoken;
The eyes that shone,
Now dimmed and gone,
The cheerful hearts now broken!
Thus in the stilly night,
Ere Slumber's chain has bound me,
Sad Memory brings the light
Of other days around me.

When I remember all
The friends, so linked together,
I've seen around me fall,
Like leaves in wintry weather,
I feel like one
Who treads alone
Some banquet hall deserted,
Whose lights are fled,
Whose garlands dead,
And all but he departed!
Thus in the stilly night,
Ere Slumber's chain has bound me,
Sad Memory brings the light
Of other days around me.

Moore.

JEANIE MORRISON.

O dear, dear Jeanie Morrison,
The thochts o' bygane years
Still fling their shadows ower my path,
And blind my een wi' tears!
They blind my een wi' saut, saut tears,
And sair and sick I pine,
As Memory idly summons up
The blythe blinks o' langsyne.

'Twas then we luvit ilk ither weel,
'Twas then we twa did part;
Sweet time, sad time!—twa bairns at schule,
Twa bairns, and but ae heart!
'Twas then we sat on ae laigh bink,
To leir ilk ither lear;
And tones, and looks, and smiles were shed,
Remembered evermair.

I wonder, Jeanie, aften yet,
When sitting on that bink,
Cheek touchin' cheek, loof locked in loof,
What our wee heads could think!
When baith bent down ower ae braid page
Wi' ae buik on our knee,
Thy lips were on thy lesson, but
My lesson was in thee.

Oh, mind ye how we hung our heads,
How cheeks brent red wi' shame,
Whene'er the schule-weans laughin' said,
We cleek'd thegither hame?
And mind ye o' the Saturdays
(The schule then skail't at noon),
When we ran aff to speel the braes—
The broomy braes o' June?

Oh, mind ye, luve, how aft we left
The deavin' dinsome toun,
To wander by the green burnside,
And hear its water croon?
The simmer leaves hung ower our heads,
The flowers burst round our feet,
And in the gloamin' o' the wud
The throssil whusslit sweet.

The throssil whusslit in the wud,
The burn sung to the trees,
And we, with Nature's heart in tune,
Concerted harmonies;

And on the knowe abune the burn
For hours thegither sat
In the silentness o' joy, till baith
Wi' very gladness grat.

O dear, dear Jeanie Morrison,
Since we were sindered young,
I've never seen your face, nor heard
The music o' your tongue;
But I could hug all wretchedness,
And happy could I dee,
Did I but ken your heart still dreamed
O' bygane days and me!

WILLIAM MOTHERWELL.

AULD LANG SYNE.

SHOULD auld acquaintance be forgot,
And never brought to min'?
Should auld acquaintance be forgot,
And days o' lang syne?
For auld lang syne, my dear,
For auld lang syne,
We'll tak a cup o' kindness yet,
For auld lang syne!

We twa hae run about the braes,
And pu't the gowans fine;
But we've wandered mony a weary foot,
Sin' auld lang syne.
For auld lang syne, my dear,
For auld lang syne,
We'll tak a cup o' kindness yet,
For auld lang syne!

We twa hae paidl't i' the burn,
Frae mornin' sun till dine;
But seas between us braid hae roared,
Sin' auld lang syne.
For auld lang syne, my dear,
For auld lang syne,
We'll tak a cup o' kindness yet,
For auld lang syne!

And here's a hand, my trusty fiere,
And gie's a hand o' thine;
And we'll take a right guid willie-waught,
For auld lang syne.
For auld lang syne, my dear,
For auld lang syne,
We'll tak a cup o' kindness yet,
For auld lang syne!

And surely ye'll be your pint-stoup,
As sure as I'll be mine;
And we'll tak a cup o' kindness yet,
For auld lang syne.
For auld lang syne, my dear,
For auld lang syne,
We'll tak a cup o' kindness yet,
For auld lang syne!

BURNS.

COME AWAY, COME AWAY, DEATH.

I.

COME away, come away, death,
And in sad cypress let me be laid;
Fly away, fly away, breath;
I am slain by a fair cruel maid.
My shroud of white, stuck all with yew,
O prepare it!
My part of death no one so true
Did share it.

II.

Not a flower, not a flower sweet,
On my black coffin let there be strewn;
Not a friend, not a friend greet
My poor corse, where my bones shall be thrown.
A thousand thousand sighs to save,
Lay me, O where
Sad true lover never find my grave,
To weep there!

SHAKSPEARE.

BLOW, BLOW, THOU WINTER WIND.

I.

BLOW, blow, thou winter wind,
Thou art not so unkind
As man's ingratitude;
Thy tooth is not so keen,
Because thou art not seen,
Although thy breath be rude.
Heigh-ho! sing, heigh-ho! unto the green holly:
Most friendship is feigning, most loving mere folly:
Then, heigh-ho! the holly!
This life is most jolly.

II.

Freeze, freeze, thou bitter sky,
That dost not bite so nigh
As benefits forgot:
Though thou the waters warp,
Thy sting is not so sharp
As friend remembered not.
Heigh-ho! sing, heigh-ho! unto the green holly:
Most friendship is feigning, most loving mere folly:
Then, heigh-ho! the holly!
This life is most jolly.

SHAKSPEARE.

UNDER THE GREENWOOD-TREE.

I.

UNDER the greenwood-tree
Who loves to lie with me,
And turn his merry note
Unto the sweet bird's throat,
Come hither, come hither, come hither:
Here shall he see
No enemy,
But winter and rough weather.

II.

Who doth ambition shun,
And loves to live i' the sun,
Seeking the food he eats,
And pleased with what he gets,
Come hither, come hither, come hither:
Here shall he see
No enemy,
But winter and rough weather.

SHAKSPEARE.

SONG.

I.

WHEN daisies pied, and violets blue,
And lady-smocks all silver-white,
And cuckoo-buds of yellow hue,
Do paint the meadows with delight,
The cuckoo then, on every tree,
Mocks married men; for thus sings he,
Cuckoo;
Cuckoo, cuckoo, — O word of fear!
Unpleasing to a married ear!

II.

When shepherds pipe on oaten straws,
And merry larks are ploughmen's clocks,
When turtles tread, and rooks, and daws,
And maidens bleach their summer smocks,
The cuckoo then, on every tree,
Mocks married men; for thus sings he,
Cuckoo;
Cuckoo, cuckoo, — O word of fear!
Unpleasing to a married ear!

III.

When icicles hang by the wall,
And Dick the shepherd blows his nail,
And Tom bears logs into the hall,
And milk comes frozen home in pail,
When blood is nipped, and ways be foul,
Then nightly sings the staring owl,
To-who;
To-whit, to-who, a merry note,
While greasy Joan doth keel the pot.

IV.

When all aloud the wind doth blow,
And coughing drowns the parson's saw,
And birds sit brooding in the snow,
And Marian's nose looks red and raw,
When roasted crabs hiss in the bowl,
Then nightly sings the staring owl,
To-who;
To-whit, to-who, a merry note,
While greasy Joan doth keel the pot.

SHAKSPEARE.

ARIEL'S SONG.

WHERE the bee sucks, there suck I:
In a cowslip's bell I lie;
There I couch when owls do cry.
On the bat's back I do fly
After summer, merrily.
Merrily, merrily, shall I live now,
Under the blossom that hangs on the bough.

SHAKSPEARE.

TELL ME WHERE IS FANCY BRED.

TELL me where is fancy bred,
Or in the heart, or in the head?
How begot, how nourished?
Reply, reply.

It is engendered in the eyes,
With gazing fed; and fancy dies
In the cradle where it lies.
Let us all ring fancy's knell:
I'll begin it, — Ding-dong, bell,
Chorus. — Ding-dong, bell.

SHAKSPEARE.

FULL FATHOM FIVE THY FATHER LIES.

FULL fathom five thy father lies;
Of his bones are coral made;
Those are pearls that were his eyes;
Nothing of him that doth fade,
But doth suffer a sea-change
Into something rich and strange.
Sea-nymphs hourly sing his knell:
Hark! now I hear them, — Ding-dong, bell.
Burden. — Ding-dong.

SHAKSPEARE.

SONG OF ECHO.

SLOW, slow, fresh fount, keep time with my salt tears;
Yet slower, yet, O faintly gentle springs:
List to the heavy part the music bears,
Woe weeps out her division, when she sings.
Droop herbs and flowers;
Fall grief in showers;
Our beauties are not ours:
O, I could still,
Like melting snow upon some craggy hill,
Drop, drop, drop, drop
Since Nature's pride is now a withered daffodil.

BEN JONSON.

SONG.

SWEET Echo, sweetest nymph that liv'st unseen
Within thy airy shell,
By slow Meander's margent green,
And in the violet-embroidered vale,
Where the love-lorn nightingale
Nightly to thee her sad song mourneth well;
Canst thou not tell me of a gentle pair
That likest thy Narcissus are?
O, if thou have
Hid them in some flowery cave,
Tell me but where,
Sweet queen of parley, daughter of the sphere!
So mayst thou be translated to the skies,
And give resounding grace to all heaven's harmonies.

MILTON.

HARK! HARK! THE LARK.

HARK! hark! the lark at heaven's gate sings,
And Phœbus 'gins arise,
His steeds to water at those springs
On chaliced flowers that lies;

And winking Mary-buds begin
To ope their golden eyes;
With every thing that pretty bin,
My lady sweet, arise;
Arise, arise.

SHAKSPEARE.

THE BUGLE-SONG.

THE splendor falls on castle walls
And snowy summits old in story:
The long light shakes across the lakes,
And the wild cataract leaps in glory.
Blow, bugle, blow, set the wild echoes flying,
Blow, bugle; answer, echoes, dying, dying, dying.

O hark, O hear! how thin and clear,
And thinner, clearer, farther going!
O sweet and far from cliff and scar
The horns of Elfland faintly blowing!
Blow, let us hear the purple glens replying:
Blow, bugle; answer, echoes, dying, dying, dying.

O love, they die in yon rich sky,
They faint on hill or field or river:
Our echoes roll from soul to soul,
And grow forever and forever.
Blow, bugle, blow, set the wild echoes flying,
And answer, echoes, answer, dying, dying, dying.

TENNYSON.

COUNTY GUY.

AH! County Guy, the hour is nigh,
The sun has left the lea,
The orange-flower perfumes the bower,
The breeze is on the sea.
The lark, his lay who trilled all day,
Sits hushed his partner nigh;
Breeze, bird, and flower confess the hour,
But where is County Guy?

The village maid steals through the shade
Her shepherd's suit to hear;
To beauty shy, by lattice high,
Sings high-born Cavalier;
The star of Love, all stars above,
Now reigns o'er earth and sky,
And high and low the influence know, —
But where is County Guy?

SCOTT.

RIVER SONG.

COME to the river's reedy shore,
My maiden, while the skies,
With blushes fit to grace thy cheek,
Wait for the sun's uprise:
There, dancing on the rippling wave,
My boat expectant lies,
And jealous flowers, as thou goest by,
Unclose their dewy eyes.

As slowly down the stream we glide,
The lilies all unfold
Their leaves, less rosy white than thou,
And virgin hearts of gold;
The gay birds on the meadow elm
Salute thee blithe and bold,
While I sit shy and silent here,
And glow with love untold.

F. B. SANBORN.

SONG FROM JASON.

I KNOW a little garden close
Set thick with lily and red rose,
Where I would wander if I might
From dewy dawn to dewy night,
And have one with me wandering.
And though within it no birds sing,
And though no pillared house is there,
And though the apple-boughs are bare
Of fruit and blossom, would to God
Her feet upon the green grass trod,
And I beheld them as before.
There comes a murmur from the shore,
And in the place two fair streams are,
Drawn from the purple hills afar,
Drawn down unto the restless sea;
The hills whose flowers ne'er fed the bee,
The shore no ship has ever seen,
Still beaten by the billows green,
Whose murmur comes unceasingly
Unto the place for which I cry.
For which I cry both day and night,
For which I let slip all delight,
That maketh me both deaf and blind,
Careless to win, unskilled to find,
And quick to lose what all men seek.
Yet tottering as I am and weak,
Still have I left a little breath
To seek within the jaws of death
An entrance to that happy place,
To seek the unforgotten face
Once seen, once kissed, once reft from me
Anigh the murmuring of the sea.

WILLIAM MORRIS.

OF A' THE AIRTS.

OF a' the airts the wind can blaw
I dearly like the west;
For there the bonnie lassie lives,
The lassie I lo'e best.
There wild woods grow, and rivers row,
Wi' mony a hill between;
Baith day and night my fancy's flight
Is ever wi' my Jean.

I see her in the dewy flowers
Sae lovely fresh and fair,
I hear her voice in ilka bird
Wi' music charm the air:

There's not a bonnie flower that springs
By fountain shaw or green;
There's not a bonnie bird that sings
But minds me o' my Jean.

BURNS.

GOLDILOCKS.

GOLDILOCKS sat on the grass,
Tying up of posies rare:
Hardly could a sunbeam pass
Through the cloud that was her hair.
Purple orchis lasteth long,
Primrose flowers are pale and clear;
O the maiden sang a song
It would do you good to hear!

Sad before her leaned the boy,
"Goldilocks that I love well,
Happy creature fair and coy,
Think o' me, sweet Amabel."
Goldilocks she shook apart,
Looked with doubtful, doubtful eyes:
Like a blossom in her heart,
Opened out her first surprise.

As a gloriole sign o' grace,
Goldilocks, ah fall and flow,
On the blooming, childlike face,
Dimple, dimple, come and go.
Give her time: on grass and sky
Let her gaze if she be fain,
As they looked ere he drew nigh,
They will never look again.

Ah! the playtime she has known,
While her goldilocks grew long,
Is it like a nestling flown,
Childhood over like a song?
Yes, the boy may clear his brow,
Though she thinks to say him nay,
When she sighs, "I cannot now.
Come again some other day."

JEAN INGELOW.

O MY LUVE'S LIKE A RED, RED ROSE.

O MY luve's like a red, red rose,
That's newly sprung in June:
O my luve's like the melodie,
That's sweetly played in tune.

As fair art thou, my bonnie lass,
So deep in luve am I:
And I will luve thee still, my dear,
Till a' the seas gang dry.

Till a' the seas gang dry, my dear,
And the rocks melt wi' the sun:
I will luve thee still, my dear,
While the sands o' life shall run.

And fare thee weel, my only luve!
And fare thee weel awhile!
And I will come again, my luve,
Though it were ten thousand mile.

BURNS.

GO, LOVELY ROSE.

Go, lovely rose!
Tell her that wastes her time and me,
That now she knows,
When I resemble her to thee,
How sweet and fair she seems to be.

Tell her that's young,
And shuns to have her graces spied,
That hadst thou sprung
In deserts where no men abide,
Thou must have uncommended died.

Small is the worth
Of beauty from the light retired:
Bid her come forth,
Suffer herself to be desired,
And not blush so to be admired.

Then die! that she
The common fate of all things rare
May read in thee, —
How small a part of time they share
That are so wondrous sweet and fair.

WALLER.

TO THE ROSE.

GOE, happy Rose, and interwove
With other flowers, bind my love.
Tell her, too, she must not be,
Longer flowing, longer free,
That so oft has fettered me.

Say, if she's fretful, I have bands
Of pearl and gold, to bind her hands;
Tell her, if she struggle still,
I have myrtle rods at will,
For to tame, though not to kill.

Take thou my blessing thus, and goe
And tell her this, but doe not so,
Lest a handsome anger flye
Like a lightning from her eye,
And burn thee up, as well as I.

HERRICK.

TAKE, O, TAKE THOSE LIPS AWAY.

TAKE, O, take those lips away,
That so sweetly were foresworn;
And those eyes, the break of day,
Lights that do mislead the morn;
But my kisses bring again, — bring again,
Seals of love, but sealed in vain, — sealed in vain.

SHAKSPEARE.

GARDEN SONG.

I.

COME into the garden, Maud,
For the black bat, night, has flown,
Come into the garden, Maud,
I am here at the gate alone;
And the woodbine spices are wafted abroad,
And the musk of the rose is blown.

II.

For a breeze of morning moves,
And the planet of Love is on high,
Beginning to faint in the light that she loves
On a bed of daffodil sky,
To faint in the light of the sun she loves,
To faint in his light, and to die.

III.

All night have the roses heard
The flute, violin, bassoon;
All night has the casement jessamine stirred
To the dancers dancing in tune;
Till a silence fell with the waking bird,
And a hush with the setting moon.

IV.

I said to the lily, " There is but one
With whom she has heart to be gay.
When will the dancers leave her alone?
She is weary of dance and play."
Now half to the setting moon are gone,
And half to the rising day;
Low on the sand and loud on the stone
The last wheel echoes away.

V.

I said to the rose, " The brief night goes
In babble and revel and wine.
O young lord-lover, what sighs are those,
For one that will never be thine?
But mine, but mine," so I sware to the rose,
" For ever and ever, mine."

VI.

And the soul of the rose went into my blood,
As the music clashed in the hall;
And long by the garden lake I stood,
For I heard your rivulet fall
From the lake to the meadow and on to the wood,
Our wood, that is dearer than all;

VII.

From the meadow your walks have left so sweet
That whenever a March-wind sighs
He sets the jewel-print of your feet
In violets blue as your eyes,
To the woody hollows in which we meet
And the valleys of Paradise.

VIII.

The slender acacia would not shake
One long milk-bloom on the tree;
The white lake-blossom fell into the lake
As the pimpernel dozed on the lea;

But the rose was awake all night for
your sake,
Knowing your promise to me;
The lilies and roses were all awake,
They sighed for the dawn and thee.

IX.

Queen rose of the rosebud garden
of girls,
Come hither, the dances are done,
In gloss of satin and glimmer of
pearls,
Queen lily and rose in one;
Shine out, little head, sunning over
with curls,
To the flowers, and be their sun.

X.

There has fallen a splendid tear
From the passion-flower at the
gate.
She is coming, my dove, my dear;
She is coming, my life, my fate;
The red rose cries, "She is near,
she is near;"
And the white rose weeps, "She
is late;"
The larkspur listens, "I hear, I
hear,"
And the lily whispers, "I wait."

XI.

She is coming, my own, my sweet;
Were it ever so airy a tread,
My heart would hear her and beat,
Were it earth in an earthy bed;
My dust would hear her and beat,
Had I lain for a century dead;
Would start and tremble under her
feet,
And blossom in purple and red.

TENNYSON.

TO ALTHEA.

WHEN Love with unconfinèd wings
Hovers within my gates,
And my divine Althea brings
To whisper at the grates;
When I lie tangled in her hair
And fettered to her eye,
The birds that wanton in the air
Know no such liberty.

When flowing cups run swiftly round
With no allaying Thames,
Our careless heads with roses crowned,
Our hearts with loyal flames;
When thirsty grief in wine we steep,
When healths and draughts go free,
Fishes that tipple in the deep
Know no such liberty.

When, linnet-like confinèd, I
With shriller throat shall sing
The sweetness, mercy, majesty,
And glories of my King;
When I shall voice aloud how good
He is, how great should be,
Enlargèd winds, that curl the flood,
Know no such liberty.

Stone walls do not a prison make,
Nor iron bars a cage;
Minds innocent and quiet take
That for an hermitage:
If I have freedom in my love,
And in my soul am free,
Angels alone, that soar above,
Enjoy such liberty.

LOVELACE.

TO CELIA.

DRINK to me only with thine eyes,
And I will pledge with mine;
Or leave a kiss but in the cup,
And I'll not look for wine.
The thirst that from my soul doth rise
Doth ask a drink divine;
But might I of Jove's nectar sup,
I would not change for thine.

I sent thee late a rosy wreath,
Not so much honoring thee,
As giving it a hope that there
It would not withered be;
But thou thereon didst only breathe,
And sent it back to me;
Since then it grows and smells, I swear,
Not of itself, but thee,

BEN JONSON.

THE NIGHT PIECE: TO JULIA.

HER eyes the glow-worme lend thee,
The shooting stars attend thee;
And the elves also,
Whose little eyes glow,
Like the sparks of fire, befriend thee.

No Will-o'-th'-Wispe mislight thee,
Nor snake nor slow-worme bite thee;
But on, on thy way,
Not making a stay,
Since ghost there's none to affright thee.

Let not the dark thee cumber,
What though the moon do slumber?
The starres of the night
Will lend thee their light,
Like tapers cleare, without number.

Then, Julia, let me wooe thee,
Thus, thus to come unto me;
And when I shall meet
Thy silvery feet,
My soule I'll poure into thee.

HERRICK.

DISDAIN RETURNED.

HE that loves a rosy cheek,
Or a coral lip admires,
Or from star-like eyes doth seek
Fuel to maintain his fires;
As old Time makes these decay,
So his flames must waste away.

But a smooth and steadfast mind,
Gentle thoughts and calm desires,
Hearts, with equal love cómbined,
Kindle never-dying fires.
Where these are not, I despise
Lovely cheeks, or lips, or eyes.

THOMAS CAREW.

LOVE.

LOVE is a sickness full of woes,
All remedies refusing;
A plant that most with cutting grows,
Most barren with best using.
Why so?
More we enjoy it, more it dies,
If not enjoyed, it sighing cries
Heigh-ho!

Love is a torment of the mind,
A tempest everlasting;
And Jove hath made it of a kind
Not well, nor full, nor fasting.
Why so?
More we enjoy it, more it dies;
If not enjoyed, it sighing cries
Heigh-ho!

SAMUEL DANIEL.

THE MANLY HEART.

SHALL I, wasting in despair,
Die because a woman's fair?
Or my cheeks make pale with care
'Cause another's rosy are?
Be she fairer than the day,
Or the flowery meads in May—
If she be not so to me,
What care I how fair she be?

Shall my foolish heart be pined
'Cause I see a woman kind;
Or a well disposèd nature
Joinèd with a lovely feature?
Be she meeker, kinder, than
Turtle-dove or pelican,
If she be not so to me,—
What care I how kind she be?

Shall a woman's virtues move
Me to perish for her love?
Or her merit's value known
Make me quite forget mine own?
Be she with that goodness blest
Which may gain her name of Best;
If she seem not such to me,
What care I how good she be?

'Cause her fortune seems too high,
Shall I play the fool and die?
Those that bear a noble mind
Where they want of riches find,
Think what with them they would do
Who without them dare to woo;
And unless that mind I see,
What care I though great she be?

Great or good, or kind or fair,
I will ne'er the more despair;
If she love me, this believe,
I will die ere she shall grieve;
If she slight me when I woo,
I can scorn and let her go;
For if she be not for me,
What care I for whom she be?

G. WITHER.

LOVE'S YOUNG DREAM.

O, THE days are gone, when Beauty bright
My heart's chain wove;
When my dream of life, from morn till night,
Was love, still love.

New hope may bloom,
And days may come,
Of milder, calmer beam;
But there's nothing half so sweet in life
As love's young dream.

MOORE.

THEKLA'S SONG.

THE clouds are flying, the woods are sighing,
A maiden is walking the grassy shore,
And as the wave breaks with might, with might,
She singeth aloud in the darksome night,
But a tear is in her troubled eye.

For the world feels cold, and the heart gets old,
And reflects the bright aspect of Nature no more;
Then take back thy child, holy Virgin, to thee!
I have plucked the one blossom that hangs on earth's tree,
I have lived, and have loved, and die.

Translated from Schiller.

THE BRIDAL OF ANDALLA.

"RISE up, rise up, Xarifa! lay the golden cushion down;
Rise up, come to the window, and gaze with all the town!
From gay guitar and violin the silver notes are flowing,
And the lovely lute doth speak between the trumpet's lordly blowing,
And banners bright from lattice light are waving everywhere,
And the tall, tall plume of our cousin's bridegroom floats proudly in the air.
Rise up, rise up, Xarifa! lay the golden cushion down;
Rise up, come to the window, and gaze with all the town!

"Arise, arise, Xarifa! I see Andalla's face —
He bends him to the people with a calm and princely grace;
Through all the land of Xeres and banks of Guadalquiver
Rode forth bridegroom so brave as he, so brave and lovely never.
Yon tall plume waving o'er his brow, of purple mixed with white,
I guess 'twas wreathed by Zara, whom he will wed to-night.
Rise up, rise up, Xarifa! lay the golden cushion down;
Rise up, come to the window, and gaze with all the town!"

The Zegri lady rose not, nor laid her cushion down,
Nor came she to the window to gaze with all the town;
But though her eyes dwelt on her knee, in vain her fingers strove,
And though her needle pressed the silk, no flower Xarifa wove;
One bonny rose-bud she had traced before the noise drew nigh —
That bonny bud a tear effaced, slow drooping from her eye —
"No, no!" she sighs — "bid me not rise, nor lay my cushion down,
To gaze upon Andalla with all the gazing town!"

"Why rise ye not, Xarifa — nor lay your cushion down —
Why gaze ye not, Xarifa — with all the gazing town?
Hear, hear the trumpet how it swells, and how the people cry:
He stops at Zara's palace-gate — why sit ye still, oh, why!"
— "At Zara's gate stops Zara's mate; in him shall I discover
The dark-eyed youth pledged me his truth with tears, and was my lover!
I will not rise, with weary eyes, nor lay my cushion down,
To gaze on false Andalla with all the gazing town!"

LOCKHART.

THE BANKS OF DOON.

YE banks and braes o' bonnie Doon,
How can ye bloom sae fresh and fair,
How can ye chant, ye little birds,
And I sae weary, fu' o' care!

Thou'lt break my heart, thou warbling bird,
That wantons thro' the flowering thorn:
Thou minds me o' departed joys,
Departed — never to return.

Aft hae I roved by bonnie Doon,
To see the rose and woodbine twine;
And ilka bird sang o' its luve,
And fondly sae did I o' mine.
Wi' lightsome heart I pu'd a rose,
Fu' sweet upon its thorny tree;
And my fause luver stole my rose,
But, ah! he left the thorn wi' me.

BURNS.

A WEARY LOT IS THINE.

A WEARY lot is thine, fair maid,
A weary lot is thine;
To pull the thorn thy brow to braid,
And press the rue for wine.
A lightsome eye, a soldier's mien,
A feather of the blue,
A doublet of the Lincoln green, —
No more of me you knew, my love;
No more of me you knew.

This morn is merry June, I trow,
The rose is budding fain;
But it shall bloom in winter snow
Ere we two meet again.
He turned his charger as he spake
Upon the river shore;
He gave his bridle-reins a shake,
Said, Adieu forevermore, my love;
And adieu forevermore.

SCOTT.

THE NIGHT-SEA.

IN the summer even,
While yet the dew was hoar,
I went plucking purple pansies,
Till my love should come to shore.

The fishing lights their dances
Were keeping out at sea,
And "Come," I sung, "my true love,
Come hasten home to me."

But the sea it fell a-moaning,
And the white gulls rocked thereon,
And the young moon dropped from heaven,
And the lights hid one by one.

All silently their glances
Slipped down the cruel sea,
And "Wait," cried the night, and wind, and storm,
"Wait till I come to thee!"

HARRIET PRESCOTT SPOFFORD.

HERO TO LEANDER.

OH! go not yet my love,
The night is dark and vast;
The white moon is hid in her heaven above,
And the waves climb high and fast.
Oh! kiss me, kiss me, once again,
Lest thy kiss should be the last.
Oh kiss me ere we part:
Grow closer to my heart,
My heart is warmer surely than the bosom of the main.

Thy heart beats through thy rosy limbs,
So gladly doth it stir;
Thine eye in drops of gladness swims,
I have bathed thee with the pleasant myrrh;
Thy locks are dripping balm;
Thou shalt not wander hence to-night,
I'll stay thee with my kisses.
To-night the roaring brine
Will rend thy golden tresses;
The ocean with the morrow light
Will be both blue and calm;
And the billow will embrace thee with a kiss as soft as mine.
No western odors wander
On the black and moaning sea,
And when thou art dead, Leander,
My soul must follow thee!
Oh! go not yet, my love,
Thy voice is sweet and low;
The deep salt wave breaks in above
Those marble steps below.
The turret stairs are wet
That lead into the sea.
The pleasant stars have set:
Oh! go not, go not yet,
Or I will follow thee.

TENNYSON.

BRIGNALL BANKS.

O, BRIGNALL banks are wild and fair,
And Greta woods are green,
And you may gather garlands there,
Would grace a summer queen.
And as I rode by Dalton Hall,
Beneath the turrets high,
A maiden on the castle wall
Was singing merrily, —
"O, Brignall banks are fresh and fair,
And Greta woods are green;
I'd rather rove with Edmund there,
Than reign our English queen." —

"If, Maiden, thou wouldst wend with me,
To leave both tower and town,
Thou first must guess what life lead we,
That dwell by dale and down.
And if thou canst that riddle read,
As read full well you may,
Then to the greenwood shalt thou speed,
As blithe as Queen of May." —
Yet sung she, "Brignall banks are fair,
And Greta woods are green;
I'd rather rove with Edmund there,
Than reign our English queen.

"I read you, by your bugle-horn,
And by your palfrey good,
I read you for a Ranger sworn,
To keep the king's greenwood."
"A Ranger, lady, winds his horn,
And 'tis at peep of light;
His blast is heard at merry morn,
And mine at dead of night." —
Yet sung she, "Brignall banks are fair,
And Greta woods are gay;
I would I were with Edmund there,
To reign his Queen of May!

"With burnished brand and musketoon,
So gallantly you come,
I read you for a bold Dragoon,
That lists the tuck of drum." —
"I list no more the tuck of drum,
No more the trumpet hear;
But when the beetle sounds his hum,
My comrades take the spear.

"And, O! though Brignall banks be fair,
And Greta woods be gay,
Yet mickle must the maiden dare,
Would reign my Queen of May!

"Maiden! a nameless life I lead,
A nameless death I'll die;
The fiend, whose lantern lights the mead,
Were better mate than I!
And when I'm with my comrades met,
Beneath the greenwood bough,
What once we were we all forget,
Nor think what we are now.
"Yet Brignall banks are fresh and fair,
And Greta woods are green,
And you may gather garlands there
Would grace a summer queen."

SCOTT.

BONNY DUNDEE.

To the Lords of Convention 'twas Claver'se who spoke,
"Ere the King's crown shall fall there are crowns to be broke;
So let each Cavalier who loves honor and me
Come follow the bonnet of Bonny Dundee.
Come fill up my cup, come fill up my can,
Come saddle your horses, and call up your men;
Come open the West Port, and let me gang free,
And it's room for the bonnets of Bonny Dundee.

Dundee he is mounted, he rides up the street,
The bells are rung backward, the drums they are beat;
But the Provost, douce man, said, "Just e'en let him be,
The gude town is weel quit of that Deil of Dundee."

With sour-featured Whigs the Grassmarket was crammed,
As if half the West had set tryst to be hanged:

There was spite in each look, there was fear in each ee,
As they watched for the bonnets of Bonny Dundee.

These cowls of Kilmannock had spits and had spears,
And lang-hafted gullies to kill Cavaliers;
And they shrunk to close-heads, and the causeway was free,
At the toss of the bonnet of Bonny Dundee.

"Away to the hills, to the caves, to the rocks, —
Ere I own an usurper, I'll couch with the fox;
And tremble false Whigs, in the midst of your glee,
You have not seen the last of my bonnet and me."

SCOTT.

SONG OF CLAN-ALPINE.

HAIL to the Chief who in triumph advances!
Honored and blessed be the evergreen Pine!
Long may the tree, in his banner that glances,
Flourish, the shelter and grace of our line!
Heaven send it happy dew,
Earth lend it sap anew,
Gayly to bourgeon, and broadly to grow,
While every Highland glen
Sends our shout back again,
"Roderigh Vich Alpine dhu, ho! ieroe!"

Ours is no sapling, chance-sown by the fountain,
Blooming at Beltane, in winter to fade;
When the whirlwind has stripped every leaf on the mountain,
The more shall Clan-Alpine exult in her shade.
Moored in the rifted rock,
Proof to the tempest's shock,
Firmer he roots him the ruder it blow:
Menteith and Breadalbane, then,
Echo his praise again,
"Roderigh Vich Alpine dhu, ho! ieroe!"

Proudly our pibroch has thrilled in Glen Fruin,
And Bannachars' groans to our slogan replied;
Glen Luss and Ross dhu, they are smoking in ruin,
And the best of Loch-Lomond lie dead on her side.
Widow and Saxon maid
Long shall lament our raid,
Think of Clan-Alpine with fear and with woe;
Lennox and Leven-glen
Shake when they hear again,
"Roderigh Vich Alpine dhu, ho! ieroe!"

Row, vassals, row, for the pride of the Highlands!
Stretch to your oars for the evergreen Pine!
O that the rosebud that graces yon islands
Were wreathed in a garland around him to twine!
O that some seedling gem,
Worthy such noble stem,
Honored and blessed in their shadow might grow!
Loud should Clan-Alpine then
Ring from her deepmost glen,
"Roderigh Vich Alpine dhu, ho! ieroe!"

SCOTT.

PIBROCH OF DONUIL DHU.

PIBROCH of Donuil Dhu,
Pibroch of Donuil,
Wake thy wild voice anew,
Summon Clan Conuil.
Come away, come away,
Hark to the summons!
Come in your war array,
Gentles and commons.

Come from deep glen and
From mountain so rocky,
The war-pipe and pennon
Are at Inverlochy.
Come every hill-plaid,
And true heart that wears one;
Come every steel blade,
And strong hand that bears one!

Leave untended the herd,
The flock without shelter;

Leave the corpse uninterred,
  The bride at the altar;
Leave the deer, leave the steer,
  Leave nets and barges:
Come with your fighting gear,
  Broadswords and targes.

Come as the winds come
  When forests are rended;
Come as the waves come
  When navies are stranded:
Faster come, faster come,
  Faster and faster,
Chief, vassal, page, and groom,
  Tenant and master.

Fast they come, fast they come;
  See how they gather!
Wide waves the eagle plume
  Blended with heather.
Cast your plaids, draw your blades,
  Forward each man set!
Pibroch of Donuil Dhu,
  Knell for the onset!

SCOTT.

THE DYING BARD.

I.

DINAS EMLINN, lament; for the moment is nigh,
When mute in the woodlands thine echoes shall die:
No more by sweet Teivi Cadwallon shall rave,
And mix his wild notes with the wild dashing wave.

II.

In spring and in autumn thy glories of shade
Unhonored shall flourish, unhonored shall fade;
For soon shall be lifeless the eye and the tongue,
That viewed them with rapture, with rapture that sung.

III.

Thy sons, Dinas Emlinn, may march in their pride,
And chase the proud Saxon from Prestatyn's side;
But where is the harp shall give life to their name?
And where is the bard shall give heroes their fame?

IV.

And oh, Dinas Emlinn! thy daughters so fair,
Who heave the white bosom, and wave the dark hair;
What tuneful enthusiast shall worship their eye,
When half of their charms with Cadwallon shall die?

V.

Then adieu, silver Teivi! I quit thy loved scene,
To join the dim choir of the bards who have been;
With Lewarch, and Meilor, and Merlin the Old,
And sage Taliessin, high harping to hold.

VI.

And adieu, Dinas Emlinn! still green be thy shades,
Unconquered thy warriors, and matchless thy maids!
And thou, whose faint warblings my weakness can tell,
Farewell, my loved Harp! my last treasure, farewell!

SCOTT.

IX.

DIRGES AND PATHETIC POEMS.

"For when sad thoughts possess the mind of man,
There is a plummet in the heart that weighs
And pulls us living to the dust we came from." — BEAUMONT AND FLETCHER.

DIRGES AND PATHETIC POEMS.

LACHRIMÆ; OR, MIRTH TURNED TO MOURNING.

Call me no more,
As heretofore,
The music of a feast;
Since now, alas,
The mirth that was
In me, is dead or ceast.

Before I went
To banishment
Into the loathèd west,
I could rehearse
A lyric verse,
And speak it with the best.

But time, ay me!
Has laid, I see,
My organ fast asleep;
And turned my voice
Into the noise
Of those that sit and weep.

Herrick.

THE NYMPH MOURNING HER FAWN.

The wanton troopers, riding by,
Have shot my fawn, and it will die.
Ungentle men! they cannot thrive
Who killed thee. Thou ne'er didst alive
Them any harm, alas! nor could
Thy death yet do them any good.
I'm sure I never wished them ill;
Nor do I for all this, nor will:
But, if my simple prayers may yet
Prevail with Heaven to forget
Thy murder, I will join my tears,
Rather than fail. But, O my fears!
It cannot die so. Heaven's King
Keeps register of every thing,
And nothing may we use in vain;
Even beasts must be with justice slain,
Else men are made their deodands.
Though they should wash their guilty hands
In this warm life-blood which doth part
From thine, and wound me to the heart,
Yet could they not be clean, their stain
Is dyed in such a purple grain.
There is not such another in
The world, to offer for their sin.

It is a wondrous thing how fleet
'Twas on those little silver feet;
With what a pretty skipping grace
It oft would challenge me the race;
And, when it had left me far away,
'Twould stay and run again and stay;
For it was nimbler much than hinds,
And trod as if on the four winds.

I have a garden of my own,
But so with roses overgrown,
And lilies, that you would it guess
To be a little wilderness,
And all the spring time of the year
It only lovèd to be there.

Among the beds of lilies I
Have sought it oft, where it should lie,
Yet could not, till itself would rise,
Find it, although before mine eyes;
For, in the flaxen lilies' shade,
It like a bank of lilies laid.
Upon the roses it would feed,
Until its lips e'en seemed to bleed,
And then to me 'twould boldly trip,
And print those roses on my lip.
But all its chief delight was still
On roses thus itself to fill,

And its pure virgin limbs to fold
In whitest sheets of lilies cold:
Had it lived long, it would have been
Lilies without, roses within.

MARVELL.

THE LABORER.

Toiling in the naked fields,
Where no bush a shelter yields,
Needy Labor dithering stands,
Beats and blows his numbing hands,
And upon the crumping snows
Stamps in vain to warm his toes.

Though all's in vain to keep him warm,
Poverty must brave the storm,
Friendship none its aid to lend, —
Constant health his only friend,
Granting leave to live in pain,
Giving strength to toil in vain.

JOHN CLARE.

LAMENT OF MARY QUEEN OF SCOTS, ON THE APPROACH OF SPRING.

Now Nature hangs her mantle green
On every blooming tree,
And spreads her sheets o' daisies white
Out owre the grassy lea:
Now Phœbus cheers the crystal streams,
And glads the azure skies;
But nought can glad the weary wight
That fast in durance lies.

Now laverocks wake the merry morn,
Aloft on dewy wing;
The merle, in his noontide bower,
Makes woodland echoes ring;
The mavis mild, wi' many a note,
Sings drowsy day to rest:
In love and freedom they rejoice,
Wi' care nor thrall opprest.

Now blooms the lily by the bank,
The primrose down the brae;
The hawthorn's budding in the glen,
And milk-white is the slae:
The meanest hind in fair Scotland
May rove their sweets amang:
But I, the Queen of a' Scotland,
Maun lie in prison strang.

I was the Queen o' bonnie France,
Where happy I hae been,
Fu' lightly rase I in the morn,
As blythe lay down at e'en:
And I'm the sov'reign of Scotland,
And mony a traitor there;
Yet here I lie in foreign bands,
And never ending care.

But as for thee, thou false woman,
My sister and my fae,
Grim vengeance yet shall whet a sword
That through thy soul shall gae:
The weeping blood in woman's breast
Was never known to thee;
Nor the balm that draps on wounds of woe
Frae woman's pitying e'e.

My son! my son! may kinder stars
Upon thy fortune shine;
And may those pleasures gild thy reign,
That ne'er wad blink on mine!
God keep thee frae thy mother's faes,
Or turn their hearts to thee;
And where thou meet'st thy mother's friend,
Remember him for me!

Oh! soon, to me, may summer suns
Nae mair light up the morn!
Nae mair, to me, the autumn winds
Wave o'er the yellow corn!
And in the narrow house o' death
Let winter round me rave;
And the next flowers that deck the spring,
Bloom on my peaceful grave!

BURNS.

THE BRAES OF YARROW.

Thy braes were bonnie, Yarrow stream,
When first on them I met my lover;
Thy braes how dreary, Yarrow stream,
When now thy waves his body cover!
Forever, now, O Yarrow stream!
Thou art to me a stream of sorrow;
Forever on thy banks shall I
Behold my love, the flower of Yarrow!

He promised me a milk-white steed,
To bear me to his father's bowers;
He promised me a little page,
To squire me to his father's towers;
He promised me a wedding-ring—
The wedding-day was fixed to-morrow:
Now he is wedded to his grave,
Alas, his watery grave in Yarrow!

His mother from the window looked,
With all the longing of a mother;
His little sister weeping walked
The greenwood path to meet her brother:
They sought him east, they sought him west,
They sought him all the forest thorough;
They only saw the cloud of night,
They only heard the roar of Yarrow.

No longer from the window look;
Thou hast no son, thou tender mother!
No longer walk, thou lovely maid;
Alas! thou hast no more a brother!
No longer seek him east or west,
No longer search the forest thorough;
For wandering in the night so dark,
He fell a lifeless corse in Yarrow.

JOHN LOGAN.

THE MURDERED TRAVELLER.

WHEN spring, to woods and wastes around,
Brought bloom and joy again,
The murdered traveller's bones were found,
Far down a narrow glen.

The fragrant birch above him hung
Her tassels in the sky;
And many a vernal blossom sprung,
And nodded careless by.

The red-bird warbled as he wrought
His hanging nest o'erhead,
And fearless, near the fatal spot,
Her young the partridge led.

But there was weeping far away;
And gentle eyes, for him,
With watching many an anxious day,
Were sorrowful and dim.

They little knew, who loved him so,
The fearful death he met,
When shouting o'er the desert snow,
Unarmed, and hard beset;

Nor how, when round the frosty pole
The northern dawn was red,
The mountain wolf and wildcat stole
To banquet on the dead;

Nor how, when strangers found his bones,
They dressed the hasty bier,
And marked his grave with nameless stones,
Unmoistened by a tear.

But long they looked, and feared, and wept,
Within his distant home;
And dreamed, and started as they slept,
For joy that he was come.

So long they looked; but never spied
His welcome step again,
Nor knew the fearful death he died
Far down that narrow glen.

BRYANT.

THE DESERTED HOUSE.

LIFE and thought have gone away
Side by side,
Leaving door and windows wide:
Careless tenants they!

All within is dark as night:
In the windows is no light;
And no murmur at the door,
So frequent on its hinge before.

Close the door, the shutters close,
Or through the windows we shall see
The nakedness and vacancy
Of the dark deserted house.

Come away: no more of mirth
Is here, or merry-making sound.
The house was builded of the earth,
And shall fall again to ground.

Come away: for Life and Thought
Here no longer dwell;
But in a city glorious,
A great and distant city, have bought
A mansion incorruptible.
Would they could have staid with us!

TENNYSON.

LAMENT FOR JAMES, EARL OF GLENCAIRN.

Ye scattered brids that faintly sing,
The reliques of the vernal choir!
Ye woods that shed on a' the winds
The honors of the aged year!
A few short months, and glad and gay,
Again ye'll charm the ear and e'e;
But nocht in all revolving time
Can gladness bring again to me.

The bridegroom may forget the bride
Was made his wedded wife yestreen;
The monarch may forget the crown
That on his head an hour has been;
The mother may forget the child
That smiles sae sweetly on her knee:
But I'll remember thee, Glencairn,
And a' that thou hast done for me!

BURNS.

HE'S GANE.

. . . .

He's gane! he's gane! he's frae us torn,
The ae best fellow e'er was born!
Thee, Matthew, nature's sel' shall mourn
By wood and wild,
Where, haply, pity strays forlorn,
Frae man exiled.

Ye hills, near neebors o' the starns,
That proudly cock your cresting cairns!
Ye cliffs, the haunts of sailing yearns,
Where Echo slumbers,
Come join, ye Nature's sturdiest bairns,
My wailing numbers!

Mourn, ilka grove the cushat kens!
Ye haz'lly shaws and briery dens!
Ye burnies, whimplin' down your glens,
Wi' todlin' din,
Or foaming strang, wi' hasty stens,
Frae lin to lin!

Mourn, little harebells owre the lea;
Ye stately foxgloves fair to see;
Ye woodbines hanging bonnilie,
In scented bowers;
Ye roses on your thorny tree,
The first o' flowers.

Mourn, ye wee songsters o' the wood;
Ye grouse that crap the heather bud;
Ye curlews calling through a clud;
Ye whistling plover;
And mourn, ye whirring paitrick brood!—
He's gane forever!

Go to your sculptured tombs, ye great,
In a' the tinsel trash o' state;
But by thy honest turf I'll wait,
Thou man of worth!
And weep the ae best fellow's fate
E'er lay in earth.

BURNS.

TO HIS WINDING-SHEET.

Come thou, who art the wine and wit
Of all I've writ;
The grace, the glorie, and the best
Piece of the rest;
Thou art of what I did intend
The all, and end;
And what was made, was made to meet
Thee, thee, my sheet;
Come then, and be to my chaste side
Both bed and bride.
We two, as reliques left, will have
One rest, one grave;

And, hugging close, we will not feare
Lust entering here;
Where all desires are dead or cold,
As is the mould;
And all affections are forgot,
Or trouble not.
Here needs no court for our request,
Where all are best;
All wise, all equal, and all just
Alike i' th' dust.
Nor need we here to feare the frowne
Of court or crown;
Where fortune bears no sway o'er things,
There all are kings.
And for a while lye here concealed,
To be revealed,
Next, at that great platonick yeere,
And then meet here.
HERRICK.

ODE.

How sleep the brave, who sink to rest,
By all their country's wishes blessed!
When Spring, with dewy fingers cold,
Returns to deck their hallowed mould,
She there shall dress a sweeter sod
Than Fancy's feet have ever trod.

By fairy hands their knell is rung;
By forms unseen their dirge is sung;
There Honor comes, a pilgrim gray,
To bless the turf that wraps their clay;
And Freedom shall a while repair,
To dwell a weeping hermit there!
COLLINS.

DIRGE.

HE is gone — is dust.
He, the more fortunate! yea he hath finished!
For him there is no longer any future,
His life is bright, — bright without spot it *was*
And cannot cease to be. No ominous hour
Knocks at his door with tidings of mishap.
Far off is he, above desire and fear;
No more submitted to the change and chance
Of the unsteady planets. O 'tis well
With *him!* but who knows what the coming hour
Veiled in thick darkness brings for us!

That anguish will be wearied down, I know;
What pang is permanent with man? from the highest
As from the vilest thing of every day
He learns to wean himself; for the strong hours
Conquer him. Yet I feel what I have lost
In him. The bloom is vanished from my life.
For O! he stood beside me, like my youth,
Transformed for me the reäl to a dream,
Clothing the palpable and familiar
With golden exhalations of the dawn.
Whatever fortunes wait my future toils,
The *beautiful* is vanished — and returns not.
COLERIDGE: *Wallenstein.*

LYKEWAKE DIRGE.

THIS ae night, this ae night,
Every night and alle,
Fire and sleet and candle-light,
And Christ receive thy saule.

When thou from hence away art past,
Every night and alle,
To Whinny-Muir thou comest at laste,
And Christ receive thy saule.

If ever thou gavest hosen and shoon,
Every night and alle,
Sit thee down and put them on,
And Christ receive thy soule.

If hosen and shoon thou never gav'st none,
Every night and alle,
The whinnes shall prick thee to the bare bone,
And Christ receive thy saule.

From Whinny-Muir when thou mayest passe,
Every night and alle,
To Purgatory fire thou comest at last,
And Christ receive thy saule.

If ever thou gavest meat or drink,
Every night and alle,
The fire shall never make thee shrink,
And Christ receive thy saule.

If meat or drink thou never gavest none,
Every night and alle,
The fire will burn thee to the bare bone,
And Christ receive thy saule.

This ae night, this ae night,
Every night and alle,
Fire and sleet and candle-light,
And Christ receive thy saule.

ANON.

SLEEPY HOLLOW.

No abbey's gloom, nor dark cathedral stoops,
No winding torches paint the midnight air;
Here the green pines delight, the aspen droops
Along the modest pathways, and those fair
Pale asters of the season spread their plumes
Around this field, fit garden for our tombs.

And shalt thou pause to hear some funeral bell
Slow stealing o'er thy heart in this calm place,
Not with a throb of pain, a feverish knell,
But in its kind and supplicating grace,
It says, Go, pilgrim, on thy march, be more
Friend to the friendless than thou wast before;

Learn from the loved one's rest serenity;
To-morrow that soft bell for thee shall sound,
And thou repose beneath the whispering tree,
One tribute more to this submissive ground; —
Prison thy soul from malice, bar out pride,
Nor these pale flowers nor this still field deride:

Rather to those ascents of being turn,
Where a ne'er-setting sun illumes the year
Eternal, and the incessant watch-fires burn
Of unspent holiness and goodness clear, —
Forget man's littleness, deserve the best,
God's mercy in thy thought and life confest.

CHANNING.

DIRGE IN CYMBELINE.

To fair Fidelé's grassy tomb
Soft maids and village hinds shall bring
Each opening sweet of earliest bloom,
And rifle all the breathing spring.

No wailing ghost shall dare appear
To vex with shrieks this quiet grove;
But shepherd lads assemble here,
And melting virgins own their love.

No withered witch shall here be seen;
No goblins lead their nightly crew:
The female fays shall haunt the green,
And dress thy grave with pearly dew!

The redbreast oft, at evening hours,
Shall kindly lend his little aid,
With hoary moss, and gathered flowers,
To deck the ground where thou art laid.

When howling winds and beating rain
In tempests shake the sylvan cell,
Or 'midst the chase, on every plain,
The tender thought on thee shall dwell;

Each lovely scene shall thee restore,
For thee the tear be duly shed;
Beloved till life can charm no more,
And mourned till Pity's self be dead.

COLLINS.

DIRGE FOR DORCAS.

COME pitie us, all ye who see
Our harps hung on the willow-tree;
Come pitie us, ye passers-by,
Who see or hear poor widows crie;
Come pitie us, and bring your eares
And eyes to pitie widows' teares.
And when you are come hither,
Then we will keep
A fast, and weep
Our eyes out all together,

For Tabitha, who dead lies here,
Clean washt, and laid out for the bier.
O modest matrons, weep and waile!
For now the corne and wine must faile;
The basket and the bynn of bread,
Wherewith so many soules were fed,
Stand empty here forever;
And ah! the poore,
At thy worne doore,
Shall be relievèd never.

But ah, alas! the almond-bough
And olive-branch is withered now;
The wine-presse now is ta'en from us,
The saffron and the calamus;
The spice and spiknard hence is gone,
The storax and the cynamon;
The caroll of our gladnesse
Has taken wing,
And our late spring
Of mirth is turned to sadnesse.

How wise wast thou in all thy waies!
How worthy of respect and praise!
How matron-like didst thou go drest!
How soberly above the rest
Of those that prank it with their plumes,
And jet it with their choice perfumes!
Thy vestures were not flowing;
Nor did the street
Accuse thy feet
Of mincing in their going.

Sleep with thy beauties here, while we
Will show these garments made by thee;
These were the coats, in these are read
The monuments of Dorcas dead:
These were thy acts, and thou shalt have
These hung, as honors o'er thy grave,
And after us, distressed,
Should fame be dumb,
Thy very tomb
Would cry out, Thou art blessed.

HERRICK.

CORONACH.

HE is gone on the mountain,
He is lost to the forest,
Like a summer-dried fountain,
When our need was the sorest.
The fount, re-appearing,
From the raindrop shall borrow,
But to us comes no cheering,
To Duncan no morrow!

The hand of the reaper
Takes the ears that are hoary;
But the voice of the weeper
Wails manhood in glory.
The autumn winds rushing
Waft the leaves that are searest;
But our flower was in flushing
When blighting was nearest.

Fleet foot on the correi,
Sage counsel in cumber,
Red hand in the foray,
How sound is thy slumber!
Like the dew on the mountain,
Like the foam on the river,
Like the bubble on the fountain,
Thou art gone, and forever!

SCOTT.

FEAR NO MORE THE HEAT O' TH' SUN.

FEAR no more the heat o' th' sun,
Nor the furious winter's rages;
Thou thy worldly task hast done,
Home art gone, and ta'en thy wages.
Golden lads and girls all must,
As chimney-sweepers, come to dust.

Fear no more the frown o' th' great,
  Thou art past the tyrant's stroke:
Care no more to clothe and eat;
  To thee the reed is as the oak:
The sceptre, learning, physic, must
All follow this, and come to dust.

Fear no more the lightning-flash,
  Nor the all-dreaded thunder-stone;
Fear not slander, censure rash:
  Thou hast finished joy and moan:
All lovers young, all lovers must
Consign to thee, and come to dust.

SHAKSPEARE.

ODE ON THE CONSECRATION OF SLEEPY-HOLLOW CEMETERY.

SHINE kindly forth, September sun,
  From heavens calm and clear,
That no untimely cloud may run
  Before thy golden sphere,
To vex our simple rites to-day
  With one prophetic tear.

With steady voices let us raise
  The fitting psalm and prayer;—
Remembered grief of other days
  Breathes softening in the air:
Who knows not Death—who mourns no loss—
  He has with us no share.

To holy sorrow—solemn joy,
  We consecrate the place
Where soon shall sleep the maid and boy,
  The father and his race,
The mother with her tender babe,
  The venerable face.

These waving woods—these valleys low
  Between these tufted knolls,
Year after year shall dearer grow
  To many loving souls;
And flowers be sweeter here than blow
  Elsewhere between the poles.

For deathless Love and blessèd Grief
  Shall guard these wooded aisles,
When either Autumn casts the leaf,
  Or blushing Summer smiles,
Or Winter whitens o'er the land,
  Or Spring the buds uncoils.

F. B. SANBORN.

ODE ON THE DEATH OF THOMSON.

IN yonder grave a Druid lies,
  Where slowly winds the stealin[g]
    wave;
The year's best sweets shall duteou[s]
    rise
  To deck its poet's sylvan grave.

In yon deep bed of whispering reed[s]
  His airy harp shall now be laid,
That he, whose heart in sorro[w]
    bleeds,
  May love through life the soothin[g]
    shade.

Then maids and youths shall linge[r]
    here,
  And while its sounds at distanc[e]
    swell,
Shall sadly seem in Pity's ear
  To hear the woodland pilgrim'[s]
    knell.

Remembrance oft shall haunt th[e]
    shore
  When Thames in summer wreath[s]
    is drest,
And oft suspend the dashing oar,
  To bid his gentle spirit rest.

And oft, as ease and health retire
  To breezy lawn, or forest deep,
The friend shall view yon whitenin[g]
    spire,
  And 'mid the varied landscap[e]
    weep.

But thou, who own'st that earth[y]
    bed,
  Ah! what will every dirge avail;
Or tears, which love and pity shed,
  That mourn beneath the glidin[g]
    sail?

Yet lives there one, whose heedle[ss]
    eye
  Shall scorn thy pale shrine glim[-]
    mering near?
With him, sweet bard, may fancy di[e],
  And joy desert the blooming yea[r].

But thou, lorn stream, whose sulle[n]
    tide
  No sedge-crowned sisters now a[t]
    tend,

Now waft me from the green hill's side
Whose cold turf hides the buried friend!

And see the fairy valleys fade;
Dun night has veiled the solemn view!
Yet once again, dear parted shade,
Meek Nature's child, again adieu!

Thy genial meads, assigned to bless
Thy life, shall mourn thy early doom;
There hinds and shepherd-girls shall dress
With simple hands thy rural tomb.

Long, long, thy stone and pointed clay
Shall melt the musing Briton's eyes:
O! vales and wild woods, shall he say,
In yonder grave a Druid lies!

COLLINS.

EPITAPH FROM SIMONIDES.

WHERE is Timarchus gone?
His father's hands were round him,
And when he breathed his life away,
The joy of youth had crowned him.
Old man! thou wilt not forget
Thy lost one, when thine eye
Gazeth on the glowing cheek
Of hope and piety.

ON THE LOSS OF THE "ROYAL GEORGE."

TOLL for the brave —
The brave that are no more!
All sunk beneath the wave,
Fast by their native shore!

Eight hundred of the brave,
Whose courage well was tried,
Had made the vessel heel,
And laid her on her side.

A land breeze shook the shrouds,
And she was overset:
Down went the "Royal George,"
With all her crew complete.

Toll for the brave!
Brave Kempenfelt is gone;
His last sea-fight is fought,
His work of glory done.

It was not in the battle;
No tempest gave the shock;
She sprang no fatal leak;
She ran upon no rock.

His sword was in its sheath;
His fingers held the pen,
When Kempenfelt went down
With twice four hundred men.

Weigh the vessel up,
Once dreaded by our foes!
And mingle with our cup
The tear that England owes.

Her timbers yet are sound,
And she may float again,
Full charged with England's thunder,
And plough the distant main.

But Kempenfelt is gone, —
His victories are o'er;
And he and his eight hundred
Shall plough the waves no more.

COWPER.

LINES.

WRITTEN AT GRASMERE, ON TIDINGS OF THE APPROACHING DEATH OF CHARLES JAMES FOX.

LOUD is the Vale! the voice is up
With which she speaks when storms are gone,
A mighty unison of streams!
Of all her Voices, One!

Loud is the Vale; — this inland Depth
In peace is roaring like the sea;
Yon star upon the mountain-top
Is listening quietly.

Sad was I, even to pain deprest,
Importunate and heavy load!
The Comforter hath found me here,
Upon this lonely road;

And many thousands now are sad —
Wait the fulfilment of their fear;
For he must die who is their stay,
Their glory disappear.

A Power is passing from the earth
To breathless Nature's dark abyss;
But when the great and good depart
What is it more than this —

That Man, who is from God sent forth,
Doth yet again to God return? —
Such ebb and flow must ever be,
Then wherefore should we mourn?

WORDSWORTH.

ODE ON THE DEATH OF THE DUKE OF WELLINGTON.

I.

BURY the Great Duke
With an empire's lamentation.
Let us bury the Great Duke
To the noise of the mourning of a mighty nation,
Mourning when their leaders fall,
Warriors carry the warrior's pall,
And sorrow darkens hamlet and hall.

II.

Where shall we lay the man whom we deplore?
Here, in streaming London's central roar.
Let the sound of those he wrought for,
And the feet of those he fought for,
Echo round his bones forevermore.

III.

Lead out the pageant: sad and slow,
As fits an universal woe,
Let the long long procession go,
And let the sorrowing crowd about it grow,
And let the mournful martial music blow;
The last great Englishman is low.

IV.

Mourn, for to us he seems the last,
Remembering all his greatness in the Past.
No more in soldier fashion will he greet
With lifted hand the gazer in the street.
O friends, our chief state-oracle is mute:
Mourn for the man of long-enduring blood,
The statesman-warrior, moderate, resolute,
Whole in himself, a common good.
Mourn for the man of amplest influ ence,
Yet clearest of ambitious crime,
Our greatest yet with least pretence,
Great in council and great in war,
Foremost captain of his time,
Rich in saving common-sense,
And, as the greatest only are,
In his simplicity sublime.
O good gray head which all men knew,
O voice from which their omens all men drew,
O iron nerve to true occasion true,
O fallen at length that tower of strength
Which stood four-square to all the winds that blew!
Such was he whom we deplore.
The long self-sacrifice of life is o'er.
The great World-victor's victor will be seen no more.

V.

All is over and done:
Render thanks to the Giver,
England, for thy son.
Let the bell be tolled.
Render thanks to the Giver,
And render him to the mould.
Under the cross of gold
That shines over city and river,
There he shall rest forever
Among the wise and the bold.
Let the bell be tolled:
And a reverent people behold
The towering car, the sable steeds:
Bright let it be with its blazoned deeds,
Dark in its funeral fold.
Let the bell be tolled:
And a deeper knell in the heart be knolled;
And the sound of the sorrowing anthem rolled
Thro' the dome of the golden cross;
And the volleying cannon thunder his loss;
He knew their voices of old.
For many a time in many a clime
His captain's-ear has heard them boom
Bellowing victory, bellowing doom:

When he with those deep voices wrought,
Guarding realms and kings from shame;
With those deep voices our dead captain taught
The tyrant, and asserts his claim
In that dread sound to the great name,
Which he has worn so pure of blame,
In praise and in dispraise the same,
A man of well-attempered frame.
O civic muse, to such a name,
To such a name for ages long,
To such a name,
Preserve a broad approach of fame,
And ever-echoing avenues of song.

VI.

Who is he that cometh, like an honored guest,
With banner and with music, with soldier and with priest,
With a nation weeping, and breaking on my rest?
Mighty Seaman, this is he
Was great by land as thou by sea.
Thine island loves thee well, thou famous man,
The greatest sailor since our world began.
Now, to the roll of muffled drums,
To thee the greatest soldier comes;
For this is he
Was great by land as thou by sea;
His foes were thine; he kept us free;
O give him welcome, this is he
Worthy of our gorgeous rites,
And worthy to be laid by thee;
For this is England's greatest son,
He that gained a hundred fights,
Nor ever lost an English gun;
This is he that far away
Against the myriads of Assaye
Clashed with his fiery few and won;
And underneath another sun,
Warring on a later day,
Round affrighted Lisbon drew
The treble works, the vast designs
Of his labored rampart-lines,
Where he greatly stood at bay,
Whence he issued forth anew,
And ever great and greater grew,
Beating from the wasted vines
Back to France her banded swarms,
Back to France with countless blows,
Till o'er the hills her eagles flew
Beyond the Pyrenean pines,
Followed up in valley and glen
With blare of bugle, clamor of men,
Roll of cannon and clash of arms,
And England pouring on her foes.
Such a war had such a close.
Again their ravening eagle rose
In anger, wheeled on Europe-shadowing wings,
And barking for the thrones of kings;
Till one that sought but Duty's iron crown
On that loud sabbath shook the spoiler down;
A day of onsets of despair!
Dashed on every rocky square
Their surging charges foamed themselves away;
Last, the Prussian trumpet blew;
Through the long-tormented air
Heaven flashed a sudden jubilant ray,
And down we swept and charged and overthrew.
So great a soldier taught us there,
What long-enduring hearts could do
In that world-earthquake, Waterloo!
Mighty Seaman, tender and true,
And pure as he from taint of craven guile,
O saviour of the silver-coasted isle,
O shaker of the Baltic and the Nile,
If aught of things that here befall
Touch a spirit among things divine,
If love of country move thee there at all,
Be glad, because his bones are laid by thine!
And thro' the centuries let a people's voice
In full acclaim,
A people's voice,
The proof and echo of all human fame,
A people's voice, when they rejoice
At civic revel and pomp and game,
Attest their great commander's claim
With honor, honor, honor, honor to him,
Eternal honor to his name.

VII.

. . . .

Remember him who led your hosts;
He bade you guard the sacred coasts.
Your cannons moulder on the seaward wall;
His voice is silent in your council-hall

Forever; and, whatever tempests lower,
Forever silent; even if they broke
In thunder, silent; yet remember all
He spoke among you, and the Man who spoke;
Who never sold the truth to serve the hour,
Nor paltered with Eternal God for power;
Who let the turbid streams of rumor flow
Thro' either babbling world of high and low;
Whose life was work, whose language rife
With rugged maxims hewn from life;
Who never spoke against a foe;
Whose eighty winters freeze with one rebuke
All great self-seekers trampling on the right:
Truth-teller was our England's Alfred named;
Truth-lover was our English Duke;
Whatever record leap to light,
He never shall be shamed.

. . . .

Hush, the Dead March wails in the people's ears:
The dark crowd moves, and there are sobs and tears:
The black earth yawns: the mortal disappears;
Ashes to ashes, dust to dust;
He is gone who seemed so great. —
Gone; but nothing can bereave him
Of the force he made his own
Being here, and we believe him
Something far advanced in State,
And that he wears a truer crown
Than any wreath that man can weave him.
Speak no more of his renown,
Lay your earthly fancies down,
And in the vast cathedral leave him.
God accept him, Christ receive him.

TENNYSON.

THE BURIAL OF SIR JOHN MOORE AT CORUNNA.

NOT a drum was heard, not a funeral note,
As his corpse to the rampart we hurried;
Not a soldier discharged his farewell shot
O'er the grave where our hero we buried.

We buried him darkly at dead of night,
The sods with our bayonets turning;
By the struggling moonbeam's misty light
And the lantern dimly burning.

No useless coffin enclosed his breast,
Not in sheet nor in shroud we wound him;
But he lay like a warrior taking his rest
With his martial cloak around him.

Few and short were the prayers we said
And we spoke not a word of sorrow,
But we steadfastly gazed on the face of the dead,
And we bitterly thought of the morrow.

We thought, as we hollowed his narrow bed,
And smoothed down his lonely pillow,
That the foe and the stranger would tread o'er his head,
And we far away on the billow!

Lightly they'll talk of the spirit that's gone,
And o'er his cold ashes upbraid him;
But little he'll reck, if they let him sleep on
In the grave where a Briton has laid him.

But half of our heavy task was done,
When the clock tolled the hour for retiring:
And we heard the distant random gun
That the foe was sullenly firing.

Slowly and sadly we laid him down,
From the field of his fame fresh and gory;
We carved not a line, we raised not a stone, —
But we left him alone with his glory.

CHARLES WOLFE.

ON SIR PHILIP SIDNEY.

SILENCE augmenteth griefe, writing encreaseth rage,
Staid are my thoughts, which loved and lost, the wonder of our age,
Yet quickened now with fire, though dead with frost ere now,
Enraged I write I know not what: dead, quick, I know not how.

Hard hearted mindes relent, and Rigor's tears abound,
And Envy strangely rues his end, in whom no fault she found;
Knowledge his light hath lost, Valor hath slaine her knight:
Sidney is dead, dead is my friend, dead is the world's delight.

Place pensive wailes his fall, whose presence was her pride,
Time crieth out, my ebbe is come, his life was my spring-tide;
Fame mournes in that she lost, the ground of her reports,
Each living wight laments his lacke, and all in sundry sorts.

He was — wo worth that word — to each well thinking minde,
A spotless friend, a matchless man, whose vertue ever shined,
Declaring in his thoughts, his life, and that he writ,
Highest conceits, longest foresights, and deepest works of wit.

He onely like himselfe, was second unto none,
Where death — though life — we rue, and wrong, and all in vaine do mone,
Their losse, not him waile they, that fill the world with cries,
Death slue not him, but he made death his ladder to the skies.

Now sinke of sorrow I, who live, the more the wrong,
Who wishing Death, whom death denies, whose thread is all too long,
Who tied to wretched life, who look for no relief,
Must spend my ever-dying days in never-ending grief.

Heart's ease and onely I, like paraleles run on,
Whose equall length, keepe equall bredth and never meete in one,
Yet for not wronging him, my thoughts, my sorrowes' cell,
Shall not run out, though leake they will, for liking him so well.

Farewel to you my hopes, my wonted waking dreames,
Farewel sometime enjoyèd joy eclipsèd are thy beams,
Farewel selfe-pleasing thoughts, which quietness brings forth,
And farewel friendship's sacred league uniting minds of worth.

And farewel mery heart, the gift of guiltless mindes,
And all sports, which for live's restore, varietie assignes,
Let all that sweet is voide? in me no mirth may dwell,
Philip the cause of all this woe, my life's content, farewel.

Now rime, the source of rage, which art no kin to skill,
And endless griefe which deads my life, yet knows not now to kill,
Go seeke that haples tombe, which if ye hap to finde,
Salute the stones, that keep the lines, that held so good a minde.

FULKE GREVILLE, LORD BROOKE.

LYCIDAS.

[In this monody, the author bewails a learned friend, unfortunately drowned in his passage from Chester on the Irish seas, 1637, and by occasion foretells the ruin of our corrupted clergy, then in their height.]

YET once more, O ye laurels, and once more
Ye myrtles brown, with ivy never sere,
I come to pluck your berries harsh and crude,
And with forced fingers rude,
Shatter your leaves before the mellowing year.
Bitter constraint, and sad occasion dear,

Compels me to disturb your season due:
For Lycidas is dead, dead ere his prime,
Young Lycidas! and hath not left his peer.
Who would not sing for Lycidas? He knew
Himself to sing, and build the lofty rhyme.
He must not float upon his watery bier
Unwept, and welter to the parching wind,
Without the meed of some melodious tear.

Begin then, Sisters of the sacred well,
That from beneath the seat of Jove doth spring,
Begin, and somewhat loudly sweep the string.
Hence with denial vain, and coy excuse;
So may some gentle Muse
With lucky words favor my destined urn,
And as he passes turn,
And bid fair peace be to my sable shroud.

For we were nurst upon the self-same hill,
Fed the same flock, by fountain, shade, and rill;
Together both, ere the high lawns appeared
Under the opening eyelids of the morn,
We drove a-field, and both together heard
What time the gray-fly winds her sultry horn,
Battening our flocks with the fresh dews of night,
Oft till the star that rose, at evening bright,
Toward heaven's descent had sloped his westering wheel.
Meanwhile the rural ditties were not mute,
Tempered to the oaten flute,
Rough Satyrs danced, and Fauns with cloven heel
From the glad sound would not be absent long,
And old Damætas loved to hear our song.

But O the heavy change, now thou art gone,
Now thou art gone, and never must return!
Thee, Shepherd, thee the woods, and desert caves
With wild thyme and the gadding vine o'ergrown,
And all their echoes mourn.
The willows, and the hazel copses green,
Shall now no more be seen,
Fanning their joyous leaves to thy soft lays.
As killing as the canker to the rose,
Or taint-worm to the weanling herds that graze,
Or frost to flowers, that their gay wardrobe wear,
When first the white-thorn blows;
Such, Lycidas, thy loss to shepherd's ear.

Where were ye, Nymphs, when the remorseless deep
Closed o'er the head of your loved Lycidas?
For neither were ye playing on the steep,
Where your old Bards, the famous Druids, lie,
Nor on the shaggy top of Mona high,
Nor yet where Deva spreads her wizard stream.
Ay me, I fondly dream!
Had ye been there — for what could that have done?
What could the Muse herself, that Orpheus bore,
The Muse herself, for her inchanting son,
Whom universal nature did lament,
When by the rout that made the hideous roar,
His gory visage down the stream was sent,
Down the swift Hebrus to the Lesbian shore?

Alas! what boots it with uncessant care
To tend the homely slighted shepherd's trade,
And strictly meditate the thankless Muse?
Were it not better done as others use,
To sport with Amaryllis in the shade,
Or with the tangles of Neæra's hair?
Fame is the spur that the clear spirit doth raise

(That last infirmity of noble mind)
To scorn delights, and live laborious days;
But the fair guerdon when we hope to find,
And think to burst out into sudden blaze,
Comes the blind Fury with the abhorrèd shears,
And slits the thin-spun life. But not the praise,
Phœbus replied, and touched my trembling ears;
Fame is no plant that grows on mortal soil,
Nor in the glistering foil
Set off to the world, nor in broad rumor lies;
But lives and spreads aloft by those pure eyes,
And perfect witness of all-judging Jove;
As he pronounces lastly on each deed,
Of so much fame in heaven expect thy meed.

O fountain Arethuse, and thou honored flood,
Smooth-sliding Mincius, crowned with vocal reeds,
That strain I heard was of a higher mood;
But now my oat proceeds,
And listens to the herald of the sea
That came in Neptune's plea;
He asked the waves, and asked the felon winds,
What hard mishap hath doomed this gentle swain?
And questioned every gust of rugged wings
That blows from off each beaked promontory:
They knew not of his story,
And sage Hippotades their answer brings,
That not a blast was from his dungeon strayed;
The air was calm, and on the level brine
Sleek Panopé with all her sisters played.
It was that fatal and perfidious bark,
Built in the eclipse, and rigged with curses dark,
That sunk so low that sacred head of thine.

Next Camus, reverend sire, went footing slow,
His mantle hairy, and his bonnet sedge,
Inwrought with figures dim, and on the edge
Like to that sanguine flower inscribed with woe.
Ah! Who hath reft (quoth he) my dearest pledge?
Last came, and last did go,
The pilot of the Galilean lake;
Two massy keys he bore of metals twain,
(The golden opes, the iron shuts amain)
He shook his mitred locks, and stern bespake;
How well could I have spared for thee, young swain,
Enow of such as for their bellies' sake
Creep, and intrude, and climb into the fold?
Of other care they little reckoning make,
Than how to scramble at the shearer's feast,
And shove away the worthy bidden guest;
Blind mouths! that scarce themselves know how to hold
A sheep-hook, or have learned aught else the least
That to the faithful herdman's art belongs!
What recks it them? What need they? They are sped;
And when they list their lean and flashy songs
Grate on their scrannel pipes of wretched straw,
The hungry sheep look up, and are not fed,
But swoln with wind, and the rank mist they draw,
Rot inwardly, and foul contagion spread;
Besides what the grim wolf with privy paw
Daily devours apace, and nothing said;
But that two-handed engine at the door
Stands ready to smite once, and smite no more.

Return, Alpheus, the dread voice is past,
That shrunk thy streams; return, Sicilian Muse,

And call the vales, and bid them hither cast
Their bells, and flowerets of a thousand hues.
Ye valleys low, where the mild whispers use
Of shades, and wanton winds, and gushing brooks,
On whose fresh lap the swart star sparely looks,
Throw hither all your quaint enamelled eyes,
That on the green turf suck the honeyed showers,
And purple all the ground with vernal flowers.
Bring the rathe primrose that forsaken dies,
The tufted crow-toe, and pale jessamine,
The white pink, and the pansy freakt with jet,
The glowing violet,
The musk-rose, and the well-attired woodbine,
With cowslips wan that hang the pensive head,
And every flower that sad embroidery wears:
Bid amaranthus all his beauty shed,
And daffodillies fill their cups with tears,
To strew the laureate hearse where Lycid lies.
For so to interpose a little ease,
Let our frail thoughts dally with false surmise.
Ay me! Whilst thee the shores and sounding seas
Wash far away, where'er thy bones are hurled,
Whether beyond the stormy Hebrides,
Where thou perhaps under the whelming tide
Visit'st the bottom of the monstrous world;
Or whether thou, to our moist vows denied,
Sleep'st by the fable of Bellerus old,
Where the great vision of the guarded mount
Looks toward Namancos and Bayona's hold;
Look homeward Angel now, and melt with ruth,
And, O ye dolphins, waft the hapless youth.

Weep no more, woful shepherds, weep no more,
For Lycidas your sorrow is not dead,
Sunk though he be beneath the watery floor;
So sinks the day-star in the ocean bed,
And yet anon repairs his drooping head,
And tricks his beams, and with new-spangled ore
Flames in the forehead of the morning sky.
So Lycidas sunk low, but mounted high,
Through the dear might of Him that walked the waves,
Where other groves, and other streams along,
With nectar pure his oozy locks he laves,
And hears the unexpressive nuptial song,
In the blest kingdoms meek of joy and love.
There entertain him all the saints above,
In solemn troops, and sweet societies,
That sing, and singing in their glory move,
And wipe the tears forever from his eyes.
Now, Lycidas, the shepherds weep no more;
Henceforth thou art the Genius of the shore,
In thy large recompense, and shalt be good
To all that wander in that perilous flood.

Thus sang the uncouth swain to the oaks and rills,
While the still morn went out with sandals gray;
He touched the tender stops of various quills,
With eager thought warbling his Doric lay;
And now the sun had stretched out all the hills,
And now was dropt into the western bay;
At last he rose, and twitched his mantle blue; —
To-morrow to fresh woods, and pastures new.

MILTON.

DEPARTED.

A SLUMBER did my spirit seal;
I had no human fears:
She seemed a thing that could not feel
The touch of earthly years.
No motion has she now, no force;
She neither hears nor sees;
Rolled round in earth's diurnal course,
With rocks, and stones, and trees.

WORDSWORTH.

THYRSIS.

[A monody to commemorate the author's friend, Arthur Hugh Clough, who died at Florence, 1861.]

How changed is here each spot man makes or fills!
In the two Hinkseys nothing keeps the same;
The village-street its haunted mansion lacks,
And from the sign is gone Sibylla's name,
And from the roofs the twisted chimney-stacks.
Are ye, too, changed, ye hills?
See, 'tis no foot of unfamiliar men
To-night from Oxford up your pathway strays!
Here came I often, often, in old days;
Thyrsis and I; we still had Thyrsis then.

Runs it not here, the track by Childsworth Farm,
Up past the wood, to where the elm-tree crowns
The hill behind whose ridge the sunset flames?
The Signal-Elm, that looks on Ilsley Downs,
The Vale, the three lone wears, the youthful Thames?—
This winter-eve is warm,
Humid the air; leafless, yet soft as spring,
The tender purple spray on copse and briers;
And that sweet City with her dreaming spires,
She needs not June for beauty's heightening.

Lovely all times she lies, lovely to-night.
Only, methinks, some loss of habit's power
Befalls me wandering through this upland dim.
Once passed I blindfold here, at any hour,
Now seldom come I, since I came with him.
That single elm-tree bright
Against the west — I miss it! is it gone?
We prized it dearly; while it stood, we said,
Our friend, the Scholar-Gypsy, was not dead;
While the tree lived, he in these fields lived on.

Too rare, too rare, grow now my visits here!
But once I knew each field, each flower, each stick,
And with the country-folk acquaintance made
By barn in threshing-time, by new-built rick.
Here, too, our shepherd-pipes we first assayed.
Ah me! this many a year
My pipe is lost, my shepherd's holiday.
Needs must I lose them, needs with heavy heart
Into the world and wave of men depart;
But Thyrsis of his own will went away.

It irked him to be here, he could not rest.
He loved each simple joy the country yields,
He loved his mates; but yet he could not keep,
For that a shadow lowered on the fields,
Here with the shepherds and the silly sheep.
Some life of men unblest
He knew, which made him droop, and filled his head.
He went; his piping took a troubled sound
Of storms that rage outside our happy ground;
He could not wait their passing, he is dead.

So, some tempestuous morn in early June,
When the year's primal burst of bloom is o'er,
Before the roses and the longest day —
When garden-walks, and all the grassy floor,
With blossoms, red and white, of fallen May,
And chestnut-flowers, are strewn —
So have I heard the cuckoo's parting cry,
From the wet field, through the vexed garden-trees,
Come with the volleying rain and tossing breeze:
The bloom is gone, and with the bloom go I.

Too quick despairer, wherefore wilt thou go?
Soon will the high Midsummer pomps come on,
Soon will the musk carnations break and swell,
Soon shall we have gold-dusted snapdragon,
Sweet-William with its homely cottage-smell,
And stocks in fragrant blow;
Roses that down the alleys shine afar,
And open, jasmine-muffled lattices,
And groups under the dreaming garden-trees,
And the full moon, and the white evening-star.

He hearkens not! light comer, he is gone!
What matters it? next year he will return,
And we shall have him in the sweet spring-days,
With whitening hedges, and uncrumpling fern,
And blue-bells trembling by the forest-ways,
And scent of hay new-mown.
But Thyrsis never more we swains shall see;
See him come back, and cut a smoother reed,
And blow a strain the world at last shall heed, —
For Time, not Corydon, hath conquered thee.
Alack, for Corydon no rival now!
But when Sicilian shepherds lost a mate,
Some good survivor with his flute would go,
Piping a ditty sad for Bion's fate,
And cross the unpermitted ferry's flow,
And unbend Pluto's brow,
And make leap up with joy the beauteous head
Of Proserpine, among whose crownèd hair
Are flowers, first opened on Sicilian air;
And flute his friend, like Orpheus, from the dead.

O easy access to the hearer's grace,
When Dorian shepherds sang to Proserpine!
For she herself had trod Sicilian fields,
She knew the Dorian water's gush divine,
She knew each lily white which Enna yields,
Each rose with blushing face;
She loved the Dorian pipe, the Dorian strain.
But ah, of our poor Thames she never heard!
Her foot the Cumner cowslips never stirred;
And we should tease her with our plaint in vain.

Well! wind-dispersed and vain the words will be,
Yet, Thyrsis, let me give my grief its hour
In the old haunt, and find our tree-topped hill!
Who, if not I, for questing here hath power?
I know the wood which hides the daffodil,
I know the Fyfield tree,
I know what white, what purple fritillaries
The grassy harvest of the river-fields,
Above by Ensham, down by Sandford, yields;
And what sedged brooks are Thames's tributaries;

I know these slopes; who knows them if not I? —
But many a dingle on the loved hill-side,
With thorns once studded, old, white-blossomed trees,
Where thick the cowslips grew, and, far descried,
High towered the spikes of purple orchises,
Hath since our day put by
The coronals of that forgotten time;
Down each green bank hath gone the ploughboy's team,
And only in the hidden brookside gleam
Primroses, orphans of the flowery prime.

Where is the girl, who, by the boat-man's door,
Above the locks, above the boating throng,
Unmoored our skiff, when, through the Wytham flats,
Red loosestrife and blond meadow-sweet among,
And darting swallows, and light water-gnats,
We tracked the shy Thames shore?
Where are the mowers, who, as the tiny swell
Of our boat passing heaved the river-grass,
Stood with suspended scythe to see us pass?
They all are gone, and thou art gone as well.

Yes, thou art gone, and round me too the Night
In ever-nearing circle weaves her shade.
I see her veil draw soft across the day,
I feel her slowly chilling breath invade
The cheek grown thin, the brown hair sprent with gray;
I feel her finger light
Laid pausefully upon life's headlong train;
The foot less prompt to meet the morning dew,
The heart less bounding at emotion new,
And hope, once crushed, less quick to spring again.

And long the way appears, which seemed so short
To the unpractised eye of sanguine youth;
And high the mountain-tops, in cloudy air,
The mountain-tops where is the throne of Truth,
Tops in life's morning-sun so bright and bare.
Unbreachable the fort
Of the long-battered world uplifts its wall;
And strange and vain the earthly turmoil grows,
And near and real the charm of thy repose,
And Night as welcome as a friend would fall.

But hush! the upland hath a sudden loss
Of quiet. Look! adown the dusk hillside
A troop of Oxford hunters going home,
As in old days, jovial and talking, ride.
From hunting with the Berkshire hounds they come.
Quick! let me fly, and cross
Into yon further field. 'Tis done; and see,
Backed by the sunset, which doth glorify
The orange and pale violet evening-sky,
Bare on its lonely ridge, the Tree! the Tree!

I take the omen! Eve lets down her veil,
The white fog creeps from bush to bush about,
The west unflushes, the high stars grow bright,
And in the scattered farms the lights come out.
I cannot reach the Signal-Tree to-night,
Yet, happy omen, hail!
Hear it from thy broad lucent Arno vale,
(For there thine earth-forgetting eyelids keep
The morningless and unawakening sleep
Under the flowery oleanders pale,)

Hear it, O Thyrsis, still our Tree is there!—
Ah, vain! These English fields, this upland dim,
These brambles pale with mist engarlanded,
That lone, sky-pointing Tree, are not for him.
To a boon southern country he is fled,
And now in happier air,
Wandering with the great Mother's train divine
(And purer or more subtle soul than thee,
I trow, the mighty Mother doth not see!)
Within a folding of the Apennine,

Thou hearest the immortal strains of old.
Putting his sickle to the perilous grain,
In the hot corn-field of the Phrygian king,
For thee the Lityerses song again
Young Daphnis with his silver voice doth sing;
Sings his Sicilian fold,
His sheep, his hapless love, his blinded eyes;
And how a call celestial round him rang,
And heavenward from the fountain-brink he sprang,
And all the marvel of the golden skies.

There thou art gone, and me thou leavest here,
Sole in these fields; yet will I not despair.
Despair I will not, while I yet descry
'Neath the soft canopy of English air
That lonely Tree against the western sky.
Still, still these slopes, 'tis clear,
Our Gypsy Scholar haunts, outliving thee!
Fields where the sheep from cages pull the hay,
Woods with anemones in flower till May,
Know him a wanderer still; then why not me?

A fugitive and gracious light he seeks,
Shy to illumine; and I seek it too.
This does not come with houses or with gold,
With place, with honor, and a flattering crew;
'Tis not in the world's market bought and sold.
But the smooth-slipping weeks
Drop by, and leave its seeker still untired.
Out of the heed of mortals is he gone,
He wends unfollowed, he must house alone;
Yet on he fares, by his own heart inspired.

Thou too, O Thyrsis, on this quest wert bound,
Thou wanderedst with me for a little hour.
Men gave thee nothing; but this happy quest,
If men esteemed thee feeble, gave thee power,
If men procured thee trouble, gave thee rest.
And this rude Cumner ground,
Its fir-topped Hurst, its farms, its quiet fields,
Here cam'st thou in thy jocund youthful time,
Here was thine height of strength, thy golden prime,
And still the haunt beloved a virtue yields.

What though the music of thy rustic flute
Kept not for long its happy country tone;
Lost it too soon, and learnt a stormy note
Of men contention-tost, of men who groan,
Which tasked thy pipe too sore, and tired thy throat—
It failed, and thou wert mute.
Yet hadst thou alway visions of our light,
And long with men of care thou couldst not stay,
And soon thy foot resumed its wandering way,
Left human haunt, and on alone till night.

Too rare, too rare, grow now my visits here!
'Mid city noise, not, as with thee of yore,
  Thyrsis, in reach of sheep-bells is my home.
Then through the great town's harsh, heart-wearying roar,
  Let in thy voice a whisper often come,
    To chase fatigue and fear:
Why faintest thou? I wandered till I died.
  Roam on; the light we sought is shining still.
  Dost thou ask proof? Our Tree yet crowns the hill,
Our Scholar travels yet the loved hill-side.

MATTHEW ARNOLD.

DION.

MOURN, hills and groves of Attica! and mourn
Ilissus, bending o'er thy classic urn!
Mourn, and lament for him whose spirit dreads
Your once sweet memory, studious walks and shades!
For him who to divinity aspired,
Not on the breath of popular applause,
But through dependence on the sacred laws
Framed in the schools where Wisdom dwelt retired,
Intent to trace the ideal path of right
(More fair than heaven's broad causeway paved with stars)
Which Dion learned to measure with delight;
But He hath overleaped the eternal bars;
And, following guides whose craft holds no consent
With aught that breathes the ethereal element,
Hath stained the robes of civil power with blood,
Unjustly shed, though for the public good.
Whence doubts that came too late, and wishes vain,
Hollow excuses, and triumphant pain;
And oft his cogitations sink as low
As, through the abysses of a joyless heart,
The heaviest plummet of despair can go —
But whence that sudden check? that fearful start!
  He hears an uncouth sound —
  Anon his lifted eyes
Saw, at a long-drawn gallery's dusky bound,
A shape of more than mortal size
And hideous aspect, stalking round and round!
  A woman's garb the Phantom wore,
  And fiercely swept the marble floor, —
  Like Auster whirling to and fro,
  His force on Caspian foam to try;
Or Boreas when he scours the snow
That skins the plains of Thessaly,
Or when aloft on Mænalus he stops
His flight, 'mid eddying pine-tree tops!

"Avaunt, inexplicable Guest! — avaunt,"
Exclaimed the chieftain . . .
But Shapes that come not at an earthly call,
Will not depart when mortal voices bid;
Lords of the visionary eye whose lid,
Once raised, remains aghast, and will not fall!

Ill-fated Chief! there are whose hopes are built
Upon the ruins of thy glorious name;
Who, through the portals of one moment's guilt,
Pursue thee with their deadly aim!
O matchless perfidy! portentous lust
Of monstrous crime! — that horror-striking blade,
Drawn in defiance of the gods, hath laid
The noble Syracusan low in dust!
Shuddered the walls, — the marble city wept, —
And sylvan places heaved a pensive sigh;
But in calm peace the appointed Victim slept,
As he had fallen, in magnanimity
Of spirit too capacious to require

That Destiny her course should change; too just
To his own native greatness to desire
That wretched boon, days lengthened by mistrust.
So were the hopeless troubles, that involved
The soul of Dion, instantly dissolved.
Released from life and cares of princely state,
He left this moral grafted on his Fate:
"Him only pleasure leads, and peace attends,
Him, only him, the shield of Jove defends,
Whose means are fair and spotless as his end."

WORDSWORTH.

HOSEA BIGLOW'S LAMENT.

BEAVER roars hoarse with melting snows,
And rattles diamonds from his granite;
Time was he snatched away my prose,
And into psalms or satires ran it;
But he, and all the rest that once
Started my blood to contra dances
Find me and leave me but a dunce
That has no use for dreams and fancies.

Rat-tat-tat-tattle through the street,
I hear the drummers making riot,
And I sit thinking of the feet
That followed once and now are quiet, —
White feet as snow-drops innocent,
That never knew the paths of Satan,
Sad ears that listened as they went,
Lifelong to hear them come will wait on.

Have I not held them on my knee?
Did I not love to see them growing,
Three likely lads as well could be,
Handsome and brave, and not too knowing?

I sit and look into the blaze,
Whose nature, just like theirs, keeps climbing
Long as it lives in shining ways.
And half despise myself for rhyming.

What's talk to them whose faith and truth
On War's red touchstone rang true metal,
Who ventured life and love and youth
For the great prize of death in battle?

To him who, deadly hurt, again
Flashed on before the charge's thunder,
Tipping with fire the bolt of men
That rived the Rebel line asunder?

Come Peace, not like a mourner bowed
For honor lost and dear ones wasted,
But proud, to meet a people proud,
With eyes that tell of triumph tasted.

Come with hand gripping on the hilt,
And step that proves you Victory's daughter!
Longing for you, our spirits wilt
Like shipwrecked men on rafts for water.

Come, while our Country feels the lift
Of a great instinct shouting Forwards,
And knows that Freedom's not a gift
That tarries long in hands of cowards.

Come, such as mothers prayed for, when
They kissed their cross with lips that quivered,
And bring fair wages for brave men,
A Nation saved, a Race delivered.

LOWELL.

OTHELLO'S LAST WORDS.

SOFT you; a word or two before you go.
I have done the state some service, and they know it:
No more of that. — I pray you, in your letters,
When you shall these unlucky deeds relate,
Speak of me as I am; nothing extenuate,
Nor set down aught in malice: then must you speak

Of one that loved, not wisely, but too well;
Of one not easily jealous, but, being wrought,
Perplexed in the extreme; of one whose hand,
Like the base Indian, threw a pearl away
Richer than all his tribe; of one whose subdued eyes,
Albeit unusèd to the melting mood,
Drop tears as fast as the Arabian trees
Their medicinal gum. Set you down this,
And say, besides, that in Aleppo once,
Where a malignant and a turbaned Turk
Beat a Venetian, and traduced the state,
I took by the throat the circumcisèd dog,
And smote him — thus. [*Stabs himself.*

SHAKSPEARE.

X.

COMIC AND HUMOROUS.

SATIRICAL.

COMIC AND HUMOROUS.

HOLY WILLIE'S PRAYER.

O THOU, wha in the Heavens dost dwell,
Wha, as it pleases best thysel',
Sends ane to Heaven, and ten to Hell,
A' for thy glory,
And no for onie guid or ill
They've done afore thee!

I bless and praise thy matchless might,
Whan thousands thou hast left in night,
That I am here afore thy sight,
For gifts an' grace,
A burning an' a shining light,
To a' this place.

What was I, or my generation,
That I should get such exaltation?
I, wha deserve such just damnation,
For broken laws,
Five thousand years 'fore my creation,
Through Adam's cause.

When frae my mither's womb I fell,
Thou might hae plunged me into Hell,
To gnash my gums, to weep and wail,
In burnin' lake,
Where damned Devils roar and yell,
Chained to a stake.

Yet I am here a chosen sample,
To show thy grace is great and ample;
I'm here a pillar in thy temple,
Strong as a rock,
A guide, a buckler, an example
To a' thy flock.

O Lord, thou kens what zeal I bear,
When drinkers drink, and swearers swear,
And singing there, and dancing here,
Wi' great and sma':
For I am keepit by thy fear,
Free frae them a'.

But yet, O Lord! confess I must,
At times I'm fashed wi' fleshly lust,
An' sometimes, too, wi' warldly trust, —
Vile self gets in;
But thou remembers we are dust,
Defiled in sin.

. . . .

Maybe thou lets this fleshly thorn
Beset thy servant e'en and morn,
Lest he owre high and proud should turn,
'Cause he's sae gifted:
If sae, thy hand maun e'en be borne,
Until thou lift it.

Lord, bless thy chosen in this place,
For here thou hast a chosen race;
But God confound their stubborn face,
And blast their name,
Wha bring thy elders to disgrace,
An' public shame.

Lord, mind Gawn Hamilton's deserts,
He drinks, an' swears, an' plays at cartes,
Yet has sae monie takin' arts,
Wi' great and sma',
Frae God's ain priests the people's hearts
He steals awa'.

An' when we chastened him therefore,
Thou kens how he bred sic a splore,
As set the warld in a roar
O' laughin' at us;—
Curse thou his basket and his store,
Kail and potatoes.

Lord, hear my earnest cry an' prayer,
Against that presbyt'ry o' Ayr;
Thy strong right hand, Lord, make it bare,
Upo' their heads;
Lord, weigh it down, and dinna spare,
For their misdeeds.

O Lord my God, that glib-tongued Aiken,
My very heart and saul are quakin',
To think how we stood sweatin', shakin',
An' swat wi' dread,
While he wi' hinging lips gaed snakin',
An' hid his head.

Lord, in the day o' vengeance try him,
Lord, visit them wha did employ him,
And pass not in thy mercy by 'em,
Nor hear their prayer:
But for thy people's sake destroy 'em,
And dinna spare.

But, Lord, remember me and mine
Wi' mercies temp'ral and divine,
That I for gear and grace may shine,
Excelled by nane,
An' a' the glory shall be thine,
Amen, Amen.

BURNS.

TO THE UNCO GUID, OR THE RIGIDLY RIGHTEOUS.

O YE wha are sae guid yoursel',
Sae pious and sae holy,
Ye've nought to do but mark and tell
Your Neebor's fauts and folly!
Whase life is like a weel-gaun mill,
Supplied wi' store o' water,
The heapet happer's ebbing still,
And still the clap plays clatter.

Hear me, ye venerable Core,
As counsel for poor mortals,
That frequent pass douce Wisdom's door,
For glaikit Folly's portals;
I, for their thoughtless, careless sakes,
Would here propone defences,
Their donsie tricks, their black mistakes,
Their failings and mischances.

Ye see your state wi' theirs compared,
And shudder at the niffer,
But cast a moment's fair regard,
What makes the mighty differ?
Discount what scant occasion gave
That purity ye pride in,
And (what's aft mair than a' the lave)
Your better art o' hidin'.

Think, when your castigated pulse
Gies now and then a wallop,
What raging must his veins convulse,
That still eternal gallop:
Wi' wind and tide fair i' your tail,
Right on ye scud your sea-way:
But in the teeth o' baith to sail,
It maks an unco leeway.

See Social Life and Glee sit down,
All joyous and unthinking,
Till, quite transmugrified, they're grown
Debauchery and Drinking:
O would they stay to calculate
Th' eternal consequences;
Or your more dreaded hell to state,
Damnation of expenses!

Ye high, exalted, virtuous Dames,
Tied up in godly laces,
Before ye gie poor Frailty names,
Suppose a change o' cases;
A dear-loved lad, convenience snug,
A treacherous inclination —
But let me whisper i' your lug,
Ye're aiblins nae temptation.

Then gently scan your brother Man,
Still gentler sister Woman,
Though they may gang a kennie wrang,
To step aside is human:
One point must still be greatly dark,
The moving *Why* they do it;
And just as lamely can ye mark
How far perhaps they rue it.

Who made the heart, 'tis He alone
Decidedly can try us,
He knows each chord — its various tone,
Each spring — its various bias:
Then at the balance let's be mute,
We never can adjust it:
What's *done* we partly may compute,
But know not what's *resisted.*

BURNS.

TO THE DEVIL.

BUT fare you weel, auld *Nickie-ben!*
O wad ye tak a thought an' men'!
Ye aiblins might, — I dinna ken,
Still hae a stake —
I'm wae to think upon yon den,
Even for your sake!

BURNS.

THE ORIGIN OF DIDACTIC POETRY.

WHEN wise Minerva still was young,
And just the least romantic,
Soon after from Jove's head she flung,
That preternatural antic,
'Tis said to keep from idleness
Or flirting, — those twin curses,—
She spent her leisure, more or less,
In writing po—, no, verses.

How nice they were! to rhyme with *far*,
A kind *star* did not tarry;
The metre, too, was regular
As schoolboy's dot and carry;
And full they were of pious plums,
So extra-super-moral, —
For sucking Virtue's tender gums
Most tooth-enticing coral.

A clean, fair copy she prepares,
Makes sure of moods and tenses,
With her own hand, — for prudence spares
A man- (or woman) -uensis;
Complete, and tied with ribbons proud,
She hinted soon how cosey a
Treat it would be to read them loud
After next day's Ambrosia.

The Gods thought not it would amuse
So much as Homer's Odyssees,
But could not very well refuse
The properest of Goddesses;
So all sat round in attitudes
Of various dejection,
As with a *hem!* the queen of prudes
Began her grave prelection.

At the first pause Zeus said, "Well sung!—
I mean — ask Phœbus, — *he* knows."
Says Phœbus, "Zounds! a wolf's among
Admetus's merinos!
Fine! very fine! but I must go;
They stand in need of me there;
Excuse me!" snatched his stick, and so
Plunged down the gladdened ether.

With the next gap, Mars said, "For me
Don't wait, — nought could be finer,
But I'm engaged at half-past three, —
A fight in Asia Minor!"
Then Venus lisped, "How very thad!
It rainth down there in torrinth;
But I *mutht* go, becauthe they've had
A thacrifithe in Corinth!"

Then Bacchus, — "With those slamming doors
I lost the last half dist—(hic!)
Mos' bu'ful se'ments! what's the Chor's?
My voice shall not be missed — (hic!)"
His words woke Hermes; "Ah!" he said,
"I *so* love moral theses!"
Then winked at Hebe, who turned red,
And smoothed her apron's creases.

Just then Zeus snored, — the Eagle drew
His head the wing from under;
Zeus snored, — o'er startled Greece there flew
The many-volumed thunder;
Some augurs counted nine, — some, ten, —

Some said, 'twas war, some, famine, —
And all, that other-minded men
Would get a precious ——.

Proud Pallas sighed, "It will not do;
Against the Muse I've sinned, oh!"
And her torn rhymes sent flying through
Olympus's back window.
Then, packing up a peplus clean,
She took the shortest path thence,
And opened, with a mind serene,
A Sunday school in Athens.

The verses? Some in ocean swilled,
Killed every fish that bit to 'em;
Some Galen caught, and, when distilled,
Found morphine the residuum;
But some that rotted on the earth
Sprang up again in copies,
And gave two strong narcotics birth, —
Didactic bards and poppies.

Years after, when a poet asked
The Goddess's opinion,
As being one whose soul had basked
In Art's clear-aired dominion, —
"Discriminate," she said, "betimes;
The Muse is unforgiving;
Put all your beauty in your rhymes,
Your morals in your living."

LOWELL.

TAM O' SHANTER.

WHEN chapman billies leave the street,
And drouthy neebors, neebors meet,
As market-days are wearing late,
An' folk begin to tak the gate;
While we sit bousing at the nappy,
An' getting fou and unco happy,
We thinkna on the lang Scots miles,
The mosses, waters, slaps, and stiles,
That lie between us and our hame,
Whare sits our sulky sullen dame,
Gathering her brows like gathering storm,
Nursing her wrath to keep it warm.
This truth fand honest Tam Q' Shanter,
As he frae Ayr ae night did canter
(Auld Ayr, wham ne'er a town surpasses,
For honest men and bonnie lasses).
O Tam! hadst thou but been sae wise,
As ta'en thy ain wife Kate's advice!
She tauld thee weel thou wast a skellum,
A blethering, blustering, drunken blellum;
That frae November till October,
Ae market-day thou was nae sober;
That ilka melder, wi' the miller,
Thou sat as lang as thou had siller;
That every naig was ca'd a shoe on,
The smith and thee gat roaring fou on;
That at the Lord's house, even on Sunday,
Thou drank wi' Kirkton Jean till Monday.
She prophesied that, late or soon,
Thou would be found deep drowned in Doon:
Or catched wi' warlocks i' the mirk,
By Alloway's auld haunted kirk.
Ah, gentle dames! it gars me greet,
To think how mony counsels sweet,
How mony lengthened, sage advices,
The husband frae the wife despises!
But to our tale: Ae market night,
Tam had got planted unco right;
Fast by an ingle, bleezing finely,
Wi' reaming swats, that drank divinely;
And at his elbow, Souter Johnny,
His ancient, trusty, drouthy crony;
Tam lo'ed him like a vera brither;
They had been fou for weeks thegither.
The night drave on wi' sangs and clatter;
And ay the ale was growing better:
The landlady and Tam grew gracious,
Wi' favors, secret, sweet, and precious:
The souter tauld his queerest stories;
The landlord's laugh was ready chorus:
The storm without might rair and rustle,
Tam did na mind the storm a whistle.
Care, mad to see a man sae happy,
E'en drowned himself amang the nappy!

As bees flee hame wi' lades o' treasure,
The minutes winged their way wi' pleasure:
Kings may be blessed, but Tam was glorious,
O'er a' the ills o' life victorious!
But pleasures are like poppies spread,
You seize the flower, its bloom is shed;
Or like the snow falls in the river,
A moment white — then melts forever;
Or like the borealis race,
That flit ere you can point their place;
Or like the rainbow's lovely form
Evanishing amid the storm.
Nae man can tether time or tide; —
The hour approaches Tam maun ride;
That hour, o' night's black arch the key-stane,
That dreary hour he mounts his beast in;
And sic a night he taks the road in,
As ne'er poor sinner was abroad in.
The wind blew as 'twad blawn its last;
The rattling showers rose on the blast;
The speedy gleams the darkness swallowed;
Loud, deep, and lang, the thunder bellowed:
That night, a child might understand,
The Deil had business on his hand.
Weel mounted on his gray mare, Meg,
A better never lifted leg,
Tam skelpit on through dub and mire,
Despising wind, and rain, and fire;
Whiles holding fast his guid blue bonnet;
Whiles crooning o'er some auld Scots sonnet;
Whiles glowering round wi' prudent cares,
Lest bogles catch him unawares;
Kirk Alloway was drawing nigh,
Whare ghaists and houlets nightly cry.
By this time he was cross the ford,
Whare in the snaw the chapman smoored;
And past the birks and meikle-stane,
Whare drunken Charlie brak's neck-bane;
And through the whins, and by the cairn,
Whare hunters fand the murdered bairn:
And near the thorn, aboon the well,
Whare Mungo's mither hanged hersel.
Before him Doon pours all his floods;
The doubling storm roars through the woods;
The lightnings flash from pole to pole;
Near and more near the thunders roll:
When, glimmering thro' the groaning trees,
Kirk Alloway seemed in a bleeze;
Through ilka bore the beams were glancing;
And loud resounded mirth and dancing.
Inspiring bold John Barleycorn!
What dangers thou canst make us scorn!
Wi' tippenny, we fear nae evil;
Wi' usquebae, we'll face the Devil!
The swats sae reamed in Tammie's noddle,
Fair play, he cared na deils a boddle.
But Maggie stood right sair astonished,
Till, by the heel and hand admonished,
She ventured forward on the light;
And, wow! Tam saw an unco sight!
Warlocks and witches in a dance;
Nae cotillion brent new frae France,
But hornpipes, jigs, strathspeys, and reels,
Put life and mettle in their heels.
At winnock-bunker in the east,
There sat auld Nick, in shape o' beast;
A towzie tyke, black, grim, and large,
To gie them music was his charge:
He screwed the pipes and gart them skirl,
Till roof and rafters a' did dirl. —
Coffins stood round, like open presses,
That shawed the dead in their last dresses;
And by some devilish cantrip slight,
Each in its cauld hand held a light, —

By which heroic Tom was able
To note upon the haly table,
A murderer's banes in gibbet airns;
Twa span-lang, wee, unchristened bairns:
A thief, new-cutted frae a rape,
Wi' his last gasp his gab did gape;
Five tomahawks, wi' blude red rusted;
Five scymitars, wi' murder crusted;
A garter, which a babe had strangled;
A knife, a father's throat had mangled,
Whom his ain son o' life bereft,
The gray hairs yet stack to the heft;
Wi' mair o' horrible and awfu',
Which even to name wad be unlawfu'.

As Tammie glowered, amazed and curious,
The mirth and fun grew fast and furious:
The piper loud and louder blew;
The dancers quick and quicker flew;
They reeled, they set, they crossed, they cleekit,
Till ilka carlin sweat and reekit,
And coost her duddies to the wark,
And linket at it in her sark!

Now Tam, O Tam! had thae been queans,
A' plump and strapping in their teens;
Their sarks, instead o' creeshie flannen,
Been snaw-white seventeen-hunder linnen!
Thir breeks o' mine, my only pair,
That ance were plush, o' gude blue hair,
I wad hae gi'en them off my hurdies,
For ae blink o' the bonnie burdies!

But withered beldams, auld and droll,
Rigwoodie hags, wad spean a foal,
Lowping and flinging on a crummock,
I wonder didna turn thy stomach.

But Tam kend what was what fu' brawlie,
"There was ae winsome wench and walie,"
That night enlisted in the core,
(Lang after kend on Carrick shore;
For mony a beast to dead she shot,
And perished mony a bonnie boat,
And shook baith meikle corn and bear,
And kept the country-side in fear,)
Her cutty-sark, o' Paisley harn,
That, while a lassie, she had worn,
In longitude though sorely scanty,
It was her best and she was vauntie. —
Ah! little kend thy reverend grannie,
That sark she coft for her wee Nannie,
Wi' twa pund Scots, ('twas a' her riches,)
Wad ever graced a dance o' witches!

But here my muse her wing maun cour;
Sic flights are far beyond her power;
To sing how Nannie lap and flang
(A souple jade she was, and strang),
And how Tam stood, like ane bewitched,
And thought his very e'en enriched;
Even Satan glowered, and fidged fu' fain,
And hotched and blew wi' might and main:
Till first ane caper, syne anither,
Tam tint his reason a' thegither,
And roars out, "Weel done, Cutty-sark!"
And in an instant all was dark;
And scarcely had he Maggie rallied,
When out the hellish legion sallied.

As bees bizz out wi' angry fyke,
When plundering herds assail their byke;
As open pussie's mortal foes,
When, pop! she starts before their nose;
As eager runs the market-crowd,
When, "Catch the thief!" resounds aloud;
So Maggie runs, the witches follow,
Wi' monie an eldritch screech and hollow.

Ah, Tam! ah, Tam! thou'll get thy fairin!
In hell they'll roast thee like a herrin!
In vain thy Kate awaits thy comin!
Kate soon will be a woefu' woman!
Now, do thy speedy utmost, Meg,
And win the key-stane of the brig;
There at them thou thy tail may toss,
A running stream they dare na cross.

But ere the key-stane she could
make,
The fient a tail she had to shake!
For Nannie, far before the rest,
Hard upon noble Maggie prest,
And flew at Tam wi' furious ettle;
But little wist she Maggie's met-
tle —
Ae spring brought off her master
hale,
But left behind her ain gray tail:
The carlin caught her by the rump,
And left poor Maggie scarce a stump.
Now, wha this tale o' truth shall
read,
Ilk man and mother's son, tak heed;
Whene'er to drink you are inclined,
Or cutty-sarks run in your mind,
Think, ye may buy the joys o'er
dear,
Remember Tam O' Shanter's mare.

BURNS.

THE WITCH OF FIFE.

"WHERE have ye been, ye ill woman,
These three lang nights frae
hame?
What gars the sweat drap frae yer
brow,
Like drops o' the saut sea-faem?

"It fears me muckle ye have seen
What gude man never knew;
It fears me muckle ye have been,
Where the gray cock never crew.

"But the spell may crack, and the
bridle break,
Then sharp yer word will be;
Ye had better sleep in yer bed at
hame,
Wi' yer dear little bairns and
me."

"Sit dune, sit dune, my leal auld
man,
Sit dune, and listen to me;
I'll gar the hair stand on yer crown,
And the cauld sweat blind yer e'e.

"But tell nae words, my gude auld
man,
Tell never a word again;
Or dear shall be your courtesy,
And driche and sair yer pain.

"The first leet night, when the new
moon set,
When all was douffe and mirk,
We saddled our nags wi' the moon-
fern leaf,
And rode frae Kilmerrin kirk.

"Some horses were of the brume-
cow framed,
And some of the green bay tree;
But mine was made of ane hemlock
shaw,
And a stout stallion was he.

"We raide the tod doune on the hill,
The martin on the law;
And we hunted the owlet out o'
breath,
And forced him doune to fa'."

"What guid was that, ye ill woman?
What guid was that to thee?
Ye would better have been in yer bed
at hame,
Wi' yer dear little bairns and
me." —

"And aye we rode, as sae merrily rode,
Through the merkest gloffs of the
night;
And we swam the flood, and we
darnit the wood,
Till we came to the Lommond
height.

"And when we came to the Lom-
mond height,
Sae lightly we lighted doune;
And we drank frae the horns that
never grew,
The beer that was never browin.

"Then up there rose a wee wee man,
From neath the moss-gray stane;
His face was wan like the colliflower,
For he neither had blude nor bane.

"He set a reed-pipe till his mouth;
And he played sae bonnily,
Till the gray curlew, and the black-
cock flew
To listen his melodye.

"It rang sae sweet through the green
Lommond,
That the night-wind lowner blew;
And it soupit alang the Loch Leven,
And wakened the white sea-mew.

"It rang sae sweet through the green Lommond,
Sae sweetly and sae shrill,
That the weasels leaped out of their mouldy holes,
And danced on the midnight hill.

"The corby crow came gledging near,
The erne gaed veering bye;
And the trouts leaped out of the Leven Loch,
Charmed with the melodye.

"And aye we danced on the green Lommond,
Till the dawn on the ocean grew:
Nae wonder I was a weary wight
When I cam hame to you." —

"What guid, what guid, my weird, weird wyfe,
What guid was that to thee?
Ye wad better have been in yer bed at hame,
Wi' yer dear little bairns and me." —

"The second night, when the new moon set,
O'er the roaring sea we flew;
The cockle-shell our trusty bark,
Our sails of the green sea-rue.

"And the bauld winds blew, and the fire-flauchts flew,
And the sea ran to the sky;
And the thunder it growled, and the sea-dogs howled,
As we gaed scurrying by.

"And aye we mounted the sea-green hills,
Till we brushed through the clouds of heaven,
Then soused downright like the stern-shot light,
Fra the lift's blue casement driven.

"But our tackle stood, and our bark was good,
And sae pang was our pearly prow;
When we couldna speil the brow of the waves,
We needled them through below.

"As fast as the hail, as fast as the gale,
As fast as the midnight leme,
We bored the breast of the bursting swale,
Or fluffed in the floating faem.

"And when to the Norroway shore we wan,
We mounted our steeds of the wind,
And we splashed the floode, and we darnit the wood,
And we left the shore behind.

"Fleet is the roe on the green Lommond,
And swift is the couryng grew;
The rein-deer dun can eithly run,
When the hounds and the horns pursue.

"But neither the roe, nor the rein-deer dun,
The hind nor the couryng grew,
Could fly o'er mountain, moor, and dale,
As our braw steeds they flew.

"The dales were deep, and the Doffrins steep,
And we rose to the skies ee-bree:
White, white was our ròad that was never trode,
O'er the snows of eternity.

"And when we came to the Lapland lone,
The fairies were all in array,
For all the genii of the north
Were keeping their holiday.

"The warlock men and the weird women,
And the fays of the wood and the steep,
And the phantom hunters all were there,
And the mermaids of the deep.

"And they washed us all with the witch-water,
Distilled frae the moorland dew,
Till our beauty bloomed like the Lapland rose,
That wild in the foreste grew." —

"Ye lee, ye lee, ye ill woman,
Sae loud as I hear ye lee!
For the worst-faured wyfe on the shores of Fyfe
Is comely compared wi' thee." —

"Then the mermaids sang, and the woodlands rang,
Sae sweetly swelled the choir;
On every cliffe a harp they hang,
On every tree a lyre.

"And aye they sang, and the woodlands rang,
And we drank, and we drank sae deep;
Then soft in the arms of the warlock men,
We laid us dune to sleep." —

"Away, away, ye ill woman,
An ill death might ye dee!
When ye hae proved sae false to yer God,
Ye can never prove true to me." —

"And there we learned frae the fairy folk,
And frae our master true,
The words that can bear us through the air,
And locks and bars undo.

"Last night we met at Maisry's cot;
Right well the words we knew;
And we set a foot on the black cruik-shell,
And out at the lum we flew.

"And we flew o'er hill, and we flew o'er dale,
And we flew o'er firth and sea,
Untill we cam to merry Carlisle,
Where we lighted on the lea.

"We gaed to the vault beyond the tower,
Where we entered free as air;
And we drank, and we drank of the bishop's wine
Till we could drink nae mair." —

"Gin that be true, my gude auld wyfe,
Whilk thou hast tauld to me,
Betide my death, betide my lyfe,
I'll bear thee company.

"Next time ye gang to merry Carlisle
To drink of the blude-red wine,
Beshrew my heart, I'll fly with thee,
If the deil should fly behind." —

"Ah! little ye ken, my silly auld man,
The dangers we maun dree;
Last night we drank of the bishop's wine,
Till near near taen were we.

"Afore we wan to the sandy ford,
The gor-cocks nichering flew;
The lofty crest of Ettrick Pen
Was waved about with blue,
And, flichtering through the air, we fand
The chill chill morning dew.

"As we flew o'er the hills of Braid,
The sun rose fair and clear;
There gurly James, and his barons braw,
Were out to hunt the deer.

"Their bows they drew, their arrows flew,
And pierced the air with speed,
Till purple fell the morning dew
With witch-blude rank and red.

"Little ye ken, my silly auld man,
The dangers we maun dree;
Ne wonder I am a weary wight
When I come hame to thee." —

"But tell me the *word*, my gude auld wyfe,
Come tell it me speedily;
For I long to drink of the gude red wine,
And to wing the air with thee.

"Yer hellish horse I willna ride,
Nor sail the seas in the wind;
But I can flee as well as thee,
And I'll drink till ye be blind."

"O fy! O fy! my leal auld man,
That word I darena tell;
It would turn this warld all upside down,
And make it warse than hell.

"For all the lasses in the land
Wald mount the wind and fly;
And the men would doff their doublets syde,
And after them would ply." —

But the auld gude man was a cunning auld man,
And a cunning auld man was he;
And he watched and he watched for mony a night,
The witches' flight to see.

One night he darnit in Maisry's cot;
The fearless hags came in;
And he heard the word of awesome weird;
And he saw their deeds of sin.

Then ane by ane, they said that word,
As fast to the fire they drew;
Then set a foot on the black cruikshell,
And out at the lum they flew.

The auld gudeman came frae his hole
With fear and muckle dread,
But yet he couldna think to rue,
For the wine came in his head.

He set his foot in the black cruikshell,
With a fixed and a wawling ee;
And he said the word that I darena say,
And out at the lum flew he.

The witches scaled the moon-beam pale;
Deep groaned the trembling wind;
But they never wist that our auld gudeman
Was hovering them behind.

They flew to the vaults of merry Carlisle,
Where they entered free as air;
And they drank, and they drank of the bishop's wine
Till they coulde drink nae mair.

The auld gudeman he grew sae crouse,
He danced on the mouldy ground,
And he sang the bonniest songs of Fife,
And he tuzzlit the kerlyngs round.

And aye he pierced the tither butt,
And he sucked, and he sucked sae lang,
Till his een they closed, and his voice grew low,
And his tongue would hardly gang.

The kerlyngs drank of the bishop's wine
Till they scented the morning wind;
Then clove again the yielding air,
And left the auld man behinde.

And aye he slept on the damp damp floor,
He slept and he snored amain;
He never dreamed he was far frae hame,
Or that the auld wives were gane.

And aye he slept on the damp damp floor,
Till past the mid-day heighte,
When wakened by five rough Englishmen,
That trailed him to the lighte.

"Now wha are ye, ye silly auld man,
That sleeps sae sound and sae weel?
How gat ye into the bishop's vault
Through locks and bars of steel?"

The auld gudeman he tried to speak,
But ane word he couldna finde;
He tried to think, but his head whirled round,
And ane thing he couldna minde:
"I cam frae Fyfe," the auld man cried,
"And I cam on the midnight winde."

They nicked the auld man, and they pricked the auld man,
And they yerked his limbs with twine,
Till the red blude ran in his hose and shoon,
But some cried it was wine.

They licked the auld man, and they pricked the auld man,
And they tyed him till ane stone;
And they set ane bele-fire him about,
To burn him skin and bone.

"O wae to me!" said the puir auld man,
"That ever I saw the day!
And wae be to all the ill women
That lead puir men astray!

"Let nevir ane auld man after this
To lawless greede incline;
Let never ane auld man after this
Rin post to the deil for wine."

The reeke flew up in the auld man's face,
And choked him bitterlye;
And the low cam up with an angry blaze,
And he singed his auld breek-nee.

He looked to the land frae whence he came,
For looks he coulde get ne mae;
And he thoughte of his dear little bairns at hame,
And O the auld man was wae!

But they turned their faces to the sun,
With gloffe and wonderous glare,
For they saw ane thing baith large and dun,
Comin sweeping down the aire.

That bird it cam frae the lands o' Fife,
And it cam right tymeouslye,
For who was it but the auld man's wife,
Just comed his death to see.

She put ane red cap on his heade,
And the auld gudeman looked fain,
Then whispered ane word intil his lug,
And toved to the aire again.

The auld gudeman he gae ane bob
I' the midst o' the burning lowe;
And the shackles that bound him to the ring,
They fell frae his arms like towe.

He drew his breath, and he said the word,
And he said it with muckle glee,
Then set his feet on the burning pile,
And away to the aire flew he.

Till ance he cleared the swirling reeke,
He lukit baith feared and sad;
But when he wan to the light blue aire,
He laughed as he'd been mad.

His arms were spread, and his heade was highe,
And his feet stuck out behinde;
And the laibies of the auld man's coat
Were wauffing in the wind.

And aye he neicherit, and aye he flew,
For he thought the play sae rare;
It was like the voice of the gander blue,
When he flees through the aire.

He lookèd back to the Carlisle men
As he bored the norlan sky;
He nodded his heade, and gave ane girn
But he never said gude-bye.

They vanished far i' the lift's blue wale,
Nae maire the English saw,
But the auld man's laughe came on the gale,
With a lang and a loud gaffaw.

May everilke man in the land of Fife
Read what the drinker's dree;
And never curse his puir auld wife,
Righte wicked altho she be.

Hogg.

COLLUSION BETWEEN A ALEGAITER AND A WATER-SNAIK.

TRIUMPH OF THE WATER-SNAIK: DETH OF THE ALEGAITER.

"There is a niland on a river lying,
Which runs into Gautimaly, a warm country,
Lying near the Tropicks, covered with sand;
Hear and their a symptum of a Wilow,
Hanging of its umberagious limbs & branches
Over the clear streme meandering far below.
This was the home of the now silent Alegaiter,
When not in his other element confine'd:
Here he wood set upon his eggs asleep
With 1 ey observant of flis and other passing

Objects: a while it kept a going on so:
Fereles of danger was the happy Alegaiter!
But a las! in a nevil our he was fourced to
Wake! that dreme of Blis was two sweet for him.
1 morning the sun arose with unusool splender
Whitch allso did our Alegaiter, coming from the water,
His scails a flinging of the rais of the son back,
To the fountain-head which tha originly sprung,
But having not had nothing to eat for some time, he
Was slepy and gap'd, in a short time, widely.
Unfoalding soon a welth of perl-white teth,
The rais of the son soon shet his sinister ey
Because of their mutool splendor and warmth.
The evil Our (which I sed) was now come;
Evidently a good chans for a water snaik
Of the large specie, which soon appeared
Into the horison, near the bank where repos'd
Calmly in slepe the Alegaiter before spoken of,
About 60 feet was his Length (not the 'gaiter)
And he was aperiently a well-proportioned snaik.
When he was all ashore he glared upon
The iland with approval, but was soon
'Astonished with the view and lost to wonder' (from Wats)
(For jest then he began to see the Alegaiter)
Being a nateral enemy of his'n, he worked hisself
Into a fury, also a ni position.
Before the Alegaiter well could ope
His eye (in other words perceive his danger)
The Snaik had enveloped his body just 19
Times with 'foalds voluminous and vast' (from Milton)
And had tore off several scails in the confusion,
Besides squeazing him awfully into his stomoc.
Just then, by a fortinate turn in his affairs,
He ceazed into his mouth the careless tale
Of the unreflecting water-snaik! Grown desperate
He, finding that his tale was fast squesed
Terrible while they roaled all over the iland.

. . . .

It was a well-conduckted Affair; no noise
Disturbed the harmony of the seen, ecsept
Onct when a Wilow was snaped into by the roaling.
Eeach of the combatence hadn't a minit for holering.
So the conflick was naterally tremenjous!
But soon by grate force the tale was bit complete-
Ly of; but the eggzeration was too much
For his delicate Constitootion: he felt a compression
Onto his chest and generally over his body;
When he ecspress'd his breathing, it was with
Grate difficulty that he felt inspired again onct more.
Of course this State must suffer a revolootion.
So the Alegaiter give but one yel, and egspired.
The water-snaik realed hisself off, & survay'd
For say 10 minits, the condition of
His fo: then wondering what made his tail hurt,
He sloly went off for to cool."

GEORGE H. DERBY.

THE DEACON'S MASTERPIECE, OR THE WONDERFUL "ONE-HOSS-SHAY."

A LOGICAL STORY.

HAVE you heard of the wonderful one-hoss-shay,
That was built in such a logical way
It ran a hundred years to a day,

And then, of a sudden, it — ah, but stay,
I'll tell you what happened without delay,
Scaring the parson into fits,
Frightening people out of their wits, —
Have you ever heard of that, I say?

Seventeen hundred and fifty-five.
Georgius Secundus was then alive, —
Snuffy old drone from the German hive.
That was the year when Lisbon-town
Saw the earth open and gulp her down,
And Braddock's army was done so brown,
Left without a scalp to its crown.
It was on the terrible Earthquake-day
That the Deacon finished the one-hoss-shay.

Now in building of chaises, I tell you what,
There is always *somewhere* a weakest spot, —
In hub, tire, felloe, in spring or thill,
In panel, or crossbar, or floor, or sill,
In screw, bolt, thoroughbrace, — lurking still,
Find it somewhere you must and will, —
Above or below, or within or without, —
And that's the reason, beyond a doubt,
A chaise *breaks down*, but doesn't *wear out*.

But the Deacon swore, (as Deacon's do,
With an "I dew vum," or an "I tell *yeou*,")
He would build one shay to beat the taown
'n' the keountry 'n' all the kentry raoun';
It should be so built that it *couldn'* break daown:
— "Fur," said the Deacon, "'t's mighty plain
Thut the weakes' place mus' stan' the strain;
'n' the way t' fix it, uz I maintain,
Is only jest
T' make that place uz strong uz the rest."

So the Deacon inquired of the village folk
Where he could find the strongest oak,
That couldn't be split nor bent nor broke, —
That was for spokes and floor and sills;
He sent for lancewood to make the thills;
The crossbars were ash, from the straightest trees;
The panels of white-wood, that cuts like cheese,
But lasts like iron for things like these;
The hubs of logs from the "Settler's ellum," —
Last of its timber, — they couldn't sell 'em,
Never an axe had seen their chips,
And the wedges flew from between their lips,
Their blunt ends frizzled like celery-tips;
Step and prop-iron, bolt and screw,
Spring, tire, axle, and linchpin too,
Steel of the finest, bright and blue;
Thoroughbrace bison-skin, thick and wide;
Boot, top, dasher, from tough old hide
Found in the pit when the tanner died.
That was the way he "put her through." —
"There!" said the Deacon, "naow she'll dew!"

Do! I tell you, I rather guess
She was a wonder, and nothing less!
Colts grew horses, beards turned gray,
Deacon and deaconess dropped away,
Children and grandchildren — where were they?
But there stood the stout old one-hoss-shay
As fresh as on Lisbon-earthquake-day!

EIGHTEEN HUNDRED; — it came and found
The Deacon's masterpiece strong and sound.
Eighteen hundred increased by ten; —
"Hahnsum kerridge" they called it then.

Eighteen hundred and twenty came;
Running as usual; much the same.
Thirty and Forty at last arrive,
And then come Fifty and FIFTY-FIVE.

Little of all we value here
Wakes on the morn of its hundredth year
Without both feeling and looking queer.
In fact, there's nothing that keeps its youth,
So far as I know, but a tree and truth.
(This is a moral that runs at large;
Take it. You're welcome. No extra charge.)

FIRST OF NOVEMBER, — the Earthquake-day. —
There are traces of age in the one-hoss-shay,
A general flavor of mild decay,
But nothing local as one may say.
There couldn't be, — for the Deacon's art
Had made it so like in every part
That there wasn't a chance for one to start.
For the wheels were just as strong as the thills,
And the floor was just as strong as the sills,
And the panels just as strong as the floor,
And the whippletree neither less nor more,
And the back-crossbar as strong as the fore,
And spring and axle and hub *encore*.
And yet, *as a whole*, it is past a doubt
In another hour it will be *worn out!*

First of November, Fifty-five!
This morning the parson takes a drive.
Now, small boys, get out of the way!
Here comes the wonderful one-hoss-shay.
Drawn by a rat-tailed, ewe-necked bay.
"Huddup!" said the parson. — Off went they.

The Parson was working his Sunday's text, —
Had got to *fifthly*, and stopped perplexed
At what the — Moses — was coming next.
All at once the horse stood still,
Close by the meet'n'-house on the hill.
— First a shiver, and then a thrill,
Then something decidedly like a spill, —
And the parson was sitting upon a rock,
At half past nine by the meet'n'-house clock, —
Just the hour of the Earthquake shock!
— What do you think the parson found,
When he got up and stared around?
The poor old chaise in a heap or mound,
As if it had been to the mill and ground!
You see, of course, if you're not a dunce,
How it went to pieces all at once, —
All at once, and nothing first, —
Just as bubbles do when they burst.

End of the wonderful one-hoss-shay.
Logic is logic. That's all I say.

O. W. HOLMES.

THE COURTIN.'

ZEKLE crep' up quite unbeknown,
An' peeked in thru' the winder,
An' there sot Huldy all alone,
'Ith no one nigh to hender.

Agin the chimbley crook-necks hung
An' in amongst 'em rusted
The ole queen's-arm thet gran'ther Young
Fetched back from Concord busted.

The very room, coz she was in,
Seemed warm from floor to ceilin',
An' she looked full ez rosy agin
Ez the apples she was peelin'.

'Twas kin' o' kingdom-come to look
On sech a blessed cretur,
A dogrose blushin' to a brook
Ain't modester nor sweeter.

But long o' her his veins 'ould run
All crinkly like curled maple,
The side she breshed felt full o' sun
Ez a south slope in Ap'il.

She thought no v'ice hed sech a swing
Ez hisn in the choir;
My! when he made Ole Hunderd ring,
She *knowed* the Lord was nigher.

An' she'd blush scarlit, right in prayer,
When her new meetin'-bunnet
Felt somehow thru' its crown a pair
O' blue eyes sot upon it.

Thet night, I tell ye, she looked *some!*
She seemed to've gut a new soul,
For she felt sartin-sure he'd come,
Down to her very shoe-sole.

She heered a foot, an' knowed it tu,
A-raspin' on the scraper, —
All ways to once her feelin's flew
Like sparks in burnt-up paper.

He kin' o' l'itered on the mat,
Some doubtfle o' the sekle,
His heart kep' goin' pity-pat,
But hern went pity Zekle.

An' yit she gin her cheer a jerk
Ez though she wished him furder,
An' on her apples kep' to work,
Parin' away like murder.

"You want to see my Pa, I s'pose?"
"Wal . . . no . . . I come dasignin'" —
"To see my Ma? She's sprinklin' clo'es
Agin to-morrer's i'nin'."

To say why gals act so or so,
Or don't, 'ould be presumin';
Mebby to mean *yes* an' say *no*
Comes nateral to women.

He stood a spell on one foot fust,
Then stood a spell on t'other,
An' on which one he felt the wust
He couldn't ha' told ye nuther.

Says he, "I'd better call agin;"
Says she, "Think likely, Mister;"
That last word pricked him like a pin,
An' . . . Wal, he up an' kist her.

When Ma bimeby upon 'em slips,
Huldy sot pale ez ashes,
All kin' o' smily roun' the lips
An' teary roun' the lashes.

For she was jes' the quiet kind
Whose naturs never vary,
Like streams that keep a summer mind
Snowhid in Jenooary.

The blood clost roun' her heart felt glued
Too tight for all expressin',
Tell mother see how metters stood,
And gin 'em both her blessin'.

Then her red come back like the tide
Down to the Bay o' Fundy,
An' all I know is they was cried
In meetin' come nex' Sunday.

LOWELL: *Biglow Papers.*

HER LETTER.

I'M sitting alone by the fire,
Dressed just as I came from the dance,
In a robe even *you* would admire, —
It cost a cool thousand in France;
I'm bediamonded out of all reason,
My hair is done up in a cue:
In short, sir, "the belle of the season"
Is wasting an hour on you.

A dozen engagements I've broken;
I left in the midst of a set;
Likewise a proposal, half spoken,
That waits — on the stairs — for me yet.
They say he'll be rich, — when he grows up, —
And then he adores me indeed.
And you, sir, are turning your nose up,
Three thousand miles off, as you read.

"And how do I like my position?"
"And what do I think of New York?"
"And now, in my higher ambition,
With whom do I waltz, flirt, or talk?"
"And isn't it nice to have riches,
And diamonds and silks, and all that?"
"And aren't it a change to the ditches
And tunnels of Poverty Flat?"

Well yes, — if you saw us out driving
Each day in the park, four-in-hand;
If you saw poor dear mamma contriving
To look supernaturally grand, —

If you saw papa's picture, as taken
By Brady, and tinted at that, —
You'd never suspect he sold bacon
And flour at Poverty Flat.

And yet, just this moment, when sitting
In the glare of the grand chandelier,
In the bustle and glitter befitting
The "finest soirée of the year," —
In the mists of a gaze de chambéry
And the hum of the smallest of talk, —
Somehow, Joe, I thought of "The Ferry,"
And the dance that we had on "The Fork;"

Of Harrison's barn, with its muster
Of flags festooned over the wall;
Of the candles that shed their soft lustre
And tallow on head-dress and shawl;
Of the steps that we took to one fiddle;
Of the dress of my queer vis-a-vis;
And how I once went down the middle
With the man that shot Sandy McGee;

Of the moon that was quietly sleeping
On the hill, when the time came to go;
Of the few baby peaks that were peeping
From under their bed-clothes of snow;
Of that ride, — that to me was the rarest;
Of — the something you said at the gate:
Ah, Joe, then I wasn't an heiress
To "the best-paying lead in the State."

Well, well, it's all past; yet it's funny
To think, as I stood in the glare
Of fashion and beauty and money,
That I should be thinking, right there,
Of some one who breasted highwater,
And swam the North Fork, and all that,
Just to dance with old Folinsbee's daughter,
The Lily of Poverty Flat.

But goodness! what nonsense I'm writing!
(Mamma says my taste still is low,)
Instead of my triumphs reciting,
I'm spooning on Joseph, — heigh-ho!
And I'm to be "finished" by travel,
Whatever's the meaning of that, —
O, why did papa strike pay gravel
In drifting on Poverty Flat?

Good-night, — here's the end of my paper;
Good-night, — if the longitude please, —
For maybe, while wasting my taper,
Your sun's climbing over the trees.
But know, if you haven't got riches,
And are poor, dearest Joe, and all that,
That my heart's somewhere there in the ditches,
And you've struck it, — on Poverty Flat.

BRET HARTE.

HIS ANSWER TO "HER LETTER."

REPORTED BY TRUTHFUL JAMES.

BEING asked by an intimate party —
Which the same I would term as a friend —
Which his health it were vain to call hearty,
Since the mind to deceit it might lend;
For his arm it was broken quite recent,
And has something gone wrong with his lung, —
Which is why it is proper and decent
I should write what he runs off his tongue.

First, he says, Miss, he's read through your letter
To the end, — and the end came too soon.
That a slight illness kept him your debtor
(Which for weeks he was wild as a loon),
That his spirits are buoyant as yours is;
That with you, Miss, he challenges Fate,
(Which the language that invalid uses
At times it were vain to relate).

And he says that the mountains are
fairer
For once being held in your
thought;
That each rock holds a wealth that
is rarer
Than ever by gold-seeker sought —
(Which are words he would put in
these pages,
By a party not given to guile;
Which the same not, at date, paying
wages,
Might produce in the sinful a
smile.)

He remembers the ball at the Ferry,
And the ride, and the gate, and
the vow,
And the rose that you gave him —
that very
Same rose he is treasuring now;
(Which his blanket he's kicked on
his trunk, Miss,
And insists on his legs being free;
And his language to me from his
bunk, Miss,
Is frequent and painful and free.)

He hopes you are wearing no willows,
But are happy and gay all the
while;
That he knows — (which this dodg-
ing of pillows
Imparts but small ease to the style,
And the same you will pardon) —
he knows, Miss,
That, though parted by many a
mile,
Yet, were he lying under the snows,
Miss,
They'd melt into tears at your
smile.

And you'll still think of him in your
pleasures,
In your brief twilight-dreams of
the past,
In this green laurel-spray that he
treasures.
It was plucked where your parting
was last.
In this specimen — but a small trifle —
It will do for a pin for your shawl;
(Which the truth not to wickedly
stifle,
Was his last week's "clean up" —
and *his all.*)

He's asleep — which the same might
seem strange, Miss,
Were it not that I scorn to deny
That I raised his last dose for a
change, Miss,
In view that his fever was high,
But he lies there quite peaceful and
pensive;
And, now, my respects, Miss, to
you;
Which, my language, although com-
prehensive,
Might seem to be freedom — it's
true.

Which I have a small favor to ask
you,
As concerns a bull-pup, which the
same —
If the duty would not overtask you —
You would please to procure for
me, *game*,
And send per express to the Flat,
Miss,
Which they say York is famed for
the breed,
Which though words of deceit may
be that — Miss,
I'll trust to your taste, Miss, in-
deed.

P. S. — Which this same interfering
In other folks' ways I despise —
Yet, if so be I was hearing
That it's just empty pockets as
lies
Betwixt you and Joseph — it follers
That, having no family claims,
Here's my pile — which it's six hun-
dred dollars,
As is, yours, with respects, —
TRUTHFUL JAMES.

BRET HARTE.

ATHEISM.

"THERE is no God," the wicked
saith,
"And truly it's a blessing,
For what he might have done with us
It's better only guessing."

"There is no God," a youngster
thinks,
"Or really if there may be,
He surely didn't mean a man
Always to be a baby."

"Whether there be," the rich man thinks,
"It matters very little,
For I and mine, thank somebody,
Are not in want of victual."

Some others also to themselves
Who scarce so much as doubt it,
Think there is none, when they are well,
And do not think about it.

But country-folks who live beneath
The shadow of the steeple;
The parson, and the parson's wife,
And mostly married people;

Youths green and happy in first love,
So thankful for illusion;
And men caught out in what the world
Calls guilt and first confusion;

And almost every one when age,
Disease, and sorrow strike him, —
Inclines to think there is a God,
Or something very like him.

A. H. Clough.

DOROTHY Q.

A FAMILY PORTRAIT.

Grandmother's mother; her age, I guess,
Thirteen summers, or something less;
Girlish bust, but womanly air,
Smooth, square forehead, with uprolled hair,
Lips that lover has never kissed,
Taper fingers and slender wrist,
Hanging sleeves of stiff brocade —
So they painted the little maid.

On her hand a parrot green
Sits unmoving and broods serene;
Hold up the canvas full in view —
Look! there's a rent the light shines through,
Dark with a century's fringe of dust, —
That was a Red-Coat's rapier-thrust!
Such is the tale the lady old,
Dorothy's daughter's daughter, told.

Who the painter was none may tell,—
One whose best was not over well;
Hard and dry, it must be confessed,
Flat as a rose that has long been pressed;
Yet in her cheek the hues are bright,
Dainty colors of red and white;
And in her slender shape are seen
Hint and promise of stately mien.

Look not on her with eyes of scorn, —
Dorothy Q. was a lady born!
Ay! since the galloping Normans came,
England's annals have known her name;
And still to the three-hilled rebel town
Dear is that ancient name's renown,
For many a civic wreath they won,
The youthful sire and the gray-haired son.

O damsel Dorothy! Dorothy Q.!
Strange is the gift that I owe to you;
Such a gift as never a king
Save to daughter or son might bring —
All my tenure of heart and hand,
All my title to house and land;
Mother and sister, and child and wife,
And joy and sorrow, and death and life!

What if a hundred years ago
Those close-shut lips had answered, No,
When forth the tremulous question came
That cost the maiden her Norman name;
And under the folds that look so still
The bodice swelled with the bosom's thrill?
Should I be I, or would it be
One-tenth another to nine-tenths me?

Soft is the breath of a maiden's Yes:
Not the light gossamer stirs with less;
But never a cable that holds so fast
Through all the battles of wave and blast,
And never an echo of speech or song
That lives in the babbling air so long!

There were tones in the voice that whispered then
You may hear to-day in a hundred men!

O lady and lover, how faint and far
Your images hover, and here we are,
Solid and stirring in flesh and bone, —
Edward's and Dorothy's — all their own —
A goodly record for time to show
Of a syllable spoken so long ago! —
Shall I bless you, Dorothy, or forgive,
For the tender whisper that bade me live?

It shall be a blessing, my little maid!
I will heal the stab of the Red-Coat's blade,
And freshen the gold of the tarnished frame,
And gild with a rhyme your household name,
So you shall smile on us brave and bright
As first you greeted the morning's light,
And live untroubled by woes and fears
Through a second youth of a hundred years.

O. W. Holmes.

CONTENTMENT.

"Man wants but little here below."

Little I ask; my wants are few;
I only wish a hut of stone,
(A *very plain* brown stone will do,)
That I may call my own; —
And close at hand is such a one,
In yonder street that fronts the sun.

Plain food is quite enough for me;
Three courses are as good as ten; —
If Nature can subsist on three,
Thank Heaven for three. Amen!
I always thought cold victual nice; —
My *choice* would be vanilla ice.

I care not much for gold or land; —
Give me a mortgage here and there, —
Some good bank-stock, — some note of hand,
Or trifling railroad share; —
I only ask that Fortune send
A *little* more than I shall spend.

Honors are silly toys, I know,
And titles are but empty names; —
I would, *perhaps*, be Plenipo, —
But only near St. James; —
I'm very sure I should not care
To fill our Gubernator's chair.

Jewels are baubles; 'tis a sin
To care for such unfruitful things; —
One good-sized diamond in a pin, —
Some, *not so large*, in rings, —
A ruby, and a pearl, or so,
Will do for me; — I laugh at show.

My dame should dress in cheap attire;
(Good, heavy silks are never dear;) —
I own perhaps I *might* desire
Some shawls of true cashmere, —
Some marrowy crapes of China silk,
Like wrinkled skins on scalded milk.

I would not have the horse I drive
So fast that folks must stop and stare;
An easy gait — two, forty-five —
Suits me; I do not care; —
Perhaps, for just a *single spurt*,
Some seconds less would do no hurt.

Of pictures, I should like to own
Titians and Raphaels three or four, —
I love so much their style and tone, —
One Turner, and no more, —
(A landscape, — foreground golden dirt;
The sunshine painted with a squirt.)

Of books but few, — some fifty score
For daily use, and bound for wear;
The rest upon an upper floor; —
Some *little* luxury *there*
Of red morocco's gilded gleam,
And vellum rich as country cream.

Busts, cameos, gems, — such things as these,
Which others often show for pride,
I value for their power to please,
And selfish churls deride; —
One Stradivarius, I confess,
Two Meerschaums, I would fain possess.

Wealth's wasteful tricks I will not learn,
Nor ape the glittering upstart fool; —
Shall not carved tables serve my turn,
But *all* must be of buhl?
Give grasping pomp its double share, —
I ask but *one* recumbent chair.

Thus humble let me live and die,
Nor long for Midas' golden touch,
If Heaven more generous gifts deny,
I shall not miss them *much*, —
Too grateful for the blessing lent
Of simple tastes and mind content!

O. W. HOLMES.

THE FIGHT OVER THE BODY OF KEITT.

A fragment from the great American epic, the Washingtoniad.

SING, O goddess, the wrath, the ontamable dander of Keitt—
Keitt of South Carolina, the clear grit, the tall, the ondaunted —
Him that hath wopped his own niggers till Northerners all unto Keitt
Seem but as niggers to wop, and hills of the smallest potatoes.
Late and long was the fight on the Constitution of Kansas;
Daylight passed into dusk, and dusk into lighting of gas-lamps; —
Still on the floor of the house the heroes unwearied were fighting.
Dry grew palates and tongues with excitement and expectoration,
Plugs were becoming exhausted, and Representatives also.
Who led on to the war the anti-Lecomptonite phalanx?
Grow, hitting straight from the shoulder, the Pennsylvania Slasher;
Him followed Hickman, and Potter the wiry, from woody Wisconsin;
Washburne stood with his brother, — Cadwallader stood with Elihu;
Broad Illinois sent the one, and woody Wisconsin the other.
Mott came mild as new milk, with gray hairs under his broad brim,
Leaving the first chop location and water privilege near it,
Held by his fathers of old on the willow-fringed banks of Ohio.
Wrathy Covode, too, I saw, and Montgomery ready for mischief.
Who against these to the floor led on the Lecomptonite legions?
Keitt of South Carolina, the clear grit, the tall, the ondaunted —
Keitt, and Reuben Davis, the ra'al hoss of wild Mississippi;
Barksdale, wearer of wigs, and Craige from North Carolina;
Craige and scorny McQueen, and Owen, and Lovejoy, and Lamar,
These Mississippi sent to the war, "*tres juncti in uno.*"
Long had raged the warfare of words; it was four in the morning:
Whittling and expectoration and liquorin' all were exhausted,
When Keitt, tired of talk, bespake Reu. Davis, "O Reuben,
Grow's a tarnation blackguard, and I've concluded to clinch him."
This said, up to his feet he sprang, and loos'ning his choker,
Straighted himself for a grip, as a bar-hunter down in Arkansas
Squares to go in at the bar, when the dangerous varmint is cornered.
"Come out, Grow," he cried, "you Black Republican puppy,
Come on the floor, like a man, and darn my eyes, but I'll show you"—
Him answered straight-hitting Grow, "Waal now, I calkilate, Keitt,
No nigger-driver shall leave his plantation in South Carolina,
Here to crack his cow-hide round this child's ears, if he knows it."
Scarce had he spoke when the hand, the chivalrous five fingers of Keitt,
Clutched at his throat, — had they closed, the speeches of Grow had been ended, —

Never more from a stump had he stirred up the free and enlightened; —
But though smart Keitt's mauleys, the mauleys of Grow were still smarter;
Straight from the shoulder he shot, — not Owen Swift or Ned Adams
Ever put in his right with more delicate feeling of distance.
As drops hammer on anvil, so dropped Grow's right into Keitt
Just where the jugular runs to the point at which Ketch ties his drop-knot; —
Prone like a log sank Keitt, his dollars rattled about him.
Forth sprang his friends o'er the body; first, Barksdale, waving-wig-wearer,
Craige and McQueen and Davis, the ra'al hoss of wild Mississippi;
Fiercely they gathered round Grow, catawampously up as to chaw him;
But without Potter they reckoned, the wiry from woody Wisconsin;
He, striking out right and left, like a catamount varmint and vicious,
Dashed to the rescue, and with him the Washburnes, Cadwallader, Elihu;
Slick into Barksdale's bread-basket walked Potter's one, two, — hard and heavy;
Barksdale fetched wind in a trice, dropped Grow, and let out at Elihu.
Then like a fountain had flowed the claret of Washburne the elder,
But for Cadwallader's care, — Cadwallader, guard of his brother,
Clutching at Barksdale's nob, into Chancery soon would have drawn it.
Well was it then for Barksdale, the wig that waved over his forehead:
Off in Cadwallader's hands it came, and, the wearer releasing,
Left to the conqueror nought but the scalp of his baldheaded foeman.
Meanwhile hither and thither, a dove on the waters of trouble,
Moved Mott, mild as new milk, with his gray hair under his broad brim,
Preaching peace to deaf ears, and getting considerably damaged.
Cautious Covode in the rear, as dubious what it might come to,
Brandished a stone-ware spittoon 'gainst whoever might seem to deserve it, —
Little it mattered to him whether Pro or Anti-Lecompton,
So but he found in the Hall a foeman worthy his weapon!
So raged this battle of men, till into the thick of the *mêlée*,
Like to the heralds of old, stepped the Sergeant-at-Arms and the Speaker.

LONDON PUNCH.

PURITANS.

OUR brethren of New England use
Choice malefactors to excuse,
And hang the guiltless in their stead,
Of whom the churches have less need;
As late it happened in a town
Where lived a cobbler, and but one,
That out of doctrine could cut use,
And mend men's lives as well as shoes.
This precious brother having slain
In times of peace an Indian,
Not out of malice, but mere zeal,
Because he was an infidel;
The mighty Tottipotimoy
Sent to our elders an envoy,
Complaining loudly of the breach
Of league held forth by brother Patch,
Against the articles in force
Between both churches, his and ours;
For which he craved the saints to render
Into his hands, or hang the offender.
But they maturely having weighed
They had no more but him of the trade,
A man that served them in the double
Capacity to teach and cobble,
Resolved to spare him; yet to do
The Indian Hogan Mogan too
Impartial justice, in his stead did
Hang an old weaver that was bedrid.

BUTLER.

THE OLD COVE.

"All we ask is to be let alone."

As vonce I valked by a dismal svamp,
There sot an Old Cove in the dark and damp,
And at everybody as passed that road
A stick or a stone this Old Cove throwed.
And venever he flung his stick or his stone,
He'd set up a song of "Let me alone."

"Let me alone, for I loves to shy
These bits of things at the passers by —
Let me alone, for I've got your tin
And lots of other traps snugly in; —
Let me alone, I'm riggin a boat
To grab votever you've got afloat; —
In a veek or so I expects to come
And turn you out of your 'ouse and 'ome; —
I'm a quiet Old Cove," says he, vith a groan:
"All I axes is — Let me alone."

Just then came along on the self-same vay,
Another Old Cove, and began for to say —
"Let you alone! That's comin' it strong! —
You've *ben* let alone — a darned sight too long; —
Of all the sarce that ever I heerd!
Put down that stick! (You may well look skeered.)
Let go that stone! If you once show fight,
I'll knock you higher than ary kite.
You must hev a lesson to stop your tricks,
And cure you of shying them stones and sticks, —
An I'll hev my hardware back and my cash,
And knock your scow into tarnal smash,
And if ever I catches you 'round my ranch,
I'll string you up to the nearest branch.

The best you can do is to go to bed,
And keep a decent tongue in your head;
For I reckon, before you and I are done,
You'll wish you had let honest folks alone."
The Old Cove stopped, and the t'other Old Cove
He sot quite still in his cypress grove,
And he looked at his stick revolvin' slow
Vhether 'twere safe to shy it or no, —
And he grumbled on, in an injured tone,
"All that I axed vos, *let me alone*."

H. H. Brownell.

JOVE AND THE SOULS.

Amazed, confused, its fate unknown,
The world stood trembling at Jove's throne;
While each pale sinner hung his head,
Jove nodding shook the heavens, and said;
"Offending race of human kind,
By nature, reason, learning, blind;
You who through frailty stepped aside,
And you who never erred through pride;
You who in different sects were shammed,
And come to see each other damned;
(So some folks told you, but they knew
No more of Jove's designs than you.)
The world's mad business now is o'er,
And I resent your freaks no more;
I to such blockheads set my wit,
I damn such fools — go, go, you're bit!"

Swift.

CHIQUITA.

Beautiful! Sir, you may say so. Thar isn't her match in the county.
Is thar, old gal, — Chiquita, my darling, my beauty?
Feel of that neck, sir, — thar's velvet! Whoa!
Steady, — ah, will you, you vixen!
Whoa! I say. Jack, trot her out; let the gentleman look at her paces.

Morgan! — She ain't nothin' else, and I've got the papers to prove it.
Sired by Chippewa Chief, and twelve hundred dollars won't buy her.
Briggs of Tuolumne owned her. Did you know Briggs of Tuolumne? —
Busted hisself in White Pine, and blew out his brains down in 'Frisco?

Hedn't no savey — hed Briggs. Thar, Jack! that'll do, — quit that foolin'!
Nothin' to what she kin do, when she's got her work cut out before her.
Hosses is hosses, you know, and likewise, too, jockeys is jockeys;
And 'tain't ev'ry man as can ride as knows what a hoss has got in him.

Know the old ford on the Fork, that nearly got Flanigan's leaders?
Nasty in daylight, you bet, and a mighty rough ford in low water!
Well, it ain't six weeks ago that me and the Jedge and his nevey
Struck for that ford in the night, in the rain and the water all round us;

Up to our flanks in the gulch, and Rattlesnake Creek just a bilin',
Not a plank left in the dam, and nary a bridge on the river.
I had the gray, and the Jedge had his roan, and his nevey, Chiquita;
And after us trundled the rocks jest loosed from the top of the cañon.

Lickity, lickity, switch, we came to the ford, and Chiquita
Buckled right down to her work, and afore I could yell to her rider,
Took water jest at the ford, and there was the Jedge and me standing,
And twelve hundred dollars of hoss-flesh afloat, and a driftin' to thunder!

Would ye b'lieve it? that night that hoss, that ar' filly, Chiquita,
Walked herself into her stall, and stood there, all quiet and dripping:
Clean as a beaver or rat, with nary a buckle of harness,
Just as she swam to the Fork, — that hoss, that ar' filly, Chiquita.

That's what I call a hoss! and — What did you say? — O, the nevey?
Drownded, I reckon, — leastways, he never kem back to deny it.
Ye see, the derned fool had no seat, — ye couldn't have made him a rider;
And then, ye know, boys will be boys, and hosses — well, hosses is hosses!

BRET HARTE.

RUDOLPH THE HEADSMAN.

RUDOLPH, professor of the headsman's trade,
Alike was famous for his arm and blade.
One day a prisoner Justice had to kill
Knelt at the block to test the artist's skill.
Bare armed, swart-visaged, gaunt, and shaggy-browed,
Rudolph the headsman rose above the crowd.
His falchion lightened with a sudden gleam,
As the pike's armor flashes in the stream.
He sheathed his blade; he turned as if to go;
The victim knelt, still waiting for the blow.
"Why strikest not? Perform thy murderous act,"
The prisoner said. (His voice was slightly cracked.)
"Friend, I *have* struck," the artist straight replied;
"Wait but one moment, and yourself decide."
He held his snuff-box, — "Now then, if you please!"
The prisoner sniffed, and, with a crashing sneeze,

Off his head tumbled, — bowled along the floor, —
Bounced down the steps; — the prisoner said no more!

O. W. Holmes.

THE FRIEND OF HUMANITY AND THE KNIFE-GRINDER.

FRIEND OF HUMANITY.

Needy knife-grinder! whither are you going?
Rough is the road; your wheel is out of order.
Bleak blows the blast; — your hat has got a hole in 't;
So have your breeches!

Weary knife-grinder! little think the proud ones,
Who in their coaches roll along the turnpike-
Road, what hard work 'tis crying all day, "Knives and
Scissors to grind O."

Tell me, knife-grinder, how came you to grind knives?
Did some rich man tyrannically use you?
Was it the squire? or parson of the parish?
Or the attorney?

Was it the squire for killing of his game? or
Covetous parson for his tithes distraining?
Or roguish lawyer made you lose your little
All in a lawsuit?

(Have you not read the Rights of Man by Tom Paine?)
Drops of compassion tremble on my eyelids,
Ready to fall as soon as you have told your
Pitiful story.

KNIFE-GRINDER.

Story! God bless you! I have none to tell, sir;
Only, last night, a drinking at the Chequers,
This poor old hat and breeches, as you see, were
Torn in a scuffle.

Constables came up for to take me into
Custody; they took me before the justice;
Justice Oldmixon put me in the parish-
Stocks for a vagrant.

I should be glad to drink your honor's health in
A pot of beer, if you will give me sixpence;
But for my part, I never love to meddle
With politics, sir.

FRIEND OF HUMANITY.

I give thee sixpence! I will see thee damned first, —
Wretch! whom no sense of wrong can rouse to vengeance, —
Sordid, unfeeling, reprobate, degraded,
Spiritless outcast!

[*Kicks the knife-grinder, overturns his wheel, and exit in a transport of republican enthusiasm and universal philanthropy.*]

George Canning.

PLAIN LANGUAGE FROM TRUTHFUL JAMES.

(TABLE MOUNTAIN, 1870.)

Which I wish to remark —
And my language is plain —
That for ways that are dark,
And for tricks that are vain,
The heathen Chinee is peculiar,
Which the same I would rise to explain.

Ah Sin was his name;
And I shall not deny
In regard to the same
What that name might imply.
But his smile it was pensive and childlike,
As I frequent remarked to Bill Nye.

It was August the third;
  And quite soft was the skies:
Which it might be inferred
  That Ah Sin was likewise;
Yet he played it that day upon William
  And me in a way I despise.

Which we had a small game,
  And Ah Sin took a hand:
It was euchre. The same
  He did not understand;
But he smiled as he sat by the table,
  With the smile that was childlike and bland.

Yet the cards they were stocked
  In a way that I grieve.
And my feelings were shocked
  At the state of Nye's sleeve;
Which was stuffed full of aces and bowers,
  And the same with intent to deceive.

But the hands that were played
  By that heathen Chinee,
And the points that he made,
  Were quite frightful to see —
Till at last he put down a right bower,
  Which the same Nye had dealt unto me.

Then I looked up at Nye,
  And he gazed upon me;
And he rose with a sigh,
  And said, "Can this be?
We are ruined by Chinese cheap labor" —
  And he went for that heathen Chinee.

In the scene that ensued
  I did not take a hand;
But the floor it was strewed
  Like the leaves on the strand
With the cards that Ah Sin had been hiding,
  In the game "he did not understand."

In his sleeves, which were long,
  He had twenty-four packs —
Which was coming it strong,
  Yet I state but the facts;
And we found on his nails, which were taper,
  What is frequent in tapers — that's wax.

Which is why I remark,
  And my language is plain,
That for ways that are dark,
  And for tricks that are vain,
The heathen Chinese is peculiar —
  Which the same I am free to maintain.

BRET HARTE.

THE COSMIC EGG.

UPON a rock yet uncreate,
Amid a chaos inchoate,
An uncreated being sate;
Beneath him, rock,
Above him, cloud.
And the cloud was rock,
And the rock was cloud.
The rock then growing soft and warm,
The cloud began to take a form,
A form chaotic, vast and vague,
Which issued in the cosmic egg.
Then the Being uncreate
On the egg did incubate,
And thus became the incubator;
And of the egg did allegate,
And thus became the alligator;
And the incubator was potentate,
But the alligator was potentator.

ANONYMOUS.

MIGNONETTE.

As I sit at my desk by the window, when the garden with dew is wet,
On the morning incense rises the breath of the mignonette,
Laden with tender memories of thirty years ago,
When she gave me her worthless promise, and we loved each other so,
Till her tough old worldly mother let her maiden charms be sold
To a miser, as hard and yellow as his hoard of shining gold.
As in Central Park I met them on their cheerful morning ride,
As she snarled at her henpecked husband who was crouching by her side,

I thought in the dust of the pathway, "I have the best of you yet!"
Far better the dream of a fadeless love in the breath of the mignonette,
And little Alice and Mabel, and the children that might have been,
Come dancing out on the paper at a twirl of the magic pen,—
Not a horrid boy among them, but a bevy of little girls
With great brown eyes, love-shining, 'mid a halo of golden curls.

They never grow old or naughty; and in them I fail to see
The slightest fault or taint of sin which could have been charged to me.
They are mine, all mine forever! No lover to them can come,
To steal away their loving hearts to grace a doubtful home.
And so, when the tender evening or morning with dew is wet,
I dream of my vanished darlings in the breath of the mignonette.

BARTLETT.

XI.

POETRY OF TERROR.

"There are points from which we can command our life,
When the soul sweeps the Future like a glass,
And coming things full freighted with our fate
Jut out dark on the offing of the mind." — BAILEY: *Festus.*

POETRY OF TERROR.

TURNER.

He works in rings, in magic rings of chance;
He knows that grand effects oft run askance,
And so he prays to Nature, color-queen.

. . . . .

He works in chaoses, — you are no artist,
You medium-man who power to write impartest;
Suffice to know he loveth Chaos old,
Because than aught created she's more bold:
And so he worketh ruleless, not to fix,
And freeze and stiffen, but to weld and mix,
That many elements thus got together
May struggle into light. —
And she loves possibility, and hence
He goes far back into Confusion's dance.
So the old Temeraire, (ah England! long
That happiness shall live within thy song,)
Lets natural ways rush through him; so may you,
If you have brain and strength and dare to do.
Believe me, there are ways of painting things
That are allied to the great Morning's wings.

J. J. G. Wilkinson.

THE TIGER.

Tiger! Tiger! burning bright,
In the forests of the night;
What immortal hand or eye
Could frame thy fearful symmetry?

In what distant deeps or skies
Burned the fire of thine eyes?
On what wings dare he aspire?
What the hand dare seize the fire?

And what shoulder, and what art,
Could twist the sinews of thine heart?
And when thy heart began to beat,
What dread hand? and what dread feet?

What the hammer? what the chain?
In what furnace was thy brain?
What the anvil? what dread grasp
Dare its deadly terrors clasp?

When the stars threw down their spears,
And watered heaven with their tears,
Did he smile his work to see?
Did He, Who made the Lamb, make thee?

Tiger! Tiger! burning bright,
In the forests of the night,
What immortal hand or eye
Dare frame thy fearful symmetry?

William Blake.

THEA.

Leaning with parted lips, some words she spake
In solemn tenor and deep organ tone:
Some mourning words, which, in our feeble tongue,
Would come in these like accents; O how frail
To that large utterance of the early Gods!

Keats.

SONG OF THE PARCÆ.

IPHIGENIA.

WITHIN my ears resounds that ancient song, —
Forgotten was it, and forgotten gladly, —
Song of the Parcæ, which they shuddering sang,
When Tantalus fell from his golden seat.
They suffered with their noble friend; indignant
Their bosom was, and terrible their song.
To me and to my sisters, in our youth,
The nurse would sing it; and I marked it well.

"The Gods be your terror,
Ye children of men!
They hold the dominion
In hands everlasting,
All free to exert it
As listeth their will.

"Let him fear them doubly
Whome'er they've exalted!
On crags and on cloud-piles
The couches are planted
Around the gold tables.

"Dissension arises;
Then tumble the feasters,
Reviled and dishonored,
In gulfs of deep midnight;
And look ever vainly
In fetters of darkness
For judgment that's just.

"But they remain seated
At feasts never failing
Around the gold tables.
They stride at a footstep
From mountain to mountain;
Through jaws of abysses
Steams towards them the breathing
Of suffocate Titans,
Like offerings of incense,
A light-rising vapor.

"They turn — the proud masters —
From whole generations
The eye of their blessing;
Nor will in the children,
The once well-beloved,
Still eloquent features
Of ancestor see."

So sang the dark sisters;
The old exile heareth
That terrible music
In caverns of darkness, —
Remembereth his children,
And shaketh his head.

GOETHE: *Trans. by Frothingham.*

CRIME.

BETWEEN the acting of a dreadful thing
And the first motion, all the interim is
Like a phantasma, or a hideous dream:
The genius and the mortal instruments
Are then in council; and the state of man,
Like to a little kingdom, suffers then
The nature of an insurrection.

SHAKSPEARE: *Julius Cæsar.*

To beguile the time,
Look like the time.

SHAKSPEARE: *Macbeth.*

REMORSE.

METHOUGHT I heard a voice cry, "*Sleep no more!*
Macbeth doth murder sleep," — the innocent sleep,
Sleep that knits up the ravelled sleeve of care,
The death of each day's life, sore labor's bath,
Balm of hurt minds, great nature's second course,
Chief nourisher in life's feast, —
Still it cried, "*Sleep no more!*" to all the house:
"*Glamis hath murdered sleep; and therefore Cawdor*
Shall sleep no more, Macbeth shall sleep no more!"

SHAKSPEARE: *Macbeth.*

Macbeth
Is ripe for shaking, and the powers above
Put on their instruments.

WHEN we in our viciousness grow hard,
O misery on't! the wise gods seal our eyes;

In our own filth, drop our clear judgments; make us
Adore our errors, laugh at us, while we strut
To our confusion.

Antony and Cleopatra.

I SEE men's judgments are
A parcel of their fortunes; and things outward
To draw the inward quality after them
To suffer all alike.

Antony and Cleopatra, iii. sc. 2.

THE gods are just, and of our pleasant vices
Make instruments to scourge us.

K. Lear.

MERCIFUL Heaven!
Thou rather, with thy sharp and sulphurous bolt
Split'st the unwedgeable and gnarlèd oak,
Than the soft myrtle; — O, but man, proud man!
Drest in a little brief authority,
Most ignorant of what he's most assured,
His glassy essence, — like an angry ape,
Plays such fantastic tricks before high heaven,
As make the angels weep.

Measure for Measure.

CLARENCE'S DREAM.

Clarence. — O, I have passed a miserable night,
So full of fearful dreams, of ugly sights,
That, as I am a Christian faithful man,
I would not spend another such a night,
Though 'twere to buy a world of happy days;
So full of dismal terror was the time.

Brakenbury. — What was your dream, my lord? I pray you, tell me.

Clar. — Methought that I had broken from the Tower,
And was embarked to cross to Burgundy;
And in my company, my brother Gloster:
Who from my cabin, tempted me to walk
Upon the hatches: thence we looked toward England,
And cited up a thousand heavy times,
During the wars of York and Lancaster
That had befallen us. As we paced along
Upon the giddy footing of the hatches,
Methought that Gloster stumbled; and, in falling,
Struck me, that thought to stay him, overboard,
Into the tumbling billows of the main.
O heaven! methought what pain it was to drown!
What dreadful noise of water in mine ears!
What sights of ugly death within mine eyes!
Methought I saw a thousand fearful wrecks;
A thousand men, that fishes gnawed upon;
Wedges of gold, great anchors, heaps of pearl,
Inestimable stones, unvalued jewels,
All scattered in the bottom of the sea.
Some lay in dead men's skulls; and in those holes
Where eyes did once inhabit, there were crept
(As 'twere in scorn of eyes) reflecting gems,
That wooed the slimy bottom of the deep,
And mocked the dead bones that lay scattered by.

Brak. — Had you such leisure in the time of death
To gaze upon these secrets of the deep?

Clar. — Methought I had: and often did I strive
To yield the ghost: but still the envious flood
Kept in my soul, and would not let it forth
To seek the empty, vast, and wandering air;

But smothered it within my panting bulk,
Which almost burst to belch it in the sea.
Brak. — Awaked you not with this sore agony?
Clar. — O, no, my dream was lengthened after life,
O, then began the tempest to my soul!
I passed, methought, the melancholy flood,
With that grim ferryman which poets write of,
Unto the kingdom of perpetual night.
The first that there did greet my stranger soul,
Was my great father-in-law, renowned Warwick,
Who cried aloud, — "What scourge for perjury
Can this dark monarchy afford false Clarence?"
And so he vanished: then came wandering by
A shadow like an angel, with bright hair
Dabbled in blood; and he shrieked out aloud, —
"Clarence is come, — false, fleeting, perjured Clarence, —
That stabbed me in the field by Tewksbury; —
Seize on him, Furies, take him to your torments!"
With that, methought, a legion of foul fiends
Environed me, and howlèd in mine ears
Such hideous cries, that with the very noise,
I trembling waked, and, for a season after,
Could not believe but that I was in hell,
Such terrible impression made my dream.

SHAKSPEARE.

HESITATION.

Lady Macbeth. — Yet do I fear thy nature;
It is too full o' the milk of human kindness,
To catch the nearest way: thou wouldst be great;
Art not without ambition; but without
The illness should attend it. What thou wouldst highly,
That wouldst thou holily; wouldst not play false,
And yet wouldst wrongly win; thou'dst have, great Glamis,
That which cries, Thus thou must do, if thou have it;
And that which rather thou dost fear to do,
Than wishest should be undone. Hie thee hither,
That I may pour my spirits in thine ear;
And chastise with the valor of my tongue
All that impedes thee from the golden round,
Which fate and metaphysical aid doth seem
To have thee crowned withal.

SHAKSPEARE: *Macbeth.*

THIS army
Led by a delicate and tender prince,
Whose spirit, with divine ambition puffed,
Makes mouths at the invisible event,
Exposing what is mortal and unsure
To all that fortune, death, and danger dare,
Even for an egg-shell.

SHAKSPEARE: *Hamlet.*

THE CORSAIR.

THERE was a laughing devil in his sneer,
That raised emotions both of rage and fear;
And where his frown of hatred darkly fell,
Hope withering fled, — and Mercy sighed farewell!

BYRON.

MANFRED.

INCANTATION.

WHEN the moon is on the wave,
And the glow-worm in the grass,
And the meteor on the grave,
And the wisp on the morass;

When the falling stars are shooting,
And the answered owls are hooting,
And the silent leaves are still
In the shadow of the hill,
Shall my soul be upon thine,
With a power and with a sign.

Though thy slumber may be deep,
Yet thy spirit shall not sleep;
There are shades which will not vanish,
There are thoughts thou canst not banish;
By a power to thee unknown,
Thou canst never be alone;
Thou art wrapt as with a shroud,
Thou art gathered in a cloud;
And forever shalt thou dwell
In the spirit of this spell.

Though thou see'st me not pass by,
Thou shalt feel me with thine eye
As a thing that, though unseen,
Must be near thee, and hath been;
And when in that secret dread
Thou hast turned around thy head;
Thou shalt marvel I am not
As thy shadow on the spot,
And the power which thou dost feel
Shall be what thou must conceal.

And a magic voice and verse
Hath baptized thee with a curse;
And a spirit of the air
Hath begirt thee with a snare;
In the wind there is a voice
Shall forbid thee to rejoice;
And to thee shall night deny
All the quiet of her sky;
And the day shall have a sun,
Which shall make thee wish it done.

From thy false tears I did distil
An essence which hath strength to kill;
From thy own heart I then did wring
The black blood in its blackest spring;
From thy own smile I snatched the snake,
For there it coiled as in a brake;
From thy own lip I drew the charm
Which gave all these their chiefest harm;
In proving every poison known,
I found the strongest was thine own.

And on thy head I pour the vial
Which doth devote thee to this trial;
Nor to slumber, nor to die,
Shall be in thy destiny;
Though thy death shall still seem near
To thy wish, but as a fear;
Lo! the spell now works around thee,
And the clankless chain hath bound thee;
O'er thy heart and brain together
Hath the word been passed — now wither!

BYRON.

MANFRED.

THE spirits I have raised abandon me —
The spells which I have studied baffle me —
The remedy I recked of tortured me;
I lean no more on superhuman aid,
It hath no power upon the past, and for
The future, till the past be gulfed in darkness,
It is not of my search. — My mother earth!
And thou, fresh breaking day, and you, ye mountains,
Why are ye beautiful? I cannot love ye.
And thou, the bright eye of the universe,
That openest over all, and unto all
Art a delight, — thou shinest not on my heart.
And you, ye crags, upon whose extreme edge
I stand, and on the torrent's brink beneath
Behold the tall pines dwindled as to shrubs
In dizziness of distance; when a leap,
A stir, a motion, even a breath, would bring
My breast upon its rocky bosom's bed
To rest forever, — wherefore do I pause?
I feel the impulse — yet I do not plunge;
I see the peril — yet do not recede;

And my brain reels — and yet my foot is firm:
There is a power upon me which withholds,
And makes it my fatality to live;
If it be life to wear within myself
This barrenness of spirit, and to be
My own soul's sepulchre, for I have ceased
To justify my deeds unto myself, —
The last infirmity of evil. Aye,
Thou winged and cloud-cleaving minister,
[*An eagle passes.*]
Whose happy flight is highest into heaven,
Well mayst thou swoop so near me; — I should be
Thy prey, and gorge thine eaglets; thou art gone
Where the eye cannot follow thee; but thine
Yet pierces downward, onward, or above,
With a pervading vision. — Beautiful!
How beautiful is all this visible world!
How glorious in its action and itself —
But we, who name ourselves its sovereigns, we,
Half dust, half deity, alike unfit
To sink or soar, with our mixed essence make
A conflict of its elements, and breathe
The breath of degradation and of pride,
Contending with low wants and lofty will
Till our mortality predominates,
And men are — what they name not to themselves,
And trust not to each other. Hark! the note,
[*The shepherd's pipe in the distance is heard.*]
The natural music of the mountain reed, —
For here the patriarchal days are not
A pastoral fable, — pipes in the liberal air,
Mixed with the sweet bells of the sauntering herd;
My soul would drink those echoes. — Oh that I were
The viewless spirit of a lovely sound,
A living voice, a breathing harmony,
A bodiless enjoyment, — born and dying
With the blest tone which made me!
Ye toppling crags of ice!
Ye avalanches, whom a breath draws down
In mountainous o'erwhelming, come and crush me!
I hear ye momently above, beneath,
Crash with a frequent conflict; but ye pass,
And only fall on things that still would live;
On the young flourishing forest, or the hut
And hamlet of the harmless villager.
The mists boil up around the glaciers; clouds
Rise curling fast beneath me, white and sulphury,
Like foam from the roused ocean of deep hell,
Whose every wave breaks on a living shore,
Heaped with the damned like pebbles. — I am giddy.

BYRON.

THE APPARITION.

I SEE a dusk and awful figure rise
Like an infernal god from out the earth;
His face wrapt in a mantle, and his form
Robed as with angry clouds; he stands between
Thyself and me — but I do fear him not.

Why doth he gaze on thee, and thou on him?
Ah! he unveils his aspect; on his brow
The thunder-scars are graven; from his eye
Glares forth the immortality of hell.
Avaunt!

BYRON.

XII.

ORACLES AND COUNSELS.

GOOD COUNSEL. — SUPREME HOURS.

"For words must sparks be of those fires they strike." — Lord Brooke.

ORACLES AND COUNSELS.

THERE is a mystery in the soul of state,
Which hath an operation more divine
Than breath or pen can give expression to.

SHAKSPEARE.

THERE is a history in all men's lives,
Figuring the nature of the times deceased;
The which observed a man may prophesy,
With a near aim of the main chance of things
As yet not come to life, which in their seeds,
And weak beginnings, lie intreasured.

SHAKSPEARE.

OPPORTUNITY.

THERE is a tide in the affairs of men,
Which, taken at the flood, leads on to fortune;
Omitted, all the voyage of their life
Is bound in shallows, and in miseries.

SHAKSPEARE: *Julius Cæsar.*

KNOWING the Heart of Man is set to be
The centre of this world, about the which
These revolutions of disturbances
Still roll; where all the aspects of misery
Predominate; whose strong effects are such
As he must bear, being helpless to redress:
And that, unless above himself he can
Erect himself, how poor a thing is man!

DANIEL.

THE recluse Hermit ofttimes more doth know
Of the world's inmost wheels, than worldlings can;
As man is of the world, the Heart of man
Is an epitome of God's great book
Of creatures, and men need no farther look.

DONNE.

O HOW feeble is man's power,
That, if good fortune fall,
Cannot add another hour,
Nor a lost hour recall;
But, come bad chance,
And we join to it our strength,
And we teach it art and length,
Itself o'er us to advance.

DONNE.

IF men be worlds, there is in every one
Something to answer in proportion
All the world's riches: and in good men this
Virtue our form's form, and our soul's soul is.

DONNE.

BEWARE.

LOOK not thou on beauty's charming,
Sit thou still when kings are arming,

Taste not when the wine-cup glistens,
Speak not when the people listens,
Stop thine ear against the singer,
From the red gold keep thy finger,
Vacant heart, and hand, and eye,
Easy live and quiet die.

SCOTT.

SATURN.

So Saturn, as he walked into the midst,
Felt faint, and would have sunk among the rest,
But that he met Enceladus's eye,
Whose mightiness, and awe of him, at once
Came like an inspiration.

KEATS.

GOOD HEART.

It's no in titles or in rank;
It's no in wealth like Lon'on bank,
To purchase peace and rest;
It's no in makin' muckle mair;
It's no in books; it's no in lear
To make us truly blest:
If happiness hae not her seat
And centre in the breast,
We may be wise, or rich, or great,
But never can be blest:
Nae treasures, nor pleasures,
Could make us happy lang;
The heart ay's the part ay,
That makes us right or wrang.

BURNS.

FAITH.

Better trust all, and be deceived,
And weep that trust and that deceiving,
Than doubt one heart that if believed
Had blessed one's life with true believing.

Oh! in this mocking world too fast
The doubting fiend o'ertakes our youth;
Better be cheated to the last
Than lose the blessed hope of truth.

MRS. KEMBLE.

THE NOBLY BORN.

Who counts himself as nobly born
Is noble in despite of place,
And honors are but brands to one
Who wears them not with nature's grace.

The prince may sit with clown or churl,
Nor feel himself disgraced thereby;
But he who has but small esteem
Husbands that little carefully.

Then, be thou peasant, be thou peer,
Count it still more thou art thine own;
Stand on a larger heraldry
Than that of nation or of zone.

What though not bid to knightly halls?
Those halls have missed a courtly guest;
That mansion is not privileged,
Which is not open to the best.

Give honor due when custom asks,
Nor wrangle for this lesser claim;
It is not to be destitute,
To have the thing without the name.

Then dost thou come of gentle blood,
Disgrace not thy good company;
If lowly born, so bear thyself
That gentle blood may come of thee.

Strive not with pain to scale the height
Of some fair garden's petty wall,
But climb the open mountain side,
Whose summit rises over all.

E. S. H.

ULYSSES AND ACHILLES.

Ulysses. — Time hath, my lord, a wallet at his back,
Wherein he puts alms for oblivion,
A great-sized monster of ingratitudes:
Those scraps are good deeds past: which are devoured
As fast as they are made, forgot as soon

As done: Persévérance, dear my lord,
Keeps honor bright: to have done is to hang
Quite out of fashion, like a rusty mail
In monumental mockery. Take the instant way;
For honor travels in a strait so narrow,
Where one but goes abreast: keep then the path;
For emulation hath a thousand sons,
That one by one pursue: if you give way,
Or hedge aside from the direct forthright,
Like to an entered tide they all rush by,
And leave you hindmost; —
Or, like a gallant horse fallen in first rank,
Lie there for pavement to the abject rear,
O'er-run and trampled on: then what they do in present,
Though less than yours in past, must o'ertop yours:
For Time is like a fashionable host,
That slightly shakes his parting guest by the hand;
And with his arms outstretched, as he would fly,
Grasps in the comer: Welcome ever smiles,
And farewell goes out sighing. O, let not virtue seek
Remuneration for the thing it was;
For beauty, wit,
High birth, vigor of bone, desert in service,
Love, friendship, charity, are subjects all
To envious and calumniating Time.
One touch of nature makes the whole world kin, —
That all, with one consent, praise new-born gawds,
Though they are made and moulded of things past;
And give to dust, that is a little gilt,
More laud than gilt o'er-dusted.
The present eye praises the present object:
Then marvel not, thou great and complete man,
That all the Greeks begin to worship Ajax;
Since things in motion sooner catch the eye,
Than what not stirs. The cry went once on thee
And still it might; and yet it may again,
If thou wouldst not entomb thyself alive,
And case thy reputation in thy tent;
Whose glorious deeds, but in these fields of late,
Made emulous missions 'mongst the gods themselves,
And drave great Mars to faction.

SHAKSPEARE.

ANTONY AND THE SOOTHSAYER.

Antony. — Say to me,
Whose fortunes shall rise higher; Cæsar's, or mine?
Soothsayer. — Cæsar's.
Therefore, O Antony, stay not by his side:
Thy daemon, that's thy spirit which keeps thee, is
Noble, courageous, high, unmatchable,
Where Cæsar's is not; but near him, thy angel
Becomes a Fear, as being o'erpowered; therefore
Make space enough between you.
Ant. — Speak this no more.
Soothsayer. — To none but thee; no more, but when to thee.
If thou dost play with him at any game,
Thou art sure to lose; and of that natural luck,
He beats thee 'gainst the odds; thy lustre thickens,
When he shines by: I say again, thy spirit
Is all afraid to govern thee near him;
But, he away, 'tis noble.
Ant. — Get thee gone:
Say to Ventidius, I would speak with him:
[*Exit Soothsayer.*]
He shall to Parthia. — Be it art, or hap,
He hath spoken true: the very dice obey him;
And, in our sports, my better cunning faints

Under his chance: if we draw lots, he speeds:
His cocks do win the battles still of mine,
When it is all to nought; and his quails ever
Beat mine, inhooped at odds.

SHAKSPEARE.

MOTHER'S BLESSING.

BE thou blest, Bertram! and succeed thy father
In manners, as in shape! thy blood, and virtue,
Contend for empire in thee; and thy goodness
Share with thy birthright! Love all; trust a few;
Do wrong to none: be able for thine enemy
Rather in power, than use; and keep thy friend
Under thy own life's key: be checked for silence
But never taxed for speech. What heaven more will,
That thee may furnish, and my prayers pluck down,
Fall on thy head!

SHAKSPEARE: *All's Well that Ends Well.*

TRUE DIGNITY.

IF thou be one whose heart the holy forms
Of young imagination have kept pure,
Stranger! henceforth be warned; and know that pride,
Howe'er disguised in its own majesty,
Is littleness; that he who feels contempt
For any living thing hath faculties
Which he has never used; that thought with him
Is in its infancy. The man whose eye
Is ever on himself doth look on one
The least of Nature's works, one who might move
The wise man to that scorn which wisdom holds
Unlawful ever. O be wiser, Thou!
Instructed that true knowledge leads to love;
True dignity abides with him alone
Who, in the silent hour of inward thought,
Can still suspect, and still revere himself,
In lowliness of heart.

WORDSWORTH.

EACH AND ALL.

HEAVEN doth with us as we with torches do,
Not light them for themselves; for if our virtues
Did not go forth of us, 'twere all alike
As if we had them not. Spirits are not finely touched
But to fine issues: nor Nature never lends
The smallest scruple of her excellence,
But, like a thrifty goddess, she determines
Herself the glory of a creditor,
Both thanks and use.

SHAKSPEARE: *Measure for Measure.*

THE flighty purpose never is o'ertook
Unless the deed go with it: from this moment,
The very firstlings of my heart shall be
The firstlings of my hand.

SHAKSPEARE: *Macbeth.*

COURAGE.

To be furious
Is to be frighted out of fear; and, in that mood,
The dove will peck the ostrich; and I see still
A diminution in our captain's brain
Restores his heart. When valor preys on reason,
It eats the sword it fights with.

SHAKSPEARE: *Antony and Cleopatra.*

Enobarbus. — Mine honesty and I begin to square
The loyalty, well held to fools, does make
Our faith mere folly;
Yet, he that can endure
To follow with allegiance a fallen lord,
Does conquer him that did his master conquer,
And earns a place in the story.

ANTONY AND CLEOPATRA.

CLEOPATRA'S RESOLUTION.

Iras. — Royal Egypt! Empress,
Cleopatra. — No more, but e'en a woman; and commanded
By such poor passion as the maid that milks,
And does the meanest chores. It were for me
To throw my sceptre at the injurious gods,
To tell them that this world did equal theirs,
Till they had stolen our jewel.
Then is it sin
To rush into the secret house of death
Ere death dare come to us?
Our lamp is spent, it's out. Good sirs, take heart:
We'll bury him: and then, what's brave, what's noble,
Let's do it after the high Roman fashion,
And make death proud to take us. Come away,
The case of that huge Spirit now is cold.

My desolation does begin to make
A better life. 'Tis paltry to be Cæsar;
Not being Fortune, he's but Fortune's knave,
A minister of her will. And it is great
To do that thing that ends all other deeds,
Which shackles accidents, and bolts up change;
Which sleeps, and never palates more the dung,
The beggar's nurse and Cæsar's.

FIRMNESS.

We must not stint
Our necessary actions in the fear
To cope malicious censurers; which ever,
As ravenous fishes, do a vessel follow
That is new trimmed; but benefit no farther
Than vainly longing. What we oft do best,
By sick interpreters, once weak ones, is
Not ours, or not allowed; what worse, as oft,
Hitting a grosser quality, is cried up
For our best act. If we shall stand still,
In fear our motion will be mocked or carped at,
We should take root here where we sit, or sit
State statues only.

SHAKSPEARE.

GUIDANCE.

Rashly, —
And praised be rashness for it. —Let us know
Our indiscretion sometime serves us well,
When our deep plots do pall: and that should teach us
There's a Divinity that shapes our ends,
Rough-hew them how we will.

SHAKSPEARE: *Hamlet.*

TRUST.

If this great world of joy and pain
Revolve in one sure track,
If Freedom, set, will rise again,
And Virtue flown, come back;
Woe to the purblind crew who fill
The heart with each day's care,
Nor gain from Past or Future, skill
To bear and to forbear.

WORDSWORTH.

HUMAN LIFE.

Our revels now are ended: these our actors,
As I foretold you, were all spirits, and

Are melted into air, into thin air;
And, like the baseless fabric of this vision,
The cloud-capped towers, the gorgeous palaces,
The solemn temples, the great globe itself,
Yea, all which it inherits, shall dissolve,
And, like this insubstantial pageant faded,
Leave not a rack behind: we are such stuff
As dreams are made of, and our little life
Is rounded with a sleep.

Tempest, act. iv. sc. 4.

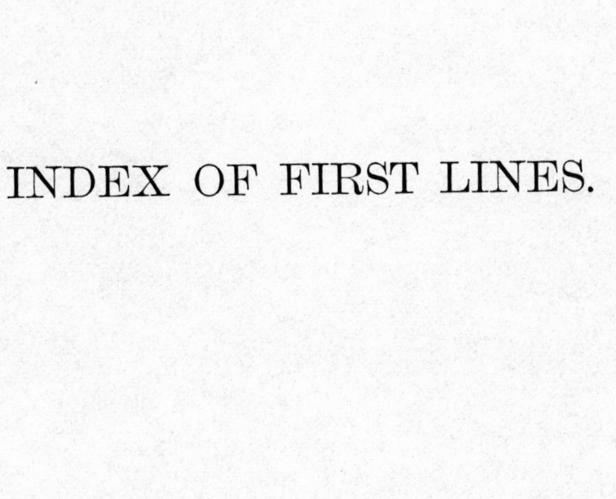

INDEX OF FIRST LINES.

INDEX OF FIRST LINES.

		Page
A barking sound the shepherd hears	Wordsworth	326
Abou Ben Adhem, may his tribe increase!	Leigh Hunt	158
A famous man is Robin Hood	Wordsworth	274
Again returned the scenes of youth	Scott	122
Ah Ben	Herrick	270
Ah, County Guy! the hour is nigh	Scott	442
Ah, God, for a man with heart, head, hand	Tennyson	198
Ah, sunflower! weary of time	W. Blake	29
A king lived long ago	Browning	282
Alas for them! their day is o'er	Charles Sprague	225
Alas! what boots the long, laborious quest	Wordsworth	221
Allen-a-Dale has no fagot for burning	Scott	363
All the world's a stage	Shakspeare	151
All things that are	Shakspeare	40
All thoughts, all passions, all delights	Coleridge	73
Along a river-side, I know not where	Lowell	237
A man prepared against all ills to come	Herrick	198
A man there came, whence none could tell	W. Allingham	158
Amazed, confused, its fate unknown	Swift	502
A mist was driving down the British Channel	Longfellow	224
An ancient story I'll tell you anon	Anonymous	352
And also, beau sire, of other things	Chaucer	96
And here the hermit sat and told his beads	W. E. Channing	7
And I shall sleep, and on thy side	Bryant	25
And on his far resounding path	G. Mellen	225
And passing here through evening dew	William Barnes	75
And sooth to say, yon vocal grove	Wordsworth	34
And whither would you lead me?	Scott	349
An empty sky, a world of heather	Jean Ingelow	80
Appeared the princess with that merry child	Henry Taylor	70
Art is long, and time is fleeting	Longfellow	149
A shadie grove not far away they spied	Spenser	30
As heaven and earth are fairer	Keats	143
As I in hoary winter's night	Robert Southwell	191
As I sit at my desk by the window	Bartlett	505
As I stood by yon roofless tower	Burns	219
As it befell	Wordsworth	17
As it fell upon a day	R. Barnefield	35
Ask ye me why I send you here?	Herrick	32
A slumber did my spirit seal	Wordsworth	471
As Memnon's marble harp, renowned of old	Akenside	99
As ships becalmed at eve	A. H. Clough	82
As unto blowing roses summer dews	D. A. Wasson	83
As vonce I valked by a dismal svamp	H. H. Brownell	502
A sweet, attractive kind of grace	Matthew Roydon	268
A sweet disorder in the dress	Herrick	87
At anchor in Hampton Roads we lay	Longfellow	239
At summer eve, when Heaven's aerial bow	Campbell	45
At the approach of extreme peril	Coleridge (Trans.)	195
At the King's gate the subtle noon	H. H.	202
Avenge, O Lord, thy slaughtered saints whose bones	Milton	195
A voice by the cedar-tree	Tennyson	72
Awake, awake, my lyre	Cowley	129
Away, ye gay landscapes	Byron	26
A weary lot is thine, fair maid	Scott	448

A wet sheet and a flowing sea . . . . . A. CUNNINGHAM . . . 39
Ay, but to die, and go, we know not where . . SHAKSPEARE 161
Ay! tear her tattered ensign down . . . . . O. W. HOLMES 226

Bankrupt, our pockets inside out . . . . . HOLMES 282
Beautiful! sir, you may say so . . . . . BRET HARTE 502
Beaver roars hoarse with melting snows . . . LOWELL 476
Before the starry threshold of Jove's court . . MILTON 104
Before thy stem, smooth seas were curled . . PUNCH 227
Behold a silly tender babe . . . . ROBERT SOUTHWELL . . 191
Being asked by an intimate party . . . . . BRET HARTE 496
Beneath an Indian palm, a girl . . . . . . MILNES 289
Below the bottom of the great abyss . . . . RICHARD CRASHAW . . 179
Be thou blest, Bertram! and succeed thy father . SHAKSPEARE 520
Better trust all, and be deceived . . . . . MRS. KEMBLE 518
Between the dark and the daylight . . . . . LONGFELLOW 57
Between the acting of a dreadful thing . . . SHAKSPEARE 510
Birdie, birdie, will you, pet . . . . . . W. ALLINGHAM 36
Blackened and bleeding, helpless, panting, prone . BRET HARTE 261
Blow, blow, thou winter wind . . . . . . SHAKSPEARE 439
Blue crystal vault and elemental fires . . . . SIR W. JONES (Trans.) . 180
Bonny Kilmeny gaed up the glen . . . . . JAMES HOGG 180
Brave Schill, by death delivered . . . . . WORDSWORTH 222
Break, Fantasy, from the cave of cloud . . . BEN JONSON 123
Breathe, trumpets, breathe slow notes . . . . GEORGE LUNT 257
Bright flag at yonder tapering mast . . . . WILLIS 51
Bury the Great Duke . . . . TENNYSON 464
Busk ye, busk ye, my bonny, bonny bride . . . HAMILTON 412
But all our praises, why should lords engross . . POPE 272
But are ye sure the news is true? . . . . . MICKLE 437
But fare you well, auld Nickie-Ben . . . . . BURNS 483
But for ye speken of such gentilesse . . . . CHAUCER 83
But I wol turn againe to Ariadne . . . . . CHAUCER 75
But souls that of his own good life partake . . HENRY MORE 173
By broad Potomac's silent shore . . . . . ANONYMOUS 226
By Nebo's lonely mountain . . . . MRS. ALEXANDER . . . 290

Call in the messengers sent from the Dauphin . SHAKSPEARE 210
Call me no more . . . . HERRICK 455
Calm and still light on yon great plain . . . TENNYSON 9
Captain or Colonel, or Knight in arms . . . . MILTON 274
Child Dyring has ridden him up under öe . . . SCOTT 336
Clothed with state, and girt with might . . . SIR PHILIP SIDNEY . . 178
Come away, come away, death . . . . . . SHAKSPEARE 439
Come into the garden, Maud . . . . TENNYSON 444
Come on, come on, and where you go . . . . BEN JONSON 493
Come on, sir, here's the place: stand still . . SHAKSPEARE 8
Come pitie us, all ye who see . . . . . . HERRICK 461
Come seeling night . . . . SHAKSPEARE 34
Come, see the Dolphin's anchor forged . . . . S. FERGUSSON 287
Come thou who art the wine and wit . . . . HERRICK 458
Come to Licöo! the sun is riding . . . . . ANONYMOUS 380
Come to the river's reedy shore . . . . . . F. B. SANBORN 442
Comrades, leave me here a little . . . . . TENNYSON 134
Consolers of the solitary hours . . . . . . S. G. W. 150

Dark fell the night, the watch was set . . . . J. STERLING 298
Dear lady, I a little fear . . . . DANIEL WEBSTER . . . 281
Dear mother Ida, harken ere I die . . . . . TENNYSON 375
Dear my friend and fellow-student . . . . . MRS. BROWNING 366
Deep in the waves is a coral grove . . . . . J. G. PERCIVAL 39
Dinas Emlinn, lament, for the moment is nigh . SCOTT 451
Drink to me only with thine eyes . . . . . BEN JONSON 445

Each care-worn face is but a book . . . . . JONES VERY 159
Ethereal minstrel! pilgrim of the sky . . . . WORDSWORTH 36
Ever a current of sadness deep . . . . . . MRS. HEMANS 130

Faintly as tolls the evening chime . . . . . T. MOORE 436
Faire Daffodills, we weep to see . . . . . . HERRICK 33
Fair pledges of a fruitful tree . . . . . . HERRICK 33
Fare thee well! and if forever . . . . . . BYRON 277
Farewell, ye lofty spires . . . . E. B. EMERSON 51
Farewell, farewell to thee, Araby's daughter . . T. MOORE 435

Far have I clambered in my mind . . . . . HENRY MORE 176
Fear no more the heat o' the sun . . . . . SHAKSPEARE 461
Fleet the Tartar's reinless steed . . . . WORDSWORTH 22
Friends, Romans, Countrymen, lend me your ears SHAKSPEARE 205
From harmony, from heavenly harmony . . . DRYDEN 127
From you have I been absent in the spring . . SHAKSPEARE 133
Full fathom five thy father lies . . . . . SHAKSPEARE 441
Full knee-deep lies the winter snow . . . . TENNYSON 24
Full little knowest thou, that hast not tried . . SPENSER 267
Full many a glorious morning have I seen . . SHAKSPEARE 6

Get up, get up for shame, the blooming morn . . HERRICK 10
Give me a spirit that on life's rough sea . . . G. CHAPMAN 198
Give me my cup . . . . BEN JONSON 269
Give me my scallop's shell of quiet . . . . SIR W. RALEIGH. . . . 160
Give place, ye ladies, and begone . . . . . HEYWOOD 65
God moves in a mysterious way . . . . . . COWPER 182
God of science and of light . . . . . . CHAUCER. 96
Goe, happy rose, and interwove . . . . . HERRICK 443
Goldilocks sat on the grass . . . . . . JEAN INGELOW 443
Go, lovely rose . . . . WALLER 443
Go, soul, the body's guest . . . . . . SIR W. RALEIGH 139
Grandmother's mother; her age I guess . . . O. W. HOLMES 498
Great God, greater than greatest . . . . . YOUNG 180
Great Ocean! strongest of Creation's sons . . . POLLOK 38
Gude Lord Graham is to Carlisle gane . . . . SCOTT 350

Hail to the chief who in triumph advances . . . SCOTT 450
Happy, happier far than thou . . . . . . MRS. HEMANS 51
Happy those early days when I . . . . . . VAUGHAN 173
Hark, hark! the lark at heaven's gate sings . . SHAKSPEARE 441
Hark, how I'll bribe you . . . . SHAKSPEARE 159
Hath this world without me wrought? . . . . F. H. HEDGE 91
Have you heard of the wonderful one-hoss-shay? . O. W. HOLMES 492
Hearken in your ear . . . . LOWELL 234
He clasps the crag with hooked hands . . . . TENNYSON 38
He is gone — is dust . . . . COLERIDGE (Trans.) . . . 459
He is gone on the mountains . . . . . . SCOTT 461
He leaves the earth, and says enough . . . . ANONYMOUS. 166
Hence, all you vain delights! . . . . . . BEAUMONT AND FLETCHER 138
Hence, loathèd melancholy! . . . . MILTON 4
Hence, vain deluding joys! . . . . MILTON. 18
Here is the place; right over the hill . . . . WHITTIER 414
Here let us live, and spend away our lives . . . CHANNING 8
Here might I pause and bend in reverence . . . WORDSWORTH 98
Her eyes the glow-worm lend thee . . . . . HERRICK 445
Her fingers shame the ivory keys . . . . . WHITTIER 380
Her finger was so small, the ring . . . . . SIR JOHN SUCKLING . . . 68
Her house is all of echo made . . . . . . BEN JONSON 101
He's a rare man . . . . JEAN INGELOW 320
He's gane! he's gane! he's frae us torn . . . . BURNS 458
He that loves a rosy cheek . . . . T. CAREW 446
He works in rings, in magic rings of chance . . J. J. G. WILKINSON . . . 509
Hope smiled when your nativity was cast . . . WORDSWORTH 42
How changed is here each place man makes or fills! MATTHEW ARNOLD . . . 471
How fresh, O Lord, how sweet and clean! . . . HERBERT 95
How happy is he born and taught . . . . . WOTTON 146
How many a time have I . . . . BYRON 21
How many thousand of my poorest subjects . . . SHAKSPEARE 160
How near to good is what is fair! . . . . . BEN JONSON 87
How oft when thou my music, music play'st . . . SHAKSPEARE 73
How pleasant were the songs of Toobonai! . . . BYRON 377
How seldom, friends, a good great man inherits . COLERIDGE 154
How sleep the brave who sink to rest . . . . COLLINS 459
How soon hath time, the subtle thief of youth . . MILTON 270
How sweet the moonlight sleeps upon the bank! . SHAKSPEARE 43
How they go by, those strange and dreamlike men! E. S. H 159
How vainly men themselves amaze! . . . . . MARVELL 25
How young and fresh am I to-night! . . . . BEN JONSON 3

I am holy while I stand . . . . HERRICK 58
I called on dreams and visions to disclose . . . WORDSWORTH 152
I came to a laund of white and green . . . . CHAUCER 97

I challenge not the oracle . . . . Sidney H. Morse . . 82
I climbed the dark brow of the mighty Helvellyn . Scott 326
If aught of oaten stop, or pastoral song . . . Collins 43
If I may trust the flattering eye of sleep . . . . Shakspeare 122
If men be worlds, there is in every one . . . Donne 517
If this great world of joy and pain . . . . . Wordsworth 521
If thou be one whose heart the holy forms . . Wordsworth 520
If thou wert by my side, my love . . . . . . R. Heber 53
If with light head erect I sing . . . . Thoreau 94
I got me flowers to strew thy way . . . . . . Herbert 192
I have done one braver thing . . . . Donne 154
I have learned to look on nature . . . . . . Wordsworth 29
I have ships that went to sea . . . . R. B. Coffin 122
I have, thou gallant Trojan . . . . Shakspeare 265
I have woven shrouds of air . . . . Channing 27
I hear thy solemn anthem fall . . . . Channing 92
I know a little garden close . . . . William Morris 442
I made a footing in the wall . . . . Byron 283
I made a posie, while the day ran by . . . . . Herbert 151
I mind it weel, in early date . . . . Burns 220
I'm sitting alone by the fire . . . . Bret Harte 495
I must go furnish up . . . . Arthur Boar 36
Inland, within a hollow vale I stood . . . . . Wordsworth 144
In sweet dreams, softer than unbroken rest . . . Tennyson 92
In the frosty season, when the sun . . . . . Wordsworth 22
In the golden reign of Charlemagne the king . . . Tuckerman 357
In the hour of my distress . . . . Herrick 186
In the summer even . . . . Harriet Prescott . . . 448
In this world, the isle of dreams . . . . . . Herrick 123
In vain the common theme my tongue would shun O. W. Holmes 232
In what torn ship soever I embark . . . . . . Donne 180
In Xanadu did Kubla Khan . . . . Coleridge 126
In yonder grave a Druid lies . . . . Collins 462
I see a dusk and awful figure rise . . . . . . Byron 514
I see before me the gladiator lie . . . . . . Byron 283
I see men's judgments are . . . . Shakspeare 511
I shall lack voice: the deeds of Coriolanus . . . Shakspeare 265
I sift the snow on the mountains below . . . . Shelley 46
I sing of brooks, of blossoms, birds, and bowers . Herrick 3
I sprang to the stirrup, and Joris and he . . . . Browning 355
Is there for honest poverty . . . . Burns 147
Is thy face like thy mother's, my fair child? . . Byron 276
It don't seem hardly right, John . . . . . . Lowell 235
It follows now you are to prove . . . . . . Ben Jonson 433
It happen that I came on a day . . . . Chaucer 60
I think not on my father . . . . Shakspeare 62
It is not to be thought of, that the flood . . . Wordsworth 223
It little profits that an idle king . . . . . . Tennyson 101
It's narrow, narrow make your bed . . . . . . Anonymous 384
It's no in titles or in rank . . . . Burns 518
It was fifty years ago . . . . Longfellow 280
It was the season, when through all the land . . Longfellow 11
It was the time when lilies blow . . . . . . Tennyson 381
It was the winter wild . . . . Milton 187
It was thy fear, or else some transient wind . . W. Congreve 133
I wandered lonely as a cloud . . . . Wordsworth 33
I watched her face, suspecting germs . . . . . Patmore 59
I wish I were where Helen lies . . . . Scott 411
I would that thou might always be . . . . . . N. P. Willis 57
I've taught me other tongues . . . . Byron 277

John Anderson, my jo, John . . . . Burns 438
John Brown in Kansas settled like a steadfast . . Stedman 227
Just for a handful of silver he left us . . . . Browning 224
Just now I've ta'en a fit of rhyme . . . . . . Burns 95

Kings, queens, lords, ladies, knights, and damsels great . . . . Spenser 293
Knowing the heart of man is set to be . . . . Daniel 517
King Ferdinand alone did stand one day upon the hill Lockhart's Spanish Ballads 300

Lady Clara Vere De Vere . . . . Tennyson 365
Lady, there is a hope that all men have . . . . Channing 153

Lately, alas! I knew a gentle boy. . . . . . . THOREAU 78
Leaning with parted lips, some words she spake . KEATS 509
Less worthy of applause, though more admired . COWPER 288
Let me not to the marriage of true minds . . SHAKSPEARE 77
Let the bird of loudest lay . . . . SHAKSPEARE 123
Life and thought have gone away . . . . . TENNYSON 457
Life, I know not what thou art . . . . . . MRS. BAUBAULD 169
Life may be given in many ways . . . . . LOWELL 258
Light-winged smoke! Icarian bird . . . . THOREAU 47
Like a poet hidden . . . . SHELLEY 36
Like as the waves make towards the pebbled shore . SHAKSPEARE 152
Like to the clear in highest sphere . . . . LODGE 72
Lithe and listen, gentlemen . . . . ANONYMOUS 307
Little I ask, my wants are few . . . . . . O. W. HOLMES 499
Little was King Laurin . . . . WARTON 126
Lochiel, Lochiel! beware of the day . . . . CAMPBELL 217
"Lo," quoth he, "Cast up thine eye" . . . . CHAUCER 45
Look not thou on beauty's charming . . . . SCOTT 517
Lord, when I quit this earthly stage . . . . WATTS 185
Lord, with what care hast thou begirt us round . HERBERT 159
Loud is the vale, the voice is up . . . . . WORDSWORTH 463
Love is a sickness full of woes . . . . . . DAVIES 446
Low-anchored cloud . . . . THOREAU 48
Lo, when the Lord made North and South . . PATMORE 58
Lo, where she comes along with portly pace . . SPENSER 67

Macbeth is ripe for shaking . . . . SHAKSPEARE 510
Man, thee behooveth oft to have this in mind . . ANONYMOUS 162
Man wants but little here below . . . . . J. Q. ADAMS 280
Men have done brave deeds . . . . E. H. 327
Merciful Heaven! . . . . SHAKSPEARE 511
Merry it is in the good green wood . . . . SCOTT 334
Methought I heard a voice say, "Sleep no more" . SHAKSPEARE 510
Methinks it is good to be here . . . . . . H. KNOWLES 167
Milton, thou shouldst be living at this hour . . WORDSWORTH 274
Mine eyes have seen the glory . . . . . . MRS. HOWE 230
Mine honesty and I begin to square . . . . . SHAKSPEARE 521
Most potent, grave, and reverend signiors . . . SHAKSPEARE 69
Motions and means, on land and sea at war . . WORDSWORTH 98
Mournfully, sing mournfully . . . . MRS. HEMANS 35
Mourn, hills and groves of Attica . . . . . WORDSWORTH 475
Much have I travelled in the realms of gold . . KEATS 94
My dear and only love, I pray . . . . . . MONTROSE 63
My gentle Puck, come hither . . . . SHAKSPEARE 124
My God, I heard this day . . . . HERBERT 143
My liege, I did deny no prisoners . . . . . . SHAKSPEARE 286
My lord, you told me you would tell the rest . . SHAKSPEARE 285
My mind to me a kingdom is . . . . BYRD 154
My mistress' eyes are nothing like the sun . . SHAKSPEARE 76
My mother, when I learned that thou wast dead . COWPER 52
Mysterious night! when our first parent knew . J. BLANCO WHITE 44

Naked on parents' knees, a new-born child . . . SIR W. JONES (Trans.) . . 56
Nature is made better by no mean . . . . . SHAKSPEARE 132
Nay, you wrong her, my friend . . . . . . JULIA C. R. DORR 64
Needy knife-grinder, whither are you going? . . CANNING 504
Night is fair Virtue's immemorial friend . . . YOUNG 94
No abbey's gloom, nor dark cathedral stoops . . CHANNING 460
No! is my answer from this cold bleak ridge . . ANONYMOUS 246
No man is lord of any thing . . . . . . SHAKSPEARE 92
No more, no more, Oh! never more on me . . . BYRON 278
Northward he turneth through a little door . . KEATS 128
No screw, no piecer can . . . . HERRICK 150
No splendor 'neath the sky's proud dome . . . PATMORE 66
Not a drum was heard, not a funeral note . . . WOLFE 466
Not mine own fears nor the prophetic soul . . SHAKSPEARE 152
Nought loves another like itself . . . . . . W. BLAKE 158
November chill blaws loud wi' angry sugh . . BURNS 53
Now deeper roll the maddening drums . . . . G. MELLEN 226
Now haud your tongue . . . . SCOTT 301
Now is the time for mirth . . . . HERRICK 269
Now is the winter of our discontent . . . . . SHAKSPEARE 211
Now Nature hangs her mantle green . . . . . BURNS 456
Now overhead a rainbow bursting through . . . BYRON 46

Now ponder well, you parents dear . . . . . Anonymous 337
Now wol I turn unto my tale agen . . . . . Chaucer 16

O Brignall Banks are wild and fair . . . . . Scott 448
O dark, dark, dark, amid the blaze of noon . . Milton 199
O dear, dear Jeanie Morrison! . . . . . . Motherwell 438
O divine star of heaven . . . . Beaumont and Fletcher 72
O draw me, Father, after thee . . . . . . John Wesley 178
O'er the glad waters of the dark blue sea . . . Byron 39
O'er western tides the fair spring day . . . . W. Allingham 77
Of a' the airts the wind can blaw . . . . . Burns 442
Of all the rides since the birth of time . . . . Whittier 304
Of Nelson and the North . . . . Campbell 220
O for my sake do you with fortune chide . . . Shakspeare 271
Often trifling with a privilege . . . . . . Wordsworth 32
Oft in the stilly night . . . . T. Moore 438
Of truth, of grandeur, beauty, love, and hope . Wordsworth 102
Oft when returning with her loaded bill . . . . Thomson 34
O heavens, if you do love old men . . . . . Shakspeare 102
O heard ye yon pibroch sound sad in the gale? . . Campbell 363
Oh, go not yet, my love . . . . Tennyson 448
Oh, have ye na heard o' the fause Sakelde . . . Scott 301
Oh, how much more doth beauty beauteous seem . Shakspeare 133
Oh, lovely Mary Donnelly, it's you I love the best . Allingham 434
O how canst thou renounce the boundless store . Beattie 3
O how feeble is man's power . . . . Donne 517
Oh, weel may the boatie row . . . . Anonymous 437
O I have passed a miserable night . . . . . Shakspeare 511
O joy hast thou a face . . . . H. H. 157
O keeper of the sacred key . . . . F. Wilson 255
O listen, listen, ladies gay . . . . Scott 414
Old wine to drink . . . . Messinger 57
O Lord, in me there lieth nought . . . . . . Sidney 178
O messenger, art thou the king, or I? . . . . H. H. 91
O my luve's like a red, red rose . . . . . . Burns 443
Once git a smell o' musk into a draw . . . . Lowell 240
Once more, Cesario . . . . Shakspeare 68
Once we built our fortress where you see . . . W. E. Channing 6
On the mountain peak . . . . W. E. Channing 7
O never rudely will I blame his faith . . . . Coleridge 120
One day, nigh weary of the irksome way . . . Spenser 85
On Linden, when the sun was low . . . . . . Campbell 223
O Proserpina . . . . Shakspeare 29
Or if the soul of proper kind . . . . Chaucer 153
Orpheus with his lute made trees . . . . . . Shakspeare 127
O Sacred Providence, who from end to end . . . Herbert 182
O than the fairest day thrice fairer night . . . William Drummond . . 190
O that last day in Lucknow fort . . . . . . Robert Lowell 311
O that we now had here . . . . Shakspeare 211
O the days are gone when beauty bright . . . . T. Moore 446
O then what soul was his, when, on the tops . . . Wordsworth 8
O then I see Queen Mab hath been with you . . . Shakspeare 125
O thou goddess . . . . Shakspeare 83
O thou who in the heavens dost dwell . . . . Burns 481
O thou that swing'st upon the waving ear . . . Lovelace 16
O! 'tis wondrous much . . . . Chapman 93
Our boat to the waves go free . . . . W. E. Channing 38
Our brethren of New England use . . . . . . Butler 501
Our bugles sang truce; for the night cloud had lowered Campbell 289
Our revels now are ended . . . . Shakspeare 521
Out upon it: I have loved . . . . Sir John Suckling . . . 139
Out upon time, who will leave no more . . . . Byron 138
O waly, waly, my gay goss-hawk . . . . . . Anonymous 361
O waly, waly, up the bank . . . . Anonymous 383
O ye wha are sae guid yoursel . . . . Burns 482
O young Lochinvar is come out of the West . . . Scott 356

Passion o' me! cried Sir Richard Tyrone . . . . Anonymous 354
Peace to all such . . . . Pope 271
Pibroch of Donuil Dhu . . . . Scott 450
Pleased we remember our august abodes . . . . Landor 40
Praise to God, immortal praise . . . . Mrs. Barbauld 183

Queen Bonduca, I do not grieve your fortune . . Beaumont and Fletcher . 213

Rabia, sick upon her bed . . . . J. F. Clarke (Trans.) . . 140
Rambling along the marshes . . . . . Channing 37
Rashly; and praised be rashness for it . . . Shakspeare 521
Reason thus with life . . . . Shakspeare 161
Remove yon skull from out the scattered heaps . . Byron 171
Ring out, wild bells, to the wild sky . . . . Tennyson 192
Rise up, rise up, Xarifa! lay the golden cushion down Lockhart 447
Round my own pretty rose . . . . T. H. Bayly 35
Royal Egypt! Empress . . . . Shakspeare 521
Rudolph, professor of the headsman's trade . . O. W. Holmes . . . 503
Ruin seize thee, ruthless king . . . . . . Gray 215
Rumble thy belly full! spit fire! spout rain! . . Shakspeare 102
Run, shepherds, run where Bethlehem blest appears William Drummond . . 190

Say to me, whose fortunes shall rise higher . . Shakspeare 519
Say, what is Honor? . . . . Wordsworth 144
Scots, wha hae wi' Wallace bled . . . . . Burns 219
See how the Orient dew . . . . Marvell 47
See living vales by living waters blest . . . Charles Sprague . . . 38
See the chariot at hand here of love . . . . Ben Jonson 73
See yonder souls set far within the shade . . . Ben Jonson 193
Send us your prisoners, or you'll hear of it . . . Shakspeare 208
Shake off your heavy trance . . . . . . Beaumont and Fletcher 433
Shall I, wasting in despair? . . . . Wither 446
She, of whose soul, if we may say, 'twas gold . . Donne 273
She's gane to dwell in heaven, my lassie . . . A. Cunningham . . . 75
She walks in beauty, like the night . . . . Byron 59
Shine kindly forth, September sun . . . . . F. B Sanborn 462
Should auld acquaintance be forgot . . . . Burns 439
Silence augmenteth grief — writing increaseth rage . Fulke Greville (Lord Brooke) 467
Silent, O Moyle, be the roar of thy water . . . Moore 126
Since I am coming to that holy room . . . . Donne 186
Since our country our God — Oh, my sire! . . . Byron 203
Since the sun . . . . Wordsworth . . . 44
Sing, and let your song be new . . . . . . Sir Philip Sidney . . 181
Sing, O Goddess, the wrath, the untamable dander of Keitt . . . . Punch 500
Sitting in my window . . . . Beaumont and Fletcher . 71
Sleep is like death, and after sleep . . . . . Allingham 94
Sleep sweetly in your humble graves . . . . . Henry Timrod 258
Slow, slow fresh fount, keep time . . . . . Ben Jonson 441
So am I as the rich, whose blessed key . . . . Shakspeare 78
So every spirit as it is most pure . . . . . Spenser 84
So fallen! so lost! the light withdrawn . . . . Whittier 227
Soft you; a word or two before you go . . . . Shakspeare 476
So Saturn, as he walked into the midst . . . . Keats 518
So, when their feet were planted on the plain . . Tennyson 294
Spring all the graces of the age . . . . . . Ben Jonson 434
St. Mark's hushed abbey heard . . . . . . Miss Palfrey 417
Star of the flowers and flower of the stars . . . J. J. G. Wilkinson . . 34
Stern daughter of the voice of God . . . . . Wordsworth 149
Still to be neat, still to be drest . . . . . . Ben Jonson 87
Sven Vonved binds his sword to his side . . . . George Borrow (Trans.) 328
Sweep ho! Sweep ho! . . . . E. S. H. 339
Sweet country life, to such unknown . . . . Herrick 15
Sweet day, so cool, so calm, so bright . . . . Herbert 147
Sweet echo, sweetest nymph that liv'st unseen . . Milton 441
Sweetness, truth, and every grace . . . . . Waller 87
Sweet peace, where dost thou dwell . . . . . Herbert 157
Sweet scented flower, who art wont to bloom . . Kirke White 32

Take along with thee . . . . Ben Jonson 196
Take, O take those lips away . . . . Shakspeare 444
Teach me, my God and King . . . . Herbert 181
Tell me not, sweet, I am unkind . . . . . . Lovelace 63
Tell me where is fancy bred . . . . Shakspeare 441
Tell us, thou clear and heavenly tongue . . . . Herrick 190
Thanks for the lessons of this spot . . . . . Wordsworth 42
That instrument ne'er heard . . . . Drayton 130
That regal soul I reverence in whose eyes . . . D. A. Wasson 198
That which her slender waist confined . . . . E. Waller 73
The Abbot on the threshold stood . . . . . Scott 415
The Assyrian came down like the wolf on the fold . Byron 282
The barge she sat in, like a burnished throne . . Shakspeare 283

The birds against the April wind . . . . . WHITTIER 246
The breaking waves dashed high . . . . . . MRS. HEMANS 225
The bush that has most briars and bitter fruit . JONES VERY 32
The clouds are flying, the woods are sighing . . (Trans.) 447
The convent-bells are ringing . . . . . . BYRON 284
The curfew tolls the knell of parting day . . . GRAY 169
The daughter of a king, how should I know? . . . H. H. 202
The despot's heel is on thy shore . . . . . J. R. RANDALL 230
The destiny, minister general . . . . . . CHAUCER 152
The earth goes on, the earth glittering in gold . . ANONYMOUS 161
The faery beam upon you . . . . BEN JONSON 125
The feathered songster Chanticleer . . . . T. CHATTERTON 343
The flighty purpose never is o'ertook . . . . SHAKSPEARE 520
The garlands wither on your brow . . . . . JAMES SHIRLEY 167
The gods are just, and of our pleasant vices . . SHAKSPEARE 511
The gods be your terror . . . . GOETHE: TRANS. BY FROTHINGHAM 510
The harp that once through Tara's halls . . . . MOORE 435
The house of Chivalry decayed . . . . . . BEN JONSON 199
The king called his best archers . . . . . ANONYMOUS 306
The king is full of grace and fair regard . . . SHAKSPEARE 267
The king is kind; and well we know . . . . SHAKSPEARE 207
The king sits in Dunfermline town . . . . . ANONYMOUS 317
The king was on his throne . . . . . . BYRON 416
The Lord descended from above . . . . . . STERNHOLD 182
The melancholy days have come . . . . . BRYANT 29
The merry world did on a day . . . . . . HERBERT 147
The minstrels played their Christmas tune . . . WORDSWORTH 197
The moon is up, and yet it is not night . . . BYRON 42
The Moorish king rides up and down . . . . BYRON 310
The muse doth tell me where to borrow . . . . GEORGE WITHER 96
The muse, nae poet ever fand her . . . . . BURNS 95
The night is come like to the day . . . . . SIR T. BROWNE 185
The night is made for cooling shade . . . . . J. T. TROWBRIDGE . . . 48
The night is passed and shines the sun . . . . BYRON 284
The old man said, "Take thou this shield, my son" S. G. W 150
The old mayor climbed the belfry tower . . . . JEAN INGELOW 340
The owl is abroad, the bat, and the toad . . . . BEN JONSON 125
The pines were dark on Ramoth hill . . . . . WHITTIER 79
There are points from which we can command our life P. BAILEY 153
There came to Cameliard . . . . TENNYSON 296
The recluse hermit ofttimes more doth know . . . DONNE 517
There in the fane a beauteous creature stands . . PROF. WILSON (Trans.) . . 58
There is a history in all men's lives . . . . SHAKSPEARE 517
There is a mystery in the soul of state . . . . SHAKSPEARE 517
There is an island on a river lying . . . . . DERBY 491
There is a pleasure in the pathless woods . . . BYRON 28
There is a stream, I name not its name . . . . A. H. CLOUGH 20
There is a tide in the affairs of men . . . . SHAKSPEARE 517
There is a Yew-tree, pride of Lorton Vale . . . WORDSWORTH 31
There like a rich and golden pyramid . . . . BEN JONSON 269
"There is no God," the wicked saith . . . . CLOUGH 497
There's a flag hangs over my threshold . . . . MRS. HOWE 236
There where death's brief pang was quickest . . . BYRON 223
There was a boy; ye know him well, ye cliffs . . WORDSWORTH 27
There was a king that much might . . . . . GOWER 265
There was a laughing devil in his sneer . . . . BYRON 512
There was a sound of revelry by night . . . . BYRON 222
There was a time when meadow, grove, and stream . WORDSWORTH 173
Ther is right at the West side of Italy . . . . CHAUCER 385
The sea rolls vaguely, and the stars are dumb . . ALLINGHAM 130
The shadow on the dial's face . . . . . . J. MONTGOMERY 151
The sky is changed; and such a change . . . . BYRON 42
The snows arise; and foul and fierce . . . . THOMSON 23
The spacious firmament on high . . . . . . ADDISON 180
The spirits I have raised abandon me . . . . BYRON 513
The splendor falls on castle walls . . . . . TENNYSON 441
The stars above will make thee known . . . . COWLEY 268
The tent-lights glimmer on the land . . . . . WHITTIER 231
The unearthly voices ceased . . . . SCOTT 218
The wanton troopers riding by . . . . . . MARVELL 455
The weather leech of the topsail shivers . . . . W. MITCHELL 40
The Wildgrave winds his bugle-horn . . . . . SCOTT 330
The wind it blew, and the ship it flew . . . . ANONYMOUS 318

The wintry west extends his blast . . . . Burns 22
The woods decay . . . . Tennyson 165
They made her a grave too cold and damp . . . T. Moore 335
They told me I was heir: I turned in haste . . H. H. 176
They that never had the use . . . . . . Edmund Waller 63
Think we King Harry strong . . . . Shakspeare 266
This ae night, this ae night . . . . . . Southwell 459
This army led by a delicate and tender prince . . Shakspeare 512
This bright wood-fire . . . . E. S. H. 56
This castle hath a pleasant seat; the air . . . . Shakspeare 6
This knight a doughter hadde by his wif . . . . Chaucer 67
This morning, timely rapt with holy fire . . . . Ben Jonson 268
Thou art not gone, being gone . . . . . . Donne 62
Thou blossom bright with autumn dew . . . . Bryant 30
Though the day of my destiny's over . . . . Byron 276
Thou hast learned the woes of all the world . . C. S. T. 95
Thou hast sworn by thy God, my Jeannie . . . A. Cunningham 66
Thou hidden love of God! whose height . . . . Wesley (Trans.). . . . 177
Thou that art our queen again . . . . . . Leigh Hunt 434
Thou that hast a daughter . . . . W. Allingham 436
Thou that hast given so much to me . . . . . Herbert 184
Thou wast not born for death, immortal bird! . . Keats 34
Thou whose sweet youth and early hopes enhance . Herbert 145
Three days through sapphire seas we sailed . . H. H. Brownell . . . 248
Three poets in three distant ages born . . . . Dryden 99
Three score o' nobles rade up the king's ha' . . Smith's Scottish Minstrel 360
Three years she grew in sun and shower . . . . Wordsworth 62
Thy braes were bonny, yarrow stream . . . . . T. Logan 456
Thy voice is heard through rolling drums . . . Tennyson 223
Tiger! Tiger! burning bright . . . . W. Blake 509
Time hath, my lord, a wallet at his back . . . . Shakspeare 518
Tired nature's sweet restorer, balmy sleep . . . Young 160
'Tis madness to resist or blame . . . . Marvell 219
'Tis night, and the landscape is lovely no more . . Beattie 3
'Tis not every day that I . . . . Herrick 93
'Tis not in battles that from youth we train . . Wordsworth 51
'Tis truth, although this truth's a star . . . . Patmore. 76
To be furious . . . . Shakspeare 520
To beguile the time . . . . Shakspeare 510
To be no more — sad cure . . . . Milton 169
To be or not to be, that is the question . . . . Shakspeare 160
To fair Fidele's grassy tomb . . . . Collins 460
To heroism and holiness . . . . Patmore 63
Toiling in the naked fields . . . . John Clare 456
To keep the lamp alive . . . . Cowper 182
To me men are for what they are . . . . . . Milnes 145
Toll for the brave . . . . Cowper 463
To the belfry one by one, went the ringers from the sun Mrs. Browning 404
To the Lords of Convention . . . . Scott 449
True bard and simple, — as the race . . . . . Moore 276
Triumphal arch, that fill'st the sky . . . . . Campbell 46
'Twas All-Souls' eve, and Surrey's heart beat high . Scott 364
'Twas at the royal feast for Persia won . . . . Dryden 130
Two went to pray — oh! rather say . . . . . Richard Crashaw . . . 180
Two voices are there; one is of the sea . . . . Wordsworth 221

Underneath this sable hearse . . . . Ben Jonson 269
Underneath this stone doth lye . . . . Ben Jonson 268
Under the greenwood tree . . . . Shakspeare 440
Upon a rock yet uncreate . . . . Anonymous 505
Uvedale, the piece of the first times . . . . Ben Jonson 269

Vane, young in years, but in sage counsel old . . Milton 271
Vex not thou the poet's mind . . . . Tennyson 133

Wail for Dædalus, all that is fairest . . . . . Sterling 132
Walking thus towards a pleasant grove . . . . Lord Herbert 272
Warriors and chiefs! should the shaft or sword . Byron 203
Wee, modest, crimson, tipped flower . . . . . Burns 279
Wee, sleekit, cow'ring, timorous beastie . . . . Burns 278
Well, honor is the subject of my story . . . . . Shakspeare 203
We must not stint . . . . Shakspeare 521
Westward the course of empire takes its way . . Berkeley 225
What is good for a bootless bene . . . . . . Wordsworth 389
What needs my Shakspeare for his honored bones . Milton 268

First line	Author	Page
When biting Boreas, fell and doure	BURNS	24
Whence is it that the air so sudden clears	BEN JONSON	9
When Chapman billies leave the street	BURNS	484
When coldness wraps this suffering clay	BYRON	172
When daisies pied and violets blue	SHAKSPEARE	440
Whene'er a noble deed is wrought	LONGFELLOW	280
When first thou didst entice to thee my heart	HERBERT	184
When Flora with her fragrant flowers	ANONYMOUS	312
When God at first made man	HERBERT	144
When I a verse shall make	HERRICK	269
When I consider how my light is spent	MILTON	271
When I do count the clock that tells the time	SHAKSPEARE	86
When I love as some have told	HERRICK	86
When Love with unconfinèd wings	LOVELACE	445
When Music, heavenly maid, was young	COLLINS	128
When spring to woods and wastes around	BRYANT	457
When the British warrior queen	COWPER	212
When the moon is on the wave	BYRON	512
When the radiant morn of creation broke	BRYANT	44
When we in our viciousness grow hard	SHAKSPEARE	510
When whispering strains with creeping wind	WILLIAM STRODE	127
When wise Minerva still was young	LOWELL	483
When with the virgin morning thou dost rise	HERRICK	185
Where dost thou careless lie	BEN JONSON	93
Where have ye been, ye ill woman?	HOGG	487
Where is Timarchus gone?	FROM SIMONIDES	463
Where like a pillow on a bed	DONNE	70
Where the bee sucks, there suck I	SHAKSPEARE	440
Where the remote Bermudas ride	MARVELL	41
Which I wish to remark	BRET HARTE	504
While from the purpling east departs	WORDSWORTH	9
While malice, Pope, denies thy page	DAVID LEWIS	272
Whither midst falling dew	BRYANT	37
Who counts himself as nobly born	E. S. H.	518
Who can divine what impulses from God	WORDSWORTH	33
Who is the happy warrior	WORDSWORTH	196
Who is the honest man	HERBERT	195
Whose are the gilded tents that crowd the way	MOORE	286
Whoso him bethoft	ANONYMOUS	162
Why fearest thou the outward foe	ANONYMOUS	154
Willie stands in his stable door	BUCHAN'S BALLADS	321
Wilt thou be gone? it is not yet near day	SHAKSPEARE	5
Winstanley's deed, you kindly folk	JEAN INGELOW	322
Within my ears resounds that ancient song	GOETHE: TRANS. BY FROTHINGHAM	510
Within the mind strong fancies work	WORDSWORTH	28
With joys unknown, with sadness unconfessed	F. B. SANBORN	59
With naked foot and sackcloth vest	SCOTT	349
With sacrifice before the rising morn	WORDSWORTH	162
Woof of the fen, ethereal gauze	THOREAU	48
Would wisdom for herself be wooed	PATMORE	146
Ye banks and braes of bonnie Doon	BURNS	447
Ye distant spires, ye antique towers	GRAY	148
Ye mariners of England	CAMPBELL	221
Ye scattered birds that faintly sing	BURNS	458
Yes, I answered you last night	MRS. BROWNING	64
Ye sigh not when the sun his course fulfilled	BRYANT	167
Yet a few days, and thee	BRYANT	168
Yet do I fear thy nature	SHAKSPEARE	512
Yet once more, O ye laurels, and once more	MILTON	467
You lay a wreath on murdered Lincoln's bier	TOM TAYLOR	254
You meaner beauties of the night	WOTTON	66
Young Jamie lo'ed me weel, and he sought me for his bride	LADY ANNE LINDSAY	383
Young Neuka plunged into the deep	BYRON	378
Your grace shall pardon me	SHAKSPEARE	207
You that can look through Heaven, and tell the stars	BEAUMONT AND FLETCHER	155
Zekle crep' up quite unbeknown	LOWELL	494